MW00979158

The Cambridge Handbook of English Corpus Linguistics

The Cambridge Handbook of English Corpus Linguistics (*CHECL*) surveys the breadth of corpus-based linguistic research on English, including chapters on collocations, phraseology, grammatical variation, historical change, and the description of registers and dialects. The most innovative aspects of the *CHECL* are its emphasis on critical discussion, its explicit evaluation of the state of the art in each subdiscipline, and the inclusion of empirical case studies. While each chapter includes a broad survey of previous research, the primary focus is on a detailed description of the most important corpus-based studies in this area, with discussion of what those studies found, and why they are important. Each chapter also includes a critical discussion of the corpus-based methods employed for research in this area, as well as an explicit summary of new findings and discoveries.

DOUGLAS BIBER is Regents' Professor of Applied Linguistics in the English Department at Northern Arizona University.

RANDI REPPEN is Professor of Applied Linguistics in the English Department at Northern Arizona University.

The Cambridge Handbook of English Corpus Linguistics

Edited by
Douglas Biber
and
Randi Reppen
Northern Arizona University

CAMBRIDGE
UNIVERSITY PRESS

University Printing House, Cambridge CB2 8BS, United Kingdom

Cambridge University Press is part of the University of Cambridge.

It furthers the University's mission by disseminating knowledge in the pursuit of education, learning and research at the highest international levels of excellence.

www.cambridge.org
Information on this title: www.cambridge.org/9781107037380

First published 2015

Printing in the United Kingdom by TJ International Ltd. Padstow Cornwall

A catalogue record for this publication is available from the British Library

Library of Congress Cataloguing in Publication data
The Cambridge handbook of English corpus linguistics / edited by Douglas Biber and Randi Reppen
Northern Arizona University.
p. cm. – (Cambridge handbooks in language and linguistics)
Includes bibliographical references and index.
ISBN 978-1-107-03738-0 (hardback)
1. Corpora (Linguistics) 2. Linguistic analysis (Linguistics) 3. Computational linguistics. I. Biber, Douglas, editor. II. Reppen, Randi, editor.
P128.C68C46 2015
420.1′88–dc23

2014035299

ISBN 978-1-107-03738-0 Hardback

We dedicate this handbook to the memory of Geoffrey Leech, one of the true pioneers of English corpus linguistics. Geoff contributed seminal research to all aspects of corpus linguistics, from corpus construction to corpus tagging and annotation, to the evaluation of corpus representativeness. But from our point of view, Geoff's most important contributions involved the application of corpus-based analysis to investigate linguistic research questions about language variation and use. Geoff contributed to nearly all major subdisciplines of English linguistics with such analyses, including pragmatics, stylistics, descriptive grammar, dialect differences, and historical change. For us personally, Geoff was a model, mentor, co-author, and friend. He will be sorely missed.

Contents

Figures

Tables

Major corpora cited in the handbook

ARCHER	*A Representative Corpus of Historical English Registers*
BNC	*British National Corpus*
Brown	*Brown Corpus*
CED	*Corpus of English Dialogues*
CEEC	*Corpus of Early English Correspondence*
CIC	*Cambridge International Corpus*
COCA	*Corpus of Contemporary American English*
COHA	*Corpus of Historical American English*
COLT	*Bergen Corpus of London Teenager Language*
ELFA	*Corpus of English as a Lingua Franca in Academic Settings*
EMEMT	*Early Modern English Medical Texts*
FLOB	*Freiburg–LOB Corpus*
FRED	*Freiburg English Dialect Corpus*
FROWN	*Freiburg–Brown Corpus*
GloWbE	*Corpus of Global Web-based English*
HKCSE	*Hong Kong Corpus of Spoken English*
ICE	*International Corpus of English*
ICLE	*International Corpus of Learner English*
LINDSEI	*Louvain International Database of Spoken English Interlanguage*
LLC	*London–Lund Corpus*
LOB	*Lancaster–Oslo–Bergen Corpus*
LOCNEC	*Louvain Corpus of Native English Conversation*
LSWC	*Longman Spoken and Written English Corpus*
LWP	*Language in the Workplace Project*
MICASE	*Michigan Corpus of Spoken Academic English*
MICUSP	*Michigan Corpus of Upper-level Student Papers*

NHCC	*Nottingham Health Communication Corpus*
T2KSWAL	*TOEFL 2000 Spoken and Written Academic Language Corpus*
Time	*Time Magazine Corpus of American English*
VOICE	*Vienna-Oxford International Corpus of English*
WrELFA	*The Written Corpus of English as a Lingua Franca in Academic Settings*

Contributors

Silvia Bernardini, Associate Professor of English Language and Translation, University of Bologna
Douglas Biber, Regents' Professor, Applied Linguistics, Northern Arizona University
Alex Boulton, Professor, English and Applied Linguistics, Université de Lorraine
Ray Carey, Researcher, ELFA Project, University of Helsinki
Winnie Cheng, Professor, English language, Hong Kong Polytechnic University
Brian Clancy, Researcher, Mary Immaculate College, University of Limerick
Thomas Cobb, Associate Professor, Applied Linguistics, Université du Québec à Montréal, Canada
Susan Conrad, Professor, Applied Linguistics, Portland State University
Jonathan Culpeper, Professor, Linguistics and English Language, Lancaster University
Mark Davies, Professor, Linguistics, Brigham Young University
Jane Demmen, Research Fellow, Linguistics and Modern Languages, University of Huddersfield
Gaëtanelle Gilquin, Research Associate, FNRS, Centre for English Corpus Linguistics, Université catholique de Louvain
Sylviane Granger, Professor, Centre for English Corpus Linguistics, Université catholique de Louvain
Bethany Gray, Assistant Professor, Applied Linguistics and Technology, Iowa State University
Stefan Th. Gries, Professor, Linguistics, University of California, Santa Barbara
Jack Grieve, Lecturer, Forensic Linguistics, Aston University
Martin Hilpert, Assistant Professor, English Linguistics, University of Neuchâtel

Marianne Hundt, Professor and Chair, English Language and Linguistics, University of Zurich

Susan Hunston, Professor, English Language and Applied Linguistics, University of Birmingham

Ken Hyland, Chair, Professor of Applied Linguistics and Director of the Center for Applied English Studies, University of Hong Kong

Daniela Kolbe-Hanna, Assistant Professor, English Studies, University of Trier

Merja Kytö, Professor, English Language, Uppsala University

Geoffrey Leech, Professor Emeritus, Linguistics and English Language, Lancaster University

Michaela Mahlberg, Professor, English Language and Linguistics, University of Nottingham

Christian Mair, Professor and Chair, English Linguistics, University of Freiburg

Anna Marchi, Linguistics and English Language, Lancaster University

Ron Martinez, Assistant Professor of English, Federal University of Paraná

Anna Mauranen, Professor of English Philology and Vice Rector, University of Helsinki

Fanny Meunier, Professor, Centre for English Corpus Linguistics, Université catholique de Louvain,

Anne O'Keeffe, Senior Lecturer, Applied Linguistics and English Language Teaching, Mary Immaculate College, University of Limerick

Magali Paquot, Postdoctoral Researcher, FNRS, Centre for English Corpus Linguistics, Université catholique de Louvain

Alan Partington, Associate Professor, Linguistics, University of Bologna

Elina Ranta, Researcher, ELFA Project University of Helsinki, University of Tampere

Paul Rayson, Director, University Centre for Computer Corpus Research on Language (UCREL), Lancaster University

Randi Reppen, Professor, Applied Linguistics and TESL, Northern Arizona University

Norbert Schmitt, Professor, Applied Linguistics, University of Nottingham

Erik Smitterberg, Researcher, English Language, Uppsala University

Shelley Staples, Assistant Professor, English, Purdue University

Benedikt Szmrecsanyi, Odysseus Research Professor, Linguistics, KU Leuven

Irma Taavitsainen, Professor, English Philology, University of Helsinki

Richard Xiao, Reader, Linguistics and English Language, Lancaster University

Introduction

Douglas Biber and Randi Reppen

Corpus linguistics is a research approach that facilitates empirical investigations of language variation and use, resulting in research findings that have much greater generalizability and validity than would otherwise be feasible. Studies carried out under the umbrella of corpus linguistics share certain research goals and distinctive analytical characteristics:

- they are empirical, analyzing the actual patterns of use in natural texts;
- they are based on analysis of a large and principled collection of natural texts, known as a 'corpus'; the corpus is evaluated for the extent to which it represents a target domain of language use;
- they make extensive use of computers for analysis, employing both automatic and interactive techniques;
- they depend on both quantitative and qualitative analytical techniques.

(see Biber, Conrad, and Reppen 1998: 4)

Corpus linguistics differs from other "hyphenated" areas of inquiry, such as sociolinguistics or psycholinguistics, in that it is not a theoretical subdiscipline of linguistics. That is, the prefixed element in hyphenated subdisciplines identifies the theoretical domain of inquiry: "socio-linguistics" is the study of language in relation to social factors; "psycho-linguistics" is the study of linguistic behavior in relation to psychological processes. But no such relation holds for "corpus linguistics." Rather, the distinctive characteristic of corpus linguistics is the claim that it is possible to actually "represent" a domain of language use with a corpus of texts, and possible to empirically describe linguistic patterns of use through analysis of that corpus. Any research question relating to linguistic variation and use can be approached from this methodological perspective.

This view of corpus linguistics is not universally accepted. For example, Stubbs (1993: 23–24) argues that "a corpus is not merely a tool of linguistic analysis but an important concept in linguistic theory," and Teubert

(2005: 2) describes corpus linguistics as "a theoretical approach to the study of language." However, this is a minority view, with most scholars focusing on the methodological strengths of corpus linguistics rather than treating it as a theoretical subdiscipline.

At the same time, nearly all scholars working in this area would agree that corpus linguistics is more than merely a methodological approach, because the analytical innovations of this approach have enabled researchers to ask fundamentally different kinds of research questions, sometimes resulting in radically different perspectives on language variation and use from those taken in previous research. Corpus linguistic research offers strong support for the view that language variation is systematic and can be described using empirical, quantitative methods. Variation often involves complex patterns of use that involve interactions among several different linguistic parameters but, in the end, corpus analysis consistently demonstrates that these patterns are systematic. In addition, corpus analyses have documented the existence of linguistic constructs that are not recognized by current linguistic theories. Research of this type – referred to as a "corpus-driven" approach – identifies strong tendencies for words and grammatical constructions to pattern together in particular ways, while other theoretically possible combinations rarely occur.

A novice student of linguistics could be excused for believing that corpus linguistics evolved in the past few decades, as a reaction against the dominant practice of intuition-based linguistics in the 1960s and 1970s. Introductory linguistics textbooks tend to present linguistic analysis (especially syntactic analysis) as it has been practiced over the past fifty years, employing the analyst's intuitions rather than being based on empirical analysis of natural texts. Against that background, it would be easy for a student to imagine that corpus linguistics developed only in the 1980s and 1990s, responding to the need to base linguistic descriptions on empirical analyses of actual language use.

This view is far from accurate. In fact, it can be argued that intuition-based linguistics developed as a reaction to corpus-based linguistics. That is, the standard practice in linguistics up until the 1950s was to base language descriptions on analyses of collections of natural texts: pre-computer corpora. Dictionaries have long been based on empirical analysis of word use in natural sentences. For example, Samuel Johnson's *Dictionary of the English Language*, published in 1755, was based on *c.* 150,000 natural sentences recorded on slips of paper, to illustrate the natural usage of words. The *Oxford English Dictionary*, published in 1928, was based on *c.* 5,000,000 citations from natural texts (totaling around 50 million words), compiled by over 2,000 volunteers over a seventy-year period (see the discussion in Kennedy, 1998: 14–15). West's (1953) creation of the *General Service List* from a pre-electronic corpus of newspapers was one of the first empirical vocabulary studies not motivated by the goal of creating a dictionary.

Grammars were also sometimes based on empirical analyses of natural text corpora before 1960. A noteworthy example of this type is the work of C. C. Fries, who wrote two corpus-based grammars of American English. The first, published in 1940, had a focus on usage and social variation, based on a corpus of letters written to the government. The second is essentially a grammar of conversation: it was published in 1952, based on a 250,000-word corpus of telephone conversations. It includes authentic examples taken from the corpus, and discussion of grammatical features that are especially characteristic of conversation (e.g. the words *well, oh, now,* and *why* when they initiate a "response utterance unit") (Fries 1952: 101–102).

In the 1960s and 1970s, most research in linguistics shifted to intuition-based methods, based on the theoretical argument that language was a mental construct, and therefore empirical analyses of corpora were not relevant for describing language competence. However, even during this period, some linguists continued the tradition of empirical linguistic analysis. For example, in the early 1960s, Randolph Quirk began the Survey of English Usage, a pre-computer collection of 200 spoken and written texts (each around 5,000 words) that was subsequently used for descriptive grammars of English (e.g. Quirk *et al.* 1972).

In fact, modern (computer-based) corpus linguistics also began during this period. Thus, work on large electronic corpora began in the early 1960s, when Kučera and Francis (1967) compiled the Brown Corpus (a 1-million-word corpus of published AmE written texts). This was followed by a parallel corpus of BrE written texts: the Lancaster–Oslo/Bergen (LOB) Corpus, published in the 1970s.

During the 1970s and 1980s, functional linguists like Prince, Thompson, and Fox also continued the empirical descriptive tradition of the early twentieth century, using (non-computerized) collections of natural texts to study systematic differences in the functional use of linguistic variants. For example, Prince (1978) compares the discourse functions of WH-clefts and *it*-clefts in spoken and written texts; Fox (1987) studied variation in anaphoric structures in conversational (versus written) texts; Fox and Thompson (1990) studied variation in the realization of relative clauses in conversation; Thompson and Mulac (1991) analyzed factors influencing the retention versus omission of the complementizer *that* in conversation.

What began to change in the 1980s was the widespread availability of large electronic corpora, and the increasing availability of computational tools that facilitated the linguistic analysis of those corpora. As a result, it was not until the 1980s that major linguistic studies based on analyses of large electronic corpora began to appear. Thus, in 1982, Francis and Kučera provide a frequency analysis of the words and grammatical part-of-speech categories found in the Brown Corpus, followed in 1989 by a similar analysis of the LOB Corpus (Johansson and Hofland 1989). Book-length descriptive studies of linguistic features began to appear in this period (e.g. Granger 1983 on passives; de Haan 1989 on nominal postmodifiers) as did the first multidimensional studies of register variation (e.g. Biber 1988). During this same period, English language learner dictionaries based on the analysis of large electronic corpora began to appear, such as the Collins *COBUILD English Language Dictionary* (1987) and the *Longman Dictionary of Contemporary English* (1987). Since that time, most descriptive studies of linguistic variation and use in English have been based on analysis of an electronic corpus, either a large standard corpus (such as the *British National Corpus*) or a smaller corpus designed for a specific study. Within applied linguistics, the subfields of English for Specific Purposes and English for Academic Purposes have been especially influenced by corpus research, so that nearly all articles published in these areas employ some kind of corpus analysis.

Goals of the handbook

Basically, any research question or application relating to language variation and/or use can be approached from a corpus-linguistic perspective. Our goals in the *Cambridge Handbook of English Corpus Linguistics* (*CHECL*) are to survey the breadth of these research questions and applications in relation to the linguistic study of English. As such, the handbook includes chapters dealing with a wide range of linguistic issues, including lexical variation, grammatical variation, historical change, the linguistic description of dialects and registers, and applications to language teaching and translation. In each case, chapters assess what we have learned from corpus-based investigations to date, and provide detailed case studies that illustrate how corpus analyses can be employed for empirical descriptions, documenting surprising patterns of language use that were often unanticipated previously.

The goals of the *CHECL* are to complement, but not duplicate, the coverage of existing textbooks and handbooks on corpus linguistics. There are many excellent textbooks in print, providing thorough introductions to the methods of corpus linguistics, surveys of available corpora, and general reviews of previous research. The *CHECL* differs from these textbooks with respect to both the target audience and goals: the handbook is written for practicing scholars and advanced students in the field, offering a critical discussion of the "state of the art," rather than an introductory overview of the field in general. As a result, the handbook includes relatively little discussion of topics that have been fully covered in existing textbooks, such as surveys of existing corpora, or methodological discussions of corpus construction and analysis. Instead, the *CHECL* focuses on a critical discussion of the linguistic findings that have resulted from corpus-based investigations: what have we learned about language variation and use from corpus-based research?

The most innovative aspects of the *CHECL* are its emphasis on critical discussion, its explicit evaluation of the state of the art in each research area, and the inclusion of an empirical case study in each chapter. Although each chapter includes a broad summary of previous research, the primary focus is on a more detailed description of the most important corpus-based studies in this area, with discussion of what those studies found and why they are especially important. Each chapter also includes critical discussion of the corpus-based methods that are typically employed for research in this area, as well as an explicit summary of the state of the art: what do we know as a result of corpus research in this area that we did not know previously? Finally, each chapter includes an empirical case study illustrating the corpus analysis methods and the types of research findings that are typical in this area of research.

Organization of the handbook

As noted above, any research question relating to language variation and use can be approached from a corpus-linguistic perspective. In our previous work, we have identified two major objectives of such research:

(1) To describe linguistic characteristics, such as vocabulary, lexical collocations, phraseological sequences, or grammatical features. These studies often attempt to account for variation in the use of related linguistic features (e.g. the choice between simple past tense versus present perfect aspect) or to document the discourse functions of a linguistic feature.
(2) To describe the overall characteristics of a variety: a register or dialect. These studies provide relatively comprehensive linguistic descriptions of a single variety or of the patterns of variation among a set of varieties.

We have structured the main body of *CHECL* around these two domains of inquiry: chapters dealing with "Corpus analysis of linguistic characteristics" in Part II and chapters dealing with "Corpus analysis of varieties" in Part III.

Part II is organized as a progression of the linguistic levels, beginning with corpus-based analyses of prosodic characteristics, moving on to chapters dealing with lexical characteristics (keywords, collocations, and phraseology), followed by chapters on grammatical features (descriptive grammar, grammatical variation, grammatical change, and the intersection of grammar and lexis), and finally concluding with chapters on the corpus-based study of discourse functions and pragmatics.

Part III, then, is organized in terms of the range of varieties that have been studied from a corpus perspective. This part begins with chapters on the corpus-based description of spoken English, written academic English, and patterns of variation (synchronic and diachronic) among a wider range of spoken and written registers. Those chapters are then followed by chapters on the use of corpus analysis to document the linguistic characteristics of other types of varieties: literary styles, regional dialects, world Englishes, English as a lingua franca, and learner English.

Preceding these two central sections, the *CHECL* has a shorter section dealing with methodological issues. As noted above, methodological issues relating to corpus design and analysis have been dealt with at length in previous textbooks. In addition, each of the chapters in *CHECL* includes discussion of the specific methodological considerations relating to their area of inquiry. However, beyond those treatments, there is need for a more general discussion of the current state of the art concerning corpus design and analysis. The three chapters included in Part I provide this discussion, dealing with current issues relating to corpus design and composition, tools and methods for the linguistic analysis of corpora, and quantitative research designs and statistical methods used to describe the patterns of use across corpora.

Finally, the *CHECL* concludes with a major section on applications of corpus-based research. Corpus linguistics has had a major influence on such applications over the past two decades, so that it is now almost impossible to find a research journal in applied linguistics, language teaching, translation studies, or lexicography that does not regularly publish articles utilizing corpus research findings. Part IV of the handbook surveys these major areas of application, including classroom applications, the development of corpus-based pedagogical materials, vocabulary studies, and corpus applications in lexicography and translation.

Internal organization of chapters

To help ensure the coherence of the *CHECL*, we have asked all authors to follow the same general organization in their chapter. While this has not always been possible, most chapters employ the same general organization. In addition to ensuring a coherent treatment across chapters, our primary goal is to provide a more sophisticated level of critical discussion than in most previous books. To achieve this goal, each chapter is composed of two major parts: a critical discussion of previous research, and presentation of an empirical case study.

Regarding the first section (the discussion of previous research), each chapter attempts to include the following:

- a general but concise survey of previous published research, briefly identifying the research topics covered by each study
- a more detailed discussion of the most important studies in this area: identifying the research questions; describing their methods; summarizing the major findings; and discussing why the study is especially important

- a critical discussion of the methods that are typically employed for research in this area, illustrated with more detailed discussions of studies that model strong research practices as well as studies that are problematic
- a summary of the state of the art for research in this area: what do we know as a result of corpus research in this area that we did not know previously? What are the major research gaps that still need to be addressed?

Regarding the second section (the empirical case study), each chapter addresses the following:

- a clear identification of the research question(s)
- motivation of the research question: why is the study important?
- a relatively detailed and critical description of methods: what are the strengths and weaknesses of the approach? Does it directly address the research questions? etc.
- a summary of the major research findings: what do we know as a result of this study that we did not know previously?

Our overall goal in requiring this strict organization across chapters is to achieve a handbook that will be of high interest to both students (with clear identification of the important research issues and discussion of strong and weak research practices) and advanced researchers (who can engage in the critical evaluations of each subfield).

Summary

In summary, the *CHECL* differs in three major ways from previous textbooks and handbooks on corpus linguistics. First, it has much more of a linguistic focus rather than a focus on the mechanics of corpus creation and analysis. Thus, most chapters in the *CHECL* deal with domains of linguistic inquiry, surveying the linguistic findings that have been achieved through corpus research.

Second, although methodological issues are important in the *CHECL*, they are addressed in each content chapter, rather than in isolation as topics in themselves. Further, these issues are addressed in a critical manner, evaluating the extent to which corpus designs and analysis techniques are in fact suitable for the linguistic research questions that are being investigated.

And third, the *CHECL* offers a more critical perspective than in most previous books. That is, rather than simply cataloging the range of research studies in an area of research, each chapter selects the most important of those studies, and describes the methods and research findings from those studies. Further, each chapter summarizes the state of the art in this area, describing what we have actually learned from corpus research. And finally, methods of corpus design and analysis are evaluated critically with respect to specific linguistic research studies, to discuss the extent to which specific empirical research methods are well suited to the research questions of interest.

In sum, our goals in the *CHECL* go beyond a simple catalog of existing corpora and research tools, and go beyond simply itemizing the range of previous publications in this area. Rather, we hope to summarize and evaluate what we have learned about language use and variation from previous corpus-based research, to identify and discuss the most important of those previous studies and research findings, and to discuss the methodologies that work best for such research.

Part I

Methodological considerations

1

Corpora: an introduction

Mark Davies

1 Introduction

Many introductions to English corpora attempt to provide a comprehensive list of the "most important" corpora currently available. While there are some advantages to such an approach, these lists are invariably outdated even before they are published, and hopelessly outdated after five to years.

In this introduction, I take a different approach. Rather than attempting to create a complete and exhaustive list, I focus on a handful of corpora (and related resources, such as text archives and the "Web as Corpus") that are *representative* of general classes of corpora. We will discuss the relative advantages and disadvantages of these *general classes* of resources, which will undoubtedly contain much better exemplars in years to come.

The types of corpora (and corpus-related resources) that we consider are the following:[1]

1. Small 1–5-million-word, first-generation corpora like the ***Brown Corpus*** (and others in the Brown "family," such as the LOB, Frown, and FLOB)
2. Moderately sized, second-generation, genre-balanced corpora, such as the 100-million-word ***British National Corpus***
3. Larger, more up-to-date (but still genre-balanced) corpora, such as the 450-million-word ***Corpus of Contemporary American English*** (COCA)[2]
4. Large text archives, such as **Lexis-Nexis**
5. Extremely large text archives, such as **Google Books**[3]
6. **The Web** as corpus, seen here through the lens of Google-based searches

[1] All of the corpora discussed in this chapter are "general" corpora, rather than corpora for a particular genre of English.

[2] See Davies 2008, 2011. [3] See Michel *et al.* 2011.

Finally, we will consider very large "hybrid" corpora, which take data from text archives or the Web, but which then deliver this data through powerful architectures and interfaces. These include:

7. The web-based corpora available through **Sketch Engine**
8. An advanced interface to Google Books, available through **googlebooks.byu.edu**.

As we discuss these different types of corpora, we will first (in Sections 2–5) see how well they can provide data for a wide range of linguistic phenomena – lexical, morphological, syntactic, and semantic. As we do so, we will consider how the quantity and quality of the data are affected by the corpus size, as well as the corpus architecture and interface. Second, in Section 6 we will consider the issue of *variation* within English, by looking primarily at genre coverage and balance in the corpora. We will also briefly consider other types of variation, such as variation in time (i.e. historical corpora) and space (i.e. corpora that provide data on dialectal variation), as well as variation at the level of individual speakers and writers. In the concluding section, we will take an (admittedly risky) "flight of fancy" and imagine what type of corpora might be available in five, ten, or twenty years.

2 Providing data on a wide range of linguistic phenomena

A typical textbook on linguistics will contain chapters on phonology, lexis, morphology, syntax, and semantics, as well as variation by speaker, by time (language change), and in space (dialects). As a result, it is probably not unreasonable to expect modern corpora to provide useful data on these types of phenomena, as shown in Table 1.1. (Note that these searches are simply representative examples of different types of searches; i.e. this is obviously not an exhaustive list.)

Too often, linguists are artificially and needlessly limited by the size or the design or the architecture of the particular corpus that they have been using for years. As a result, they are in a sense "blind" to the full range of phenomena that can be studied with other robust, well-designed corpora. For this reason, we will consider in some detail in the following sections (with many concrete examples) how the quantity and quality of the data that we obtain from corpora (for the phenomena listed above) are a function of corpus size, architecture, and genre balance.

3 Corpus size (Brown, BNC, COCA)

In this section, we will consider the importance of corpus size, and we will attempt to answer two questions. First, how do the data from

Table 1.1 *Types of phenomena*

Lexical
1. Frequency and distribution of specific words and phrases
2. Lists of all common words in a language or genre

Morphology
3. Processes involving word formation (e.g., nouns formed with suffixes like **ism* or **ousness*)
4. Contrasts in the use of grammatical alternatives, such as *HAVE + proven/proved*, or *sincerest/most sincere*

Grammar/syntax
5. High-frequency grammatical features, like modals, passives, perfect or progressive aspect
6. Less frequent grammatical variation, such as choices with verb subcategorization (*John started to walk / walking; she'd like (for) him to stay overnight*)

Phraseological patterns
7. Collocational preferences for specific words (e.g., *true feelings* or *naked eye*)
8. Constructions, e.g. *[V NP into V-ing] (they talked him into staying)* or [V POSS *way* PREP] (*he elbowed his way through the crowd*)

Semantics
9. Collocates (generally) as a guide to meaning and usage (e.g. with *click* (n), *nibble* (v), or *serenely*)
10. Semantic prosody, e.g. the types of words preceding the verb *budge* or nouns following the verb *cause*.

"first-generation" corpora like the Brown Corpus (1 million words in size) compare to those from second-generation corpora (which have anywhere from 100 to 500 million words), in terms of providing enough occurrences of different linguistic phenomena? Second, is there much of a difference between a 100-million-word corpus (e.g. BNC) and a nearly 500-million-word corpus (COCA), or is 100 million words adequate?

We will examine these two questions empirically, by looking in turn at each of the ten phenomena presented in Table 1.1.[4] (Note that these numbers are probably a bit cryptic at this point, but they will be explained – phenomenon by phenomenon – in the discussion that follows.)

3.1 Lexical

Even for some moderately frequent words, a one-million-word corpus like Brown does not provide enough data for useful analyses. For example, 83 of the 1,000 most frequent adjectives in COCA occur five times or less in Brown, including such common words as *fun, offensive, medium, tender, teenage, coastal, scary, organizational, terrific, sexy, cute, innovative, risky, shiny, viable, hazardous, conceptual*, and *affordable* (all of which occur 5,000 times or more in COCA). Of the top 2,000 adjectives in COCA, 425 occur five times or less in Brown, and this rises to 2,053 of the top 5,000 and 5,106 of the top

[4] Note that the COCA data are based on the 450-million-word version from 2012, but counts for later years will be higher, since COCA grows by 20 million words a year. The BNC and Brown, on the other hand, are static.

Table 1.2 *Frequency of different phenomena in COCA, BNC, and Brown (numbers explained in detail in Sections 3.1–3.5)*

		COCA (450 m)	BNC (100 m)	Brown (1 m)
1	Lexical: individual	(See discussion in Section 3.1 above)		
2	Lexical: word lists	100,705	43,758	3,956
3	Morphology: substrings	*-ousness* 112 *-ism* 512	*-ousness* 25 *-ism* 278	*-ousness* 1 *-ism* 6
4	Morphology: compare	*prove{n/d}* 2,616 + 3,001 *sincere* 85 + 65	*prove{n/d}* 82 + 1,169 *sincere* 11 + 12	*prove{n/d}* 3 + 7 *sincere* 1 + 0
5	Syntax: high frequency	modals 5,794k perfects 1,837k *be* passives 2,900k	modals 1,421k perfects 446k *be* passives 890k	modals 14k perfects 4k *be* passives 10k
6	Syntax: low frequency	*love* 12,178 + 5,393 *hate* 3,968 + 1,773 *for* 931	*love* 1,192 + 351 *hate* 389 + 475 *for* 103	*love* 10 + 2 *hate* 8 + 2 *for* 0
7	Phraseology: words	*true feelings* 654 *naked eye* 175	*true feelings* 148 *naked eye* 53	*true feelings* 2 *naked eye* 0
8	Phraseology: constructions	*way* 251v : 15,868t *into* 275v : 2,160t	*way* 83v : 3,533t *into* 111v : 358t	*way* 15v : 44t *into* 6v : 6t
9	Semantics: collocates	*riddle* (n) 57 *nibble* (v) 96 *crumbled* (j) 33 *serenely* (r) 24	*riddle* (n) 0 *nibble* (v) 13 *crumbled* (j) 1 *serenely* (r) 4	*riddle* (n) 0 *nibble* (v) 0 *crumbled* (j) 0 *serenely* (r) 0
10	Semantics: prosody	*budge* (v) 1,427 *cause* (v) 1,344	*budge* (v) 164 *cause* (v) 358	*budge* (v) 3 *cause* (v) 0

10,000 (all of which occur 120 times or more in COCA). In addition, a Brown-based frequency list (for all words in the corpus) would be quite sparse. For example, only 3,956 lemmas occur 20 times or more in Brown, but this rises to more than 43,000 lemmas in the BNC and 100,000 lemmas in COCA. (Note that this is not due to norming, but rather it is the number of word types.)

3.2 Morphology

Morphologists are interested in morpheme ordering in English (see Hay and Baayen 2005), and it is therefore useful to look for the frequency of words with multiple suffixes, such as **ous+ness*. In COCA, there are 112 different forms that end in **ousness* and that have more than 10 tokens (e.g. *consciousness*, *seriousness*, *nervousness*, *righteousness*, *graciousness*, *dangerousness*), and this decreases to 25 in the BNC and just one in Brown (*consciousness*). In COCA, there are 512 words ending in **ism* with more than 20 tokens, 278 in the BNC, and only 6 in Brown (*communism*, *criticism*, *nationalism*, *mechanism*, *realism*, *anti-Semitism*). Morphologists are also interested in variation in competing word forms, such as *have* + *proven* or *proved*, because of insights that these give into how we process language (e.g. single or dual-route model). In COCA, there are 2,616 tokens of *have proven* and 3,001 for *have* *proved* in COCA. The BNC has 82 *have proven* and 1,169 *have proved*, and Brown has only 3 *have proven* and 7 *have proved*. Comparing adjectival forms (*sincerest* vs. *most sincere*), there are 85 and 65 tokens (respectively) in COCA, 11 and 12 in the BNC, and only 1 and 0 in Brown.

3.3 Syntax

High-frequency syntactic constructions are perhaps the one type of phenomenon where Brown provides sufficient data.[5] For example, there are 14,080 tokens of modals, 4,288 perfect constructions, and 9,985 *be* passives. In the BNC this increases to approximately 1,421,000 modals, 446,000 perfect constructions, and 890,000 *be* passives. And in COCA it is of course even more: 5,794,000, 1,837,000, and 2,900,000 tokens, respectively. But even for something as frequent as the *get* passive (*John got fired last week*) there are only 58 tokens in Brown, whereas there are about 9,000 in the BNC and in 70,000 in COCA. There are very few tokens of less common syntactic constructions (such as verbal subcategorization) in Brown. For [*to* V / V-*ing*] (*John hated* [*to buy*/ *buying*]), COCA has 12,178 tokens of [*love* to VERB] and 5,393 tokens of [*love* V-ing], and 3,968 + 1,773 tokens with *hate*. The BNC has 1,162+351 with *love* and 389+475 with *hate*. Brown, on the other hand, has only 10+2 with *love* and 8+2 with *hate* – too few to say much about this construction. With the ±*for* construction (when it is "optional," e.g. *I want* (*for*) *you to leave*) there are 931 tokens in COCA, 103 in the BNC, and 0 in Brown.

3.4 Phraseology

Specific words and phrases: Sinclair (2004a: 30–36) discusses the patterning of two different phrases: *naked eye* and *true feelings*. COCA has a robust 654 and 175 tokens (respectively), while the BNC has 148 and 53 tokens. Such an investigation of phraseology would be quite impossible in Brown, however, where there are only 2 and 0 tokens, respectively. Constructions: in COCA, there are 251 distinct verbs and 15,868 tokens for the "*way* construction," e.g. *make his way to*, *find their way into*, *push his way through*, *bluster their way out of*. This decreases to 83 verbs and 3,533 tokens in the BNC and only 15 verbs and 44 tokens in Brown – probably too few for an insightful analysis. With the "*into* V-*ing*" construction (e.g. *talk him into going*, *bribe her into getting*, *lure me into buying*), there are 275 distinct matrix verbs and 2,160 tokens in COCA, which decreases to 111 verbs and 358 tokens in the BNC, and only 6 verbs and 6 tokens in Brown – again, too few for any insightful analyses.

[5] For this reason, it is perhaps no surprise that the Brown family of corpora has been used for a number of insightful analyses of high-frequency grammatical phenomena in English, e.g. Leech *et al.* (2009).

3.5 Semantics

Collocates can provide useful insight into meaning and usage, following Firth's insight that "you shall know a word by the company it keeps" (1957: 11). But collocates are very sensitive to corpus size. For example, there are 15 distinct ADJ collocate lemmas of *riddle* (NOUN) that occur three times or more in COCA (span = 1L/0R), e.g. *great, ancient, cosmic*; 96 distinct NOUN collocate lemmas of *nibble* (VERB) occurring three times or more (span = 0L/4R), e.g. *edges, grass, ear*; 33 distinct NOUN collocate lemmas of *crumbled* (ADJ) occurring three times or more (span = 0L/2R), e.g. *cheese, bacon, bread*; and 24 distinct VERB collocate lemmas of *serenely* occurring three times or more (span = 3L/3R), e.g. *smile, float, gaze*. Because collocates are so sensitive to size, we find that these numbers decrease dramatically from 15, 96, 33, and 24 in COCA to 0, 13, 1, and 4 (respectively) in the BNC, and a dismal 0, 0, 0, 0 in Brown. An interesting use of collocates is their role in signaling "semantic prosody" (see Louw 1993), in which a word occurs primarily in a negative or positive context. For example, *budge* is nearly always preceded by negation (*it wouldn't budge, they couldn't budge it*), and *cause* takes primarily negative objects (e.g. *death, disease, pain, cancer, problems*). In order to see such patterns, however, we need large corpora. In COCA, there are 1,427 tokens of *budge* and 1,344 different object noun collocates of *cause* that occur at least 10 times each (span = 0L/4R). This decreases to 164 tokens of *budge* and 358 noun collocates of *cause* in the BNC, and just 3 tokens of *budge* and 0 noun collocates of *cause* (occurring ten times or more) – again, simply not enough for insightful analyses.

3.6 Accuracy of annotation in small and large corpora

As we have seen, large corpora have certain advantages in terms of providing data on a wide range of phenomena. But it is also true that there are some challenges associated with large corpora. This is particularly true in terms of the accuracy of annotation – both at the word level (e.g. accurate part of speech tagging) and the document level (e.g. accurate metadata for all of the texts in the corpus). And this is especially true when the corpus is created by a small team and with limited resources.

Consider first the issue of accuracy in document-level metadata. The Brown Corpus is composed of just 500 texts, and it is very easy to achieve 100 percent accuracy in terms of metadata. COCA, on the other hand, currently has more than 180,000 texts and the 400-million-word COHA historical corpus has more than 100,000 texts.[6] Even if COHA is 99.9 percent accurate in terms of metadata, there are potentially 50 or 100 texts that might have the wrong date, title, author, or genre classification. If one is researching the very first occurrence of a word or phrase or a

[6] COHA = *Corpus of Historical American English* – a historical, "companion" corpus for COCA; see Davies 2012a, 2012b, forthcoming.

construction with just 5–10 tokens, then even one text with the wrong metadata can cause serious problems. But in the case of a construction with 700 or 1,000 tokens, then 99.9 percent accuracy in metadata (with perhaps one errant token) should be sufficient.

Consider also word-level annotation, such as part-of-speech tagging. Suppose that we want to study the use of *for* as a conjunction (*, for had we known that . . .*). As Hundt and Leech (2012) point out, there are few enough tokens in the Brown Corpus (just 121 in all) that researchers have been able to manually examine each one of these to check the PoS tagging, and we see a clear decrease in *for* as a conjunction over time. COCA, on the other hand, has about 16,500 tokens of *for* that have been tagged as a conjunction and COHA has another 80,000 tokens for the period from the 1810s to the 1980s, which is far too many to examine manually.

And yet because of the sheer number of tokens, I would argue, in this particular case we can still have confidence in the data. Consider Figures 1.1 and 1.2 which show nicely the decrease in *for* as a conjunction from the 1810s to the 2000s (COHA)[7] and then in the 1990s to the 2000s (COCA).[8]

In nearly every decade in COHA since the 1890s, *for* as a conjunction is less frequent than the preceding decade. And in COCA, it has decreased in every five-year period since 1990, and the decrease is still ongoing (as of 2012). So in this particular case, where Hundt and Leech (2012) suggested that there might be a problem with large corpora, it looks as though the large corpus works quite well. Further discussion and examples of other phenomena are addressed in Davies (2012b).

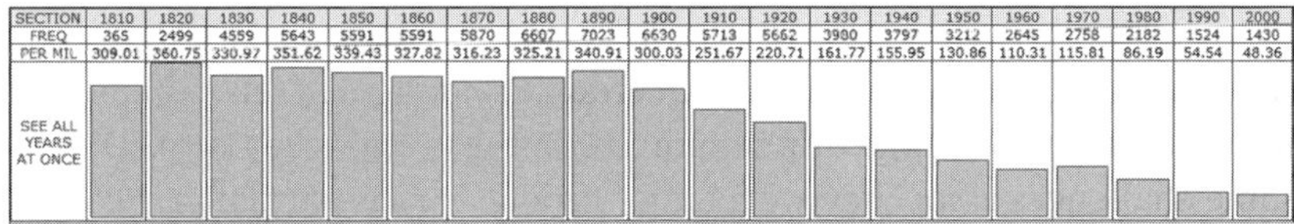

SECTION 1810 1820 1830 1840 1850 1860 1870 1880 1890 1900 1910 1920 1930 1940 1950 1960 1970 1980 1990 2000
FREQ 365 2499 4559 5643 5591 5591 5870 6607 7023 6630 5713 5662 3980 3797 3212 2645 2758 2182 1524 1430
PER MIL 309.01 360.75 330.97 351.62 339.43 327.82 316.23 325.21 340.91 300.03 251.67 220.71 161.77 155.95 130.86 110.31 115.81 86.19 54.54 48.36
SEE ALL YEARS AT ONCE

Figure 1.1 Decrease in *for* (as conjunction in COHA), 1810s–2000s

SPOKEN	FICTION	MAGAZINE	NEWSPAPER	ACADEMIC	1990-1994	1995-1999	2000-2004	2005-2009	2010-2012
2013	5917	3293	2151	3124	4209	3804	3570	3290	1625
21.06	65.43	34.46	23.45	34.30	40.47	36.77	34.68	32.24	31.30

Figure 1.2 Decrease in *for* (as conjunction in COCA), 1990s–2012

[7] See http://corpus.byu.edu/coha/?c=coha&q=24684721

[8] See http://corpus.byu.edu/coca/?c=coca&q=24684733

There are of course additional questions, such as whether recall is as good as precision - since, by definition, we would have to manually look through large masses of (initially) incorrectly tagged tokens to improve precision. In addition, although precision may be 99 percent or higher in the case of *for* as a conjunction, there are undoubtedly other cases where POS tagging is more problematic. What is probably needed is a systematic study of accuracy of POS tagging for a wide range of phenomena in a number of (otherwise similar) small and large corpora, to determine just how much of an issue this might be.

4 Text archives and the Web[9]

Based on our analysis in the preceding section, it might appear that "bigger is always better." Of course, this is not the case. We have already discussed some of the challenges inherent in the creation of large corpora, in terms of accurate metadata and word-level annotation. In this section, we will consider several types of resources that dwarf traditional corpora in terms of their size, but which have limited use in researching many of the phenomena presented above in Table 1.1.

As an introduction to this section, we should remember that the usefulness of a corpus for end users is a function of at least

text (e.g. sentences and paragraphs in the corpus) +
annotation (e.g. document and word-level) +
architecture and interface

Just because a corpus is larger (number of words of text), it may have limited use if it is not annotated for parts of speech, or if the architecture is weak, or if the interface does not allow a wide range of linguistically relevant queries.

In this section, we will consider three examples of text archives - Lexis-Nexis (representing a wide range of similar text archives, such as ProQuest or EBSCO archives, other newspaper archives, or archives like Literature Online or Project Gutenberg), the Web (via Google), and Google Books. Table 1.3 shows how well these different resources do as far as allowing for the different types of research. Note that the checkmark in parentheses means that the search is probably only possible with (often significant) post-processing; i.e. it is not possible via the standard Web interface.

[9] In this section, we will discuss Web *as* Corpus, rather than Web *for* Corpus – an important discussion that is considered in some detail in Fletcher (2011). In Section 5, we will discuss Web *for* corpus.

Table 1.3 *Phenomena that can be researched with three text archives / Web*

		Lexis-Nexis	Web (via Google)	Google Books
1	Lexical: individual	(✓)	(✓)	(✓)
2	Lexical: word lists			
3	Morphology: substrings			
4	Morphology: compare forms	(✓)	(✓)	(✓)
5	Syntax: high frequency	(✓)	(✓)	(✓)
6	Syntax: low frequency	(✓)	(✓)	(✓)
7	Phraseology: words	(✓)		
8	Phraseology: constructions	(✓)	(✓)	(✓)
9	Semantics: collocates			
10	Semantics: prosody			

4.1 Lexical

There is no way to create frequency listing from text archives, at least via the standard interfaces for these resources. Nevertheless, with all three types of resources, it is certainly possible to see the frequency of an exact word or phrase, and of course the number of tokens will typically be much larger than with a 100- or 500-million-word corpus. For example, the adjectives in Table 1.4 – which shows their frequency in these text archives[10] – occur 20 times in COCA.

For some lexically oriented searches, there is really no alternative to an extremely large text archives, because of their sheer size. As can be seen, even COCA provides only relatively meager data for the words shown in Table 1.4. And this is even more pronounced for still-infrequent neologisms, where there may not be any tokens at all in a well-structured, half-billion-word corpus.

Nevertheless, there are a number of problems with the figures from text archives, shown in Table 1.4. First, in some cases the interface blocks access to more than a certain number of hits and it will not show the total number, as in the case of words with a frequency of 990–999 in Lexis-Nexis. Second, in text archives the numbers typically refer to the number of texts containing the word, rather than the total number of tokens. Third, as Kilgarriff (2007) notes, we need to be very skeptical of the numbers from (at least) Google. In the case of phrases, particularly, the numbers can be off by several orders of magnitude.[11] Fourth, in the case of Google Books, at present it is difficult to see (or extract) the number of tokens for a given word or phrase (see Figure 1.4). The results are displayed primarily as a "picture" of the frequency over time, and the actual raw number of tokens is deeply embedded in the HTML code for the web page.

[10] The average for these ten adjectives will of course be different from that of another set of adjectives, but it nonetheless lets us get a general sense of these resources. The size (lower row) in each case is calculated by finding the ratio with COCA, where the word occurs 20 times in 450 million words. We know that Google Books (English) is actually about 250 billion words, so the 232-billion-word estimate there is fairly accurate.

[11] For example, a search of the phrase *would be taken for a* shows 1,610,000 hits in Google, but after paging through the results, one finds that there are actually only 528 hits (accessed February 2013).

Table 1.4 *Frequency of very infrequent words in BNC, COCA, and three text archives / Web*

	BNC	COCA	Lexis-Nexis	Google Books	Web (Google)
accentual	19	20	168	26,155	244,000
biggish	40	20	999	4,577	504,000
coloristic	0	20	992	6,853	141,000
consummatory	1	20	71	25,710	109,000
disassociative	0	20	580	1,108	178,000
folkloristic	0	20	542	11,209	195,000
freckly	6	20	999	1,178	505,000
ivied	1	20	776	13,166	187,000
Kennedyesque	2	20	987	512	62,100
unbruised	3	20	995	3,240	86,500
Average	7.2	20	711	10,355	221,160
Size (??)	100 m	450 m	15 billion	232 billion	5 trillion

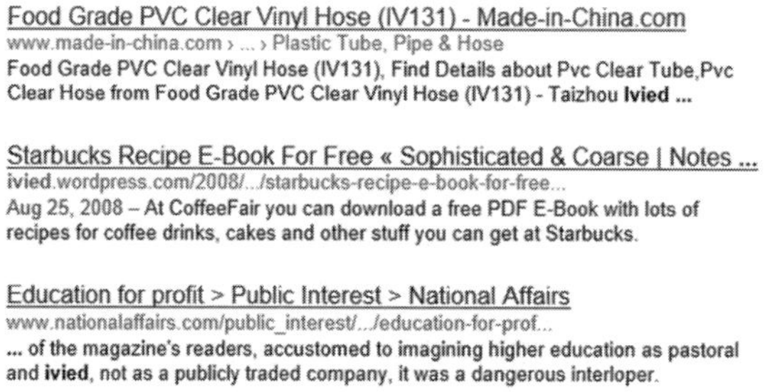

Food Grade PVC Clear Vinyl Hose (IV131) - Made-in-China.com
www.made-in-china.com › ... › Plastic Tube, Pipe & Hose
Food Grade PVC Clear Vinyl Hose (IV131), Find Details about Pvc Clear Tube,Pvc Clear Hose from Food Grade PVC Clear Vinyl Hose (IV131) - Taizhou **Ivied** ...

Starbucks Recipe E-Book For Free « Sophisticated & Coarse | Notes ...
ivied.wordpress.com/2008/.../starbucks-recipe-e-book-for-free...
Aug 25, 2008 – At CoffeeFair you can download a free PDF E-Book with lots of recipes for coffee drinks, cakes and other stuff you can get at Starbucks.

Education for profit > Public Interest > National Affairs
www.nationalaffairs.com/public_interest/.../education-for-prof...
... of the magazine's readers, accustomed to imagining higher education as pastoral and **ivied**, not as a publicly traded company, it was a dangerous interloper.

Figure 1.3 "Snippet" view in Google (Web)

Another challenge with text archives is working with the often limited interface. For example, consider the output from Google in Figure 1.3 (Lexis-Nexis and Google Books have similar displays). Unlike the interfaces for many structured corpora, where it is possible to display nicely sorted KWIC (Keyword in Context) lines, in the case of text archives one would have to write a script to extract the data in a usable format.

4.2 Morphology

Via the standard web interfaces, it is typically not possible to search by substrings. It is however, possible to compare competing word forms, such as *HAVE* + *proven* / *proved*. In Lexis-Nexis, this is straightforward. In Google (Web), one must remember that the frequency of strings can be wildly inaccurate (see note 11), so the comparison of these two numbers can also be very inaccurate. Finally, in Google Books it is possible to compare alternate forms, as in Figure 1.4. But again the actual raw numbers are very hard to extract (they are displayed primarily as cryptic "percentage" figures, as shown in Figure 1.4).

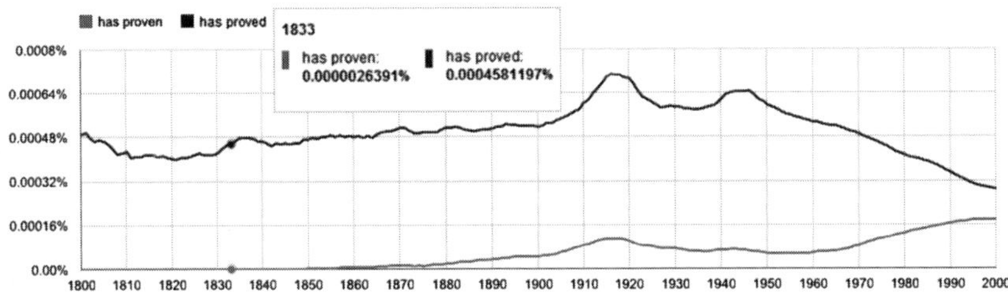

Figure 1.4 Frequency chart in Google Books

4.3 Syntax

Syntactically oriented queries present a real challenge for the often simple interfaces of text archives. Take for example the high-frequency *be* passive or the less frequent case of verbal subcategorization [*to* V / V-*ing*]. Text archives typically do not allow searching by part of speech (or even by lemma), so we would need to search for hundreds or thousands of matching strings one by one, e.g. *start to see*, *started to see*, *started to notice*, etc. One option would be to write a script to serially carry out many searches and then store the results for each search. But such queries are certainly not possible for most users, natively via the interface.

4.4 Phraseology

In cases like *true feelings* or *naked eye*, again one could write a script to parse through hundreds of "snippet" entries (as in Figure 1.3 above), and then store the snippets (and the accompanying metadata) in a KWIC format that can be analyzed with another piece of software. But even in Lexis-Nexis, which has the best KWIC-oriented display, it is cumbersome at best to try to use the output from the web interface, without additional processing. In cases like the "*way* construction" (e.g. *pushed his way through the crowd*) or the "*into* V-*ing*" construction (e.g. *he talked her into staying*), one is faced with the same problem as with the syntactically oriented searches in Section 4.3 above. Users would have to write a program to serially input thousands or tens of thousands of exact strings (e.g. *talk her into going*, *talk him into staying*, *coax Fred into doing*, etc.), and then store the results.

4.5 Semantics

In order to extract the collocates using the native interface for these text archives, one would (again) have to write a program to parse through the simple "snippet" output and save each snippet, and then post-process these data to extract collocates. However, even this would probably not be possible, since most text archives severely limit the number of "snippets" for a given search (e.g. 1,000 in Lexis-Nexis, Google (Web), and Google Books). With only 1,000 tokens per word or phrase, it is impossible to create a robust dataset to extract collocates.

4.6 Summary

Text archives are initially quite appealing, because of their sheer size. For certain types of lexically oriented queries (e.g. very low-frequency words or neologisms), they may be the only option, and they may also be sufficient for comparisons of alternating word forms (e.g. *have* + *proven/proved*, or *he snuck/sneaked*). But for virtually all other types of searches, the simplistic interface simply cannot generate the desired data, without significant post-processing.

5 Hybrid "corpora": text archives + full-featured architecture and interface

We saw in Section 3 that size is crucial: small 2–4-million-word corpora are at times limited in terms of the range of data that they can provide. But as we have seen in Section 4, size is not everything – most text archives have such a simplistic interface that they also are very limited in the range of queries that they offer. As we will see in this section, the best solution may be to take the texts from a text archive or the Web (containing billions of words of data), and then combine this with a robust corpus architecture.

As examples of this "hybrid" approach, in this section we will consider two sets of corpora. First, we will look at the corpora from Sketch Engine (www.sketchengine.co.uk). All of the corpora in Sketch Engine that are publicly accessible and that are more than a billion words in size are based on web pages, and there are currently three corpora of English that contain more than a billion words of text. Second, we will consider the different "corpora" that are available from googlebooks.byu.edu, which are based on the n-grams from books.google.com/ngrams/, and which range in size from 45 to 155 billion words.

As Table 1.5 shows, both of these hybrid corpora offer a wide range of searches.

Table 1.5 *Phenomena that can be researched with two "hybrid" corpora*

		Sketch Engine	googlebooks.byu.edu
1	Lexical: individual	✓	✓
2	Lexical: word lists	✓	✓
3	Morphology: substrings	✓	✓
4	Morphology: compare forms	✓	✓
5	Syntax: high frequency	✓	(✓)
6	Syntax: low frequency	✓	(✓)
7	Phraseology: words	✓	
8	Phraseology: constructions	✓	(✓)
9	Semantics: collocates	✓	(✓)
10	Semantics: prosody	✓	(✓)

5.1 Lexical

Both corpora allow users to search for a particular word or phrase, and to see the frequency of the word in the different sections of the corpus. For example, Figures 1.5 and 1.6 show the frequency of *tidy* in different web pages in the 3.2-billion-word enTenTen08 corpus from Sketch Engine (Figure 1.5) and in each decade from the 1810s to the 2000s in the 155-billion-word American English dataset from Google Books (BYU) (Figure 1.6).

5.2 Morphology

With both corpora, it is possible to generate word lists, including words that contain particular substrings. For example, the common words ending in **ism* in the Sketch Engine enTenTen08 corpus (about 3 billion words, from web pages) are *terrorism* (126,534 tokens), *mechanism* (95,034), *criticism* (92,190), *capitalism* (47,624), *journalism* (44,863), *racism* (43,451), *tourism* (37,552), *baptism* (33,774), *socialism* (28,717), and *organism* (23,629). In the Google Books (BYU) corpora, we can also see the distribution by decade (Figure 1.7).

Since we can easily search for strings in these corpora (see Section 5.1 above), we can also easily compare word forms, e.g. *he sneaked/snuck*. Figure 1.8 shows the frequency by decade in Google Books (BYU) (note the increasing use of *snuck* over time).

	doc.url	Freq	Rel [%]
p/n	http://www.cs.yale.edu/homes/dvm/papers/owl-s-gram.html	44	4933.1
p/n	http://www.irt.org/articles/js192/index.htm	37	6214.4
p/n	http://www.geocities.com/terry_teague/tidy.html	31	25052.3
p/n	http://us.geocities.com/terry_teague/tidyhist.html	26	13813.6
p/n	http://itre.cis.upenn.edu/~myl/languagelog/archives/2005_03.html	22	348.8
p/n	http://www.chami.com/html-kit/plugins/feedback/default.html	17	1678.9
p/n	http://www.irt.org/articles/js138/index.htm	16	5970.0

Figure 1.5 Lexical frequency: Sketch Engine

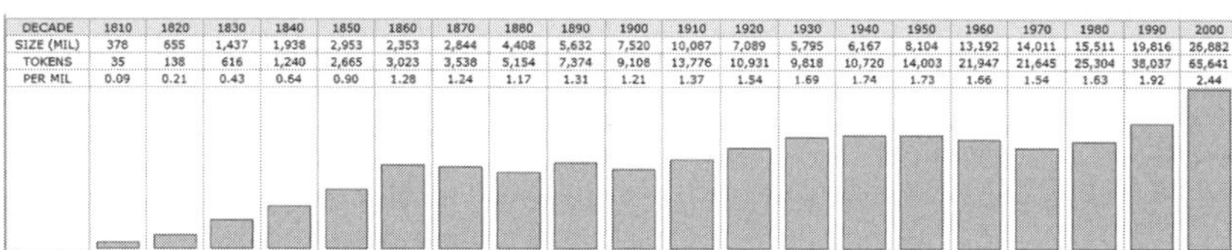

DECADE	1810	1820	1830	1840	1850	1860	1870	1880	1890	1900	1910	1920	1930	1940	1950	1960	1970	1980	1990	2000
SIZE (MIL)	378	655	1,437	1,938	2,953	2,353	2,844	4,408	5,632	7,520	10,087	7,089	5,795	6,167	8,104	13,192	14,011	15,511	19,816	26,882
TOKENS	35	138	616	1,240	2,665	3,023	3,538	5,154	7,374	9,108	13,776	10,931	9,818	10,720	14,003	21,947	21,645	25,304	38,037	65,641
PER MIL	0.09	0.21	0.43	0.64	0.90	1.28	1.24	1.17	1.31	1.21	1.37	1.54	1.69	1.74	1.73	1.66	1.54	1.63	1.92	2.44

Figure 1.6 Lexical frequency: Google Books (BYU)

	WORD(S)	CHARTS	TOTAL	1810	1820	1830	1840	1850	1860	1870	1880	1890	1900	1910	1920	1930	1940	1950	1960
1	criticism	G B	5426220	5120	7951	17160	26366	42630	39076	52769	105656	169341	247386	346591	280083	245163	240566	333238	618744
2	mechanism	G B	4885909	1327	2517	7553	9308	15781	11640	19417	34598	52826	84166	177370	145663	130122	168694	271249	501658
3	organism	G B	2756106	25	70	395	4646	14857	16213	31312	56855	97622	159625	273762	177318	136206	133460	205589	318576
4	metabolism	G B	2071179	5			5		2	89	2054	7616	40725	99471	67019	53494	61063	105554	199693
5	Judaism	G B	1460561	910	1163	3461	7539	9545	9986	14113	21564	46153	36752	50449	30322	36567	44855	81562	131255
6	capitalism	G B	1427387	1		2	18	5	3	9	522	1628	7820	22454	29741	74921	75324	72496	155756
7	baptism	G B	1369446	19435	16361	49645	85027	91912	51318	69473	70753	73932	80670	80490	38122	28353	34589	51327	87642
8	socialism	G B	1181815	5	3	3	258	917	666	1262	7143	21972	33349	55803	44682	50694	61740	82035	187268
9	patriotism	G B	1175726	5406	10802	21882	31023	43202	42091	34389	54712	74093	93479	137359	83007	56389	48937	49261	94320

Figure 1.7 Word forms (**ism*) in Google Books (BYU)

	WORD(S)	CHARTS	TOTAL	1810	1820	1830	1840	1850	1860	1870	1880	1890	1900	1910	1920	1930	1940	1950	1960	1970	1980	1990	2000
1	he sneaked	G B	7483		10	23	76	84	106	73	148	297	325	522	372	385	441	455	599	572	692	961	1342
2	he snuck	G B	1734								2	2		5	5	27	22	14	32	72	156	381	1016

Figure 1.8 Morphological variation in Google Books (BYU)

5.3 Syntax

The Sketch Engine corpora are tagged with TreeTagger and they are searched via Corpus Query Language (CQL), a widely used corpus architecture and search engine. This allows us to find constructions like the [*END up* V-*ing*] construction (e.g. *you'll end up paying too much*).[12]

Google Books (BYU) is a bit more problematic, in terms of syntactic searches. The version of the Google Books n-grams that it uses does not include part of speech or lemma. As a result, in a search like "[*end*] *up* [v?g*]," it creates the search "on the fly," based on COCA data. It finds all forms of the lemma *end* from COCA, followed by the word *up*, followed by any word in COCA that is tagged [v?g*] (e.g. *watching, knowing*) at least 50 percent of the time (50 percent is the default value, and it can be any number 1–100). Nevertheless, for most queries this works quite well. For example, Figure 1.9 shows the first entries for "[*end*] *up* [v?g*]," and these 400,000+ tokens are retrieved from the 155 billion words (*n*-grams) in about two seconds.

5.4 Phraseology

In just a couple of seconds, Sketch Engine can provide users with concordance lines for words, phrases, or even syntactic strings, which can be re-sorted, thinned, and so on. Google Books (BYU) cannot generate these concordance lines, because it is based just on n-grams. The actual text is in the Google Books "snippets" (e.g. Figure 1.3), and users would have the same problems extracting data for concordance lines from these snippets as they would in using Web data generally, as was discussed above in Section 4.1. Sketch Engine can search quite nicely for the patterns in which constructions occur – the same as it does for advanced syntactic searches generally, as seen in Section 5.3 above. For example, for the [VERB NP *into* V-*ing*] construction, Sketch Engine finds about 3,900 tokens (Figure 1.10),[13] and Google Books (BYU) finds about 30,200 tokens[14] (Figure 1.11).[15]

	WORD(S)	CHARTS	TOTAL	1810	1820	1830	1840	1850	1860	1870	1880	1890	1900	1910	1920	1930	1940	1950	1960	1970	1980	1990	2000
1	end up being	G B	33429								1		1	2		10	45	170	680	1955	3874	8418	18273
2	ended up being	G B	20784													1	15	46	223	840	1897	5056	12706
3	ends up being	G B	13223														2	63	256	685	1586	3477	7154
4	end up doing	G B	11205								1				4	6	25	86	307	791	1466	2926	5593
5	end up having	G B	10174														15	52	209	579	1155	2511	5653
6	end up paying	G B	7963									1					7	35	141	617	1013	2004	4145
7	ended up doing	G B	7340													4	12	48	156	438	888	1909	3885
8	ended up having	G B	7318													17	9	16	84	276	731	1879	4306
9	end up getting	G B	7114												1		7	39	126	398	796	1741	4006
10	ended up getting	G B	6193														5	16	58	215	572	1568	3759

Figure 1.9 Probabilistic POS tagging in Google Books (BYU)

[12] [lemma = "end"] [word = "up"] [tag = "VVG"], which yields about 52,000 tokens.

[13] [tag = "VV."] [tag = "PP"] [word = "into"] [tag = "VVG"]

[14] Google Books (BYU) is based on the Google Books n-grams, which only include n-grams that occur 40 times or more in the corpus. This creates complications for a search like *[vv*] [p*] into [v?g*]*, where because of all of the different verbs, the vast majority of unique strings (e.g. *they bamboozled us into recapping*) will not occur 40 times or more, and will therefore not appear in the "corpus."

[15] [vv*] [p*] into [v?g*]

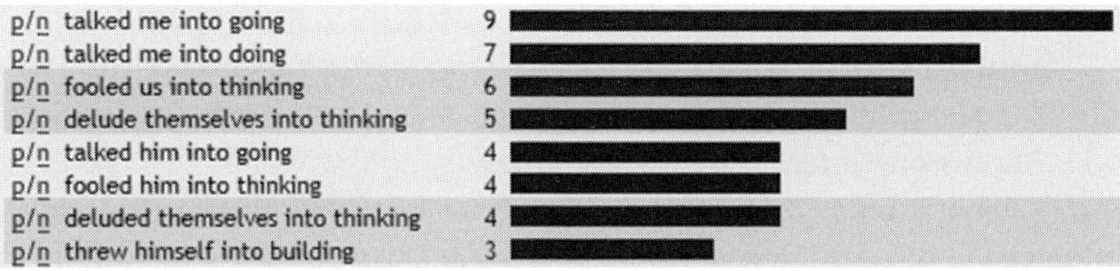

Figure 1.10 Syntactic searches in Sketch Engine

	WORD(S)	CHARTS	TOTAL	1810	1820	1830	1840	1850	1860	1870	1880	1890	1900	1910	1920	1930	1940	1950	1960	1970	1980	1990	2000
6	delude ourselves into believing	G B	616							4	3	9	9	21	17	24	29	40	72	90	60	130	108
7	talk me into going	G B	519												6	9	14	21	30	35	71	162	171
8	talk him into going	G B	491										4	2	2	12	18	20	40	46	62	104	181
9	delude himself into believing	G B	468						2				19	18	27	24	43	41	71	70	47	40	66
10	resolves itself into finding	G B	443			1			2	1	15	28	36	99	68	38	45	39	39	20	9	2	1
11	deceive themselves into believing	G B	430			7		4		2	2	27	11	34	29	22	28	7	23	27	59	77	71
12	brings them into being	G B	384			2		2	3	8	7	10	4	11	8	17	22	29	48	42	49	66	56
13	deceive ourselves into believing	G B	374				1				1	6	7	47	24	12	21	24	50	36	27	55	63
14	talk him into coming	G B	358				1								1	1	1	13	20	29	47	89	156

Figure 1.11 Syntactic searches in Google Books (BYU)

5.5 Semantics

As we saw above in Section 3.5, collocates are extremely sensitive to corpus size. Table 1.6 shows the number of collocates (with a minimum lemma frequency of at least three tokens) for four different searches.

It is interesting, however, that for some words at least, there appears to be a "diminishing return" with corpus size. Although the number of collocates between the BNC and COCA (4–5 times as large as the BNC) is striking, in a corpus like enTenTen12 from Sketch Engine (which is 25 times as large as COCA), for some words (e.g. *nibble* or *serenely*) there is not nearly as significant a yield in collocates. We will discuss some possible explanations for this in the following section, as we discuss the composition of the corpora.

Table 1.6 *Number of collocates in different corpora*

		coll:span	Brown	BNC	COCA	SketchEng[b]	GB: BYU
Genre[a]	node word	Size	1 m	100 m	450 m	11.2 b	155 b
FIC, ACAD	*riddle* (N)	J: 1L/0R	0	0	15	228	188
FIC, MAG	*nibble* (V)	N: 0L/4R	0	13	99	~90[c]	~58[d]
MAG	*crumbled* (J)	N: 0L/1R	0	1	28	115	92
FIC	*serenely* (R)	V: 3L/3R	0	4	28	36	54

[a] This is the genre of COCA in which the word is the most frequent, which ends of being important as we talk about genre balance in Section 6.
[b] The Sketch Engine *enTenTen12* corpus – currently 11,192,000,000 words in size
[c] Sketch Engine groups collocates by grammatical relation, so it separates for example direct object (*nibble the cheese*) from object of preposition (*nibble on the cheese*). We have done our best to group the collocates from different relations and calculate their total frequency, but 90 is an approximate number.
[d] Collocates in Google Books (BYU) work differently than the other BYU corpora, like COCA or COHA, since Google Books is based on *n*-grams. As a result, these numbers are an approximate. Remember also the issue with the 40 token threshold, explained in note 14.

6 Accounting for and describing variation: genre, historical, dialect, and demographic

6.1 The importance of genre variation

Hundreds of studies over the past decade or two have shown the crucial importance of genre in describing language. Perhaps the best example of this is Biber *et al.* (1998), which shows how very different the language is in different genres – in terms of syntax and morphology (with somewhat less attention given in the book to lexis and semantics).

We will here provide just a few pieces of data from COCA – a robust, well-balanced corpus – to show the importance of genre. First, consider Figure 1.12, which shows verbs that are much more common in fiction (left) than newspapers (right). Imagine that we had a corpus composed only of newspapers (which are very easy to obtain). In this case, words like those on the left would be almost completely absent in the corpus, while those on the right would be massively over-represented.

Figures 1.13–1.17 show extreme variation between genres in COCA for other phenomena as well. Figure 1.13 shows how much more common *-al* adjectives are in academic (adjectives that are at least ten letters in length). Figures 1.14–1.17 show a number of grammatical phenomena where there are significant variations between genres: preposition stranding with *to* (e.g. *the man I was talking to*), the *get* passive (e.g. *John got fired from his job*), the quotative *like* (e.g. *and I'm like, what's the problem?*), and *real* instead of *really* before adjectives (e.g. *he was real sick*).

The important differences between genres extend to meaning as well. For example, Figure 1.18 shows collocates that are much more common

SEC 1: 90,429,400 WORDS

	WORD/PHRASE	TOKENS 1	TOKENS 2	PM 1	PM 2	RATIO
1	FUCK	984	0	10.88	0.00	1,088.14
2	PISS	389	8	4.30	0.09	49.32
3	WHIMPER	90	2	1.00	0.02	45.64
4	HISS	84	3	0.93	0.03	28.40
5	SHRIEK	114	5	1.26	0.05	23.12
6	FIDGET	65	3	0.72	0.03	21.98
7	SNORE	86	4	0.95	0.04	21.81
8	GLARE	170	8	1.88	0.09	21.55
9	THROB	101	5	1.12	0.05	20.49
10	SOB	238	12	2.63	0.13	20.12
11	UNDRESS	213	11	2.36	0.12	19.64
12	TREMBLE	485	26	5.36	0.28	18.92
13	PEE	465	26	5.14	0.28	18.14
14	CRUMPLE	52	3	0.58	0.03	17.58
15	UNZIP	67	4	0.74	0.04	16.99

SEC 2: 91,717,452 WORDS

	WORD/PHRASE	TOKENS 2	TOKENS 1	PM 2	PM 1	RATIO
1	RE-SIGN	201	1	2.19	0.01	198.18
2	REFINANCE	214	3	2.33	0.03	70.33
3	REZONE	62	0	0.68	0.00	67.60
4	BLITZ	53	0	0.58	0.00	57.79
5	REDEVELOP	92	2	1.00	0.02	45.35
6	TELEVISE	89	2	0.97	0.02	43.88
7	OUTPERFORM	79	2	0.86	0.02	38.95
8	OVERCOOK	71	2	0.77	0.02	35.00
9	RESTRUCTURE	278	8	3.03	0.09	34.26
10	PRIVATIZE	169	5	1.84	0.06	33.33
11	DEREGULATE	61	2	0.67	0.02	30.07
12	DIVERSIFY	263	9	2.87	0.10	28.81
13	RETOOL	82	3	0.89	0.03	26.95
14	LEGALIZE	147	6	1.60	0.07	24.16
15	TOUT	138	6	1.50	0.07	22.68

Figure 1.12 Lexis of fiction and newspapers in COCA

SPOKEN	FICTION	MAGAZINE	NEWSPAPER	ACADEMIC
142906	54665	234038	193870	642274
1,495.38	604.50	2,449.15	2,113.77	7,052.83

Figure 1.13 **al*.[j*]

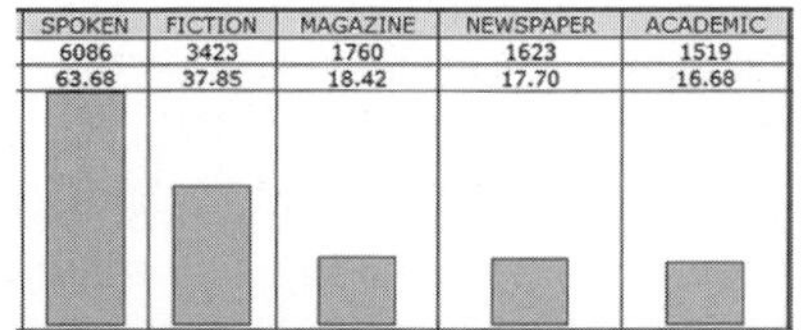

SPOKEN
FICTION
MAGAZINE
NEWSPAPER
ACADEMIC
6086
3423
1760
1623
1519
63.68
37.85
18.42
17.70
16.68

Figure 1.14 [vv*] *to*

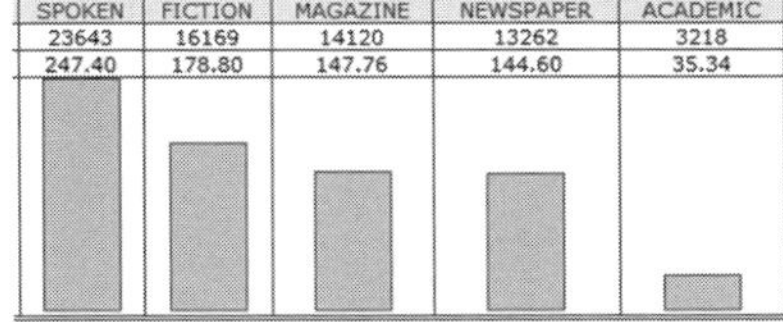

SPOKEN FICTION MAGAZINE NEWSPAPER ACADEMIC
23643 16169 14120 13262 3218
247.40 178.80 147.76 144.60 35.34

Figure 1.15 *get* passive

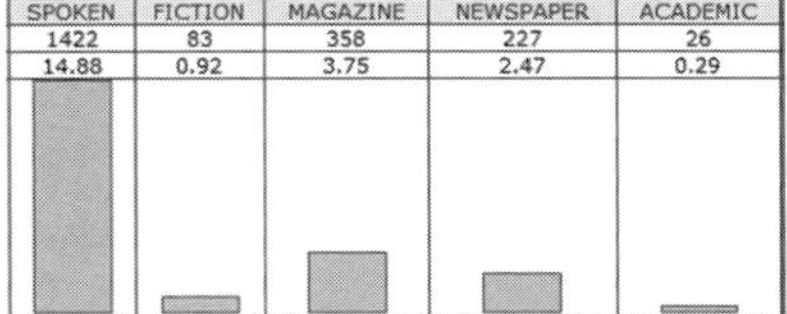

Figure 1.16 quotative *like*: [c*] [p*] [*be*] *like*,|

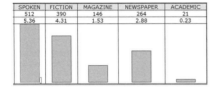

SPOKEN	FICTION	MAGAZINE	NEWSPAPER	ACADEMIC
512	390	146	264	21
5.36	4.31	1.53	2.88	0.23

Figure 1.17 [*be*] *real* [j*] [y*]

SEC 1: 90,429,400 WORDS

	WORD/PHRASE	TOKENS 1	TOKENS 2	PM 1	PM 2	RATIO
1	STRAIGHT	48	0	0.53	0.00	53.08
2	HEAVY	42	1	0.46	0.01	42.60
3	STRAIGHTER	32	0	0.35	0.00	35.39
4	UNCOMFORTABLE	32	0	0.35	0.00	35.39
5	NEAREST	32	0	0.35	0.00	35.39
6	OPPOSITE	30	0	0.33	0.00	33.18
7	HIGH-BACKED	65	2	0.72	0.02	32.96
8	HARD	65	2	0.72	0.02	32.96

SEC 2: 91,717,452 WORDS

	WORD/PHRASE	TOKENS 2	TOKENS 1	PM 2	PM 1	RATIO
1	VICE	59	1	0.64	0.01	58.17
2	DEMOCRATIC	27	1	0.29	0.01	26.62
3	NATIONAL	18	0	0.20	0.00	19.63
4	HONORARY	18	2	0.20	0.02	8.87
5	PAST	12	2	0.13	0.02	5.92
6	AMERICAN	10	3	0.11	0.03	3.29
7	ELECTRIC	112	86	1.22	0.95	1.28
8	ENDOWED	10	9	0.11	0.10	1.10

Figure 1.18 Collocates of *chair* in fiction and newspapers in COCA

with *chair* in fiction than in newspapers (left) and those that are much more common in newspapers than in fiction (right). Again, if our corpus is composed of one easily obtainable genre (like newspapers), we see only one very narrow "slice" of the language.

Even more than with newspapers, it is very easy to create extremely large corpora that are based solely on web pages. It is no surprise that virtually all of the corpora over 100 million words in size in Sketch Engine, for example, are based exclusively on web pages. But the question is – how representative are web pages of the full range of variation in the language?

Consider Table 1.7, which compares the lexis of the "traditional" genres to the web-only corpora. In this case, we compare word frequency in COCA and the BNC to the 2-billion-word *Corpus of Global Web-based English* (GloWbE),[16] which is just based (like Sketch Engine) on web pages. Here we see how many words in a 100,000 word list of English[17] have roughly the same normalized frequency in the (entire) GloWbE as in different genres of COCA and the BNC. For example, there are 13,386 words (from among the 100,000 total in the list) whose normalized frequency in COCA newspapers is roughly the same as that of GloWbE – i.e. the ratio is between 0.8 and 1.2.

[16] http://corpus2.byu.edu/web/ [17] www.wordfrequency.info

Table 1.7 *Similarity of lexis in web-based GloWbE and genres in COCA and BNC*

COCA	No. words	BNC	No. words
NEWSPAPER	13,836	MAGAZINE	8,743
MAGAZINE	13,349	NEWSPAPER	8,677
ACADEMIC	11,828	ACADEMIC	7,032
SPOKEN	10,793	FICTION	6,335
FICTION	8,804	SPOKEN	4,667

As can be seen, at least in terms of lexis, the web-only corpus is most like newspapers and magazines, but "web" lexis does a much poorer job of representing the lexis of the academic genre, or especially fiction and spoken. This may be why at times even very large web-only corpora do not improve significantly on the data from a well-balanced corpus (like COCA or the BNC). As we saw in Table 1.6, even a corpus like the 11.2-billion-word Sketch Engine *enTenTen12* corpus (25 times as large as COCA) provides only minimally better data for words that are most common in genres like fiction (e.g. *nibble* or *serenely*).

If we compare certain morphological and syntactic phenomena in the web only corpora to more balanced corpora, the situation becomes even more confusing. For example, the normalized frequency of *-al* adjectives[18] is 2,244 per million words in GloWbE-US,[19] which places it between COCA magazines and newspapers (see Figure 1.13 above). But the normalized frequency of the *get* passive ([get] [vvn*]; *John got fired last week*) is (at 239 tokens per million words) the most similar to spoken (see Figure 1.15 above). And strangely enough, the normalized frequency of *real* + ADJ ([be] real [j*] [y*]; *he was real smart*) is 0.77 in GloWbE-US, which is most like COCA Academic (see Figure 1.17). As we see, depending on the particular phenomena that we are studying, the web corpora are "all over the map" in terms of which of the "traditional" genres they best represent. As a result, it would be difficult to know ahead of time – for any particular phenomena – how representative of other genres a web-only corpus would be.

In summary, virtually all corpora with more than 1 billion words are composed of just web pages. But these large web page-based corpora do not represent particularly well the full range of variation that we see in genre-balanced corpora like the 100-million-word BNC, the 440-million-word *Bank of English*, or the 450-million-word (and growing) *Corpus of Contemporary American English* – which is currently the largest publicly available, genre-balanced corpus of English.

[18] *-al* adjectives that are at least ten letters long, e.g. *environmental* or *educational*.

[19] The 400 million words from the United States in the 2-billion-word GloWbE corpus.

6.2 Other types of variation

Besides genre-based variation, other important types of variation are change over time, variation between dialects, and variation at the level of the individual speaker.

In terms of historical variation, I have suggested at some length in other studies that perhaps the only historical corpus of English that is currently available, which can account for a full range of lexical, morphological, phraseological, syntactic, and semantic variation over the past 200 years (e.g. items 1–10 of Table 1.1) is the 400-million-word *Corpus of Historical American English* (COHA; see Davies 2012a, 2012b, forthcoming). I have also suggested that for very recent changes in English, the only reliable monitor corpus – which maintains the same genre balance from year to year (a crucial factor, which virtually all previous studies seem to have overlooked) and which is large enough to study a wide range of phenomena – is the *Corpus of Contemporary American English* (COCA; see Davies 2011).

In terms of dialectal variation, the International Corpus of English (Greenbaum 1996; Hundt and Gut 2012) can describe the range of variation about as well as other 1-million-word corpora, as we discussed in Section 3. The 1.9-billion-word *Corpus of Global Web-based English* (GloWbE) can account for the full range of linguistic phenomena shown in Table 1.1, since it uses the same architecture and interface as COCA and COHA. This includes queries that show variation between dialects, and which allow us to compare one dialect (or set of dialects) to another. But we must remember that this corpus – as is the case with virtually all corpora of its size – is based solely on web pages from these twenty countries – with the accompanying limitations discussed in Section 6.1 above. One other option is to use a corpus interface like that of the BYU corpora, which allow side-by-side comparisons of a wide range of phenomena in corpora from different countries (e.g. BNC for British English, COCA for American English, and the Strathy Corpus for Canadian English).[20]

Finally, in terms of demographic variation – variation at the level of the speaker (e.g. gender or age) – the *British National Corpus* is currently the only corpus that was designed, constructed, and annotated in such as way that it is possible to compare at the level of the individual speaker – *and* which is large enough to enable research on the full range of linguistic variation (items 1–10 of Table 1.1). But the degree to which end users can use this information is dependent on the corpus interface for the BNC. BNCweb[21] is currently the best interface for the BNC, in terms of researching demographic variation.[22]

[20] See http://corpus.byu.edu/comparing-corpora.asp for a wide range of side-by-side comparisons of the BNC and COCA, including lexical and syntactic frequency, collocates (to examine semantic contrasts), and so on.

[21] http://bncweb.lancs.ac.uk/ [22] See www.natcorp.ox.ac.uk/docs/URG/BNCdes.html

7 Some concluding remarks (and a crystal ball)

In this introductory chapter on "corpora," rather than attempting to discuss all of the important English corpora that are currently available (an impossible task), we have focused instead on different *types* of corpora (with just a few examples of each), and we have paid particular attention to *general* issues of size (Section 4), architecture (Section 5), and variation (Section 6). We have seen that there are relatively few corpora (perhaps limited to just the BNC, the *Bank of English*, and COCA and COHA) that (1) are large, (2) allow a wide range of searches, and (3) provide data from a wide range of genres.

Even at this level of abstraction, some of what we have considered will still be outdated almost as soon as this chapter published, and much of this will be hopelessly outdated within five to ten years. This is due in part to dramatic changes that I believe are on the verge of taking place, particularly in terms of data from social media. For example, Twitter already provides real-time "fire hose" access to every single tweet[23] – hundreds of millions of words of data each day – and Facebook and other social media sites may soon do so as well.

Imagine the situation five, ten, or twenty years from now, when researchers will be able to download billions of words of data *every day* from Facebook or other social media sites. For each status update or post that comes through, they will have accompanying metadata that show the gender, general age range, and approximate geographical location of the author. Assume further that because of advances in technology, they are able to efficiently process hundreds of billions of words of data at a rate that is hundreds or thousands of times as fast as today. One can therefore imagine a scenario – in the not-too-distant future – in which a researcher can examine the use of a particular word, or phrase, or syntactic construction – virtually in real time, and with incredible detail (gender, age, and location).

For example, researchers could examine two competing syntactic constructions (e.g. +/– *to* with *help: help Mary clean the room, help Mary to clean the room*), and see which of the two is more common in the US or the UK, between men and women, between different age groups, as a function of the embedded verb, or in data from this year compared to data from last year. Even the largest "structured" corpora from the present time (e.g. Sketch Engine corpora, GloWbE, COCA, or the BNC) cannot provide this degree of granularity. And this one example from the domain of syntax can be multiplied endlessly for other variations in syntax, or in lexis, morphology, phraseology, or meaning. At this point, I suspect that many of us will look back with nostalgia on the "quaint" 100- or 500-million-word corpora

[23] See https://dev.twitter.com/docs/streaming-apis/streams/public

that we currently have available, and wonder how we were able do so much with so little.

While this is an admittedly hypothetical scenario, what is probably beyond dispute is that the corpora that will be available to us in a decade or two will be truly revolutionary, at least from our current vantage point. The only question, then, is whether we will take advantage of the new resources that are certain to come our way.

2

Computational tools and methods for corpus compilation and analysis

Paul Rayson

1 Introduction

The growing interest in corpus linguistics methods in the 1970s and 1980s was largely enabled by the increased power of computers and the use of computational methods to store and process language samples. Before this, even simple methods for studying language such as extracting a list of all the different words in a text and their immediate contexts was incredibly time consuming and costly in terms of human effort. Only concordances of books of special importance such as the Qur'an, the Bible, and the works of Shakespeare were made before the twentieth century and required either a large number of scholars or monks or a significant investment in time by a single individual, in some cases more than ten years of their lives. In these days of web search engines and vast quantities of text that is available at our finger tips, the end user would be mildly annoyed if a concordance from a 1-billion-word corpus took more than five seconds to be displayed.

Other text-rich disciplines can trace their origins back to the same computing revolution. Digital humanities scholars cite the work of Roberto Busa working with IBM in 1949, who produced his Index Thomisticus, a computer-generated concordance to the writings of Thomas Aquinas. Similarly, lexicographers in the nineteenth century used millions of handwritten cards or quotation slips, but the field was revolutionized in the 1980s with the creation of machine-readable corpora such as COBUILD and the use of computers for searching and finding patterns in the data.

The survey presented in this chapter was supported by the ESRC Centre for Corpus Approaches to Social Science, ESRC grant reference ES/K002155/1.

This chapter presents an introductory survey of computational tools and methods for corpus construction and analysis. The corpus research process involves three main stages: corpus compilation, annotation, and retrieval (see Rayson 2008). A corpus first needs to be compiled via transcription, scanning, or sampling from online sources. Then, the second stage is annotation, through some combination of manual and automatic methods to add tags, codes, and documentation that identify textual and linguistic characteristics. A snapshot of tools and methods that support the first and second stages of the corpus research process are described in Sections 2.1 and 2.2.

Retrieval tools and methods enable the actual linguistic investigations based on corpora: i.e. frequency analysis, concordances, collocations, keywords and *n*-grams. These tools are introduced in Section 2.3, together with a brief timeline tracing the historical development of retrieval tools and methods and the current focus on web-based interfaces for mega-corpora. Corpus tools and methods are now being applied very widely to historical data, learner language, and online varieties (Usenet, Emails, Blogs, and Microblogs), so I also consider the effect of non-standard or "dirty data" on corpus tools and methods, e.g. where spelling variation affects their robustness. Although the focus in this chapter and the handbook is on tools and methods for English corpus linguistics, I highlight issues of support for other languages and corpora and tools that support multiple languages where they are relevant.

Corpus linguistics as a discipline has matured in parallel with the development of more powerful computers and software tools. In Section 2.4, I will reflect on the question of whether corpus linguistics is now tool-driven, i.e. whether researchers can only ask the research questions that are supported by the existing tools and methods, and whether other important questions are not tackled due to a lack of tool support. I highlight some limitations of the existing tools and methods, which include for example limited support of manual categorization of concordance lines and categorization of key words. The empirical study presented in Section 3 will investigate the relative strengths and weakness of tools and methods for studying *n*-grams, also called lexical bundles (Biber *et al.* 1999), recurrent combinations (Altenberg 1998) or clusters (Scott).[1] This will serve to highlight practical analysis problems such as the vast quantity of *n*-grams that are extracted from a corpus, and overlaps between shorter 2-grams that form part of longer 3-, 4-, or 5-grams. An approach called *c*-grams (collapsed-grams) will be presented alongside other proposed solutions to this problem.

Finally, the chapter will conclude in Section 4 with a peek into the future, taking some current tools, describing what research gaps need to be addressed and what tools and methods might look like in the future.

[1] www.lexically.net/wordsmith/

Improvements in speed and usability of corpus tools are important as well as interoperability between the tools. In addition, the sheer scale of mega-corpora such as those derived from online varieties of language suggests that better support for the visualisation of results would be beneficial.

2 Survey of tools and methods

Corpus linguistic research differs from most research in theoretical linguistics in that the language sample analyzed, and the methods used for that analysis, are central concerns. As a result, most research articles in corpus linguistics include discussion of corpus compilation, annotation, and/or the computational methods used to retrieve linguistic data. To illustrate this, I have undertaken a small quantitative analysis of recent papers published in the field and how often they discuss each of the three considerations. The source data for this analysis are the academic papers published in four leading corpus linguistics journals:

- *International Journal of Corpus Linguistics* published by John Benjamins[2]
- *Corpora* published by Edinburgh University Press[3]
- *Corpus Linguistics and Linguistic Theory* published by De Gruyter[4]
- *ICAME Journal* published by UCREL, Lancaster University[5]

The analysis considers papers published in 2012, and for the *International Journal of Corpus Linguistics* it includes only the first two issues for that year since these were the ones published at the time of writing (early 2013). A total of 32 papers in the four journals have been categorized into the three main areas in the survey: compilation, annotation, and retrieval. Although the vast majority of studies refer to corpus data as would be expected, I have only counted a paper in the compilation set where it refers to new corpus compilation activity rather than the use of a pre-existing corpus.

Table 2.1 provides the results of the survey. Each paper could count toward any or possibly all three of the categories; therefore the figures in the total column do not add up to 32 since some papers can fall into multiple categories.

Table 2.1 shows that of the 32 papers published in the four journals in 2012, there are 27 (84%) which describe some sort of retrieval tool or method; 12 (38%) papers describe some new corpus compilation activity and only 8 (25%) include tools or methods related to corpus annotation. Although this is just a small snapshot and the results would no doubt change if another year's worth of published papers were considered, it does illustrate the focus of recent work in the field and serves to justify the

[2] http://benjamins.com/#catalog/journals/ijcl/main [3] www.euppublishing.com/journal/cor
[4] www.degruyter.com/view/j/cllt [5] http://icame.uib.no/journal.html

Table 2.1 *Quantitative analysis of papers published in 2012*

	IJCL	Corpora	CLLT	ICAME	Total
Compilation	5	5	2	0	12
Annotation	1	3	3	1	8
Retrieval	8	6	9	4	27
No computational methods	0	1	1	0	2
Number of papers	9	8	11	4	

choice of the three categories presented in this chapter. The survey also throws up another interesting result. In the vast majority of cases, the software tools used in these papers are employed off-the-shelf, pre-built rather than tools which researchers have created themselves or programming languages and environments such as R where corpus methods can be implemented by the corpus researcher directly. Such approaches are described elsewhere in this handbook (see Chapter 3) and in other publications (Mason 2000; Gries 2009). Therefore in this chapter, I will focus on these pre-existing software tools that implement the methods that are described.

Many similar computational methods and tools would be seen if areas such as content analysis, Computer Assisted Qualitative Data Analysis (CAQDAS), digital humanities, and text mining had been considered. However, in this chapter, the scope needs to be limited carefully to computational methods and tools employed for corpus linguistics research. The following subsections will focus in turn on tools and methods related to the three key phases of corpus linguistics methodology that have already been highlighted, i.e. compilation, annotation, and retrieval. After that I will reflect on the current state of the art in corpus tools and methods.

2.1 Compilation

Unless the corpus linguist is planning to use an existing off-the-shelf corpus, the first thing they need to do is to compile one of their own. Unfortunately, considering the plethora of textbooks in the field, it is the practical aspects of this process that are dealt with least out of the three key phases of corpus-linguistics methodology. Kennedy (1998: 70) states that there are three stages to corpus compilation: "corpus design, text collection or capture and text encoding or markup" and reminds us of the importance of a catalogue which is needed along with safe backup and storage. Adolphs (2008: 21) also says there are three stages in the compilation process: "data collection, annotation and mark-up, and storage" and the overlap between these two definitions can be clearly seen although Adolphs includes the annotation step as well, which I discuss separately below. This chapter is not the place to launch into detailed descriptions about the many issues and ongoing discussions related to the design and representativeness of corpora since that will be dealt with elsewhere (see Chapter 1 this volume). In this section, I will focus on general methods more than specific software tools that will very quickly go out of date, but inevitably this part of the survey will reflect the state of the art at the time of writing. In the corpus compilation stage, there are few tools and methods aimed specifically at the corpus linguist. Processes such as transcription, scanning, OCR, encoding, and documenting tend to be supported by software that is used in many other document-handling arenas. Conversely, for corpora of web, online, or other computer-mediated communication (CMC) language varieties there is more software support. The new paradigm of web-as-corpus has only recently started to be presented in the textbooks in the field, e.g. Cheng (2012: 36).

Creating a machine-readable corpus can be a very costly and time-consuming exercise. The accuracy of any transcription and scanning is a primary consideration. In the next few paragraphs I will focus in turn on spoken, written, and web-based language sampling and examine compilation issues specific to each type.

For spoken corpora, hardware and software recorders can be used for data collection. It is clearly important to obtain as high-quality recording as possible and digital recorders are available quite cheaply. Next, transcription-editing software is used to create a word-level transcript alongside the audio data. Systems such as Voicewalker was used for the Santa Barbara corpus and SoundScriber was used for compiling the *Michigan Corpus of Academic Spoken English* (MICASE). Praat can be employed for phonetic analysis. Unfortunately, speech recognition software is not yet accurate enough to automatically create text from sound recordings unless they are of broadcast quality. Even then, significant manual checking is required to prepare the high-quality, error-free transcriptions required for linguistic analysis. Some online sources of spoken data from broadcasters do include subtitles that may be extracted. Spoken corpora are often multimodal, incorporating a video stream as well, e.g. SCOTS and SACODEYL, so this entails the recording, editing, and processing of video data. Ideally the transcription that is produced by these different methods would be aligned with the audio and video streams using software such as EXMARaLDA and the NITE XML Toolkit.

The considerations for written corpora are quite different. If the source material is available in hardcopy form, e.g. a printed book or magazine, then a scanner is required in order to turn the printed version into a digital image and then OCR software creates a machine-readable version of the text contained in the image. A significant investment of time may be needed to manually check the OCR output and correct mistakes made by the software. Where the printed material is not of good clarity or the image has degraded over time, perhaps from a large newspaper sheet printed from a microfilm archive or photocopied from an original source, then OCR software may struggle to correctly block out multiple columns and recognize characters. In these cases, it may be better to resort to conversion by keyboarding of the original. This also applies to historical material or where the original is handwritten, e.g. children's school projects or diaries. The approach taken by the *Early English Books Online* (EEBO) Text Creation Partnership (TCP) is to have an original book manually keyboarded by two different individuals. Then these two versions are compared and a third editor manually intervenes when differences arise. Such processes are vital in order to ensure that the machine-readable text is as accurate as possible. Depending on the type of corpus and the age of the sources, it may be possible to find corpus material in electronic form already and then the keyboarding or scanning stages can be avoided. Out-of-copyright texts are more readily available, otherwise publishers need to be contacted to secure access and obtain copies of the data. Most corpus tools require plain text versions with optional XML encoding, so where material is sourced in another form, some format conversions will be in order. There are many tools available to assist in the conversion of Word, RTF, and PDF file formats to TXT. These vary in quality and it is obviously important for later linguistic analysis to check that the original text flow has been preserved, especially where the source has multiple columns or tabular formatting.

With the advent of the web and online data sources, it is easier to obtain electronic copies of written material. For example, the BE06 corpus (Baker 2009) contained published British English written material that was sourced from the web to match the sampling model of the LOB/Brown family. Sites such as Project Gutenberg[6] contain large quantities of out-of-copyright or self-published books. In addition, text is made available online in such plentiful and continually growing quantities that linguists have started using the web as a source of corpus data directly, resulting in the so-called web-as-corpus (WaC) paradigm. In contrast to the other areas of corpus compilation described above, there are a number of computational tools and methods to support the use of WaC data that are aimed at the corpus linguistic community. A typical WaC study involves a number of steps. First, you require a web crawler or downloader to collect the raw data, followed by language identification and filtering tools, then tools to aggregate multiple pages and clean them of superfluous or boilerplate material such as navigation bars and adverts. It may also be necessary to detect duplicate pages or content and determine domain and genre information in order to select the most appropriate material for the corpus. Fortunately, most of these processes have been combined into simple tools such as BootCat (Baroni and Bernardini 2004), WebBootCat (Baroni *et al.* 2006), and the WebGetter utility in *WordSmith Tools*.[7] Other types of online

[6] www.gutenberg.org/ [7] www.lexically.net/wordsmith/

or CMC data can also be collected and cleaned in similar ways, e.g. Usenet newsgroups (Hoffmann 2007) although specific collections will require new tools to be developed.

Whether the corpus contains written, spoken, or online varieties, computational tools and methods for record keeping, cataloging, and documenting the results are largely general purpose. Tools such as spreadsheets, databases, and word processors are usually sufficient here although the relevant information may be stored alongside the corpus data itself for later retrieval in headers encoded within the files. In this case, XML editing software may be required to simplify the process and check for consistency of the results.

For further reading in the area of corpus compilation, Meyer (2002: 55–80) describes in detail the process of collecting and computerizing data, although some of the technical details have changed in the ensuing decade. Good summaries of the basic design, practical collection, and mark-up issues in compiling written and spoken corpora are covered by three chapters in the handbook by O'Keeffe and McCarthy (2010): Reppen (2010a), Nelson (2010), and Adolphs and Knight (2010). The collection edited by Wynne (2005) covers issues of character encoding, archiving, distribution, and preservation that are out of scope for this survey. Finally, legal and ethical issues of corpus construction and use are described in more detail in McEnery and Hardie (2012: 57–70).

2.2 Annotation

After a corpus has been collected, compiled, and marked-up as described in the previous section, the second stage of the typical corpus linguistics methodology is to annotate the data. This can take many forms depending on the linguistic features that are to be investigated: morphological, lexical, syntax, semantic, pragmatic, stylistic, or discoursal. Annotation can also be applied using manual (human-led) and/or automatic (machine-led) methods. Adding annotation allows the researcher to encode linguistic information present in the corpus for later retrieval or extraction using tools described in the next section. If the text is annotated or corrected by hand then this could form the basis of a training corpus for an automatic tagging system which can then learn from the human annotators in order to attempt to replicate their coding later on larger amounts of data. Part of the manually annotated dataset could also be used as a gold-standard corpus against which to compare the output of the automatic tagging system in order to evaluate its accuracy. Computational methods and tools for corpus annotation therefore take two forms. First, intelligent editors to support manual annotation and second, automatic taggers which apply a particular type of analysis to language data.

Focusing on the first kind for a moment, it would be possible of course to manually annotate texts using any standard word processor, but here it is useful to have software tools that check annotation as it is added, e.g. to ensure that typos in tags or category labels do not occur, and to allow standard mark-up formats (such as XML) to be employed consistently and correctly in the resulting corpus, e.g. as in the Dexter software.[8] In addition, such editors may be coupled with a central database or web server to allow teams of researchers to collaborate on a large-scale manual corpus annotation effort, e.g. the eMargin software.[9] Intelligent editors and manual tagging tend to be used for levels of linguistic annotation that are currently not feasible through automatic means, usually at the discourse level. A first example of this would be coreference annotation in which relationships between pronouns and noun phrases are marked up allowing the cohesion in a text to be studied. The Xanadu editor (Garside 1993) was created for the manual mark-up of anaphor/cataphor and antecedent/postcedent relationships and other related features. Further examples of annotation that are carried out manually are pragmatic (speech or dialogue act) and stylistic (speech, thought, and writing presentation) annotation, although these do not tend to be directly supported by tailor-made software tools. Tagging of errors in learner corpora also proceeds at multiple linguistic levels and is generally carried out by hand although some automatic computational tools are now beginning to assist in this research for spelling and grammar-level errors.

Now, turning to the automatic taggers which apply annotation without human intervention, many such systems exist and it is only possible to scratch the surface in a short survey. Annotation can be carried out automatically and with high levels of accuracy at the level of morphology (prefix and suffix), lexical (part-of-speech and lemma), syntax (parsing), and semantics (semantic field and word sense). For annotation in English and other major world languages, many of these tools are well developed and mature, but for other languages where corpus resources are scarce, basic language resource kits (BLARKs) are now becoming available. The commonest form of corpus annotation is part-of-speech (POS) tagging, where a label (tag) is assigned to each word in the text representing its major word class and further morpho-syntactic information. POS tagging is essential for the study of grammatical change in language but also forms the basis of other levels such as parsing and semantic annotation as well as collocation analysis. In POS tagging as in other types of automatic corpus annotation, different computational methodologies have emerged with varying degrees of success. Rule-based methods rely on large manually constructed knowledge-bases encoding linguistic information such as the possible POS tags that a word or suffix may take and templates giving contexts where specific POS tags are ruled in or out. Statistical approaches draw their information from large corpora and use probabilities to calculate which POS tag

[8] www.dextercoder.org/ [9] http://emargin.bcu.ac.uk/

is most likely in a given context. The most successful taggers employ a combination of the two kinds to provide robust results across multiple types of text e.g. CLAWS.[10]

For further information about the corpus annotation process and computational tools and methods that support it, the reader is referred to Garside *et al.* (1997), Mitkov (2003), and McEnery *et al.* (2006: 29–45).

2.3 Retrieval

Once a corpus has been compiled and annotated using the methods and tools described in the previous two subsections, it is ready for the third stage, i.e. retrieval. Retrieval methods and tools are those most commonly and prototypically associated with the corpus user's toolbox because many linguists use pre-existing corpora and so can skip the first two stages. Central amongst these methods is the concordance, which displays all examples of a particular linguistic feature retrieved from the corpus and displayed in context, usually presented as one example per line, with a short section of surrounding text to the left and right of the example itself as shown in Figure 2.1.

All concordance tools provide for searching by a simple word and some tools permit searching for suffixes, multiple word phrases, regular expressions, part-of-speech tags, other annotation embedded within the corpus, or more complex contextual patterns. The idea of such a concordance arrangement predates the computer by quite a significant margin and scholars have in the past created concordances by hand for significant texts such as the Qur'an and the Bible. For example, Cowden-Clarke (1881) took sixteen years to manually produce a complete concordance of all words (apart from a small set of words considered insignificant and occurring frequently such as *be*, *do*, and *have*) in Shakespeare's writings. The

```
o that banks pay for the financial  support  they have received , until such tim
ehave responsibly . And we need to  support  and develop new ways of financing g
sk or offers rewards for failure .  Support  the establishment of Local Enterpri
 their own part of the country and  support  the development of new products fro
a Liberal Democrat government will  support  them in doing so . Liberal Democrat
re existing RDAs have strong local  support  , they may continue with refocused
 be covered in company reporting .  Support  public investment in the roll-out o
ing up opportunities and providing  support  and help when needed . a fair deal
ing up opportunities and providing  support  and help when needed . Despite incr
ovide for after-school and holiday  support  . This will allow an average primar
sed Graduate Teacher Programme and  support  the expansion of Teach First to att
e medium-sized firms that need the  support  . The money saved will Prime Minist
dent commission , with cross-party  support  , to develop proposals for long-ter
 directly to prevention measures .  support  a ban on below-cost selling , and a
ent has failed to provide adequate  support  for those affected by the contamina
 Paralympic Games in 2012 , and we  support  bids for other high-profile events
ic funding and dominant position .  Support  a diverse regional and local media
elieve every family should get the  support  it needs to thrive . a fair deal fo
elieve every family should get the  support  it needs to thrive , from help with
```

Figure 2.1 Concordance example for the word *support*

[10] http://ucrel.lancs.ac.uk/claws/

concordance arrangement with the search item aligned centrally in the middle of each line provides the main window on to the underlying text for a corpus linguist.

Alongside the concordance method, a further four methods have emerged as central to the work of the corpus user: frequency lists, keywords, n-grams, and collocations. Frequency lists, usually of words, provide a list of all the items in the corpus and a count of how often they occur and in some cases how widely dispersed the items are across multiple sections of a corpus. Again, this is something the computer is really good at doing efficiently and accurately. Different software tools do, however, produce slightly different frequency information and word counts for the same corpus data due to the way words are defined and delimited, e.g. whether punctuation is counted, capitalization is significant, and contractions are counted as one item or two. The keywords approach is a method to compare two word frequency lists using statistical metrics in order to highlight interesting items whose frequency differs significantly between one corpus that is being analyzed and a much larger reference corpus. The keywords method can also be extended by comparing three or more word frequency lists representing distributions in a larger number of corpora. The keyness metric (usually chi-squared or log-likelihood) provides complementary information to word frequency alone and gives an indication of the aboutness of a text, or what items are worthy of further investigation. The next method in the expanding corpus toolbox is usually referred to in the computational linguistics community as *n*-grams. In the corpus linguistics field, it is also known as lexical bundles, recurrent combinations or clusters. This method is fairly simple, is easy for the computer to calculate, and represents the ability to count repeated phrases or continuous word sequences that occur in corpus data. *N*-grams of different lengths are counted separately, i.e. repeated sequences of pairs of words are counted as 2-grams, three-word sequences as 3-grams and so on. These lists can be seen as extensions of the simple word frequency list which is identical to a 1-gram list. An important variant of the *n*-gram approach is referred to as concgrams since they are derived from concordances and *n*-grams. Concgrams are repeated sequences of words that may be discontinuous and in any order, and this allows the user to find possibly interesting phraseological patterns in text which contain optional intervening items. In addition, the keyness method and the *n*-gram method can be combined in order to highlight key clusters, i.e. repeated sequences whose frequency differs significantly in one corpus compared to a reference corpus. I will return to consider *n*-grams in more detail in Section 3.

The final method in the corpus toolbox is collocation. In Firthian terms, collocation refers to the relationship between a word and its surrounding context where frequent co-occurrence with other words or structures helps to define the meaning of the word. In practical terms, collocation as a method refers to the counting of the co-occurrence of two words in a corpus depending on their relative proximity to one another, and usually includes the calculation of a statistic or metric to assign significance values to the amount or type of co-occurrence relationships. Unlike the previous four methods, where some minor operational differences that exist in tokenization for frequency lists, concordances, keywords, and *n*-grams could produce slightly different results in different tools, the collocation method itself is less tightly defined. Results can vary greatly depending on the parameters and metrics chosen. Many different statistics can be selected to determine the significance of the difference in the frequency of a word that occurs in close proximity to the node word against its frequency in the remainder of the corpus, e.g. simple frequency, Mutual Information, log-likelihood, Z-score, T-score, MI2 or MI3. Altering the span of the window around the node word where possible collocate words are considered can also significantly affect the results. Further typical options include whether to consider punctuation as a boundary to collocation window spans or impose minimum frequencies on collocates or node words.

The five methods described above have all been defined in relation to words contained in a corpus. They can equally well apply to tags within a corpus, if any levels of annotation have been applied. For instance, a concordance can be produced for a certain part-of-speech tag, a frequency list of lemmas, key semantic tags, and calculate collocation statistics for which semantic tags relate to a given word.

The discussion so far in this subsection has been deliberately focused on general methods rather than specific software tools, but it is useful to include a brief timeline describing the development of retrieval tools in order to put them into context alongside the methods. The historical timeline of corpus retrieval software can be divided into four generations. In the first generation that developed alongside machine-readable corpora, software tools running on large mainframe computers simply provided concordance or key-word-in-context (KWIC) displays, and separate tools were created in order to prepare frequency lists, e.g. as used by Hofland and Johansson (1982). These tools were usually tied to a specific corpus. In the second generation, applications such as the Longman Mini-Concordancer, Micro-Concord, Wordcruncher, and OCP were developed to run on desktop computers. These were capable of dealing with multiple corpora and extra features to sort concordance lines by left and right context were added. Increased processing capabilities of PCs and laptops in the 1990s led to the third generation of retrieval software with systems such as WordSmith, MonoConc, AntConc, and *Xaira* being developed. They were able to deal with corpora of the order of tens of millions of words, containing languages other than English, and they included implementations of the other methods outlined above in one package rather than as separate tools. The fourth generation of corpus retrieval software has moved to web-based interfaces. This allows developers to exploit much more powerful server machines and database indexes, provide a user-friendly web interface and host corpora that cannot otherwise be distributed for copyright reasons. Most of the web-based interfaces only permit access to pre-existing corpora rather than texts that the users collect themselves. For example, Mark Davies' corpus.byu.edu interface permits access to very large corpora: 450 million words of the *Corpus of Contemporary American English* (COCA), 400 million words of the *Corpus of Historical American English* (COHA), 100 million words of the *Time* Magazine Corpus, and 100 million words of the *British National Corpus*. Other systems tend to rely on the Corpus Query Processor (CQP) server (part of the Open Corpus Workbench) or Manatee server. Their well-known web-facing front ends are BNCweb (providing access to the *British National Corpus*), SketchEngine (aimed at lexicographers), and CQPweb (based on the BNCweb design but suitable for use with other corpora). Other web-based tools in a similar mold are Intellitext (aimed at humanities scholars), Netspeak, and ANNIS. The web-based Wmatrix software (Rayson 2008) allows the user to perform retrieval operations but it also annotates uploaded English texts with two levels of corpus annotation: part-of-speech and semantic field. For further information on the four generations of corpus retrieval tools, a good survey can be found in McEnery and Hardie (2012: 37–48).

2.4 Critical reflection

Although I have presented corpus software as distinct tools used for the three stages of compilation, annotation, and retrieval, it needs to be highlighted that the separation between these stages is not always clear cut. As mentioned, Wmatrix performs both automatic annotation and retrieval. Other tools, such as WordSmith and BNCweb, permit the user to manually categorize concordance lines and this can be viewed as a form of corpus annotation. It should therefore be clear that a specific piece of corpus software cannot always be pigeonholed into one of these three categories.

Looking back on the brief survey in the preceding three subsections, it can be seen that a wide range of computational methods and tools are available to the corpus linguist. Updated versions of corpus software are being delivered on a regular basis; however, the corpus toolkit is in need of a methodological overhaul on a number of fronts. Words of caution have been expressed over the use of the keywords technique (Kilgarriff 1996; Baker 2004; Rayson 2008; Culpeper 2009) related to the choice of reference corpus, the statistic used in the calculation, the sometimes overwhelming number of significant results, the use of range and dispersion measures, and the focus on lexical differences rather than similarities. As discussed in the next section, *n*-gram results as currently presented can be large in number and difficult to analyze. Concordance software does not fully support linguists' requirements for the manual categorization of concordance lines (Smith *et al.* 2008). The use of different software and methods sometimes produces different analyses (Baker 2011). And finally, the methodology for the study of large-scale diachronic datasets is just beginning (Hilpert and Gries 2009) and lacks good tool support.

One notable issue is the goodness of fit of current annotation and retrieval software where the corpus data is non-standard or "noisy". Vast quantities of historical data are now being digitized, and billions of words are available on the web or in online social networks. In both these cases, automatic tagging tools have been shown to be less accurate and robust. In particular, spelling variation causes problems for POS tagging, concordancing, keywords, *n*-grams, and collocation techniques. Even simple frequency counting is more difficult for the computer since multiple spelling variants will disperse the counts across different surface forms. Fortunately, tools such as VARD[11] have been developed in order to counter this problem by pre-processing the corpus data and linking standard forms to spelling variants.

As described in the introduction, corpus linguistics matured following hardware and software developments in computers and text processing methods. These developments have enabled much larger corpora to be collected and analyzed. However, it could be argued that corpus linguistics is now very tool-driven (Rayson and Archer 2008), in other words we are "counting only what is easy to count" (Stubbs and Gerbig 1993: 78) rather than what we would like to count. There are some areas of linguistic study where automatic annotation tools are not yet accurate enough or not available at all, and so studies have to proceed with manual corpus annotation e.g. at the discourse, stylistic, or pragmatic levels with very little computational tool support. Finally, as has been seen, corpus retrieval software in general does not permit the concordancing of audio and video material apart from in some notable cases, e.g. the SCOTS corpus.

3 Empirical study

Following on from the critical reflection about the limitations of computational methods and tools in corpus linguistics, this section will zoom in on one of the standard methods and illustrate some of the potential problems with it for corpus linguists and some possible solutions. As described in the previous section, the computational *n*-grams method appears under various guises in corpus linguistics. Biber *et al.* (1999) name the outputs of the *n*-gram method as *lexical bundles*, Altenberg (1998) refers to them as *recurrent combinations*, and Scott calls them *clusters* in WordSmith Tools.[12] All these

[11] http://ucrel.lancs.ac.uk/vard/ [12] www.lexically.net/wordsmith/

names refer to the results of the same procedure which counts continuous multiword sequences and produces frequency lists very much like a word frequency list. The simple word frequency list consists of *n*-grams of length one, but *n*-grams of length 2, 3, 4, and 5 are usually counted. Longer sequences occur in larger corpora but are less frequent than their shorter counterparts.

Let us now consider some example lists in a short empirical study to consider the usefulness of the n-gram method itself. The *n*-gram procedure was applied to the full text of *Alice's Adventures in Wonderland* (one of the most frequently downloaded texts from the Internet Archive and Project Gutenburg)[13] using Ted Pedersen's *N*-gram Statistics Package (NSP).[14] The text is only 26,400 words long but it produces 1,810 2-grams, 737 3-grams, 192 4-grams and 51 5-grams that occur three times or more. This illustrates the first problem with the *n*-gram method, since even with a small text such as this, a large number of results is generated. Table 2.2 shows the top 10 *n*-grams of length between 2 and 5, and their frequencies.

Unsurprisingly, the top 2-grams often are dominated by high-frequency words such as *the*, *of*, *in*, and *it*. In the 3-gram list there are potentially more useful entries, depending on the research question in mind, which contain information about the main characters of the story. Higher-order clusters

Table 2.2 *Top 10* n-*grams from* Alice's Adventures in Wonderland

	2-gram	Freq.	3-gram	Freq.
1	said the	210	the mock turtle	53
2	of the	133	the march hare	30
3	said alice	116	i don t	30
4	in a	97	said the king	29
5	and the	82	the white rabbit	21
6	in the	80	said the hatter	21
7	it was	76	said to herself	19
8	the queen	72	said the mock	19
9	to the	69	said the caterpillar	18
10	the king	62	she went on	17
	4-gram	**Freq.**	**5-gram**	**Freq.**
1	said the mock turtle	19	will you won t you	8
2	she said to herself	16	won t you will you	6
3	a minute or two	11	the moral of that is	6
4	you won t you	10	you won t you will	6
5	said the march hare	8	as well as she could	6
6	will you won t	8	and the moral of that	5
7	said alice in a	7	as she said this she	5
8	i don t know	7	the dance will you won	4
9	well as she could	6	you will you won t	4
10	in a great hurry	6	dance will you won t	4

13 www.archive.org/details/alicesadventures00011gut

14 www.d.umn.edu/~tpederse/nsp.html

may be more useful for analysis as they correspond to longer phrasal or clausal-like fragments and help to disambiguate and contextualize some frequent words. The top frequencies of 3-grams and 4-grams are much lower and a total of only 51 5-grams are reported with a frequency of three or more. In terms of practicalities for analysis and categorizing these items, it would be useful to look further into concordances but that is beyond the scope of this small case study. Especially at the 2-gram level there are too many patterns (1,810) to analyze by hand, so some further filtering would be required. These lists are already reduced to patterns occurring three or more times, but the dispersion or range information across chapters might also be considered in order to remove *n*-grams which only occur in one or two chapters. When the *n*-gram method is applied to larger texts, significantly many more results are produced and the practical analysis problems are only exacerbated, so much more stringent filtering will be required. For example, Biber *et al.* (1999: 992) used a frequency cut-off of 10 occurrences per million words in a register and the occurrences must be spread across at least five different texts in the register. A second option is to use the keyness calculation in a similar way to how it is applied to a word frequency list. A p-value or log-likelihood value cut-off or sorting of results could then be applied in order to filter or rank key clusters in terms of keyness. For example, Mahlberg (2007, also see Chapter 19 this volume) examines key clusters in a Dickens corpus compared against a similar-sized corpus of other nineteenth-century authors and this allows her to home in on more interesting *n*-grams more quickly.

Despite the practical issues reported here, *n*-grams in the form of lexical bundles have been used very successfully to differentiate registers by comparing their frequency of occurrence, lexico-grammatical type, and typical discourse function across different texts. Biber (2009) puts the *n*-gram method in the corpus-driven category in order to distinguish it from other approaches which put more emphasis on the structures informed by linguistic theory and phraseology such as formulaic and idiomatic expressions. The obvious conclusion from looking at *n*-gram lists such as those in Table 2.2 is that there are few meaningful, structurally complete or idiomatic phrases that have been extracted by this method. Some manual work needs to be done in order to match the *n*-grams to grammatical or clausal elements or fragments of elements. In practice, a common approach is to combine the automatic, simple, corpus-driven techniques with the linguistically informed corpus-based methods. Hence, collocation statistics and collocational frameworks can be combined, possibly with the addition of POS templates in order to filter out *n*-gram patterns that are not of interest. A further extension, as mentioned briefly before, is to use concgrams to allow more flexibility in the order and placement of unspecified elements of the phrases or chunks (O'Donnell *et al.* 2012). The kfNgram software tool also allows discovery of phrase-frames which are groups of *n*-grams that are identical except for a single word.[15]

Returning to the example text and the results above, it can be observed that there is a further cause of redundancy in the *n*-gram lists. This redundancy emerges if the patterns from multiple *n*-gram lists are compared. For example, the most frequent 2-gram *said the* also appears in four of the top 10 3-grams *said the king, said the hatter, said the mock*, and *said the caterpillar* and two of the top 10 4-grams *said the mock turtle* and *said the march hare*. The 3-gram *said the mock* overlaps with the 4-gram *said the mock turtle*. Further overlaps can be seen for *in a, the king, and the, the march hare*, and others. The practical upshot of this recursion would be a duplication of effort considering and investigating these patterns in turn, or worse still, missing the occurrence of shorter or longer overlapping recurrent sequences if a study is limited to one length of *n*-grams as quite often happens for reasons of time. In addition, partial overlaps can be seen between the end of one pattern *dance will you won t* and another *you won t you will*. Given the small size of this text such things are relatively easy to spot, but some automatic tool support is required to facilitate this process for larger corpora. One approach adopted in the Wmatrix software (Rayson 2008) is to provide *c*-grams or "collapsed grams" which combine these overlaps and subsequences into one tree view. An example of this can be seen in Table 2.3 for the 2-gram *and the*.

This tree view shows longer *n*-grams indented and arranged underneath shorter *n*-grams that they contain. With software support, this tree view can be expanded or collapsed in order to focus on the important details. When linking to concordance views, if the user clicks on *and the* they

Table 2.3 *C-gram tree view for* and the

and the	82
and the queen	5
and the moral	5
and the moral of	5
and the moral of that	5
and the little	4
king and the	4
the king and the	4
and the other	4
and the words	3
duchess and the	3
the duchess and the	3
and the gryphon	3
gryphon and the	3
the gryphon and the	3
and the baby	3

[15] www.kwicfinder.com/kfNgram/kfNgramHelp.html

can choose whether to include or exclude longer patterns identified elsewhere. Such an approach significantly reduces the manual labor required to analyze *n*-grams.

Similar motivations lay behind the proposal for an adjusted frequency list (O'Donnell 2011), where clusters and single words appear alongside each other in a single cluster-sensitive frequency list. Rather than use frequency or collocation statistics to rank or filter *n*-grams, Gries and Mukherjee (2010) recommend the use of the measure of lexical gravity which employs type (rather than token) frequencies. Their method also considers *n*-grams for multiple *n* at the same time rather than separate lists, i.e. rather than fixing the length in advance, they use a collocational measure to determine the most appropriate length for the *n*-grams. It is now abundantly clear from this short empirical excursion into *n*-grams that there is much still to learn about how this computational method can be used for corpus linguistics and that accompanying software tools need further development to enable us to find and filter results more accurately and efficiently.

4 Conclusion

This chapter has very briefly surveyed the three stages in the corpus research process: compilation, annotation, and retrieval. To survey this whole area in one chapter is an almost impossible task and pointers to further book-level treatments of each of these areas were provided. It would also have been possible to widen out this survey of computational tools and methods to include very similar approaches undertaken elsewhere. There are at least three groups of tools and their related disciplines which are relevant. First, tools which provide Computer Assisted Qualitative Data Analysis (CAQDAS), such as ATLAS.ti, NVivo, QDA Miner, and Wordstat, incorporate some very similar methods to those described here but are not widely used in corpus linguistics. Their application tends to be in areas other than linguistics research but where language, texts, or documents are key sources, e.g. for political text analysis or other social science research questions. Second, tools such as Linguistic Inquiry and Word Count (LIWC) are used in psychology for counting emotional and cognitive words and other psychometric properties of language. Third, another similar set of tools is employed in the field of digital humanities for text mining of language properties in order to answer traditional humanities research questions and the formation of new research questions that are more difficult to answer with small-scale manual text analysis. Software tools such as Voyant and MONK are designed to allow large quantities of text to be searched, analyzed, and visualized alongside other tools such as Geographical Information Systems (GIS) and Social Network Analysis (SNA). However, here the focus has been on the tools and methods used in the field of (English) corpus linguistics. I uncovered some limitations of the current crop of computational tools and methods and reflected on whether corpus linguistics could be said to be becoming tool-driven.

Methods and tools for corpus linguistics have developed in tandem with the increasing power of computers and so it is to the computational side that I look in order to take a peek into the future of corpus software. In order to deal with the increasing scale of mega corpora derived from the web or historical archives, significantly more processing power is needed. Cloud computing may offer a solution here where (possibly multiple) virtual machines are used to run software tasks in parallel thereby making the results quicker to retrieve. For example, the GATE system (General Architecture for Text Engineering) now runs in the cloud, and on a smaller scale, so do Wmatrix and CQPweb. In order to analyze and automatically tag a 2-billion-word Hansard dataset consisting of data from 200 years of the UK parliament,[16] we recently estimated that it would take forty-one weeks of computer time. However, using a High Performance Cluster (multiple connected computers running small batches of text) at Lancaster, we were able to complete the task in three days.[17] A similar approach was taken by Oldham *et al.* (2012) to apply corpus methods to a vast collection of scientific articles in synthetic biology. Other computational projects offer a wider distributed approach where tools and corpora are connected across Europe in a large research infrastructure, e.g. CLARIN[18] and DARIAH.[19]

The sheer scale of corpora and the consequential numbers of results obtained from keyness and *n*-gram analyses are becoming increasingly hard to analyze by hand in a sensible timescale. This suggests that better visualization techniques would be beneficial in order to home in on interesting results, and simple histograms or bar charts to utilize frequency, range or dispersion data and display large collocation networks are no longer sufficient. Another visualization approach is to use a Geographic Information System (GIS) to locate corpus results on a map and this may enable the analysis of texts in literature, history, and the humanities via computational techniques to extract place names.

Finally, gazing into a crystal ball, it is possible to see corpus linguistics techniques spreading not just to other areas within linguistics (e.g. stylistics) but also to other disciplines, e.g. psychology, history, and the social sciences in general where large quantities of text are used in research.[20] Following the four generations of corpus retrieval software discussed in Section 2.3, this development will form the fifth generation where the specific disciplinary needs of the end user will need to be taken into account and greater interoperability between different software tools will be vital to facilitate the research.

[16] www.gla.ac.uk/schools/critical/research/fundedresearchprojects/parliamentarydiscourse/

[17] This work was implemented by Stephen Wattam, currently a PhD student at Lancaster University.

[18] www.clarin.eu [19] www.dariah.eu

[20] This is beginning to take place in initiatives such as CASS, the ESRC Centre for Corpus Approaches to Social Science (http://cass.lancs.ac.uk/).

3

Quantitative designs and statistical techniques

Stefan Th. Gries

1 Introduction

As is well known, corpus linguistics is an inherently distributional discipline: corpora really only contain strings of elements – letters/characters in the typical case of corpora as text files, phonemes, or gestures in the growing segments of auditory or multimodal corpora. That means that analysts can determine their frequency of occurrence, frequency of co-occurrence, or their dispersion/distribution in corpora and analysts have to operationalize whatever they are interested in – meaning, communicative function/intention, speaker proficiency, . . . – in terms of how this will be reflected in such frequencies of (co)-occurrence or dispersions/ distributions. From this perspective, it is obvious that knowledge of the discipline involving the analysis of frequencies/distributions – a.k.a. statistics – should form a central component of corpus linguists' methodological knowledge. However, compared to other social sciences (e.g. psychology, communication, sociology, anthropology, . . .) or branches of linguistics (e.g. psycholinguistics, phonetics, sociolinguistics . . .), most of corpus linguistics has paradoxically only begun to develop this methodological awareness. For now, let's assume that corpus-linguistic methods can be categorized, in terms of how much context of the occurrence(s) of a linguistic phenomenon they consider, into

(i) a group of methods in which the, say, word or pattern under consideration is not studied involving (fine-grained) contextual analysis: if one only wants to know which of the inflectional forms of the verb *give* is most frequent, one does not need to look at the contexts of these verb forms. These methods involve core corpus-linguistic tools such as frequency lists, collocations, dispersions, and statistics computed directly on these.

(ii) a group of methods in which the word or pattern under consideration is studied by means of a detailed analysis of its context. This usually involves the inspection of concordance lines of an element and their annotation for various linguistic and/or contextual features: if one wants to determine when speakers will use the ditransitive (V $NP_{Recipient}$ $NP_{Patient}$) and when the prepositional dative with *to* (N $NP_{Patient}$ $PP_{to\text{-}Recipient}$), one needs to inspect the whole sentence involving these two patterns and their larger contexts to determine, for instance, the lengths of the patient and the recipient, whether the clause denotes transfer or not, etc. Such data are usually analyzed with general statistical tools, i.e. methods that are applied in the same way as they are in psychology, ecology, and so on.

Corpus linguistics needs to "catch up" with regard to both of these groups. With regard to the former, for instance, corpus linguists have used different association measures to quantify, typically, how much two words are attracted to each other or how much a word is attracted to a grammatical pattern, but critical methodological analysis of the commonly used association measures is relatively rare. With regard to the latter, for example, with very few exceptions (such as Biber's multidimensional analysis or Leech, Francis, and Xu's (1994) multivariate exploration of the English genitive alternation) corpus linguistics has only begun to explore more advanced quantitative tools in the last fifteen years or so – compare that to psycholinguistics, which has discussed more advanced linear models and how to deal with subject-specific and lexical item-specific findings at least since Clark (1973).

In this overview, I will discuss statistical tools in corpus linguistics. Section 2 is devoted to the "first group," i.e. statistics directly involving corpus-linguistic tools; Section 3 then turns to the "second group," i.e. statistics that are usually applied to the annotation of concordances. In each section and subsection, I will first discuss some commonly used methods to provide an easier overview of common questions and methods; then I will provide some pointers to more advanced and/or currently under-utilized methods, whose exploration or wider use would benefit the field. Section 4 will conclude with more general comments.

2 Statistics on core corpus-linguistic methods

In this section, I will be concerned with statistical methods that apply "directly" to the methods of frequency lists, collocations, and dispersion.

2.1 Frequencies of occurrence

2.1.1 Frequency lists

Frequencies of occurrence are the most basic statistic one can provide for any word or pattern. They come as either token or type frequencies and typically in one of the following three forms:

- raw frequencies: *give*'s frequency in the spoken component of the ICE-GB is 297;
- normalized frequencies: *give*'s frequency in the spoken component of the ICE-GB is ≈0.46575 ptw (per thousand words) or ≈465.75 pmw (per million words);
- logged frequencies: the natural log ln of *give*'s frequency in the spoken component of the ICE-GB is ln 297 = 5.693732 (natural logs are computed to the base of $e = 2.7182818$, and $e^{5.693732}=297$).

Raw frequencies are easiest to interpret within one corpus, normalized frequencies are most useful when frequencies from differently sized corpora are compared, and logged frequencies are useful because many psycholinguistic manifestations of frequency effects operate on a log scale. For example, if words *a* and *b* occur 1,000 and 100 times in a corpus, *a* will be recognized faster than *b*, but not $^{1000}/_{100}=10$ times as fast but maybe $^{\log 1000}/_{\log 100}=1.5$ times as fast.

Most often, the frequencies that are reported are word frequencies in (parts of) corpora. However, many studies are also concerned with frequencies of morphemes, grammatical constructions, words in constructions, or *n*-grams/lexical bundles. Examples abound in

- learner corpus research, to document potential over-/underuse by learners compared to native speakers;
- language acquisition corpora, to document how children acquire patterns as they increase the number of different verbs (i.e. the type frequency) filling a slot in a particular construction;
- historical linguistics, to document the in-/decrease of use of particular words or constructions over time.

In spite of the straightforwardness of the above, there are still several underutilized methods and desiderata. One is concerned with the fact that words can theoretically have identical type and token frequencies, but may still be very differently distributed. Consider Figure 3.1, which

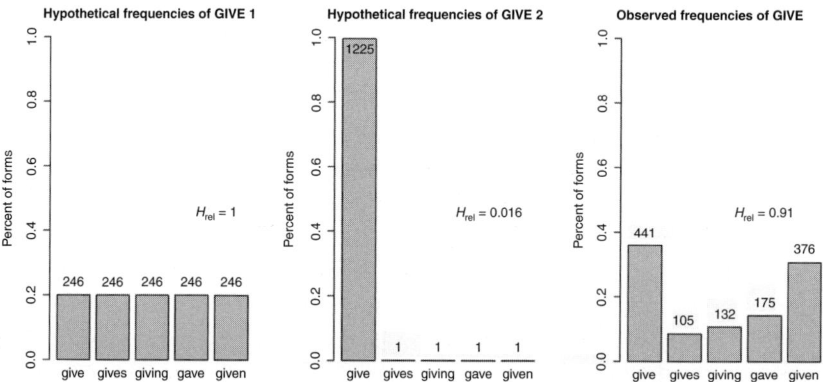

Figure 3.1 Hypothetical and actual frequencies of the forms of GIVE in the ICE-GB and their relative entropies (H_{rel})

shows frequency distributions of the lemma GIVE in the ICE-GB, two hypothetical ones (left and middle panels) and the actual one (from Gries (2010b) in the right panel). While all three distributions have the same token frequency (1,229 instances of GIVE) and type frequency (5 different verb forms), they are obviously very different from each other, which means one should not just report type and token frequencies. One way to quantify these differences is with relative entropy H_{rel} as defined in (1) and plotted into Figure 3.1.

(1) a. $$H = -\sum_{i=1}^{n} p(x) \cdot \log_2 p(x), \text{with } \log_2 0 = 0$$

b. $$H_{\text{rel}} = {}^{H}/_{H_{max}} = {}^{H}/_{\log_2} \text{number of categories}$$

(2) $$H_{\text{rel}} \text{ for } give = -\left(\frac{441}{1229} \cdot \log_2 \frac{441}{1229} + \ldots + \frac{376}{1229} \cdot \log_2 \frac{376}{1229}\right) \div \log_2 5 \approx 0.91$$

Entropies and related information-theoretic measures (e.g. surprisal; see Jaeger and Snider 2008) are not only useful to just descriptively distinguish different frequency distributions as above, but also to questions of language learning or ease of processing in online production.

Even more interesting for frequency lists of words or *n*-grams is the question of what the word or *n*-gram to be counted is or should be. In some corpora one can make use of multi-word unit tags. For example, the *British National Corpus* (BNC) has annotation that shows the corpus compilers considered *of course*, *for example*, *for instance*, *according to*, *irrespective of*, etc. to be one lexical item each, which means one would count *of course*, not *of* and *course* separately. However, in unannotated corpora, the situation is more complicated. Several strategies are possible: first, one can regard spaces and/or other characters as word delimiters and retrieve words or *n*-grams of a particular *n* using these word delimiters. The identification of word delimiter characters is not completely uncontroversial – what does one do with apostrophes, hyphens, etc.? – but far from insurmountable. However, even then the choice of *n* is bound to be arbitrary. To find *according to*, *in spite of*, *on the other hand*, *be that as it may*, and *the fact of the matter is*, one would need to set *n* to 2, 3, 4, 5, and 6 respectively, but typically studies just set *n* to 4 and proceed from there.

A more interesting but unfortunately rarer approach is to let the data decide which *n*-grams to consider. While very useful, these approaches become quite complicated. In one of the first studies to address this problem, Kita *et al.* (1994) proposed to use a cost-reduction criterion, which essentially quantifies how energy (cost) one saves processing a corpus *n*-gram by *n*-gram (where *n* can be any number greater than 0). For each word sequence α, one determines its length in words and its frequency $freq_\alpha$ and len_α in the corpus. From these, one computes the cost

Table 3.1 *The frequencies of several* n*-grams in the untagged Brown corpus*

1-gram	Freq	2-gram	Freq	3-gram	Freq	4-gram	Freq
in	21,428	*in spite*	55	*in spite of*	54	*in spite of all*	3
spite	57	*spite of*	54			*in spite of the*	20
of	36,484	*in* ___ *of*	625			*in spite of this*	6

reduction *K*(*a*) first defined as in (3) and then extended to (4) since word sequences are not mutually disjoint and any shorter *n*-gram α will be part of a longer *n*-gram β.

(3) $K(\alpha) = (len_\alpha - 1) \cdot freq_\alpha$

(4) $K(\alpha) = (len_\alpha - 1) \cdot (freq_\alpha - freq_\beta)$ for non-disjoint *n*-grams such as *in spite* / *in spite of*

Then, all word sequences are sorted by *K*(*a*) and the top *n* elements are considered individual elements of the vocabulary. Finally, one iterates and repeats these steps with the new inventory of individual elements. Consider as an example the *n*-gram *in spite of* and its parts as well as three 4-grams it is a part of and their frequencies in the Brown Corpus in Table 3.1.

Assuming that *in spite* is a unit is not useful given that, whenever one sees *in spite*, one nearly always also sees *of* as the next word, so the corresponding *K*-values are very small (see (5); it would be better to assume that *in spite of* is a unit). Correspondingly, assuming that *in spite of* is a unit leads to much higher *K*-values (see (6)). Thus, this measure quantifies the fact that there is little variation after *in spite*, but a lot more after *in spite of*.

(5) $K(in\ spite(of)) = (2 - 1) \cdot (55 - 54) = 1$

(6) a. $K(in\ spite\ of(all)) = (3 - 1) \cdot (54 - 3) = 102$
b. $K(in\ spite\ of(the)) = (3 - 1) \cdot (54 - 20) = 68$
c. $K(in\ spite\ of(this)) = (3 - 1) \cdot (54 - 6) = 96$

One approach towards the same goal is Gries and Mukherjee's (2010: Section 2.2) implementation of lexical gravity *G*, which also leads to the notion of lexical stickiness – the degree to which words like to occur in *n*-grams (cf. Sinclair's 1991 idiom principle) rather than on their own (cf. Sinclair's 1991 open-choice principle). The most sophisticated approaches in corpus linguistics so far, however, seem to be Brook O'Donnell's (2011) "adjusted frequency list" and Wible and Tsao's (2011) hybrid *n*-grams. The former adjusts frequencies of units on the basis of larger units they occur in (not unlike Kita *et al.*'s work); the latter enriches the study of *n*-grams with lemma and part-of-speech information (see also the 2010 special issue of *Language Resources and Evaluation* on multi-word units). Other approaches in computational linguistics, which may well inform corpus-linguistic research

Table 3.2 *Damerau's (1993) relative frequency ratio*

	Corpus *T*	Corpus *R*
Perl	249	8
All words	6,065	5,596

in this area, are Nagao and Mori (1994), Ikehara, Shirai, and Uchino (1996), Shimohata, Sugio, and Nagata (1997), and da Silva *et al.* (1999).

2.1.2 Key words

A widespread application of frequency lists is the comparison of frequency lists of two corpora, often one (larger and/or more general) reference corpus *R* and one (smaller and/or more specialized) target corpus *T*. This is useful, for instance, in applied linguistics contexts: if one wants to teach the English of engineering, it would be useful to have a list of words that are more frequent in an engineering context than they are in general English. However, one cannot use a simple frequency list of an English engineering corpus, because its most frequent words would still be *the*, *of*, *in*, ... – these are frequent everywhere. One of the earliest ways to compare the frequencies of words $w_{1,\ldots,n}$ in *R* and *T* to determine which words are "key" to *T* compared to *R* involves Damerau's relative frequency ratio. For example, if the word *Perl* occurs in *T* and *R* 249 and 8 times respectively and *T* and *R* contain 6,065 and 5,596 word tokens respectively, then this can be summarized as in Table 3.2. The relative frequency ratio is the odds ratio of this table, i.e. it is computed as $(^{249}/_{6,065}) \div (^{8}/_{5,596}) \approx 28.72$ and if it is larger/smaller than 1, *Perl* prefers/disprefers to occur in corpus *T* relative to its frequency in corpus *R*. Here we obtain a value much larger than 1, which means *Perl* strongly prefers to occur in *T*.

Another approach towards identifying key words involves G^2, which has been popularized by Dunning (1993) and Scott (1997). For the above data, G^2=270.71, a value indicating very high keyness of *Perl* for corpus *T*.[1]

2.2 Frequencies of co-occurrence

For many linguistic questions, the frequency of occurrence of a word/patterns *P* alone is not sufficient – rather, what is required is the frequency of *P* co-occurring with some other linguistic element *S*, *T*, ... Typically, when *P*, *S*, *T*, ... are words, this co-occurrence is referred to as *collocation* (and *P*, *S*, *T*, ... are *collocates*); when *P* is a construction/pattern, this co-occurrence is referred to as *colligation* or *collostruction* (and *S*, *T*, ... are called *collexemes* of *P*). In both cases, a central concern is being able to rank

[1] Many corpus linguists seem to use Paul Rayson's log-likelihood calculator (at http://ucrel.lancs.ac.uk/llwizard.html) but cite Dunning (1993) for the formula, which actually uses a different formula. The above result uses the general G^2 formula in statistics, i.e. the one mentioned by Dunning.

Table 3.3 *Schematic co-occurrence table of token frequencies for association measures*

	S	not *S*	Totals
P	*a*	*B*	*a+b*
not *P*	*c*	*d*	*c+d*
Totals	*a+c*	*b+d*	*a+b+c+d*

collocates/collexemes *S*, *T*, ... in terms of their direction and strength of association with *P*: the words *strong* and *powerful* are near synonyms, but which of them is more likely to be used with *tea* and how much so? Or, the words *alphabetic* and *alphabetical* seem to be very similar semantically, but can we glean how they differ by identifying the words they "like to co-occur with," such as *order* and *literacy*?

More than eighty different measures have been discussed; see Wiechmann (2008) and Pecina (2010) for overviews, and even those do not cover the most recent developments (e.g. Zhang *et al.* 2009 and studies discussed below). Nearly all these measures derive from a 2×2 co-occurrence table such as Table 3.3 (of which Table 3.2 is a reduced version in that it omitted the not-*P* row). If one studied the collocation *alphabetical order*, then (i) *P* could represent *alphabetical*, *S* could be *order*, and not-*P* and not-*S* would represent all other words, and (ii) the frequency *a* would represent the frequency of *alphabetical order*, which one is interested in, *b* would represent the frequency of *alphabetical* without *order*, *c* would represent the frequency of *order* without *alphabetical*, and *d* would represent all bigrams with neither *alphabetical* nor *order*.

Typically, association measures involve computing the frequencies one would expect to see in cells *a*–*d* if the distribution in the table followed straightforwardly from the row and column totals (see Gries 2013a: 182). (7) lists a few widely used association measures for the frequencies for *alphabetical order* in the BNC: $a=87$, $b=145$, $c=33{,}559$, and $d=99{,}966{,}209$. From this, it follows that $a_{\text{expected}}=(87+145)\cdot(87+33{,}559)/(100{,}000{,}000)=$ 0.078, etc.

(7) a. $\textit{pointwise Mutual Information} = \log_2 \frac{87}{0.078} \approx 10.12$

b. $z = \frac{a - a_{expected}}{\sqrt{a_{expected}}} \approx 311.11$ and $t = \frac{a - a_{expected}}{\sqrt{a}} \approx 9.32$

c. $G^2 = 2 \cdot \sum_{i=1}^{4} obs \cdot \log \frac{obs}{exp} \approx 1{,}084.84$

It is impossible to single out one association measure as "the best" since they often produce quite different rankings of collocates/collexemes. In the domain of collocation, *Mutual Information* is known to inflate with low expected frequencies, *t* is known to prefer more frequent collocations, and G^2 is a quasi-standard. In the domain of collostructions, the $-\log_{10}$ *p*-value of the Fisher-Yates exact test is used most often (because it is probably the most precise test and a good reference; see Evert 2008: 1235); it remains to be hoped that collocation studies adopt this exact test more.

In spite of the large number of proposed measures, the field still has much to explore. Two areas are particularly noteworthy. The first of these is only concerned with collocations and is concerned with the range of words around a word *P* that are included. Just as with *n*-grams, practitioners usually seem to make an arbitrary choice, and frequent choices are 4, 5, or 10 words to the left and to the right, yielding context windows of 8, 10, or 20 words. However, Mason (1997, 1999) has provided a much better solution to this problem, which is unfortunately hardly ever used. He proposes to explore larger contexts of words around *P* and then for each slot before or after *P* he computes the entropy of the frequency distribution of the collocates in that slot (along the lines of Section 2.1.1 above). The lower the entropy value, the more a slot deserves attention for the unevenness of its distribution. Table 3.4 exemplifies this approach: the most frequent collocates of *the* in a small corpus are shown in the first column together with their frequencies around *the* in columns 2–4 (3-left, 2-left, 1-left) and 6–8 (1-right, 2-right, 3-right). For example, the circled frequency shows the word *program* occurs 57 times in the position 1-right of *the*. Column 9 shows the entropies of each collocate's frequency distribution and column 10 shows the mean position of the collocate: for *you* and *on*, those are ≈-1, which means these prefer to show up one word before *the*; for *program* and *software*, they are ≈1, which means these prefer to show up one word after *the*. Finally, the last row exemplifies Mason's approach by showing the entropies for the collocate columns (computed on more data than are shown here), and one can see a frequent pattern:

Table 3.4 *Toy example for 3L-3R collocations of* the *with row and column entropies*

Word/Pos	3L	2L	1L	NODE	1R	2R	3R	H_{rel}	Mean
the	9	3	0	194	0	3	9	0.70	0.00
of	0	6	30		0	27	11	0.68	0.61
program	1	2	2		(57)	1	0	0.25	0.79
to	6	9	16		0	6	10	0.86	−0.21
or	4	8	0		0	14	1	0.62	0.11
is	6	3	0		0	12	4	0.69	0.48
and	5	3	3		0	8	5	0.86	0.29
you	4	11	0		0	4	2	0.67	−0.95
on	2	3	13		0	1	1	0.61	−1.00
a	10	0	0		0	2	5	0.52	−0.65
software	1	1	0		6	9	0	0.58	1.12
H_{rel}	0.75	0.75	0.64		0.60	0.67	0.72		

entropies grow with the distance from the node word, which is the technical way of saying that the more slots away one gets from the word of interest, the less systematic patterning one will find.

The second area in need of additional research is concerned with the nature of the association measures per se: just about all – and all that are regularly used – have two potentially undesirable characteristics: they are

- bi-directional, i.e. they assign a value to, say, the collocation *of course* and do not distinguish whether the association of *of* to *course* is greater/less than that of *course* to *of*;
- based on token frequencies of, again, say, *of* and *course* alone and do not take into account how many different words these two words co-occur with (let alone the entropies of these type frequencies; see Gries 2012a, 2014).

There are two measures, each of which addresses one of these problems, but both need much more exploration and no single measure addresses both problems. As for the former, Ellis (2007) was the first to mention a specifically bi-directional association measure, ΔP from the associative learning literature, in corpus linguistics, which was then used in Ellis and Ferreira-Junior (2009). ΔP is ≈ 0 when no association is present and greater/less than 0 if one word attracts/repels the other (with +1 and –1 being the maximum and minimum values respectively). Consider Table 3.5 with frequency data on *of course* and the two ΔPs (*of* → *course* in (8a) and *course* → *of* in (8b)) as an example.

(8) a. $\Delta P_{course|of} = p(course|of) - p(course|\text{other})$

$$= \frac{5,610}{174,548} - \frac{2,257}{10,235,320} \approx 0.032$$

b. $\Delta P_{of|course} = p(of|course) - p(of|\text{other}) = \frac{5,610}{7,867} - \frac{168,938}{10,402,001} \approx 0.697$

Clearly, the word *of* does not attract *course* much – many words can and do occur after *of* – but the word *course* attracts *of* strongly – not many other words occur frequently before *course*. See Michelbacher, Evert, and Schütze (2011) for a discussion of conditional probabilities and ranks of association measures (the latter are promising but come with a huge computational

Table 3.5 *Co-occurrence table for* of *and* course *in the spoken component of the BNC*

	course: present	other	Totals
of: present	5,610	168,938	174,548
other	2,257	10,233,063	10,235,320
Totals	7,867	10,402,001	10,409,898

effort) and Gries (2013b) for a validation of ΔP using multiword units and control 2-grams.

As for the latter problem, lexical gravity *G* (see Daudaravičius and Marcinkevičienė 2004) is an interesting attempt to include type frequencies of collocations in association measures. This measure takes into consideration how many different word types make up a token frequency. Using Table 3.5 as an example again, nearly all association measures would only "note" that there are 2,257 instances of *course* that are not preceded by *of*, but they would not consider how many different words these 2257 tokens represent. The most extreme possibilities are that these 2,257 tokens would be

- 2,257 different word types, which means that *course* was preceded by altogether 1 (*of*) + 2,257 (other) = 2,258 different word types;
- 1 word type only, which means that *course* was preceded by altogether 1 (*of*) + 1 (other) = 2 different word types.

All other things being equal, the first scenario would lead to a higher *G*-value because, anthropomorphically speaking, in both cases *of* managed to sneak into the slot before *course* 5,610 times, but in the first case, it would have managed that although *course* was so promiscuous in terms of allowing many different types in front of it, and this is what *G* would "reward" with a higher value. These and other developments are all in dire need of investigation.

2.3 Dispersion

Another topic that is even more important but at least as understudied is the notion of dispersion, the degree to which any (co-occurrence) frequency of *P* is sensitive to how evenly *P* is distributed in a corpus. For example, if one explores which verbs "like to occur" in the imperative on the basis of the ICE-GB, then many of the most attracted verbs are what one would expect: *let, see, look,* go, *come*, and others – however, two verbs returned as highly attracted stick out: *fold* and *process* (see Stefanowitsch and Gries 2003). Closer inspection reveals that these are fairly frequent in the imperative (esp. given their overall rarity), but occur in the imperative in only a single one of all 500 files of the ICE-GB. Thus, while their association measures suggest *fold* and *process* are strongly attracted to the imperative, their dispersion throughout the corpus suggests that this is such a highly localized phenomenon that it is hardly representative of how *fold* and *process* are used in general.

Ever since some early work in the 1970s (see Gries 2008 for the most comprehensive overview, data for several corpora, and R functions), researchers have attempted to develop (i) dispersion measures that indicate how (un)evenly an item *P* is distributed in a corpus or (ii) adjusted frequencies, i.e. frequencies that are adjusted (downwards) for elements that are unevenly distributed. For instance, both *amnesia* and *properly* occur 51 times in the ICE-GB but one would probably not ascribe the same importance/centrality (e.g. for foreign-language learners) to both: *amnesia* and *properly* occur in 2 and 47 files of the ICE-GB respectively so adjusted frequencies proposed by Juilland for both are ≈14 and ≈43.5 respectively, which underscores what, here, is intuitively clear: *amnesia* is much more specialized.

Unfortunately, this problem is a very general one: *any* statistic in corpus linguistics is ultimately based on frequencies in parts of corpora, which means that both dispersion and the notion of corpus homogeneity should always be considered potential threats to our studies. Gries (2006) exemplifies (i) how even the simplest of phenomena – frequencies of present perfects – can exhibit large variability across different divisions of a corpus and (ii) how the degree to which speakers' unconscious linguistic choices can be explained can differ hugely between different corpus parts; his recommendation is to always explore and quantify the homogeneity of the corpus for the pertinent phenomenon and at a certain level of granularity.

Given the straightforward logic underlying the notion of dispersion, the huge impact it can have, and the fact that dispersion can correlate as strongly as frequency with experimental data (see Gries 2010c), dispersion and corpus homogeneity should be at the top of the to-do list of research on corpus-linguistic statistics.

3 General statistics

In this section, I will now turn to statistical tools that are often applied to annotation of corpus data, i.e. to data that emerge from the description – linguistic, contextual, or otherwise – of concordance data; Section 3.1 is concerned with confirmatory statistics (and mentions descriptive statistics in passing); Section 3.2 with exploratory statistics.

3.1 Confirmatory/hypothesis-testing statistics

Confirmatory statistics can be classified according to two main characteristics:

- the number of independent variables, or predictors (often, the suspected causes of some observed effect). A design can be *monofactorial*, which means one analyzes the relation between one predictor and one response/effect (see Section 3.1.1), or it can be *multifactorial*, which means one analyzes the relation between two or more predictors and one response/effect (see Section 3.1.2);
- the nature of the dependent variable(s), or effect(s)/response(s), which is usually either *categorical* (e.g. a constructional choice: ditransitive or prepositional dative) or *numeric* (e.g. a reaction times in ms) and which, thus, affects the choice of statistic chosen: categorical responses usually lead to frequencies whereas numeric responses often lead to averages or correlations.

Table 3.6 *The distribution of different types of NPs across subject/non-subject slots (Aarts 1971: table 4.5)*

	Pronouns/names	±Determiner + head	Totals
Subject	5,821	928	6,749
Non-subject	2,193	2,577	4,770
Totals	8,014	3,505	11,519

3.1.1 Monofactorial statistics

Monofactorial statistical analyses have been relatively frequent in corpus linguistics for quite a while; the most frequent test is probably a chi-squared test for independence, which tests whether an observed distribution is different from a random distribution. Aarts (1971) is a classic early case in point. She studies the distribution of NP types in English clauses to explore, for instance, what kinds of NPs occur in subject slots. As Table 3.6 shows, subject slots prefer structurally lighter NPs: subjects are pronouns/names 86.2 percent of the time ($^{5,821}/_{6,749} = 0.862$) whereas non-subjects are pronouns/names 46 percent only of the time ($^{2,193}/_{4,770} = 0.4,597$); according to a chi-squared test (see Gries 2013a: section 4.1.2.2), this is extremely unlikely if there is no correlation between subjecthood and NP lightness.

Another well-known application of chi-squared tests is Leech and Fallon's (1992) study of what word frequency differences between the Brown and the LOB corpus might reveal about cultural differences between the USA and the UK. Predating Damerau's relative frequency ratio, they use a difference coefficient and chi-squared tests to identify words that are more/less frequent in AmE/BrE than one would expect if there was no difference between the varieties. As a final example, Mair *et al.* (2002) compare part-of-speech frequencies between the 1960s LOB corpus and its 1990s counterpart FLOB; using G^2 they find that frequencies of nouns increase considerably over time.

Turning to other monofactorial explorations, Schmitt and Redwood (2011) is an example of the use of correlations. They used the Pearson product-moment correlation r to address the question of whether English-Language Learners' knowledge of phrasal verbs (numeric scores in tests) is related to the verbs' frequency in the BNC and find a significant positive correlation: on the whole, the more frequent the phrasal verb, the higher the performance of learners. In addition, they use a *t*-test to see whether learners' reception and production scores differ, and they do.[2] Another example from the same domain is Durrant and Schmitt (2009), who compare the use of adjective–noun and noun–noun collocations by learners

[2] Unfortunately, their characterization of their statistical test does not reveal which *t*-test they used. Also, while they *t*-test whether learners perform differently well in productive and receptive tests, they do not test what learner corpus researchers might actually be most interested in: whether corpus frequency has different effects on production and reception, for which multifactorial methods of the kind discussed in Section 3.1.2 would have been required.

with that of native speakers, which were extracted from essays and whose strength was quantified using different association measures. The values of the association measures were classified into bands respectively so the authors could explore native and non-native speakers' use of collocations of particular strengths with *t*-tests. One kind of result suggests that non-native speakers make greater use of collocations in terms of tokens but not when type variability is considered as well. As a last example, Wiechmann (2008) explores how well corpus-linguistic association measures (on the association of verbs to NP/S complementation patterns) predict the results of eye-tracking experiments. Again using a correlational measure (R^2 s of (quadratic) regression models), he finds that, apart from the theoretically problematic measure of Minimum Sensitivity (see Gries 2012a: 491f.), the association measure of $p_{\text{Fisher-Yates exact test}}$ predicts the experimental data best.

While I will provide more detailed suggestions regarding how statistics in corpus linguistics can generally be improved below, two comments may already be pertinent here. One is that corpus linguists often do not seem to explore in detail whether the assumptions of tests are met. Many common significance tests require particular shapes or properties of the data studied, but usually there is little mention of whether these assumptions were tested let alone met. With observational data, normality especially is very rare, which means that alternative tests (e.g. Kendall's τ or the *U*-test as in Borin and Prütz's 2004 study of *n*-gram type frequencies of native speakers and learners) or more general tests, such as the under-used Kolmogorov–Smirnov test, may often be more appropriate; see Gries (2013a) for discussion of these tests.

The other general point is that corpus linguists need to be more aware that no linguistic phenomenon is ever monofactorial. Any monofactorial test can only be a (dangerous) shortcut, given that what is really required for confirmatory statistics is a kind of analysis that combines three characteristics (see Gries and Deshors 2014):

- they are multifactorial in the above sense: they consider multiple causes for linguistic choices (such as the choice of an *of* vs. an *s*-genitive) into consideration;
- they involve interactions between the linguistic predictors so that one can determine whether a particular predictor (is the possessor of a genitive construction specific or non-specific?) has the same effect regardless of other predictors (is the possessor singular or plural?): maybe specific possessors make it more likely that speakers would produce an *s*-genitive, but only (or especially) when the possessor is also singular . . .;
- they involve interactions between linguistic predictors on the one hand and data-type predictors on the other. Data-type predictors include, for example, L1 (is the speaker a native speaker or a learner of some variety?), REGISTER (which register/genre is a data point from?), TIME

Table 3.7 *Hundt and Smith's (2009) observed frequencies of English present perfects and simple pasts in LOB, FLOB, Brown, and Frown*

	LOB	FLOB	Brown	Frown	Totals
Pres. perfect	4,196	4,073	3,538	3,499	15,306
Simple past	35,821	35,276	37,223	36,250	144,570
Totals	40,017	39,349	40,761	39,749	159,876

(which time period is a data point from?) etc. Including such interactions is necessary if one wants to determine whether the linguistic predictors have the same effect in each L1/variety, in each register, at each time period, etc.: maybe specific possessors make it more likely that speakers would produce an *s*-genitive, but only (or especially) when the speaker is a Chinese learner (as opposed to a German learner or a native speaker) of English ...

Unfortunately, multifactorial analyses taking all this into consideration, which are usually regression models (see Gries 2013a: ch. 5), are still in the minority. Tono (2004) is a rare exemplary study that takes especially the third characteristic into consideration. Mostly, studies either run no statistics at all and only report observed frequencies, or they run (many) monofactorial statistics on datasets regardless of whether the data are mono- or multifactorial. Table 3.7 represents an example.

Table 3.7 suggests a monofactorial perspective because it seems as if the choice of tense (in the two rows) is dependent on the corpus (the four columns), but the dataset is in fact multifactorial: the frequencies of tenses can depend on the times the corpora represent, the variety, and a potential interaction as shown in a schematic regression equation in (9), in which the tilde means "is a function of."

(9) TENSE ~ VARIETY (AmE vs. BrE) + TIME (1960s vs. 1990s) + VARIETY:TIME

Hundt and Smith (2009: 51) state, among other things, that "[simple pasts] have also decreased over time" but appropriate multifactorial analysis with a binary logistic regression (see the following section) shows that the slight change of frequencies of past tenses is insignificant. In fact, the only significant effect in this data set is VARIETY – there is no diachronic effect of TIME and no interaction of VARIETY with TIME. As for this effect of VARIETY, Hundt and Smith (2009: 51) state that "we are – again – dealing with stable regional variation," which is correct, and the exact result (present perfects are more likely in BrE than in AmE) is represented in Figure 3.2. However, if one calculates effect sizes (see Section 4 below) the effect is so weak (Nagelkerke R^2=0.0017, C=0.524) that it is hardly worth mentioning (and dangerously close to what one might just obtain from variation due to sampling rather than a real varietal difference).

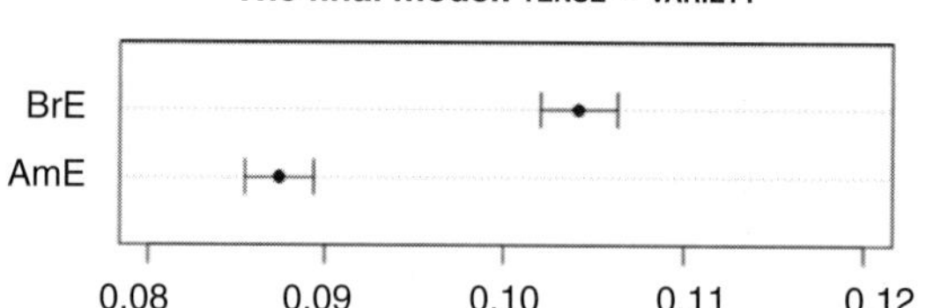

Figure 3.2 The effect of VARIETY on TENSE

Unfortunately, similar examples of multifactorial datasets that are not analyzed multifactorially abound, which is why the recognition that corpus-linguistic statistics has to go multifactorial is maybe *the* most important recommendation for the field's future development.

3.1.2 Multifactorial statistics

Perhaps the most important tool in confirmatory statistics in corpus linguistics is, or should be, the generalized linear model and its extensions, a family of regression models, which serve to model a response/dependent variable as a function of one or more predictors. Crucially, in the GLM and its extensions, the dependent variable can be of different kinds: they can be

- numeric (as when one models, say, numeric test scores as in the above discussion of Schmitt and Redwood 2011), in which case the GLM boils down to "regular" linear regression models;
- ordinal (as when one tries to predict the etymological age of a verb on the basis of characteristics of the verb; see Baayen 2008), in which case one might compute an ordinal logistic regression;
- binary or categorical, in which case one might compute a binary logistic regression (as when above the choice of a tense was modeled on TIME and VARIETY) or a multinomial regression (or a linear discriminant analysis);
- frequency counts (as when one tried to predict how particular frequency disfluencies happen in particular syntactic environments), in which case one might compute a Poisson regression.

In the same way, predictors can also be numeric, ordinal, binary or categorical variables (or any interactions between such variables, see above), and the results of such regressions are predictions (either raw values for linear and Poisson regression or predicted probabilities of outcomes for logistic regressions as in Figure 3.2 and multinomial regressions). The earliest such confirmatory studies that I am aware of – see below for earlier multivariate exploratory methods – are Leech, Francis, and Xu's (1994) use of loglinear analysis to explore the alternation between *of*- and *s*-genitives and Gries's (2000, published 2003a) use of linear discriminant analysis to study particle placement, the alternation of *John picked up the squirrel* and *John picked the squirrel up*. Following these studies and various replications and extensions – see Gries (2003b) and Kendall, Bresnan, and van Herk (2011) on the dative alternation, Diessel and Tomasello (2005) on particle placement in child language acquisition, Szmrecsanyi (2005) on analytic/synthetic comparatives, particle placement, and future tense, Hinrichs and Szmrecsanyi (2007) on genitives, etc. – such regression analyses have become adopted more frequently, though, see above, not widely enough.

Most of these applications involve binary logistic regressions, i.e. speaker choices of one of two alternatives, but multinomial regression is also slowly becoming more mainstream. Buchstaller (2011) explores the use of multiple quotation markers (*say* vs. *go* vs. *be like* vs. *be all*, and others) in a diachronic corpus of Tyneside speech and finds that the effects of AGE, SOCIALCLASS, TENSE, and NARRATIVE on the choice of quotation marker change over time. Similarly, Han, Arppe, and Newman (forthcoming) model the use of five Shanghainese topic markers on the basis of TOPICLENGTH, TOPICSYNTCAT, GENRE, and other variables. An example for ordinal logistic regression is Onnis and Thiessen (2012), who model levels of syntactic parse depths in English and Korean as a function of *n*-gram frequencies and two conditional probabilities and show, e.g. that cohesive phrases tend to be more frequent and that "the patterns of probability that support syntactic parsing are clearly reversed in the two languages." As a final example, Tono (2004) uses a method that is essentially equivalent to Poisson regressions, namely log-linear analysis, to explore differences between the acquisition of verb subcategorization frames in an EFL context.[3]

While the more widespread adoption of the above tools would already constitute huge progress, there is still a variety of additional improvements that would be useful. First, regressions can be followed up in a variety of ways. One very important one of these is referred to as general linear hypothesis (GLH) tests (see Bretz, Hothorn, and Pestfall 2010). While some scholars now routinely follow Occam's razor and do a regression model selection in which they eliminate insignificant independent variables (as was done above, when, for instance, the interaction VARIETY:TIME was discarded from the discussion of Hundt and Smith's data), what is much rarer is the use of GLH tests to determine whether, say, keeping all levels of a categorical predictor distinct is merited. For example, one might study whether the animacy of a possessor affects the choice of an *s*-genitive and annotate possessors in concordance lines for the following six levels of animacy: abstract vs. concrete/inanimate vs. plants vs. animals vs. superhuman beings vs. humans. However, even if animacy of the possessor were

[3] Interestingly, Tono (2004) changes numeric predictors – target and interlanguage frequencies – into categorical (or, strictly speaking) ordinal factors with three levels (low vs. medium vs. high). This kind of discretization of numeric variables is a not infrequent strategy but, as Baayen (2010) has shown, incurs some loss of power in the statistical analysis. Had Tono done a Poisson regression, this step would not have been necessary; however, this minor issue must not detract from the otherwise very informative statistical analysis.

to play a significant role in the decision for an *s*-genitive, this does not mean that it would be necessary to distinguish all these levels – maybe choices of genitives can be sufficiently well explained even if one just distinguishes two levels: a low-animacy group (conflating abstract, concrete/inanimate, and plants) and a high-animacy group (animals, superhuman beings, and humans). GLH tests can be a very powerful tool for studing such questions, discerning structure in data, or disproving analyses; see Gries (forthcoming) for a small GLH-based re-analysis of corpus data first discussed by Hasselgård and Johansson (2012).

Second, such regression analyses can be fruitfully combined. Gries and Deshors (2014) develop what they call the *MuPDAR* approach (for *Multifactorial Prediction and Deviation Analysis with Regressions*). This approach is designed to advance learner corpus research and involves three steps and two regressions:

i. a regression R_1 in which some phenomenon *P* is studied in native speaker data with a logistic or multinomial regression;
ii. the computation of native-speaker-based predictions for learner data;
iii. a regression R_2 which tries to model where the learners did not make the choices the native speakers would have done and why.

Gries and Deshors apply this approach to the use of *may* and *can* by native speakers and French and Chinese learners of English. First, their R_1 determines which factors govern native speakers' use of *may* and *can*. Second, they apply these results to the learner data and predict for each learner use of *may* and *can* which of the two modals a native speaker would have chosen. Third, they explore the cases where the learners did not do what the native speakers would have done to determine what features of the modals the learners still have (the most) difficulties with.

Third, a range of other interesting statistics can help corpus linguistics tackle other statistical challenges. One example is the approach of Structural Equation Modeling, which is designed to help identify causal effects from correlational effects; see Everitt and Hothorn (2011) for an applied introduction. Also, the approach of mixed-effects modeling enjoys a growing popularity in (corpus) linguistics. This method augments the traditional regression methods from above with the ability to include random effects – e.g. subject-, file- or word-specific effects – into the analysis, which has three advantages: (i) it addresses the problem that many statistical techniques assume that the individual data points are independent of each other, which is usually not the case in corpus data where one speaker/writer may provide many concordance examples; (ii) this approach can handle the kind of unbalanced data that corpora provide much better than traditional methods; (iii) since these models help account for, say, subject- or word-specific variability, their results are usually much more precise. Once a variety of uncertainties that still accompany this approach are addressed (see Gries 2013a: 335f.), this will be one of the most powerful tools in corpus linguistics; see Bresnan *et al.* (2007) for perhaps the inaugural application of this method (to the dative alternation) in corpus linguistics, Baayen (2008: ch. 7 for illustration), and the technique of generalized estimation equations as a potentially more flexible alternative.

Other examples are methods that can help corpus linguists handle the kinds of noisy/skewed data that often violate the assumptions of regression approaches but that are still quite rare in corpus linguistics; examples include classification and regression trees, conditional inference trees, or Random Forests, which, with some simplification involve the construction of flowchart-like tree structures based on successively more fine-grained binary splits of the data; see Hastie, Tibshirani, and Friedman (2009) for technical discussion, Torgo (2011) for more applied discussion, and Bernaisch, Gries, and Mukherjee (2014) for a recent corpus-linguistic application. In addition, the whole field of robust statistics provides a huge array of tools to handle the kind of skewed and outlier-ridden data corpus linguists face very day. Nonlinearities in data may be studied using generalized additive models; see Zuur *et al.* (2009). Finally, the most interesting alternatives to regressions that I have seen in many years are Baayen's (2011) naïve discriminative learning algorithm and Theijssen *et al.*'s use of Bayesian Networks / memory-based learning, both of which have the potential to revolutionize the field in how they provide psycholinguistically more motivated statistics than regression models and allow researchers to build causal models on data that do not meet the usual requirements of regressions (lack of collinearity, for instance).

3.2 Exploratory / hypothesis-generating statistics

Apart from the many confirmatory approaches discussed so far, there is also a large range of so-called exploratory tools, i.e. methods which usually do not test hypotheses and return *p*-values but that detect structure in data that the analyst must then interpret. One of the most widely known methods is of course Biber's multidimensional analysis (MDA); see Biber (1988, 1995) for the most comprehensive treatments. In a nutshell, performing an MDA involves

i. annotating a corpus for a large set of relevant linguistic characteristics;
ii. generating a table of normalized frequency counts of each linguistic feature in each part of the corpus;
iii. computing a factor analysis (FA) on this table, which is a method that will group together those annotated linguistic features that behave similarly in the different corpus parts;
iv. interpreting the co-occurrence patterns in terms of the communicative functions that the co-occurring features perform.

Table 3.8 *Dimensions of variation in Biber (1988)*

Factor	High positive loadings	High negative loadings
1: involved vs. informational production	private verbs, *that* deletion	nouns, long words
2: narrative vs. non-narrative discourse	past tense verbs, third person pronouns	present tense verbs, attribute adjectives
3: situation-dependent vs. elaborated reference	time and place adverbials	*wh*-relative clauses on object and subject positions, pied-piping
4: overt expression of argumentation	infinitives, prediction modals	–
5: abstract vs. non-abstract style	conjuncts, agentless passives	–

Biber (1988) identified five dimensions of variation, which are selectively summarized in Table 3.8. MDA has been one of the most influential quantitative methods in corpus linguistics and has spawned a large number of follow-up studies and replications, many of which used MDA results for the characterization of new registers. In addition, MDA has probably been a main reason why FA, and its statistical sibling, principal component analysis (PCA), have become popular in corpus-linguistic circles long before regression modeling has; see Biber (1993) for an application to word sense identification.

Other exploratory tools that are widespread are cluster-analytic approaches. Just like FA/PCA, cluster-analytic approaches try to identify structure in multivariate datasets, but unlike FA/PCA, they do not require the data to be numeric and they return their results in an intuitively interpretable tree-like plot called a dendrogram (see Figure 3.3). Many different kinds of cluster analysis can be distinguished but the most frequent in corpus linguistics is hierarchical agglomerative cluster analysis, which approaches datasets containing *n* items such that it tries to successively amalgamate the *n* items into larger and larger clusters until all items form one cluster; it is then the researcher's task to determine how many clusters there are and what, if anything, they reflect. Other techniques are phylogenetic clustering, which is more flexible than hierarchical clustering in that it does not require all elements to form one cluster at some point; *k*-means clustering, where the analyst defines the desired/suspected number *k* of clusters, and the analysis returns the *n* items grouped into *k* clusters for interpretation; and others.

Given their flexibility, cluster analyses can be and have been applied in very many contexts where large and potentially messy datasets were explored for possibly complex correlational structures that would remain invisible to the naked eye; Moisl (2009) provides a general overview, three recent applications are Divjak and Gries (2006, 2008), who apply cluster analysis to finely annotated co-occurrence data for nine synonymous

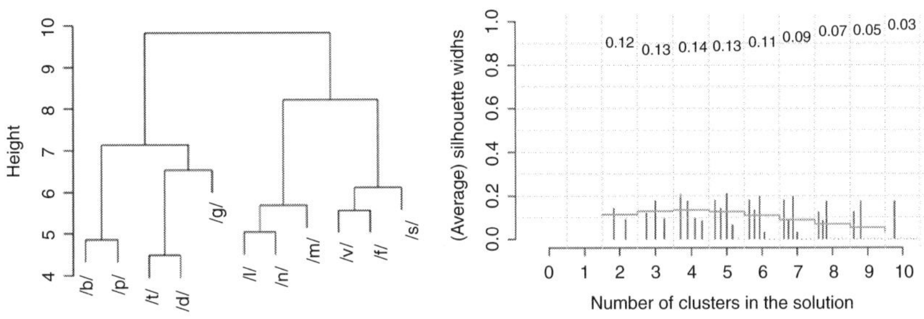

Figure 3.3 Cluster-analytic results for English consonant phonemes (from Gries 2013a)

Russian verbs meaning "to try," Szmrecsanyi and Wolk (2011), who use clustering and other tools within quantitative corpus-based dialectometry, and Hilpert and Gries (2009), who discuss a specific kind of clustering, Variability-based Neighbor Clustering, which can identify temporal stages of development in diachronic corpus data such as longitudinal language acquisition data or historical corpora.

While cluster analysis is not uncommon in contemporary corpus linguistics, there is a variety of follow-up methods that have not been widely adopted yet. These methods can help researchers identify how many clusters to assume for a given dendrogram. For example, it is not immediately obvious how many clusters the dendrogram of English consonant phonemes in the left panel of Figure 3.3 represents: any number between two and five seems possible. The right panel exemplifies one approach to this question, a statistic called average silhouette widths, which quantifies how similar elements are to the clusters which they are in relative to how similar they are to other clusters; in this case, this statistic "recommends" that four clusters should be assumed.

Many more exploratory statistical tools are only used occasionally at this point. Examples include (multiple) correspondence analysis (see Greenacre 2007 for technical details and implementation and Glynn 2010 for an application to the distributional behavior of *bother*) or multidimensional scaling (see Sagi, Kaufmann, and Clark 2011 on how collocates of *docga/dog* and *deo/deer* document semantic broadening and narrowing respectively).

4 Discussion and concluding remarks

In spite of having discussed many techniques and desiderata, this chapter could only scratch the surface of quantitative analysis and design in corpus linguistics – most quantitative applications/tools would easily merit an article on their own. As just one example, consider studies concerning the productivity of linguistic elements: Baayen's (1993, 1994) work broke the ground on studies of morphological productivity with applications ranging from linguistic theory to literary scholarship on vocabulary richness, and Zeldes (2012) is a recent extension of this work to syntax, but lack of space precludes more detailed discussion of these and other works. In addition to the many pointers for future research and exploration above, I will conclude with a few more basic comments and recommendations.

First, in addition to the mere knowledge of what techniques are available, we also need firm guidelines on what is important in statistical analysis, what is important to report, and how methods and results should be reported (see again note 2). Other fields have had long and intense discussions about these things – corpus linguistics, unfortunately, has not. We should be prepared to be inspired by how other disciplines with similar kinds of questions and data have come to grips with these challenges; from my point of view, ecology and psychology are most relevant to us, and Wilkinson and the Task Force on Statistical Inference (1999) provide many essential tips (e.g. to always include effect sizes to distinguish significance from effect size and make analyses comparable).

Let me briefly adduce an example of what happens if even elementary rules of statistics are not followed, in this case the rule that, if one computes many significance tests on one and the same dataset, then one needs to adjust one's significance level (see Gries 2013a: 273f.). The point of this example is not to bash a particular linguist or study – it is only by being able to point out very concrete dangers in existing studies that we learn. The case in point is Egan (2012), who discusses translations of *through* and reports a table (see Table 3.9) in which eight senses of *through* are contrasted in 28 pairwise chi-squared tests.

However, this analysis is quite problematic. One very minor problem is what is presumably just a typo, but since Egan does not provide any actually observed frequencies, there is no way to know whether the comparison between *Channel* and *Means* resulted in 3.4 or 34. Much more importantly, Egan seems to have adopted a critical chi-squared value

Table 3.9 *Chi-squared values with 2* df *for pairwise comparisons (Egan 2012: table 1; figures in italics represent chi-squared values with* p >= *0.05 acc. to Egan)*

	Perc	Space	Channel	Other	Means	Idiom	Time	Clause
Perc		9	6.2	20.9	20.1	54.6	35.5	53.4
Space	9		*0.2*	11	8.8	76	20.3	37.8
Channel	6.2	*0.2*		*2.3*	*3.4*	15.5	6.7	17.3
Other	20.9	11	*2.3*		*5.6*	10	*4.1*	17.6
Means	20.1	8.8	*34*	*5.6*		24	*2.6*	6.6
Idiom	54.6	76	15.5	10	24		17.2	37.6
Time	35.5	20.3	6.7	*4.1*	*2.6*	17.2		7.4
Clause	53.4	37.8	17.3	17.6	6.6	37.6	7.4	

of ≈5.99, the chi-squared value for p=0.05 at df=2. However, Egan did not adjust his critical chi-squared value for the fact that he runs 28 tests on a single dataset. Thus, while he reports 22 significant contrasts out of 28, an adjustment (Hommel's method) results in only 14 significant contrasts, and since it is the "significant" differences upon which his possible network of *through* is based, this network essentially collapses: *perception* senses are not significantly different from all other senses. Similar problems are common: see Gries (forthcoming) for a discussion of a similar flaw in Laufer and Waldman (2011) and Gries (2005b) on how corrections for multiple testing address the issue of too many significant values in keywords analyses. Thus, corpus linguists need to be more aware of the fairly straightforward notion of the multiple-testing problem and ways to address it with corrections and especially corrections that are more powerful than the Bonferroni correction (such as corrections recommended by Holm 1979, Hochberg 1988, or Hommel 1988).

Given all of the above, it may seem as if corpus linguists are supposed to spend quite some time on learning a large number of sometimes quite complex statistical tests. That perception is accurate. As I have asked elsewhere, why is it that corpus linguists look at something (language) that consists of distributional/frequency-based probabilistic data and is just as complex as what psychologists, cognitive scientists, etc. look at, but most of our curricula do not contain even a single course on statistical methods? If we want to make serious headway in our analyses of corpus data, then, given the complexity of our data, we must commit to learning statistical methodology, and hopefully the above succeeded at least in providing an overview of foundational and useful tools that, if adopted, can help us advance our discipline.

Part II

Corpus analysis of linguistic characteristics

4

Discourse intonation: a corpus-driven study of prominence on pronouns

Winnie Cheng

1 Introduction

Not everyone agrees on what exactly is covered by the term "prosody." Prosody is considered to be all of the suprasegmental features which include changes in pitch, "loudness, timing (including pauses) and voice quality" (Wichmann 2000: 8). According to Reed (2006: 3), prosody includes intonation, pitch, loudness, and time, with loudness and time being realized "in the form of duration, tempo, speech rate, rhythm and pause," but excludes voice quality. The reason for excluding voice quality is because voice quality is optional, and therefore paralinguistic, in the sense that a speaker uses a change in her "normal voice quality for interactionally motivated reasons" (Reed 2006: 10). Cauldwell (2013: 325) offers a rather open-ended definition of prosody, namely a "collective term for the variations in pitch, loudness, tempo, rhythm and other features of the sound substance of speech."

There is no a general agreement on what prosody is, and the same is true for intonation, a subset of prosody. Pickering (2012: 5437) provides both a narrow and a broad definition of intonation. The narrow definition is "the linguistically significant use of pitch movement at the suprasegmental level"; the broader definition includes "the alignment of the pitch contour with phrasal or clausal groups separated by pauses." Cauldwell (2013: 325), taking the discourse intonation perspective, defines intonation as the "overall shape of a stretch of speech as created by a speaker's use of prominence, non-prominence, key and tone."

The intonation system in English has been investigated from different approaches, depending on linguistic schools and countries (Chun 2002).

A grammatical or syntactic approach to intonation views intonation as segmental (see, for example, Chomsky and Halle 1968; Liberman and Prince 1977; Pierrehumbert 1980; Pierrehumbert and Hirschberg 1990) in which the functions of intonation are inherently linked to grammatical relationships. This approach sees rule-driven generative phonology as a natural, or inevitable, way of viewing such prosodic features based on their notion of generative grammar. It is grounded on the notion that tones align with specific syntactic structures. Thus, the case is made that a rise tone is employed with yes/no questions, and a fall tone with commands, statements, and *wh*-questions. There have been attempts by generative phonologists to assign meanings to intonation (for example, Pierrehumbert and Hirschberg 1990), but the fact that their data are typically experimental in nature has not helped to advance their case.

Another approach considers the relation among syntax, information structure, and intonation (Halliday 1967). Halliday's (1967) model of intonational meaning views intonational features as being "coextensive with information units, syntactic clauses, or both" (Pickering 2012: 5437). In Halliday's (1963, 1967) phonological typology based on meaning-making grammatical choices, intonation is highly structured, with three hierarchical systems: tonality, tonicity, and tone. Tonality is the division of speech into intonation/tone groups. Each tone group has one unit of information and conveys a speaker's perception and management of the whole message. Tonicity is the assignment and realization of the most prominent word in a tone group which indicates the focus of information. Lastly, tone refers to the contrasting pitch movements in each tone group and expresses different speech functions plus the status of information. Halliday's (1967) model of intonational meaning views intonational features being "coextensive with information units, syntactic clauses, or both" (Pickering 2012: 5437). In Calhoun's (2010: 1130) study, syntactic variation of spoken discourse is driven by information structure which places "focal material in prosodically prominent positions."

The third approach is based on the primacy of the affective or attitudinal role of intonation (O'Connor and Arnold 1973; Crystal 1975, 1995; Cruttenden 1997). As stated by O'Connor and Arnold (1973: 4) in their study of colloquial English, "a major function of intonation is to express the speaker's attitude, at the moment of speaking, to the situation in which he or she is placed." They describe the attitudinal meanings associated with ten tone groups when spoken in combination with four kinds of utterance: statements, questions, commands, and interjections. In a similar vein, Cruttenden (1997: 97–99) describes the rise tone as conveying the attitudinal meaning of "reassuring" with *wh*-questions, but either "non-committal" or "grumbling" with declaratives. The rise–fall tone means "impressed" with yes/no question and declaratives, and "challenging" with "clauses of any syntactic type" (Cruttenden 1997: 92–93).

The last approach covered here, discourse intonation, is derived from a discourse analysis perspective which views intonation as performing discourse functions (Chun 2002). The role played by discourse intonation is "related to the function of the utterance as an existentially appropriate contribution to an interactive discourse" (Brazil 1994: 46). Studies have examined discourse functions, including the speaker signaling topic structure with the use of pitch variation and pause length and the listener identifying major discourse boundaries by referring to pause length and pitch variation (Cutler, Dahan, and van Donselaar 1997; cited in Pickering 2012: 5437), and interlocutors communicating the extent of context-specific new and shared information.

The term "discourse intonation" is also used to refer to the model of discourse intonation proposed by David Brazil (1985/1997). In Brazil's model, the choices made by speakers are from four systems – prominence, tone, key, and termination – and these choices add additional layers of real-time situation-specific interpersonal meaning to what is spoken. Discourse intonation accounts for "speakers' moment-by-moment context-referenced choices" (Cauldwell 2007). While intonation has long been seen as simply a speaker's pitch variations on a continuous scale, in Brazil's systems of discourse intonation, intonation is a finite set of meaningful intonational oppositions. The communicative value of the utterance is affected by intonational variations on the basis of "a small set of either/or choices," and these choices are a "distinctive sub-component of the meaning-potential of English" (Brazil 1997: 2). In Brazil's discourse intonation, syntax and intonation (Chomsky and Halle 1968; Liberman and Prince 1977; Pierrehumbert 1980; Pierrehumbert and Hirschberg 1990) are considered to be "separate areas of choice," without any "'normal' relationship between tone units and clauses" (Cauldwell 2007). Attitudinal meanings, such as surprise, irony, and grumpiness, are not the product of any tone choice directly, but are determined locally (Cauldwell and Hewings 1996; Cruttenden 1997; Brazil 1997).

While British approaches to intonation are concerned with tone groups or tone units and pitch contours, American approaches to intonation tend to focus on a phonemic or levels approach to intonation (Chun 2002). Bloomfield (1933), for example, regards "differences of pitch . . . as secondary phonemes." In Pike's (1945) system, there are four levels of pitch, extra-high, high, mid, and low, for describing all the contours that distinguish meanings. Intonation contours are characterized by sequences of pitch height (Pike 1945). The ToBI framework, developed at the Ohio State University, is an intonation transcription system based on two relative levels, i.e. high and low (Beckman, Hirschberg, and Shattuck-Hufnagel 2005). It is used "for developing community-wide conventions for transcribing the intonation and prosodic structure of spoken utterances in a language variety . . . (e.g., tonally marked phrases and any smaller prosodic constituents that are distinctively marked by other phonological means)" (ToBI, n. d.).

2 The discourse intonation framework

In the prosodic transcription system developed by Brazil (1997), speakers can select from four independent systems: prominence, tone, key, and termination within a tone unit. Below is a summary of the descriptive categories used in discourse intonation.

1. Used language is divided into "tone units."
2. The tone units of used speech normally have either one or two "prominent syllables."
3. The last prominent syllable in each tone unit is the 'tonic syllable' and it carries one of the five tones.
4. At all prominent syllables, there is a possibility of choice in a three-term system of pitch level: high, mid, or low. The pitch level of the first prominent syllable in a tone unit establishes key, and the pitch level on the last prominent syllable establishes termination. In a tone unit with only one prominent syllable, key and termination are selected simultaneously.

(Brazil 1995: 240–246)

A tone unit is taken to mean a stretch of speech with one tonic segment comprising at least a tonic syllable, but which may extend from the first prominent syllable to the final prominent syllable (Hewings 1990: 136). Each of the independent systems is a source of "local meaning" (Brazil 1997: xi) and constitutes moment-by-moment choices made by speakers based on their ongoing assessment of the current state of understanding between the participants. The discourse intonation systems and choices are described, as follows:

System	Choice
Prominence	prominent/non-prominent syllables
Tone	rise–fall, fall, rise, fall–rise, level
Key	high, mid, low
Termination	high, mid, low

(Adapted from Hewings and Cauldwell 1997: vii, in Brazil 1997)

Brazil (1997) states that prominence distinguishes words which are situationally informative. In his framework, assigning prominence is not on the basis of grammar or word-accent/stress; it is a choice made by the speaker in context. Speaker decisions within the prominence system are based on the speaker considering the status of individual words (Brazil 1997). The other three systems in discourse intonation, tone, key, and termination, are not attributes of individual words but of the tonic segment (i.e. the section of the tone unit between the first and the last prominent syllable).

In Brazil's discourse intonation, a particular communicative value is associated with each of the five possible tones. A tone is the pitch movement that begins at the tonic syllable (i.e. the last prominent syllable in a tone unit). Any spoken discourse unfolds based on the shared knowledge between the discourse participants (Brazil 1997), and it is for the speaker to decide on a moment-by-moment basis whether what s/he is saying is shared or not. Speaker–hearer convergence is not something which a speaker can be certain of, and so speakers make their choices on the basis of what they assume the common ground to be at any particular point. Speakers, according to Brazil, basically have a choice between fall–rise/rise tones and fall/rise–fall tones. Brazil (1997) calls the former referring tones and the latter proclaiming tones. When a speaker chooses the referring tones, s/he indicates that this part of the discourse will not enlarge the common ground assumed to exist between the participants. Choice of a proclaiming tone, on the other hand, shows that the area of speaker–hearer convergence is about to be enlarged. The finer distinctions (Brazil 1997: 86–98) between these tones are given below:

fall–rise tone	indicates that this part of the discourse will not enlarge the common ground assumed to exist between the participants
rise tone	reactivates something which is part of the common ground between the participants
fall tone	shows that the area of speaker–hearer convergence is about to be enlarged
rise–fall tone	indicates addition to the common ground and to speaker's own knowledge at one and the same time.

There is a fifth tone, the level tone, in the tone system which is associated with "truncated" tone units and tone units which precede an encoding pause (Brazil 1997: 146).

According to Brazil (1997), speakers can choose from a three-tier system (high, mid, and low) in terms of the relative "key" at the onset of a tone unit which is the first prominent syllable in a tone unit. The choice of key is made on the first prominent syllable and the selection of high, mid, or low will affect the meaning of what is said. High key has contrastive value, mid key additive value, and low key has equative value, in the sense of "as to be expected" (Brazil 1997).

Lastly, Brazil states the speaker also chooses pitch level again at the end of the tonic segment on the tonic syllable; that is, the last prominent syllable in the tone unit which is underlined in the transcripts, and he terms this system "termination" (Brazil 1997: 11). Again, this is a three-tier system of high, mid, and low. This choice signals that the speaker seeks to constrain the next speaker to respond if s/he selects high or mid termination and, due to the seeming preference for "pitch concord" (Brazil 1985: 86) found in spoken discourse across turn boundaries, the next speaker frequently "echoes" the termination choice of the previous speaker in her/his choice of key. If the speaker chooses low termination, no attempt to elicit a response is made by the current speaker and this choice then leaves the next speaker to initiate a new topic or for the discourse to come to a close.

The local meaning of selecting high or mid termination varies according to the functional value of what is being said and can be briefly summarized based on three broad scenarios. In the case of yes/no questions (Brazil 1997), the choice of high termination carries the meaning that adjudication is invited and mid termination seeks concurrence from the hearer. In *wh*-type questions (Brazil 1997: 56), high termination carries the meaning that "an improbable answer is expected," and mid termination is a "straightforward request for information," while in declaratives, the choice of high termination denotes the meaning "this will surprise you" and mid-termination the meaning "this will not surprise you" (Brazil 1997: 58).

Cauldwell (2013: 309–310) distinguishes two approaches to the study of speech: first, careful speech that is rule-governed and tidy, in which differences that are important in grammar are audible with tones carrying meaning, and second, spontaneous speech that is unruly and messy, in which differences that are important in grammar may be inaudible with tones co-occurring with meaning. The second approach to speech is conducive for applying Brazil's discourse intonation system.

3 Prosodically transcribed corpora

Generally speaking, we all speak more than we write, but corpora consisting of naturally occurring spoken texts have been largely neglected in favor of those comprised of written ones. Most corpora are solely made up of written texts and those which are a mixture of written and spoken data texts are still overwhelmingly written. To date, the largest corpora of the English language, *Global Web-based English* (GloWbE) (1.9 billion words), *Bank of English* (550 million words), and *Corpus of Contemporary American English* (COCA) (450 million words) contain relatively small amounts of spoken English, from 0 to 20 percent. Exceptions to these are the few specialized spoken corpora that are being compiled around the world. For example, the *Cambridge and Nottingham Corpus of Discourse in English* (CANCODE) is a collection of 5 million words of spoken English recorded between 1995 and 2000 (see, for example, Carter and McCarthy 1997). The *Michigan Corpus of Academic Spoken English* (MCASE) (Simpson, Briggs, Ovens, and Swales 2002) has 1.7 million words of academic spoken texts. In China a 500-hour spoken Chinese corpus of situated business discourse in the

Beijing area (SCCSD BJ-500) has been compiled (Gu 2002). In the UK, the *Cambridge Nottingham Business English Corpus* (CANBEC) has one million words from a variety of semi-formal and informal corporate contexts (Handford 2010: 1–2). Importantly, none of these large corpora have attempted to include details of the speakers' prosody. The sheer size of these corpora, coupled with the time and expense of including prosodic features in the transcriptions, is, one must assume, prohibitive given that none of the compilers argue that prosody is excluded because it is unimportant in spoken language.

What are some of the well-known prosodically annotated spoken corpora? One of the first prosodically transcribed corpora is the 500,000-word *London–Lund Corpus of Spoken English* (LLC), which has been available for use since the 1970s (Svartvik 1990). Two versions of transcription, full and reduced, are available. In the full transcription, there are tone unit boundaries, the location of the nucleus, the direction of the nuclear tone, varying lengths of pauses, varying degrees of stress, varying degrees of loudness and tempo, modifications in voice quality, and paralinguistic features such as whisper, creak, and speaker-utterance overlap. In the reduced transcription, the basic prosodic features of the full transcription are retained but all paralinguistic features and certain indications of pitch and stress are omitted (Svartvik 1990). The *Lancaster/IBM Spoken English Corpus* (SEC) contains 52,637 words, or 339 minutes of recordings (Leech 1996; Knowles, Wichmann, and Alderson 1996; Wichmann 2000). Prosodic features represented in the SEC are tone groups, stressed and accented syllables, pitch direction, simple and complex tones, high and low tones, and significant changes of pitch not covered by the tone markings (Taylor 1996: 28–29). A representative sample of 150,000 words of the 0.5-million-word *Bergen Corpus of London Teenage Language* (COLT) is prosodically transcribed. The prosodic features are nucleus, tone (fall, rise, fall–rise, rise–fall, level) and tone unit boundary. In the *Intonation Variation in English* (IViE) Corpus, about twelve hours of speech data are transcribed in terms of rhythmic structure, acoustic–phonetic structure, and phonological structure (Grabe and Post 2002). The C-ORAL-ROM *Corpus for Spoken Romance Languages* (300,000 words for each of the languages: Italian, French, Spanish, and Portuguese) (Cresti and Moneglia 2005) is prosodically tagged for terminal and non-terminal breaks only. A terminal break marks an utterance and a non-terminal break marks "the internal prosodic parsing of a textual string which ends with a terminal break" (Cresti & Moneglia 2005: 25–26). Another corpus is the C-PROM corpus with 70 min of speech of seven spoken genres (Lacheret, Simon, Goldman, and Avanzi 2013: 97), designed to "develop an annotation tool in the Praat software" and "build an open data-base to train algorithms for semi-automatic prominence detection in French." By adopting a corpus-based approach, Lacheret *et al.*'s (2013) study examined the relationship between grammatical constraints (content and function words) and perception of prominences in French continuous speech.

A recently released prosodically annotated corpus is the SPICE-Ireland corpus that contains the annotation of tunes (Kallen and Kirk 2012).

In Hong Kong, almost half (900,000 words) of the 2-million-word *Hong Kong Corpus of Spoken English* (HKCSE) has been prosodically transcribed and is known as the HKCSE (prosodic) (Cheng, Greaves, and Warren 2008). The HKCSE (prosodic) is the first large-scale attempt to use the categories and conventions of discourse intonation (Brazil 1985/1997) in its transcription. This descriptive framework was chosen to prosodically transcribe the corpus because it was considered to be best suited to account for the ways in which intonation impacts pragmatic and situated meanings in interactive discourse (Cheng *et al.* 2008: 11). Other studies (see, for example, Goh 1998, 2000; Chun 2002; Hewings 1986, 1990; Cauldwell 2007; Pickering 2001) have used discourse intonation to analyze and describe a variety of genres and different languages. Brazil's discourse intonation framework has also been shown to be a useful framework to apply to English language teaching and English language learning materials (see, for example, Cauldwell 2003a, 2003b).

The HKCSE (prosodic) is unique in that it can be searched using specially designed software which enables the user to search for tone unit boundaries, the number of words in the tone units, frequencies of each of the tones, prominence, key, and termination across the corpus or a variety of subcorpora. The subcorpora are based on gender, gender plus mother tongue, domains of interaction (i.e. conversation, academic, business, and public), and genres. This makes it possible to compare, for example, the use of the rise tone by Hong Kong Chinese women in conversation versus Hong Kong Chinese women in business meetings. The results can then be displayed in the concordance format familiar to corpus linguistics with the search feature (e.g. rise tone or low key) centered in the concordance. The iConc software also allows the user to enter combinations of words or phrases with one or more discourse intonation features in the search function. In order for the software to search the corpus, the research team devised a notation system which allowed all of the possible combinations of discourse intonation features to be retrieved automatically (Cheng *et al.* 2008).

4 Corpus-based research on prosody

In this section, examples of recent corpus-based studies of prosody are described to provide a sense of the types of current work that are underway. Dehé & Wichmann (2010) examined the prosodic marking of epistemic parentheticals, such as *I think* and *I believe*, in the British Component of the International Corpus of English (ICE-GB, version 3.0; see Nelson, Wallis, and Aarts 2002), which amounts to 640,000 words of various spoken text types. They searched for comment clauses and identified 156 comment clauses in sentence-medial or sentence-final positions to be processed by PRAAT. Of the 156 clauses, 113 instances of epistemic parentheticals were clause medial and the rest clause final. Dehé and Wichmann (2010: 57) found that accent status is related to information status, and that the unstressed tokens are formulaic markers with a "falling tone decomposed into a high tone associated with an accented syllable," signaling that the proposition is the view of the speaker. They also found that the prosodic marking of epistemic parentheticals is based on a continuum from propositional to formulaic, reflecting the impact of grammaticalization. Thus prosodic separation and prominence were found with semantic transparency when the function was propositional. There was prosodic integration and deaccentuation when semantic bleaching had taken place, and, finally, when the epistemic parenthetical signaled disfluency and hesitation (i.e. it was functioning as a filler) and was non-prominent, the utterance was spoken with level tone (p. 20). Dehé and Wichmann (2010: 24) therefore concluded that prosody played an important role in "semantic disambiguation."

In another study, Flamson, Byrant, and Barrett (2011) examined the prosody of spontaneous humor in a small corpus of 4.75 hours of conversation collected on a Brazilian farm using PRAAT in order to compare the baseline and set-up utterances, the baseline and punchline utterances, and the set-up and punchline utterances. They found that of the 40 separate recordings, 16 were discarded because they had a lot of overlapping speech and so could not be processed by the software. Findings included that the speakers did not prosodically mark a joking "frame" (2011: 248) with the exceptions that speakers increased the loudness of their voice relative to the baseline loudness during the set-up of a joke and that speakers tended to narrow the pitch range of their voices when producing the punchline. The latter was thought to be a strategy to penetrate the laughter of the audience as they foresaw the upcoming punchline and began to laugh before it was even delivered (Flamson *et al.* 2011).

Calhoun (2010) analyzed the Switchboard corpus (Godfrey, Holliman, and McDaniel 1992) from which the researcher used 18 telephone conversations, totaling 2.5 hours and 10,143 words, involving 33 speakers. The corpus was analyzed on two levels: accent prediction and acoustic features of accents to find out how informativeness and prosodic factors act as constraints on the "probabilistic mapping of words onto metrical prosodic structure" (Calhoun 2010: 1130). Findings showed that a "higher level prosodic structure (including nuclear accent and major pause breaks) is based on information structure" (2010: 1130); as a result, prosodic requirements can influence the syntactic structure used to convey the message, ensuring that foci align with nuclear accents and the nuclear accent occurs late in the phrase. These findings are in line with earlier studies (see, for example, Halliday 1968) which showed that syntactic variation is driven by information structure which places "focal material in prosodically prominent positions" (Calhoun 2010: 1130).

In Cole, Mo, and Baek's (2010) study, the relationship between the syntactic form of an utterance and the perception of prosodic phrase structure by 97 untrained listeners was investigated with the use of spontaneous speech taken from the Buckeye corpus. In the study, three aspects were examined, namely variability by listener and speaker, the relationship between syntactic properties of an utterance and perceived prosody, and the role of acoustic duration, if any, as a cue to syntactic or prosodic phrases. Findings indicated that ordinary listeners' judgments show a close relationship between perceived boundaries and syntactic structure and they perceive prosodic boundaries in conversational speech in real time. Cole, Mo, and Baek (2010: 1174) concluded that in their perception of prosody, listeners are guided by both "acoustic cues and syntactic context," with the effect of syntactic context "partly independent of the effect due to final vowel duration," which is "the primary acoustic cue to prosodic phrase boundaries."

5 Corpus-based research on prominence

Two research studies examining the characteristic features of Singapore English (Goh 2000; Brown and Deterding 2005) suggest that different varieties of English might have different tendencies when it comes to speakers' choice of prominence. The findings from these studies provide evidence that speakers of Singapore English select prominence on pronouns more often than speakers of British English. Based on these studies, the HKCSE (prosodic) was examined by Cheng *et al.* (2008: 113–115) to see whether the same pattern exists among the HKC when compared with the NES. A study of spoken French confirmed that "perceptual illusion (i.e. perception of a prominence where the acoustics show a low degree of prominence) is far more frequent for content words than for function words" (Lacheret *et al.* 2013: 105). The finding was similar to that of Cole, Mo, and Hasegawa-Johnson's (2010), who studied English language and formulated the opposition "between *signal-driven prominence perception* and *expectation-driven hypothesis*" (Lacheret *et al.* 2013: 105).

In the following, the focus of discussion is on HKCSE (prosodic), prosodically transcribed using Brazil's discourse intonation system, and its tailor-made corpus-linguistic software called iConc (Cheng *et al.* 2008). iConc was designed specifically to enable the user to search for single or multiple discourse intonation features, combinations of these forms, or combinations of words/phrases and forms of discourse intonation. With the use of iConc, the more typical analyses associated with corpus linguistic studies, for example, frequency lists of prosodic features and concordances displaying prosodic features, can be carried out in addition to more qualitative forms of analysis.

In the following, an example analyzing the use of prominence is taken from Cheng *et al.* (2008) to compare the frequencies and percentages of occurrence of prominence on personal pronouns, possessive pronouns, and possessive determiners used by Hong Kong Chinese (HKC) and native English speakers (NES) in the HKCSE (prosodic). It also illustrates the kinds of findings uncovered by searching the HKCSE using the iConc software. This study addresses the research question: how do the two groups of speakers (HKC and NES) compare in the use of prominence on different pronouns in their spoken discourses?

6 Use of prominence on pronouns in HKCSE (prosodic)

The HKCSE (prosodic) was first searched for personal pronouns (*I*, *me*, *you*, *one*, *he*, *him*, *she*, *her*, *it*, *we*, *us*, *they*, and *them*) and possessive determiners and possessive pronouns (*my*, *mine*, *your*, *yours*, *his*, *her*, *hers*, *its*, *our*, *ours*, *their*, *theirs*, and *one's*) to examine the frequencies with which the HKC and NES select prominence on these words (Cheng *et al.* 2008: 114–115). The number of words spoken by the HKC in the corpus is 643,286, and that by the NES is 227,894, i.e. 2.8: 1. The discussion in the following does not, however, compare the relative proportion of use of different pronouns by the HKC and NES in the corpus. Rather, it is concerned with the two groups of speakers' respective use of prominence on different pronouns, in terms of percentages of prominence use, as opposed to non-use, on pronouns. Table 4.1 shows the frequencies of use of thirteen personal pronouns, and the use of prominence on each of the personal pronouns, by the two groups of speakers.

Table 4.1 *Personal pronouns in HKCSE (prosodic)*

Personal pronoun	HKC use of pronoun	HKC use of prominence on pronoun	NES use of pronoun	NES use of prominence on pronoun
1. I	14,092	4,552 (32.3%)	6,857	1,566 (22.9%)
2. me	1,152	281 (24.4%)	471	97 (20.6%)
3. you	15,014	2,681 (17.9%)	7,429	1,273 (17.1%)
4. one	17	12 (70.6%)	8	3 (37.5%)
5. he	1,494	404 (27.0%)	943	161 (17.1%)
6. him	212	70 (33.0%)	155	27 (17.4%)
7. she	695	246 (35.4%)	1,723	115 (6.7%)
8. her	288	71 (24.7%)	172	26 (15.1%)
9. it	9,176	1,321 (14.4%)	5,787	434 (7.5%)
10. we	8,228	1,689 (20.5%)	2,709	443 (16.4%)
11. us	769	239 (31.1%)	225	45 (20.0%)
12. they	4,629	1,403 (30.3%)	2,315	523 (20.6%)
13. them	961	236 (24.6%)	510	30 (5.9%)

Table 4.2 *Possessive pronouns in HKCSE (prosodic)*

Possessive pronoun (possessive determiners and possessive pronouns)	HKC use of possessive pronoun	HKC use of prominence on possessive pronoun	NES use of possessive pronoun	NES use of prominence on possessive pronoun
1. my	1,621	524 (32.3%)	543	138 (25.4%)
2. mine	34	32 (94.1%)	21	14 (66.7%)
3. your	1,746	298 (17.1%)	765	114 (14.9%)
4. yours	22	20 (90.1%)	15	12 (80.0%)
5. his	294	61 (20.7%)	155	17 (11.0%)
6. her	288	71 (24.7%)	172	26 (15.1%)
7. hers	0	0 (0%)	1	0 (0%)
8. its	329	46 (14.0%)	64	4 (6.3%)
9. our	2,304	521 (22.6%)	287	77 (26.8%)
10. ours	13	11 (84.6%)	2	2 (100.0%)
11. their	1,053	210 (20.0%)	290	54 (18.6%)
12. theirs	2	2 (100.0%)	0	0 (0%)
13. one's	6	4 (66.7%)	0	0 (0%)

Table 4.1 shows that across all the thirteen personal pronouns, HKC select prominence on personal pronouns proportionately more often than NES, especially in the cases of *one* (70.6% vs. 37.5%), *she* (35.4% vs. 6.7%), *them* (24.6% vs. 5.9%), and *him* (33.0% vs. 17.4%). For some personal pronouns, the two sets of speakers use prominence with similar percentages, particularly *you* (17.9% vs. 17.1%), *we* (20.5% vs. 16.4%), and *me* (24.2% vs. 20.6%).

Table 4.2 shows the frequencies of use of thirteen possessive pronouns, and the use of prominence on each of the possessive pronouns, by the two groups of speakers.

While the same phenomenon is seen Table 4.2, it is less consistent. In the case of *ours* (100% vs. 84.6%) and *our* (26.8% vs. 22.6%), it is NES who are more likely to select prominence. HKC select prominence proportionally more frequently than NES in all the other eleven possessive pronouns, the more notable ones being *theirs* (100% vs. 0%), *one's* (66.7% vs. 0%), and *mine* (94.1% vs. 66.7%).

The above discussion illustrates Brazil's (1997) view that prominence distinguishes words which are situationally informative. In this comparative study of patterns of prominence use on the 26 personal and possessive pronouns, HKC and NES are found to make differing contextual choices regarding their perception of the status of individual pronouns as situationally informative or otherwise. The finding that overall HKC speakers tend to select prominence on a range of pronouns much more frequently than NES speakers concurs with those of Goh (2000) and Brown and Deterding (2005) that the tendency for speakers of Singapore English to select prominence on pronouns is higher than for speakers of British English. Another finding is that there is a very wide range across all of the pronouns examined in terms of the speakers in general selecting prominence. Excluding non-occurrences (0%), the percentages range from 5.9% (*them* by NES) and 6.3% (*its* by NES) to 100% (*ours* by NES and *theirs* by HKC).

In Cheng *et al.*'s (2008) discussion of the relationship between the frequency of a word in the HKCSE (prosodic) and the number of times speakers make it prominent, they concluded that for all word classes there is "an apparent connection between low relative frequency in the HKCSE (prosodic) and prominence ... the more frequent a word is in the HKCSE (prosodic), the less likely it is to be spoken with prominence (and, of course, vice versa)" (2008: 120). This explains why the more frequently used pronouns, such as *its* (393) and *it* (14,963), are less likely to be assigned prominence by all the speakers than the much less frequent ones, such as *ours* (15) and *theirs* (2).

Cheng *et al.* (2008) further argue that Sinclair's (2004a) notion of the "phraseological tendency" in language use, whereby meanings created not by individual words but by the co-selection of words, offers an explanation for the inverse relationship described above. The more frequent a word is, the more functions it typically performs, and so the more likely its contribution to meaning when it is co-selected along with other words (Sinclair 1996). Thus when, for example, nouns or adverbs are modified, Cheng *et al.* (2008) show that they are less likely to be made prominent (see Figures 4.1 and 4.2, adapted from Cheng *et al.* 2008: 121–122).

Nouns and adverbs, such as *people* and *only*, often collocate with other words, such as *many, more*, and *most*, and *just* and *not*, respectively. Figures 4.1 and 4.2 show sample concordance lines for *most* + *people* and *just* + *only*. When words such as *people* and *only* are modified, it reduces the likelihood that these words are spoken with prominence, and prominence is more likely to be selected for the preceding modifier. In the HKCSE (prosodic),

1 \ [BEIjing] < auTHOrities > } {\ i [THINK] **MOST people** would < acKNOWledge > } { \ that in th

2 { \ [< MM >] } a4: { \ [< _ YEAH >] } { \ [**MOST] people** < aGREE > } { = we [< DON'T >] hav

3 { \ [OR] you < WON'T > get it } { \ but [^ **MOST] people** < GET > it } { = they [< ^ ARE >]

4 { \ [< ^ sucCESS >] } * { = but after all [^ **MOST] people** < HERE > } { \ [< ARE >] } { = i m

5 SEE > er } (.) {\ you [< KNOW >] } (.) { = [**MOST] people** have < GOT > } { ? [< TEL >] } { /

6 { = i [< THINK >] in } { = [< IN >] } { = [**MOST] people**'s < MIND > } { \ [parTIcularly] in

7 { \ [BUT] in their HEART of < ^ HEARTS > } { \ **most [PEOple**] < WANT > } (.) { \ they [< WANT >]

8 minutes < LATE > } { = [< AND >] er } {\ [^ **MOST] people** would have <THOUGHT > } { ? it's o }

9 > } { V to [< SAY >] } { = that [< **MOST >] people**} { = are [NOT] < aWARE > } { = o

10 > it yeah } { = like [< MOST >] of } { = [< **MOST >] of the people** that we } { = [< HANG >] }

Figure 4.1 Sample concordance lines for *most* + *people*

1 ngs you [< ^ CAN'T >] } a: * { \ she's**just** [< **ONly** >] } A: ** { = you [< KNOW >] she's just like }
2 * { / [< ^ NO >] } A: ((laugh)) a: { \ [**JUST**] **only**< ^ WORking > } A: ((laugh)) { \ [< OH >] } { \
3 of the [< CHILD >] } { \ if they have [**JUST**] **only** < ONE > } * { = so [^ ALL] the time i am enCOUr
4 [< WE >] } { ? [< JUST >] } b1: { = [**JUST**] **only** < ONE > night } x: { = [< YES >] } b1: { = [
5 ? but [^ SOMEtimes] < WHEN > you } { = [**JUST**] **only** eat the < SANDwich > } { = [< WHEN >] } { = [<
6 { \ [THIS] < SYStem > } { = is not [<**JUST** >] **only** for } { \ [toDAY'S] < USE > } { \ [< oKAY >] }
7 < ^ SOMEtimes >] } a: { = cos i'm [<**JUST** >] **only** s } { = [< SEE >] her only } * { \ [ORder] t
8 \ [< FACtors >] } (.) { = [THERE] is < **JUST** > **only** } { = [< _ ER >] } { \ [< PENnington >] } b2:
9 < LIKE >] } { = we [ACtually] SAID it's **JUST only** a < beGINning > } { / it's a [< LONG >] } { =
10 ** { ? so [< WE >] } b: { \ [WE] have **JUST only** about < STUdents >} { = [Okay] * NOW it's < T

Figure 4.2 Sample concordance lines for *just* + *only*

Cheng *et al.* (2008) found 60.92 percent of the instances of *people* are made prominent of the time, but when co-selected with *most*, this falls to 31.37 percent. Similarly, *only* is made prominent in 46.83 percent of the instances, but when co-selected with *just*, this falls to a mere 6.66 percent of the instances of *only*.

7 Conclusion

This chapter has outlined a brief review of research studies in prosody, primarily in intonation and other prosodic features including loudness, tempo, and voice quality, with a focus on a discussion of a few recent corpus studies in prosody, including a corpus-driven study of discourse intonation (Cheng *et al.* 2008), the intonational phrasing of parenthetical insertions (Dehé 2009), the effect of prosodic prominence on informative words in an utterance (Calhoun 2010), the role of syntactic structure in guiding prosody perception (Cole, Mo, and Baek 2010), the semantic–pragmatic meanings of epistemic parentheticals (comment clauses such as *I think*, *I believe*) realized by prosodic cues; for example, prosodic separation versus integration and prominence versus deaccentuation (Dehé and Wichmann 2010), and the prosodic feature of loudness in spontaneous humor (Flamson *et al.* 2011). The chapter has also examined the methods that are employed in prosodic research with a view to highlighting the strengths of corpus methods in the description of the features of tone of voice in naturally occurring spoken discourses. It has also discussed the findings of a corpus-driven study that has compared how different groups of speakers, HKC and NES, use prominence on different pronouns, namely personal pronouns, possessive pronouns, and possessive determiners, in their spoken discourses (Cheng *et al.* 2008).

The future directions for research in the prosody of large speech corpora, as noted by Lacheret *et al.* (2013: 95), could focus on establishing a single, simple, and common prosodic notation or transcription system that "would allow easy data exchange, comparison of annotations and analyses, and automatic processing," and would "form the basis for non-expert manual annotation, and be used for linguistic teaching and research." While the feasibility of having a common prosodic notation system is doubtful, given the range of approaches to, and frameworks of, the study of the prosody of speech, concerted efforts made by researchers and scholars in corpus linguistics and speech prosody will be most contributive to the advancement of the education and research in "the stream of speech" (Cauldwell 2013: 2).

5

Keywords

Jonathan Culpeper and Jane Demmen

1 Previous research on keywords

1.1 An introductory survey

The term "keyword" has considerable currency outside corpus linguistics, but there it is usually understood in a different sense. Raymond Williams's ([1976] 1983) book, entitled *Keywords*, was not the first to discuss keywords (see, for example, Matoré 1953). However, it has done more than any other publication to popularize the idea that some words – such as *democracy*, *private*, or *industry* – are "key" because they capture the essence of particular social, cultural, or political themes, thoughts or discourses. In fact, Williams's work has given rise to a journal: *Keywords: A Journal of Cultural Materialism*. Such words are deemed key on the basis of "readings" of their role in representing and shaping culturally important discourses. In corpus linguistics, a keyword has a quantitative basis: it is a term for a word that is statistically characteristic of a text or set of texts. The advantages of this basis are twofold. First, it is less subject to the vagaries of subjective judgments of cultural importance. Second, it does not rely on researchers selecting items that might be important and then establishing their importance, but can reveal items that researchers did not know to be important in the first place.

However, we would not want to argue that the two different kinds of keyword, qualitatively defined and quantitatively defined, are completely separate. Quantitatively defined keywords can indeed be of social, cultural, or political significance if they are characteristic of social, cultural, or political texts. That significance can be established by conducting qualitative analyses of the keywords identified through initial quantitative analysis. This has been the tactic of the bulk of studies applying the quantitative notion of keywords to particular texts, in a wide range of genres. These include, for example, Baker (2004) on gay and lesbian texts and Baker (2009b) on parliamentary debates, Fairclough (2000) and Jeffries and Walker (2012) on newspaper representations of New Labour, Johnson *et al.* (2003) on newspaper political correctness discourse, McEnery (2009) on books by social activist and campaigner Mary Whitehouse, Gerbig (2010) on travel writing, and Warren (2010) on engineering texts. Studies of literary texts include Archer and Bousfield (2010) and Culpeper (2002) on characters in Shakespeare's plays, Fischer-Starcke (2009) on Jane Austen's novels, Tribble (2000) on romantic fiction and, in the area of present-day drama, Bednarek (2010) on TV situation comedy and McIntyre (2010) on film dialogue. Research into languages other than English includes Fraysse-Kim (2010) on Korean school textbooks and Philip (2010) on Italian political speeches and press releases.

An important strand of work has focused on the nature of keywords (henceforth, the term *keyword(s)* will always refer to quantitatively defined items, unless specified otherwise). Discussions of keywords can most clearly be traced back to work in stylistics, particularly statistical stylistics, one of the early pioneers being Guiraud ([1954] 1975), but also to frequency-oriented discussions of style, notably that of Nils Erik Enkvist (e.g. 1964) on "style markers" (see Section 1.2). However, it was not until the advent of computer programs, and especially Mike Scott's *WordSmith Tools* (1996–2013), that we saw an explosion in studies, such as those listed in the previous paragraph. Notable research includes Scott's own, culminating in especially Scott and Tribble (2006) (see Section 1.3). By the mid 2000s, the field of keyword study had reached a certain maturity, with scholars having grappled with the notion of a keyword, applied it in analyses of discourses, and tackled methodological problems. Baker (2004) is a good example of a study that both performs a keyword analysis of a particular set of texts and reflects on the nature of that analysis. In the area of stylistics, Stubbs (2005) demonstrates the advantages of extending the analysis of keyness from single words to multi-word units (see Section 1.4). Following some reflections on landmark studies in keyness, we provide a more focused discussion of keyness methodology, in Section 1.5. At the end of Section 1, we sum up the state of the art in keyness research (in Section 1.6), and in Section 1.7 we highlight two relatively new approaches to investigating key items other than single words: key parts of speech (POS) and key semantic domains. In Section 2 we present a case study of the application of key POS and key semantic domains from Culpeper (2009b), which evaluates the benefits they offer in addition to an analysis of keyness at the word level.

1.2 Early history

Some notion that relatively frequent words can characterize particular literary styles, notably authorial styles, has been around for centuries, especially in French stylistics (Ullmann 1973: 72–73 cites authors from as far back as 1832). But it is studies in the area of statistical/computational stylistics or stylometry that present the clearest line of descent to the notion of a keyword used in corpus linguistics today. Perhaps the first to use the term "keyword" ("mot-clés") for this particular concept was Pierre Guiraud ([1954] 1975). Guiraud (1975: 64–66) contrasts "mots-clés" (based on relative frequency) with "mots-thèmes" (based on absolute frequency):

> Toute différente est la notion de *mots-clés*, qui ne sont plus considérés dans leur fréquence absolue, mais dans leur fréquence relative; ce sont les mots dont la fréquence s'écarte de la normale.
>
> [Wholly different is the notion of *mots-clés* (keywords), which are not considered in terms of their absolute frequency, but their relative frequency; these are the words whose frequency diverges from the normal.]

Simply being relatively statistically significant is not in itself the important point of interest. That lies in the link between keywords and style, but it is not articulated by Guiraud. Although he does not use the label "keywords," this link is clearly articulated by Nils Erik Enkvist (1964). In the following quotations, Enkvist defines style in terms of "frequencies," "probabilities," and "norms," and goes on to define "style marker":

> Style is concerned with frequencies of linguistic items in a given context, and thus with *contextual* probabilities. To measure the style of a passage, the frequencies of its linguistic items of different levels must be compared with the corresponding features in another text or corpus which is regarded as a norm and which has a definite relationship with this passage. For the stylistic analysis of one of Pope's poems, for instance, norms with varying contextual relationships include English eighteenth-century poetry, the corpus of Pope's work, all poems written in English in rhymed pentameter couplets, or, for greater contrast as well as comparison, the poetry of Wordsworth. Contextually distant norms would be, e.g., Gray's *Anatomy* or the London Telephone Directory of 1960. (1964: 29, original emphasis)
>
> We may . . . define style markers as those linguistic items that only appear, or are most or least frequent in, one group of contexts. In other words, style markers are contextually bound linguistic elements . . . style markers are mutually exclusive with other items which only appear in different contexts, or with zero; or have frequencies markedly different from those of such items. (1964: 34–35)

Enkvist's concept of style markers as words whose frequencies differ significantly from their frequencies in a norm corresponds precisely to what keywords are. Repetition is the notion underlying both style markers and hence keywords, but not all repetition, only repetition that statistically deviates from the pattern formed by that item in another context.

1.3 Establishment in corpus linguistics

It is in the context of corpus linguistics that the notion of keywords and the practice of keyword analysis has been developed and popularized, notably by Mike Scott through the KeyWords facility of WordSmith Tools (Scott

1996–2013), a program making it a relatively easy and rapid task for a researcher to calculate the incidences of each and every single word in the target data as well as a comparative dataset, undertake statistical comparisons between incidences of the same words in order to establish significant differences, and see the resulting keywords ranked according to degrees of significance of difference.

Scott and Tribble (2006: chapter 4) call attention to some of the most crucial issues in keyword analysis. They emphasize the nature of the comparative textual data, specifically the choice and type of "reference corpus" (see Section 1.5). They also argue that (apart from proper nouns, which often tend to appear), keywords tend to be of two main types: those relating to the text's "aboutness" or content, and those which are related to style (see further Scott 2013: 196). Scott (2000: 155) links aboutness to Halliday's (e.g. 1994) ideational metafunction, and also suggests that aboutness keywords are those that we would be "likely to predict" (Scott 2000: 160). Scott and Tribble's (2006: 60) analysis of Shakespeare's play *Romeo and Juliet* reveals the following as such keywords: *love*, *lips*, *light*, *night*, *banished*, *death*, and *poison*. But their analysis also shows that some items – exclamations, *thou*, *art*, and the pronoun *she* – do not fit the notion of aboutness, for which they propose the label "style" as a cover term (ibid.) (see Culpeper 2009b: 39 for an alternative categorization).

Scott and Tribble (2006) also illustrate the dispersion of keywords (see further Section 1.5). They examine the distribution of keywords in *Romeo and Juliet*, partly with the aim of demonstrating a "dispersion plot" (2006: 65–70). Figure 5.1 is generated by WordSmith Tools. Vertically, it displays

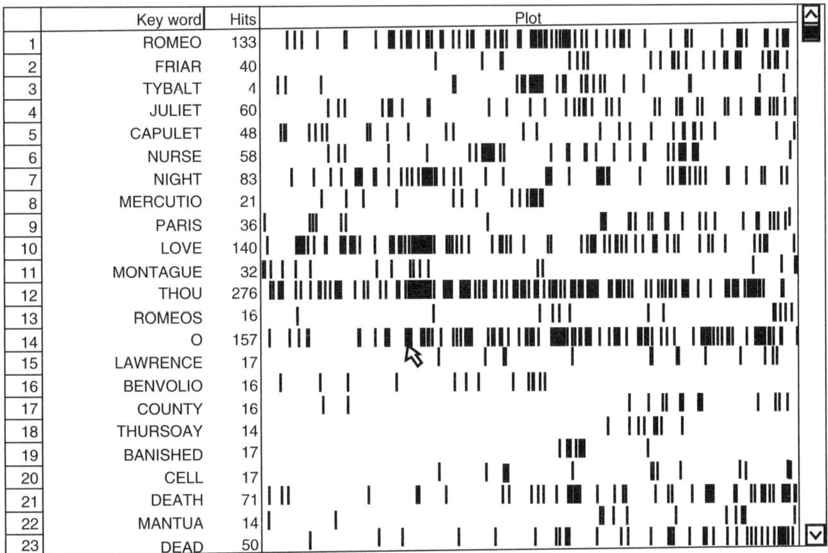

Figure 5.1 A keyword dispersion plot of *Romeo and Juliet* generated by *WordSmith Tools* (reproduced from Scott and Tribble 2006: 65)

keywords from the play in order of keyness; horizontally, the plot shows a small virtual line for every instance of the keyword, ordered from the beginning of the play on the left to the end of the play on the right.

The utility of this tool is obvious: a visual map of keyness enables us to see whether or not the keywords are likely to be general features of the play or concentrated at particular points. Scott and Tribble (2006: 66) make a distinction between "global" keywords, such as *thou*, which appears to be more or less evenly spread throughout the play, and "local" keywords, such as *banished*, which is mostly confined to a narrow area (Act III Scene ii, where the impact of Romeo's banishment is felt).

Connected with the issue of dispersion, Scott and Tribble (2006: 66–70) explore the idea that some keywords are not only key within a particular text but share collocational space with other keywords. For example, other keywords that collocate with the keyword *Romeo* within a 10-word collocational span (5 words to the left and 5 words to the right) are: *Benvolio*, *Juliet*, *banished*, *night*, *Tybalt*, *art*, *dead*, *O*, *thou*, and *is*. This suggests that there is a "natural association" (2006: 68) amongst the keywords. Thus, Romeo is friends with Benvolio, a lover of Juliet, banished by Capulet, meets at night, kills Tybalt, and so on. Scott and Tribble (2006: chapter 5) go on to explore linkages between keywords, in more detail, showing how these can be used to profile genres. They use the *British National Corpus* (BNC; see Aston and Burnard 1998) to investigate "key keywords" (keywords that are key in many texts) and "associates" (the co-key items associated with key keywords found in a number of texts) (see also Scott 1997). It should be noted that these notions can only be explored with a very large number of texts. Scott and Tribble (2006: 70–72) also analyze 1,000 randomly selected BNC texts in order to consider the POS characteristics of keywords. They report that four word classes (nouns, determiners, prepositions, and pronouns) account for 57 percent of keyword types, and that interjections, pronouns, alphabetical symbols, proper nouns, possessive *-s*, the verb *be*, and nouns are the most likely sources of keywords. They leave it for further research to investigate the reasons for this intriguing finding.

1.4 Further keyword developments

In his (2004) analysis of gay and lesbian texts, Baker discusses some of the major pitfalls in interpreting keywords. He shows the risks of overgeneralizing or overstating what keyness implies, emphasizing that "keywords only focus on lexical differences, rather than semantic, grammatical, or functional differences" (2004: 354). Baker not only points out that keywords may be unevenly dispersed in a corpus, and accounted for by only a minority of texts, but that keyness may involve only one of several possible senses of a word. The word *session*, for example, has a particular sexual meaning in the gay texts, which accounts for its keyness when compared to the lesbian texts, but if instances with this meaning are excluded then *session* would not be a keyword (2004: 354–55). Baker airs the pros and cons of lemmatizing or annotating data, adjusting the settings of corpus tools to constrain the numbers of results generated, and looking at multi-word units (see below and Section 1.5). He notes that a problem with moving beyond the word level to, for example, semantic categories is that it involves making subjective choices about the categories (2004: 353).

As a way of finding keywords which are not concentrated in only a minority of texts, Baker (2004: 350–351) also investigates key keywords. He argues that key keyword results include "keywords that we could have probably made a good educated guess at in advance," for example that the lesbian texts contains "more female pronouns and more words relating to female parts of the body and clothing" than the gay texts. Baker considers this a limitation of key keywords (2004: 350), though it is worth pointing out that empirical evidence which supports intuitions about corpora can be useful, particularly if one is not very familiar with the data or text-type. Baker (2004: 349) also makes the important point that keywords are oriented to differences between texts, and argues that similarities should not be overlooked. Despite this, most studies utilizing keyness have not sought to contextualize differences by looking at empirically-based language similarities. Baker's (2011) more recent concept of "lockwords" offers a possible way forward (see also the brief comments in Section 1.6).

Other scholars have focused specifically on the benefits of looking at key multi-word units in addition to single words. Various terms are adopted for multi-word linguistic units, such as "lexical bundles" (Biber *et al.* 1999), "word clusters" (the items generated by Scott's program WordSmith Tools) and "n-grams," sometimes under a general heading of "phraseology." As might be expected, there are issues of compatibility, depending on the program and/or parameters used. Multi-word units are often structural fragments rather than complete units. They are best considered as recurring word sequences which have collocational relationships. Investigating key multi-word units has been particularly fruitful in the area of stylistics, and popularised by Stubbs' (2005) analysis of Joseph Conrad's novel *Heart of Darkness*. Stubbs argues that looking at single (key)words offers limited prospects for analysis, pointing out that words occur in recurrent "lexico-grammatical patterns" (2005: 15–18) and that "collocations create connotations" (2005: 14). Stubbs illustrates that recurrent multi-word units provide evidence of recurrent metaphors and/or intertextuality (2005: 13–14) which may not be discernible from single-word results, and that they can reveal pragmatic and discoursal aspects of dialogue and narrative. Other linguists with an interest in literary texts who have made notable contributions to key multi-word unit research include Mahlberg (e.g. 2007), who shows how some of the memorable characters in Charles Dickens' novels are created through recurrent localized word clusters, and Fischer-Starcke (e.g. 2009), who investigates how frequent phrases in Jane Austen's novels contribute to the construction of characters, and places such as the city of Bath.

1.5 Methodology

To generate a list of keywords, corpus linguistic software programs such as WordSmith Tools, AntConc, and WMatrix conduct statistical comparisons between the words in one dataset (also called the "target" corpus) and another (the comparative or "reference" corpus). This is done by first generating a "word list" of the lexical items in the dataset and the reference corpus, using the appropriate program function. The keyness tool is then run, which makes a series of frequency-based comparisons using a statistical significance test, typically Dunning's (1993) log-likelihood test or the chi-square test. The tool ranks the results in a list showing the keyness value (statistical significance) of each word. Positive keywords are those with comparatively high frequency, and negative keywords are those with comparatively low frequency (Scott e.g. 2013: 196).

The ease and rapidity of keyness analysis afforded by the programs mentioned above is the major boon. This boon is also apparent when one considers other methods designed to reveal styles. Using data comprising three genres (conversation, monologic speech, and academic prose), Xiao and McEnery (2005) compare a multidimensional analysis of the type conducted in Biber (1988) with a keyword analysis. The results they obtain are "similar" for both methods (Xiao and McEnery 2005: 76), but the keyword analysis was "less demanding" (2005: 77), for the reason that multidimensional analysis first involves some relatively complex algorithms for the extraction of certain grammatical features from the corpus, and then further relatively complex statistical analysis. However, the downside of the comparative ease of keyword analysis is the potential for performing studies in a relatively mechanical way without a sufficiently critical awareness of what is being revealed or how it is being revealed. Below, we will briefly dwell on some important considerations for the analyst seeking to generate maximally useful keyword results.

1.5.1 The reference corpus

Scott and Tribble (2006) conclude that "while the choice of reference corpus is important, above a certain size, the procedure throws up a robust core of KWs [keywords] whichever the reference corpus used" (2006: 64). Of course, a set of data which has no relationship whatsoever with the data to be examined is unlikely to reveal interesting results regarding the characteristics of that data (as Enkvist (1964) notes with regard to comparing a poem by Pope with a telephone directory; see Section 1.2 above). What if one selects a huge multi-genre corpus, such as the BNC, as indeed other studies have done (e.g. Johnson *et al.* 2003; Tribble 2000)? We can readily hypothesize that some genres within that corpus have a relatively close relationship with the data to be examined, whilst other genres have a relatively distant relationship. The choice of the reference corpus will affect the potential for acquiring keyword results that are relevant to the particular aspect of the text(s) one is researching (see also Scott 2013: 197).

For example, Johnson *et al.* (2003) are interested in what characterizes the discourse in which political correctness expressions appear in different newspapers. Some of the keywords they retrieve simply reflect the fact that it is newspaper discourse, and have nothing specifically to do with political correctness.

Reference corpora are typically the same size as the target corpus, or very much larger. Scott and Tribble (2006: 58) suggest that the reference corpus "should be an appropriate sample of the language which the text we are studying . . . is written in," and that "appropriate sample" "usually means a large one, preferably many thousands of words long and possibly much more." Precisely what counts as large enough is still a matter of debate. Scott's (2009) findings indicate that the content of the reference corpus is more crucial than the size, where only one register or text type is under investigation. Xiao and McEnery (2005: 70) compare two reference corpora, the 100-million-word BNC and the one-million-word Freiburg–LOB Corpus (see Hundt *et al.* 1998), and achieve almost identical keyword lists, thus concluding that "the size of reference corpus is not very important in making a keyword list."

1.5.2 Minimum frequency

The minimum frequency cut-off parameter can be used to exclude words that will be identified as unusual simply because they happen not to have occurred, or have occurred very infrequently, in either the dataset or the reference corpus. Proper nouns, for example, are often amongst these one-off occurrences. This is not to say that such phenomena – which are referred to as "hapax legomena" – are uninteresting (see, for example, Hoover 1999: chapter 4). The problem is that in a list of keyword results, mixing frequent items with very infrequent items often means mixing generalized phenomena with phenomena that are extremely localized, making an account of the keyword list problematic (see the following subsection for a statistical technique designed to reduce this problem). It is advisable to experiment with different minimum frequency cut-off points to minimize this problem, whilst ensuring that sufficient results are generated (if the dataset is small). A further point of good practice is to provide the raw frequencies of each keyword, in addition to its keyness value (log-likelihood or chi-square) when keyword lists are given.

1.5.3 Statistical significance

The significance test calculates the significance of the difference in frequency between the word in the target data and in the reference corpus. Some programs offer a choice of statistical tests (e.g. WordSmith Tools offers both chi-square and log-likelihood), while others do not (Wmatrix, for example, offers only log-likelihood). Culpeper (2009b: 36) conducts keyword analyses using both tests and discovers that the "same results were revealed with only minor and occasional differences in the ranking of keywords, differences which had no effect on the overall picture revealed by the keywords." According to Scott (2013: 199), log-likelihood "gives a better estimate of keyness, especially when contrasting long texts or a whole genre against your reference corpus," although he also suggests that "where the notion of risk is less important than that of selectivity, you may often wish to set a comparatively low *p* value threshold such as 0.000001 (one in 1 million) . . . so as to obtain fewer keywords" (2013: 195–196). The *p* value is a number between 0 and 1 used in log-likelihood and chi-square tests. It indicates the probability of a key result occurring by chance; see e.g. Scott (2013: 203–204). Rayson (2003), evaluating various statistical tests for data involving low frequencies and different corpus sizes, favors the log-likelihood test "in general" and, moreover, a 0.01% significance level "if a statistically significant result is required for a particular item" (2003: 155). Further information on significance levels and cut-off thresholds is given on the website http://ucrel.lancs.ac.uk/llwizard.html, which also offers a log-likelihood calculator.

Alternative or additional statistical manipulations have been proposed. In brief, these are:

Bayes Factors. Wilson (2013) argues that the interpretation of the significance test in keyword analyses is often erroneous, notably because of the role of the null hypothesis. The *p*-value is a conditional probability: it is based on a range of statistics conditional upon the null hypothesis being true (i.e. there is no actual difference in the frequency of this word between the larger populations from which the samples are drawn). Wilson's solution is to use Bayesian statistics which focus on the weight of evidence against the null hypothesis (i.e. against there being no true difference between the populations from which the samples were drawn). One of the benefits of this technique is that it more accurately pinpoints the items that are highly key in the list.

The Cochran rule. Expected frequencies, as opposed to observed frequencies (i.e. the number of cases that actually occur), are calculated in the background by keyword programs. They are important because they influence statistical reliability; expected frequencies below 5 have been shown to render chi-square statistics unreliable (Oakes 2009: 165–166; Rayson *et al.* 2004b: 928). The Cochran rule (Cochran 1954) has been proposed as a method for eliminating items with expected frequencies with low statistical reliability, and has been extended by Rayson *et al.* (2004b) on the basis of numerous experiments with different corpus sizes, word frequencies, and statistical cut-off levels (see also Walker 2012). However, the advantages of the Cochran rule may vary according to the kind of analysis applied to keywords, and, as with Bayes Factors, at the present time it needs to be applied manually.

Bonferroni's correction. It is also possible to apply additional statistical methods to adjust the *p* value in order to control for the fact that a keyword list is a set of multiple statistical comparisons, the argument being that the probability of a result occurring by chance increases with the number of comparisons performed. See for example Gries (2003a: 82–87), with regard to the Bonferroni correction, and for further discussion Gelman *et al.* (2012).

1.5.4 Dispersion

Uneven dispersion makes the interpretation of keywords difficult (Leech *et al.* 2001; Gries 2008). We have already discussed the notion of dispersion in Section 1.3, where we showed how a keyword plot gives a visual representation of dispersion. Eyeballing such a representation is not a precise method. Some scholars have proposed that the dataset and its reference corpus should be divided into parts, and then two-sample tests such as the *t*-test (Paquot and Bestgen 2009) or the Wilcoxon-Mann-Whitney test (Kilgarriff 1996) should be deployed.

We would concur with Baker (2004) that the best general approach to settings for keywords is to determine them by testing various possibilities and, in most cases, choosing a combination that results in: (1) a sufficient number of results to meet one's research goals, (2) a not overwhelming number of words to analyze, (3) an adequate dispersion of at least some keyword instances, and (4) any one-off or extremely rare word types being minimized. It may be possible for future research to produce more precise guidelines, though settings cannot be reduced to a simple mathematical formula for the reason that different research purposes and contexts have different requirements. Minimally, all studies should declare the settings that are deployed.

1.6 The state of the art

Keywords and other key items have become established in corpus linguistics as useful methods for identifying the lexical characteristics of texts. It is recognized that the notion of exactly what qualifies as key in any study is influenced by the settings and parameters of the program used, and by the comparator texts (in the reference corpus). Keyness in corpus linguistics is but the first statistical step in the analysis of texts. As Scott emphasises, keyness is context-dependent, and keywords "are pointers, that is all" (2010: 56).

Relatively new software tools, notably Paul Rayson's web-based WMatrix (Rayson 2003, 2008, 2009), enable users to annotate their datasets for both grammatical and semantic categories relatively easily and rapidly, and then to identify which categories are key. Studies include: Jones *et al.* (2004) on key POS categories in a spoken corpus of English for Academic Purposes, Afida (2007) on semantic domains in business English, and Archer *et al.* (2009) on semantic domains in Shakespeare's plays (see http://ucrel.lancs.ac.uk/wmatrix for further references on Wmatrix). We examine the added value of POS and semantic domain analyses to word-level keyness in Section 2.

The contributors to Bondi and Scott (2010) explore some current issues surrounding the theoretical nature of keyness, provide new perspectives on different aspects of keyness, and extend the existing boundaries of keyness methods in examining specific text-types. Stubbs, for example, discusses the relationship between the concept of "keywords" in corpus linguistics (as a textual feature) and ideas of sociocultural "keywords" (see Section 1.1), arguing that "[s]ocial institutions and text-types imply each other: they are different way of thinking about the same thing" (2010: 40). He points out that the findings from corpus studies of keyness address research questions in particular discourse contexts, but do not yet extend to bigger "cognitive and social questions" (ibid.).[1] Groom focuses on closed-class keywords in a corpus of academic history journal articles, arguing that they "may actually be preferable over their open-class counterparts as objects of corpus-driven discourse analysis because they offer much greater coverage of the phraseological data in a specialized corpus in both quantitative and qualitative terms" (2010: 73). Warren (2010) airs the matter of aboutness, using "concgrams" (Greaves 2009; see also Scott 2013: 332) and "aboutgrams" to investigate two different engineering texts, a process he derives from Sinclair (2006). Gerbig (2010) uses keywords as a starting point, and extends her analysis of a diachronic corpus of travel writing to key keywords and associates, extended lexical units, key phrases, and phrase frames.

Other recent developments include McIntyre and Archer's (2010) use of key semantic domains to investigate mind style in a play, and the partial automation of metaphor analysis, also using key semantic domains (Archer *et al.* 2009; Koller *et al.* 2008; Deignan and Semino 2010). Finally, Baker (2011) puts forward the concept of a "lockword," a potential means of addressing similarities between texts, bearing in mind that keyness is oriented to differences (Baker 2004: 349). Baker argues that lockwords are words with the most similar high frequency, statistically, across several corpora, and that these can be considered the opposite of keywords (2011: 73; see Taylor 2013 for further exploration of lockwords and the "locking" concept).

1.7 The value of going beyond keywords: key parts of speech and semantic categories

Rayson (2008: 543) puts forward two arguments for conducting key POS and semantic analyses *in addition* to keyword analyses. He argues, firstly, that they present fewer categories for the researcher to grapple with. Whilst it may well be the case that fewer keywords can be produced by tweaking program settings, it is also the case that by conducting key POS

[1] A recent linguistic pragmatics study by Bigi and Greco Morasso (2012) investigates keywords which trigger or activate cognitive frames in argumentation, using a psychologically salient concept of a "keyword," i.e. a sociocultural concept not a statistical concept.

and semantic analyses one can get clues to patterns that exist in a large set of keywords. Second, Rayson argues that POS and semantic categories can group lower-frequency words which might not appear as keywords individually and could thus be overlooked. In the case study in Section 2, we assess what added value the researcher can gain from the application of keyness methods to POS and semantic domains, in addition to single words, by presenting some data and analysis from Culpeper's (2009b) research.

2 Case study: evaluating key part of speech and semantic domain analysis

2.1 Introduction

Culpeper (2009b) addresses the following research question: by extending keyness analysis to grammatical or semantic tags, precisely what do we gain beyond what we could have learnt from a keyword analysis alone? Importantly, he sought to quantify what additional findings would be reached through the investment of time and effort in the further analytical steps of investigating key POS and key semantic domains. The results illuminate how and where these newer keyness techniques can most usefully be deployed. We present these here in order to assist researchers in making informed choices about the kinds of key linguistic structures that will most usefully serve their aims. The continuing development of keyness tools means that scholars have ever-widening choices to make about which techniques and programs to deploy from those that are now available, yet time and other resources are inevitably finite. Limited space means that we present a selection of results and analysis only, in Section 2.3, following an outline of the methodology used (in Section 2.2).

2.2 Methodology

Culpeper's (2009b) study built on the keyword analysis of Shakespeare's *Romeo and Juliet* reported in Culpeper (2002), using the same data, sourced from the 1914 Oxford edition of the plays edited by W. J. Craig. The data comprise the speech of the six characters who speak the most (their total speech varying from 1,293 to 5,031 words) plus reference corpora devised for each character containing the speech of all the others. Keywords were derived using *WordSmith Tools*. The statistical criteria used are a log-likelihood value of 6.63 or higher, which is equivalent to $p < 0.01$, and a raw frequency value of five or more. These same criteria are maintained for all the analyses in Culpeper (2009b). To illustrate, the positive (over-used) keywords derived for Romeo were (in rank-order of strength of keyness): *beauty* (10), *love* (46), *blessed* (5), *eyes* (14), *more* (26), *mine* (14), *dear* (13), *rich* (7), *me* (73), *yonder* (5), *farewell* (11), *sick* (6), *lips* (9), *stars* (5), *fair* (15), *hand* (11), *thine* (7), *banished* (9), *goose* (5), and *that* (84).

Culpeper (2009b) focused on three characters: Romeo, Mercutio, and the Nurse, whose keywords he determined to be characterized by different functions (see Halliday e.g. 1994): ideational (Romeo), textual (Mercutio) and interpersonal (the Nurse). Texts containing the speech of Romeo, Mercutio, and the Nurse were then uploaded into WMatrix, which automatically ran them through a number of programs. The Constituent Likelihood Automatic Word-tagging System (CLAWS) applies POS tags (see further Garside 1987; Leech *et al.* 1994). The UCREL (University Centre for Computer Corpus Research on Language) Semantic Analysis System (USAS) tool applies semantic tags, and is an annotation program designed for automatic dictionary-based content analysis (see Rayson *et al.* 2004a).[2] Needless to say, neither POS nor semantic tagging achieves a perfect result (semantic tagging is claimed to achieve an accuracy rate of 91 percent with present-day English by Rayson *et al.* 2004a). Each and every resulting key item was checked manually, in order to assess whether or not that item accounted for a textual pattern or style that had also been accounted for in the other analyses (and also, in the case of the grammatical and semantic analyses, whether or not that item was simply a tagging error).

2.3 Results of key part of speech analysis

Below, we briefly introduce some of the POS and semantic category results and discussion for Romeo (based on Culpeper 2009b). Table 5.1 displays

Table 5.1 *Romeo's parts-of-speech rank-ordered for positive keyness (i.e. relative overuse) (keywords are in bold text)*

Grammatical category (and tag code and frequency)	*Items within the category (and their raw frequencies) up to a maximum of ten types if they are available (excluding clear tagging errors in square brackets)*
Nominal possessive personal pronoun (e.g. *mine, yours*) (PPGE) (17)	**mine** (8), hers (4), **thine** (3), [his (1)], yours (1)
Comparative after-determiner (e.g. *more, less, fewer*) (DAR) (16)	**more** (15), less (1)
1st person sing. objective personal pronoun (i.e. *me*) (PPIO1) (73)	**me** (73)
General adjective (JJ) (328)	**fair** (14), good (10), **dear** (10), sweet (8), **rich** (7), dead (6), holy (5), true (5), heavy (5), **blessed** (4)
1st person sing. subjective personal pronoun (i.e. *I*) (PPIS1) (144)	I (144)
Than (as conjunction) (CSN) (16)	than (16)

[2] Both CLAWS and USAS were developed at Lancaster University. More information about the CLAWS tagger can be found at: www.comp.lancs.ac.uk/ucrel/claws, and further details about the USAS tagger at http://ucrel.lancs.ac.uk/usas/.

the grammatical categories that are key in Romeo's speech. Insecure items, mostly because of tagging errors, are in square brackets.

With the exception of the category General adjective (JJ), all the key grammatical categories in Table 5.1 are dominated by a single item. This is because such categories have high frequencies of tokens but a relatively limited range of types. The category General adjective (JJ) stands in contrast, because it is a more contentful lexical category including a broader and more even group of items. The more grammatical categories tend to contain items which have already occurred in the keyword results, since those categories are mainly populated by high-frequency items that are also likely to appear in a keyword analysis. Four of the most frequent words for each of the six categories (*mine*, *more*, *me*, *fair*) also occur as keywords. Note that among them is the category General adjective (JJ), although the status of this whole category is questionable because most of the instances of *good* and *dear* occur in vocative expressions. In contrast, in the more grammatical categories, the first-person singular subjective personal pronoun (*I*; PPIS1) and *than* (as conjunction; CSN), do *not* include members which are keywords at the significance level used in this paper (i.e. $p < 0.01$).[3] Therefore, we cannot say that the prevalence of a limited number of high-frequency items in grammatical categories means that they will also occur in a keyword list, although this tends to be the case.

Table 5.2 displays the semantic categories that are key in Romeo's speech. In Table 5.2, very few lexical items in the semantic categories also occur as keywords. The top two categories, Relationship: Intimate/sexual (S3.2) and Liking (E2+), are, of course, closely linked semantically. Considered overall, the appearance of these categories as most key is very well motivated; as we might expect, the findings confirm Romeo's role of one of the lovers in the play. The contents of the third-ranked category, Colour and colour patterns (O4.3), are rather less predictable. In some cases Romeo describes literal light, e.g.: "But, soft! what *light* through yonder window breaks?" (II.ii). However, the terms are more often used metaphorically, e.g.: "More *light* and *light*; more *dark* and *dark* our woes" (III.v). Such metaphors are quite conventional: *light*/*dark* to mean happiness/unhappiness, *greenness* to mean envy, and *redness*/*whiteness* to mean life/death. The semantic tagger does not (currently) make a distinction between literal and metaphorical meanings. Despite this, metaphorical patterns surface in some of the semantic categories which occur as key.

To reach a more definite general conclusion about what is to be gained from extending a keyness analysis to POS categories or semantic

[3] In the keyword analysis, the word forms *I* scores and *than* achieve log-likelihood of 5.52 and 6.18, respectively, both of which are lower than the critical value of 6.63 for $p < 0.01$. These single items may occur as key in grammatical categories but not as *keywords* because the more items that populate a category, the harder it is for differences in frequency between items in that category to surface. Differences relating to a specific item in that category could be averaged out by other items.

Table 5.2 *Romeo's semantic categories rank-ordered for positive keyness (i.e. relative overuse) (keywords are in bold text)*

Semantic category (and tag code and frequency)	*Items within the category (and their raw frequencies) up to a maximum of ten types if they are available (excluding clear tagging errors in square brackets)*
Relationship: Intimate/sexual (S3.2) (48)	**love** (34), kiss (5), lovers (3), kisses (2), paramour (1), wantons (1), chastity (1), in love (1)
Liking (E2+) (38)	**love** (15), **dear** (13), loving (3), precious (2), like (1), doting (1), amorous (1), [revels (1)], loves (1)
Colour and colour patterns (O4.3) (33)	light (6), bright (4), pale (3), dark (3), green (2), stained (2), black (2), golden (1), white (1), crimson (1)
Education in general (P1) (9)	teach (3), [course (2)], philosophy (2), school (1), schoolboys (1)
Business: Selling (I2.2) (19)	sell (4), [bid (4)], shop (2), hire (2), buy (1), sold (1), [stands (1)], [bade (1)], [stand (1)], [store (1)], merchandise (1)
Thought, belief (X2.1) (26)	think (7), feel (3), devise (2), believe (2), [take thence (1)], thinking (1), thought (1), engrossing (1), dreamt (1), [found (1)], in thine eyes (1), in mind (1)
Affect: Cause/Connected (A2.2) (20)	[hence (7)], reason (2), [spurs (2)], depend (1), for fear of (1), provoke (1), excuse (1), effect (1), consequence (1), to do with (1), appertaining (1), prompt (1)
Avarice (S1.2.2+) (7)	envious (3), [mean (1)], tempt (1), jealous (1), sparing (1)
The universe (W1) (21)	world (8), [word (6)], **stars** (5), moon (2)
Money: Affluence (I1.1+) (7)	**rich** (7)

categories, Culpeper (2009b: 53–54) quantifies the benefits of each type of analysis for the three characters. Although the raw frequencies are low, in percentage terms 75 percent of the POS categories are mainly populated by one or two words which also occur as keywords, and 66.6 percent of the semantic categories mainly constitute one or two words which also occur as keywords. Therefore, although the tests clearly need to be replicated on bigger datasets, the findings indicate that a key*word* analysis led to most of the conclusions. At face value, the difference between 75 percent and 66.6 percent appears to be of little or no consequence. It is notable, though, that the POS and semantic domain results for Romeo overlapped rather less with the keyword analysis: 66 percent for the POS categories and 40 percent for the semantic categories. When keyword lists are mainly populated by those which are ideational, which reflect the 'aboutness' of the text, the POS, and particularly the semantic keyness analyses can make a more valuable contribution, taking the analysis to a level beyond that which emerges from the keywords. The likely explanation for this is that more grammatical items, and also discourse markers, tend to occur as a relatively limited range of types, each with frequent tokens. This means that, if categories constituting these kinds of items are identified as key in the POS or semantic analyses (as they are for the Nurse and Mercutio), then such items are also very likely to occur in the keyword analysis.

The outcomes of Culpeper (2009b) lend support to Rayson's (2008: 543) arguments for conducting key POS and semantic domain analyses *in addition* to keyword analyses, given at the start of this section. In particular, Rayson's claim that POS and semantic categories can group lower frequency words, which might not appear as keywords individually and could thus be overlooked, is confirmed in the analyses included in this chapter. Examples include general adjectives and Romeo's (metaphorical) colour terms. These kinds of results are not easy to predict, but closer analysis indicates that they are well motivated. It should be noted, though, that the added value obtained from these analyses is more specific than indicated by Rayson, as it applies only to more lexical, more ideational categories.

3 Conclusion

In addition to charting the history and development of keyword research (in Section 1), our discussions have been designed to emphasize that key lexical items should be used as a *guide* for what to analyze qualitatively, and not considered the end product in themselves. We have emphasized (particularly in Section 1.5) that the usefulness of key items, and the quality of analyses and conclusions based upon them, relies on careful and explicit manipulation of the keyword tools settings as well as interpretation. Finally, our case study in Section 2 aimed to demonstrate that, given the availability of new and varied techniques for investigating keyness in different kinds of linguistic structures, it is necessary to consider and test out which one(s) will most usefully target the language features the researcher wishes to uncover.

The future of work involving keyness looks bright. We can expect developments in three directions. First, there is scope for methodological improvements. As discussed in Section 1.5, statistical refinements have been suggested, some of which have yet to be integrated into mainstream programs (e.g. log ratio as a means of taking effect size into consideration in the ranking of keyword results is being incorporated into a number of programs). Second, the extension of keyness analysis to POS and semantic categories need not stop there. In principle, any computer-readable form or user-supplied tag could be interrogated. For example, styles of punctuation could be thus investigated. Third, we are only just beginning to see the deployment of keyness analyses in academia (currently, many studies have focused on literary texts). The full potential of keyness analyses across the humanities and social sciences has yet to be realized.

6

Collocation

Richard Xiao

1 Introduction

While the study of recurrent co-occurrence of words dates back to as early as the mid eighteenth century, which saw the publication of Alexander Cruden's concordance of the Bible (Kennedy 1998: 14), serious linguistic research on collocation only started in the 1950s with the British linguist John Firth, who introduced the concept of collocation into modern linguistics. Collocation is one of the linguistic concepts "which have benefited most from advances in corpus linguistics" (Krishnamurthy 2000: 33–34). Indeed, corpus linguistics has not only redefined collocation but has also foregrounded collocation as a focus of research by neo-Firthian linguists as well as those of other traditions.

This chapter aims to provide a critical account of corpus-based collocation research. Following this brief introduction, Section 2 explores the state of the art in collocation research, on the basis of which Section 3 presents a cross-linguistic study of the collocational behavior and semantic prosodies of a group of near synonyms in English and Chinese. Section 4 concludes the chapter by summarizing the research.

2 State of the art in collocation research

This section starts with discussions of the definitional and methodological issues in collocation analysis (Sections 2.1 and 2.2), and then explores the meaning arising from collocation (Section 2.3) and collocational phenomena beyond lexical level (Section 2.4), which is followed by a discussion of the importance of collocation in language use (Section 2.5).

2.1 Definitional issues

The term "collocation" was first used by Firth (1957: 194) when he said "I propose to bring forward as a technical term, meaning by *collocation*, and apply the test of *collocability*." While collocation has been studied in linguistics for more than half a century, there is little consensus on the definition of the term. According to Firth (1968: 181–182), "collocations of a given word are statements of the habitual or customary places of that word." However, the meaning of "habitual or customary" is vague and has been interpreted and operationalized differently in different areas of linguistic research. For example, in traditional discourse analysis, Halliday and Hasan (1976: 287) use collocation as "a cover term for the cohesion that results from the co-occurrence of lexical items that are in some way or other typically associated with one another, because they tend to occur in similar environments," as exemplified by word pairs such as *letter*, *stamp*, and *post office*, or *hair*, *comb*, *curl*, and *wave*. This kind of conceptually based associations between lexical items have been called "coherence collocation," as opposed to "neighbourhood collocation" in corpus linguistics (Scott 2012), i.e. words that actually co-occur with a word in text (e.g. the co-occurrence of *my*, *this*, and *a* with *letter*). In spite of its name, coherence collocation, which takes a conceptual approach, differs clearly from Firth's (1957: 196) notion of collocation: "Meaning by collocation is an abstraction at the syntagmatic level and is not directly concerned with the conceptual or idea approach to the meaning of words." Coherence collocations are hard to measure using a statistical measure. In contrast neighborhood collocations can be retrieved using the computational method developed by Sinclair (1966: 415):

> We may use the term node to refer to an item whose collocations we are studying, and we may then define a span as the number of lexical items on each side of a node that we consider relevant to that node. Items in the environment set by the span we will call collocates.

In addition to coherence and neighborhood collocations, the term has also been used in computational linguistics to refer to a phrase that is semantically non-compositional and structurally non-modifiable and non-substitutable (Manning and Schütze 1999: 184), which, according to Evert (2008), has become better known now as "multiword expression." It is important to note, however, that a multiword expression as commonly understood is not necessarily non-compositional, non-modifiable, or non-substitutable as defined in Manning and Schütze (1999). This phraseological notion of collocation has been investigated under different names including, for example, "lexical bundle" and "word cluster" in corpus linguistics, "multiword unit" and "*n*-gram" in natural language processing, and "formulaic expression" in language education. Unfortunately, collocation has been used to refer to all three different types of recurrent co-occurrence which may or may not overlap with one other.

While collocation analysis has traditionally been concerned with contiguous word associations, recent developments in corpus linguistics have also made it possible to analyze the so-called "concgrams," i.e., sequences of associated words, whether consecutive or non-consecutive, which allow constituency variation (i.e. AB, ACB) and/or positional variation (i.e. AB, BA) (Cheng, Greaves, and Warren 2006: 413–414).

2.2 Methods used in collocation analysis

While some examples of collocation can be identified intuitively, "particularly for obvious cases of collocation" (Greenbaum 1974: 83), intuition is typically a poor guide to collocation. Greenbaum recognized this, and tried to address this problem by eliciting data on collocation from a number of informants "to provide access to the cumulative experience of large numbers of speakers" (ibid.). In those introspection-based elicitation experiments, he found it quite unsurprising that "people disagree on collocations" (ibid.). Intuition, as noted, may not be reliable, "because each of us has only a partial knowledge of the language, we have prejudices and preferences, our memory is weak, our imagination is powerful (so we can conceive of possible contexts for the most implausible utterances), and we tend to notice unusual words or structures but often overlook ordinary ones" (Krishnamurthy 2000: 32–33). Partington (1998: 18) also observes that "there is no total agreement among native speakers as to which collocations are acceptable and which are not." As Hunston (2002: 68) argues, whilst "collocation can be observed informally" using intuition, "it is more reliable to measure it statistically, and for this a corpus is essential." This is because a corpus can reveal such probabilistic semantic patterns across many speakers' intuitions and usage, to which individual speakers have no access (Stubbs 2001a: 153).

As noted earlier, the terms like "habitual" and "customary" as used by Firth (1957) are vague and impressionistic; they rely on the simple frequency counts of co-occurrence (Krishnamurthy 2002). This approach to collocation analysis, which is also adopted by neo-Firthian linguists, is labeled as "collocation-via-concordance" as opposed to "collocation-via-significance" in McEnery and Hardie (2012: 126–127). This latter approach depends on more rigorous inferential statistical tests than simple frequency counts and is now extensively used in collocation analysis. Indeed, the role of statistical tests in collocation analysis was well recognized decades ago, when Halliday (1966: 159) argued that "[the] occurrence of an item in a collocational environment can only be discussed in terms of probability," while Hoey (1991: 6–7) used the term collocation only if a lexical item co-occurs with other items "with greater than random probability in its (textual) context."

A number of statistical formulae are commonly used in corpus linguistics to identify statistically significant collocations, e.g. mutual information (MI), *t*-test, *z*-score test, and log-likelihood test. The MI score is computed by dividing the observed frequency of the co-occurring word in the defined span for the node word by the expected frequency of the co-occurring word in that span and then taking the logarithm of the result, as shown in equation (1):

$$\mathrm{MI} = \frac{\log(F_{n,cN}/F_{nF_c}S)}{\log 2} \tag{1}$$

In the equation, N stands for the total number of words in a corpus (e.g. 98,313,429 words in the BNC via BNCweb), $F_{(n)}$ for the frequency count of the node (e.g. *sweet* occurs 3,460 times in the BNC), $F_{(c)}$ for the frequency of the collocate (e.g. *nothings* occurs 37 times in the BNC), $F_{(n,c)}$ for the frequency of the node and collocate co-occurring within the defined span (e.g. within 4 words to the left and 4 words to the right of the node, with S=8), or 16 in the BNC example, while log2 is a constant roughly equivalent to 0.301. Based on equation (1), the MI score for the collocation of *sweet* with *nothings* within the 8-word span in the BNC is 10.58.

The MI score is a measure of collocational strength as well as the direction of association (i.e. attraction or repulsion between two lexical items). The higher the MI score, the stronger the association between two items; the closer to 0 the MI score gets, the more likely it is that the two items co-occur by chance. The MI score can also be negative if two items tend to shun each other. Conventionally an MI score of 3.0 or above is taken as evidence that two items are significant collocates (Hunston (2002: 71). In our example above, *nothings* can be said to be a statistically significant collocate of *sweet*.

However, as Hunston (2002: 72) suggests, collocational strength is not always reliable in identifying meaningful collocations. We also need to know the amount of evidence available for a collocation. This means that the corpus size is also important in identifying how certain a collocation is. In this regard, the *t*-test is useful as it takes corpus size into account. The *t*-test is based on the mean and variance of a sample in comparison with the expected mean when the null hypothesis holds. The *t*-score is calculated on the basis of the difference between the observed and expected means, scaled by the variance, to determine the probability of a particular sample of that mean and variance with the assumption of the normal distribution of the dataset, as expressed in equation (2).

$$t\text{-score} = \frac{\overline{x} - \mu}{\sqrt{\frac{s^2}{N}}} \tag{2}$$

In the equation, $\overline{x}$ and μ respectively represent the mean of the sample and the expected mean, S^2 is the sample variance while N refers to the sample size. In the BNC, for example, the frequency counts of *sweet* and *smell* are 3,460 and 3,508 respectively in N (98,313,429) tokens, and the two words co-occur 90 times within the 8-word span. Then the mean $\overline{x}$ can be expressed as $\frac{90}{98313429}$, i.e. 9.155×10^{-7}; the expected mean can be computed using the formula μ = P(*sweet*)P(*smell*), i.e. $(\frac{3460}{98313429})*(\frac{3508}{98313429})$, roughly equivalent to 1.2547×10^{-9}. The sample variance S^2 = P(1–P), and for a very small P value, it is roughly equivalent to P, namely $\overline{x}$ in this case. Based on equation (2), the *t*-score for the co-occurrence of *sweet* and *smell* within the 8-word span can be obtained as 9.4.

Conventionally a *t*-score of 2.576 or above is considered to be statistically significant, which means that in our example above, *smell* is a significant collocate of *sweet*. While the MI test measures the strength of collocations, the *t*-test measures the confidence with which we can claim that there is some association (Church and Hanks 1990). As the *t*-test assumes the normal distribution of the population, which can rarely be guaranteed in language use, it is inappropriate to use the *t*-test if the data are known to be skewed. Collocations with high MI scores tend to include low-frequency words, whereas those with high *t*-scores tend to show high-frequency pairs as demonstrated by *nothings* and *smell* in the above examples, which are both among the most significant collocates of *sweet* identified on the basis of the two statistical measures.

The *z*-score test provides a measure of how far a sample is from the mean and in what direction. The test compares the observed frequency with the frequency expected if only chance is affecting the distribution. The *z*-score test is a measure which adjusts for the general frequencies of the words involved in a potential collocation and shows how much more frequent the collocation of a word with the node word is than one would expect from their general frequencies. It can be obtained using equation (3).

$$z\text{-score} = \frac{F_{n,c} - E}{\sqrt{E(1-P)}} \tag{3}$$

In the formula, $F_{n,c}$ and E are respectively the observed and expected frequency counts of co-occurrence while P refers to the probability of the collocate occurring where the node does not occur. P is expressed as $\frac{F_c}{N-F_n}$ and E as $P\,F_nS$, where F_n and F_c are the frequency counts of the node and collocate while N and S stand for the size of the corpus (i.e. token number) and the collocation span respectively. In the above example of *sweet* and *nothings* from the BNC, F_n, F_c and $F_{n,c}$ are 3,460, 37 and 16 respectively, while N and S remain the same. Based on equation (3), the *z*-score for the collocation between *sweet* and *nothings* is 156.78, which is considerably greater than 1.96, the critical value of a *z*-score (absolute value) that can be taken as evidence for significant collocations.

It can be seen from the above that in terms of the procedures of computation, the *z*-score is quite similar to the *t*-score, whereas in terms of output, the *z*-score is more similar to the MI score. A higher *z*-score indicates a greater degree of collocability of an item with the node word. As Dunning (1993) observes, the *z*-score assumes that data are normally distributed, an assumption which is not true in most cases of statistical text analysis unless either enormous corpora are used, or the analysis is restricted to only very common words (which are typically the ones least likely to be of interest). As a consequence, the *z*-score measure, like MI, can substantially overestimate the significance of infrequent words (see Dunning 1993). For lexicographical purposes, these are interesting (e.g. *sweet nothings* and *sweet marjoram*) and should be treated in a general-purpose dictionary. However, for pedagogical purposes, these expressions are of secondary importance compared with more basic collocations.

The solution Dunning proposes for this problem is the log-likelihood (LL) test. The LL measure does not assume the normal distribution of data. For text analysis and similar contexts, the use of LL scores leads to considerably improved statistical results. Using the LL test, textual analysis can be done effectively with much smaller amounts of text than is necessary for statistical measures which assume normal distributions. Furthermore, this measure allows comparisons to be made between the significance of the occurrences of both rare and common features (Dunning 1993: 67).

The log-likelihood test is probably the most complex of the four collocation statistics discussed in this chapter. The LL score is calculated on the basis of a contingency table, as shown in Table 6.1, by adding every cell in the table to the logarithm of that cell and applying the same to multiple combinations of table cells, with the final result multiplied by 2, as indicated in equation (4). In our example of *sweet* and *smell*, the calculated LL score is 688, which is much greater than 3.84, the critical value for statistical significance.

$$\begin{aligned}\text{LL} = {} & 2 * (a * \log(a) + b * \log(b) + c * \log(c) + d * \log(d) \\ & - (a+b) * \log(a+b) - (a+c) * \log(a+c) - (b+d) * \log(b+d) \\ & - (c+d) * \log(c+d) \; + \; (a+b+c+d) * \log(a+b+c+d)\,) \qquad (4)\end{aligned}$$

Of the four association measures discussed above, the LL test produces consistently better results in collocation extraction by including both common and rare lexical items as collocates. While it is known that MI scores may unduly overvalue infrequent words, it is certainly used widely as an alternative to the LL and *z*-scores in corpus linguistics because of its cognitive relevance for collocations (see McEnery and Hardie 2012: 206, 224). While a standard statistics software package such as SPSS can be used to calculate the statistical test scores discussed above, many popular

Table 6.1 *Contingency table*

	Word A (e.g. *sweet*)	NOT Word A (e.g. *sweet*)
Word B (e.g. *smell*)	a	c
NOT word B (e.g. *smell*)	b	d

corpus analysis tools, both web-based and standalone, also include such statistical measures as built-in functions. For example, the Wordsmith Tools and BNCweb include all of these statistical tests in addition to other options, while AntConc includes MI and *t*-score, and Xaira includes MI and *z*-score.[1]

2.3 Collocational meaning

Shifting from form to meaning, Stubbs (2002: 225) hypothesizes that "there are always semantic relations between node and collocates, and among the collocates themselves." The collocational meaning arising from the interaction between a given node and its typical collocates is known as "semantic prosody," "a form of meaning which is established through the proximity of a consistent series of collocates" (Louw 2000: 57). Both individual words and phrases can have semantic prosodies (cf. Schmitt and Carter 2004: 7). The primary function of semantic prosody is to express speaker/writer attitude or evaluation (Louw 2000: 58). Semantic prosodies are typically negative, with relatively few of them bearing an affectively positive meaning. However, a speaker/writer can also violate a semantic prosody condition to achieve some effect in the hearer – for example irony, insincerity or humor can be explained by identifying violations of semantic prosody (see Louw 1993: 173).[2]

It would appear, from the literature published on semantic prosody, that it is at least as inaccessible to a speaker's conscious introspection as collocation is (see Louw 1993: 173; Partington 1998: 68; Hunston 2002: 142). Yet as the size of corpora has grown, and tools for extracting semantic prosodies have been developed, semantic prosodies have been addressed much more frequently by linguists. Table 6.2 gives some examples of semantic prosodies that have been investigated in the literature.[3]

Semantic prosody that belongs to an item is the result of the interplay between the item and its typical collocates. On the one hand, the item does not appear to have an affective meaning until it is in the context of its typical collocates. On the other hand, if a word has typical collocates with an affective meaning, it may take on that affective meaning even when used with atypical collocates. As the Chinese saying goes, "he who stays near vermilion gets stained red, and he who stays near ink gets stained black" – one takes on the color of one's company – the consequence of a word frequently keeping "bad company" is that the use of the word alone

[1] BNCweb can be accessed at http://bncweb.lancs.ac.uk/bncwebSignup/user/login.php

[2] This view put forward by Louw (1993) is recently challenged by Wei and Li (2014), who distinguish between the Major Patterning and the Minor Patterning, thus calling into question the practice of treating counter-examples as exploiting so-called default prosody of a word for ironical purposes.

[3] A word in small capitals refers to the lemma of the word, including its morphological variations. For example, *CAUSE* refers to *cause, causes, caused*, and *causing*.

Table 6.2 *Examples of semantic prosodies*

Author	Negative prosody	Positive prosody
Sinclair (1991)	BREAK out	
	HAPPEN	
	SET in	
Louw (1993, 2000)	bent on	BUILD up a
	BUILD up of	
	END up *verb*ing	
	GET oneself *verb*ed	
	a recipe for	
Stubbs (1995, 1996, 2001a, 2001b)	ACCOST	career PROVIDE
	CAUSE	
	FAN the flame	
	signs of	
	underage	
	teenager(s)	
Partington (1998)	COMMIT	
	PEDDLE/peddler	
	dealings	
Hunston (2002)	SIT through	
Schmitt and Carter (2004)	bordering on	

may become enough to indicate something unfavorable (see Partington 1998: 67).

In Stubbs's (2002: 225) comment cited above, the meaning arising from the common semantic features of the collocates of a given node word can be referred to as "semantic preference," which is defined "by a lexical set of frequently occurring collocates [sharing] some semantic feature" (ibid.: 449). For example, Stubbs (2001b: 65) observes that *large* typically collocates with items from the same semantic set indicating "quantities and sizes" (e.g. *number(s), scale, part, quantities, amount(s)*). A more detailed study of *large* and its near synonyms such as *big* and *great* is undertaken by Biber, Conrad, and Reppen (1998: 43–53), who compare and contrast these words with respect to their semantic preferences shown by their collocates in a 5.7-million-word sample from the Longman–Lancaster Corpus. Partington (2004: 148) also notes that "absence/change of state" is a common feature of the collocates of maximizers such as *utterly, totally, completely*, and *entirely*.

Semantic preference and semantic prosody are two distinct yet interdependent collocational meanings. Partington (2004: 151) notes that semantic preference and semantic prosody have different operating scopes: the former relates the node word to another item from a particular semantic set whereas the latter can affect wider stretches of text. Semantic preference can be viewed as a feature of the collocates while semantic prosody is a feature of the node word. On the other hand, the two also interact. While semantic prosody "dictates the general environment which constrains the preferential choices of the node item," semantic preference "contributes powerfully" to building semantic prosody (ibid.).

2.4 Beyond lexical collocation

While collocation has commonly been viewed as a phenomenon of the association between individual words, whether in their orthographic or lemma forms, this does not need to be the case. Rather collocational phenomena can occur beyond word level to involve the characteristic co-occurrence between words and phrases with certain grammatical categories and syntactic contexts. Colligation is a type of this kind of higher-level abstraction, which refers to the relationship between words at grammatical level, i.e. the relations of "word and sentence classes or of similar categories" instead of "between words as such" as in the case of collocation (Firth 1968: 181). In other words, while collocation relates to the association between a lexical item and other lexical items (e.g. *very* collocates with *good*), colligation is concerned with the relationship between a lexical item and a grammatical category (e.g. *very* colligates with adjectives). According to Sinclair (1996, 1998) and Stubbs (2001b), the relationship between lexical units can be characterized at four different levels from the lowest to the highest: collocation (the relationship between a node and individual words), colligation (the relationship between a node and grammatical categories), semantic preference (semantic sets of collocates), and semantic prosody (affective meaning of a given node with its typical collocates).

Firth's (1968) definition of colligation has often been applied in a loose sense to refer not only to significant co-occurrence of a word with grammatical categories as noted above but also to significant co-occurrence of a word with grammatical words (e.g. Krishnamurthy 2000). On the other hand, colligation can also mean a word's syntactic preferences or its characteristic co-occurrence with syntactic contexts instead of particular grammatical categories. For example, the word *consequence* is typically used as the head rather than a modifier in a noun phrase (Hoey 2005: 48–49); the adjectives *alone* and *lonely* also display different colligational properties: the former functions as a complement whereas the latter is used as an attributive modifier. Further studies of such lexico-grammatical patterns can be found in Francis, Hunston, and Manning (1996, 1998) and Biber *et al.* (1999).

A specific approach that has been developed to study colligation in this latter sense, i.e. the interaction between lexical items and grammatical structures, is collostructional analysis (Stefanowitsch and Gries 2003). The term *collostruction* is a blend of *collocation* and *construction*, suggesting that this approach is largely concerned with the co-occurrence between lexical items and constructions. Starting with a particular construction, collostructional analysis uses statistical measures to determine the degree to which particular slots in a grammatical structure attract or shun particular lexical items (ibid.: 211). This new approach has certainly provided a useful tool in colligation analysis in its broad sense.

2.5 The importance of collocation in language use

Collocation is part of word meaning. Because of the "mutual expectancy" between two words, "You shall know a word by the company it keeps!" (Firth 1968: 179, 181), as illustrated by Firth's (1957: 196) example: "One of the meanings of *night* is its collocability with *dark*." In language comprehension and production, collocation plays an important role in disambiguating a polysemous word, and together with semantic prosody, helps the language user to choose near synonyms appropriately. Making use of collocation is also considered as a useful strategy that helps the language user to convey complex ideas efficiently (Bartsch 2004: 18–19). This is because, according to Hoey's (2005: 13) lexical priming theory, words are "primed" to co-occur with other particular words (i.e. their collocates), together with their semantic prosody, in the same context.

While a good command of collocation is an important indicator of native-like proficiency and fluency (Bartsch 2004: 20), even a native speaker's intuition is a poor guide to collocation and collocational meanings (see Section 2.2). Hence, not only has the development of corpus linguistics greatly facilitated collocation analysis but corpus-based collocation research over the past decades has also revealed a range of interesting findings that have hitherto been largely overlooked in previous non-corpus-based language descriptions.

First, while collocation analysis had been undertaken on specific texts such as the Bible before corpus linguistics was established (see Section 1), it is the growing number of large representative corpora and the development of increasingly sophisticated collocation statistics that have enabled large-scale collocation analysis and foregrounded collocation in linguistic research (e.g. Williams 2001; McEnery 2006a; Baker, Gabrielatos, and McEnery 2013), language teaching (e.g. Nattinger and DeCarrico 1992; Nesselhauf 2003), and natural language processing (NLP) tasks such as word sense disambiguation, parsing, computational lexicography, terminology extraction, language generation, and machine translation (see Manning and Schütze 1999; McKeown and Radev 2000). In discourse analysis, for example, collocation and collocational network (i.e. lexical items that are collocationally related), which provide a powerful way of visualizing collocation relationships, are a major form of analysis in McEnery's (2006a) book-length exploration of discourses about bad language in English. Collocation has proven to be a useful tool in discourse analysis because it can not only reveal patterns of lexical association but also show how a word can acquire meaning in context, which may differ from or even contradict its literal meaning (e.g. semantic prosody). Collocation has also been recognized as playing a central role in language learning and in NLP because the collocational approach treats words not as words in isolation but as large lexical units.

Second, collocation information in dictionaries, if any, has traditionally been provided in the form of illustrative examples. Benson, Benson, and Ilson's (1986/2010) *BBI Dictionary* is probably the best-known dictionary of word combinations in the English language, and is considered a "monumental work" in the field of lexicography (Williams 2001: 63). Apart from specialized collocation dictionaries such as this, however, corpus-based collocation research has helped to produce better dictionaries in general and learner dictionaries in particular, in such a way that collocation information, together with frequency band and authentic examples, is routinely used in dictionaries published since the 1990s, particularly in dictionaries for language learners (Benson 1990; Walker 2009), including for example the *Longman Dictionary of Contemporary English* (3rd or later edition), *Oxford Advanced Learner's Dictionary* (5th or later edition), and *Cambridge International Dictionary of English*.

Third, corpus research has provided more reliable empirical evidence than intuition that facilitates the identification of collocational behavior and semantic prosody of an extensive range of lexical items that have until recently been hidden from intuition. Such knowledge is essential in improving language descriptions in general and in detecting subtle differences between near synonyms in particular (see Sections 2.2 and 3 for further discussion). Explicit teaching of collocation and semantic prosody also has an important role to play in language education (see Nesselhauf 2005).

On the other hand, corpus research on collocation needs to address two important gaps. The first relates to the collocation-via-significance approach. While a variety of statistical formulae are currently available to extract significant collocates, the lists of collocates extracted using different statistics differ sharply (see Section 2.2). Furthermore, existing statistical measures are based on the assumption of random distribution, which is not true in language use (Kilgarriff 2005); the distribution of words of different frequency is also skewed, as indicated by Zipf's law (Evert 2008). For these reasons there is a need to develop more scientific statistical models to address such issues in collocation research.

Second, corpus-based collocation studies have so far focused on, or indeed have largely been confined to, the English language. There has been little work done on collocation and semantic prosody in languages other than English. Still less work has been undertaken which contrasts collocation and semantic prosody in different languages (but see Sardinha 2000; Tognini-Bonelli 2001: 131–156; Xiao and McEnery 2006; Ebeling, Ebeling, and Hasselgård 2013); yet findings yielded by this kind of research can be particularly valuable in language typology, language education, contrastive linguistics, and translation studies.

As such, the case study to be presented in the section that follows will explore collocation and semantic prosody in two genetically distant languages, English and Chinese in this case, from a cross-linguistic perspective rather than in a monolingual context.

3 Collocation and semantic prosody of near synonyms in English and Chinese

By "near synonyms" we mean lexical pairs that have very similar cognitive or denotational meanings, but which may differ in collocational or prosodic behavior (Partington 1998: 77). As such, synonymous words are not collocationally interchangeable (see Conzett 1997: 70–87; Tognini-Bonelli 2001: 34). For example, Halliday (1976: 73) observes that tea is typically described as *strong* rather than *powerful* whereas a car is more likely to be described as *powerful* than *strong*, even though the two modifiers share similar denotational meanings. Likewise, while *weak* and *feeble* have similar cognitive meanings, native speakers of English prefer to say *weak tea* rather than *feeble tea* (Mackin 1978: 150). In addition to different collocational behavior, near synonyms can also differ in semantic prosodies, e.g. *fickle* is negative whereas *flexible* is positive (Tognini-Bonelli 2001: 18–24).

This section explores, from a cross-linguistic perspective, the collocational behavior and semantic prosodies of near synonyms, drawing upon data from two distinctly different languages, English and Mandarin Chinese. The near synonyms selected for cross-linguistic contrast in this study denote *consequence* because these words have been studied in English (Hoey 2005; Stewart 2009) and we want to move from the established patterns of English to investigate the patterns occurring in Chinese by examining the collocational behavior and semantic prosodies of the close equivalents of the words in question in Chinese, with the aim of addressing the following two research questions:

1. Does Chinese exhibit semantic prosody and semantic preference as English does?
2. How different (or similar) are the collocational behavior and semantic prosody of lexical items with similar denotational meanings (i.e. near synonyms) in genetically distant languages such as English and Chinese?

Before these questions are answered, it is appropriate to introduce the corpora and data analysis method used in this study (Section 3.1), which is followed by a discussion of the collocation and semantic prosodies of the chosen group of near synonyms in English (Section 3.2) and a contrastive analysis of the Chinese group (Section 3.3).

3.1 Corpora and data analysis method

As intuition is usually an unreliable guide to patterns of collocation and semantic prosody, this study takes a corpus-based approach to addressing these research questions. The principal corpus data used in this study are the FLOB corpus of British English (Hundt, Sand, and Siemund 1998), the Frown corpus of American English (Hundt, Sand, and Skandera 1999), and the *Lancaster Corpus of Mandarin Chinese* (LCMC; McEnery, Xiao, and Mo 2003). Each of these corpora follows the same corpus design, containing approximately one million words of samples collected from fifteen written text categories published around 1991. FLOB/Frown and LCMC are, as far as is practically possible, comparable corpora well suited for contrastive language research. However, there were points in our research when these corpora were not large enough to provide a reliable basis for quantification. On such occasions a supplementary group of data was also used to extract significant collocates, including the 100-million-word *British National Corpus* (BNC) for English and the *People's Daily* corpus (PDC2000) for Chinese, which covers one year's newspaper texts published in the *People's Daily* in 2000, totaling approximately 15 million words. As the supplementary corpora are not comparable either in sampling period or coverage, we clearly indicate where they are used in this study. These corpora were only used to add further weight to observations made in small comparable corpora.

In collocation analysis we chose to use the MI measure because it is built into the corpus tools we used, WordSmith and Xaira. Both tools allow users to set the minimum co-occurrence frequency of an item to be considered as a collocate of a given node word so that the drawback of the MI measure as noted in Section 2.2 can be partly offset. Given the size of the comparable corpora used, we set the minimum co-occurrence frequency to 3. Within a 4–4 window span, items which had a minimum co-occurrence frequency of 3 and a minimum MI score of 3.0 were accepted as the collocates of a node word. When using additional data from the BNC and PDC2000 corpora, the minimum co-occurrence frequency was set at 20. As we will see from the collocates extracted in Sections 3.2–3.3, these adjustments have allowed us to use the MI score safely.

In our analysis of semantic prosody the positive, neutral, and negative meaning categories correspond to Partington's (2004) favorable, neutral, and unfavorable prosodies. We evaluated each case in context. A pleasant or favorable affective meaning was labeled as positive while an unpleasant or unfavorable affective meaning was judged as negative. When what occurred was completely neutral, or the context provided no evidence of any semantic prosody, the instance was classified as neutral. Note that in the collocate lists presented in Sections 3.2–3.3, items with an unfavorable affective meaning are underlined and those with a favorable affective meaning are emboldened.

3.2 The CONSEQUENCE group of near synonyms in English

In English there are a number of words that mean "anything that is due to something already done," e.g. *result, outcome, consequence*, and *aftermath*. Table 6.3 shows the distribution of CONSEQUENCE across meaning categories in FLOB/Frown. It is clear from the table that while fixed expressions such

Table 6.3 *Distribution of* CONSEQUENCE *across meaning categories in FLOB/Frown*

Pattern	Negative	Neutral	Positive
as a consequence	6	7	4
in consequence (of)	8	3	1
consequence	27	7	6
consequences	85	20	1
consequent(ly)	15	73	5

as *as a consequence* and *in consequence (of)* can be negative, neutral, or positive, depending upon their contexts, *consequence* and *consequences* show a strong tendency towards a negative semantic prosody. The plural form *consequences* is even more likely to be used negatively. In the BNC, for example, collocates indicating the nature of consequences include, in the order of their co-occurring frequencies, <u>*serious*</u>, ***important***, <u>*disastrous*</u>, <u>*adverse*</u>, <u>*dire*</u>, <u>*far-reaching*</u>, <u>*damaging*</u>, <u>*negative*</u>, *profound*, <u>*unintended*</u>, *major*, <u>*unfortunate*</u>, <u>*tragic*</u>, <u>*fatal*</u>, *new*, <u>*severe*</u> and ***significant***. All of the underlined items express an unfavorable affective meaning.

In FLOB and Frown, significant collocates of *consequences* include (ranked by co-occurring frequency):

- Nature: **important**, <u>adverse</u>
- Affected target: social, financial, economic, ethical, moral, individual, public
- Action: HAVE, (there) BE, ACCEPT

Of the collocates indicating the nature of consequences, *important* is positive while *adverse* is negative. Interestingly, all instances of *important consequences* in FLOB/Frown collocate with *HAVE/there BE* to denote a positive pattern meaning. This observation is confirmed in a larger corpus. Of the 68 instances of *important consequences* in the BNC, 54 occurrences follow *HAVE* and one instance follows *there BE*. All 54 examples are positive while the remaining cases may be either positive or neutral.

When they are modified by collocates indicating an affected target, *consequences* are typically negative. As such, actions associated with them normally include *accept*, *alleviate*, *avoid*, *face*, *meet*, *minimize*, *offset*, *(be) responsible*, *(take) responsibility*, *suffer*, and *sustain*.[4] *Consequences* sometimes collocates with verbs such as *REAP*, as in (1):

(1) These officials generally attributed their problems to: [...] Some critics charged, though, that states were reaping the consequences of profligate spending during the growth years of 1984–1989. (Frown: H)

[4] In this list only *accept* is a significant collocate as defined in this study. In the BNC significant collocates indicating actions include *AVOID, ACCEPT, BE, CAUSE, CONSIDER, FACE, FOLLOW, HAVE*, and *SUFFER*.

REAP typically collocates in its literal meaning with names of crops and *harvest*, or metaphorically with words with a positive meaning such as *benefit(s)* and *rewards* (the three significant collocates are from the BNC). It seems that the apparently paradoxical combination of *REAP* and *consequences* in this example carries the implication that "you reap as you sow": the officials were suffering as a result of their own profligate spending.

In comparison with *consequence(s)*, *aftermath* displays an even more pronounced tendency towards the negative pole of the semantic continuum. In FLOB and Frown, 14 occurrences of *aftermath* were found, mostly in the expression *in the aftermath of*. There is only one significant collocate indicating what causes the state of affairs referred to by *aftermath*. It is *war*. As the low frequency may result in unreliable quantification, we consulted the BNC, which provides 687 instances of *aftermath*. Significant collocates in the BNC typically include *war(s)*, *world* (as in *World War I*) and *Gulf* (as in the *Gulf War*). Clearly these words are negative in their contexts.

Further away from the negative pole of the semantic continuum are *result* and *outcome*. *Result* is significantly more common than *outcome* (with 677 and 86 occurrences respectively in FLOB/Frown). It appears that both words are associated with a favorable affective meaning, e.g. *a good result, a great result, an excellent result, a brilliant result, a successful outcome* (see Hoey 2004a), as reflected by their significant collocates which indicate the nature of a result or outcome:

- Result: **better**, different, early, end, final, similar, direct, empirical, likely, experimental, **good**, negative, **desired**
- Outcome: likely, **positive, successful**

It is of interest to note that *negative* appears on the collocation list of *result*. A close examination of the concordances shows that in all of the three instances *negative* should be interpreted in a mathematical or medical sense, which has no impact upon affective meaning. The discussion above shows that the four near synonyms can be arranged, from positive to negative, on a semantic continuum as follows: *outcome/result, consequence*, and *aftermath*.

3.3 A contrastive analysis of the Chinese group of near synonyms

Shifting to consider these words in contrast, the Chinese translation equivalent of *result/outcome* commonly found in a bilingual dictionary is *jiéguǒ* "result" while the translation equivalent for *consequence/aftermath* is *hòuguǒ* "consequence." In addition, there are a number of obviously positive synonyms such as *chéngguǒ* "achievement" and *shuòguǒ* "great achievement," and negative synonyms including *kǔguǒ* "a bitter pill to swallow" and *èguǒ* "evil consequence."

There are 240 instances of *jiéguǒ* in LCMC, which are distributed across different meaning categories as follows: positive 33, neutral 129, and negative 78. Significant collocates of *jiéguǒ* include:

- Modifiers: *dàxuǎn* "general election," *bìrán* "inevitable," *shìyàn* "experiment," *diàochá* "investigation," *kěnéng* "possible," *jīngjì* "economic," ***hǎo*** "good"
- Actions: *biǎomíng* "show," *zàochéng* "cause," *zēngjiā* "increase," *chǎnshēng* "give rise to; arise," *yǒu* "have"

There are both similarities and differences in the distribution of *result* and its Chinese translation equivalent *jiéguǒ* across meaning categories. On the one hand, like its English counterparts *result* and *outcome, jiéguǒ* typically does not express a negative evaluative meaning. The semantic prosody of *jiéguǒ* is dependent upon its collocates. For example, when it collocates with *zàochéng* "cause," it indicates an unfavorable result; conversely, when it collocates with *chǎnshēng* "bring about," the result is evaluated favorably. The neutral use of *jiéguǒ* was mainly found in academic prose. As there are inherently positive synonyms in Chinese (e.g. *shuòguǒ* and *chéngguǒ*), as noted above, *jiéguǒ* is less frequently used than English *result* to indicate a positive semantic prosody.

In relation to *jiéguǒ, hòuguǒ* is typically negative, though it can be used neutrally, because in some instances there is no evidence of semantic prosody in its context. Of the 22 occurrences of *hòuguǒ* in LCMC, 19 are used negatively, with the remaining three being neutral. The only significant collocate of *hòuguǒ* in LCMC is *yánzhòng* "serious, grave." When the consequences are specified, they typically refer to undesirable situations such as "increasingly intensifying contradictions," "unsold goods piling up in stock," and "inflation." When the consequences are not made clear, there are usually modifiers expressing value judgments or indicating the nature of the consequences. These modifiers normally share a negative semantic preference including, for example, *yánzhòng* "serious, grave," *bùkānshèxiǎng* "too ghastly to contemplate," *bùkěwǎnhuí* "irrecoverable," *bùliáng* "adverse," *xiāojí* "negative," *náncè* "dubious," and *bùyánzìyù* "self-evident." In fact, *hòuguǒ* keeps bad company so frequently that simply using this word alone is usually sufficient to indicate some unfavorable result, as exemplified in (2):[5]

(2) a. nǐ xiǎngxiang nà huì yǒu zěnyàng de hòuguǒ (LCMC: G)
you think-think that will have what GEN consequence
'Just imagine what consequences will result.'

b. hng-hng, nà hòuguǒ, qǐng xiānsheng zìjǐ hǎoshēng
Humph then consequence please sir self carefully

[5] In the grammatical glosses of Chinese examples, ASP stands for *aspect marker*, BA for *ba*-construction, CL for *classifier*, GEN for *genitive*, and PRT for *particle*.

xiǎngxiang ba (LCMC: N)
think-think PRT
"Humph! Then you must think carefully of the consequences."

A more marked contrast was observed in the supplementary Chinese newspaper corpus PDC2000, where 472 instances of *hòuguǒ* were found. Of these, 470 instances show a negative affective meaning, with the remaining two being neutral. The PDC2000 corpus shows two collocates with a minimum co-occurring frequency of 20, *yánzhòng* "serious, grave" and *zàochéng* "cause."

Like English *consequences*, all of the neutral occurrences of *hòuguǒ* in LCMC were found in academic prose (e.g. 3a). *Hòuguǒ* was also found to occur in contexts where an option between a desirable effect (e.g. "peace") and an unpleasant consequence (e.g. "disaster") is available, as shown in (3b). Note, however, that whilst *hòuguǒ* can be used neutrally, the pattern meaning is quite unambiguous – a negative evaluation – when it collocates with verbs like *zàochéng/dǎozhì/zhìshǐ* "cause" (see Xiao and McEnery 2006).

(3) a. shēn céngcì rènshi de hòuguǒ biāozhì-zhe
deep level knowledge GEN consequence mark-ASP
gètǐ yìngfù yìngjī de nénglì (LCMC: J)
individual cope-with emergency GEN ability
"Deep level knowledge allows an individual to cope with emergencies."
b. qí yǐnqǐ de hòuguǒ jiāng bù shì hépíng,
they cause GEN consequence will not be peace
ér shì zāinàn (PDC2000)
but be disaster
"The consequences caused by any of such words and deeds will not be peace but a disaster."

In contrast to the typically positive *jiéguǒ* and the typically negative *hòuguǒ*, *shuòguǒ*, and *chéngguǒ* are inherently positive whereas *kǔguǒ* and *èguǒ* are inherently negative, regardless of genre. There are 4,572 instances of *chéngguǒ* and 109 instances of *shuòguǒ* in LCMC and PDC2000. The typical collocates of *chéngguǒ* include ***fēngshuò*** "rich and great," ***jiǎng*** "award," *zhuǎnhuà* "transform, turn into," *kējì* "sci-tech," *yánjiù* "research," *qǔdé* "gain," ***yōuxiù*** "excellent," ***gòngxiàn*** "contribution," and *shēngchǎnlì* "productivity." The significant collocates of *shuòguǒ* include *léiléi* "heaps of" and *jiéchū* "yield." *Chéngguǒ* is significantly more frequent than *shuòguǒ*, reflecting the fact that in the real world, results that can be labeled as *shuòguǒ* are considerably fewer than those labeled as *chéngguǒ*. *Kǔguǒ* occurs 32 times and *èguǒ* 42 times in the two Chinese corpora. All of these are negative, but no significant collocate was found for the two node words.

Like the synonyms of *result* in English, the six near synonyms of *jiéguǒ* in Chinese can be arranged on a semantic continuum, from positive to negative, as follows: *shuòguǒ, chéngguǒ, jiéguǒ, hòuguǒ*, and *kǔguǒ/èguǒ*. Our contrastive analysis of the collocational behavior and semantic prosodies of the two sets of near synonyms in English and Chinese suggests that *result/outcome* in English and *jiéguǒ* in Chinese can be considered cross-linguistic near synonyms; likewise *consequence/aftermath* in English versus *hòuguǒ* in Chinese are cross-linguistic near synonyms. In relation to English, it appears that Chinese is more sharply divided between the clearly negative and positive ends of the continuum so that the Chinese words *shuòguǒ* and *chéngguǒ* (both highly positive) and *kǔguǒ* and *èguǒ* (both highly negative) can hardly find their cross-linguistic near synonyms in English at lexical level. It is also important to note that unlike English, in which different forms of a lemma may have different collocates and semantic prosodies (e.g. *consequence* vs. *consequences*), Chinese does not have a rich morphology which can affect collocation and semantic prosody in this way.

Our contrastive analysis shows that semantic prosody and semantic preference are as observable in Chinese as they are in English. As the semantic prosodies of near synonyms and the semantic preferences of their collocates are different, near synonyms are normally not interchangeable in either language. It can also be seen from the case study that the semantic prosody observed in general domains may not apply to technical texts. While English and Chinese are genetically distant and distinctly unrelated, the collocational behavior and semantic prosodies of near synonyms are quite similar in the two languages. This observation echoes the findings which have so far been reported for related language pairs, e.g. English vs. Portuguese (Sardinha 2000), English vs. Italian (Tognini-Bonelli 2001: 131–156), and English vs. German (Dodd 2000).

While the corpus-based approach can only reveal but not explain such cross-linguistic similarity, at least part of the explanation, in our view, can be found in the common basis of natural language semantics – "the conceptual system that emerges from everyday human experience" (Sweetser 1990: 1). However, as different languages can have different ranges of near synonyms, near synonyms and their close translation equivalents in different languages may also demonstrate, to some extent, different collocational behavior and semantic prosody. A more general difference between English and Chinese is that collocation and semantic prosody may be affected by morphological variations in English but not in Chinese, which lacks such variation.

4 Conclusion

This chapter has sought to provide a critical account of the current debates in corpus-based collocation research. The first main section (Section 2) explores the state of the art in collocation analysis, covering definitional and methodological issues, meaning arising from collocation, collocational phenomena beyond lexical level, as well as the importance of collocation in language use. The review in this section demonstrates that corpus linguistics has enabled large-scale collocation analysis and foregrounded collocation in linguistic research while corpus-based collocation studies over the past decades have uncovered a range of interesting collocational behavior and semantic prosody which have been hidden from intuition and can only be revealed by examining a large amount of attested data simultaneously. Such findings have not only helped to achieve improved language descriptions, but they also have an important role to play in practical applications such as language teaching, translation, and natural language processing. This review section concludes with a brief discussion of two major gaps to be addressed in future research, namely development of improved statistical measures and cross-linguistic research. To demonstrate the kind of research called for, the second main section in this chapter (Section 3) presents a contrastive study of collocation and semantic prosody in English and Chinese, via a case study of a group of near synonyms denoting *consequence* in the two languages, which suggests that, in spite of some language-specific peculiarities, even genetically distant languages such as English and Chinese display similar collocational behavior and semantic prosody in their use of near synonyms.

7

Phraseology

Bethany Gray and Douglas Biber

1 Introduction

There has been widespread interest over the last three decades in the use of multi-word prefabricated expressions (e.g. *in a nutshell*, *if you see what I mean*). This research argues that a good portion of the language we use every day is composed of prefabricated expressions, rather than being strictly compositional (see, e.g., Pawley and Syder 1983, and Nattinger and DeCarrico 1992; also see the reviews of earlier research in Howarth 1996; Wray and Perkins 2000; and Wray 2002).

Such multi-word sequences have been investigated under a variety of labels and definitions, including "lexical phrases," "formulas," "routines," "fixed expressions," "prefabricated patterns" (or "prefabs"), *n*-grams, and "lexical bundles." Regardless of label, however, these studies share a focus on how words combine into more and less fixed combinations. Most early studies were primarily theoretical in nature, comparing the various perspectives and approaches to multi-word units, proposing new frameworks for analysis, and calling for further research. Hakuta (1974), Yorio (1980), Pawley and Syder (1983), Weinert (1995), Howarth (1996, 1998a, b), and Wray and Perkins (2000) are good examples of this type.

Beginning in the 1990s, most research on phraseological patterns has been empirical, utilizing corpus analysis. Weinert (1995: 182) identifies two basic issues for such research: the best way to define and identify fixed multi-word units, and analysis of the discourse functions that these multi-word units perform. While there have been dozens of empirical studies carried out since then, these issues are still two of the most important considerations motivating current studies.

We would like to thank Christopher Gray, who helped construct the database and offered tutorials on how to write SQL queries and integrate them into programs to extract the data from the database.

Table 7.1 *Major design parameters of corpus-based and corpus-driven studies of phraseology*

A. Research goals	B. Nature of multi-word units
Scope and methodological approach 1. explore the use of pre-selected lexical expressions (corpus-based approach) vs. 2. identify and describe the full set of multi-word sequences in a corpus (corpus-driven approach)	*Idiomatic status* 1. fixed idiomatic expressions vs. 2. non-idiomatic sequences that are very frequent
Role of register 3. comparisons of phraseological patterns across registers vs. 4. focus on patterns in a single register vs. 5. focus on general corpora with no consideration of register	*Length* 3. relatively short combinations: 2–3 words vs. 4. extended multi-word sequences: 3+ words
Discourse function 6. consideration of discourse functions vs. 7. no consideration of discourse functions	*Continuous/discontinuous* 5. continuous (uninterrupted) sequences vs. 6. discontinuous sequences with variable "slots"

With respect to the first issue, two general approaches have been employed to identify and analyze important multi-word units: corpus-based and corpus-driven (see Tognini-Bonelli 2001: 84–87). In corpus-based studies of formulaic language, the researcher pre-selects multi-word expressions that are perceptually salient or theoretically interesting, and then analyzes the corpus to discover how those expressions are used (e.g. Moon 1998). In contrast, "corpus-driven" research is inductive, with the lexical phrases themselves being identified from the analysis of a corpus (see also Biber 2009 for additional discussion on corpus-driven phraseology research).

In addition to that distinction, there are several other important differences among corpus-based and corpus-driven studies of phraseology, including their overarching research goals, the role of register in the analysis, and the nature of the multi-word units (see Table 7.1).

First, studies differ in their research goals: some focus on the use of a few important lexical expressions, while others set out to identify and describe the full set of multi-word sequences in a corpus (with a focus on characterizing the multi-word sequences, or on characterizing language variety according to the extent to which is it composed of patterned units). A related consideration is whether a study includes register comparisons: some studies compare phraseological patterns across two or more registers; others focus on phraseological patterns in a single register; while some studies analyze a general corpus and disregard the influence of register altogether. Finally, there are differences in the nature of the lexical sequences targeted for analysis, including fixed idiomatic expressions versus non-idiomatic sequences of frequent words; relatively short sequences of 2–3 words versus extended multi-word sequences; and sequences of contiguous words (e.g. *in the middle of*, *in the rest of*) versus discontinuous lexical frames in which one or more "slot" in the pattern is variable (e.g. *in the * of*).

In the following section, we undertake a survey of some of the most important corpus investigations of phraseology carried out to date, grouped according to the considerations introduced above. Sections 2.1 and 2.2 contrast studies based on their major methodological approaches, distinguishing between corpus-based studies of pre-selected lexical expressions versus corpus-driven studies to identify the full set of important multi-word sequences in a corpus. Section 2.3 discusses two additional factors: the role of register and discourse function in analyses of lexical phrases. Section 2.4 turns to research on discontinuous, rather than contiguous, word patterns. Then, in Section 3 we take a step back to consider the state of the art of phraseological research in corpus linguistics, considering some of the core issues still being debated within the field. Finally, in Section 4, we briefly present a case study illustrating the application of large-scale corpus analysis to investigate the types of discontinuous lexical frames found in spoken and written registers of English.

2 A survey of major approaches and research findings

2.1 Corpus-based studies of lexical phrases

Collocational research is typically restricted to relations between two words; it can be regarded as a hybrid approach that employs both corpus-based and corpus-driven methods: the researcher begins with a theoretically interesting target word (or a set of roughly synonymous target words), and then explores the corpus to identify the collocates that frequently occur in the context of the target words. Research of this type is discussed in detail in Chapters 6 (Xiao), 12 (Partington and Marchi), and 25 (Paquot).

In this chapter, we focus instead on phrases that might be regarded as extended collocations: lexical expressions involving three or more words. Different frameworks and studies have adopted a range of terminologies to represent such extended collocations (e.g. "lexical bundles," "*n*-grams," "prefabricated expressions," "formulaic sequences," etc.). For the purposes of this chapter, we refer to the general construct of phraseological patterns of three or more words as "lexical phrases." The range of specific terms, and how they are theoretically and methodologically distinct, will be discussed in the sections that follow.

There is a fairly long tradition of intuitive research on phraseology, noting the importance of prefabricated expressions in discourse (e.g. Pawley and Syder 1983) and even proposing lists of important lexical phrases (e.g. Nattinger and DeCarrico 1992). Although these early studies have indirectly motivated numerous corpus investigations of phraseology, there have been few corpus-based studies to investigate the specific lexical phrases proposed by earlier researchers, mostly because corpus linguists have not been convinced of the validity of the phrase lists proposed on an intuitive basis. Rather, most corpus investigations of continuous lexical phrases have applied some form of corpus-driven research.

2.2 Corpus-driven studies of lexical phrases

While there have been relatively few corpus-based studies of lexical phrases, there have been numerous corpus-driven studies. The main distinguishing characteristic of corpus-driven studies of phraseological patterns is that they do not begin with a pre-selected list of theoretically interesting words or phrases. Rather, the corpus itself is analyzed, inductively and typically automatically, to identify the lexical phrases that are especially noteworthy. The corpus analysis involves recording all multiword combinations with specified characteristics that appear in a corpus, usually tracking the frequency with which each combination occurs.

In some cases, corpus-driven analysis requires intensive reading and coding by human analysts, as in the study of idioms in academic speech by Simpson and Mendis (2003). The main methodological challenge encountered in that study was the identification of idioms (relatively fixed expressions with meanings that cannot be predicted from the meanings of the individual words). Simpson and Mendis argued that the existing lists of idioms were not reliable, and thus they set out to inductively identify the set of idioms that occurred in the MICASE corpus (the *Michigan Corpus of Academic Spoken English*). However, because idiomatic expressions cannot be reliably identified automatically, Simpson and Mendis manually analyzed half of MICASE to make their list of idioms. They then searched for those idiomatic expressions in the full corpus, to analyze their quantitative distributions and functions. (Thus, a corpus-driven analysis of a subcorpus was used to create the list of academic idioms, while a corpus-based analysis of the full corpus was used to describe the distribution of those idioms.) This study found that idioms are not especially prevalent in academic spoken discourse: only 32 idiomatic expressions occurred four or more times in MICASE, and even the most common expressions (e.g. *the bottom line*) occurred only *c.* ten times per million words (see Simpson and Mendis 2003: 436). However, Simpson and Mendis argue that these particular idioms do serve important discourse functions and are important for ESL students in academic contexts.

In contrast to the Simpson and Mendis study, most corpus-driven investigations of lexical phrases have used automatic techniques to investigate the use of recurrent lexical sequences. These studies set frequency thresholds and dispersion requirements in order to identify the lexical phrases that are prevalent in the target corpus.

One of the earliest corpus-driven studies of this type was Salem's (1987) analysis of repeated lexical phrases in a corpus of French government resolutions. In the late 1990s, corpus-driven studies of recurrent lexical phrases in English registers began to appear. Altenberg (1998) was perhaps the first study to investigate frequently occurring lexical phrases in spoken English, identifying 470 three-word sequences that occurred at least ten times in the *London-Lund Corpus*. Altenberg then classified these lexical sequences according to their grammatical characteristics (independent clauses, dependent clauses, and clause constituents) and discussed some of the major discourse functions served by these expressions (e.g. as interactional responses, epistemic tags, and comment clauses).

Around the same time, the *Longman Grammar of Spoken and Written English* (Biber *et al.* 1999: chapter 13) reported on the most common "lexical bundles" in conversation and academic writing. Lists are provided for common four-word, five-word, and six-word lexical bundles, defined as sequences of words that occurred at least ten times per million words in the target register, distributed across at least five different texts. These bundles were interpreted in structural/grammatical terms (e.g. main clause fragments like *have a look at*, question fragments like *do you want to*, dependent clause fragments like *know what I mean*, and noun phrase or prepositional phrase fragments like *the end of the*). These structural correlates were surprising in two respects: (i) most lexical bundles are not complete structural units, and (ii) most bundles bridge two different structural units (e.g. a main clause plus the start of an embedded complement clause, like *I don't know why*; or a head noun phrase plus the start of an embedded prepositional phrase, like *the nature of the*). A further surprising finding was that almost none of these most frequent lexical phrases were idiomatic in meaning, although they could be interpreted as serving important discourse functions. Numerous subsequent studies have employed a "lexical bundle" framework to describe the lexical expressions typical of different registers, focusing on both frequency and discourse function (see Sections 2.3 and 2.4 below).

2.3 Register variation and discourse functions of lexical phrases

As noted in the last section, most corpus-linguistic phraseological studies begin by identifying the set of lexical phrases that are especially prevalent in a corpus. However, they often have the ultimate goal of describing the phraseological characteristics of a register (or describing phraseological variation among multiple registers), and describing the discourse functions served by different types of lexical phrases.

For example, Biber, Conrad, and Cortes (2004) compare the distribution and functions of lexical bundles in four registers: conversation, university classroom teaching, university textbooks, and published academic research writing. That study found systematic differences at all levels. Overall, lexical bundles are much more common in speech than in writing (i.e. more tokens), and there are also more different bundles (i.e. more types) used in speech. Conversation uses bundles consisting mostly of verbs and clause fragments (including dependent clause fragments), while academic writing uses lexical bundles consisting of noun phrase and prepositional phrase fragments. Spoken classroom teaching is especially interesting because it combines both the conversational and written-academic patterns – using both clausal and phrasal bundles – and because both types of bundle occur much more frequently in teaching than in either conversation or academic writing. Lexical bundles also vary in their discourse functions, being used to express "stance," "discourse organization," and "referential" meanings. In addition, registers differ in the extent to which they use lexical bundles for each of these functions: conversation uses bundles especially for stance functions, while academic writing uses bundles especially for referential functions. Here again, the corpus analysis shows that the register of classroom teaching is particularly interesting, frequently using lexical bundles for all three major functions.

Subsequent lexical bundle studies keep these same research objectives, applied to other discourse domains. For example, Biber and Barbieri (2007) describe the use of lexical bundles in other spoken and written university registers (e.g. written course syllabi and spoken advising sessions), describing the specialized discourse functions that bundles serve in those registers (e.g. as directives). Nesi and Basturkmen (2006) similarly undertake a more detailed study of lexical bundles in university monologic lectures, focusing especially on the cohesive functions that bundles serve in those speech events. Csomay (2013) is also especially interested in the distribution of lexical bundle types within spoken lectures. In that study, lectures are first segmented into discourse units, based on their use of shared sets of content words. Then, Csomay investigated the typical discourse functions of lexical bundles found in different parts of the lectures: stance bundles are especially common in the opening phases of a lecture, while referential bundles are less common. However, when the lecturer shifts to the instructional phases, this preference is reversed: stance bundles become less common, while referential bundles become more prevalent. Topic-introducing discourse organizing bundles have important functions in these lectures, but further research is required to document their functions within particular discourse units.

Hyland (2008b) and Cortes (2013) document the functions of lexical bundles in written academic registers. Hyland focuses primarily on variation across four academic disciplines: electrical engineering, biology, business, and applied linguistics. This study also analyzes discourse functions in terms of three general categories, but with slightly different labels and emphases: "participant-oriented" (including stance bundles), "text-oriented" (including transition and framing signals), and "research-oriented" (e.g. regarding location, procedures, quantification, etc.). While, noun phrase + *of* bundles were the most common in all four disciplines, there were also disciplinary differences. For example, bundles with passive verbs (e.g. *is shown in Figure*) were especially common in engineering and biology, while bundles with prepositional phrases + *of* (e.g. *on the basis of*) were considerably more common in the social sciences.

The disciplines also varied in their reliance on bundles for different discourse functions: science and engineering preferred bundles with research-oriented functions, while participant-oriented bundles were proportionally more important in the social science disciplines. Text-oriented bundles, though, were important in all four disciplines.

Cortes (2013) undertakes a more direct investigation of the discourse functions of lexical bundles in the Introductions to published research articles, by first segmenting those texts into discourse "moves" and "steps." Lexical bundles are then analyzed for their internal distribution across moves. Cortes finds that some bundles have particular functions tied to specific moves and steps; for example, the bundles *one of the most important* and *play an important role in the* are both associated exclusively with the "claiming the relevance of the field" step (Move 1). Bundles like *it is necessary to* and *it should be noted that* have a strong association with the expression of the "gap" in the second move. And bundles like *the aim/objective of this paper/study* are associated strongly with the third move, announcing the purpose of the study. At the same time, other bundles with more general discourse functions are distributed across moves and steps, such as *the fact that the* and *the nature of the*. The studies by Cortes and Csomay are both noteworthy in that they take the investigation of discourse function one step further than previous research, showing how lexical bundles function within spoken and written texts and serve particular discourse functions related to the internal organization of discourse.

As this review of research illustrates, there has been a particular interest in lexical phrases in academic registers, perhaps because much corpus research on lexical phrases has been motivated by applied concerns related to language teaching and learning. For example, Cortes (2004) compared the use of lexical bundles by university students and published researchers in history and biology, while several studies have compared the use of bundles by native-English versus non-native-English writers (e.g. Nekrasova 2009; Chen and Baker 2010; Ädel and Erman 2012; Staples *et al.* 2013). These studies document the different bundles used by native and non-native groups, and debate the question of whether non-native speakers have an under-reliance on bundles (because they have not yet learned them) or an over-reliance on bundles (because they are convenient chunks of discourse).

In a second line of applied research, Simpson-Vlach and Ellis (2010) had a different objective: to develop a list of academic formulas that could be used for language teaching. As the basis for this list, they assembled an academic corpus including spoken and written registers, by combining resources from several available corpora (e.g. MICASE, BNC, and Hyland's corpus of research articles). Simpson-Vlach and Ellis were concerned with the psycholinguistic validity of the lexical phrases in their lists, so they employed several different quantitative approaches, and directly evaluated the perceptual status of the phrases identified through corpus analysis (see also Ellis *et al.* 2008). The corpora were originally analyzed to extract all three-, four-, and five- word sequences that occurred at least ten times per million words, and were distributed across the majority of academic disciplines included in the corpus. Then, log-likelihood measures were used to identify the phrases that were especially frequent in academic corpora, by comparison to a non-academic reference corpus. Finally, mutual information scores (MI) were computed to identify phrases in which the words have a strong collocational association. Simpson-Vlach and Ellis contrast the results of a simple frequency approach and an MI approach (2010: 494–495), and in the end, opt for an approach that combines the two measures. They then go on to present three lists: one for lexical phrases typical of academic speech (e.g. *the idea of*), phrases typical of academic writing (e.g. *in the form of*), and phrases typical of both speech and writing (*the idea that*). Those phrases are then categorized for discourse functions, using the framework developed in Biber *et al.* (2004). Overall, this study is exemplary in the attention given to methodological considerations, and in the attempt to validate the results of quantitative corpus analysis by reference to the judgments of human raters.

2.4 Corpus studies of discontinuous lexical frames

The research studies surveyed above have all focused on *continuous* sequences of words. However, researchers have also been interested in *discontinuous* sequences of words. One approach to these phenomena focuses on the ways in which two words collocate at a distance (e.g. *PLAY* and *ROLE*; see Cheng *et al.* 2006, 2008). Several other studies have focused on fixed discontinuous phrases: recurrent words forming a "frame" for variable slots (e.g. *too* ___ *to* ___). Most early studies of this type were corpus-based, describing the use of pre-selected frames that the authors had noticed in texts. Renouf and Sinclair (1991) were probably the first to carry out a corpus-based analysis of the variable fillers in discontinuous lexical sequences, referred to as "collocational frameworks." Renouf and Sinclair examined seven specific collocational frameworks (e.g. *a* + ? + *of*), investigating the common fillers that occur in each frame. Butler (1998) adopts a similar approach to undertake a much more ambitious study of 28 different discontinuous frames in Spanish (e.g. *un* ___ *de; de* ___ *por*). Butler uses a range of statistical methods (including MI scores, Pearson correlations, and type–token ratios) to identify the important lexical fillers in these discontinuous frames, and to compare the quantitative distribution of frames and fillers across spoken and written registers in Spanish. Although the primary focus of that article is to present quantitative patterns, Butler also includes some functional interpretation, classifying the filler nouns into semantic classes (e.g. measure nouns versus human nouns).

Eeg-Olofsson and Altenberg (1994) was probably the first corpus-driven study to investigate discontinuous lexical frames, based on analysis of the

London–Lund Corpus. This is a highly innovative study, exploring a number of new computational and statistical techniques for the analysis of phraseological combinations in a corpus. The analysis identifies 197,580 different two-word frames (with the middle slot of one to two words being variable), although 88 percent of those frames occurred only once or twice in the corpus. The 1,000 most common frames are further analyzed with respect to the type–token ratios of the filler words, "entropy" (how predictable the frame filler is), and MI score for the frame words. There is no functional analysis of the frames, but the authors do provide some generalizations, noting that the highest-frequency frames are composed mostly of function words; medium-frequency frames tend to consist of abstract/ general lexical words; and lower-frequency frames have more lexical words, with fillers that are less variable.

More recently, Biber (2009) began with the 234 most frequent continuous lexical sequences ("lexical bundles") in conversation and academic writing (see Sections 2.2 and 2.3 above), and then analyzed each word in the bundle to determine the extent to which it was fixed or variable. The primary goal of the study was to compare the differing ways in which spoken and written discourse are constructed of extended lexical phrases, by characterizing phraseological patterns as relatively fixed sequences (bundles) versus discontinuous frames with a variable slot (frames). For example, written academic discourse relies primarily on frames with intervening variable slots (e.g. 1*34, 12*4, 1*3*); fixed slots are typically filled by content words while variable slots are typically filled by function words. In contrast, conversational discourse relies more on continuous lexical sequences, and both fixed and variable slots are typically filled with function words. Gray and Biber (2013) extend that study by undertaking a genuinely bottom-up (corpus-driven) approach to the identification of discontinuous frames; we briefly present part of that study in our case study below (Section 4). Finally, Römer (2010) applies a similar methodological approach to analyze 280 frequent discontinuous lexical sequences ("p-frames") in a corpus of academic book reviews. That paper includes extensive methodological discussion, illustrating the application of available software packages for analyses of this type (especially *kfNgram*, developed by William Fletcher; see www.kwicfinder.com/kfNgram/ kfNgramHelp.html). In the discussion, this article illustrates how discontinuous lexical frames are distributed in systematic ways and serve particular rhetorical functions within book reviews.

2.5 Summary

As the review of research in this section has shown, corpus-linguistic studies of extended lexical sequences have addressed the nature of patterned language from a variety of perspectives, under a range of rubrics, and with varying goals and methodologies. Table 7.2 summarizes how a

Table 7.2 *Research studies of extended lexical sequences*

			Research goals		Research goals			Nature of multi-word units					
			Scope		Role of register			Idiomatic status		Length		Continuous vs. discontinuous	
Study	Phraseological label	Corpus-based (CB) vs. corpus-driven (CD)	pre-selected lexical expressions	full set of multi-word sequences	cross-register comparisons	single-register	general corpora (no register consideration)	fixed idiomatic	non-idiomatic but frequent	short: 2-3 words	extended: 3+	continuous	discontinuous
Simpson & Mendis (2003)	Idioms	hybrid CD / CB	X	X		X		X		(X)	(X)	X	
Altenberg (1998)	recurrent word combinations	CD		X		X			X	X		X	
Biber *et al.* (1999), Biber *et al.* (2004), Biber & Barbieri (2007), Hyland (2008b), Cortes (2013)	lexical bundles	CD		X	X				X		X	X	
Nesi & Basturkmen (2006), Csomay (2013)	lexical bundles	CD		X		X			X		X	X	
Renouf & Sinclair (1991), Butler (1998)	collocational frameworks	CB	X				X		X	X			X
Eeg-Olofsson & Altenberg (1994)	discontinuous frames	CD		X			X		X	X			X
Biber (2009)	lexical bundles and frames	hybrid CD / CB	X	X	X				X		X		X
Römer (2010)	phrase-frames (p-frames)	hybrid CD / CB	X	X		X			X		X		X
Gray & Biber (2013)	lexical frames	CD		X	X				X		X		X

sample of the studies discussed in Section 2 can be characterized along these parameters.

3 State of the art and current issues

Taken together, corpus investigations over the last few decades have greatly extended our understanding of phraseological lexical sequences in English discourse. As shown by the research studies surveyed above, for example, we now know that lexical phrases serve important discourse functions relating to the expression of stance, discourse organization, and local referential framing (related to research orientations in academic writing). Previous research has also shown that lexical phrases have systematic distributions within texts, and serve as important signals to the internal discourse structure of spoken and written registers. We know that idioms are not common in natural discourse, and that instead most frequent lexical phrases have non-idiomatic meanings. There are major differences in the typical grammatical correlates of lexical phrases as well as in the typical discourse functions of lexical phrases across registers. Spoken registers generally prefer lexical sequences composed of verbs and clauses, often serving stance-related functions; written registers (especially academic written registers) generally prefer lexical phrases composed of nouns and phrases, often with referential functions.

However, research practices in this domain of inquiry could be further improved through consideration of some basic methodological issues. For example, one current issue for the study of phraseology in corpus linguistics concerns the best methods to be used for the identification of the most important lexical phrases in a corpus. More specifically, at issue is the quantitative measures used to identify important lexical phrases: simple frequency and dispersion, versus measures of collocational association (like mutual information). Biber (2009) has argued that frequency-based measures and statistical measures (like mutual information) identify fundamentally different types of lexical patterns. Gries and Mukherjee (2010) provide a very useful discussion of these issues, proposing the measure of lexical gravity as an alternative approach. Lexical gravity considers both token frequencies as well as type frequencies (i.e. the number of different words that can occur in a given position of a lexical sequence) to evaluate relative importance. Still other measures (e.g. entropy, type–token ratios, *t*-scores, etc.) have been proposed for discontinuous frames. However, more experiments are required to make sense of the different types of information.

A related consideration involves the length of lexical phrases. Lexical bundles research has consistently demonstrated that longer bundles occur with lower frequencies than shorter bundles (e.g. Biber *et al.* 1999). Thus, since frequency cutoffs are commonly one (and often the primary) criterion used for identifying the set of important lexical phrases, consideration of the length of phrases being analyzed is required when establishing frequency criteria. However, to date there is a lack of specific recommendations to address this issue. Most studies have used a predetermined length (e.g. three words or four words) to limit the scope of the analysis; thus, this decision is based on practical rather than theoretical considerations. Other studies (e.g. Simpson-Vlach and Ellis 2010) include lexical sequences of different lengths in the same analysis, although it is not clear how those studies adjust for the necessarily higher frequencies of shorter lexical sequences.

A third current issue is the analysis of phraseology in languages other than English, particularly non-European languages. English is typologically unusual in that it has an incredibly rich inventory of function words. As a result, corpus-driven studies of lexical phrases (both continuous and discontinuous) have shown that lexical patterning is ubiquitous in English, and basic to the discourse structure of both spoken and written texts. These lexical sequences and frames consist mostly of different combinations of function words. However, it is not entirely clear whether these patterns should be taken to show a universal reliance on prefabricated phrases, or whether they reflect the typological characteristics of English grammar.

Although the focus of this handbook is on corpus-based investigations of English language texts, a few of the studies reviewed here have addressed the issue of phraseology in other languages. Salem's (1987) study of lexical phrases in French is an early example of this type, and Butler's (1998) study of discontinuous lexical frames in Spanish is also noteworthy. Cortes (2008) also focused on Spanish, comparing the distribution and functions of academic-writing lexical bundles in English versus Spanish. Kim (2009) explores the types of lexical bundles found in Korean, and Biber, Kim, and Tracy-Ventura (2010) compare the phraseological patterns of use in English, Spanish, and Korean. These last two papers make the important point that quantitative phraseological tendencies will be strongly influenced by the typological linguistic characteristics of a language (especially the distinction between agglutinative and isolating languages). For this reason, any claims about the universal importance of lexical phrases should be treated with caution. At present, it is not even clear how to go about defining formulaic lexical phrases in a highly agglutinative language. For example, a lexical phrase like *in the case of* might correspond to one lexical stem with morphological affixes (marking definiteness and case), together with a single morphological affix marking case from an adjacent word. At present, we do not have methods capable of identifying formulaic chunks of this type. Thus, there is currently great need for developing new methods and carrying out empirical investigations of phraseological patterns in languages other than English.

A final issue has received very little attention in corpus-driven studies of phraseology: the extent to which specific lists of lexical phrases are reliable (i.e. can they be replicated in analyses of another corpus), and the influence of corpus design on the identification of important lexical phrases. It is clear that corpus composition must have an influence on the identification of important lexical phrases. Even if register is controlled, the set of lexical phrases identified in a large corpus (containing more words) will probably be different than the set of phrases identified in a small corpus. But the total number of words is not the only important factor here: the number of different texts (and the average length of texts) is equally important. This is because different texts deal with distinct, specific topics, and as a result those texts use different words. Thus, a corpus with a greater number of different texts is likely to result in a greater number of different lexical phrases than a comparable corpus with fewer texts. Of course, these potential influences on the identification of lexical phrases become even more problematic if there are considerable register and/or topic variations between the corpora that are being compared. These methodological considerations are generally disregarded in corpus-driven studies of phraseology. While there has been considerable discussion of the best statistical methods to identify important phrases within a corpus, there has been almost no discussion of the replicability of phraseological findings, or the ways in which corpus design and composition influence the results of this kind of research. Thus, this is a key methodological concern that must be addressed in future research.

4 Case study on discontinuous lexical sequences in conversation and academic writing

4.1 Introduction

As noted above, corpus research on lexical phraseology has been carried out across the full continuum of corpus-based to corpus-driven research. For example, at the corpus-based extreme, Renouf and Sinclair (1991) began with a few lexical frames that they had noticed in texts (e.g. *a ___ of*), and then they carried out corpus research to describe the distribution and functions of those frames. At the other extreme, Biber, Conrad, and Cortes (2004) carried out corpus-driven research to identify the most commonly occurring lexical sequences in their corpus, and then interpreted those sequences in functional terms.

Studies like Biber (2009) and Römer (2010) could be considered intermediate, or hybrid, on this continuum: they begin with corpus-driven research to identify the most frequent continuous lexical sequences in a register (the "*n*-grams" or "lexical bundles"), and then carry out a corpus-based analysis of those sequences, identifying sequences that have variable slots and can thus be considered discontinuous lexical frames. This approach relies on an underlying assumption that all high-frequency discontinuous frames will correspond to at least one moderately frequent continuous sequence. For example, an analysis of the frequent lexical bundle *on the basis of* reveals that the third slot ("basis") is variable, and thus the frame *on the * of* is identified (which happens to be highly frequent).

Both the corpus-based and hybrid approaches can be contrasted with a strict corpus-driven approach to this issue, which would directly identify the thousands of possible discontinuous lexical frames in a corpus (e.g. *the * of the*, *in the * of*). Each sequence in the initial list of potential lexical frames can then be analyzed to determine its frequency, the words that can occur in the slot, and the extent to which the internal slot is variable or fixed. This fully corpus-driven approach is rather resource-intensive, yet is theoretically important because it makes it possible to account for frequent discontinuous sequences of words that are not associated with a moderately frequent lexical bundle. This situation can theoretically arise if the internal slot is so variable that there is no corresponding continuous sequence that gets identified as a lexical bundle. The goal of the case study here is to explore that methodological possibility by comparing the list of highly frequent lexical frames that result from a hybrid corpus-based study of discontinuous sequences (Biber 2009) with results from a fully corpus-driven approach. We briefly summarize our methods and major findings here, while referring readers to Gray and Biber (2013) for a fuller discussion.

4.2 Corpora

The academic writing and the American English conversation subcorpora from the *Longman Spoken and Written Corpus* were used in the case study (see Biber *et al.* 1999: 24–35). The academic writing subcorpus (150 texts, *c.* 5.3 million words) is composed of academic books and research articles, while the American English conversation (717 texts, *c.* 4.9 million words) contains everyday conversation. The use of these corpora, which were also analyzed by Biber (2009), allows us to directly compare a hybrid and a fully corpus-driven approach to discontinuous sequences. That is, as a hybrid approach, Biber (2009) first identified common lexical bundles and then analyzed those bundles to determine if they represented discontinuous frames based on the variability of the words making up the frame. In contrast as a fully corpus-driven approach, the present case study directly identifies the full set of frames in the corpora.

4.3 Database construction and analysis procedures

Because of the computational resources required to process and store all potential discontinuous sequences (frames) in large corpora (*c.* 10 million

Table 7.3 *Summary of lexical bundles and frame patterns investigated in the case study*

4-Word patterns	Examples
1234	*in the case of, I don't know if*
1*34	*be * by the, and * was like*
12*4	*it is * to, I was * to*

words in total) from a strictly corpus-driven approach, we used a MySQL database to store all possible four-word sequences in the two subcorpora (specifically all four-word sequences that did not cross (a) punctuation boundaries in the written corpus, and (b) turn boundaries in the spoken corpus).

MySQL database queries were then integrated into specialized computer programs written in Perl to identify all frequently recurring lexical combinations, including continuous lexical bundles and discontinuous lexical frames. To restrict the scope of our investigation, we considered only four-word patterns, and lexical frames with only one internal variable slot. Table 7.3 lists the patterns included in the present study (* indicates the variable slot). While the focus of this analysis is on discontinuous lexical frames, continuous lexical bundles were also included for comparison. In this study, a pattern was considered frequently recurrent if it occurred more than forty times per million words and in at least five texts in the subcorpus.

For discontinuous frames, the program additionally analyzed the number of distinct fillers occurring in the variable slot, which was used to compute a type–token ratio that measured the internal fixedness of each frame, where *type* is the number of distinct lexical items occurring in the variable slot and *token* is the total raw number of occurrences of the frame. For example, a frame occurring 200 times with 25 distinct fillers would have a type–token ratio of .125 (25 ÷ 200). The type–token measure has been used by previous collocational framework studies (i.e. Renouf and Sinclair 1991; Eeg-Olofsson and Altenberg 1994; Butler 1998; Marco 2000; Römer 2010), and represents the degree to which the slot is relatively fixed or variable. A type–token ratio approaching 1 indicates a high degree of variability (i.e. that nearly as many different words occur in the variable slot as there are occurrences of the frame). For example, in the academic writing corpus, the frame *the * may be* has 366 distinct fillers attested in its 485 instances, resulting in a type–token ratio of .75. In contrast, a type–token ratio approaching 0 indicates a relatively fixed pattern with fewer possible fillers. For example, the frame *do you * to* occurs 1,058 times in the conversation corpus with only 29 different fillers, resulting in a low type–token ratio of .03.

Following Biber (2009), the final measure used in this study is "predictability," calculated as the percentage of the total occurrences of a frame in which the most frequent filler occurred.[1] For example, *use* occurs 55 times in the 3,434 occurrences of the frame *of the * of* in the academic writing subcorpus. Thus, the predictability measure for this frame is 2 percent (55 ÷ 3434 × 100), indicating that the frame is not highly predictable.

4.4 Distribution of discontinuous lexical frames versus continuous lexical bundles

If a corpus is analyzed for all lexical combinations, rather than only those combinations meeting minimum frequency and/or dispersion requirements, we would logically assume that there will be more continuous sequences (pattern 1234) than discontinuous sequences. That is, logically, as we introduce variable slots, multiple continuous sequences (e.g. *explore this methodological possibility* and *explore this theoretical possibility*) will combine into a single discontinuous sequence (*explore this * possibility*), and result in fewer distinct discontinuous sequences (frames) than continuous sequences (bundles).

Figure 7.1 displays the total number (in millions) of distinct patterns that occur one or more times (raw) in our corpora. These findings show that the logical expectations are borne out by corpus analysis: there are more continuous sequences identified than discontinuous patterns when no frequency or dispersion criteria to specify levels of recurrence are applied to the data.

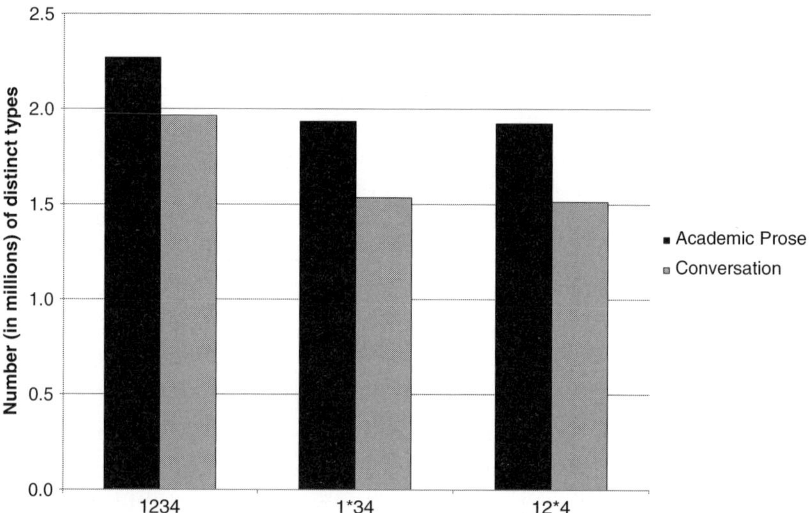

Figure 7.1 Number of distinct four-word combinations occurring at least once (with no dispersion restriction)

[1] Biber (2009: 292) illustrates this measure through discussion of the bundle *on the other hand*. For example, to determine the fixedness of slot 1, we can divide the number of times the first slot contained the word *on* (550) with the total number of occurrences of ** the other hand* (567) to find that *on* fills the first slot 97 percent of the time. Thus, slot 1 in the bundle *on the other hand* is quite fixed.

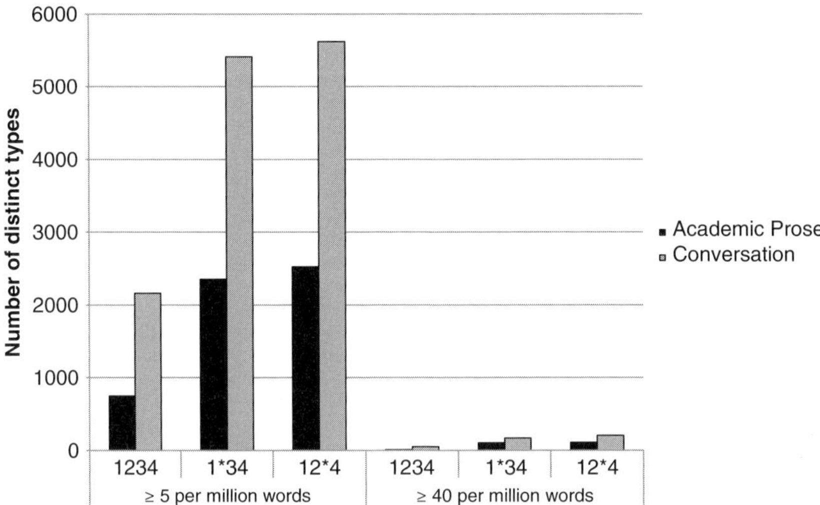

Figure 7.2 Number of distinct four-word pattern types occurring at two frequency levels (range = 5 texts)

However, when frequency and dispersion limits are set, the opposite quantitative trend appears: there are many fewer recurrent continuous sequences than discontinuous frames. Figure 7.2 displays the number of four-word sequences that are identified at two frequency levels (forty times per million words and five times per million words), with a range requirement that the sequence occurs in at least five texts. For both conversation and academic writing, many more discontinuous frames are identified than continuous lexical bundles.

At a certain point, the trend shown in Figure 7.2 reverses itself to produce the trend shown in Figure 7.1. Surprisingly, though, the greater number of discontinuous sequence types persists to extremely low levels of recurrence. While Figure 7.2 displays the results for patterns that recur only five times per million words (a quite low frequency cutoff for most formulaic language studies), the same trend is found as low as one time per million words (or about five raw occurrences for corpora of this size).

The trend shown in Figure 7.2 is important because, as noted in Section 4.1 above, previous empirical studies of discontinuous lexical frames (e.g. Biber 2009 and Römer 2010) first identify the most frequent lexical bundles, and then analyze that set of bundles to locate sequences that contain variable slots (and thus constitute discontinuous frames). This approach is based on the assumption that all high-frequency discontinuous frames will be recoverable from at least one moderately frequent continuous sequence.

In contrast, the approach taken here is to directly identify and analyze the full set of discontinuous sequences, bypassing the bundles stage, and allowing for the possibility that there are common recurrent discontinuous frames that are not associated with a common lexical bundle. Our

Table 7.4 *12*4 Frames identified in the present study in academic writing (frames that were also identified in Biber (2009) are marked by ✓)*

Frame	Biber (2009)	Frequency per million words	Type–token ratio	Predictability measure	Most frequent filler
in the * of	✓	1,002	.21	9%	case
of the * of	–	649	.38	2%	use
to the * of	✓	546	.36	2%	development
and the * of	–	394	.44	2%	development
on the * of	✓	371	.34	16%	basis
it is * to	✓	356	.13	17%	possible
of the * and	–	322	.65	2%	body
for the * of	–	297	.39	3%	purpose
at the * of	✓	292	.14	21%	end
with the * of	–	280	.44	4%	exception
by the * of	–	253	.43	5%	end
that the * of	–	244	.51	2%	number
it is * that	✓	240	.12	10%	possible
is the * of	–	214	.44	3%	number
as a * of	✓	213	.20	27%	result

results indicate that there are numerous such sequences. To illustrate, we compare the frames identified by Biber (2009) and the frames identified by the fully corpus-driven approach. Table 7.4 lists all most frequent 12*4 frames (occurring >200 times per million words in the academic writing corpus) identified in the present study, compared with the frames identified by Biber (2009).[2] Each frame with a checkmark was also identified in Biber (2009), while the remaining frames were not. Thus, 8 of these 15 discontinuous frames were *not* identified by the hybrid corpus-based and corpus-driven approach used in Biber (2009), despite the high rate of occurrence for these frames (over 200 times per million words).

Table 7.4 also details the distributional characteristics of each 12*4 frame in terms of the normed frequency, type–token ratio, predictability measure, and the word that most commonly fills the variable slot. The predictability measure is especially interesting here. All lexical frames that had a predictability of > *c.* 10 percent were identified in Biber (2009); that is, the most common filler in these frames occurred frequently, and so there was a frequent lexical bundle associated with the discontinuous frame. In contrast, most frames that have a low predictability score (< 5 percent) are not associated with a high-frequency lexical bundle, and thus they failed to be identified in the earlier study.

Figure 7.3 shows this same information graphically: the frames from Table 7.4 are plotted by their measures of predictability (percentage of most frequent filler) on the *y*-axis, and variability (type–token ratio) on the

[2] The comparison to Biber (2009) only considers the patterns he identified with internal variable slots (and not the patterns with a beginning or ending variable slot, e.g., *234, 123*, *23*).

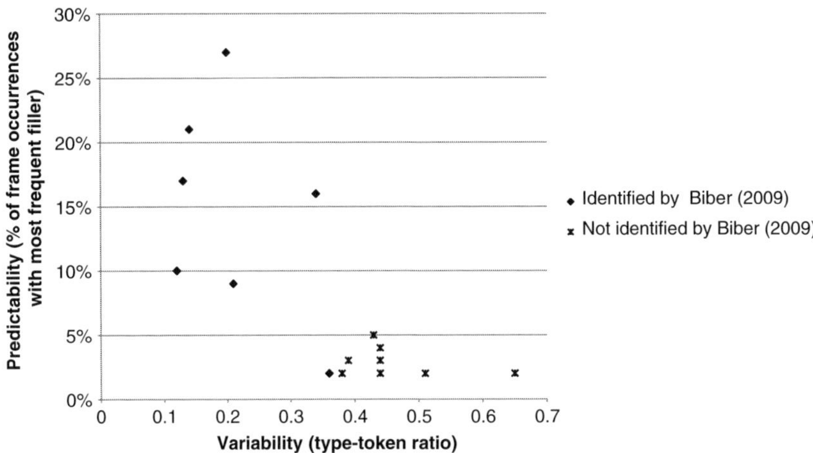

Figure 7.3 Relationship between variability and predictability for 12*4 frames occurring more than 200 times per million words in academic prose

x-axis. This scatterplot shows that most frames with higher type-token ratios and low predictability rates were not captured by Biber's (2009) bundles-to-frames approach. Thus, it is clear that identifying frames from bundles misses discontinuous patterns which are highly variable.

The fully corpus-driven approach employed in this case study shows that some of the gaps in previous findings were simply an artifact of the corpus-based methodology at the first stage of the research. For example, both Biber (2009) and the present study identified four academic-writing frames of the pattern *preposition + the * of*: *in the * of, to the * of, on the * of, at the * of*. However, the corpus-driven study further shows that this same pattern is generalizable to other prepositions, as four additional high-frequency frames with the same structure (*of the * of, for the * of, with the * of, by the * of*) were also identified in the present study. These four patterns are equally important as frames, but they are not associated with any single high-frequency filler. As a result, they are not associated with a high-frequency lexical bundle and thus would not be identified by a corpus-based analysis of lexical bundle patterns.

In summary, the direct corpus-driven approach – identifying all possible discontinuous sequences, and then determining which of those are recurrent – results in a considerably more complete analysis than the previously used approach in which discontinuous sequences are identified from frequent continuous sequences (lexical bundles).

5 Summary and conclusion

In this chapter, we have surveyed the large body of corpus research on phraseology. Unlike many other areas of linguistics, there is a fairly clear difference between corpus-based and corpus-driven research on phraseology, and both approaches have been applied productively. Corpus-based studies begin with lexical expressions (e.g. idioms or discontinuous frames) that researchers noticed before setting out on their investigations, and then they explore a corpus to learn more about the use of those expressions. Corpus-driven studies begin by analyzing a corpus to identify the set of important lexical phrases, and then study further the use of those phrases in discourse contexts to interpret the initial results.

In our case study, we illustrated how this distinction is not absolute: some previous studies of discontinuous lexical frames (like Biber 2009 and Römer 2010) are intermediate along this continuum, beginning with a corpus-driven approach to identify a set of continuous lexical sequences, but carrying out the corpus-based investigation of only those sequences, to analyze the extent to which they occur as discontinuous frames. In contrast, the exploratory investigation that we present in our case study employs a corpus-driven approach to directly identify the important discontinuous frames in speech and writing. The analysis has shown that the mixed methodological approach applied in previous studies fails to capture the full set of important (i.e. highly frequent) lexical frames. Rather, many lexical frames are so variable, with no individual filler being frequent enough to be captured in any individual frequent lexical bundle. Thus, an approach that analyzes lexical bundles to determine the extent to which they are fixed or variable will fail to reveal these highly variable lexical frames. However, these frames can be identified through direct corpus-driven analysis.

Future research is required for many research questions related to the study of phraseology. These include specific questions relating to our case study (e.g. the functional correlates of the discontinuous frames identified in this study; see Gray and Biber 2013), as well as more basic theoretical issues, such as:

- Exploration of more sophisticated quantitative methods for the identification of lexical phrases, and a better understanding of the types of phrases identified by each approach
- Exploration of the influence of corpus design and composition on the identification of important lexical phrases
- Assessment of the extent to which corpus analyses of phraseology are replicable, and development of new methods to achieve findings with higher reliability
- Exploration of phraseological patterns in typologically different languages
- Exploration of the extent to which (and ways in which) discourse can be regarded as formulaic across registers and across languages.

In summary, there have been huge advances over the last twenty years in our knowledge of the types and functions of phraseological language, resulting from numerous and diverse analyses of corpora. But there are still many basic aspects of phraseology that have yet to be investigated, making this a highly promising domain of inquiry for future research.

8

Descriptive grammar

Geoffrey Leech

This chapter, as the first of a series of four chapters dealing with grammar in this handbook, will take a rather general approach to the topic, beginning by looking back in history at the treatment of grammar from the beginning of the electronic era to the recent past. As studies of grammar have progressed and proliferated enormously through the development and exploitation of corpora, I will confine this survey to the grammar of one language - English - and will inevitably consider only a selection of publications.

The term "descriptive" in my title is, in a sense, redundant. All corpus studies of grammar inevitably make use of the evidence of grammatical usage as observed in corpora in order to arrive at some kind of description of what the corpus attests about some area(s) of grammar. In this context, "descriptive" is frequently contrasted with "prescriptive" grammar, which reflects attitudes in favor of certain usages and against others, rather than what is found to be evidenced by usage. "Descriptive" is also contrasted, often less favorably, with "theoretical." It is sometimes supposed that corpus linguists are content "merely" to "describe" what is found in a corpus, for example by describing the structures found and their frequencies, rather than to show how their findings advance understanding in terms of some theoretical framework(s) of how grammar works. I think this view is mistaken, and that description and theory are mutually dependent - see McEnery and Hardie (2012: 171–176); Gries (2010a, 2012b); also many contributions to the journal *Corpus Linguistics and Linguistic Theory*.

However, accounts of grammar can be differentiated as being *more* theory-oriented or *more* description-oriented than others. Another interpretation of the term "descriptive" here is that the descriptive grammarian aims to achieve unbiased objectivity through the principle of *total accountability*:

I am grateful to the following for their very helpful recommendations on how to write this chapter: Bas Aarts, Bengt Altenberg, Doug Biber, Ron Carter, Susan Conrad, Hilde Hasselgård, Marianne Hundt, Graeme Kennedy, Christian Mair, and Nick Smith. Regrettably, I was not able to include all their suggestions for reasons of space.

ideally[1] making use of all relevant data from the corpus, as formulated by Quirk in 1960 (cf 1968: 70–87), and examining "*all* the linguistic features of a text as well as the way these features interrelate in context" (Aarts 1999: 5). One consequence of this is that a descriptive linguist cannot ignore corpus data that do not fit his/her view of grammar, as theoretically oriented grammarians have sometimes done in the past.

1 Historical review

The principle of total accountability was first enunciated in the early days of modern corpus linguistics – although the term "corpus linguistics" was not used at that time – by Quirk, planning the first attempt to build a representative corpus of contemporary English. This attempt was also associated with another way of understanding total accountability: as the attempt to build a *comprehensive* corpus-informed description of the grammar of a language – eventually embodied in the "mega-grammar" of Quirk *et al.* (1985) and its forerunner Quirk *et al.* (1972). I say "attempt" because no grammatical account of a language is totally comprehensive, just as no dictionary is ever complete. "Comprehensiveness," like "representativeness," still remains an object of aspiration rather than of achievement.

Quirk's Survey of English Usage project, which formed the basis of the 1972 and 1985 grammars, was in a sense continuing a much older tradition, the continental "great tradition" of Jespersen (1909–1947), Poutsma (1929), and Kruisinga (1909–1911/1931–1932) among others, whose grammars of English were substantially based on datasets in the form of collections of examples recorded on paper slips – mainly from written texts of varying dates, though also from spoken examples that happened to be noted by the grammarian. The paper slips, which could be annotated and could be shuffled at will, provided the nearest thing to the present-day corpus linguist's "sort" button. These examples, rather like the citations in a dictionary, formed a corpus of sorts, but a "citation corpus"[2] rather than a corpus of continuous textual materials. The notion of corpus grammar was also pioneered by Fries (1940, 1952), who in the later publication based his English grammar on his own recorded corpus of speech. The innovation of Quirk was to build a corpus of continuous texts and spoken transcriptions, selected so as to capture a wide range of contemporary text types and spoken genres – thereby representing the use of the language in

[1] In practice, where scrutiny of individual examples is needed, "total accountability" is not achievable with large modern corpora, as their size often provides too many examples. However, most modern corpus search software provides the option of "thinning," or automatically reducing the set of examples to be examined by random selection, thus preserving the principle through unbiased sampling across the whole range of data.

[2] Perhaps "shoe box corpus" would be a better term than "citation corpus," as Jespersen was famous for keeping his data in shoe boxes (Lindquist 2009: 2), a more primitive and more vulnerable analogue of the fire-proof filing cabinets in which Quirk kept his corpus data.

terms of time and variety more strictly and consistently than had been achieved in earlier periods.

A year or two after Quirk's Survey of English Usage (SEU) project began in London, Nelson Francis and Henry Kučera at Brown University began the first electronic corpus of present-day English. They finished and released their corpus, the Brown Corpus of edited written English "for use with digital computers," in 1964, before Quirk (concentrating on detailed spoken transcription) had completed as much as a quarter of his. These two corpora inaugurated the modern age of corpus linguistics, although both suffered from limitations: the Brown Corpus was restricted to written, printed material; and the SEU corpus remained on paper until the mid 1970s, when most of the spoken part of it was computerized by Jan Svartvik and became the *London–Lund Corpus* (LLC). Nevertheless, they provided a rich source of data for an increasing number of grammatical studies in the 1970s and 1980s. Most such studies focused on individual areas of grammar, such as modal auxiliaries, relative clauses, the comparison of *will* and *be going to*, and the choice between contractions and full forms of verbs. Important early publications were the studies by Svartvik (1966) on the passive and Greenbaum (1969) on adverbials.

Such studies can be seen as a continuation of a slightly different corpus tradition (particularly associated with graduate theses in northern Europe) whereby the researcher collected his/her own corpus typically in the form of printed material, and searched it manually for instances of the grammatical phenomenon under scrutiny (e.g. Behre 1955; Van Ek 1966; Wekker 1976). A major advantage Svartvik, Greenbaum, and their like enjoyed over these studies was that the corpus was a "standard" resource representing a wide range of comparable genres, and (in the age of computerized corpora) could be searched automatically for the phenomenon to be studied, if it could be orthographically recognized – thereby dispensing with the tedium of manual searches. Further advantages were the use of a corpus which was "publicly" available such that results were in principle replicable, and the increasing availability of corpus data consisting of spoken transcriptions.

The benefits of using computer corpora for grammatical studies became more obvious when automated *grammatical tagging* (now usually called *POS-tagging*) became feasible (Greene and Rubin 1971). Once tagging had developed, associating each word and punctuation mark with a category (singular common noun, past tense lexical verb, etc.), the searches for tokens of a grammatical phenomenon became more powerful, and it became a relatively simple matter to extract from a tagged corpus a large majority of instances of abstract categories such as the progressive aspect or the passive voice.

POS-tagging is generally thought of as the basic level of corpus annotation, as a foundation for more abstract and complex levels of annotation, by which to carry out more sophisticated and abstract grammatical corpus queries. Beyond POS-tagging, the most important level of annotation for grammar is obviously the syntactic level, which allows the investigator the means to extract tokens of particular constituent structure configurations. Automatic corpus parsing, however, has proved a more difficult nut to crack than POS-tagging. The conversion of a corpus into a database of syntactic tree structures or a *treebank* remains a problematic and laborious task, which is associated with error or failure rates far greater than those associated with taggers.

Nevertheless, treebanks have become available over the last twenty years: examples are the Penn treebank (Marcus, Santorini, and Marcinowicz 1993) and the parsed ICE-GB, the latter distributed with the sophisticated ICECUP software (see Nelson, Wallis, and Aarts 2002), which enables the researcher to use syntactic templates termed *fuzzy tree fragments* to retrieve syntactic patterns of variable levels of specificity.[3] Since major constituent boundaries are identifiable in a parsed corpus, the ICE-GB enables us to search, for instance, for unusual constituent orderings (e.g. in clefts, extraposition, and topicalization) which would be virtually impossible to extract using queries based only on words and POS-tags. If we use the ICE-GB corpus as an example of a parsed corpus, however, there are disadvantages to balance against the great advantage of syntactically coded information. The ICE-GB, by recent standards, is not very large (about a million words), and yet many person-years went into its machine-aided compilation. The corpus is consequently relatively expensive to obtain on license, and understandably the ICECUP software, requiring knowledge of the grammatical system of ICE-GB (based on that of Quirk *et al.* 1985), is more difficult to learn to use than other kinds of corpus search tools.

This background explains why advances in corpus-based grammar research have been in some ways less impressive than advances in some other areas – particularly research on phraseology and collocation, which is less dependent on complex structure-dependent search mechanisms. One negative result of the relative lack of accurately annotated treebanks has been, as pointed out by Gilquin (2002), that corpus grammarians have a tendency to choose topics for research that can be investigated through relatively simple corpus searches, rather than those requiring a high level of abstract structure. In this sense corpus study (say) of modal auxiliaries is much easier to conduct than a study of constituent ordering or subject-verb agreement in the clause. It is also worth mentioning that many grammatical corpus studies are dependent on the identification of semantic or pragmatic characteristics, which often require the grammarian's "manual" coding of individual examples. In this context, the value of parsed corpora such as ICE-GB gains significance.

[3] Mention should also be made of historical treebanks, particularly the *Penn–Helsinki Parsed Corpus of Early Modern English* (PPCEME) and the *Penn–Helsinki Corpus of Middle English*, 2nd edition (PPCME2). Details of these and other corpora are found at www.helsinki.fi/varieng/CoRD/corpora/index.html.

It should be pointed out, however, that there are other means of extracting syntactic patterns (or rather, lexical + grammatical patterns) than relying on parsed corpora. One of these is to write small-scale customized programs to identify individual grammatical features of texts, the method used by Biber (1988), also applied in Biber *et al.* (1999). Another is to extend the functionality of search software by providing the ability to use patterns or templates constructed on the basis of regular expressions and/or CQP query syntax (see Hofmann *et al.* 2008). This means that the query language incorporates its own grammar, enabling it to retrieve complex lexico-syntactic patterns even where the corpus itself has no such structured information "built in," i.e. provided by annotation. Enough has been said to show how much of the progress in corpus grammar depends on advances in the annotation and searchability of corpora.

2 Extending the range and power of grammatical description: the many contributions of corpus linguistics

We move on now to some key advantages of corpus grammar in extending the range of grammatical description.

2.1 Unexpected findings

Perhaps the most memorable contributions of corpus grammar arise when the corpus linguist discovers something new and striking. Thus Hudson (1994) came up with the eye-catching title: "About 37% of word-tokens are nouns." At first glance, this might be dismissed as one of the boring quantitative results from corpora that are "descriptive" in a bad sense. But Hudson had discovered a new regularity: that (in general) all varieties of written English show a fixed percentage of "nominals": and that more than one in three word tokens belong to this category, so the frequency of referring items in a text is not only very high but more or less constant. The catch here is that "nouns" are taken to include not only common nouns and proper nouns, but also pronouns.[4] Considered as distinct classes, nouns and pronouns have markedly different distributions in speech and writing, and this difference also shows up strongly even in written corpora: Hudson notes that in the Brown Corpus pronouns are only 7 percent of word tokens in informational texts, but 14 percent in imaginative texts. It is their combination that approximates to a constant.

[4] Conflation of pronouns with nouns is a linguistically justifiable move – adopted, for example, by Huddleston and Pullum in their reference grammar (2002), which is not only in many areas more detailed than Quirk *et al.* (1985), but is regarded by many as the best comprehensive grammar of English at the present time.

Another example of a surprising corpus finding is the discovery by Tottie and Hoffmann (2006) that tag questions are nine times more common in BrE conversation than in AmE conversation – a vast discrepancy for which no convincing explanation has apparently yet been found.

2.2 Peripheral areas of grammar that corpus linguistics has opened up

Theoretically oriented grammarians often ignore areas of grammar which are not "interesting" from their theoretical viewpoint. Corpus-based grammatical research (following the principle of total accountability) cannot ignore such areas, and often finds that they are by no means uninteresting – rather the opposite. I will illustrate this from two related areas: adverbials and discourse markers.

Adverbs and adverbials have been virtually ignored by theoretical grammarians. Even the most comprehensive of grammars written by transformational grammarians, Stockwell, Schachter, and Partee (1973), had little to say about them. But, in contrast, one of the longest chapters in the corpus-informed grammars of Quirk *et al.* (1972, 1985) was the chapter on adverbials. Likewise, in the corpus-based grammar Biber *et al.* (1999) the adverbial chapter was actually the longest. Following Greenbaum's (1969) monograph, these chapters draw a major distinction between adjuncts – the more central and frequent category of adverbials – and disjuncts and conjuncts – more peripheral categories, which were previously little studied. In case it should be supposed that these long chapters, coupled with Greenbaum's book (1969), tell us all that is to be known about English adverbials, a more recent in-depth study of adjuncts by Hasselgård (2010) builds on them in providing quantitative and functional (qualitative) analyses, showing how the variability of position and combination of adjuncts reflect functional considerations such as the demands of information processing.

Closely related to the adverb/adverbial category is the even more grammatically peripheral category of discourse markers, also termed pragmatic markers, discourse particles, and the like. Discourse markers were not recognized as a part of speech in traditional grammars, and even in the present day they are an uncertain category, straddling the border between grammar, pragmatics, and discourse analysis. The early tagging systems of the Brown and LOB corpora made no provision for discourse markers. However, the compiling of the LLC in the mid 1970s gave considerable impetus to the study of the grammar of spoken language, where the frequency and conversational role of certain discourse markers (e.g. *actually*, *really*, *well*, *by the way*, *you know*) cannot be ignored. The work of Karin Aijmer has been particularly important in this field – see Aijmer (2002).

2.3 Investigating spoken English

I have already implied that the unprecedented opportunity provided by spoken corpora for the detailed study of speech phenomena was a major breakthrough for corpus-based grammar. Grammar has traditionally focused on the written language,[5] to the extent that the spoken language was largely ignored up to the invention of tape-recorders in the mid twentieth century, when it became practical to record and study spoken language in detail for the first time. The computerization (with prosodic transcription) of Quirk's spoken texts of the SEU provided the impetus for a flowering of spoken English research (e.g. Aijmer 2002a, Altenberg 1998, Stenström *et al.* 2002), but there was a time lag before the spoken data were sufficiently exploited to feature substantially in the work of grammarians. Perhaps the most regrettable limitation of the Quirk *et al.* grammars (1972, 1985) was that they still adhered to the traditional focus on written data, although they moved in the direction of speech in subjecting to close examination such spoken features as tag questions and situational ellipsis. Later, with the inception of very large corpora such as the *British National Corpus* (BNC), the *Bank of English*, and the *Cambridge International Corpus* (CIC) with a substantial component of speech, prominence was given to the grammar of spoken English as a topic of great interest.

Among studies focusing on the differences between speech and writing, a leading place should be given to Biber (1988) – see further Section 2.4 below – and to Tottie (1991), the latter a book on negation. Negation is an important topic in English grammar, and corpus analysis afforded the opportunity for a comparison of spoken and written negation data, which apparently no previous studies had undertaken. Tottie made the unexpected discovery that negation is (roughly) twice as common in speech as in writing. She used qualitative analysis of the LLC and LOB corpora to explain why this should be. The phenomena particularly associated with spoken negation were largely connected with the interactive, involved nature of speech: (i) use of mental verbs, as in *I don't think*; (ii) use in explicit denial; (iii) use in questions; (iv) use as supports; (v) use in repetition; and (vi) use in rejections.

It became obvious in the last two decades of the millennium that certain phenomena were characteristic of speech, and other phenomena that were virtually absent from written data had been seriously neglected by the grammatical tradition. They include expletives, vocatives, ellipsis phenomena, and the discourse markers mentioned above – all reflecting the interactive nature of conversation, and all part of the prevalence of non-clausal, verbless material in spoken language. Carter and McCarthy (1995) also made a strong case for grammatical structures that are unique to speech and need to be analyzed in their own terms. For example, utterances such as the following have their own kind of complexity:

[5] Significantly, the etymology of *grammar* and *grammatical* in classical Greek relates to written symbols and the art of reading and writing.

| A----------------| | B------------------| | C-------------------|

North and south London – they're different worlds – aren't they, in a way?

where the chunks marked "A," "B," and "C" can be characterized as *pre-clause*, *clause*, and *post-clause*, forming a pattern that has no place in the standard grammar of written sentences. The orthodox clausal structure of B, which would be normal in written communication, can be extended by non-clausal elements such as A and C, which can be added initially and finally.

Carter and McCarthy, in this landmark article, argued (following a similar line taken by Brazil in 1995) that the grammar of spoken English needed a "new broom" approach, and could in principle be described independently of the grammar of the written language.[6] A contrasting position was taken by Leech (2000), who agreed that corpus evidence showed the grammar of speech and of writing to be very different, but argued that this difference lay largely in the observed frequency of features of grammar, some of which are (highly) typical of speech, and some of writing. But the two varieties, according to this "holistic" viewpoint, are still using virtually the same grammatical system. From the "holistic" viewpoint, it is also maintained that in terms of patterns of usage, the difference between spoken and written language is a continuum, rather than an absolute dichotomy.[7]

The first large-scale grammar of English to give full priority treatment to conversational data is Carter and McCarthy (2006), unique as a grammar in which (after an introductory A–Z dictionary-like section) a detailed grammatical account of phenomena of the spoken language (pp. 164–265) precedes the more structure-based treatment of "core topics" such as the noun phrase and the verb phrase. Although in giving precedence to the spoken language this is to be applauded as counteracting the age-old priority given to written texts, it does lead to a "cart-before-the-horse" phenomenon whereby Carter and McCarthy make use of cardinal grammatical terms like *noun phrase, non-finite clause*, and *complement* in the spoken sections before explaining them in the subsequent "core grammar" chapters.

2.4 The value of statistical methodologies

The two chapters on grammatical variation and grammatical change, which follow this chapter, will give more attention to the statistical modeling of grammatical phenomena. However, in this chapter it will also be

[6] McCarthy goes so far as to argue a tabula rasa approach to describing spoken grammar: "Spoken grammar must always be elaborated in its own terms, using spoken data. If, at the end of the exercise, spoken and written are shown to have features in common, then this is a convenience to be thankful for, and not something that can be prejudiced without careful research" (McCarthy 1989: 20).

[7] This scalar view of the spoken–written contrast is also accepted later by Carter and McCarthy (2006: 165).

appropriate to consider how quantitative methods add value to descriptive grammar.

It is worth recalling that in the fifty years following Chomsky's *Syntactic Structures* (1957), probabilities and statistical methods were assumed by the leading school of linguistics, the generative school, to have no role in explaining or describing the grammar of a language (see Chomsky 1962/1964). On the other hand, it is arguably the most important spin-off from corpus building that we have an empirical basis for frequency statements about language.

Relatively simple statements about frequency already have implications for descriptive grammar. For example, the decision to treat the "preterite modals" *would*, *could*, *should*, and *might* as the past-tense forms of *will*, *can*, *shall*, and *might* in contemporary English (as adopted, for instance, by Huddleston and Pullum 2002: 106–108) is appealing both historically and logically (because it makes the modals seem less anomalous), but is undermined by the fact that a recent corpus study shows *shall* to be four times less frequent than *should*, and reveals that less than 5 percent of *shoulds* can be semantically considered to be past/remote forms of *shall* (Leech 2003: 233). The argument for *should* being the past tense of *shall* in PDE is minimal. From the same corpus study, we see that *need/needn't*, constructed as a modal auxiliary, is rare and becoming rarer, such that a 2.5-million-word corpus of American conversation provided no example of *needn't*. Hence it is hardly tenable for Huddleston and Pullum to maintain (2002: 183) that *You needn't attend the lectures* is "perfectly acceptable to all speakers."[8] Where corpora attest to extreme infrequency, there is reason to take account of this in synchronic description. With the recent gain in influence of usage-based cognitive models of language (see e.g. Bybee 2007), we at last have the motivation as well as the ability to elucidate grammar in quantitative terms. Observations about the relative frequency of grammatical features under various conditions are no longer to be considered an epiphenomenon of no relevance to language theorizing.

The first major demonstration of the value of corpus methods in statistical modeling is found in Biber (1988) – and its predecessor Biber (1986), significant, I believe, for being the first corpus-based article[9] to be accepted on a grammatical topic in the LSA's world-leading journal *Language* (at a time when for leaders of opinion in linguistics, corpus work was a "no-go area"). These multidimensional, multifeature, multitext studies, to be followed by many others by Biber and co-authors, used factor analysis to identify six dimensions of variation on the basis of a wide range of linguistic features and their patterns of co-occurrence. (Biber 1988 used 67

[8] Huddleston and Pullum (2002), for all its impressive depth of analysis, shows very little use of corpus data. The point worth making here is that if corpora had been consulted more, the grammar would have been even more impressive.

[9] It is true that Quirk (1965) – see below – had already been published in *Language*, but its use of corpus data was peripheral. It was corpus-informed rather than corpus-based.

linguistic features, of which 65 were grammatical categories.)[10] The resulting model of variation was able to provide a description of the distinctive grammatical characteristics of any spoken or written text, and of the degree of similarity between any two texts. The model demonstrated how the simple dichotomy between speech and writing had been misleading, and how many of the contradictory conclusions reached in previous research on speech and writing could be reconciled. These studies were thus transformative in showing how sophisticated multifactorial language modeling can be undertaken on the basis of grammatical phenomena in corpora. The chapters on grammar which follow the present one give more recent instances of the way corpus-based statistical models have advanced the study of grammar.

2.5 Gradience and multifactorial analysis

Frequency and probability, when applied in grammar, lead to the view that not all categories and structures are of equal status, but that some are more significant or salient than others. Similarly, grammar becomes a matter of "more or less" rather than "either/or" when consideration is given to the much-discussed notion of gradience (Aarts 2007) – the idea that membership of two (or more than two) categories is differentiated not by a strict dichotomy, but by a scale of similarity and difference. The concept of gradience entered linguistic terminology with Bolinger (1961), but it competed with alternative terms such as cline (Halliday 1961), serial relationship (Quirk 1965), and squish (Ross 1973). Quirk's article was inspired by his work on the SEU corpus, and made a breakthrough in providing a practical way of describing gradience by means of a two-dimensional matrix in which each cell is filled with a "+," a "–," or occasionally a "?." These three symbols may be explicated as "membership of category A," "non-membership of category A," and "membership not determined." The basic idea is that, unlike Aristotelian categories, grammatical categories are often recognized by a set of properties, such that not all properties are present in each instance of category membership, and not all properties are of equal centrality or importance.

Gradience can be recognized either between members of different categories (what Aarts 2007 calls intersective gradience) or between members of the same category (what he calls subsective gradience). The latter type of gradience fits well with the notion of prototype categories (Rosch 1975, 1976) which has been influential in grammatical description, although it has often been vaguely used to refer to the grammarian's sense that some members of a category are more central than others, and that the boundaries of categories are often unclear and fuzzy (Zadeh 1965). The benefit of corpus grammar is that it helps the analyst to map the phenomenon of

[10] The two non-grammatical features out of the 67 were word length and type–token ratio.

gradience more precisely – using, for example, the "plus and minus" matrix method – and can also use frequency data to give substance to the idea that some members or subtypes of a category are more typical or cognitively central than others.

In the past theoretical linguists, relying on their own language intuition and the occasional well-picked example, have found little need to recognize gradience, which can complicate rather than clarify their grammatical models. However, the corpus linguist, analyzing and classifying real data, soon discovers that gradience is a reality. An early example of corpus-based gradience was provided by Svartvik's study of the passive (1966), where he found that the distinction between the passive verb construction of (1) and the copular *be* + Adjective construction of (2) was far from a simple dichotomy:

(1) A total of £130 was *stolen* (by . . .). [BNC K4 W 1441]
(2) Claire was (very) *excited*. [BNC A0D 1592]

It is possible to distinguish the passive of (1) from the adjectival construction of (2) by the simple test of the acceptable insertion of a *by*-agent in (1) and the acceptable insertion of *very* in (2). However, a number of intermediate variants need to be recognized. One possibility is the blend of adjectival and passive constructions where both *very* and the *by*-agent co-occur: *I was very surprised by the King's reply* [BNC FPV 672]. More than a hundred examples of this are found in the BNC. Another possibility is the "statal" passive, where a participial dynamic verb is used in reference to a state of completion, in which case it is hardly possible for the *by*-agent to occur:

(3) An unusually low price might mean the car *is stolen*. [BNC ARA 510]

The corresponding active sentence here would not have a corresponding meaning, unless *steals* were changed into *has stolen*:

(4) An unusually low price might mean [someone] *has stolen* the car.

Qualitative analysis of corpus examples enables a matrix table to be built up, whereby criteria showing resemblance to the *be* + adjective category or to the passive category can be plotted against numbers of tokens, and degrees of similarity to and difference from the passive can be established.

It must be admitted, however, that the analysis of gradience is a laborious affair, and even corpus grammarians have been known to shy away from it. Quirk *et al.* (1985), as a corpus-informed grammar, differs from its rival Huddleston and Pullum (2002) in acknowledging the existence of gradience as a grammatical phenomenon, and yet in its 1,779 pages only about 30 examples of gradience are discussed. These include some well-known borderline phenomena in English grammar, such as the fuzzy boundaries between subordinators, conjuncts, and coordinators (*for* and *so* are particularly borderline); between auxiliaries and main verbs; and between complex prepositions (e.g. *in spite of*) and free combinations (e.g. *on the shelf by*).

To illustrate the case of complex prepositions, corpus analysis can demonstrate the degree of fixedness of the sequence Prep 1 + Noun + Prep 2 by a number of criteria, of which Quirk *et al.* (1985: 671–672) propose nine:

a. Prep 2 can be varied: *on the shelf at (the door)* vs. **in spite for*
b. Noun can be varied between singular and plural: *on the shelves by* vs. **in spites of*
c. Noun can be varied in respect of determiners: *on shelves by* vs. **in a/the spites of*
d. Prep 1 can be varied: *under the shelf by (the door)* vs. **for spite of*
e. Prep 2 + complement can be replaced by a possessive: *on the surface of the table* ~ *on its surface* vs. *in spite of the result* ~ **in its spite.*
f. Prep 2 + complement can be omitted: *on the shelf* vs. **in spite.*
g. Prep 2 + complement can be replaced by a demonstrative: *on that shelf* vs. **in that spite*
h. The noun can be replaced by nouns of related meaning: *on the ledge by (the door)* vs. **in malice of*
i. The noun can be freely modified by adjectives: *on the low shelf by (the door)* vs. **in evident spite of*

These and similar criteria of fixedness can be related to the diachronic process of grammaticalization, a topic explored by Hoffmann (2005) and Smith (2013).

Corpora also allow us to investigate the set of factors which determine the choice between apparently synonymous alternatives. An example of this is the choice between the English *s*-genitive and the (often semantically equivalent) *of*-construction. Using data from the LOB Corpus, Leech, Francis, and Xu (1994) employed logistic modeling to calculate the odds in favor of the genitive [X's Y] as contrasted with [the Y of X], taking account of four factors which were assumed to condition the choice: (a) the semantic category of X (human, inanimate, etc.); (b) the semantic relation between X and Y (possessive, partitive, etc.); and (c) the genre of text (press, learned, fiction). The model established that all three factors were significant variables in making the genitive the more likely choice. The order of significance, moreover, was (a), (c), (b). Within each factor, the variants could also be ordered in terms of their degree of preference or dispreference for the genitive. For example, in (a) "X is human" favored the genitive most strongly, whereas "X is inanimate (apart from place)" favored it least. In factor (b) the relation "X is the origin of Y" favored the genitive most strongly, whereas "X is the object of Y" favored it least. In factor (c), fictional texts favored the genitive most, whereas learned (academic) texts favored it least. Whereas these findings may not be particularly surprising, it is good to know that such results can be obtained inductively from corpus data, once the texts have been humanly annotated with the categories concerned. This

tracking recent historical changes relating to tense, aspect, modality, voice, and verb complementation.

(c) Lexico-grammar

One of the ways in which corpus linguistics has changed our view of language, I believe, is in the now widespread recognition that grammar and lexis are not separate components of language, but that they interpenetrate. The view was put forward by Michael Halliday as early as 1961, that there is a "cline" rather than a dichotomy between lexis and grammar, and the inseparability of "lexico-grammar" is now widely recognized particularly through the work of John Sinclair (1991), and has been supported strongly by construction grammar and usage-based models of language acquisition, as well as by corpus linguistics. The advantage of corpus linguistics in this domain, of course, is the ability to search large corpora for patterns of collocation and colligation which were formerly only imagined or intuited, but can now be demonstrated through statistical measures of "bondedness" such as MI (mutual information).

How does this affect corpus-based grammar? It has long been held that grammatical patterns, although abstract in themselves, are realized through lexical as well as grammatical choice. Even traditional grammars contain an admixture of lexical and grammatical information: for instance, patterns of complementation with lexical verbs. But in addition, large corpora have proved game-changing in providing frequency information on the interaction of lexis and grammar, as new statistical modeling techniques have developed: pattern grammar (Hunston and Francis 2000); collostructions; (Stefanowitsch and Gries 2003); word sketches (Kilgarriff and Tugwell 2002); concgrams (Cheng *et al.* 2006).

The three areas discussed under (a)–(c) above can be described as "leading edge," as they are leading, and will lead, to further advances in the understanding of language in the future. Thanks to them, descriptive grammar will continue to have a role in corpus linguistics.

9

Grammatical variation

Daniela Kolbe-Hanna and Benedikt Szmrecsanyi

1 A discussion of previous research in this area

In this chapter, we use a fairly liberal definition of "grammatical variation," including both genuinely variationist research – where grammatical variants are modeled as competing against each other – and text-linguistic research that explores variable text frequencies of particular grammatical constructions in corpora.

Corpus-based research on grammatical variation is a wide research area, so the review we are offering is somewhat selective. By and large, research along these lines can be categorized into five groups:

1. *Variationist sociolinguistics*. Researchers in this tradition are typically interested in how linguistic variation is conditioned by language-internal and language-external factors. Although early studies largely relied on the researcher's personal notes taken while listening to the audio recordings, state-of-the-art work is usually based on corpora consisting of fully transcribed sociolinguistic interviews (see Tagliamonte 2007). The bulk of this literature is concerned with phonological variation; however, grammatical variation has been subject to study since at least the 1980s (Torres Cacoullos and Walker 2009a; MacKenzie 2013; Poplack and Dion 2009; Poplack and Tagliamonte 1996; Scherre and Naro 1991; Tagliamonte and Temple 2005; Travis 2007; Weiner and Labov 1983).
2. *Diachronic linguistics*. In this department we find work exploring grammatical variation with regard to resultant grammatical change – short-term or long-term, completed or in progress – on the basis of historical corpora (Biber and Gray 2011; Gries and Hilpert 2010; Hinrichs and Szmrecsanyi 2007; Hundt 2004; Nevalainen 1996; Raumolin-Brunberg 2005; Taylor 2008; Wolk *et al.* 2013).
3. *Register/genre/text type analysis*. Work in this tradition is often focused on lexis, but many studies include features that come within the remit of

grammatical variation (e.g. Biber 1988; Biber and Finegan 1989; Hundt and Mair 1999). Some analysts are exclusively concerned with grammatical variation (see Grafmiller 2014; and the papers in Dorgeloh and Wanner 2010). The *Longman Grammar* (Biber *et al.* 1999) backs up its comprehensive grammatical description of English with information about text type variation.

4. *Dialectology*. While dialectology, by and large, is phonology-focused and atlas-based, corpus-based research into grammatical variation within or between dialects, or regional varieties, of a language has become increasingly popular since relatively recently (Anderwald 2009; Grieve 2012; Steger and Schneider 2012; Szmrecsanyi 2013; Tagliamonte and Smith 2002, and the contributions in Kortmann *et al.* 2005; Hernández, Kolbe, and Schulz 2011).
5. *Knowledge, processing, cognition*. Grammatical variation has also been the subject of corpus-based psycholinguistic research (Gries 2005a; Jaeger 2006; Reitter, Moore, and Keller 2010), of work in cognitive linguistics (De Smet and Cuyckens 2005; Grondelaers and Speelman 2007; Hilpert 2008), and of research concerned with the nature of linguistic knowledge (Bresnan *et al.* 2007; Adger and Smith 2010).

In what follows, we discuss five studies, each one exemplifying one of the categories defined above.

Variationist sociolinguistics. Weiner and Labov (1983) is a comparatively dated study, but it illustrates well the variationist sociolinguistic approach to grammatical variation. It draws on a corpus of agentless sentences produced in sociolinguistic interviews (this "corpus" may not live up to contemporary standards of corpus compilation, but it comes within the remit of our notion of corpus linguistics). The paper is concerned with a syntactic variable, the alternation between agentless passives, as in (1a), and generalized, "empty" actives, as in (1b), in spoken English:

(1) a. The liquor closet got broken into.
 b. They broke into the liquor closet. (Weiner and Labov 1983: 34)

As is customary in the variationist sociolinguistic literature, Weiner and Labov assume semantic interchangeability between the two variants. Using a private corpus containing sociolinguistic interviews attesting 1,489 relevant constructions, Weiner and Labov conduct, among other things, multivariate Variable Rule (Varbrul) analyses to determine the influence of several external and internal factors on the choice of generalized actives or agentless passives in their corpus. The language-external conditioning factors studied are careful vs. casual style, sex, and social class; the language-internal constraints subject to study are information status, parallelism in surface structure, and whether or not a passive was used anywhere in the five preceding clauses. Weiner and Labov find, in short, that the single most powerful factor influencing the choice of actives vs. passives is repetition of previous structure.

Diachronic linguistics. Gries and Hilpert (2010) draw on the syntactically parsed Corpus of Early English Correspondence (PCEEC) to explore morphological variation during the transition period, between 1417 and 1681, from third-person singular *-(e)th* (as in *he giveth*) to *-(e)s* (as in *he gives*). From the parsed data source, Gries and Hilpert extract about 20,000 relevant observations of *-(e)th* or *-(e)s*. They use a variant of cluster analysis to derive periods in a bottom-up fashion, using text frequencies of the variant suffixes to derive a similarity measure. Thus, based on the structure of the dataset, Gries and Hilpert distinguish five intervals: 1417–1478, 1479–1482, 1483–1609, 1610–1647, and 1648–1681. This periodization is one of the explanatory variables that is subsequently fed into a mixed-effects regression analysis that models the change from *-(e)th* to *-(e)s* considering both language-external factors (such as bottom-up periods, or author gender) and language-internal constraints (e.g. does the following word begin with a fricative?) to predict the observable variation, which the model does with a 95 percent success rate. The model also takes care of author idiosyncrasies and verb lemma effects by treating these independent variables as random effects. Crucially, Gries and Hilpert check for interactions between the periodization they use and the language-internal constraints considered in the model to establish if and to what extent particular language-internal constraints are fluctuating diachronically. Along these lines it turns out, for instance, that certain phonological factors play a role only in some periods but not in others.

Register/genre/text type analysis. Hundt and Mair (1999) explore the original Brown family of corpora, a set of four one-million-word parallel corpora sampling Standard written British and American English from the 1960s and 1990s. The Brown corpora cover a variety of written text types, and Hundt and Mair propose a continuum of openness to innovation ranging from "agile" to "uptight" genres. Specifically, Hundt and Mair compare the press and academic prose sections of the Brown corpora, and demonstrate that the two genres differ in terms of innovativeness and conservativeness: press is an "agile" genre, and academic prose is "uptight." On the methodological plane, Hundt and Mair investigate features that are suspected to contribute to the growing "colloquialization" of the norms of written English. Such features include first- and second-person pronouns, sentence-initial conjunctions, contractions, phrasal and phrasal-prepositional verbs, passive constructions, abstract nouns ending in *-tion*, *-ment*, *-ness*, *-ity*, usage of the progressive construction, usage of bare infinitives after *help*, and usage of the preposition *upon*. For example, phrasal verbs (as in *he made the story up*) are considered the colloquial variant of more bookish Latinate verbs, such as *invent*. This is why Hundt and Mair explore text frequencies of phrasal verbs with *up*, implicitly assuming that frequency increases are at the expense of more bookish alternatives. It turns out that in press writing, both the type and token frequency of phrasal verbs have increased between the 1960s and the 1990s – in academic writing, by contrast, type and token frequencies are rather stable or even decreasing.

Dialectology. Szmrecsanyi (2013) explores the extent to which grammatical variation in British English dialects is structured geographically – and thus, is sensitive to the likelihood of social contact. The study draws on a methodology ("corpus-based dialectometry") that combines corpus-based variation studies with aggregative-dialectometrical analysis and visualization methods. It is proposed that this synthesis is desirable for two reasons. First, multidimensional objects, such as dialects, call for aggregate analysis techniques. Second, compared to linguistic atlas material, corpora yield a more trustworthy frequency signal. Against this backdrop, Szmrecsanyi calculates a joint measure of dialect distance based on the discourse frequency of dozens of morphosyntactic features, such as multiple negation (e.g. *don't you make no damn mistake*), non-standard verbal *-s* (e.g. *so I says, What have you to do?*), or non-standard weak past tense and past participle forms (e.g. *they knowed all about these things*) in data from the 2.7-million-word *Freiburg Corpus of English Dialects* (FRED), which covers dialect interviews all over Great Britain. The ultimate aim is to reveal large-scale patterns of grammatical variability in traditional British English dialects. The study shows, for example, that it is impossible to find a clearly demarcated Midlands dialect area on grammatical grounds, and that travel time is a better predictor of linguistic distance than as-the-crow-flies geographic distance.

Knowledge, processing, cognition. Bresnan *et al.* (2007) explore the well-known dative alternation, viz. the syntactic variation between the double object structure, as in (2a), and the prepositional dative structure, as in (2b):

(2) a. He gave the children toys
    b. He gave toys to the children

Bresnan *et al.* calculate several logistic regression models that all correctly predict more than 90 percent of the actual dative outcomes in the Switchboard collection of recorded telephone conversations and in a corpus of *Wall Street Journal* texts. Bresnan *et al.*'s models draw on a wide range of explanatory variables to account for speakers' dative choices: semantic class, accessibility of the recipient, accessibility of the theme, pronominality of the recipient, pronominality of the theme, definiteness of the recipient, definiteness of the theme, animacy of the recipient, person of the recipient, number of the recipient, number of the theme, concreteness of the theme, structural parallelism in dialogue, and length difference between theme and recipient. In addition, the study employs bootstrapping techniques and mixed-effects modeling to investigate issues such as the role of idiolectal differences and the validity of cross-corpus generalizations. Besides showing that intuitions are a poor guide to understanding the dative alternation, Bresnan *et al.* conclude (i) that "linguistic data are more probabilistic than has been widely recognized in theoretical linguistics" (Bresnan *et al.* 2007: 91); (ii) that naturalistic corpus data can be married to sophisticated statistical analysis techniques to address issues in linguistic theory; and (iii) that probabilistically constrained linguistic variation is every bit as interesting as categorical patterns.

1.1 Discussion of methods

Most of the research in the variationist sociolinguistic tradition is based on studies of "private" (D'Arcy 2011: 55) corpora. These kinds of corpora comprise data that were gathered specifically for a project, such as in Weiner and Labov (1983). The particular text type sampled is usually sociolinguistic interviews, which more often than not are conducted in order to analyze a specific variable. Unfortunately, the data are not usually made public or generally available to other researchers. Studies that draw on publicly available corpora, such as the *Corpus of Early English Correspondence* (CEEC) in Gries and Hilpert (2010), are arguably more reliable and replicable, as anyone interested in the topic is able to repeat the analysis, and to add and remove variables as fits their own research interest. This increases the transparency of research.

Rich grammatical annotation in corpora such as the parsed version of the CEEC employed in Gries and Hilpert (2010) enables researchers to conduct feature extraction and annotation more easily, relying on decisions made in the process of parsing. Dealing with corpora that are not parsed makes extraction and annotation more laborious. Any decisions on assigning a category are left solely to the researcher and are thus more subjective. Very often, however, there is no choice left if the corpus subject to analysis is not parsed. Sometimes it might also seem beneficial to ignore existing parsing to have control over all of the data input.

Traditionally the focus has been on determining the conditioning of grammatical variation, so studies such as Bresnan *et al.* (2007) consider variation as explanandum: how can we explain regularities in variation? What are the factors that favor usage of one or the other variant – for example, which factors favor the prepositional dative structure? In another line of research, however, grammatical variation is seen as explanans, so that the aim is not to show the causes, but the effects of variation. For example, Szmrecsanyi (2013; see Grieve 2012 for a similar approach) is interested in how micro-variation in dozens of grammatical features "gangs up," as it were, to create the big picture – that is, dialect areas and dialect continua. In a similar vein, in much register-analytic research (consider, for example, Biber 1988) the question is how grammatical variation, which is seen as having functional motivations, creates register differences. When studies observe the constraints and conditions of variation, some rely on univariate analyses that assess the effect of one independent factor at a time on the variable in question (e.g. Hundt 2004). Other (multivariate) studies analyze the joint impact of a multitude of independent variables on a dependent variable (e.g. Bresnan *et al.* 2007). Since many grammatical variables have proved to be conditioned by a multitude of factors, analysts should attempt to include as many of these factors as possible. For certain variables, however, this might not be possible (very little is known, for instance, about the choice between *if* and *whether* in interrogatives).

As far as analysis tools are concerned, Varbrul has dominated the market in Labov-type variationist sociolinguistics in particular. Varbrul is designed to calculate the stochastic influence of multiple independent variables on grammatical variation (e.g. Weiner and Labov 1983). Recently, however, the dominance of Varbrul in variationist linguistics has been challenged by competitors such as the open source software R, which makes possible sophisticated mixed-effect modeling (as implemented, for instance, in the package lme4), which has the following advantages over Varbrul: first, unlike Varbrul, it can take care of non-repeatable nuisance factors such as idiolectal differences; thus, it can control for the fact that individual speakers may deviate strongly from average behavior and are not representative of the population. Second, unlike Varbrul, R can handle continuous independent predictors, while predictors in Varbrul must be discrete and categorical. A continuous variable or predictor is, for instance, mean length (in orthographic characters) of words. By contrast, categorical variables consist of distinct (discrete) categories such as "male" versus "female." In a Varbrul analysis, mean word length would have to be transposed into discrete categories such as < 3 characters vs. ≥ 4 characters – a kind of data reduction that is more often than not, not desirable. Third, unlike Varbrul, R can also handle interaction effects, such as the interaction between speaker age and speaker sex, i.e. differences in behavior between older (or younger) men vs. women. Varbrul, however, can handle influence of a speaker's sex and a speaker's age separately, but not in interaction. We hasten to add that the Varbrul software has been refurbished in the form of Rbrul (Johnson 2008), but it is not clear to us why variationist sociolinguists would need an idiosyncratic software tool, given that lme4 is available and widely used in the social sciences at large.

In any event, it has been a hallmark of variationist linguistics to study relative frequencies or usage rates of a variant vis-a-vis another variant that it competes with (e.g. Weiner and Labov 1983; Gries and Hilpert 2010); the level of granularity is such that individual linguistic choices take center stage. By contrast, corpus linguists often adopt a text-linguistic perspective, investigating absolute frequencies of a phenomenon per, for instance, million words of running text (see, for example, Hundt and Mair 1999; Szmrecsanyi 2013). Biber *et al.* (forthcoming) offer an in-depth discussion of the differences between the two approaches.

In conclusion, corpus-based research has shown that grammatical variation, like phonological variation, can be sociolinguistically conditioned. Also, we now know that we can trace back the development from variation to language change in historical corpora, as do, for instance, Gries and Hilpert (2010). Further, although some scholars have suggested that grammatical variation is not sensitive to geography, recent research (e.g. Szmrecsanyi 2013) has demonstrated that grammatical variation can provide a geolinguistic signal, especially when joining many variables at a time to paint a larger picture.

It also turns out that speakers implicitly know about (probabilistic) aspects of grammatical variation. For instance, in a series of experiments Joan Bresnan (Bresnan 2007) has shown that the intuitions which native speakers have about the acceptability of dative structures (double object versus prepositional dative) in particular contexts correlate significantly with the probabilities that corpus models calculate (such as the ones reported in Bresnan *et al.* 2007), given the same co(n)text.

An interesting issue that remains to be resolved would be to link up the variation-as-explanandum approach and the variation-as-explanans approach. An example will be provided in our case study in Section 2, which models constraints on complementizer *that* deletion (variation-as-explanandum), but then goes on to utilize part of the probabilistic output of this analysis to explore how complementizer *that* variation engenders dialectological differences (variation-as-explanans). Wolk (2014) is a study that more systematically explores this interface between the two approaches, integrating the aggregational approach to language variation as exemplified by dialectometry (for example, Szmrecsanyi 2013), and the probabilistic modeling of language variation customarily utilized by probabilistic grammarians (Bresnan *et al.* 2007). Another important aspect to keep in mind is that any results can only be as good as the corpora they are based on. When we use statistic models created for representative samples we must make sure to establish clear criteria of what counts as a representative corpus.

2 Case study: variation in the use of the complementizer *that*

Our case study is an exercise in variationist analysis: we investigate grammatical variation in the use of the complementizer in *that* clauses, such as in (3), where speakers have the choice between retaining the explicit complementizer *that*, and omitting it. The latter option is also referred to as the use of the zero variant.

(3) We think (that) these worries are common.

While many factors have proved to be influential in variable *that* omission, only a few studies have included language-external factors (e.g. Staum

2005). We add this additional perspective to previous research and explore how language-internal and language-external factors interact to engender linguistic variation. In this endeavor, we use data from FRED (the *Freiburg English Dialect Corpus*), which samples dialect speech from all over Great Britain. Following our typology in Section 1, our study is situated at the intersection between variationist sociolinguistics, dialectology, and research on knowledge, processing, and cognition.

On the technical plane, we employ multivariate analysis, in particular mixed-effects logistic regression as implemented in the lme4 package, to include as many factors as possible known to condition this variation, and to compare the strength of each factor with the strength of each other factor. We also account for the lack of repeatability in certain independent variables by treating them as random effects. This means that rather than calculating the strength of influence of these variables, the model adjusts the calculation according to the bias of these variables (see Baayen 2008: 241–242). A typical random effect is variation by subject, which, in our case, is equal to variation by speaker. A new sample of the same population would result in a different set of speakers with different idiosyncratic preferences, so the set of speakers in the dataset is random. Since individual speakers may have very strong preferences for *that* or its omission that are not representative of the whole population, by-subject variation may skew the results. It is therefore useful to fit a model that takes this skewing into account. In contrast, fixed variables, such as verb morphology, are repeatable and not random, because they would be the same in a different sample – one would always assign the same value (past, base form, etc.) to the same form of a verb.

2.1 Previous research on the retention or omission of *that*

The variation in the use of the *that* complementizer has been the object of an abundance of linguistic research. Research in cognitive linguistics as well as in psycholinguistics has shown that the cognitive complexity of an utterance plays an important role in a speaker's choice to use or not to use the explicit complementizer. This choice reflects speakers' effort to find a balance between explicitness and economy. While the retention of *that* explicitly marks the subsequent clause as an embedded clause and is thus more precise, the omission of the complementizer reduces the production effort by rendering a shorter utterance. Consequently, the omission of *that* is in general preferred in linguistically less complex environments, where less explicitness is needed to signal that the following linguistic material is a complement clause (Rohdenburg 1996, 1999; Jaeger 2006: 74–89; Hawkins 2003). Whereas cognitive complexity is a language-internal issue, Kolbe (2008: 90–129) shows that language-external factors such as age, sex, and dialectal preference may also influence a speaker's choice between zero and *that* (see Staum 2005).

2.2 Data and methods

FRED consists of roughly 2.7 million words of dialect speech (Hernández 2006; see Szmrecsanyi and Hernández 2007 for the publicly available sampler version). As the retention or omission of *that* is determined by many cognitive factors, spoken language is a crucial resource for examining the influence of those factors. The texts in FRED derive from interviews with speakers from England, Wales, and Scotland. The corpus files mostly consist of transcripts of oral history interviews and thus offer a style of speech that is casual and adapted to the interview format (Hernández 2006).

We chose to restrict attention to the complement-taking predicates *think*, *say*, and *know* – the most common matrix verbs of embedded *that* clauses (Biber *et al.* 1999: 668) – to obtain a large sample of clauses. Note that we are fully aware of the fact that these verbs commonly occur with omitted *that*. Based on a Perl script identifying these verbs in FRED, the beginning and the end of each embedded *that* clause following these verbs was coded manually by the two authors. Tests for inter-coder reliability in samples of clauses showed that the two coders agreed in 83 percent of all cases.[1] We then used another Perl script to extract the *that* clauses identified in this manner, their matrix verb phrase(s) and the corresponding metadata (speaker, local origin, file name, etc.).

Drawing on previous research on the choice between the omission and the retention of *that* (see above), we identified as independent variables those aspects of each embedded clause and its matrix clause that are likely to influence a speaker's choice between explicit and zero *that*. Szmrecsanyi (2006) shows that grammatical variants tend to persist in speech, so that speakers are more likely to use the variant they have used before. We therefore investigate how far this is true for the use of explicit *that*. The following section (2.2.1) provides a description of all variables used in this study.

2.2.1 Variables

The dependent variable in our study is binary: retention or omission of the complementizer *that*. The independent variables in our annotation layer are detailed in the following.

Language-external factors

As Kolbe (2008) and Staum (2005) observe, sociolinguistic factors may influence a speaker's choice of complementizer. Based on the FRED metadata (see Hernández 2006 and Szmrecsanyi and Hernández 2007), we included the variables TEXT, AREA, COUNTY, and SPEAKER.

[1] Differences between the assessments of clause length typically result from different perceptions on whether or not a chunk was still embedded in the previous clause.

- TEXT indicates the corpus file (e.g. SFK_018 or IOM_002) where the token occurred.
- AREA codes the nine dialect areas as specified in FRED. These are Hebrides, Isle of Man, English Midlands, Northern England, Scottish Highlands, Scottish Lowlands, Southeast England, Southwest England, and Wales.
- COUNTY specifies the county in which the speaker lived at the time of recording.
- SPEAKER renders the current speaker's ID (as defined in the FRED manual).

Information on speakers' age is unavailable for 1,124 cases in the database, or more than 20 percent. Since the inclusion of age would thus result in substantial data loss, we did not include speakers' age in the analysis. We also did not include information on speakers' sex, since the sample in FRED is skewed: of the 5,296 utterances, only a quarter (1,389 instances) is produced by female speakers. While this decision simplifies model building, it partly undermines our aim to study the influence of language-external factors, in omitting factors that play an important role in traditional variationist studies.

Language-internal factors

According to Rohdenburg's "complexity principle" (1996, 1999) more explicit variants are preferred in cognitively more complex environments. Most of our independent linguistic variables are related to the cognitive complexity of an utterance.

1 Features of the matrix clause

As previous research has shown (Torres Cacoullos and Walker 2009b; Jaeger 2006: 88–89; Dor 2005; Biber 1999: 681), the choice of matrix verb strongly affects the likelihood of the retention of *that*: speakers tend to omit the complementizer after using a matrix verb that frequently controls embedded *that* clauses. The variable VERB thus specifies which matrix verb is used (*think*, *say*, or *know*). All three verbs are highly frequent and they frequently function as matrix verbs of *that* clauses (Biber *et al.* 1999: 668). However, *think* and *say* are by far the most frequent matrix verbs of *that* clauses in British English and their use strongly favors the omission of *that* (Torres Cacoullos and Walker 2009b: 19–20; Biber *et al.* 1999: 681, Thompson and Mulac 1991: 244–245).

Further features of the verb phrase in the matrix clause that affect a speaker's choice between zero and *that* are the morphology of the verb and whether the verb phrase contains an auxiliary. The less complex the verb phrase is, the less likely that *that* will occur (see Torres Cacoullos and Walker 2009b: 24–27; Biber *et al.* 1999: 681–682; Rohdenburg 1996: 161; Thompson and Mulac 1991, 246). These features are captured in the variables VERBMORPH, MATRIX_NEGATION, and MATRIX_AUXILIARY.

- VERBMORPH codes whether the matrix verb occurs as base form, as third-person singular present tense, as past (tense or participle), or as *-ing* form.
- MATRIX_NEGATION specifies whether the matrix verb is negated.
- MATRIX_AUXILIARY states whether the matrix verb is preceded by a modal auxiliary (e.g. *should, could, would, will, 'll, shall, must, can* + negated forms).

A third feature of the matrix clause that has an impact on a speaker's choice of complementizer is its subject. When the matrix clause subject is *I* or *you*, the omission of *that* becomes more likely (Torres Cacoullos and Walker 2009b: 24–25; Thompson and Mulac 1991: 242–243). The appearance of the matrix subject is determined by MATRIX_SUBJECT_TYPE, which distinguishes between *I, you, it*, and any other subject.

If the matrix clause is *I think*, the retention of *that* is highly unlikely. This clause not only comprises all features that favor the omission of *that* (subject *I*, simple verb morphology, highly frequent verb lemma that very often controls *that* clauses), it also functions as a comment clause or epistemic parenthetical (see, for example, Thompson and Mulac 1991). For reasons that will be discussed in more detail in Section 2.4, we consider it a matrix clause, but we use the variable I_THINK to distinguish this matrix clause from other ones.

The variables MORPHID and VERBID combine features of the matrix verb that are potentially relevant to grammatical persistence as discussed in Szmrecsanyi (2005, 2006). They check whether or not a matrix verb has the same morphology, respectively verb lemma, as the previous verb.

2 Features of the embedded *that* clause

Whether speakers choose to retain or omit a *that* complementizer has also proved to depend on features of the embedded clause itself. The cognitive complexity of the embedded clause is gauged by means of the following variables:

- EMB_CL_LENGTH specifies the number of words in the embedded clause (excluding the complementizer when present), since speakers use the explicit complementizer more often in longer clauses (Jaeger 2006: 85; Rohdenburg 1996: 164). In the analysis, we use a logarithmic transformation, LOG_EMB_CL_LENGTH, to reduce skewing and outliers in the data, as is customary in quantitative modeling (see Baayen 2008: 31).
- Material between matrix verb and beginning of the embedded clause: *that* is more often retained if any linguistic material occurs between matrix verb and embedded clause (Rohdenburg 1996: 160; Hawkins 2003: 178–179). We distinguish between INTERV_MATERIAL_MACL_EMBCL, which specifies the number of orthographic words between the matrix verb and the start of the embedded clause, and ADV_BEGINNING, which specifies whether an adverbial (*in, because, cause, if, since, when, after, before, during*) occurs at the beginning of the embedded clause. We also included ADV_AFTEREND,

which shows whether an adverbial (*in, because, cause, if, since, when, after, before, during*) occurs after the end of the embedded clause.

- COMPLEMENT_SUBJECT states whether the first element in the embedded clause is a pronoun, in which case previous research has shown a stronger tendency to omit *that* (Torres Cacoullos and Walker 2009b: 24, 28; Rohdenburg 1996: 162).
- SAME_VERB_IN_EMBD_CL indicates if the exact same verb as the matrix verb occurs in the embedded clause, which we assume to be a possible factor to decrease cognitive complexity.
- HORROR_AEQUI checks whether the embedded clause after the complementizer (explicit or zero) starts with *that*, as in *I think that that man is his father*. There is evidence from non-finite clauses that speakers avoid using identical forms consecutively (Kolbe 2008: 217–218, 222–224).

3 Features across clauses

The scope of the following variables goes beyond clause boundaries:

- Speech perturbations: Jaeger shows an effect of disfluency on a speaker's choice of complementizer (2006: 91–92). "Production difficulties" increase the likelihood of *that* retention. In terms of cognitive complexity this relates to the speaker's need to make the relationship between two clauses more explicit when complexity has already led to production difficulties. Jaeger speculates that speakers use the complementizer to signal production difficulties. In our study, EHMS_ETC_NARROW counts the number of speech perturbations in the immediate context from three words before the matrix verb to the end of the embedded clause. EHMS_ETC_BROAD counts the number of speech perturbations in the wider context from 100 words before the matrix verb to the next finite verb.
- Grammatical persistence: as speakers tend to reuse a form they have used previously (Szmrecsanyi 2005, 2006), we take into account grammatical persistence by including three variables: ALPHA_PERSISTENCE_50 checks whether an explicit *that*-complementizer occurs up to 50 words before the complementizer; ALPHA_PERS_DISTANCE specifies the textual distance (in words) to the last occurrence of an explicit *that*-complementizer (from matrix verb to matrix verb); and BETA_PERS_DISTANCE indicates the textual distance (in words) to the last occurrence of any *that*.
- Increased complexity of a sentence may also derive from a high type-token ration, so the variable TTRPASSAGE renders the type-token ratio divided by 10 in a context of -50/+50 words around the matrix verb slot.

2.3 Determinants of the choice between explicit and zero-complementizer

In order to explore the influence of the independent variables mentioned above on a speaker's choice between explicit *that* and its omission ("zero"), we analyzed their effects in a logistic regression analysis with mixed effects, i.e. one that takes into account both random and fixed effects for the reasons stated above (see Baayen 2008: 195–208 and 278–284).

The dependent variable is the choice between the zero-complementizer and its explicit form. As FRED consists of spoken data only and "[i]n conversation, the omission of *that* is the norm, while the retention of *that* is exceptional" (Biber *et al.* 1999: 680), the predominant value of the complementizer is its omission, which occurs in 91 percent of all embedded clauses in the database.

We included four independent variables, or factors, as random effects (i.e. adjustments to the intercept), since their influence is non-repeatable. VERB lemma, SPEAKER, TEXT, and COUNTY are non-repeatable effects, as a second study relying on randomly chosen verbs, speakers, texts, and counties would result in a different sample. VERB can be seen as a classical by-item effect, whereas SPEAKER is the classical by-subject effect. TEXT and COUNTY are directly connected to SPEAKER, because they represent a particular interview with a speaker who lived in a specific county at the time. The model adjusts the intercept for each of these non-repeatable effects, to avoid skewing the results in the direction of their deviation.

At first, we created a maximal model that included all independent variables listed in Section 2.2.1. Subsequently, the model was simplified by removing factors lacking significant explanatory power (such as MORPHID and VERBID). We started the pruning process with the least significant factors, moving to more significant ones in a stepwise fashion. Explanatory power of categorical factors with more than two levels was assessed via likelihood-ratio tests. Our final model (the "minimal adequate model") comprises the minimal amount of factors showing maximal results and the best possible fit to the data. It correctly predicts 92.4 percent of all outcomes, which is a modest but significant (p=0.01) increase over the baseline percentage at 91.0 percent, which represents the percentage of zero-complementizers in the database.[2] Although the model is thus validated, the predictive bonus of the model is not exactly breathtaking. This may well be caused by the predominance of the zero variant, since a baseline percentage of already 91 percent is very difficult to increase. Somers' Dxy, a rank correlation coefficient between predicted outcome probabilities and observed binary outcomes, is 0.77, which indicates that the model discriminates fairly between complementation types.

The fixed effects that turned out to be significant predictors of the choice between zero and explicit complementizers concern ten variables:

- matrix verb morphology (VERBMORPH)
- the subject of the matrix clause (MATRIX_SUBJECT_TYPE)

[2] Multicollinearity is not an issue, as the model's condition number ($\kappa = 12.5$) is below the customary threshold of 15. The model was bootstrapped (sampling with replacement, 10 runs, the confidence intervals did not include zero) and the exclusion of outliers was analyzed and consequently rejected.

- the presence of an auxiliary in the matrix verb phrase (MATRIX_AUXILIARY)
- whether the embedded clause is controlled by *I think* (I_THINK)
- HORROR_AEQUI
- the presence of an adverbial after the end of the embedded clause (ADV_AFTEREND)
- whether the subject of the embedded clause is a pronoun or not (COMPLEMENT_SUBJECT)
- the logarithmically transformed length of the embedded clause (LOG (EMB_CL_LENGTH))
- the occurrence of *that* within 50 words before the complementizer (ALPHA_PERSISTENCE_50)
- the number of speech perturbations in the immediate context of the complementizer (logarithmically transformed as LOG(EHMS_ETC_NARROW +1)).[3]

Table 9.1 contains a detailed summary of the model. The strength of each of the predictors is indicated by the value in the columns "Coefficient." These are the estimated coefficients of the respective factors, to be added or subtracted from the intercept. Negative numbers show a negative (disfavoring) influence of this predictor on the use of explicit *that*; positive numbers represent an increase in the likelihood of the retention of *that* if the respective predictor level applies. A larger estimate's value represents a stronger effect. The figures in the column "Odds Ratio" render the same influence in a different, more interpretable form. An odds ratio of 1 would mean that the odds for the use of *that* are 1:1, or 10:10. If *that* is less likely to be used with a certain predictor, the odds ratio for this predictor ranges between 0 and 1 (e.g. 2:10 = 0.2), while odds ratios larger than 1 (e.g. 10:2 = 5) indicate that the complementizer is more likely to be retained. The column "*p*" (probability) indicates statistical significance, which does not refer to the strength of a predictor but its statistically reliability in the

[3] In FRED overall, the complementizer is omitted in 89 percent of all *that* clauses (n=5,945) controlled by typical matrix verbs of *that* clauses (*think, say, know, see, feel, find, believe, show, suggest,* and *guess*; see Biber 1999: 668). This study therefore not only includes a vast majority of all *that* clauses in FRED, the percentage of *that* omission in our sample (91 percent) is also very close to its actual occurrence. The distribution of retention and omission of *that* after *see* is available in data from Kolbe (2008; total n: 181, 60.8 percent omission); percentages after *feel, find,* and *believe* were counted manually in concordance results (total n: 57, 225, 162, 39%, 10%, 46% omission respectively). The vast majority of *that* clauses (n=3,394) are controlled by *think* and the complementizer is retained in merely 4.5 percent of them. The average percentage of *that* omission after the remaining matrix verbs in FRED is at 80 percent. Note that the treatment of choice of verb as a random effect in the presented model takes account of this fact. However, in order to exclude effects of the extreme frequency of *think, that* clauses controlled by the least frequent matrix verbs *show, suggest,* and *guess* were also coded and added to a second data set together with clauses controlled by *know* and *say*. This "control" data set contains 82.8 percent *that* clauses with omitted complementizer. A logistic regression model run on this data set manages to actually increase the percentage of correctly predicted cases to 86.3 percent, but is a lot weaker in terms of explained variance (Somers Dxy = 0.69). It also retains most of the predictors for the choice of complementizers, except that the influence of an adverbial at the end of the embedded clause is not significant anymore, and beta persistence (the use of any *that*) is more important than alpha persistence (the use of the complementizer *that*). As most of the embedded *that* clauses in FRED are controlled by *think*, the model presented is thus more representative of actual language use.

Table 9.1 *Logistic regression model with fixed and random effects in complementation choice. Predicted odds are for the retention of the* that-*complementizer*

Fixed effects	Coefficient	Odds Ratio	p	
(Intercept)	-3.37	0.03	<0.001	***
VERBMORPH (default: base form)				
VERBMORPH: 3sg	-0.73	0.48	0.071	.
VERBMORPH: past	-0.35	0.71	0.022	*
VERBMORPH: *ing*	1.07	2.92	<0.001	***
MATRIX_SUBJECT_TYPE (default: other)				
MATRIX_SUBJECT_TYPE: *I*	-1.48	0.23	<0.001	***
MATRIX_SUBJECT_TYPE: *it*	1.42	4.13	0.005	**
MATRIX_SUBJECT_TYPE: *you*	-0.99	0.37	0.001	**
HORROR_AEQUI: yes	-1.04	0.35	0.001	**
ADV_AFTEREND: yes	0.42	1.52	0.032	*
MATRIX_AUXILIARY: yes	0.72	2.05	<0.001	***
COMPLEMENT_SUBJECT: pronoun	-0.53	0.59	<0.001	***
I_THINK: yes	-0.70	0.49	<0.001	***
ALPHA_PERSISTENCE_50: yes	1.07	2.92	<0.001	***
LOG(EMB_CL_LENGTH)	1.08	2.95	<0.001	***
LOG(EHMS_ETC_NARROW+1)	0.79	2.21	0.001	**
Random effects	**N**	**Variance**	**Standard deviation**	
speaker	331	0.54	0.74	
verb lemma	3	0.09	0.30	
text	310	0.17	0.42	
county	38	0.33	0.57	
Model summary				
Somers' Dxy	0.77			
Correctly predicted	92.4%	(91.0 baseline)		

Significance levels:
. marginally significant ($p < 0.1$), * significant ($p < 0.05$), ** very significant ($p < 0.01$), *** highly significant ($p < 0.001$)

model. The lower *p* is for any value, the more reliable the effect is. A value of *p* that is less than 0.05 by convention denotes statistical significance. For categorical variables (e.g. VERBMORPH or HORROR_AEQUI), the model relies on identifying one category as the constant or default value, with which the other values are compared. The default category in VERBMORPH is "base" – the verb used in its base form (e.g. *say*).

Within VERBMORPH the use of *that* becomes less likely when the matrix verb is in the third-person singular present tense or in the past tense (estimates -0.73 resp. -0.35) than when it is used in its base form (the default value). Although the influence of the third-person singular present-tense form is not significant at the conventional threshold of 0.05, we consider it to be marginally significant because its *p*-value at 0.1 means that there is a 90 percent chance that its effect is not due to chance. An *-ing* participle, however, increases the likelihood of the use of zero *that* (1.07).

The form of the matrix subject (MATRIX_SUBJECT_TYPE) also has a significant effect on the retention of *that*. When the matrix subject is *I* or *you* (–1.48 and –0.99 respectively), the retention of *that* is less likely than with *it* or the default category of any other subject. When *it* is the matrix subject, speakers use *that* more readily (1.42).

Moreover, the form of the subject of the embedded clause influences a speaker's choice significantly. When it is or begins with *that* speakers avoid the use of the explicit complementizer, to avoid the sequence *that that* (*horror aequi*, estimate –1.04). In addition, speakers tend to omit *that* if the subject of the embedded clause is a pronoun (–0.53), as well as after *I think* (–0.70).

The following conditions increase the probability of the retention of the complementizer *that*: the persistence of a *that*-complementizer, i.e. when it has been used within 50 words before this slot (1.07), an auxiliary in the matrix verb phrase (0.72), and an adverbial at the end of the embedded clause (0.42). The longer the embedded clause is and the more speech perturbations there are between matrix and embedded clause, the more likely speakers are to choose *that* (LOG(EMB_CL_LENGTH): 1.08; (LOG (EHMS_ETC_NARROW + 1): 0.79).

The strongest factor increasing the likelihood of a *that* is noted for the matrix subject *it* (1.42). The strongest factor decreasing the probability of the retention of *that* is the use of *I* as matrix subject (–1.48). Another way to express the influence of these factors is in odds ratios, which are calculated by raising *e* to the power of the regression coefficient. An odds ratio (OR) of 1 indicates that a predictor has no effect whatsoever. An OR larger than 1 indicates that a predictor increases the odds for explicit *that* (there is no upper limit). An OR from 0 to 1 indicates that a predictor decreases the odds that *that* will be retained. Compared to the default category "other," which comprises the pronouns *he, she, we, they*, and any non-pronominal matrix subject, retention of *that* turns out to be over four times more likely if the matrix subject is *it* (OR 4.13). If the matrix subject is *I*, however, the odds for the retention of *that* decrease by a factor of 0.23, i.e. by 77 percent.

As regards the random effects, SPEAKER and COUNTY result in the strongest adjustments (standard deviations of 0.74 and 0.57 respectively). *Think* favors zero-complementizers most strongly of the three matrix verbs (of 3,394 instances of *think*, only 152, or 4.5 percent, control an explicit *that* clause), so the adjustment of the intercept is negative (–0.27) for this matrix verb, while the intercept adjustment for *know* is 0.37 and the adjustment for *say* is 0.15. It is not feasible to report all intercept adjustments for each of the 300+ speakers and texts. In the extremes, FRED speaker MlnJH favors explicit complementation least (intercept adjustment: -0.87; *that* retained in 4.3 percent), while speaker SRLM_HM likes it most (1.33; 48 percent *that* retained). FRED interview MLN_007 is least

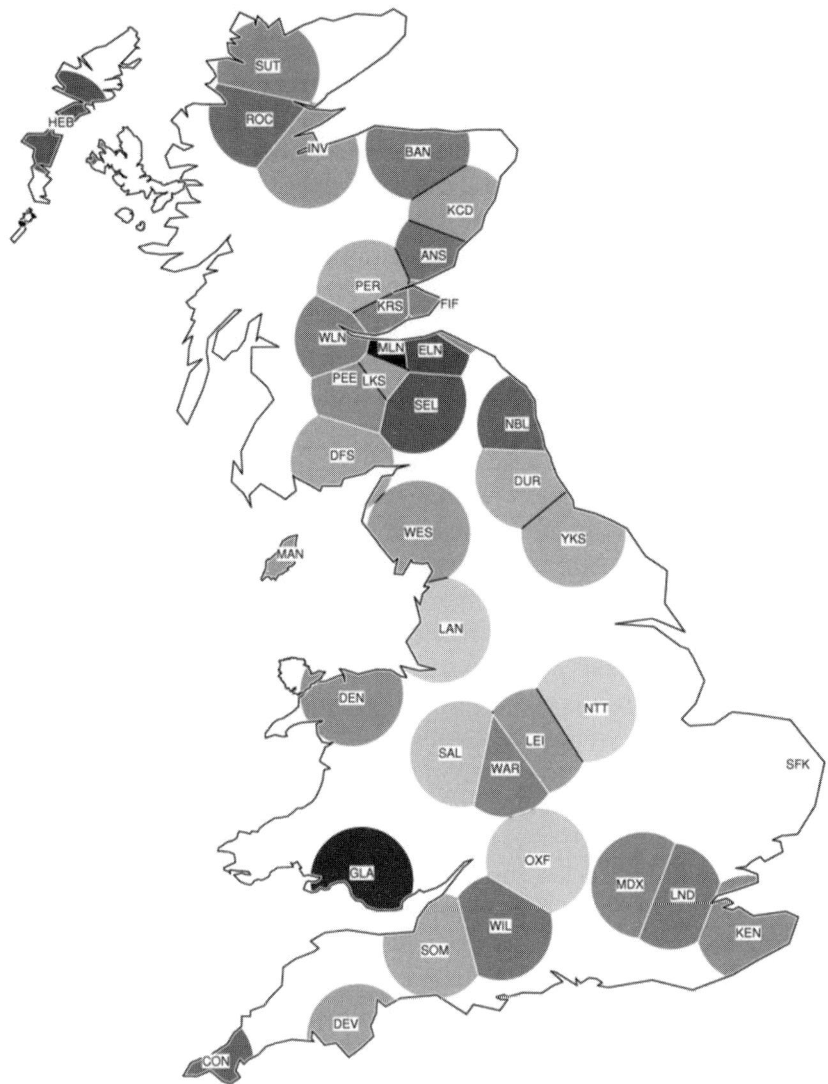

Figure 9.1 Projection of intercept adjustments to geography. Darker shades indicate positive intercept adjustments (i.e. more hospitality towards explicit *that*), lighter shades indicate negative intercept adjustments (i.e. less hospitality towards explicit *that*).

hospitable towards explicit *that* (–0.28; 4.3 percent *that*), and interview KEN_010 is most hospitable (0.45, 24 percent *that*).

The geographical distribution of complementizer choice according to county is illustrated in Figure 9.1. This map, which translates our analysis into the sort of geolinguistic visualization customary in dialectology and dialectometry, projects intercept adjustments to geography: it shows how frequently complementizer *that* is retained in particular counties in Great Britain. In other words, Figure 9.1 highlights how hospitable dialect speakers are towards *that* in which county. Darker shades indicate more hospitality towards explicit that (i.e. positive intercept adjustments), lighter shades indicate less hospitality towards explicit *that* (i.e. negative intercept adjustments). Thus, we see more omission of *that* in Central England (including Lancashire) and more retention of *that* in Southern Wales, in Edinburgh and to its south (East Lothian, Midlothian, and Selkirkshire), and on the Outer Hebrides, which corresponds to the findings in Kolbe (2008: 112, 120–121). In general, in southern Great Britain *that* is less likely to be retained; notable exceptions are southern Wales and Cornwall.

2.4 Summary of findings

Most of the factors that significantly influence a speaker's choice between zero and explicit *that* are concerned with cognitive complexity. The complementizer is more likely to be omitted in less complex environments, in which it is easier for the listener to infer that material following the matrix clause will be an embedded *that* clause. These cognitively less complex environments are typically the more frequent patterns, which makes the syntactic structure of the utterance more predictable (Roland *et al.* 2006). That, for instance, *you think* will be followed by an embedded *that* clause is predictable for listeners because this is the most frequent case, so that the relationship between the clauses need not be explicated by the retention of *that*. Cognitively more complex contexts increase the need to mark the embeddedness of the following clause explicitly by retaining *that*. In our study this proves to be the case especially if the matrix subject is *it* or the longer the embedded clause is.

As *I think* is a very frequent comment clause that can occur nearly everywhere in a sentence (see, for example, Kaltenböck 2008), it is disputable whether this clause actually functions as matrix in sentence-initial position. It is nearly exclusively followed by zero-*that* clauses in our data (in 97 percent, viz. 66 out of 2,258 occurrences). The variable I_THINK captures this distribution so that the negative influence of the matrix subject *I* on the use of *that* mostly concerns the use of *I* as subject of other verbs, such as *say*, *know*, *said*, *knew*, but also in clauses such as *I would think* or *I was thinking*, which have similar discourse functions as *I think* (van Bogaert 2010). In addition, clauses such as *I don't know* take on discourse functions (e.g. as "utterance launcher"; see Biber *et al.* 1999: 1002–1004). It therefore seems impossible to maintain a distinction between "grammatical" matrix clauses and constructions with discourse functions that are not actual matrix clauses.

One factor increasing the probability of explicit *that* is not related to cognitive complexity of the current clauses, namely the persistence of *that*. Speakers are more likely to use explicit *that* if they did so the last time they had a choice and if that choice occurred within 50 words of the present slot. Although this factor is not related to the cognitive complexity of the current locus of variation, it is linked to a speaker's processing load in general, since *that* is repeated simply because it prevails in the speaker's working memory (see, for example, Szmrecsanyi 2005, 2006).

Some of our results come as a surprise: it was not to be expected that the occurrence of an adverbial at the end of the embedded clause would turn out to be a significant factor, whereas an adverbial between matrix and embedded clause did not.

Many of the independent variables accounted for in our original dataset (for example, INTERV_MATERIAL_MACL_EMBCL) have proved to be less influential factors than the ones actually included in the final, minimal model. This does not mean that they are not relevant to the choice between zero and explicit *that* at all, but that for the speakers in our dataset they are less decisive than other factors. Further similar studies on grammatical variation should take into account as many variables as feasible, since the interplay of determinants of variation needs to be re-examined for each dataset.

In sum, our little case study is a corpus-based exercise in variationist (socio)linguistics because it investigates linguistic choices between the use of an overt complementizer and zero, drawing on modern multivariate analysis techniques; it is concerned with knowledge, processing, and cognition thanks to the inclusion of factors such as *horror aequi*; and it falls within the remit of dialectology because it considers the effect that geography has on linguistic choices (see Figure 9.1).

10

Grammatical change

Martin Hilpert and Christian Mair

1 Introduction

This chapter is concerned with phenomena of grammatical change in the English language, and with the question of how these phenomena can be studied in corpus-based analyses. To start out, we clarify briefly what we mean by the terms grammar, grammatical change, and corpus-based analyses. In the words of Huddleston and Pullum (2002: 3), the term grammar "describes the principles or rules governing the form and meaning of words, phrases, clauses, and sentences." More specifically, the grammar of English is a set of regularities that captures, amongst other things, how noun phrases and verb phrases are formed, how new words may be coined through word-formation processes, and how clauses can be combined to form complex sentences. Grammatical change, on this understanding of grammar, is a change in the regularities that characterize a language system at a given point in time. This is a very general definition which, of course, glosses over the fact that grammatical change can manifest itself at very different levels. The most straightforward type of grammatical change is when an altogether new option emerges in the system of grammatical forms as the outcome of grammaticalization (Hopper and Traugott 2003). An example of grammaticalization in English is the emergence of the passive progressive (e.g. *the meat is being cooked*), which was added to the older passival (i.e. active form with passive meaning, as in *the meat is cooking*) from the eighteenth century onwards. We also consider as grammatical change a development in which there is no change with regard to the available choices in the system, but a significant statistical shift in the frequencies with which they are used. For example, possessive *have* allows auxiliary and main-verb negation in English (*I haven't the time – I don't have the time*). Both these options were available in 1900, as they are today, but the first one has declined in frequency during this period whereas the second one has increased. There are, finally, some grammatical constructions whose use is closely linked to particular genres. For example, passive constructions are typical of formal written styles, in particular academic and scientific English. If diachronic fluctuations in the frequency of a construction remain confined to a particular genre, or a small set of genres, it is probably best to consider them as style change, that is as change in the stylistic norms governing writing or speaking practices in particular textual genres or communicative domains. To illustrate, D'Arcy (2012) studies different quotatives in New Zealand English, reporting diachronic frequency changes which suggest that the practice of quoting speech as a whole has become more common in informal conversation. The dividing line between grammaticalization, frequency change, and style change is not always sharp, but assessment is helped decisively by the analysis of corpus data.

But of course there is a far more general reason why corpus data are of particular importance for the study of grammatical change. Until quite recently in the history of linguistics, changes in grammar could only be observed indirectly, through the comparison of analogous examples from different historical periods (Bloomfield 1933: 347). Consider the following line from the Old English version of the Lord's Prayer.

(1) and forgyf us ure gyltas swa swa we forgyfað urum gyltendum
and forgive us our sins so as we forgive our debtors

Quite evidently, a number of grammatical changes have taken place between the times of Old English and today. For instance, the two uses of the verb *forgive* show that some of the verbal inflections of Old English have disappeared. Likewise, the two uses of the possessive determiner *our* document the loss of nominal case endings. Comparisons of older and more recent stages of language use thus allow, in a rather straightforward fashion, the identification of grammatical changes. At the same time, these comparisons do not yield answers to the questions of how, when, and why these changes happened. If a researcher is interested in these questions, it becomes necessary to undertake a corpus analysis that goes beyond the pointwise comparison of single examples. The hallmark of a corpus-based analysis, as understood in this chapter, is that a grammatical phenomenon is studied in its entirety, such that all relevant examples of a phenomenon are exhaustively retrieved from a corpus. Johansson (1985) and Leech (1992) invoke the concept of "total accountability" for approaches of this kind. An exhaustive representation of a grammatical phenomenon allows the researcher to analyze how that phenomenon varies across different contexts (see Chapter 9 this volume), and crucially, given the subject matter of this chapter, how the phenomenon changes across different historical periods. A necessary prerequisite for such an undertaking is of course a corpus, or a set of corpora, representing comparable types of language use across different periods of time. For the English language, numerous resources of this kind are in existence, covering different time spans, different varieties, and different genres (Claridge 2008). Most recently, even diachronic corpora of spoken language (Wallis *et al.* 2006) and protocols of spoken language (Huber 2007) have been made available, while corpora representing the recent past have grown to match the size of synchronic mega-corpora (Davies 2007, 2008, 2010). As a result, these are interesting times for linguists working on grammatical change in English.

This chapter surveys a number of studies in which different aspects of grammatical change have been approached from a corpus-based perspective. This survey includes grammatical domains such as complementation patterns, modal auxiliaries, verbal inflections, and argument structure constructions. In keeping with the other contributions in this handbook, the final part of the survey discusses a more detailed case study, focusing on a change in word formation. Throughout, the chapter highlights the ways in which corpus-based analyses can reveal aspects of change that would otherwise remain unnoticed, or less fully understood.

2 A survey of corpus-based studies on grammatical change

This section presents different corpus-based approaches to grammatical change that are unified by a common thread: they focus on the grammar of English verbs. Characteristic grammatical behaviors of verbs concern their ability to inflect, their co-occurrence with complements, and their role as the central element in larger syntactic constructions. This section discusses these characteristics one by one in order to showcase a spectrum of current analytical approaches and to show how processes in the verbal grammar of English illustrate the different types of change that were outlined above.

2.1 Change in complementation

Many English verbs function as complement-taking predicates, that is, they project a syntactic structure such as a *that*-clause, an *ing*-clause, or a *to*-infinitive, amongst several other options, as one of their arguments. Quite commonly one and the same verb takes different kinds of complement with different relative frequencies, such that one type is preferred and other ones are more marginal. Over time, these frequencies may undergo shifts as relative preferences change or new complementation patterns enter the picture. This subsection reports on studies that have analyzed this particular kind of frequency change.

Mair (2002) uses the Brown family of corpora, a set of four corpora that represent standard British English and standard American English from the 1960s and the 1990s respectively. Researching the same grammatical

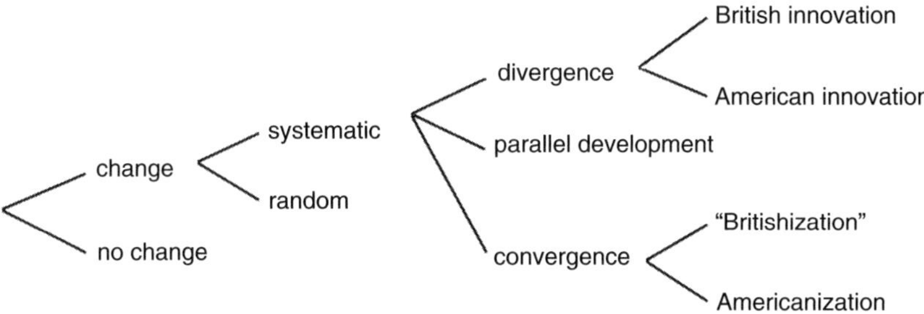

Figure 10.1 Possible results for analyses of the Brown family of corpora

phenomenon across this set of corpora yields contrasts of language use across time and across varieties. For any given phenomenon, it can thus be determined whether there is diachronic stability or whether there has been a change. More interestingly, it can be determined whether an attested process of change represents divergence or convergence between British and American English. Cases of divergence represent innovations that take place either in British English or in American English. Cases of convergence illustrate either Americanization or, as is less often the case, "Britishization." Figure 10.1 summarizes the different kinds of scenario that may be found.

Mair (2002: 112) reports a case of British innovation in the complementation behavior of the verb *prevent*, which occurs with patterns that differ in the presence of the element *from*, as illustrated in the following examples.

(2) a. This prevented me from leaving early.
  b. This prevented me leaving early.

The latter variant is almost completely absent from twentieth-century American corpora, but its relative frequency in the British corpora rises from 17 percent in the 1960s to 50 percent in the 1990s. A similar tendency can be observed with the semantically related verb *stop*. Conversely, a case of American innovation can be observed with the complementation patterns of *begin* and *start* (Mair 2002: 117). Both verbs occur with *to*-infinitives as well as with *ing*-clauses, but whereas the variation between these options remains stable in British English, *ing*-clauses gain ground in American English between the 1960s and the 1990s, from 19 to 32 percent with *begin* and from 51 to 65 percent with *start*. In this development, the genre of press texts is leading the way. A case of convergence, more specifically Americanization, is illustrated by the development of the verb *help*, which occurs with both *to*-infinitive complements and bare infinitive complements (Mair 2002: 122). In the Brown family of corpora, the diachronic shift towards bare infinitives is more pronounced in the British corpora, from 22 to 61 percent, whereas the American corpora develop in parallel but already start out with a fairly high ratio, going from 69 to 82 percent. Since the shift towards a more compact complementation pattern coincides with an increase in text frequency and with semantic broadening, the overall development of *help* follows a common grammaticalization path from a lexical verb to a grammaticalized auxiliary verb. Mair (2002: 125) offers examples of bare infinitive *help* with inanimate subject referents that illustrate the increasing semantic breadth of the verb. Contrary to this idea, Lohmann (2011: 512) presents the results of a synchronic multivariate study of *help* and its complements which show that animate subjects have a tendency to occur with bare infinitives, rather than *to*-infinitives. At the same time, Lohmann's analysis shows that cases with implicit subjects, as in *She is eager to help them succeed* or *She was involved in helping them succeed* favor the bare infinitive even more strongly, which is in line with the idea that *help* is currently undergoing grammaticalization.

Another diachronic study of verbal complementation examines the developments of 44 complement-taking predicates, such as *expect*, *hope*, *enjoy*, and *suggest* in the recent 150 years of American English (Hilpert 2011).[1] The analysis was done on the basis of COHA, the *Corpus of Historical American English* (Davies 2010). Like Mair (2002), Hilpert identifies differences in the relative frequencies of different complementation patterns over time, differentiating between six construction types.

(3) full clauses --------------- I suggest we do nothing.
that-clauses --------------- I hope that John will win.
ing-clauses --------------- I enjoy knitting sweaters.
to-infinitives -------------- I expect to hear from John.
subject-to-object raising --- I want John to be our next president.
noun phrases ------------- I hate broccoli.

Each of the verbs under analysis exhibits different relative preferences for these complementation patterns. The verb *expect* shows a high ratio of *to*-infinitives; *enjoy* frequently occurs with noun phrases and *ing*-clauses; and *hope* commonly takes *that*-clauses and full clause complements. Hilpert (2011: 451) uses multidimensional scaling to assess the differences in complementation behavior between the 44 verbs over time. For this kind of analysis, the relative frequencies of all six complementation patterns are determined for all of the 44 verbs for all of the time periods under analysis. The complementation profiles of *expect*, *hope*, and *enjoy* in the 1860s are thus not only compared against all other verbs during the 1860s, but against *expect*, *hope*, *enjoy*, and all other verbs during the 1870s, 1880s, and all following decades. Such an analysis reveals whether there are groups of similarly behaving verbs, how this configuration of groups has changed over time, and whether individual verbs exhibit

[1] The verbs under investigation were the following: *acknowledge, admit, affirm, appreciate, await, believe, cherish, claim, concede, confirm, consider, continue, declare, demand, deny, despise, disclose, discuss, dislike, doubt, enjoy, expect, fear, find, forget, hate, hope, imagine, know, like, love, mention, miss, need, order, prefer, promise, remember, request, suggest, suspect, think, try,* and *want*.

developments that go against larger trends in the system. More concretely, the results show that the 44 verbs can be broadly classified into three groups: one that consists of verbs such as *suggest*, *remember*, and *demand*, which primarily take *that*-clauses and full clause complements; another group that includes *try*, *want*, or *like*, which occur with a high ratio of *to*-infinitives; and third, a small cluster of verbs that take a large share of nominal complements, among them *miss*, *appreciate*, and *await*. From the 1860s to the 2000s, the configuration of these three groups stays recognizable, but it exhibits a number of changes both on the level of individual verbs as well as on the systemic level (Hilpert 2011: 455). Notably, the verbs *confirm* and *dislike* transform their behavior between the 1860s and the 2000s. Until the 1920s, the verb *confirm* is found among other verbs that predominantly take noun phrase complements. From the 1930s onwards, it is increasingly used with *that*-clauses. The verb *dislike* initially behaves like verbs such as *try* and *want*, which mostly occur with *to*-infinitives. In the final decades of the twentieth century, the analysis places *dislike* next to verbs such as *enjoy* or *remember*. This movement reflects an increasingly higher ratio of *ing*-clauses and a marked decrease in the ratio of *to*-infinitive complements. There are even signs of systemic developments. The fact that several verbs show a growing preference for *ing*-clauses can be seen as a reflection of the so-called "great complement shift" (Vosberg 2006), a long-term change in the English complementation system that replaces *to*-infinitive complements with *ing*-clauses across many contexts.

In summary, corpus-based studies of verbal complementation show that this part of English grammar is currently in a period of change. Certain changes can be identified as instances of grammaticalization; beyond that, we see a broad range of frequency changes. While the studies reviewed here have dealt with comparatively recent data, the origins of the developments under study can be traced back at least to Early Modern English, in some cases even to Middle English (de Smet 2012b). Corpus data are of central importance for the analysis of this kind of change because, in some cases, the change manifests itself only in shifting relative frequencies of forms that have been co-existing all along. In such an event, point-wise comparisons of analogous examples from different periods do not provide answers to the most pressing questions. Furthermore, only corpus-based studies can address the question whether any long-term developments are to be seen as systemic grammatical changes (Vosberg 2006; Rudanko 2006), or whether we are in fact dealing with a multitude of mutually unrelated frequency changes on a smaller scale.

2.2 Change in the modal auxiliaries

Another domain of English grammar that is currently undergoing change is the domain of modality, specifically the modal auxiliaries. In the most general of terms, the situation is that several of the core modal auxiliaries

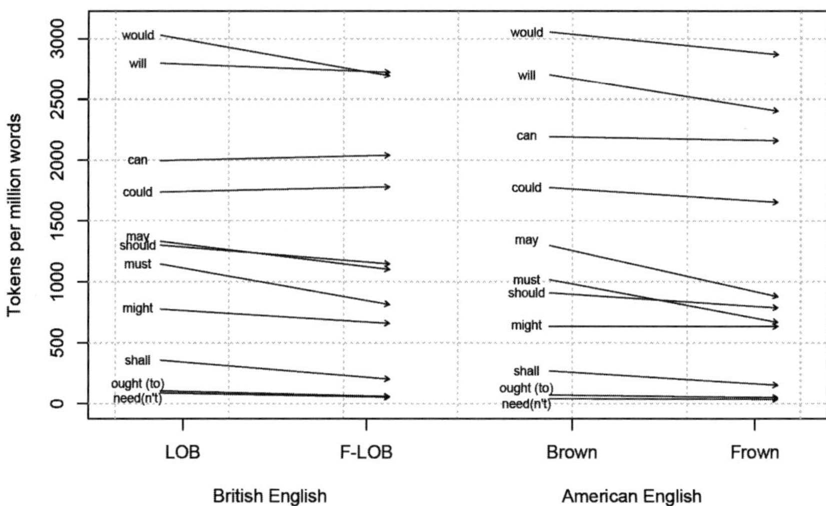

Figure 10.2 The decline of the modal auxiliaries (based on Leech 2003: 228, table 3)

are declining in text frequency (Leech 2003; Mair 2006), while at the same time new quasi-modal elements are undergoing grammaticalization (Krug 2000). The result is a dynamic situation that raises a number of questions. For instance, it has been asked why certain forms are in decline whereas others are on the upswing. Is there a relation between these developments, and if so, how do we assign the roles of cause and effect?

Leech (2003: 228) documents the decline of the core modals in the Brown family of corpora. Figure 10.2 shows the text frequencies of eleven modal auxiliaries across the four corpora, revealing a parallel frequency change across British and American English. Parallel cross-variety declines are particularly in evidence for the modals *would*, *may*, *should*, *must*, and *shall*.

Leech examines the possibility that newly grammaticalizing modal forms may be responsible for the observed decline. An analysis of forms such as *be going to*, *have to*, *got to*, *need to*, and several others does not, however, lend credence to this idea. Not all of these forms increase in frequency, and those that do, notably *need to* and *want to*, are relatively low in text frequency and hence do not match the declining numbers of core modals such as *will* or *would*. So if competition does not explain the decline, what does? Mair (2006: 100) further discusses the cases of *must* and *shall*, arguing that the recent demise of *shall* is merely the continuation of a development that has been going on for a considerably longer time. Mair points out that the remaining uses of *shall* mostly appear in contexts in which the modal functions as a text-structuring device, i.e. in phrases such as *as we shall see* or *I shall discuss this further in chapter 4*. This is further corroborated by Hilpert (2008: 37), who finds that typical verbal collocates of *shall* in the *British National Corpus* are the explicitly metalinguistic verbs *consider*, *examine*, *discuss*, and *argue*. The decline of *shall* is thus to be seen as a retraction into a highly specific communicative genre. With regard to the decline of *must*, Mair (2006: 104) reconsiders the possible competitive role of *have to*, *got to*, and *need to*. Spoken data from the *Santa Barbara Corpus of Spoken American English* indeed shows that *have to* and *need to* currently surpass *must* in text frequency, so that the idea of competition in the modal domain should not be discarded out of hand.

In a study that is based on the *Time* magazine corpus (Davies 2007), Millar (2009) tracks the frequency of the modal auxiliaries in American English press writing. He finds that *shall*, *must*, and *ought* are declining between the 1920s and the 2000s, but that interestingly, *can*, *could*, and *may* are undergoing substantial frequency increases and *will*, *might*, and *should* show at least small increases (Millar 2009: 205). One explanation for the discrepancies between the tendencies in the Brown family of corpora and in the *Time* corpus is the composition of the respective corpora. Whereas the Brown corpora represent a balanced set of genres, the *Time* corpus represents a single text type. To test whether genre differences explain the discrepancies, Millar (2009: 207) compares his *Time* results against an analysis of the press genres in the Brown and Frown corpora, finding, however, no satisfactory convergence between the two. Millar thus invokes sampling error as an explanation, which is criticized by Leech (2011a), who replicates the results from the Brown family of corpora on the basis of the balanced diachronic mega-corpora COCA and COHA (Davies 2008, 2010). These results leave the frequency increases of *can*, *could*, and *may* in *Time* in need of an explanation, for which Leech (2011a: 557) suggests a genre-specific style change in journalistic writing.

As the previous paragraphs illustrate, different kinds of corpora can yield complementary, though hopefully not contradictory, perspectives on the ongoing developments of the English modals, which illustrate the problems that are associated with interpreting observed shifts in frequency either as frequency change or as style change. In this regard, increasing the size of the corpus that is used will not automatically solve the problem. Depending on the phenomenon to be analyzed and the particular needs of the analyst, the statement that "bigger is better" need not always be true: Hundt and Leech (2012) summarize some of the advantages that may come from using highly comparable small corpora.

2.3 Change in verbal inflections

Whereas loss of inflectional categories is a phenomenon that is first and foremost a characteristic of the transition from Old English to Middle English, later historical periods do also offer examples of this type of grammatical change. Gries and Hilpert (2010) focus on a case of inflectional change that took place between Late Middle English and Early Modern English. Between the mid fifteenth and the late seventeenth centuries, a change affected the third-person singular form of the present tense. Specifically, this change led from a state of variability between two pronunciation variants, one the interdental fricative *-(e)th*, the other the alveolar fricative *-(e)s*, to a state of invariability, as the latter variant gradually ousted its competitor. A corpus analysis can determine how a variable system turned into a fixed state, particularly with an eye to change in the factors governing the variation, i.e. the choice between two forms such as *writeth* and *writes*. Gries and Hilpert used the *Corpus of Early English Correspondence* (CEEC), which is a corpus of personal letters that comes with some annotation of language-external variables, such as the gender of writer and addressee and the mutual familiarity between the two. Gries and Hilpert retrieved all verbs in the third-person present-tense form and annotated these forms for a number of explanatory factors that previous work on this change (Kytö 1993, Nevalainen and Raumolin-Brunberg 2003) had identified as important. These factors are summarized below and further discussed in the subsequent paragraphs.

(4) dependent variable *-(e)th* vs. *-(e)s*
explanatory factors lexical vs. grammatical verb
stem ending in sibilant vs. ending in another element
following word beginning in *s*, *th*, or another element
previous occurrence of *-(e)th* or *-(e)s*
gender of author and recipient
mutual familiarity

The factors that govern speakers' choices between *-(e)th* and *-(e)s* include a distinction between lexical and grammatical verbs (*write*, *sing*, etc. vs. *do*, *have*), phonological characteristics of the verb (stem ending in a sibilant vs. stem ending in some other sound), and phonological characteristics of the following word (beginning with an *s*, a *th*, or some other element). It is furthermore of importance which of the two variants was used in the preceding context. Language-external factors that play a role include the gender of author and recipient and their mutual familiarity. In order to investigate whether the respective impacts of these factors had changed over time, each corpus example was tagged for the time period during which it had been produced. For the purpose of annotating this variable, Gries and Hilpert divided the corpus into five sequential stages, using Variability-based Neighbor Clustering (see Section 3 below). Gries and Hilpert used logistic regression to analyze the change, finding that all factors listed in (4), except for familiarity, have a measurable effect, either on their own or in an interaction with other factors. Of particular interest are interactions that involve the factor of time, because such effects show that the relative impact of a conditioning factor has changed diachronically. The analysis reveals several interaction effects of this kind. First, there is a transient effect of cross-gender communication: writers use the *-(e)s* variant more often when writing to the opposite sex, but this effect is only measurable in the third of the five periods. Likewise, a stem-final sibilant, as in the verb *curse*, induces a *horror-aequi* effect that leads speakers to avoid the *-(e)s* suffix, but this effect is only statistically significant in period 4. Third, the older *-(e)th* variant is most entrenched with high-frequency grammatical forms (*doth*, *hath*), and, as expected, this effect is strongest towards the tail end of the change, in periods 4 and 5.

What this study illustrates is that corpus data allow very detailed analyses of how a given change proceeded. The analysis not only reveals which explanatory factors have a role to play in that change, it also assesses the relative strength of these factors and, most importantly, the time window during which a factor was most powerful. This type of analysis is furthermore relevant for the identification of given changes such as frequency change, style change, or grammatical change. If time as a variable interacts significantly with the explanatory factors that condition the use of a grammatical form, this can be taken to be a tell-tale sign of grammatical change.

2.4 Change in argument structure constructions

Like verbal complementation, argument structure is a domain of grammar that concerns the structures that are projected by verbs. The work of Goldberg (1995) has popularized the idea of argument structure constructions, that is, syntactic patterns that can be argued to carry meaning in themselves. Examples such as *John sneezed the napkin off the table* famously illustrate the fact that an intransitive verb such as *sneeze* may, given the right syntactic context, convey the meaning "to move by means of sneezing." Diachronic analyses of argument structure constructions are investigating how such patterns come into being and evolve over time.

The inception of a construction is studied by Israel (1996). Using data from the *Oxford English Dictionary* (*OED*), Israel tracks the formal and semantic development of the so-called *way*-construction that in modern usage gives rise to examples such as *How to fake your way through a wine tasting*. The meaning that this construction conveys is that an agent moves along a path, typically a metaphorical one, that is strewn with obstacles. This traversion is accomplished by the means of action that is specified by the verb. In the case of the above example, a wine tasting is thus portrayed as a difficult task. Getting through that task requires the agent to fake knowledgeable assessments of the wines' qualities.

Historically, the construction originated in literal descriptions of movement that included verbs of motion and path creation, as in the following examples (Israel 1996: 221).

(5) a. The kyng took a laghtre, and wente his way. (1412)
    b. He lape one horse and passit his way. (1375)

The subsequent development of the construction involves two types of change. First, the construction undergoes a formal change in which the presence of an oblique object expressing a path becomes obligatory. Examples without such an oblique, which are illustrated by the examples above, become increasingly rarer with time, whereas examples like the following become the norm (Israel 1996: 227).

(6) She started up, and fumbled her way down the dark stairs. (1801)

Second, the construction shows a type-frequency increase in its verbs. Israel identifies analogical extension as the driving force behind this increase. Initially, verbs that encode laborious or winding motion such as *plod*, *totter*, or *worm* enter the construction. The construction further branches out to include verbs of sound emission. Verbs such as *crunch*, *crash*, or *buzz* encode the sound that accompanies certain kinds of motion. Also verbs that describe the creation of a path enter the picture: *cut*, *pave*, and *fight* give rise to further analogical extensions that find their endpoint in metaphorical uses of the construction such as the following.

(7) a. Not one man in five hundred could have spelled his way through a psalm. (1849)
    b. Addison wrote his way with his Whig pamphlets to a secretaryship of state. (1890)

Israel's study demonstrates that the *OED*, with its database of precisely dated quotations, is a highly useful resource for corpus linguists. Its wide temporal coverage and large scope of lexical types make the *OED* an ideal basis for studies that investigate diachronic type frequency changes in phenomena such as the *way*-construction.

In a study of change in argument structure constructions, Wolk *et al.* (2013) demonstrate how smaller corpora can also be fruitfully used for this kind of analysis. Using the ARCHER corpus, Wolk *et al.* investigate variability in alternative genitive and dative constructions over time. The discussion here will focus exclusively on the latter. In a nutshell, Wolk *et al.* analyze whether and how the factors that lead speakers to choose one of the following examples over the other have changed during Late Modern English.

(8) a. I wrote my sister a letter. (the ditransitive construction)
    b. I wrote a letter to my sister. (the prepositional dative construction)

The alternation of these two constructions in Present-day English has been extensively studied (e.g. Bresnan *et al.* 2007 and references therein); factors such as the animacy of the recipient, the length of theme and recipient, and the discursive givenness of theme and recipient largely explain speakers' choices. Wolk *et al.* set out to analyze how the present system of interacting factors has changed over the past centuries. Using a set of alternating verbs, they search the ARCHER corpus for instances of the ditransitive construction and the prepositional dative construction, annotating each example for the following variables.[2]

(9)	dependent variable:	ditransitive vs. prepositional dative construction
	explanatory factors:	time, i.e. century of production
		variety, i.e. British or American English
		length of theme and recipient
		animacy of theme and recipient
		definiteness of theme and recipient

A logistic regression analysis establishes that all of the explanatory factors have an effect in the direction that synchronic studies of dative variability have found. This indicates that this area of grammar has been relatively stable in the recent past. However, with regard to diachronic change, the analysis shows that inanimate recipients, as in *The herbs gave the soup a nice flavor*, have become more acceptable in the ditransitive construction in the twentieth century.

Wolk *et al.*'s study exemplifies how diachronic corpus studies can precisely document changes in grammatical structure and simultaneously address issues of speakers' knowledge of language. Synchronic studies of the dative alternation have yielded converging evidence between corpus studies and experimental studies: statistical models that capture under what conditions the ditransitive construction and the prepositional dative construction occur in corpus data (Bresnan *et al.* 2007) correlate very well with experimental data in which speakers choose either one or the other (Bresnan 2007; Bresnan and Ford 2010; Lorenz 2012). This convergence suggests that probabilistic analyses of corpus data can be taken to represent speakers' knowledge of language. Assuming that the general cognitive mechanisms that underlie speakers' behavior in the present have been the same in the past, corpus-based studies of constructional alternations in diachronic data allow the putative reconstruction of what grammatical knowledge must have been like for earlier generations of speakers.

[2] The mixed-effects logistic regression model that Wolk *et al.* fit to the data includes also the variables of Text ID, theme, the verb lemma, and the corpus register of the text as random factors.

3 A case study: the life and death of *-ment*

This section turns to grammatical change in the area of morphology, presenting a case study of the development of the English derivational suffix *-ment* on the basis of data from the *Oxford English Dictionary* (Hilpert 2013).

3.1 Motivation: why study *-ment*?

The overall story of *-ment* is one of rise and fall: the suffix entered the English language through multiple loans from French, a productive word-formation process established itself, but its productivity began to wane soon after. Dalton-Puffer (1996: 108) adduces evidence from the Helsinki Corpus to show that the origins of *-ment* as a productive nominalizing suffix lie in the years between 1250 and 1350. In forms such as *judgment*, *parliament*, or *payment*, which were borrowed from Norman French, the initial stem was transparently verbal. At some point, enough nouns of this kind had entered the language that speakers began to use the suffix with Germanic stems. Accounts vary with regard to the subsequent decline of *-ment*, but it is certain that speakers of English today do not produce new coinages with the suffix on a regular basis. Studying *-ment* thus offers the opportunity to come to terms with the full life cycle of a word-formation process.

Hilpert's study builds on two previous analyses of *-ment* that have utilized the *OED* as a corpus, namely Anshen and Aronoff (1999) and Bauer (2001). Following these studies, Hilpert used the *OED* online interface to collect a list of entries that identify the suffix *-ment* in their etymology section. This search procedure returned a list of 1,245 types. Examples not instantiating the target construction, notably adverbs such as *malheureusement* and spelling variants such as *disgreement* [sic], were excluded. To cast a wider net, the full text of the *OED*, including its quotation base, was searched for a list of other *ment*-types that was collected from the COCA corpus (Davies 2009). The types that were retrieved in this way increased the overall number of types to 1,407. Figure 10.3 (adapted from Hilpert

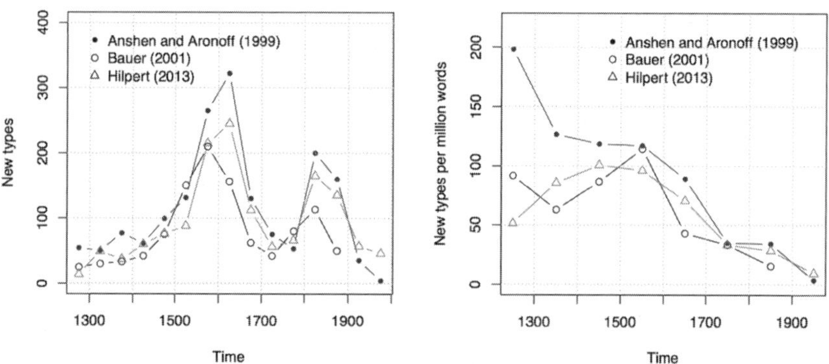

Figure 10.3 Absolute and normalized frequencies of new types with *-ment* in the *OED*

2013: 126) shows the absolute and normalized frequencies of new types per half-century, comparing them to the figures that had been offered by the two previous studies. The measurements are in broad agreement, although Anshen and Aronoff (1999) find relatively more early types, whereas Hilpert collects more modern ones that may have entered the online *OED* as recent updates. However, all three studies show that the normalized rate of new types has been in decline from the sixteenth century onward.

It is important to note that neither absolute type frequencies nor normalized type frequencies can reliably settle the question of whether and how *-ment* changed in productivity. Absolute type frequencies are trivially related to corpus size, with larger corpora yielding larger type frequencies, all other things being equal. Normalized type frequencies are problematic to compare across corpora because the relationship between type frequency and corpus size is not linear, furthermore exhibiting different slopes across productive and unproductive word-formation processes (Evert and Lüdeling 2001). In order to arrive at an account of the life and death of *-ment*, Hilpert (2013) therefore adopts a different methodology.

3.2 Methods

Hilpert's analysis has three parts. In a first step, a quantitative measure of productivity is computed for successive time slices in the development of *-ment*. This step is meant to answer the question of how the productivity of *-ment* changed over time. In a second step, the resulting curve of changing productivity is used to divide the development into diachronic stages. The resulting time intervals can be further investigated to answer the question of how *-ment* was used in different ways at different points in time. The third analytical step addresses this question with a quantitative analysis that compares formations with *-ment* across the diachronic stages with regard to several structural and semantic variables.

3.2.1 Measuring change in productivity

In order to investigate how *-ment* changed in productivity over time, a measure of productivity is needed that gets around the problems associated with absolute and normalized type frequencies. In pursuit of such a measure, Hilpert searched the *OED* quotations for all *ment*-types in the database, retrieving a concordance of 91,908 lines and approximately 655,000 words in total. Since each quotation in the *OED* is tagged with its historical date, the concordance could be binned into fifty-year increments, which form the basis for subsequent assessments of productivity. Several corpus-based measures of productivity are available, but the measure of expanding productivity (Baayen 1993) was used here. This measure of productivity is calculated in terms of a ratio, comparing for each slice of the data how many *hapax legomena* are found in total, and how many of

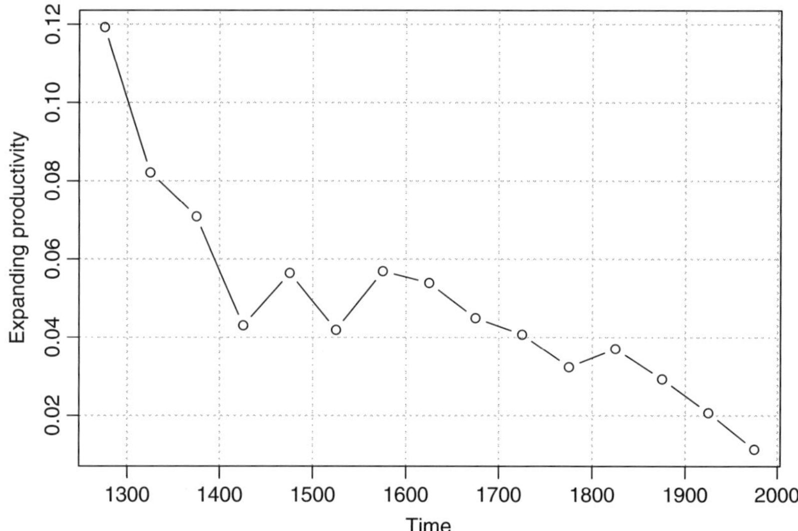

Figure 10.4 Changes in the expanding productivity of *-ment* in the *OED* (Hilpert 2013: 131)

these *hapax legomena* are forms with the suffix *-ment*. The logic of such a comparison is that relatively productive word-formation processes will account for a higher ratio of hapaxes than relatively unproductive ones. Comparisons over time thus indicate how the productivity of *-ment* has developed over time. The resulting curve of expanding productivity closely matches the normalized frequency decline of new types that was seen in Figure 10.3 above. Figure 10.4 shows that from 1550 onwards, there is a steady decline in expanding productivity.

3.2.2 Dividing the database into stages

The second methodological step in the analysis is the division of the decreasing productivity curve into stages. For this task, Hilpert used Variability-based Neighbor Clustering (Gries and Hilpert 2008), which is an iterative clustering algorithm that operates on a sequence of measurements, comparing degrees of similarity from one step to the next. The two neighboring measurements that are most similar to one another are joined together, so that successive reiterations turn a sequence of measurements into a hierarchically ordered clustering structure on the basis of which the data are divided into periods. For the data at hand, the algorithm suggests the division into five periods, as shown in Table 10.1 (Hilpert 2013: 134).

What is this periodization into five periods good for? Quite simply, it forms the basis for a comparison that investigates how formations with *-ment* developed structurally and semantically across the past centuries. An analyst can compare the types found in period 2 against the types found in period 3 and determine whether there are meaningful differences

Table 10.1 *Periods identified through VNC*

Period	Time	Number of new types
1	1250–1299	13
2	1300–1399	86
3	1400–1649	686
4	1650–1899	525
5	1900–2000	97
Total		1,407

between the two sets. In more technical terms, the periods allow mutual comparisons through the use of multivariate quantitative techniques, as described in the following subsection.

3.2.3 Analyzing the stages

Each type in the database is annotated in terms of a time stamp and five variables that pertain to the form as well as the meaning of the *ment*-types in the database. The variables and their possible values, including corpus period, are summarized in (10) below; the following paragraphs discuss each variable in turn.

(10) time: period 1, 2, 3, 4, 5
source: borrowed vs. derived
stem type: verb, adjective, noun
branching: binary, left, right
transitivity: transitive, intransitive
meaning: activity, result, means, remainder

A first distinction that is fundamental to the analysis of the suffix concerns the etymological sources of the attested types. Is a given type borrowed or natively derived? All elements in the database were classified by checking their etymologies in the *OED*; unclear cases were coded as borrowed. A second variable concerns the word class of the host to which the *-ment* suffix attaches. In the overwhelming majority of cases the host is verbal. Forms such as *funniment* and *scholarment* illustrate deviations from that tendency. Cases with ambicategorical stems (*debatement*, *securement*) were decided with recourse to the etymology sections in the *OED*. Types such as *segment* or *nugament*, which are morphologically opaque to present-day speakers, were analyzed into the parts of speech that they originally represented, so that all stems in the database were categorized as either adjectival, nominal, or verbal. Thirdly, the *ment*-types in the database vary with regard to their internal branching structure. In the simplest case, exemplified by forms such as *puzzlement*, the types exhibit a bipartite structure. A form such as *bedevilment* unites a complex stem with the suffix *-ment* and is thus to be seen as left-branching. Conversely, the type *non-attachment* illustrates the prefixation of a bipartite *ment*-type, resulting in a right-branching structure. Importantly, the appearance of a right-branching type does not testify to the productivity of the suffix *-ment*, but rather to the productivity of the respective prefix. Right-branching types were retained in the database in order to test whether diachronically, right-branching forms account for a progressively greater share of new formations as the productivity of the suffix wanes. The fourth variable that informs the analysis classifies the *ment*-types as either transitive or intransitive. Transitivity describes the ability of a verb to take a direct object. A clear case of a transitive *ment*-type would be *punishment*; a clear case of an intransitive type is *settlement*. Problematic are types with ergative stems such as *move* or *shatter*, which were resolved using the *OED* entries once more: higher and historically prior entries were taken as definitive. Even more problematic are forms with adjectival or nominal stems, for which it was determined whether they encoded a transitive or an intransitive event. By that logic, *merriment* is classified as intransitive, *desightment* as transitive. The fifth and final variable concerns the overall meanings of the *ment*-types in the database. In the default case, a noun ending in *-ment* denotes an activity, as in *disagreement* "the act of disagreeing." By contrast, an *assortment* of chocolates does not refer to the act of assorting; rather, it refers to the chocolates themselves. Dalton-Puffer (1996: 109) identifies four semantic classes of *ment*-types that Hilpert (2013) adopts. Besides "the act of V-ing" (*disagreement*), Dalton-Puffer identifies "the result of V-ing" (*impairment*), "the means for V-ing" (*steadiment*), and a remainder category (*abutment*).

These five variables enter an analysis that also takes the passage of time into account. What the annotated database allows one to investigate is whether formations with *-ment* have changed over time with regard to the formal and functional variation that is captured by the five variables. The analytical technique that Hilpert uses is called Hierarchical Configural Frequency Analysis (HCFA), which is a procedure that is based on the chi-squared test, but which allows the analysis of data that is annotated in terms of more than just two categorical variables (von Eye 1990). The analysis was carried out using a script for the open-source software R (HCFA 3.2, Gries 2004). Like the chi-squared test, HCFA compares expected frequencies against observed frequencies and determines whether a difference between the latter and the former is statistically significant. The basic question that can be investigated with this method is whether there are certain configurations of variable values in formations with *-ment* that occur more frequently than expected, and whether different historical periods are characterized by different configurations. A comparison of such configurations, which are called "types," i.e. typical, frequent configurations, can inform our understanding of how this particular word-formation process evolved over time. In more concrete terms, the raw data that go into an HCFA have the format that is shown in Table 10.2, which shows, in alphabetical order, the first entries from the database.

Table 10.2 *Input data for a HCFA*

Type	Etymology	Stem	Branching	Meaning	Transitivity	Period
abandonment	borrowed	verb	binary	activity	transitive	3
abasement	borrowed	verb	binary	activity	transitive	3
abashment	borrowed	verb	binary	result	transitive	3
abatement	borrowed	verb	binary	activity	transitive	2
abhorment	borrowed	verb	left	activity	transitive	3
abjurement	borrowed	verb	left	activity	transitive	3
ablandishment	borrowed	verb	left	activity	transitive	4
abodement	derived	verb	binary	result	transitive	3
abolishment	borrowed	verb	binary	activity	transitive	3
...	...	...	...	...	...	...

Every type in the database exhibits a certain configuration of features: for instance, the type *abhorment* instantiates a configuration of a borrowed transitive verbal stem, a left-branching structure, the meaning of an activity, and a diachronic origin in the third corpus period. Is this configuration a type? An HCFA tests systematically for all possible configurations whether they are observed more or less frequently than expected. While the configuration of *abhorment* does occur more often than expected in the third corpus period (o = 75, e = 52.4), this difference is not large enough to be statistically significant, so that the configuration of *abhorment* is not a type. By contrast, there are other configurations that are found significantly more often than expected in their respective corpus periods. Specifically, the statistical analysis returns ten types that are summarized in Table 10.3 and discussed in the following subsection.

3.3 Results

Type 1 (o = 11, e = 3.2), which characterizes early instantiations of *-ment*, is borrowed and verbal as expected. The verbs that act as stems are transitive. This type can be seen as the prototype of the early borrowings with which the word-formation process originated. The second period is characterized by two types. Both types represent borrowed forms that encode means, type 2 (o = 10, e = 0.8) with transitive verbal stems, type 3 with nominal stems (o = 3, e < 0.1). The former of these reappears in the third period (o = 22, e = 5.4), whereas the latter was too infrequent to establish itself as a longer-lasting pattern. The third period further marks the entrance of two natively derived types. Type 5 (o = 174, e = 121.9) represents the most common pattern overall: in this type the suffix combines with a complex verbal stem that encodes a transitive action. The popularity of this type continues into the fourth period (o = 150, e = 93.3). Type 6 (o = 6, e = 0.3) in the third period is to be seen as a short-lived fad, namely the use of native adjectival stems to construct forms such as *funniment* or *dreariment*.

Table 10.3 Results for types of *-ment* formation

1250–1299	1300–1399	1400–1649	1650–1899	1900–2000
1: Borrowed, verbal stem, transitive *judgment, pavement, imprisonment*	2: Borrowed, verbal stem, binary branching, transitive, means *ointment, battlement* 3. Borrowed, nominal stem, binary branching, transitive, means *monument, vesselment*	4: Borrowed, verbal stem, binary branching, transitive, means (=2) *garnishment, medicament*		
		5: Derived, verbal stem, left-branching, transitive, action *disbursement, embitterment, enlargement*	7: Derived, verbal stem, left-branching, transitive, action (=5) *dismemberment, enthronement, interminglement*	
		6: Derived, adjectival stem, binary branching, intransitive, action *dreariment, jolliment*		
			8: Derived, verbal stem, right-branching, transitive, action *disembodiment, maltreatment, overenrichment*	9: Derived, verbal stem, right-branching, transitive, action (=8) *antiestablishment, ecomanagement* 10: Derived, verbal stem, right-branching, transitive, result *malnourishment, misalignment, noninvolvement*

The fourth period sees the ascent of right-branching forms, which indirectly signals that the suffix *-ment* is waning in its productivity. Type 8 (o = 41, e = 18.9), exemplified by formations such as *disembodiment*, subsumes all the features of the overall prototype (types 5, 7), except for the fact that it consists of prefixed forms that merely cannibalize on the high frequency of types 5 and 7. In the fifth period, the analysis detects two types. Type 9 (o = 25, e = 3.4) is identical to type 8. Type 10 (o = 19, e = 1.7), a second right-branching type, is structurally identical, but encodes a result rather than an action, in formations such as *malnourishment*. On the whole, the information offered in Table 10.2 shows that the development of *-ment* is not merely a story of rise and fall that could be captured in a simple line graph of waning productivity. Instead, it is a story that has several by-lines and something of an aftermath. The general lesson that the analysis provides is that a word-formation process may be less unified a phenomenon than is usually taken for granted. The overall productivity of any given suffix represents an average that obtains across several subtypes of a word-formation process. Whether it truly makes sense to average across these subtypes is a question that only a qualitative analysis can settle. From the perspective of a linguistically informed observer, it may be more sensible to re-conceptualize a process of productivity loss, as in the case of *-ment*, as a story of how its subtypes emerge, hold out, but ultimately disappear.

4 Summary and concluding remarks

In a loose sense, much classical philological work on grammatical change was corpus-based. When, for example, Otto Jespersen (1909–1949: IV, 177) compared successive translations of the Bible into English to illustrate the increase in the frequency of the progressive from the Middle English period onwards, this was a way of comparing matching corpora in the pre-digital era. In the era of computer-aided corpus linguistics, the amount, quality, and diversity of the available data and the power of our analytical tools have increased massively, with important consequences. The case studies that were presented in this chapter illustrate how the use of corpus data allows researchers to go beyond the mere statement that a grammatical change happened, and to address the questions of **when** and **how** something happened. The corpora and the analytical techniques that are currently available have turned the corpus-based study of grammatical change into an expanding and rapidly evolving area of research. The key to success remains the use of ever better corpora and advanced analytical techniques in conjunction with state-of-the-art models of grammatical change in usage-based linguistics, such as grammaticalization theory (Mair 2011).

In the early stages of corpus-based research on grammatical change, digital language corpora and the software for data analysis were powerful tools which enabled linguists to perform traditional tasks in a much more efficient and systematic way. This is illustrated, for instance, by the problem of identifying early attestations of a grammatical innovation. In the pre-digital era, apart from consulting reference works such as the *Oxford English Dictionary*, the only way to find them was through educated guesswork, by consulting likely sources. Today, searches in large corpora and the even larger masses of text stored in digital archives will do the same job much more effectively, and numerous ante-datings are in fact reported regularly. As the results of corpus-based research on grammatical change accumulate and as the methods of analysis become more sophisticated, the corpus ceases to be merely a tool and becomes an active ingredient in the further development of usage-based theoretical models. This is evident, for example, in language-historical periodization, where statistical analysis of corpus data serves to generate linguistically coherent periods in a bottom-up process (Gries and Hilpert 2008), which complements, and sometimes corrects, our traditional system of periodization, which combines language-internal and language-external criteria in sometimes problematical ways (Curzan 2012).

One central aim for future investigations would be to focus on a question that is considerably harder than the "when" and the "how": can the analysis of corpora yield explanations for *why* a given process of grammatical change happened? In order to address this question, historical corpus linguists need to intensify collaborations with researchers in sociolinguistics and psycholinguistics, who have long been concerned with the social and cognitive processes that shape grammar and that ultimately also shape grammatical change. A growing recent interest displayed by historical corpus linguists in notions such as "persistence" and "priming" in discourse (Szmrecsanyi 2006, Traugott 2008), "salience" (Brems 2011) or "actualization" (de Smet 2012a) seems a promising beginning on the long path towards truly integrated and comprehensive usage-based models for diachronic grammar.

11

Lexical grammar

Susan Hunston

1 Introduction

This chapter discusses a body of research in corpus linguistics that describes and theorizes a strong connection between lexical words and the grammatical features with which they co-occur. There is no consistent terminology to describe research of this kind, but the phrase "Lexical Grammar" directs us to the combination of lexis and grammar embodied in it. This chapter examines the research in terms of: innovation in observation (seeing associations and patterning that have not been seen before); innovations in methodology (finding new ways of making those observations); and innovations in theory (using observations to confirm theories of language or to generate new theories). After a brief survey of the research context, four specific studies are discussed in some detail, two under the heading of "grammar to lexis" and two under the heading of "lexis to grammar." Then a short account is given of an empirical case study in the field of lexical grammar.

2 Research context

The argument that the grammar of a language and its lexicon are not separate entities is consistent with a functional rather than a formal view of language, which prioritizes observation of actual language use over a reliance on instances of idealized language drawing on a speaker's intuition (McEnery and Hardie 2012: 168) and predates the development of corpus linguistics. The availability of large, searchable corpora, however, has led to a number of major advances in this area. On the one hand, statistical packages that can handle large quantities of data facilitate reliable statements about the frequency of co-occurrences and the significance of comparative frequencies. On the other hand, software that targets key-word-in-context, collocations, recurring phrases, and the like encourages the observation of lexical patterning and details of phraseology. Each set of developments co-occurs with a different perspective on lexical grammar (Biber 2012). A tradition that might be called the "grammar-to-lexis" viewpoint takes grammatical categories as prior and notes the lexis that occurs disproportionately frequently in each category (e.g. Biber *et al.* 1999; Stefanowisch and Gries 2003; Nesselhauf and Römer 2007). The alternative tradition, that might be called the "lexis-to-grammar" viewpoint, takes lexis as prior and notes the frequently occurring grammatical contexts of each word (e.g. Sinclair *et al.* 1995; Francis *et al.* 1996, 1998; Herbst *et al.* 2004).

For the "lexis-to-grammar" tradition, the challenge is to generalize from what can be an unwieldy mass of data; if the unit of analysis is the individual word, then the description of language consists of at least as many statements as there are words. Earlier corpus studies often focused on the patterning of a small number of individual words (e.g. Sinclair 1991; Stubbs 1996; Kennedy 1998; Tognini-Bonelli 2001), taking into account collocations, grammatical context, and pragmatics. From those raw descriptions come attempts to systematize the mass of detail that can be found therein. One such attempt is to look at recurring co-occurrences of lexical and grammatical words (e.g. Renouf and Sinclair 1991). Research into phrases, variously defined, is now extensive and includes phraseological profiling (Römer 2010), bundles, and P-frames (Biber *et al.* 2003, 2004; Gray and Biber 2013). Pattern grammar, to be considered in greater detail below, systematizes the grammar of individual words by identifying a finite set of grammatical elements (noun phrase, *that*-clause, etc.) and a finite set of patterns that they combine to form. Each word can then be described in terms of the patterns it occurs with, and each pattern can be described in terms of the words that occur with it (Francis *et al.* 1996, 1998; Hunston and Francis 1998, 2000).

The descriptions of lexical and grammatical patterning find explanations in a range of existing theoretical approaches to language. Valency grammar, for example, has much in common with pattern grammar (Herbst 2009). There is a range of work drawing on a systemic–functional background that studies specialized corpora from the point of view of the intersection of lexis and process type (e.g. Goatly 2004; Holtz 2007; Miller 2006; Mulderigg 2011). The lexis-to-grammar work has also generated approaches of its own, most notably Sinclair's (1991, 2004a) concept of the Idiom Principle and units of meaning, which sees language in use as comprising series of "single choice" semi-fixed phrases that are indeterminate in extent and restricted in terms of lexis, grammar, and functional meaning. Integration of these concepts into broader linguistic theory is carried out by Stubbs (2001b, 2009) and, in a rather different way, by Hoey (see discussion below).

With the exception of Hoey, the lexis-to-grammar tradition sketched above is agnostic with regard to psycholinguistic theories. Other studies of lexis and grammar draw on theories of phraseology (e.g. Wray 2002) and on usage-based theories of grammar (e.g. Kemmer and Barlow 2000; Schulze and Römer 2009) and are informed by empirical research in second language acquisition (e.g. Ellis *et al.* 2008). Most saliently, the concept of Construction Grammar is used as the cognitive model that most satisfactorily accounts for observations of the intersection of lexis and grammar (Fillmore 1985; Goldberg 1995, 1999, 2006). Construction Grammar argues that instead of a set of syntactical rules, the mental grammar comprises a series of constructions, ranging from quite general ones (e.g. the question construction), to ones that have some lexical restrictions (e.g. the ditransitive construction), to ones that are very specific lexically (e.g. the *waiting to happen* construction). Construction Grammar is also used as the basis for a set of related concepts: collexemes (the words found in constructions) and collostructions (word and construction combined). A significant part of the research on Construction Grammar is the development of statistical methods to establish the strength of association between construction and collexeme.

As might be expected, much of the research on lexis and grammar stems from applied linguistic concerns. Reference grammars and dictionaries with this focus are often designed for learners of English (e.g. Sinclair *et al.* 1990, 1995; Biber *et al.* 1999; Herbst *et al.* 2004; Carter and McCarthy 2006). Moving beyond the learner, it is reasonable to suppose that varieties of English might use patterns/constructions somewhat differently. Mukherjee and others (Mukherjee 2009; Hoffman and Mukherjee 2007; Mukherjee and Gries 2009) study the range of verbs used in a set of constructions in new varieties of English, especially Indian English. Studies of diachronic language change are sometimes based on words and constructions (e.g. Noël and Colleman 2010).

The close association between pattern/construction and meaning is exploited by using pattern/construction to investigate discourse. A key example of this is the use of patterns/constructions associated with stance. Patterns/constructions exemplified by *believe/argue that, dismiss something as, a demonstration of, it is likely that, it is questionable whether* are routinely used to express stance in academic discourse, but their frequency varies across disciplines. Biber (2006b) includes these in studies of stance, but Charles (2006a, 2006b) and Hiltunen (2010) do so more explicitly from the standpoint of pattern and construction respectively.

3 Grammar-to-lexis

This section will discuss in detail some key publications which have in common that they take grammatical categories as prior and populate accounts of grammar with information about lexis.

3.1 *The Longman grammar of spoken and written English* (Biber *et al.* 1999)

The *Longman Grammar of Spoken and Written English* (*LGSWE*) is based on the model of English developed by Quirk *et al.* (1972), but populates that model with reference to a corpus of 40 million words. The corpus is annotated to enable the occurrence of features identified in the grammatical model to be quantified, and it is divided into four register-specific corpora representing fiction, conversation, news reportage, and academic prose, so that the frequencies of occurrence in the different registers can be compared (Biber *et al.* 1999: 24–40). Throughout the book individual words that are significant to particular grammatical categories are identified and quantified.

The result is a rich description of English that extends the previous model substantially by the inclusion of comparative frequency information. To give just one example, verb phrases across the four registers are compared in terms of the frequency of present tense, past tense, and modal verb (ibid.: 456). This allows a comparison between verb phrase types in each register and between the registers. In both conversation and academic prose, for example, present tense is much more frequent than past tense or modal, whereas in fiction past tense dominates and present and past occur about equally in news reportage. Modal verbs are less frequent than either of the verb tenses, but they are most frequent in conversation. A subsequent discussion (ibid.: 457–458) accounts for the differences in terms of the context of each register, pointing out, for example, that present tense plays a very different role in the each of the two registers (conversation and academic prose) in which it is the dominant tense. Turning to lexical grammar, the book then gives a brief list of verbs that are statistically associated with each tense, in the sense that over 70 percent or 80 percent of their total occurrences are in the relevant tense.

This particular quantitative information about lexis and grammar suggests a complex interaction of grammar, lexis, register, and phraseology in relation to frequency (ibid.: 459). The verbs occurring most frequently with present tense are those associated with particular functions in conversation (*I bet, I doubt whether, you know, it doesn't matter*), and those occurring most frequently in past tense are largely associated with fictional narrative.

In some other sections of *LGSWE* the information about lexis is more extensive. To take one example from many, there is a fairly lengthy section on verbs that control *wh*-clauses. The most frequent verbs (*know, see, tell, wonder, ask*, and *understand*) are identified, and a further 100+ verbs are listed in six semantic domains (e.g. "speech act," "cognition," "perception") (ibid.: 686). The relative frequency of the most frequent verbs in this structure is given in each of the four registers (ibid.: 689). This shows that, for example, *tell* occurs more frequently in conversation and fiction than in news reportage or academic prose, and that, conversely, in conversation and fiction *tell* is more frequent than the other verbs listed. None of the speech act verbs occurs more than twenty times per million words in academic prose except *explain*. This verb, conversely, occurs most frequently in academic prose and in news reportage. There is, then, a dual perspective on each word listed: which register(s) it occurs in most frequently, and how it compares to the other words in each register.

One of the strengths of *LGSWE* is its sense of completeness. Because it is based on a finite and comprehensive account of English grammar, there is a sense that every key aspect of English has been covered, and there are useful additional chapters about the lexical and grammatical special features of academic prose and of conversation. Other obvious key points are the unique quantitative information and the focus on register distinctions, an important theme in all of Biber's work.

It is, however, possible to see the model that is the foundation of *LGSWE* as a limitation as well as a structure. Lexis is examined only insofar as it fits within the chosen grammatical description. Also, the focus on very high-frequency words, or those with a high frequency within a particular category, means that relatively few individual words are featured in the book. The book's complement, or reverse image, can be found in the Pattern Grammar books discussed below.

3.2 Collostructions (Stefanowitsch and Gries 2003)

This paper proposes units termed collostructions, which are composed of constructions and the lexical items that significantly occur in them (collexemes). The term "construction" comes from Construction Grammar (Goldberg 1995, 1999, 2006), and it refers to "any linguistic expression … that is directly associated with a particular meaning or function, and whose form or meaning cannot be compositionally derived" (Stefanowitsch and Gries 2003: 212). It is important that constructions are essentially psycholinguistic constructs, that is, they articulate what the mental representation of a language consists of.

Examples of constructions include very general ones such as the ditransitive construction, which is associated with the meaning of "transfer," as in "*give* someone something" (straightforward transfer) or "*tell* someone a story" (metaphorical transfer). Other examples are more specific, such as the "N *waiting to happen*" construction, as in *an accident waiting to happen* or *a new industrial revolution is waiting to happen*, which has a meaning of "currently obvious that something will occur" (ibid.: 220). Perhaps midway is the "*into*-causative" construction (e.g. *talk someone into doing something*), whose meaning might be glossed as: "person *a* talks to person *b* and as a result person *b* does something" (ibid.: 224–225). The paper (one of many on this topic by these and other authors) describes the concept of collostructions, explains how collostructions are identified, and gives a series of case studies indicating how the identification of collostructions might support, modify, or challenge other views of language.

Central to the paper is an account of the methodology used to establish a defensible connection between a word and a construction. The authors use the Fisher exact test, whose advantages, they argue, include an avoidance of the false assumptions about word distribution that lie behind, for example, *t*-score. The Fisher test is used to establish "collostruction strength" by comparing the number of times a word (e.g. *tell*) occurs in a given construction (e.g. the ditransitive) with the total other occurrences of *tell* and the total other occurrences of the ditransitive, and the total number of other words and other constructions in the corpus. The collexemes can then be placed in order of collostruction strength. In some instances, the collostruction strength coincides with raw frequency. For example, *accident* co-occurs with *waiting to happen* more frequently than any other word, and it has the strongest association with that construction. On the other hand, in the "*into*-causative" construction ("verb someone *into* doing something"), the verb *force* occurs most frequently but the verb *trick* has the highest collostruction strength.

The paper presents its findings as a number of case studies, moving from a study based on a single lemma, *cause*, to ones based on grammatical categories such as the imperative and the past tense. The study of *cause* follows up the point made by Stubbs (1996) that this verb co-occurs with words with a negative evaluative meaning, such as *problem*, *damage*, or *injury*. This paper, however, takes the argument a stage further and shows that the collexemes occur differentially in the constructions of which *cause* is a part. For example, whereas the transitive construction (*cause damage/injury*) is used with nouns indicating external events, the ditransitive construction (*cause* someone *distress/hardship*) is used with nouns indicating negative states of mind or subjective interpretations of experience. This is a useful reminder of the sensitivity of lexis to structure, but a more radical interpretation might be that meaning is associated with combinations of lexis and grammar – with units of meaning – rather than with lexis or grammar alone.

Another example is the construction "*think nothing of* doing something." An interpretation of concordance lines (as reported in Sinclair *et al.* 1995) suggests that the "doing something" will be "difficult or strange," as in the examples cited in Stefanowitsch and Gries's paper: *think nothing of mortgaging themselves* ... or *think nothing of abandoning his wife* ... Simply listing collocates of *think nothing of* provides little evidence for this interpretation, as no verbs occur frequently in the "mortgaging/abandoning" slot and many of the ones that occur appear to be innocuous (*walk, hear, bring, call*). However, the verbs can be ranked according to collostruction strength and then it is seen that the strongest do indeed associate with risk (*mortgage, leap, fly*) or with actions that might be considered undesirable (*abandon, beat*).

The final case study included in the paper is the ditransitive construction ("*give* someone something" or "*tell* someone something"). The collostruction strength analysis places frequent and expected verbs at the top of the list: *give, tell, send, offer, show, cost, teach, award, allow, lend, deny*, and so on. The authors make the point that this collostruction strength explains why most people intuitively identify these verbs as "basically" ditransitive, even though they are not limited to the ditransitive construction and the construction is not limited to them.

The construct of "collostruction strength" is extremely important, but the sophistication of the calculations it embodies needs to be kept in mind to avoid misinterpretation. Collostruction strength combines two calculations of relative frequency: the number of times a word occurs in a construction compared with the total instances of the word (answering the question "how important is this construction to this word?"); and the number of times a word occurs in a construction compared with the total instances of the construction (answering the question 'how important is this word to this construction?'). As Biber (2012) notes, it is important in interpreting the numbers attached to this construct to remember that the frequencies so described are relative only. In other words, a word+construction combination with a high collostruction strength in a given corpus may actually not occur particularly frequently.

It may be useful to think of collostruction strength as a measurement of prototypicality. It offers a quantitative explanation for intuitions that do not necessarily match absolute frequency information: why some verbs "feel" ditransitive even though they regularly occur in other constructions, or why a construction such as "think nothing of *-ing*" "feels" negative in spite of the counterexamples found in the construction. It may not, however, be the only explanation for such intuitions. In many instances of *THINK nothing of*, for example, the negativity associated with the construction is found in the broader phraseology rather than in the verb itself, as in . . . *some loonies think nothing of making death threats to players* . . . The same is true when the construction indicates "something contrary to expectation" rather than "something negative." Examples include *thinks nothing of spending a couple of grand in the shops* . . ., *studying complex subjects later on in life* . . ., *getting up at five o'clock in the morning* . . . In other words it can be argued that the prototypical meaning of the "think nothing of" construction does not derive from the relative frequency of individual verbs in the construction, and cannot therefore be captured by calculating this; rather, a true calculation needs to take into account the relative frequency of other indications of "unexpectedness" in a much broader context.

4 Lexis to grammar

In this section we look at the other side of the coin and discuss studies that begin with lexis and investigate grammatical aspects of their context. Two studies are examined in some detail below, though others would deserve inclusion if space permitted. For example, the *Valency Dictionary of English* (Herbst *et al.* 2004) incorporates corpus-based observations of pattern into a valency model of grammar and populates a dictionary of English with the resulting information about each word sense. Also of importance are studies which specify form–meaning mappings in the context of individual words. The most longstanding of these is the Framenet project (Fillmore *et al.* 2003). This assigns each word to a meaning frame, which in turn specifies core and peripheral elements of meaning to be mapped on to grammatical elements in the co-text of the target word. For example, the "commercial transaction" frame includes a purchaser, a vendor, an owned item, and an amount of money. These occur in different configurations depending on the verb used. For example, *Amy sold the book to Charles for $10* follows the grammatical sequence "noun phrase + SELL + noun phrase + *to* + noun phrase + *for* + noun phrase" and the meaning sequence "vendor + SELL + owned item + *to* + purchaser + *for* + amount of money." Similar approaches to meaning–grammar mapping can be found in local grammars developed by Barnbrook (2002), Bednarek (2008), and Hunston and Sinclair (2000) and in the Corpus Pattern Analysis project described in Hanks (2013).

4.1 The "Pattern Grammar" project

The concept of Pattern Grammar (PG) came out of the COBUILD project, a large-scale lexicographical exercise that was unique when it began, in that the compilers relied on a very large (for its time) corpus of English to identify frequent usages and phraseologies of words. The project produced a large number of publications, including an early grammar book (Sinclair *et al.* 1990) that takes a "grammar-to-lexis" approach somewhat similar to that in *LGSWE*, though without the register focus. The first two COBUILD dictionaries (Sinclair *et al.* 1987; Sinclair *et al.* 1995) include grammar codings for each sense of each headword. In the second of these publications, grammatical categories such as "object," "complement" are abandoned in favor of "pattern" notation: a sequence of elements that specifies the words, word classes, clause or phrase types that are dependent on the headword. For example, the verb *consider* is shown as having three senses, the first associated with four patterns including "V n *as* adj" ("verb + noun phrase + as + adjective": *consider jogging as unnatural*), the second associated with two patterns including "V n" ("verb + noun phrase": *consider a plan*), the third associated with two patterns including "V *-ing*" ("verb + clause beginning with *-ing* form of verb": *consider hiring a lifejacket*). It should be noted that, in contrast to constructions, as noted above, patterns are conceived as a purely observational phenomenon, and the researchers are agnostic as to whether they reflect mental constructs or not.

Patterns were identified manually, and although semi-automatic pattern annotation is possible, it is not entirely straightforward, because a sequence of elements does not unambiguously constitute a pattern. One example is the sequence "provide + noun phrase + *to* + noun phrase," which may be an example of the pattern "verb + noun + *to* + noun," where the preposition *to* is dependent on the verb, or an example of "verb+noun" and "noun + *to* + noun," where *to* is dependent on the noun. An example of the first is *provide useful information to the learner*. An example of the second is *provide clues to changes in sea level*. Another example is the sequence "train + *for* + noun phrase," which may be an example of "verb + *for* + noun," if the noun phrase is dependent on the verb, as in *train for the priesthood* (priesthood is the end point of the activity). Where *for* introduces an adverbial of time, however, as in *train for three weeks*, there is no such dependency and the pattern relating to *train* is simple "verb" (i.e. this is an intransitive verb).

The two "Pattern Grammar" books present all the patterns identified and for each pattern list all the verbs (Francis *et al.* 1996) and all the nouns and adjectives (Francis *et al.* 1998) that are included in Sinclair *et al.* (1995) and used with that pattern. Although the books cannot claim to be entirely complete in their listings, they do comprise the most comprehensive descriptions of their kind to date, with 700 verb patterns and 100 noun and adjective patterns identified and associated with 9,000 verb senses and 10,000 nouns and adjectives. Because pattern and meaning are connected (see above, for example, the different senses of *consider* distinguished by pattern), the words occurring with each pattern are not a random collection but can be divided into rough "meaning groups." These groups list together the words that are found to occur with the relevant pattern and that share an element of meaning. For example, the pattern "V *in* n/*-ing*" ("verb + *in* + noun phrase or *–ing* clause": *assist in safeguarding; revel in their new freedom, believe in coincidences, deal in antiques*) is shown as having 16 meaning groups, including "assist or take part" (*aid, collaborate, help*, etc.), "enjoy" (*delight, glory, rejoice*, etc.), "believe" (*believe, concur, trust*, etc.) and 'deal' (*deal, trade, traffic*, etc.). The different relationships between the elements of the pattern (e.g. *assist in safeguarding, believe in God, deal in stocks and shares*) help to distinguish the groups, but the books make less of these distinctions than of the meanings.

A number of publications discuss Pattern Grammar, notably Hunston and Francis (1998, 2000). Themes in these publications include: the concept of "pattern"; the association between pattern and meaning; the challenges of providing structural descriptions (Subject, Object, etc.) for patterns; and how patterns map on to segments of naturally occurring interaction, showing routine and creative usage.

Possibly the most significant feature of the Pattern Grammar study lies in the comprehensive listings given in Francis *et al.* (1996, 1998). Although many dictionaries, including Herbst *et al.* (2004), give grammatical information about each individual word, these reference books are the only ones to collect that information into a book organized in terms of grammar. This allows the connection between meaning and pattern to be demonstrated in the organization of lists of words into "meaning groups." In addition, the PG books offer an insight into what a description of English based on lexis rather than grammar looks like, and how it differs from a traditional grammar.

As noted above, *LGSWE* and the PG books have complementary approaches: *LGSWE* views lexis through the lens of grammar; the PG books arrive at grammar through a study of lexis. It is not surprising, then, that they also have almost directly complementary strengths and weaknesses. *LGSWE* is more explicit about its methodology, which is based on the annotation of a corpus with the categories used in the book. The PG books treat methodology less explicitly. *LGSWE* distinguishes registers; the PG books do not. *LGSWE* includes quantitative information; the PG books do not. On the other hand, where the two publications give similar information, for example listing verbs governing non-finite clauses, the PG books give a more exhaustive list than *LGSWE* does. Thus the PG books are more comprehensive in terms of lexis but *LGSWE* covers more topics in terms of grammar. Arguably, the PG books break more new ground than *LGSWE*, but do so at some cost in terms of lack of coverage.

Another area of complementarity involves patterns and constructions. Given that in many of the examples cited the only distinction is nomenclature, the question arises as to whether these are the same phenomenon with a different name. However, the essential feature of constructions is that they are taken to be mental constructs, whereas no such claim is made for patterns. One proposal, then, would be to use the term "construction" to refer to the mental construct and the term "pattern" to refer to aspects of language output. In addition, the notion of construction includes many items not considered to be patterns. Patterns are identified only when there are lexical restrictions on their use. For example, the ditransitive construction appears as the pattern "verb phrase + noun phrase + noun phrase," but the interrogative construction has no pattern equivalent because there are no restrictions on the lexis with which it occurs. In this case the construction is too general to be considered a pattern. Conversely, some constructions are considered too specific to be patterns. The "noun *waiting to happen*" construction and the "*THINK nothing of*" construction are more specific lexically than patterns are. One consequence of this specificity is that the number of constructions is potentially vast. A practical advantage of patterns is that simple principles lie behind them, and they can be listed (Francis *et al.* 1996; 1998). This is not just a matter of practicality, however. The discussion of the "*THINK nothing of*" construction above suggested that the salient aspect of the phraseology was not the construction and its participant lexeme but in the wider immediate context. In other words, I would suggest that phenomena such as "something waiting to happen" and "think nothing of doing" are better considered as units of meaning (Sinclair 2004a) than as constructions.

4.2 Lexical priming (Hoey 2004b)

This paper is an articulation of Hoey's theory of lexical priming, which has two main facets. The first is that the phenomenon of the unequal distribution of lexis accounts for much more about naturally occurring text than might be expected from reading any of the papers discussed so far. The second is a hypothesis about how language is stored in the brain and made available for use in everyday interaction, though this concept is less fully explained in this paper than in Hoey (2005).

Hoey uses a corpus of 100 million words, mainly consisting of texts from the *Guardian* newspaper. He tests the relative frequency of target items in contrasting contexts. For example, *consequence* is noted as occurring in a definite noun group in 67 percent of all occurrences, whereas *result* occurs in a definite noun group in 94 percent of all occurrences. The "semantic associations" of the two words are also studied: *consequence* is described as associating strongly with "inevitability," "negative evaluation," and "significance," while *reason* associates strongly with "positive evaluation," "accuracy," and "sameness/difference." Statistical corroboration for these associations is not given in this paper, but reference is made to Hoey (2005) where this aspect of the methodology is explained in more detail. Most of this paper is devoted to an argument around the opening sentence of Bill Bryson's book *Neither Here nor There* (Bryson 1991): *In winter Hammerfest is a thirty-hour ride by bus from Oslo, though why anyone would want to go there in winter is a question worth considering.* Hoey compares aspects of this sentence with his *Guardian* corpus, to identify ways in which the sentence as written is more natural than other expressions with an apparently similar content would be. He demonstrates this by comparing Bryson's actual sentence with a grammatically correct but less idiomatic invented sentence.

In comparing his two sentences, Hoey finds that many two-word combinations in Bryson's original sentence occur frequently also in the 100-million-word *Guardian* corpus. He also finds that the two-word combinations "interlock." For example, *bus* and *ride* co-occur in the corpus, as do *ride* and *hour*, and *thirty* and *hour*. The relative frequency (in percentage terms) of these co-occurrences is greater than equivalent frequencies in the invented sentence. Using the concept of semantic association, measures of "typicality" increase. For example, whereas *thirty-hour ride* is rare, *hour* occurs regularly in similar phrases (*a half-hour drive, a four-hour flight, a two-hour trip*, etc.) (ibid.: 44).

In a further extended argument, Hoey contrasts the phrase *in winter* with similar phrases: *in the winter, during the winter*, and *that winter*. He finds that *in winter* co-occurs with a meaning of "timeless truth" (as in Bryson's opening sentence, and as opposed to a "specific event") proportionally more frequently than the other phrases do. Similarly, *in winter* occurs in a present-tense clause proportionally more frequently than the other phrases do. In the sample sentence, *in winter* is "thematised," and Hoey shows that this phrase when occurring in Theme position collocates in his corpus with the verb *be*, and with the names of places, again proportionally more frequently than the alternative phrases.

Hoey's paper is an important statement of what makes even creative language sound "natural" and "idiomatic." He shows that establishing "typicality" involves going beyond word–word collocation, but also beyond lexis–grammar colligation into the identification of recurring sequences of meaning elements, or "textual colligation." It also goes beyond each individual observation; what makes the Bill Bryson sentence "idiomatic" is the intersection of the various typical uses it embodies. Hoey discusses this in terms of what he calls "priming prosody" (ibid.: 53). He argues that this prosody "occurs when the collocations, colligations, semantic associations and textual colligations of lexical items in an utterance chime with each other in such a way that they reinforce each other." In other work, most notably Hoey (2005), the argument is made that language users store a version of co-occurrence frequencies, based on their own experience of language, and this "mental corpus" heavily influences each instance of language use.

5 Empirical study

A recurring theme in this chapter is the importance of phraseology to the study of lexical grammar. It has been argued that an explanation for co-occurrence of lexeme and structure may sometimes be found in the more extensive co-text. Inevitably, studies of co-text and phraseology are "messier" than those of lexeme and structure alone. The unit of investigation is not predetermined, and salient items are not easily identified automatically.

In this section I follow up this theme by reporting a study of the co-occurrence of verbs and *wh*-clauses (e.g. *decided whether*, *discovered what*) (Hunston 2003, 2011). The starting point for the study was a simple observation from concordance lines showing the verb DECIDE followed by either a *that*-clause or a *wh*-clause. Each clause type appeared to co-occur disproportionately with one word form: *that*-clauses with *decided* and *wh*-clauses with *decide*. This was in line with Sinclair's (1991) comment that it cannot be assumed that all forms of a lemma will have identical collocational or grammatical profiles, an observation confirmed by Rice and Newman (2008). The first task was to test the initial observation. Is it the case that *that*-clauses co-occur disproportionately with the *-ed* form and *wh*-clauses with the base form? Does this apply to any verb similar in meaning to DECIDE? A total of 25 verb lemmas were selected from the total list of verbs with the two patterns given in Francis *et al.* (1996). For each word form in each lemma, three percentage figures were calculated: what proportion of the total instances of the lemma is accounted for by the word form; what proportion of all the instances of the lemma followed by a *that*-clause is accounted for by the word form; and what proportion of all the instances of the lemma followed by a *wh*-clause is accounted for by the word form. In each case, to what extent do the figures show a differential between the overall word form distribution, the *that*-clause distribution, and the *wh*-clause distribution? Because the corpus used in study was POS tagged but not parsed, *that*-clauses were identified by counting instances of *that* following the word form in question and *wh*-clauses by counting instances of *what, why, whether*, etc. As this inevitably led to inaccuracies, a manual study of 100 concordance lines for each verb was used to estimate the accuracy of the initial figures, and adjustments made where necessary.

The results showed that in general terms the prediction was met: *that*-clauses co-occur disproportionately with *-ed* forms and *wh*-clauses with base forms. Not all lemmas behave the same, though, and this drew attention to phraseology and to the meanings behind the forms. In general, *that*-clauses construe "facts" whereas *wh*-clauses construe "possibilities." For example, *decided that* ... reports a decision that has been taken and now exists. On the other hand, *decide whether* ... reports a decision still to be taken. This is reflected in the fact that the word form *decided* mostly occurs as a finite form whereas *decide* mostly does not, but instead occurs in sequences such as *should decide whether* ..., *had to decide whether* .... This pattern is not true for all verbs, however. The lemma MENTION has a very different distribution pattern from DECIDE, with *mention that* being proportionately more frequent than *decide that*. On further scrutiny of the concordance lines, it was found that *mention that* is largely used to report a negative: someone *did not mention* or *failed to mention* a fact. This highlights a key difference between DECIDE + *that*-clause and MENTION + *that*-clause. In the first case, the act of deciding brings into being the decision reported in the *that*-clause. In the second, the fact in the *that*-clause exists independently of its mention. So whereas *I failed to mention that* ... is unmarked and relatively frequent, *I failed to decide that* ... is marked and is less frequent in relative terms. In other cases, differences in frequency distribution can be accounted for by frequently occurring semi-fixed phrases. For example *figure out that* occurs more frequently than might be expected if DECIDE is taken as the norm. However, the phrases *it doesn't take [an expert] to figure out that* and *you don't have to be [expert] to figure out that* account for this difference.

All this suggests that the original observation regarding DECIDE and its complementation pattern does not reflect arbitrary behavior on the part of English verbs but is a consequence of what typically needs to be said about decisions, things that are mentioned, and so on. Another unexpected observation from the 2003 study was that when the base form of a verb occurs with a *wh*-clause, the word *to* occurs very frequently indeed before the verb. In turn, *to* forms the final element in phrases such as *have to, need to, wanted to, told [someone] to, took a long time to, found it difficult to, make it possible to*, etc. This suggested that the co-occurrence of base form and *wh*-clause was actually part of a more extensive phraseology consisting of "meaning of obligation or difficulty or possibility" followed by "meaning of creating a construct through thought" followed by "construed possibility." The term "semantic sequence" was coined to express a series of meanings of this kind. Whereas a "semantic sequence" is in part an expression of lexical grammar, it goes beyond notions of construction or pattern towards a much looser concept of a sequence of meanings. It suggests that it is the presence of the sequence of meanings that leads to the co-occurrence of lexis and grammar. In other words, just as collocation is a by-product of the existence of units of meaning, so patterns are a by-product of frequently occurring semantic sequences.

In Hunston (2011) there is further work on how modal-like expressions might be identified and on how verbs that disproportionately attract modal meaning might be distinguished from those that do not. Although the outcomes of the study are somewhat speculative, there are some potentially important implications. Establishing that some verbs attract modal meaning (including but not restricted to modal auxiliary verbs) more than others, and that some complementation patterns attract modal meaning more than others, would extend still further Hoey's concept of a "priming" effect of lexis. An attraction of this kind is unlikely to be unique, and other sequences of meaning and lexis can be identified. This concept of semantic sequences can be used to document "what is often said" in English in general or in specific genres.

Having said that, there are considerable difficulties in demonstrating that modal meaning occurs with a particular set of verbs, and these difficulties are apparent in Hunston (2011). The chapter offers a number of individual studies that are indicative of possibilities, but each needs to be taken further and made more robust statistically. There is, for example, no established baseline of frequency of word form distribution or of co-occurrence of modal modification and individual verbs. Without this baseline, skewed frequencies cannot reliably be identified. For example, in the study of ten (base-form) verb sequences (*speculate wh*, *persevere in*, *wonder about*, *agonize over*, *ponder on*, etc.), selected to be representative of the patterning associated with verbs indicating "concerted mental process," eight of the verbs occur relatively infrequently as finite present tenses (the exceptions are *wonder about* and *agonize over*) and in more than half their occurrences are preceded by modal verbs or modal-like expressions indicating obligation, necessity, or possibility. What is not known, however, is to what extent the high incidence of modal meaning or the high incidence of present tense is the norm for the base form of verbs.

6 Conclusion

In this chapter, a number of different approaches to lexical grammar have been outlined, based on Biber's (2012) distinction between "grammar-to-lexis" and "lexis-to-grammar." The various strengths of the different approaches have been discussed, as well as their weaknesses. The implication is that it would be misleading to consider any one approach to have found all the answers. Rather, it is important to consider a number of questions as still open. Whereas combinations of lexis and grammar can be identified, and confirmed statistically, what kind of phenomenon that combination represents should not be taken for granted.

The methodologies used in these sample papers incorporate a number of procedures that are highly valued by corpus linguists. These include: establishing statistical evidence for register variation (Biber *et al.* 1999); making frequency counts meaningful through co-text comparisons (Stefanowitsch and Gries 2003); close attention to patterning going beyond expected feature categories (Hoey 2004). They suggest that corpus output needs to be interpreted both as a set of numbers and as a collection of instances of language.

All the studies seek a balance between rigor (in numbers) and detail (in language). The potential conflict can be illustrated with the pattern/construction "verb + someone + *into* + doing something." Stefanowitsch and Gries's paper lists the thirty verbs with the greatest collostruction strength in this construction. Francis *et al.* (1996) list, without frequency information, those thirty verbs and a further forty-five found to occur with the pattern in the Bank of English corpus. The comprehensive (though statistically uninformative) listing throws up other points of interest that the shorter (though statistically exact) listing misses. For example, Stefanowitsch and Gries include *shame* in their list; other similar verbs found in the pattern are: *frighten*, *scare*, *shock*, *terrify*, and *embarrass*. A sub-construction, then, might be said to be paraphrased as "make someone do something by making them feel and act on an emotion." If the frequency figures for this set of verbs were combined, different quantitative information would be available. Questions have always arisen about which words should be treated as "the same" when calculating frequency. Acts of interpretation such as these lie behind more solid quantitative evidence. In Hoey's study the interpretation (of instances as constituting similarity) is transparent. In *LGSWE* it is less explicit but present in the annotation process that underpins the project.

Studies in lexical grammar are currently pulling in two directions, and any research project has to find a balance between the two. One direction is the refinement of methods to obtain increasingly delicate statistical information. The other is the broadening of the scope of studies into co-occurrences that move beyond grammar, strictly speaking, and into what Hoey calls "textual colligation" (a measure of "naturalness") or what Hunston calls "semantic sequences." Studies of this kind increase the number of variables to be taken into account in calculating relative frequency. Balancing the detail associated with the phraseology of open-class words with the rigor of statistical analysis is a challenge for research into lexical grammar.

12

Using corpora in discourse analysis

Alan Partington and Anna Marchi

1 Introduction: an outline of corpus-assisted discourse studies (CADS)

In the linguistics literature, "discourse" is often defined in two, not mutually exclusive, ways, namely, structurally, for instance, "language above the sentence or above the clause" (Stubbs 1983: 1) and functionally, for example, "language that is doing some job in some context" (Halliday 1985: 10). We shall privilege the functional viewpoint here, though analyzing the structures of discourses is important for shedding light on the jobs being done. It has to be stressed that discourse is not a special form of language, but a perspective upon it, language described not only as a set of interacting units and systems, but also precisely that implied by Halliday, as an instrument put to work. The work which it does is the attempt by one participant or set of participants to influence the ideas, opinions, and behavior of other participants. Such work can be studied in a single text or in a number of tokens of similar texts to try to infer generalities of behaviors and responses (which may well then in turn serve as background to studying particular language events for particular, special meanings).

Most forms of traditional non-corpus-assisted discourse analysis have practiced the close-reading (that is, "qualitative analysis") of single texts or a small number of texts in the attempt to highlight both textual structures and also how meanings are conveyed. Some types, such as much work in critical discourse analysis (CDA), use few concepts from linguistics proper, tending to rely on the analyst's knowledge and experience (and prejudices) of similar texts, in a manner reminiscent of literary analysis (though with a politically driven purpose). Other traditional discourse analysis is more linguistically grounded. Thompson (1996a: 108–112), for instance, demonstrates the power of functional grammar, in particular transitivity analysis, in displaying how meanings, including what we might call *non-obvious* meanings, are communicated. Analyzing a nursing recruitment advertisement, he demonstrates how the grammar itself in subtle ways positions the reader as a certain type of personality (caring and compassionate) and that, as a nurse, your transitivity role, as actor/agent would be to "help patients recover their [own] normal transitivity roles (their normal function as human beings)" (1996a: 112), but without neglecting that a nurse must also have a sensible role as Mental Senser with regard to the real-world Phenomenon of money: "So what sort of money can you expect as a nurse?" (1996a: 111, 112).

In what follows we will attempt to outline ways in which corpus-assisted discourse studies (CADS) can help build upon traditional qualitative linguistic analysis, what "added value" it can bring. We contend that it can contribute in two ways. First, by combining close reading with statistical "overview" analysis, very generally of a large number of tokens of the discourse type under scrutiny, which can enable the analyst to build up a detailed picture of how work is typically performed in that type of discourse. Second, by integrating into the analysis a number of insights into how discourses function which have developed within the field of corpus linguistics.

The three most commonly employed statistical overview techniques are the following. First, frequency listing of words and clusters (that is, strings of words which "are found repeatedly together in each other's company" (Scott 2004), also known as *n*-grams and lexical bundles), which tells us which items and clusters are common in a particular set of texts of a certain discourse. Second, keyword and key-cluster listing, which tells us which items and clusters are more or less frequent in one set of texts, representative of one discourse type, relative to another set, perhaps of another discourse type or of "general," that is, heterogeneric, English (or any other language). Finally, the concordance which searches through large quantities of texts and can collect together and display recurring patternings of words surrounding the search (or "node") item stipulated by the analyst.

The main linguistic insights arising from or developed using corpus-linguistic research include the lexical grammar notion of co-selection, the psychological but also textual theory of lexical priming, and, finally, evaluative cohesion.

The principle of co-selection or co-occurrence states that a far greater proportion of the language of most discourse types is made up, not of the accretion of individual items chosen from the mental lexicon, but of prefabricated or semi-prefabricated collections of items; "chunks" if we prefer. These include simple collocations (defined as two items which regularly co-occur in texts), such as *roaring fire*, proper names like *the Houses of Parliament*, set phrases like *as a matter of fact*, *by all means*, idioms like *never a dull moment*, semi-idiomatic templates, for instance, LIVE *to a [ripe/grand] old age* (Stubbs 2000: 2–3), templates containing fixed parts but also elements of considerable variability, for example, (Locality A) BE *a* number + time-word + vehicle + (*journey, trip, voyage, flight,* etc.) *from* (Locality B), which can be realized as *a twenty-minute bus ride from, a two-hour train journey from, a five-day bike-hike from,* and so on (Hoey 2005: 16–17), and also other abstract items which have what we might call lexical-grammatical satellites orbiting around them, such as *brook* + negative + modal, which can be realized in a wide variety of ways *will brook no . . ., determined not to brook,* and so on (Sinclair 2004a: 36–37). The case study in Section 3 below examines how participants can use such chunking in discourse production to their own ideological advantage.

Lexical priming (Hoey 2005) is a self-reproducing *mental* phenomenon whereby the normal language user learns, by repeated acquaintance with a lexical item and by processes of analogy with other similar items, the typical behavior of that item in interaction. In particular, we learn which other lexical items it co-occurs with regularly (*collocation*), which semantic sets it occurs with (*semantic association*; other authors would favor the term *semantic preference*; see Sinclair 2004a: 32–33, 142), which grammatical categories it co-occurs with or avoids and which grammatical positions it favors or disfavors (*colligation*), which positions in an utterance or sentence or paragraph or entire text it tends to prefer or to avoid occurring in (*textual colligation*), and whether it tends to participate in cohesion or not.

The user then reproduces this behavior in their own linguistic performance. By metaphorical extension, the lexical item itself is said to be primed to behave in these particular ways, and so lexical priming is also regarded as a *textual* phenomenon. Thus, for example, the item *winter* is said to be primed to collocate with *in, that, during the,* etc. As regards colligational behavior, Hoey's most complex examination is of the colligational behaviour of the item *consequence*. He looks at 1,809 occurrences in his corpus data (a 100-million-word corpus of *Guardian* newspaper texts) and discovers first of all that it displays a clear aversion to appearing as part of the object of a sentence (4% of occurrences) but no such aversion to appearing as part of a verb complement (24%). Given that, exactly as with many types of research, the relevance of such individual findings can only be evaluated by comparison with the behavior of other items, he also looks at four other abstract nouns, *question, preference, aversion,* and *use*, none of which exhibits the same absence from object position (occurring there, respectively, on 27%, 38%, 38%, and 34% of occurrences).

The principle of evaluative cohesion, very closely associated with coselection, states that, in normal circumstances, speakers and writers will attempt to maintain consistency or "harmony" of evaluation – of the evaluative polarity, good or bad – at local moments in discourse production. Evaluation is here intended as "the indication of whether the speaker thinks that something (a person, thing, action, event, situation, idea, etc.) is good or bad" (Thompson 1996a: 65). It is not difficult to demonstrate how items with the same evaluation tend to cluster together. The item *fraught with* is normally chosen precisely because it "fits" with other items of negative evaluation and a concordance offers the following illustrations of clustering of items of similar (negative) evaluation (examples from the SiBol newspaper corpus, see Section 2):

(1) The seven-year journey from that dazzling sales pitch in the Far East to the reality of 2012 will be *complicated* and *arduous*, and after Thursday we must *fear* it will be **fraught with** the *rawest of hazards* for ordinary citizens. (SiBol 05)

(2) But *appearances can be deceptive* – these funds can be **fraught with** *danger*. The managers buy *riskier* bonds to add to the mix to boost the income. (SiBol 05)

Such evaluative harmony is normally taken for granted and only becomes apparent when, for dramatic or ironic effect, a speaker/writer chooses to upset it by combining items of opposing evaluative polarity within the same text, for example, *an outbreak of honesty, the onslaught of goodwill and attention* (SiBol), when both *outbreak of* and *onslaught of* very generally co-occur with negative items. The concordancer is an excellent way of locating examples of such prosodic clash. It has also proved invaluable, through its ability to collect large numbers on instances of use in context, as a means of uncovering the evaluative polarity of many items which was not previously apparent to the naked eye, such as *set in, dealings, utterly, potentially, sit through, orchestrate, true feelings*, and *par for the course* (generally negative) and *flexible, persevere, provide, career, my place, make a difference*, and *brimming with* (generally positive).

The main function of evaluative cohesion and the consistency of evaluation at local points in the discourse is to help maintain comprehensibility for the listener, since it meets rather than upsets primed expectations. A discourse needs to make sense not only ideationally but also at the evaluative level.

Both lexical priming and evaluation will be highly relevant to the case study in Section 3.

2 A survey of previous CADS research

2.1 Corpus-assisted studies of sociopolitical discourses: (im)migration, race, gender

In this survey we concentrate on sociopolitical CADS, that is, a branch of linguistics in which corpora are employed to help study how social and political phenomena are represented and constructed in the cultural products of a society. A pioneer in the formulation of this type of research is Stubbs (1996 and 2001b), who was one of the first scholars to propose and promote the synergic use of corpus linguistics and discourse analysis. The core idea is that a mixed-approach "has the empirical data and the hermeneutic methods to try out some new approaches to long-standing problems, and should therefore try to move from the descriptive to explanatory adequacy" (Stubbs 2006: 34).

Comparative analysis of lexical patterns is a powerful tool to investigate how social, cultural, and political representations, such as gender or race, are constructed and reinforced by the accumulation of linguistic patterns. Scholars have used collocation analysis to study the discourse of sexual and gender difference. Stubbs (1996) analyzes striking differences in Baden-Powell's messages to guides and scouts and shows, for example, how the former are "full of references to men," as well as family (*husband, children*), whilst the latter make "no mention of women" or family (1996: 84). Pearce (2008) examines the differences between the lemmas *man* and *woman* in the BNC, classifying their collocates in semantic domains, including physical appearance, attitudes and interests, psychological traits, social relations, and occupations, and finding in all domains a reinforcement of gender stereotypes. Baker (2006 and 2008) compares the terms *spinster* and *bachelor*, also in the BNC and shows, for example, the cultural stigmatization of spinsters that emerges from the collocates, for instance, we find *eligible* bachelors, but *frustrated* spinsters.[1] Baker (2010) looks at gendered terms (such as *girl* and *boy* and male and female pronouns and titles) in the four British diachronic corpora of the Brown family, demonstrating the usefulness of diachronic corpora for getting social snapshots of an age. Taylor (2013) examines differences and similarities in the representation of *boy/s* and *girl/s* in the British press over time, from 1993 to 2010. The representation of females in infantilized/sexualized ways was seen to be a continuous feature of newspaper discourse over the time period but she also found that *boy/s* were increasingly characterized in these ways over time. Macalister (2011) examines gender constructions in children's books over a ninety-year period. Whilst he finds confirmation of the gender stereotypes which emerged in previous research he also registers an increased visibility and emphasis on individuality regarding girls. Baker (2005) compares the discourses surrounding *gay(s)* and *homosexual(s)* and other related terms in various corpora, including parliamentary debates and articles from two politically opposed British tabloids, the *Daily Mail* and the *Mirror*, and transcripts of the sit-com *Will & Grace*. Examining the collocates of *gay(s)* and *homosexual(s)*, he shows how the word *gay* presents an element of self-definition that is not there in the term (of medical derivation) *homosexual*. He also argues, through a review of collocates, that homosexuality in general is presented as a behavior (and a definitely negative one) rather than an identity in the tabloid press.

Other collocational research has focused on the representation of minorities. In his seminal paper Krishnamurthy (1996) analyzes how the words *ethnic, racial*, and *tribal* are used, juxtaposing three different kinds of

[1] This does not imply that *bachelor* is characterized in a univocally positive way. Baker highlights also how the term (and consequently the identity) is, for instance, associated with a man's inability to take care of himself and with loneliness.

materials: individual newspaper articles, dictionaries, and a large corpus of English. What is particularly interesting in Krishnamurthy's paper in terms of CADS methodology is the combination of perspectives and windows onto the data. He begins with the close reading of newspaper articles that inspire the analysis, then looks at dictionary definitions, and finally he examines the collocational profiles of the target words in a general corpus. From the comparative profile of collocates, we learn, for example, that *ethnic* and *tribal* tend to be associated with specific groups, with the second focusing on a particular group's members, while *racial* is used in a more abstract way. The main activity related to *racial* is *discrimination*, where the *race* is the "Done-to"; with *ethnic* it is *violence*; and with *tribal* the violence is made specific as with *killing* – in both of the latter cases the named group is more likely to be "Doer."

A further influential example of corpus-assisted discourse analysis, also related to ethnicity, is the Lancaster University project on the representation of refugees, asylum seekers, and immigrants (or RASIM). Baker and McEnery (2005) looked at the discourses surrounding refugees and asylum seekers in two kinds of texts, UK newspaper articles and United Nations documents. Rather than comparing the corpora directly (for instance, using keywords analysis) the researchers analyzed collocational patterns in the two sets of texts, they identified categories of how RASIM were portrayed, such as "quantification," "movement," "tragedy," "aid," and "crime," and they compared findings for the two corpora. This kind of analysis of collocates (that is, of commonly co-occurring lexis) makes similarity visible as well as difference and allows for a comprehensive view of the representation of identities, that are often complex and intertwined. This research was followed up and expanded in the project *Discourses of Refugees and Asylum Seekers in the UK Press 1996–2006*,[2] where two groups of scholars, one consisting of corpus linguists and the other of critical discourse analysts (see Section 1 above) attempted to combine theoretical backgrounds and methods traditionally associated with their respective fields (Baker *et al.* 2008). The study fails to fulfill its promise of methodological integration between CDA and corpus linguistics given that, during the course of the research, the two teams operated largely independently from one another. While not a convincing example of "synergy," the RASIM work is, nevertheless, particularly interesting from a methodological point of view because it describes a variety of ways of entering the data and adopts a range of different perspectives, such as looking at diachronic change or stability of representations, at political stance differences and comparing styles between quality and popular newspapers (Gabrielatos and Baker 2008). The researchers used a number of tools: they traced the temporal distribution of RASIM stories, identifying "spikes" and "troughs" of press interest; they performed an extensive

[2] For further details see www.ling.lancs.ac.uk/activities/285/.

collocation analysis of the target terms and grouped collocates into semantic categories and they looked at "consistent-collocates" (that is, collocates that remain stable over time and are therefore unlikely to be the product of a particular event), showing how some discourses are progressively confirmed and reinforced. Among the discourses reinforced by repeated co-occurrence there is, for example, a moral panic about quantity prompted by the widespread use of negative metaphors of *flooding, streaming, pouring*, or the discourse of illegality created by collocates such as *caught, detained, smuggled*.

While in the case of RASIM the researchers track the evolution of discourses over a continuous period of time, another series of diachronic studies compares corpora from different points in time in order to identify change or stability. An instance of this is the SiBol set of CADS which employs comparable newspaper corpora from 1993, 2005, and 2010 (see Partington 2010a; Partington *et al.* 2013). Since the SiBol corpora contain the whole output of the newspapers for their years, a wide range of different topics can be researched, sociolinguistic as well as purely linguistic (lexical and grammatical), and since the particular newspapers were the left-leaning *Guardian*, the right-leaning *Telegraph*, and the centrist *Times*, sociopolitical issues can be viewed and contrasted from different perspectives. Partington (2010b) identifies which social concerns were labeled "moral panics" by the left and by the right in 1993 and then in 2005, to see which ones remained (for example, juvenile crime), which disappeared (for example, lone parents, trade unions, abortion), and appeared (for example, immigration, binge-drinking, obesity). Duguid (2010a) examines the word prefix *anti* in order to track the changes in the items it premodifies and the changes in social and political concerns they reflect, noting, for instance, the rise in mentions of *anti-capitalism, anti-money*, and *anti-globalisation*, and also of *anti-gun, anti-bullying*, and *anti-slavery*. Taylor (2010) uses the same corpora to look at the ways *science* is represented in the press over time, observing how the "other" to science projected by the UK press changes from "culture" and "the arts" in 1993 to "religion" in 2005. Marchi (2010) looks at what the press portrays as pertaining to the moral domain and how this changes over time. She finds a general decrease in the use of the label *moral*, a growing reference to the notion of *moral relativism*, and a tendency to see *morality* as belonging to the personal rather than social sphere. She also highlights how the inductive data-driven "funnelling" process commonly used in CADS, which consists of looking at the data, finding patterns, restricting the analysis to that phenomenon/portion is prolific in generating new questions (2010: 164). Partington (2012) examines discussions of anti-Semitism. In the earlier material it was seen largely as a historical phenomenon or restricted to Eastern Europe but concerns about a resurgence of the phenomenon in certain religious and political circles in Western Europe are widespread in the recent data. Duguid (2010b) analyzes the evolution of UK broadsheet journalistic style over time, noting an increase both in informal style (for instance, use of vague lexis) and in overt expressions of evaluation (for example, a much greater use of hyperbole and positive evaluation, very probably reflecting an ever-growing inclusion of PR material in the magazine sections), all evidence that the so-called "quality" press is increasingly adopting linguistic practices typical of their tabloid rivals.

2.2 Comparison across discourse-types

Discourse analysis is, of course, inherently comparative; it is only possible to both uncover and evaluate the particular features of a discourse type by comparing it with others. We are not deontologically justified in making statements about the relevance of a phenomenon observed to occur in one discourse type unless, where it is possible, we compare how the phenomenon behaves elsewhere. Several corpus techniques, for example, keyword and key-cluster tools, have the specific aim of facilitating comparison. We can compare between corpora or within a corpus (for example, for different speaker roles such as questioner and responder) and we can compare a specialized corpus to a general (or "heterogeneric") one. We have discussed diachronic comparisons, but the parameters and entities to be compared can be various. Bondi (2008), for example, analyzes the role played by stance markers in academic journals for two different disciplines, namely history and economics. Bednarek (2006) compares the evaluation of the European constitution in the British broadsheets and tabloids, finding pervasive and consistent negative evaluation of the EU in the latter, while encountering a less monolithic and not univocally Eurosceptic attitude in the former. We can also compare across languages and/or different geographical and political entities. Bayley *et al.* (2012) also examines attitudes towards the EU, focusing on the semantic construction of citizenship and identity in the British, French, and Italian media, where the researchers confirm the stronger sense of "Europeness" and sometimes perhaps acritical positive evaluation of European citizenship expressed in the press in France and Italy compared to the UK. If the corpus is compiled and marked-up to identify speaker turns, we can compare different speakers, as in Taylor (2009) on friendly and hostile examination in the Hutton Inquiry, or Bachman (2011) on the debate in the British Parliament over same-sex marriage where speeches in favour and speeches against are compared. In addition to comparison between corpora and subcorpora, we can also compare different words within a corpus, for example, near-synonyms (e.g. *climate change, global warming*, and *greenhouse effect* in Grundman and Krishnamurthy 2010), or related concepts, as in the previously mentioned research on gender. Undoubtedly the most influential work in corpus-assisted comparative discourse analysis is Biber *et al.* (1999), which describes in systematic and exhaustive detail the lexical-grammatical features of four very different macro-discourse types, namely conversation, fiction, newspaper language, and academic prose, and uses the analyses to infer a general grammar of English. It is the most data-grounded and data-rich description of the language every produced.

Other CADS work looks at the interaction between discourse types. Duguid (2009) investigates that between political discourse and news discourse by analyzing the presentation of "voices" in a multi-genre corpus[3] about the Iraq war in 2003. Employing Thompson's (1996b) framework, she studies how speech events are embedded in one another by means of attribution and, following the traces of speech representation, she demonstrates empirically how messages move from the political arena via the media to the public.

From Stubbs on, several CADS researchers have found it useful to combine linguistics with other disciplines and Bednarek's recent work on TV dialogue (Bednarek 2010) and on language in different news media (see Bednarek and Caple 2012) integrates notions from the fields of semiotics, media studies, and sociolinguistics in the study of multimodal data (vision and speech). Cotter (2010) is an interdisciplinary study of journalistic language from the perspective of the newsworkers, combining linguistics and newsroom ethnography, and it employs a wide range of data, ranging from news stories themselves to interviews with news practitioners and episodes of communication among them. By integrating input from different sources as well as combining analytical tools, Cotter offers a comprehensive account of the context of newsmaking and bridges the gap between traditional analysis of the message (discourse as product) and production research (discourse as process).

2.3 Reflections on the methodologies of corpus-assisted discourse studies

According to Johnson's (2012) content analysis of the *International Journal of Corpus Linguistics*, the interest in using corpora to study discourse has grown in recent years. There is also increasing reflection on methodological aspects, with studies addressing issues of accuracy, accountability, and potential research shortcomings, a discussion on good practices that seems particularly important for a territory of research in expansion. Taylor (2013) points out that there is an embedded tendency in CADS research to focus on difference, while overlooking similarity. Critics of corpus linguistics claim that corpus research is not well equipped to identify what is absent; Taylor (2012) illustrates ways to overcome this potential failing. Some experimental work on replicability (Marchi and

[3] The *CorDis* corpus: an XML marked-up collection of subcorpora, including sources of news creation (British House of Commons and US House of Representatives debates), negotiation between news creators and news mediators (White House press briefings), news messages (British and American TV news programs, news reports, and comment articles from British and US quality and popular press), and the Hutton judicial inquiry (Morley and Bayley 2009).

Taylor 2009 and Baker 2011) has been carried out in order to investigate ways of ensuring that corpus-assisted procedures, given the sometimes very large numbers of text tokens it handles, are as transparent and as accessible to other researchers as possible. Stubbs (2001b: 124) and Partington (2009: 293–294) discuss the question of what the latter terms *para-replicability*, that is, the replication of an analysis with either a fresh set of texts of the same discourse type or of a related discourse type, "in order to see whether [findings] were an artefact of one single data set" (Stubbs 2001b: 124) or whether they can be considered more generally valid, clearly an important scientific procedure in the analysis of features of any discourse type.

3 A case study: *forced primings* in White House briefings

By means of this case study on political discourse we wish to demonstrate a number of ways in which "added value" can be brought to discourse analysis by the integration of corpus techniques. In particular, we wish to show first how the concordancer's ability to collect examples of a similar linguistic phenomenon, as contained in repeated word strings or clusters, can lead to insights into the intentions of discourse participants, second how corpus techniques can enable the tracking of discourse features over time, and third how, contrary to charges from some quarters, corpora can shed light on what is absent from a dataset under examination and what this might signify. At the same time we will illustrate the typical CADS methodology of moving back and forth between statistical overview analysis (keywords and concordancing in this case) and close textual reading.

The overall topic is a study of the discourse type of White House press briefings during the opening period of the Arab Uprisings. It examines both the phenomenon of *forced primings* (Duguid 2007) – that is, the strategic flooding by linguistic means of messages favorable to speakers or their clients into an ongoing discourse – and also the related phenomenon of competition amongst speakers to have their messages, their reading of events, accepted by either interlocutors or an audience of beneficiaries (the party for whom the language event is taking place; Halliday 1994: 144; Partington 2003: 57–58). "Priming" is of course a term borrowed from Hoey (2005), who argues that individuals are primed to ingest a semi-conscious knowledge of the properties and meanings of lexical items by repeated exposure in interaction with others (Section 1 above). We contend that a roughly similar priming process can occur when individuals are repeatedly exposed to clusters and word patterns expressing the same underlying meaning, and that the process can be effected deliberately, a form of semi-subliminal persuasion.

3.1 The corpus used in the analysis: White House press briefings

White House press briefings are press conferences held on a regular basis, in normal times, daily. They are a particular type of *institutional talk* (Drew and Heritage 1992), which is defined as talk between professionals and lay people, but the definition can be stretched, as here, to include talk between two groups of professionals with an audience of lay persons (the TV and internet audience). Briefings are a particularly fascinating genre of institutional talk in that they combine features of informal talk, given that the participants meet so often and know each other well, and confrontational or "strategic" talk. The two parties involved – the spokesperson or Podium (officially known as the White House Press Secretary) and the press – have very different interests and aims, which are in conflict on several levels. The Podium wishes to project his political ideas and particular view of the world, the press to test that view, often suggesting more critical alternatives. The press hopes to uncover ever more information, including any evidence of weakness, malpractice, internal dissension, and so on, whereas the Podium ideally wants to give as little away as possible outside the official line of his employers (Partington 2003). Moreover, the stakes are very high. Not only are the Podium's words often treated by the press as White House policy, but they risk interpretation by non-American bodies as official US policy. Since they are broadcast both on television and on the internet, "any misstep can be beamed instantaneously around the world" (*CNN-allpolitics*).

The corpus of briefings employed here is called WH-Obama, and contains all the briefings of the Obama administration in the year from December 2010 to the end of November 2011 (*c.* 1,300,000 words, compiled by Franconi 2011). For comparison purposes, we also use WH-Bush, containing briefings from the George W. Bush administration (*c.* 3,400,000 words, compiled by Riccio 2009).

3.2 Asserting the administration's message, imposing primings in briefings

From the point of view of the White House, the whole raison d'être of briefings, the reason they were instituted in the first place, is to affirm the administration's favored view of events to the press and through them to the public. To this end, the Podium's discourse is replete with repeated phrases, often with minor variation. This was first noted in earlier research whilst both watching briefings, broadcast by C-Span public service TV, and by reading a good number of transcripts (Partington 2003). To study this phenomenon, we prepared lists of relatively long clusters – 4, 5, 6, and 7 items in length – using the WordSmith Wordlist Tool. Individual items which reoccurred in these clusters could then be concordanced in the hope of throwing light on the nature of messages being launched. For instance, the concordance of *realize* in the WH-Bush corpus yields

25 occurrences of HELP *the Iraqi people realize a better future / a better and brighter future / a free and peaceful future*. A concordance of *job* in the same corpus reveals how the Podium uses it to praise some party, typically some member of the government or service personnel abroad. Of the 250 occurrences, 23 are of the form, *do* an* [intensifier] *job* (for instance, the President / Secretary Rice / our troops are *doing an outstanding/superb/terrific job*). Others are of the form *we greatly appreciate the job they are doing* or we will *make sure our troops have all the tools/resources they need to get the job done / do their job*. This use of *job* in expressing messages of praise – of positive evaluation for some person or people – is entirely absent from the press's language; indeed commendation of any kind is much rarer in journalists' turns.

In the first six months of the WH-Obama corpus, on the other hand, in times of severe economic crisis, *job* collocates 101 times in the Podium's speech with *grow* and *growth* in constructions like [our aim is to] *drive / increase job creation and economic growth* and, in fact, *grow the economy and increase job creation* is the most common long cluster in the corpus.

It is true that, as Biber *et al.* remark, spoken discourse is particularly characterized by an abundance of (semi-)prefabricated phrases (see Section 1):

> Time pressure makes it more difficult for speakers [compared to writers] to exploit the full innovative power of grammar and the lexicon: instead they rely heavily on well-worn, prefabricated word sequences, readily accessible from memory. *(Biber* et al. *1999: 1049)*

But the kind of repeated sequences we see here are very often longer and syntactically more complex than Biber *et al.*'s examples of prefabs (or "lexical bundles," as they term them) from conversation, such as, *Can I have a . . . ?, Do you know what . . . ?*

The cluster lists of WH-Obama contained several clusters containing WORK and concordancing this item showed that, in the same six months, the Podium uses *we* + WORK a total of 198 times, often accompanied by a positively evaluating intensifier: *we are working avidly, we have worked assiduously / diligently / aggressively / very hard / every day*. In a keyword list comparing WH-Obama with the one-million-word spoken section of the BNC Sampler (a collection of diverse discourse types) the following items all appeared among the top 200 keywords: *continue* (as in *continue our efforts, continue to work on . . .*), *forward* (*move the economy forward, as we go forward to create an America that . . .*), *action, progress, effort/efforts, measures, steps, commitment, decision/decisions*. The attempt is made to portray and evaluate the White House and their political affiliates generally as active to the point of workaholism. However, the impression (and positive evaluation) is not shared by at least one journalist in the room:

(1) Q: Why does the Congress and the President and Washington generally act like a college kid and wait until the last minute to get everything done? (20/12/2010)

It is sometimes possible, moreover, with the benefit of corpus techniques, to observe how White House messages evolve, how the exact nature of the primings flooding into the discourse changes over time, which provides strong evidence of deliberate attempted linguistic engineering. This temporal tracking is possible since each briefing is contained in a separate file which is named by date.

For instance, in a study of how the Arab revolts were debated in the briefings, the first step was to concordance the names of some of the countries involved, namely, *Libya/Libyan(s)*, *Syria/Syrian(s)*, and *Egypt/Egyptian(s)*, along with the names of the countries' leaders, *Qaddafi*, *Assad*, and *Mubarak*. In January 2011, *Libya* or *Libyan* is not mentioned in the briefings room. In February, both the Podium and press are comfortable in discussing the Libyan *government*, which is mentioned 32 times, but in March only 9 times, and after that never at all (except a couple of times in the context of freezing Libyan government assets). In the same February, there are 6 mentions of the Libyan *regime* and 6 of the *Qaddafi regime*. By March, however, *regime* is used a total of 58 times, 37 co-occurring with *Qaddafi* and 21 with *Libyan*. In the final six months of the year, we find only *Qaddafi* with *regime* and never *Libyan*. The evaluatively neutral *Libyan government* has rapidly been replaced in briefings discourse with the negative *Qaddafi regime* in a priming shift to create diplomatic distance between the White House and the Libyan administration. Perhaps the most interesting aspect is that *Libyan government* disappears from the journalists' speech almost as quickly as from the Podium's. They clearly acquiesce to the White House's message and evaluations on this issue or, if we prefer, the administration's priming flooding has been successful.

There is a similar process of diplomatic distancing regarding Syria in WH-Obama, but the process is slower and not complete. In the first six months of 2011, we find 48 occurrences of *Syrian government* and only 3 of *Syrian regime*. In the second six months, there are 34 references to *Syrian*

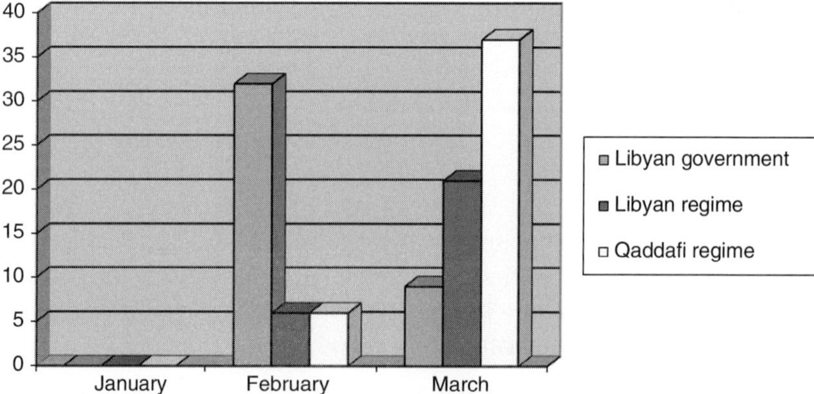

Figure 12.1 How the briefings participants refer to the Libyan administration in the first three months of 2011

regime but it is still called *government* 18 times, all by the Podium. The Podium's language towards the Syrian leader is also gentler than that used about Qaddafi. Throughout the year he continues to be called "*President* Assad," whilst Qaddafi moves from "*Colonel*" or "*Muammar* Qaddafi" to predominantly just "Qaddafi." When the White House in August 2011 finally deems the Syrian leader to have *lost his legitimacy*, he is asked to *step aside* (previously simply to *change course* or *cease the violence*) and there is no talk of *remove/removal* from power, as for Qaddafi.

There is also an evolution in the administration's evaluative messages regarding Egypt, but once again a different one. The administration in general and the Podium in particular are clearly wrongfooted and embarrassed by events. The item *Mubarak* was concordanced month by month (this is possible since, we might recall, each briefing is contained in a separate file which is named by date). Although occasionally simply "Mubarak" for the press, the Podium refers throughout the year to "*President* Mubarak." We then passed from the concordance to close reading of the co-text around occurrences of *Mubarak*, a very common process in corpus-assisted discourse studies. He is initially praised as "a close and important partner with our country" (27/01/2011) and the President even praises the Egyptian army just before news breaks of its failure to protect protestors (02/02/2011). The Podium cannot bring himself to condemn the President:

(2) Q: And as you stand today, you still back President Mubarak?
MR.: GIBBS Again Egypt is a strong ally. (26/01/2011)

As the violence grows, much of it reportedly committed by supporters of the President, the Podium is asked the straight question:

(3) Q: Do you think Mubarak is a dictator?

Realizing this phrasing might afford the Podium some room for footing evasion (perhaps "it's not important what I think"), the journalist switches the target or *recipientship* (Partington 2003: 51) of the question to the President:

(4) Q: More importantly does the President think Mubarak is a dictator?

But they are still not obliged with a straight answer:

(5) The administration believes that President Mubarak has a chance to show the world exactly who he is by beginning this transition which is so desperately needed in his country and for his people now. (02/02/2011)

Instead the Podium's repeated message is that of urging (maximum) *restraint/nonviolence*, sometimes *on all sides*. One journalist at least becomes frustrated at this priming flooding:

(6) Q: "Deeply concerned," "urging restraint" – to this point, from my knowledge, no US official has come out and condemned the violence. Is it time to condemn the violence?

This seems indeed to shame the Podium into slightly stronger language:

(7) MR GIBBS: Let's be clear Mike. Urging restraint and then seeing violence is obviously very counter to what we believe should be had. And we would strongly condemn the use of violence on either side during this situation, absolutely. (28/01/2011)

But note *on either side*. And *condemn the violence* is not the same as directly condemning the perpetrators of the violence. At this point, we concordanced month-by-month the items *violence* and *side(s)* and the co-text of the resulting occurrences were read. No mention is forthcoming, regarding Libya, about the violence committed by opponents of the regime, nor reference to condemning violence *on both/all/either side(s)*, as was the case with Egypt. In fact a concordance of *restraint* and another of *violen** in an 8-word span of *on either/both/all sides* yielded altogether 18 results, all of them contained in the Podium's turns. The countries where, according to the White House Podium, *both* sides in a conflict – that is, the government/regime and its opponents – need to refrain from violence and exercise restraint are principally Bahrain (7 occurrences) and Yemen (5).[4] The message is, in contrast, used twice about Egypt, just once about Syria, and is completely absent in discourses about Libya, where there is only *one* side seen as perpetrating violence, as the following typical statement implies:

(8) MR CARNEY: Well, let me just say that the President strongly condemns [...] the bloodshed perpetrated by the Libyan government in Libya. (23/02/2011)

This is an indication (admittedly limited given the small sample) that the administration is unwilling to take sides against the comparatively "friendly" governments of Bahrain and Yemen, but exhibits no such qualms about the rulers in Libya and Syria, who had long been seen as less than congenial by many in the West.

By the beginning of February, alongside *restraint* in Egypt, the White House also begins to flood the discourse with calls for (*orderly*) *transition* (67 occurrences in the month) which at times must *begin now*, and for *progress, change* and *free and fair elections* (this last phrase is used by the Podium 39 times, from 28 January to the end of February):

(9) MR GIBBS [...] I think this underscores precisely what the President was speaking about last night, and that is the time for a **transition** has come and that time is **now**. The Egyptian people need to see **change**. We know that that **meaningful transition** must include opposition voices and parties being involved in this process as we move toward **free and fair elections**. But that process must **begin now**. (02/02/2011)

[4] The remaining three refer not to Arab Spring protests but to the Israelis and Palestinians.

Analysis of keywords and key-clusters lists, using WH-Bush as reference corpus, reveals other repeated Middle East foreign policy messages. The Podium affirms that in Libya, Syria, and Egypt *people* have *legitimate aspirations* (19), *legitimate grievances* (16) (but "Bahrain is a very different case," 21/03/2011). Because a *humanitarian crisis* is unfolding in Libya, the US provides *humanitarian assistance/relief*, which includes, rather bizarrely, *non-lethal* humanitarian relief:

(10) MR DONILON: [...] And again, it would have to be worked out with the opposition group that control various aspects in the east, but they could also be air provisions of non-lethal humanitarian relief. (10/03/2011)

This would make air provisions of *lethal* humanitarian relief an intriguing euphemism indeed, a very novel evaluative clash (see end of Section 1). To stress that the US is not acting alone, in the keyword lists we find *partners, allies, together with, international, coalition*, and *multilateral*, but to avoid any accusation of lack of initiative or of weakness, also *US leadership*. Finally, *each/every country* co-occurs 40 times with *different*, for example:

(11) MR. CARNEY: Well Dan, as we've said, **each country** that has been affected by this unrest is **different. Each country** in the region is **different. Each country** has **different** traditions, political systems and relationships with the United States and other countries around the world. (24/02/2011)

This illustrates the Podium's stock response to questions on why the administration's evaluative reaction to the various regional uprisings was so different, from bombing in Libya, to diplomatic pressure in Egypt, to kid gloves over Syria and Bahrain (see also Franconi 2011).

Throughout this section, the methodology followed is the recursive "shunting" between concordancing and close reading then back to concordancing salient items noted during the close reading, very common practice in CADS work.

3.3 Institutions and forced priming

Our knowledge, use, and expectations of language are, of course, determined by our exposure to language in context but, as we see in briefings, not all exposure is the result of random personal experience. The above episodes constitute what we have called *forced priming*. Frequently repeated phraseologies – *getting the job done, each country is different*, and so on – result in evaluative messages being deliberately flooded into the discourse for a particular purpose. Institutions and enterprises spend considerable investment in encouraging priming through planned repetition, a process Fairclough has called the "technologisation" of discourse (1996: 71–83), and for this reason it can be illuminating to employ concordancing and key-item comparison to examine frequency data in institutional discourse.

In an age of mass communication and near instant reproduction of multimedia material, there is increased care and attention paid by institutions to how their desired messages are conveyed. Those who have the information gatekeeping role, including the Podiums in the White House, as well as government special advisers (Duguid 2009; Taylor 2009), are, of course, professional discourse technicians.

3.4 Tracking appearance and disappearance of items: governments and regimes in White House briefings

There is a general methodological point which emerges from these investigations. It has been claimed by non-corpus-assisted discourse analysts that "the corpus-based analysis tends to focus on what *has* been explicitly written, rather than what *could have been* written but was not" (Wodak 2007 quoted in Baker *et al.* 2008: 296). However, it is only by having this set of briefings texts compiled into a corpus and accessible to keyword and concordancing software that we were able first of all to assert with some confidence the complete absence of discussions of these countries prior to a certain date or that, say, Assad is never referred to as a "dictator" in the entire SiBol 2010 newspaper datasets (see Section 2 on SiBol).

Indeed, corpus linguistics techniques actually allow us to cross-compare the discourses around the different countries and their leaders and, furthermore, to *identify* absences, to *quantify* the relative absence or presence of certain messages, and to *track over time* how certain messages can move into or out of the ongoing discourse between the White House and the press.

For example, we were able to identify the absence of any mention of Libya or Qaddafi in the briefings before February 2011; it just was not on the press's map.

We were able to track changes in the denomination of the various Arab country administrations and in the honorifics or dishonorifics applied to the leaders, for instance that *Libyan government* rapidly disappears – becomes absent – whilst *Qadaffi regime*, previously absent, becomes the normal appellation.

In terms of quantifying *relative* absence versus presence we can contrast the fact that the *Colonel* of *Colonel Qaddafi* quickly disappears – becomes absent – whilst the honorific *President* continues over the period to be applied to *Mubarak*. The concordance of all/both *sides* allowed us to identify the countries where both government and opposition were urged to *show restraint* and those where only the government was being blamed for the violence.

One general observation is also highly pertinent here. In the first part of this study outlining forced priming keyword and key-cluster analyses were conducted contrasting WH-Obama with both the BNC and WH-Bush. Of course the entire raison d'être of keywording, a vital tool in the corpus linguistic kit, is to ascertain and quantify the relative presence in and absence from a target corpus of lexical items – that is what "keyness" means – usually as a first step in investigating what that relative presence/absence may infer.

It is hard to see how, without the corpus techniques or some extremely time-consuming substitute for them, any firm, objective statements on these matters could be made. Before debating "what is implied, inferred, insinuated or latently hinted at" (Baker *et al.* 2008: 296), one needs to ascertain what actually *was* and *was not* said or written, and the corpus-assisted discourse analyst would appear to be in a good position to do so.

4 Conclusion

The most obvious advantage of integrating corpus resources into discourse analysis is the potential it offers for analyzing large numbers of tokens of any particular discourse type, which enables the analyst to study typical discourse structures, typical ways of saying things, and typical messages, alongside the local structures, meanings, and messages available to traditional close reading. It also provides a way of locating potentially interesting linguistic features – for instance, sites of unusual evaluation – in a large body of texts, which the analyst can then home in upon. Additionally, it facilitates comparison among discourse types, highlighting the relative frequency and the possible different roles of the linguistic features they display, for instance, differences in collocational patterning or "profile" of the "same" lexical item or set of items.

There remains one final methodological-theoretical consideration. As in all research, there is much in corpus linguistics that is subjective, including the choice of research question and of the procedures and software to employ, not to mention the interpretation of the output data. However, there is one phase at least, namely the statistical analyses performed by the machine, where the analyst cannot either consciously or unconsciously predetermine the output and, when it arrives, s/he must deal with whatever it contains, including, and especially, things previously unexpected. These latter may include "known unknowns"; for instance, Marchi (2010) knew that some issues would be discussed in moral terms in the UK press in 1993 and 2005, but she did not, until the data analysis, know which. Or they may include "unknown unknowns"; for example, Duguid's (2010b) discovery of large numbers of explicitly evaluative keywords in the 2005 SiBol newspaper data, as compared to that of 1993 (see above), was entirely unanticipated, and an explanation needed to be sought and categorizations of the lexis developed. In this sense then corpus-assisted research, including that into discourse, is partly data-driven; intuitions themselves deriving serendipitously from data observation can often direct the course of the research, especially by encountering the unexpected, including counterexamples which challenge the initial research hypothesis. It is very generally when the possible insights of the analyst – their chances of finding things – are not entirely predetermined, and therefore constrained, by his or her initial theoretical framework and also perhaps by the paucity of data available, that advances in knowledge can be made.

13

Pragmatics

Brian Clancy and Anne O'Keeffe

1 Introduction

Corpus pragmatics is a methodological framework that allows for the interpretation of spoken or written meaning, with an emphasis on providing empirical evidence for this interpretation (see O'Keeffe *et al.* 2011). It is a relatively recent development within the field of corpus linguistics and interest in this "subfield" has blossomed as spoken corpora have become more readily available. Meaning is an elusive concept to say the least but what is clear is that participants in interaction, especially those engaged in spoken discourse, negotiate meaning through a series of sometimes almost barely perceptible "clues" that are supplied by the participants themselves, their shared knowledge (both personal and cultural) and the situation in which the interaction takes place. Given that classical pragmatics has its roots in the philosophy of language, traditionally, the study of pragmatics has employed an interpretative methodology in order to account for this negotiation of meaning. Therefore, many of the illustrative examples are invented rather than "attested" or "in use." Corpus linguistics has emerged as a sympathetic methodological companion for the study of pragmatics providing researchers with representative samples of real-life language in use, and an attendant empirical tradition.

Corpus pragmatics is distinct from other fields in corpus linguistics. However, in common with other fields, corpus pragmatics investigates the co-textual patterns of a linguistic item or items, which encompasses lexico-grammatical features such as collocation or semantic prosody. However, where corpus pragmatics' "added value" lies is in its insistence that these patterns be considered in light of the *context* – the situational, interpersonal, and cultural knowledge that interactional participants share. Through an iterative process, corpus pragmatics therefore moves beyond important but surface observations of lexico-grammatical patterns to allow a more nuanced interpretation of these patterns taking into consideration who uses them, where they were used, for what purposes, and how this use has changed over time. In this way, corpus pragmatics has retained in part its original interpretative nature but has endeavored to supply this interpretation with objective supporting evidence.

We contend that the studies critically examined here exemplify many of the strengths of corpus pragmatics. We examine some of the current concerns of the field in key concept areas such as speech acts, pragmatic markers, and pragmatics and power. Although the majority of the research concentrates on pragmatic features of spoken language, we also include studies that highlight the importance of corpus pragmatics to the written context.

2 The state of the art in corpus pragmatics

The blend of corpus linguistics and pragmatics, though a relatively recent development, is a mutually beneficial one. Therefore, the area is ripe with research opportunities. One of the latest (and most fruitful) synergies of pragmatics and corpus linguistics is the area of *historical corpus pragmatics* which is primarily concerned with the diachronic study of speech acts (see, for example, Jucker and Taavitsainen's 2008a edited volume). This research has proven especially beneficial in addressing some of the difficulties associated with using a corpus-based methodology. Primary among these is that speech act form and function do not directly correlate and, therefore, speech acts are not automatically retrievable through the use of corpus software (see Adolphs 2008; Rühlemann 2010). The pragmatic tagging of corpora would be a major advancement, and this is underway. Recent historical corpus pragmatic research has seen the development of sophisticated methodologies (Kohnen 2008) and pragmatic annotation schemes (Wichmann and Culpeper 2003) which allow for the examination of utterance-by-utterance interaction between conversational participants. Moreover, the release of corpora such as SPICE-Ireland (Kallen and Kirk 2008), a pragmatic and discourse-annotated version of the Irish component of the *International Corpus of English*, opens up a wealth of research paths given that, amongst other advantages, it is one of the first corpora to provide a searchable system where prosodic and pragmatic information sit side-by-side. The application of these annotation schemes in other corpora and other contexts, and also an examination of their robustness, is one area of potential research.

There is also a substantial body of research building up within corpus pragmatics around the area of pragmatic markers. Much of the seminal work in this area has been led by Karin Aijmer. Aijmer (2013) focuses on pragmatic marker variation with regard to social, cultural, and regional factors. Her rationale for exploring the variability of these markers in the ICE-GB corpus (the British component of the *International Corpus of English*) is to contribute to the discussion surrounding the influence of context on the function and meaning of pragmatic markers. A possible focus for future research in this area is the continued development of the cross-cultural analysis of the functions of pragmatic markers. For example, Clancy and Vaughan (2012) highlight how corpus pragmatics can be employed to characterize a language variety's pragmatic system. They found that the marker *now* was markedly more frequent in Irish English than in British English due to the fact that it has additional pragmatic functions in Irish English – it is used as both a pragmatic marker and deictic presentative. It is also important to note that research on pragmatic markers is not limited to native-speaker usage. Aijmer and Simon-Vandenbergen (2006) bring together a volume focusing cross-linguistically on pragmatic markers, while Fung and Carter (2007) explored the use of pragmatic markers in two pedagogical corpora – a corpus of learners of English in Hong Kong, and the pedagogic subcorpus from the *Cambridge and Nottingham Corpus of Discourse in English* (CANCODE). Fung and Carter found that markers, while present in the student corpus, are generally less frequent than in British English, especially in relation to those whose function is interpersonal, for example, *you know, well, sort of,* or *yeah.*

Corpus pragmatics is also to the forefront in exploring the link between language, power, and ideology. Baker and McEnery (2005: 223) highlight the usefulness of corpus pragmatics for critical social research. They point out that corpora are beneficial to fields of study such as Critical Discourse Analysis as "by looking at the collocational strength of lexical items in a corpus of general language, we are given an objective sense of the themes and associations that are embedded in words due to their continual pairing with other words." This research yielded, amongst other findings, the co-occurrence of *refugee* with metaphors associated with the movement of water such as *flood, stream,* or *swell* – words that frequently have negative connotations in normative patterns of language use. In relation to power and the workplace, Holmes and Stubbe (2003) explore the tension associated with the need to get things done at work while maintaining good collegial relationships. Using the Language in the Workplace Corpus, they examine a number of speech acts typical of the context, such as advice and instruction, in addition to aspects of workplace discourse such as humor and small talk. On humor, Vaughan and Clancy (2011: 51) suggest it is a "powerful, polyvalent pragmatic resource" and that it requires much more focused research in the realm of corpus pragmatics and power relations.

Corpus pragmatics has also advocated the synergy of corpus linguistics and conversation analysis in order to investigate the organizational level of pragmatics, that which explores turn-taking phenomena such as pauses, overlaps, interruptions, or backchannels (Schneider 2012). Clancy and McCarthy (2015) have focused on the benefits of corpus linguistics in the study of the co-construction of speaker turns. Co-construction is an inherently pragmatic activity given that the concept "hinges on the notion that meaning is created through the interaction itself, in the specific context of that interaction" (Kereckes 2007: 1943). Three high-frequency items identified as traditionally involved in the co-constructions process, *if, when*, and *which*, were identified and their patterns explored through an examination of concordance of these in turn-initial position based on their reported tendency to occur at points of co-construction. Corpus researchers habitually "enter" a corpus using items identified as high frequency on the corpus frequency list. Wichmann (2004) presents a potential avenue for future research when she suggests that researchers need to focus on low-frequency phenomena in addition to high-frequency items.

Finally, in relation to deixis, personal pronouns feature prominently in corpus frequency lists, especially spoken ones. Personal pronouns are strongly associated with deictic reference: a system of reference that facilitates contextual orientation. The use of personal pronouns to negotiate identity has received some attention in corpus pragmatics. O'Keeffe (2006) looks at deictic centering and othering in corpora of media discourse, particularly through the pronouns *we* and *they*. Vaughan and Clancy (2013) examine the complexity of reference of *we* in establishing community identity in both workplace and family discourse. Hyland (2002a, b) explores the use of first-person pronouns in two academic written corpora – an "expert" corpus and a "novice" corpus. He finds that academic writing is not impersonal or faceless, as it has often been portrayed in textbooks and style guides, and that expert writers use first-person pronouns three times more frequently than novice writers. He cautions against novice writers avoiding these pronouns as it may result in them not establishing an effective authorial identity. However, in saying this, deixis remains, as noted by Levinson (2004: 97), "one of the most empirically understudied core areas of pragmatics" and, although there remains much work to be done, researchers in corpus pragmatics appear to be at the forefront of the efforts to redress this discrepancy.

With the state of the art in corpus-pragmatic research established, we now turn to a more fine-grained discussion of exemplar studies in the areas outlined above.

3 A critical discussion of previous research at the forefront of corpus pragmatics

3.1 Speech acts

The study of speech acts outside the field of corpus pragmatics has predominantly been based on elicited data generated from discourse completion tasks (DCTs) or role plays (O'Keeffe *et al.* 2011). As already stated, corpus pragmatics is characterized by the analysis of real-life language in use. The use of corpus-pragmatic approaches has led to a reconsideration of the results produced by elicited data in light of corpus-based findings. For example, in a study of DCTs and corpus data, Schauer and Adolphs (2006) compare and contrast the results yielded by corpus data, in this case CANCODE, and DCTs in relation to speech acts of gratitude in order to determine if they can be used in conjunction with one another to inform teaching materials. At an "actional level"[1] (Schneider 2012: 1027), in both the DCT and corpus data, expressions of gratitude involving the *thank* stem and the item *cheers* were the most frequent. Where the results diverge, however, is at an interactional level, i.e. "how speech acts combine into larger units of discourse ranging from adjacency pairs to conversational phrases" (ibid.). At this level, the corpus data demonstrates how *cheers* is not employed primarily as an expression of gratitude but as a response to an expression of gratitude, "used in this way it is difficult to determine whether it actually marks gratitude or whether it functions as a discourse marker that signals the end of the encounter or discourse episode" (Schauer and Adolphs 2006: 125). This possible discourse-marking function is absent in the DCT data due to the non-interactive nature of the data they produce. Another difference noted between corpus and DCT data is the length of speaker turn in which the expression of gratitude was produced. The corpus data highlighted, in addition to expressions of gratitude most frequently used, that these expressions tend to cluster across extended speaker turns as part of a process of collaborative negotiation, and that this pragmatic use of *thanks*, for example, is often found in gatekeeping encounters such as service encounters. Finally, the corpus data highlighted the importance of the ability to produce an expression of gratitude twinned with a polite refusal, a *thanks but no thanks*, which was very infrequent in the DCT data but flagged by Schauer and Adolphs as "one of the main skills that students may need to possess in a native speaker context" (2006: 129). Although we are not suggesting here that DCTs are unsuitable for the study of pragmatics, we are once again highlighting the suitability of corpus linguistics as a complementary methodology due to the nature of the data contained in corpora.

3.2 Pragmatic markers

As outlined in Section 2 above, pragmatic markers have received a large amount of attention. The study we have chosen here illustrates the complementary use of large and small corpora to investigate the pragmatic markers *I would say* and *I'd say*. Farr and O'Keeffe's (2002) first step was to examine the occurrences of *I would say* and *I'd say* at a dialectal level using three large spoken corpora: the *Limerick Corpus of Irish English* (LCIE), CANCODE, and a corpus of American spoken data from the *Cambridge International Corpus* (CIC). Using purely quantitative data in the form of

[1] Schneider's (2012) "actional level" represents the level of speech act analysis.

frequency lists, they found that, at this level, Irish speakers seem to be twice as "hedgy" as their American counterparts. However, an intervarietal, quantitative study such as this, is, they maintain, "restrictive in its insightfulness" (p. 29), in that it does not further any understanding we have of how, where, or why *would* is used as a hedge.

Farr and O'Keeffe recommend that the use of *would* as a hedge is investigated at the level of register in order to more fully appreciate its use. Therefore, its occurrence in two small corpora – a 55,000-word corpus of radio phone-in data and a 52,000-word corpus of post-observation teacher trainee interaction – was examined. They discovered, through an exploration of colligational and collocational patterns, that *would* is used in these institutional domains to redress asymmetry, to mitigate face-threatening acts or to "transpose" the focus of the talk to a hypothetical "safe band" (2002: 41). This treatment of *would* in small corpora at the level of register also demonstrated the different levels of context that have an influence on the use of a marker in that the results for *would* in the institutional context of the two small corpora are rooted in their sociocultural context – in this case within Irish society. Farr and O'Keeffe suggest that forwardness is not valued in Irish culture and that Irish society, in general, "does not place a high value on powerful or direct speech" (2002: 42), something that has been borne out in subsequent research into the Irish system of pragmatic marking (see Vaughan and Clancy 2011; Clancy and Vaughan 2012). Of particular note here are the contextual insights provided by the use of small corpora in corpus-pragmatic research. These insights could not have been retrievable using a larger, more general corpus where the user usually has little contextual information of any depth. The effectiveness of small corpora in corpus pragmatics will be echoed in our empirical study presented below.

3.3 Language, power, and ideology

Critical discourse analysis (CDA) has successfully utilized corpus linguistics as a complementary methodology. The purpose of CDA is to show how language in use is often constructed and shaped by various social forces (see Fairclough 1989). Although it can also be applied to the study of spoken language, it is particularly associated with written language, especially media discourse. CDA has employed corpus linguistics to engage with texts such as newspapers (as per the example presented here) in order to bring to the fore how power is enacted through "inferred and indirect linguistic devices" (Wodak 2007: 204), such as the pragmatic concepts of *presupposition* and *implicature* (see Archer *et al.* 2012: Unit A12). Both implicature and presupposition rely on the determination of meaning through inference, i.e. beyond linguistic form. This is a process exemplified by Baker *et al.*'s (2008) analysis of the semantic prosody of *POSE as* presented here.

Baker *et al.* (2008) analyzed a 140-million-word corpus of UK tabloid and broadsheet newspapers, composed of daily and Sunday papers, both local and national, to investigate linguistic representations of, and attitudes toward, refugees, asylum seekers, immigrants, and migrants (RASIM). Corpus linguistics enabled them to map these data, "pinpointing areas of interest for a subsequent close analysis" (2008: 284). CDA has traditionally focused on grammatical features such as passivization or metaphor; however, one of the benefits of corpus linguistics for CDA is that it facilitates a focus on lexical patterns also. Once these lexical patterns had been identified quantitatively by, for example, keyword lists or cluster analysis, concordance lines were generated to allow subsequent qualitative examination. Take, for example, their corpus analysis of the semantic prosody of the multi-word item *POSE as*. Semantic prosody refers to a process of implicature through the tendency of words to "appear in particular environments in such a way that their meaning, especially their connotative and evaluative meaning, is spread over several words ... words might tend to occur in overwhelmingly positive or negative environments" (O'Keeffe *et al.* 2007: 14). A detailed analysis of the concordance lines in relation to *POSE as* revealed eight frames of use of the type "Actor(s) pose as X to achieve Y," which revealed that the item can have a negative, positive, or neutral semantic prosody according to the actor and the context. For example, "RASIM posing as doctors/sports fans/tourists in order to gain entry/find work/receive benefits," represents a negative prosody whereas "reporters posing as RASIM in order to investigate their plight in an asylum system" has a positive prosody. Baker *et al.* found that despite the tabloids using *POSE as* almost eight times more frequently in relation to RASIM, the traditional stereotype that tabloid newspapers are more negative in their portrayal of RASIM than broadsheets did not hold true. Generally, what they found was that tabloids do adopt a negative stance in their reporting of issues related to RASIM and broadsheets tend to adopt a more balanced perspective, which does, however, combine both positive and negative reporting. In this way, corpus linguistics assists CDA researchers in quantifying notions like bias. Therefore, it is the synergy of the methodologies that lends this study its analytic strength.

3.4 The organization of discourse

Corpus pragmatics has also successfully combined the methodological field of conversation analysis (CA) with that of corpus linguistics in order to provide a much more fine-grained analysis of spoken language than would be possible if each were used in isolation. This synergy of methodologies allows linguistic items to be examined at both a structural (syntactic) and interpersonal (pragmatic) level and enables us to understand how "words, utterances and text combine in the co-construction of meaning" (Walsh, 2013: 37). In one study of this type, McCarthy (2003) analyzes the occurrence of a number of non-minimal response tokens in two corpora; 3.5 million words of the CANCODE corpus and a similarly sized sample of the CIC corpus. The corpus results provide a profile of the most frequent tokens used, for example, *right, wow, true, exactly*, or *sure*, thereby pointing toward these as salient items for further analysis. These results also indicate a shared set of non-minimal response tokens that occur within the core 2,000-word frequency lists for both British and American English. The more fine-grained, up-close view provided by the more qualitative CA approach means that we can determine their role in discourse and McCarthy demonstrates how examining non-minimal response tokens in their local context of use reveals how this role is essentially pragmatic in nature. On the structural level, he presents the accepted view that response tokens function structurally to design and organize discourse, however, he also reveals their role as "indexes of engaged listenership" (2003: 59). This is particularly the case when tokens occur as doublets or triplets (for example, *Lovely. Terrific.* or *Good. Good. Good.*). These patterns do not simply signal discourse boundaries but "inject a strong relational element of response to the situation (one of satisfaction, agreement and positive social bonding)" (2003: 54). In this way, listeners can be seen to be attending to pragmatic concerns – both social and affective – in their responses perhaps before attending to structural concerns such as taking the turn for themselves.

3.5 Deixis

The final corpus-pragmatic work that we examine here is Rühlemann's (2007) unique study of the conversational subcorpus of the BNC. This study is significant because it analyzes frequent conversational features that previously had not been systematically researched using corpus linguistics. Furthermore, the study positions deixis as one of the cornerstones of the analysis. Rühlemann argues that conversation is characterized by a much greater wealth of shared context than most written language situations. In order to quantitatively and qualitatively prove this, Rühlemann examines, amongst other features, person, place, and time deixis – shared-context phenomena that are manifest in spoken corpora in general. One of the most obvious and frequent manifestations of person deixis is personal pronouns. Regarding the distribution of these pronouns, Biber *et al.* (1999: 333) have shown that *I* and *you* are far more common in casual conversation than in other registers such as academic prose. Rühlemann (2007: 66–69) posits four reasons for the preferred use of *I* and *you* in casual conversation; (i) *I* is prone to repetition (*I* is repeated at a frequency of about 200 times per million words in conversation (see Biber *et al.*, 1999: 334)); (ii) *I* and *you* have a high frequency of collocation, especially with cognitive verbs, for example, *I think* and *you know*; (iii) speakers in conversation show a clear tendency to prefer a direct mode than an indirect mode and, importantly for studies in corpus pragmatics, (iv) conversation is co-constructed, with speakers taking turns and each new turn requiring the reconstruction of the new speaker's deictic system. Based on the evidence provided by personal pronouns, but also on the analysis of the role of deixis in the tense system, speech reporting, and vocatives, Rühlemann concludes that our deictic system demonstrates a "remarkable flexibility" (2007: 221), with participants seamlessly projecting, oscillating and varying their deictic centers.

In addition to exploring verbal shared context, Rühlemann also uses corpus techniques to examine non-verbal pragmatic items. In modern spoken corpora in general, a wealth of paralinguistic information is tagged, such as coughing or door slamming, much of which is of little importance; however, some of these features, such as laughter, are of significance to corpus pragmatics. Rühlemann uses frequency counts to demonstrate the importance of laughter to conversation, for example, if "between-speech laughter" is considered as a linguistic item in and of itself, it would be placed in 29th position on the BNC conversational subcorpus frequency list. A closer inspection of the contexts in which laughter occurs demonstrates that it fulfills core pragmatic functions. According to Rühlemann, it functions as a backchannel, and, as such, is an indicator of engaged listenership akin to McCarthy's (2003) non-minimal response tokens. It also has a discourse deictic function as a discourse marker which signals that word choices should not be understood too literally. Laughter is not always associated with humorous contexts but is concomitant with incongruity. The frequency of laughter in the BNC, Rühlemann argues, demonstrates the intrinsic importance of this incongruity to human interaction.

Although these studies illustrate the state of the art in corpus pragmatics and showcase the field's methodological and analytical rigor, corpus pragmatics is, however, not without its thorns. As already mentioned, corpus linguistics has been criticized in relation to its suitability for the study of speech acts. Moreover, if corpus pragmatics is concerned with the interpretation of meaning in context, another disadvantage associated with the relationship between corpus linguistics and pragmatics is that many larger corpora are impoverished both textually and contextually (Rühlemann 2010). Koester (2010: 66–67) points out that in large corpora it is "very difficult, if not impossible" to connect what is said with its original context. In terms of spoken language, one of the main contributing factors is that in order to analyze conversation, corpus builders first "translate" spoken language into writing in the form of transcripts, many of which exclude important contextual features such as prosody. This results in what Rühlemann (2007: 13) refers to as a "written-speech paradox." One solution to these challenges has emerged from the increasing use of small corpora in corpus pragmatics. We strongly advocate small corpora as ideally suited for corpus pragmatics given their "constant interpretative dialectic between features of texts and the contexts in which they are produced" (Vaughan and Clancy 2013: 70). Researchers working with these corpora are frequently both compiler and analyst (and, indeed, often participant), which gives them a unique insight into context. Small corpora also allow every instance of the item(s) under investigation to be mined, as illustrated by our case study here, resulting in refined and nuanced pragmatic profiles of the items under investigation.

4 Case study: a corpus-pragmatic analysis of vocative function

This corpus-based investigation of vocative use focuses on two small corpora in an Irish English context. The results presented here are a combination of those from McCarthy and O'Keeffe (2003) and Clancy (forthcoming). The first of the two corpora utilized is a 55,000-word corpus of a daily Irish radio program *Liveline* which is broadcast on the national broadcaster RTÉ and has a listenership of approximately 10 percent of the Irish population. The second corpus, the 12,500-word *SettCorp*, represents the conversations of a six-member (father, mother, two boys, and two girls) middle-class Irish family. Interaction in radio phone-in takes place between people who very often do not know one another, and although the speaker relationship is hierarchical (the media persona has the power), a "pseudo-intimacy" (O'Keeffe 2006) is maintained in order that a greater level of disclosure might be achieved. In contrast, family discourse is characterized by an unequal intimacy (Blum Kulka 1997) – there exists in the family an in-built hierarchy where the parents have more conversational power than the children. Therefore, this case study is concerned with comparing and contrasting the use of vocatives among intimates in family discourse and those who simulate intimacy in radio phone-in. The goal of the study is to contrast how vocatives function within the two corpora, one in an intimate family context, and the other in a pseudo-intimate institutional (radio phone-in) context, in order to better understand how vocatives contribute to the creation and maintenance of intimacy and whether this is replicated in a pseudo-intimate context.

Vocatives, terms of address (Ervin-Tripp 1971), and forms of address (Brown and Gilman 1960) are, according to Leech (1999: 107), "closely related topics which are easily confused." He points out that a term of address "is a device used to refer to the addressee(s) of an utterance" whereas a vocative is a particular kind of address term: "a nominal constituent loosely integrated with the rest of the utterance." Formally, a vocative has a number of guises: endearments (*honey, baby, love*, etc.), kin titles (*Mammy, Daddy*, etc.), familiarizers (*mate, man, folks*, etc.), first names familiarized (*Brad, Jen*, etc.), full first names (*Bradley, Jennifer*, etc.), title and surname (*Mr. Holmes, Dr. Watson, Professor Moriarty*, etc.), honorifics (*sir, ma'am*, etc.) and a group called "other" which includes nicknames in addition to some complex noun phrases (*Those of you who want to bring your pets along*, please sit in the back of the space ship … (Leech 1999: 111)). Functionally, a vocative behaves peripherally in an utterance in a similar way to, for example, a discourse marker. Pragmatically, a vocative performs a range of functions and it is these functions that this empirical study is concerned with. Leech (1999) identifies three pragmatic functions of vocatives: (1) summoning attention, (2) addressee identification, and (3) establishing and maintaining social relationships between conversational participants. Subsequently, McCarthy and O'Keeffe (2003) developed Leech's (1999) functional categories and derived a more nuanced framework containing six functional categories: *relational, topic management, badinage, mitigation, turn management*, and *summons*. Relational vocatives establish and/or maintain social relations rather than transmit information or services. This category includes compliments and other positive face boosters, general evaluations, phatic exchanges, and ritualistic offers and thanks. Topic management refers to the occurrence of a vocative in an utterance or set of utterances that launch, expand, shift, change, or close a topic. Included here also is what McCarthy and O'Keeffe (2003: 162) have termed *topic validation*, whereby a speaker calls on another conversational participant by name to validate or confirm an assertion. Badinage refers to the use of a vocative in instances of humor, irony, and general banter among participants. Mitigators include those vocatives that help soften or downtone a potential threat to positive or negative face (Brown and Levinson 1987). Turn management vocatives select the next speaker or disambiguate possible recipients in multi-party talk. Summons concerns the use of a vocative to directly summon a conversational participant (these categories are illustrated with examples below). However, we stress that the vocatives themselves might not perform the function but they occur as a "signal of that utterance's intent" (Wilson and Zeitlyn 1995: 8).

4.1 Research question and methodology

This study sets out to answer the following question: what are the similarities and differences in pragmatic function between family discourse and radio phone-in, that is, between their use in real intimate relationships and pseudo-intimate relationships? This examination of the function of vocatives is important for a number of reasons. First, it vividly illustrates, through the application of a corpus-based, bottom-up methodology, the close interrelationship between pragmatic function and context. In doing so, it showcases the usefulness of small corpora for pragmatic research, particularly with regard to how their investigation can deepen our understanding of the descriptive framework for spoken genres. One of the criticisms of small corpus research is that a small corpus does not allow for generalization. However, the encouraging aspect of this research is that the findings from a number of small corpora in similar contexts can be used to generalize if a number of features emerge as constant. For example, small corpora in institutional contexts, such as those used by McCarthy (2000), O'Keeffe (2006), and Vaughan (2007), have all demonstrated a "blurring of the lines" through the presence of relational talk in this context. Another fundamental benefit of small corpora in pragmatic research is that they allow the researcher to maintain close contact between authentic, naturally occurring language and its context of use (Vaughan and Clancy 2013). Moreover, Leech (1999: 107) notes that vocatives are a "surprisingly neglected" aspect of English grammar and, although it can be argued that there is a robust research tradition in relation to the broader *term of address*, it is still true now that studies utilizing a corpus-based approach to the study of vocatives are under-represented, relatively speaking, especially in comparison to say hedging research (notable exceptions include, however, Shiina 2005 and Busse 2006).

In terms of the methodology utilized, in the case of both corpora, the data were read manually and every vocative classified. Hence, this methodology, if transferred to a larger dataset, needs to employ a sampling strategy so as to arrive at a manageable amount of vocatives. This in itself poses a challenge as vocatives are not normally tagged. In these studies, the vocatives in the datasets were categorized according to vocative type (for example, endearments, kin titles, etc.) and function (relational, summons, etc.) and, although not discussed here, position (initial, medial, or final). Concordance lines were then generated using the categories as the search items so that the function and position of the vocative is placed in relief. Figure 13.1 illustrates a random sample of the concordance lines for the kin title *mam* (node word in bold) in SettCorp where Wordsmith Tools™ has been used to resort the concordance lines two words to the right (2 R) and three words to the right (3 R):

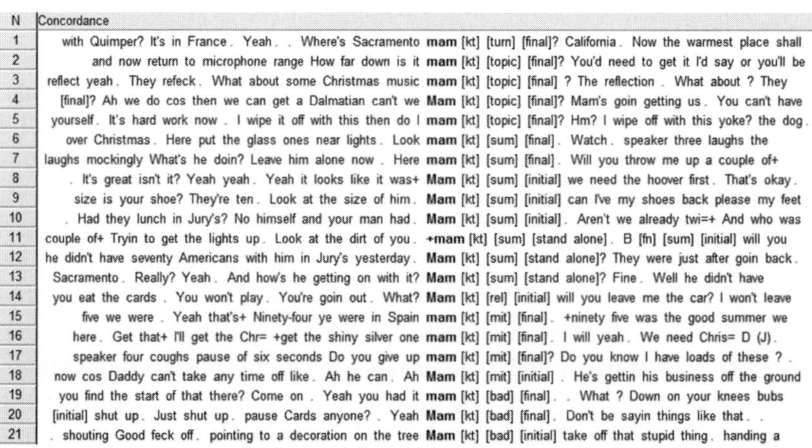

N	Concordance
1	with Quimper? It's in France. Yeah. . Where's Sacramento **mam** [kt] [turn] [final]? California. Now the warmest place shall
2	and now return to microphone range How far down is it **mam** [kt] [topic] [final]? You'd need to get it I'd say or you'll be
3	reflect yeah. They refeck. What about some Christmas music **mam** [kt] [topic] [final] ? The reflection . What about ? They
4	[final]? Ah we do cos then we can get a Dalmatian can't we **Mam** [kt] [topic] [final]? Mam's goin getting us. You can't have
5	yourself. It's hard work now . I wipe it off with this then do I **mam** [kt] [topic] [final]? Hm? I wipe off with this yoke? the dog.
6	over Christmas. Here put the glass ones near lights. Look **mam** [kt] [sum] [final]. Watch. speaker three laughs the
7	laughs mockingly What's he doin? Leave him alone now . Here **mam** [kt] [sum] [final]. Will you throw me up a couple of+
8	. It's great isn't it? Yeah yeah. Yeah it looks like it was+ **Mam** [kt] [sum] [initial] we need the hoover first. That's okay.
9	size is your shoe? They're ten. Look at the size of him. **Mam** [kt] [sum] [initial] can I've my shoes back please my feet
10	. Had they lunch in Jury's? No himself and your man had. **Mam** [kt] [sum] [initial]. Aren't we already twi=+ And who was
11	couple of+ Tryin to get the lights up. Look at the dirt of you. **+mam** [kt] [sum] [stand alone]. B [fn] [sum] [initial] will you
12	he didn't have seventy Americans with him in Jury's yesterday. **Mam** [kt] [sum] [stand alone]? They were just after goin back.
13	Sacramento. Really? Yeah. And how's he getting on with it? **Mam** [kt] [sum] [stand alone]? Fine. Well he didn't have
14	you eat the cards . You won't play. You're goin out. What? **Mam** [kt] [rel] [initial] will you leave me the car? I won't leave
15	five we were . Yeah that's+ Ninety-four ye were in Spain **mam** [kt] [mit] [final]. +ninety five was the good summer we
16	here. Get that+ I'll get the Chr= +get the shiny silver one **mam** [kt] [mit] [final]. I will yeah. We need Chris= D (J).
17	speaker four coughs pause of six seconds Do you give up **mam** [kt] [mit] [final]? Do you know I have loads of these ? .
18	now cos Daddy can't take any time off like. Ah he can. Ah **Mam** [kt] [mit] [initial] . He's gettin his business off the ground
19	you find the start of that there? Come on . Yeah you had it **mam** [kt] [bad] [final]. . What ? Down on your knees bubs
20	[initial] shut up. Just shut up. pause Cards anyone? . Yeah **Mam** [kt] [bad] [final]. Don't be sayin things like that. .
21	. shouting Good feck off. pointing to a decoration on the tree **Mam** [kt] [bad] [initial] take off that stupid thing. handing a

Figure 13.1 Concordance lines for *mam* in SettCorp (sorted 2R then 3R)

Table 13.1 *Occurrences of vocatives in* Liveline *and SettCorp, normalized to 10,000 words (raw results in brackets)*

	Liveline	SettCorp
Total vocatives	42 (232)	129 (161)

Figure 13.1 demonstrates that tagging and sorting the concordance lines in this manner demonstrates that *mam* functions primarily as a summons vocative [sum] and is, to a lesser extent, involved in topic management [topic], mitigation [mit], and badinage [bad]. In terms of vocative position, 12 of the 21 occurrences are in final position. All topic management functions are final, for example, as are the majority of mitigators, and this perhaps indicates the relationship between these functions and their position in an utterance. Therefore, despite there being only 21 concordance lines, there is evidence of the pragmatic behavior of this vocative (see below for further analysis).

4.2 Findings

Table 13.1 illustrates the initial frequency results for vocatives in the two datasets. For the purposes of comparability, these are normalized to occurrences per 10,000 words. This finding illustrates that despite the pseudo-intimacy simulated in the radio phone-in context, vocatives are more frequent in intimate casual conversation. Interestingly, this runs contrary to Leech's (1999: 117) findings which note that vocatives do not occur among what he terms "close associates," his study includes mother–daughter and wife–husband interactions, where, he maintains, neither the addressee identification nor the social relationship function is necessary. One of the crucial analytical aspects of corpus pragmatics is to offer compelling quantitative evidence in support of automatically generated, frequency data. Not only this, automatically generated frequency data can be sorted and categorized in order to generate a more in-depth and nuanced quantitative interpretation of the results in Table 13.1, so a functional analysis of all vocatives in the two corpora was conducted, as illustrated in Figure 13.2.

Figure 13.2, perhaps unsurprisingly, reveals a contrast in vocative function between the two datasets. The starkest difference in the contextual functional categories is between their use as mitigators in family discourse and call management in radio phone-in. While it is not surprising that vocatives occur frequently in the context of call management on a radio phone-in and that this has no occurrence in the family data, it is striking that their use in the context of mitigation is so low in radio phone-in. It is here that we move to the second step in the analytical process. We have

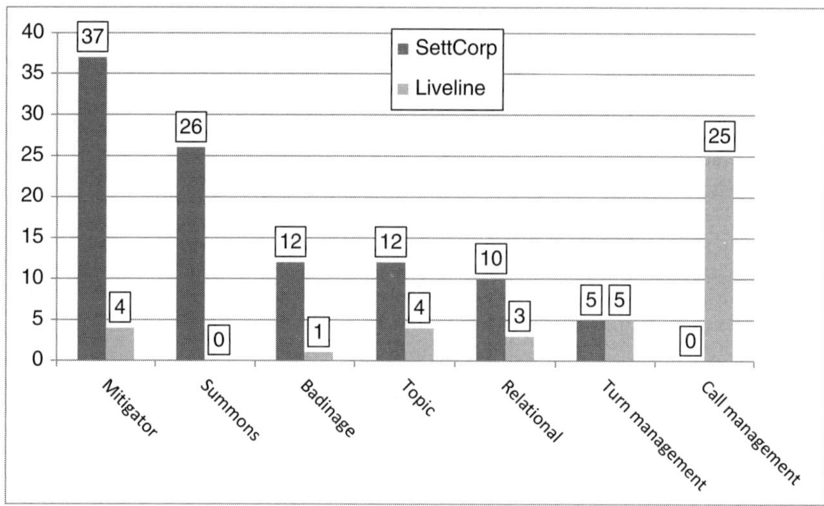

Figure 13.2 Functions of vocatives in *Liveline* and SettCorp (normalized to 10,000 words)

already extracted telling quantitative evidence and now we can synthesize these quantitative insights by taking a qualitative approach. Extract 1 is illustrative of a typical use of a vocative in the context of call management where the radio host identifies the next speaker and cues them to speak by means of a vocative, thus initiating the next caller and his tale:

Extract 1

[Introducing a caller whose son narrowly escaped death from meningitis]

<$1> Now to a couple that had very very difficult Christmas this year however all's well that ends well ah Austin good afternoon to you.
<$2> Good afternoon Marian.
<$1> Your little boy went back to playschool yesterday?
<$2> Yesterday that's right.

Mitigation, the most frequent context of use in family data, accounting for 36 percent of all vocatives in that dataset, is typified by the following example where the family is decorating the Christmas tree:

Extract 2

<Son> Oh look the state of the one that mam hate mam hates that because they're+
<Mother> It's awful.
<Daughter> It's rotten.
<Mother> Don't put it up.
<Daughter> It's rotten Jimmy.
<Mother> It's all dirty and everything.

The son locates one particular decoration and it is reasonable to surmise, judging by speaker reactions, that the mother and daughter dislike it. He is then instructed, in the form of an unmitigated parental directive, not to put the decoration on the tree. The daughter, in the consecutive utterance, mitigates the directive by giving a reason why and softens it further by using a mitigating vocative in the form of a first name familiarized. McCarthy and O'Keeffe (2003) also noted the high frequency of vocatives in the context of mitigation in CANCODE casual conversation data, saying that they are neither syntactically nor semantically necessary and they function solely as pragmatic downtoners of challenges, adversative comments, and disagreements. However, adversarial situations are relatively uncommon in the *Liveline* radio phone-in data. The interaction is usually between the radio host and the caller. However, there are a few instances where two adversaries give their opposing view on a conflictual situation and in these contexts, we can find some examples of vocatives used when mitigating the force of a challenge, etc., as in extract 3:

Extract 3

[Two callers, Colm and Máirtín, are in a heated dispute]

<$3> Oh Colm come on . . . pull the other one.

The other difference of note in the two datasets is in relation to the use of vocatives in summons. Again this is very context specific. It would suggest that families frequently use vocatives to summon other family members. However, we note that McCarthy and O'Keeffe (2003) found only four 4 percent of vocatives in the context of summons in the casual conversation data between family and friends. This is in contrast to 25 percent of vocatives being used to summon in the Irish family discourse in this study. There are a variety of reasons why this may be the case – for example, there may be a differing age profile in the datasets and this can have an impact as younger children generally demand more attention from their parents than older children. The sampling process could also have a role to play in that if the conversations were recorded in situations where everyone was already present, such as dinner time, then there would be less need to summon. In order to ascertain this, further cross-cultural analysis using data from CANCODE family-only contexts would be needed.

Identified as the largest functional category by McCarthy and O'Keeffe (2003: 160), the relational function in the family data is surprisingly low, accounting for 10 percent of all uses:

Extract 4

<Son 1> Yeah. That's exactly what I did. Cards anyone?
<Son 2> No thank you Jimmy.

However, the fact that the discourse takes place in this intimate context, coupled with fixed and pre-established speaker relationships and the "politeness license" (Blum-Kulka 1997; Clancy 2005) granted to families,

e.g. historical speech act studies (Arnovick 1999; Jucker and Taavitsainen 2008a; Taavitsainen and Jucker 2007, 2008; Valkonen 2008). The problem is that they allow only lexical searches, but it is not possible to retrieve relative frequencies or to apply more advanced statistical methods. Yet there are other corpora with literary materials that can be studied with more advanced corpus-linguistic methods. The *Late Modern English Corpus* (CLMET by de Smet, Diller, and Tyrkkö 2013) is a case in point. The newest version includes search parameters to help researchers find appropriate data for their study questions.[3] The *Historical Thesaurus of English* (HT hereafter) has also proved a useful tool for historical pragmatic research.

4.3 Developing corpora for corpus-linguistic applications

Besides corpus compilation projects, corpus linguists have profited greatly from recent advances in automatic normalization of spelling variants that make possible the application of advanced linguistic methods to historical data. The Variant Detector program, VARD 2 (by Baron, see www.comp.lancs.ac.uk/~barona/vard2/) has been developed for Early Modern English to improve the reliability of data sources. Corpus development has already taken the normalized versions on board. *Early Modern English Medical Texts* (EMEMT) is the first corpus that in addition to the authentic texts includes normalized versions of corpus text to be used in corpus-linguistic applications of keywords, clusters, and *n*-grams, but researchers go back to the originals for citing examples (see Lehto *et al.* 2010). Corpus annotation is in a dynamic phase. Corpus compilers have come up with innovative solutions for integrating metadata, detailed background information about sociolinguistic parameters, and pragmatic units like speech acts. The goal is to allow corpus users direct access to relevant material (see e.g. Archer 2014).

5 Historical pragmatic studies with corpus-linguistic methodology

In this section I shall outline some of the most important subfields of historical pragmatics where corpus-linguistic methods have yielded novel insights into central research questions. Researchers are well provided for with rich data resources and exciting new software programs.

5.1 Processes of language change

Research in the area of language change has been active since the 1980s, at first from the morphosyntactic and semantic point of view, but pragmatic

[3] In addition, there are new tools like the Ngram Viewer that can be used for overviews of developments. It contains data from millions of books from 1500 to 2000 scanned by the Google Books project (see Michel *et al.* 2011).

motivations and the interface beween semantics and pragmatics have received increasing attention since the 1990s (e.g. Traugott 1982, 2003, 2010, and Traugott and Dasher 2005). Processes of language change lend themselves readily to corpus linguistic assessments, as lexical items serve as search words to retrieve data from electronic corpora. The direction of study is from form to function (see Jacobs and Jucker 1995): the linguistic form provides the point of departure and studies aim at revealing the functional profiles of these items. Such studies represent the top-down methodology with the applications of KWIC concordances and contextual micro-assessments of meanings in context. Of the branches of historical pragmatics, this is the one that overlaps most with historical linguistics (see Taavitsainen 2012). How context is assessed makes the difference, as the researcher may focus on syntactic changes or go beyond to the communicative functions and motivations in studies where negotiability of meaning is central. Related processes of linguistic change pertinent to historical pragmatics include subjectification and intersubjectification, pragmaticalization, and discoursization (see López-Couso 2010; Claridge and Arnovick 2010).

Traugott (2003: xv) defines grammaticalization as "the change whereby lexical items and constructions come in certain contexts to serve grammatical functions and once grammaticalized, continue to develop new grammatical functions." Brinton (2007) takes the above definition as her point of departure in an article called "The development of *I mean*: Implications for the study of historical pragmatics" that discusses the development of this parenthetical pragmatic marker. This article illuminates the methodology in an excellent way. Brinton sets out with a research question that asks whether grammaticalization is indeed the process that underlies the development of pragmatic markers; alternative processes could be pragmaticalization, lexicalization, or idiomaticization. She takes present-day functions of *I mean* as her point of departure. It is used metacommunicatively in prefacing repair, reformulation, or explication, it can reveal speaker attitude or modify speaker meanings, but it has also gained interpersonal meanings. Brinton starts with the generally accepted assumption that frequency distributions across various electronic and online corpora provide evidence for semantic and syntactic developments, but concludes that pragmatic meanings are more elusive, and can only be caught by studying the historical contexts. By micro-analyses it is possible to detect how these various meanings first arose, how they relate to one another and how they continue in use. Contexts of metacommunicative uses can be revealed by "translations" with equivalent expressions like *namely* or *in other words*; the less frequent interpersonal, hearer-directed functions are revealed by second-person pronouns, vocatives, and imperatives in the vicinity of *I mean* (2007: 61). Brinton concludes in favor of grammaticalization, and agrees with Traugott that pragmaticalization is a subspecies of it, not a distinct process (2007: 64).

In a more recent article "Interjection-based delocutive verbs in the history of English" Brinton (2015) assesses a reverse change by which a grammatical word (e.g. a second-person pronoun used as a verb *to thou*) or an interjection becomes a lexical word (*to boo*). The point of departure is a novel set of research questions about delocutive verbs, with reference to a locutionary act of uttering *x*. The tokens are rare but types quite numerous, and the low frequency makes it impossible to establish a sequence of semantic development. The core of the category is verbs based on interjections expressing emotive states. Brinton points out the long diachrony of such verbs, and traces the development of interjection-based delocutives in several corpora from Middle English to the Early Modern and the Late Modern English periods from dictionaries and traditional corpora to electronic resources and literary databases. She noticed a significant increase in these items in Early Modern and Late Modern English periods. The linguistic cotext and surrounding discourse context are considered, and the findings related to larger patterns of various processes of change like lexicalization and degrammaticalization. In particular, Brinton wants to find out to what extent these verbs have undergone lexicalization (rather than conversion), and whether interjection-based delocutives have undergone degrammaticalization involving grammatical "upgrading" – a shift from more minor to more major part of speech. She considers various possibilities and concludes in favor of neologisms and states that the verbs arise through conversion or by back formation from the gerund as they first appear in the *-ing* form.

5.2 Studies on styles of stance

The second set of case studies represents a different point of departure and method that relies on a large repertoire of linguistic features that work together to express styles of stance, i.e. speaker's or writer's epistemic or attitudinal comments on propositional information. The linguistic features to be studied are chosen on the bases of previous studies, also representing the top-down methodology, but instead of form-to-function studies, it is related to the multidimensional method that reveals continuous scales of variation (Biber 1988). English has a rich array of devices for stance marking, as described in the *Longman Grammar of Spoken and Written English* (*LGSWE*, Biber *et al.* 1999). The study investigates the entire system to verify the underlying patterns of change. *LGSWE* provides the basis for the selection of linguistic features, and it also gives the point of comparison as the synchronic patterns of expressing stance, in various registers of Present-day English (conversation, fiction, news reports, and academic writing) are established in it. The aim of Biber's article "Historical patterns of grammatical marking of stance: A cross-register comparison" (2004) is to map the development of expressions of stance across various registers in the ARCHER corpus (drama, letters, newspapers, and medical prose) over three centuries (1650–1990) and to trace historical change in the ways in which a wide selection of devices, including (semi-)modals, adverbials, and complement clause constructions with specific grammatical devices, are used. The texts were tagged and frequency counts conducted, and the results are represented with various graphs that indicate the developments in a clear way. The article shows that fine-tuned descriptions of styles of stance are possible. Some overall changes in the grammatical system for the expression of stance emerge: there is a decline in the use of modal verbs, and an increase in the use of semi-modals and complement clause constructions. Register diversification grows over time, with particular stance devices taking on more specialized uses in particular registers. Drama and letters favor semi-modals and stance adverbials, while news reports employ complement clauses, and medical prose infrequently uses most of these devices. Some semantic specialization can also be verified as epistemic uses increase while affect and attitude remain more constant. The results indicate a general shift in the cultural norms over the three centuries: speakers and writers are more willing to express stance in recent periods. The article concludes with suggestions for future research.

The same topic, styles of stance, and the same method were developed in a new direction and applied to the more specific research task of stance marking with EMEMT data (Gray, Biber, and Hiltunen 2011). The purpose was to detect possible innovations in the new medium, the *Philosophical Transactions* (*PT* hereafter), the first scientific journal established for new communicative purposes and targeted at a new discourse community of the Royal Society. The rest of the contemporary medical literature (1650–1700) served as a reference corpus.[4] New genres of writing were created for new purposes, and the article focuses on reports, letters, and book reviews published in the journal. The data were tagged for this purpose, and the study conducted much in the same way as the previous one, but the KWIC concordances were analyzed manually with respect to the controlling word and stance category. A second computer program was made to parse the KWIC files and to create counts for each item and category, and the findings were normalized to 1,000 words. The results did not show any overall differences between *PT* and the other texts, but interesting trends emerged from a comparison of the three genres within the new scientific journal. Letters contain high frequencies of stance markers, but reports, treatises on specialized topics, regimens, and surgical texts came close; book reviews and recipes had the fewest stance markers. However, a trend connected with a stylistic innovation was detected, as *that*-complement clauses were more prevalent in *PT* than in the reference corpus, and in book reviews they were particularly striking. This feature reflects more explicit evaluation,

[4] The corpus is divided into the following categories based on the topics of texts: 1. General treatises or textbooks 2. Treatises on specific topics 3. Recipe collections 4. Regimens and health guides 5. Surgical and anatomical treatises 6. *Philosophical Transactions* 7. Appendix: Medicine in society.

and is in accordance with the new purpose of the scientific journal. This study shows how we can probe into essential features and accurately pin-point innovative uses with statistical computerized methods combined with qualitative assessments. It also shows how corpus-linguistic methods can be tailored to answer very specific research questions.

5.3 Historical speech act studies

The language practices of common people have attracted increasing attention, for example, in historical speech act studies, where greetings and farewells, thanks and apologies, requests, and other everyday practices are highlighted. Speech act studies represent function-to-form mapping, which is more difficult to deal with than the form-to-functions direction of fit with corpus-linguistic methods. Some steps towards diachronic speech act analysis were taken in the inaugural issue of the *Journal of Historical Pragmatics* where Bertuccelli Papi (2000) posed the question "Is a diachronic speech act theory possible?" It was followed by tentative positive answers in qualitative studies. Corpora were used to locate relevant examples, but the identification of speech acts proved problematic. Insults are particularly difficult as they depend on the perlocutionary effect and cannot be directly searched in electronic corpora (Jucker and Taavitsainen 2000).

In principle, three methods can be used. The first relies on Illoctionary Force Indicating Devices (IFIDs), and many of the present-day IFIDs also work for historical texts too, e.g. *sorry* and *thank you*, but there is no one-to-one fit between the present and the past, and there may be other expressions typical of the period that could go unnoticed. Such was the case, for example, in eighteenth-century thanking as *I am obliged* and similar phrases are very much in accordance with the politeness ideals of the period (Taavitsainen and Jucker 2010). The second way of identifying speech acts is through routine realizations of speech acts other than IFIDs. Examples of typical search strings for compliments include positive adjectives, but more unusual and creative manifestations do not easily lend themselves to corpus searches (Taavitsainen and Jucker 2008). The researcher's own familiarity with the data guides him or her to detect to recurrent patterns of "hidden manifestations" of speech acts (Kohnen 2008). Different solutions have been suggested (see below), but qualitative reading and manual inspection are needed for reliable results. The third method of identification is the metacommunicative expression analysis that reveals how the speech act was understood in its time, but the actual words may not be recorded. The research task of insults was modified to instances of verbal aggression that could be searched with the help of HT and speech act labels (Taavitsainen and Jucker 2007) and developed further in subsequent studies (Jucker *et al.* 2012; Jucker and Taavitsainen 2014b; see also Jaworski *et al.* 2004; Culpeper 2011; Busse and Hübler 2012).

We have come a long way forward, and scholars are actively testing new possibilities, even automatic retrieval of speech act manifestations, but they present problems. One such study is Jucker *et al.* (2008). Its point of departure is the statement by Manes and Wolfson (1981: 115) that American compliments (collected by the diary method or participant observation) display "almost total lack of originality," and Holmes (1988: 480) confirms that according to her studies "compliments are remarkably formulaic." These statements were tested with search strings translated into syntactic query language and applied to the 100-million-word *British National Corpus* in order to improve the methodology so that it could be applicable to historical studies in the future. Severe problems of both precision in finding the relevant examples and recall, i.e. retrieving examples with appropriate structure but not appropriate function, were encountered. The retrieved examples were analysed manually by two independent raters, which confirmed the statement that speech acts are fuzzy notions with a subjective element, and that contextual qualitative analysis is needed to tell apart, for example, sincere and ironical examples with identical wordings (Jucker and Taavitsainen 2000). The conclusion was that results of the corpus-linguistic searches can be improved by manual annotation but for practical reasons this cannot be done with very large corpora.

Valkonen (2008) and Kohnen (2007b, 2008, 2009) have also made attempts to develop the methods of speech act identification in historical corpora. Valkonen tested speech act retrieval in unannotated corpus material by commissive speech act verbs (*promise, swear, vow*, etc.). He used a section of ARCHER as a training corpus and then applied the method to Chadwyck-Healey eighteenth-century prose texts. Problems of recall and precision were obvious, and he concluded that the recall was not good enough to serve as a reliable basis for quantitative studies, but nevertheless it provided a useful basis for qualitative analysis. Kohnen relied on a more "philological" bottom-up method. The first step in his model was to make an inventory of various manifestations of directives by hand, the second was to repeat the procedure in different genres, and the third to test the manifestations in larger corpora. Indirect manifestations proved most problematic as they cannot be caught in this way and it is the researcher's familiarity with the data that guarantees the best results.

5.4 Discourse studies on ideology

Corpus-linguistic applications are newcomers in the field of discourse studies in general as discourse studies have traditionally relied on qualitative assessments. The development has been rapid and sophistication has increased greatly in recent years. McEnery's (2006b) article "The moral panic about bad language in England, 1691–1745" shows how the new applications of corpus-linguistic methodology can reveal subtle aspects of meaning-making processes in historical texts. In the late seventeenth and early eighteenth centuries bad language was associated with a wide range of sins and sinful acts, and societies were founded to abolish it and legally charge its users. A special corpus, the Society for the Reformation of Manners Corpus, was compiled for this study, and the *Lampeter Corpus* of contemporary shorter tracts and pamphlets served as the reference corpus. WordSmith was used to define positive and negative keywords, i.e. words that were significantly more or less frequent in the assessed corpus than in a reference corpus. The program ranks the keywords and gives them a keyness score that denotes the scale from the strongest to the weakest negative and positive keywords. In general, keywords are of three kinds: names, topic words, and grammatical items. Most keywords fall into the topic area, but often it is the function words that prove most interesting. In this case, the first non-register positive keyword *and* has a main function in creating spirals of signification, as it tied objects of offence in coordinated noun phrases. These Societies developed a particular obsessive and moralistic discourse style that made use of "spirals of signification" by associating bad language with other sources of moral offence. Keywords served to distinguish these texts from general English, or even texts written in a similar register/genre but not conveying moral panic. Moral panic was shown to occur in clusters, and the collocations with their complex networks contributed to a signification spiral. For example, *swear* was collocated with *blaspheme, curse, damn, game, hector*, and *rant. Swearing* was systematically coordinated with disapproved verbal acts, lawlessness, frivolous pursuits, and sexual activity. Negatively loaded collocates are frequent, and by this mechanism moral panic becomes amplified with a strong negative semantic prosody. The keyword method was able to demonstrate in a detailed way the discursive construction of "moral panic" about language use and it revealed the mechanism of manipulating readers' conceptions of ideological issues. This pioneer study was followed by an article on the mid-seventeenth-century Glencairn Uprising, a military rebellion by Scottish Highlanders against the English government (Prentice and Hardie 2009). The focus is on the presentations of the opposing sides of the conflict in the contemporary London newspaper data, and the dichotomy of "us" and "them" is statistically verified with WordSmith tools, mainly KWIC concordances.

6 Negotiating pragmatic meanings: a case study of general nouns, vagueness, and specificity

Negotiability is one of the defining features of pragmatic approaches to language use (Verschueren 1999: 59–61). It is the context that determines how meanings are made, how they are intended and how they are interpreted. Both speaker meanings and the recipients' understandings depend on shared cultural background and the practices of discourse communities need to be considered. One of the core questions in the history of science is what continued and what changed (Crombie 1995). Medieval science was scholastic, and the new thought-style of empiricism is usually ascribed to the Royal Society period: authorities lost their status as the holders of truth and reliance on their writings gave way to observation. But changes in thought-styles are long processes, and most medieval genres and styles of writing continue in the early modern period, but undergo modifications. New uses emerge as features typical of the earlier scholastic style gain new uses. Evidence for more detailed knowledge of the change comes from my earlier study (Taavitsainen 2009) which shows how the mechanisms of change can be assessed in detail with corpus-linguistic tools, but qualitative reading is also needed to interpret the statistical results. The point of departure was a list of authorities, obtained by a previous study on late medieval materials (Taavitsainen and Pahta 1998) and complemented by the EMEMT word lists, and assessed with the KWIC concordance function of Wordsmith.[5] Treatises on specific topics (Category 2) contained several texts with clusters of references to authorities. A further study was conducted with keyword analysis of single texts with the rest of the same category as a reference corpus. A declining frequency scale of authorities emerged but a microanalysis was needed to indicate a core group of texts worth more attention. The plot view of WordSmith revealed *loci* for qualitative assessment. Passages like the following reveal the medieval commentary style at the turn of the seventeenth century with features typical of scholasticism: deontic modality (*to wit*), passive-voice sentences but a clear authorial voice, code switching to Latin, definitions, and an enumerative text strategy.[6]

> PHlebotomy is the letting out of bloud by the opening of a vayne, for the preuenting or curing of some griefe or infirmitie. I take in this place bloud, not as it is simple and pure of it self, but as it is mingled with other humours, to wit, fleame, choler, melancholy, and the tenue serum, which all (as Fernelius sheweth) as they are conteined together in the vaynes, are by one word vsually called by the name of bloud. And although it still fall out that other humours are also by Phlebotomy euacuated out of the whole body, yet (as Fuchsius doth proue out of Galen) it is properly the remedy of those diseases, ... There are foure seuerall sorts and vses of letting of bloud. The first is called, euacuatio: The second is called, and of Montanus ciscutatio: The third, revulsio: The fourth, deriuatio. (EMEMT Harward, *Phlebotomy* 1601, page 1)

General nouns indicating vagueness were also included in the study. In EMEMT they occurred in all kinds of writing, but most commonly in the

[5] The list included Galen, Hippocrates, Aesculapius, Avicenna, Albucasis, Rhazes, Haly Abbas, Averroes, Aristotle, Plato, and Ptolemy.

[6] Late medieval vernacular texts did not achieve the same clarity of expression as the register was new and the language had not developed to express abstract scientific notions.

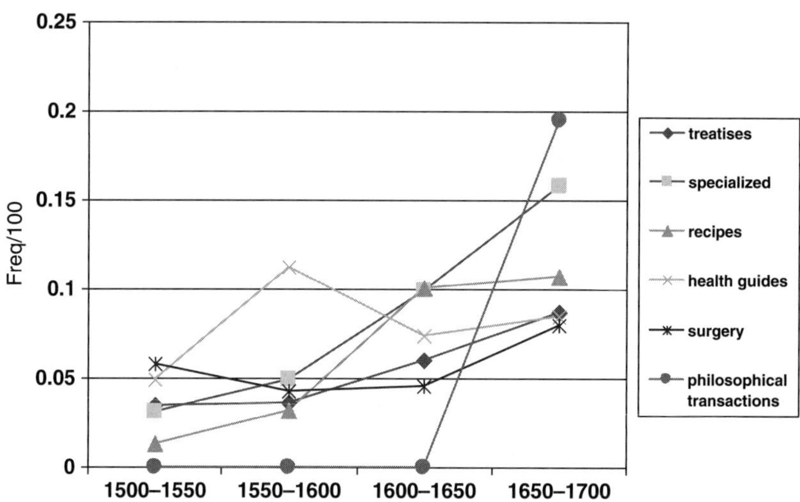

Figure 14.1 General references in the text categories of EMEMT 1500–1700 (according to Taavitsainen 2009)

remedy book tradition. In EMEMT they were rare at first, but increased greatly in the last decades.

Generic references mark a shift in the locus of scientific knowledge in the early modern period, and an interesting development emerged. The discourse community and its members' role in creating new knowledge became enhanced. Earlier vague references gain new functions and implicit meanings: they become specific in the sense that all members of the discourse community knew who the general nouns referred to. The following passage deals with a conflict. The author has a clear role in controlling the text and refers to the parties of the dispute known to all with general nouns:

> THO I have been much solicited, to shew my Opinion, about the Debate betwixt the two Physicians, concerning ... and violently oppos'd by a certain Club of Physicians; ... And whether or not by the vain Fears of Friends and By-standers, a Faithful and Expert Physician may be blunder'd, and a good Method disgrac'd? And whether dallying and triffling with a Fever, tho less exceptionable, be not more dangerous, and often of more fatal consequence, than Plentiful Purging? ... These I take to be the most material Points in this Debate, which seems to be handled with a little more Heat and Humour, than is consistent either with the Import of the Matter, or Dignity of the Members of so Judicious a Society, who would be expected to treat all their Matters, and seek to advance the Improvement of Medicine, in Candor, Amity, and Peace. (EMEMT; Brown, *The Epilogue* 1699, page 3)

7 Future trends

The new data sources have brought historical pragmatics to a new phase as one branch is heading to multimodal assessments with digital images of manuscript and book pages (see Taavitsainen and Suhr 2012). For example, book printers' types can reveal the intended audiences, whether elementary black letter type or the more demanding Roman type, and illustrations in early printed books convey additional meanings. Book history and palaeography can also be viewed from a pragmatic angle (see Meurman-Solin and Tyrkkö 2013). With EEBO and ECCO new research agendas have already been created. The interface between semantics and pragmatics has been invigorated by the electronic version of HT (see Jucker *et al.* 2012). Thus it is not only the traditional corpora but the other electronic resources that enhance the potentials for innovative work. Historical pragmatics is also extending to completely unstudied areas, with early speech recordings. They have been pointed out as a potential sources for study (Jucker and Taavitsainen 2013), but the work has hardly begun. It seems likely that the European "perspective view" will extend to phonetics/phonology, which is a new area to be added to morphology, syntax, and semantics for historical pragmatic studies.

English linguistics has undergone a change with corpus-linguistic methods, but for historical pragmatics, the change is less dramatic as corpus-linguistic methods have been used from the beginning. Sophistication has increased greatly from the early years and the methods have developed from frequency counts and assessments of distributional patterns to tailor-made research algorithms and refined investigations revealing ideological underpinnings. New software tools allow researchers to probe into more subtle aspects of meaning-making processes and it is possible to gain deeper insights into past communication of earlier historical periods. In some areas, like historical discourse pragmatics, progress has been considerable, but it has also been noticed that all branches of historical pragmatics do not lend themselves easily to corpus studies. Researchers have become aware of the problems and they are trying out new solutions. The field offers plenty of challenging and rewarding research opportunities for the future.

CORPORA (For a more complete list of historical corpora, see CoRD, www.helsinki.fi/varieng/CoRD/corpora/index.html)

ARCHER *A Representative Corpus of Historical English Registers* www.llc.manchester.ac.uk/research/projects/archer/

CEEC Corpora of *Early English Correspondence*, see www.helsinki.fi/varieng/CoRD/corpora/CEEC/index.html.

CEEM Corpus of *Early English Medical Writing*, see Taavitsainen and Pahta (eds.). 2010. www.helsinki.fi/varieng/CoRD/corpora/CEEM/index.html

CED	*Corpus of English Dialogues* www.engelska.uu.se/Research/English_Language/Research_Areas/Electronic_Resource_Projects/A_Corpus_of_English_Dialogues/
CETA	*A Corpus of English Texts on Astronomy*. See Moscovich and Crespo (eds. 2012)
	Chadwyck-Healey Literature Collections, Online (LION) at http://lion. chadwyck.com/
CLMET	*Corpus of Late Modern English* Texts. Compiled by Hendrik De Smet, Hans-Jürgen Diller, and Jukka Tyrkkö. https://perswww.kuleuven.be/~u0044428/
CoER	*Corpus of Early English Recipes*. See Alonso Almeida *et al.* (2012).
COERP	*Corpus of English Religious Prose*. Compiled by Thomas Kohnen, Tanja Rütten, Ingvilt Marcoe, Kirsten Gather, and Dorothee Groeger. www.helsinki.fi/varieng/CoRD/corpora/COERP/
COHA	*The Corpus of Historical American English*, http://corpus.byu.edu/coha/
CSC	*Corpus of Scottish Correspondence*, see www.helsinki.fi/varieng/CoRD/corpora/CSC/index.html
ECCO	*Eighteenth Century Collections Online*. ProQuest LLC.
EEBO	*Early English Books Online*. ProQuest LLC. http://eebo.chadwyck.com/home
ETED	*An Electronic Text Edition of Depositions 1560–1760*. See Kytö *et al.* (eds.). 2011.
HC	*The Helsinki Corpus of English Texts* see www.helsinki.fi/varieng/CoRD/corpora/HelsinkiCorpus/index.html
LC	*The Lampeter Corpus of Early Modern English Tracts*, see www.helsinki.fi/varieng/CoRD/corpora/LC/index.html
	The Málaga Corpus of Late Middle English Scientific Prose. Forthcoming. See Miranda-García Antonio and Javier Calle-Martín.
	The Old Bailey Corpus www.uni-giessen.de/oldbaileycorpus
ZEN	*The Zurich English Newspaper Corpus*, see http://www.helsinki.fi/varieng/CoRD/corpora/ZEN/index.html

Part III

Corpus analysis of varieties

15

Spoken discourse

Shelley Staples

1 Introduction

Spoken corpora have long been of interest to researchers but also more challenging to compile than written corpora. It should be noted that early "corpora" (those developed before the 1980s when corpora became computerized) were more often based on spoken rather than written language, but were quite small and focused primarily on the study of phonetic features (Ling 1999: 240, qtd. in McEnery, Xiao, and Tono 2006: 3). Such corpora were rightly criticized for being "skewed" as they could not claim to be representative of speech as a whole or even in particular domains due to their small size and inability to be analyzed quantitatively (McEnery, Xiao, and Tono 2006: 4).

Modern spoken corpora consist of much larger, transcribed texts stored on computers, which enables researchers to use quantitative methods of analysis. However, some of the remaining issues include: (1) consent for gathering spoken data, particularly in more sensitive domains such as legal and medical interactions; (2) the time-consuming nature of transcription; (3) lack of reliable automatic analysis tools for some spoken features, such as prosodic features.

Due to particularly the first two limitations, spoken corpora are less numerous than written corpora and also have tended to focus on more limited domains. There are a number of available spoken corpora that contain face-to-face conversation, for example, the *London–Lund Corpus* (LLC), *Cambridge and Nottingham Corpus of Discourse in English* (CANCODE), the *British National Corpus* (BNC), the *Lancaster/IBM Spoken English Corpus* (SEC), and the *Santa Barbara Corpus of Spoken American English* (SBCSAE).

While these corpora also contain other spoken registers, face to face conversation forms the bulk of the texts in the spoken sections. However, a growing number of spoken corpora focus on other more specialized registers of speech. From the corpora that are publicly available, two useful examples are COCA and MICASE. Although COCA simply calls its spoken subcorpus "speech," it is important to note that it consists primarily of transcripts of news programs and talk shows, not face-to-face interaction. MICASE includes examples from various spoken registers found in an academic setting (e.g. lectures, study groups, presentations). Other examples include the *Corpus of Professional Spoken American English* (press conferences; faculty meetings and committee meetings related to national tests) and COLT (*Bergen Corpus of London Teenage Language*). Other specialized corpora tend to be unavailable to the public. These include T2KSWAL, which contains a variety of registers found in academic settings (e.g. classroom teaching, study groups, and office hours), the *Nottingham Health Communication Corpus* (NHCC), which consists of interactions between nurses, pharmacists, NHS Direct health advisers, a hospital chaplain, and patients, and the *Language in the Workplace Project* (LWP) corpus, which contains workplace interactions in a variety of settings (e.g. government departments, meetings, and factory settings). Other more specialized corpora include Friginal (2009), a corpus of call center interactions and Staples (2014), a spoken corpus of nurse–patient interactions.

A number of spoken corpora also focus on different varieties of English. The *International Corpus of English* in particular represents ten varieties of spoken English (e.g. Great Britain, South Africa, India). The BNC is probably the most well-known corpus focused on a national variety. The *Wellington Corpus* (New Zealand) and *Limerick Corpus of Irish English* are two other national corpora with spoken English represented.

Finally, a growing number of corpora focus on the language of learners. LINDSEI (*Louvain International Database of Spoken English Interlanguage*) contains interviews from L2 English learners of eleven different language backgrounds (e.g. Spanish, Chinese, Polish). One limitation of this and most other learner corpora is that most of the interviews are not rated for proficiency level.

In addition to the challenges in creating spoken corpora, another important consideration is that many corpora are aging. The LLC was gathered in the 1980s, and the BNC between 1980 to 1993. Most corpora (spoken and written) are sampled corpora (meaning that they are sampled from a specific period of time). One monitor corpus that allows us to see changes in spoken corpora and also provides more current spoken data is COCA. However, as mentioned above, one limitation of this corpus is that it is composed of transcripts from news programs and talk shows and thus the speech is likely to be more scripted or more carefully produced than informal registers of spoken English.

The following sections highlight key advancements within corpus linguistics on the study of speech, starting with characteristics that differentiate speech from writing (Section 2), and then moving to characteristics of particular spoken registers (Section 3), and specific individual features associated with speech (Section 4). New directions and challenges for spoken corpus research is the focus of Section 5, including research on fluency, prosody, and non-verbal behavior in spoken corpora, dialect studies, and discourse-level investigations. After a summary of the advancements and future directions for spoken corpora (Section 6), the seventh and final section will focus on a case study that brings together some of themes and innovations highlighted in the previous sections. The case study investigates stance features in nurse-patient interactions, a lesser-studied discourse domain, and also highlights differences within the interactions and across speaker groups (nurses and patients).

2 Distinctive features of speech in comparison with writing

The earliest studies investigating spoken corpora used corpora of both speech and writing to identify key linguistic features associated with different modes of communication. While characteristics differentiating speech and writing were discussed by many scholars in the 1980s (see, e.g., Tannen 1985), the first study to investigate these differences empirically, in a large corpus, was Biber (1988). Biber (1988) identified features that were used more frequently in spoken registers. A factor analysis of 67 linguistic features identified 6 factors of co-occurring linguistic features. Although no factor (referred to hereafter as Dimension) was entirely divided between speech and writing, Dimension 1 of Biber (1988), "Informational vs. Involved Production," showed the sharpest division between the two modes, with most spoken registers using many more features associated with involvement (e.g. first- and second-person pronouns). This was particularly the case for dialogic spoken discourse (telephone conversations, face-to-face conversation, and interviews). This study also introduced a novel method of linguistic analysis, multidimensional analysis (MD analysis), which allowed for the examination of a wide range of co-occurring linguistic features (see Chapter 17 this volume for an explanation of MD analysis). As discussed in the 2013 special issue of *Corpora*, this study laid the groundwork for much of the quantitative investigation of spoken and written discourse to follow.

After this landmark study, a number of others examined spoken language in relation to written language, using MD analysis. These studies examined more specific domains than those included in the Biber (1988) study, as well as speakers of different language backgrounds or dialects. Reppen (1994) investigated the spoken and written language used and consumed by elementary school children. A similar first dimension was identified in this corpus, "Edited informational discourse" and "On-line informational discourse," which showed divisions in written and spoken registers. The "on-line informational discourse" used more adverbials and pronouns while the written registers contained more nouns and noun modifiers. In a somewhat related study, Biber (2006a) examined differences across speech and writing within university contexts. Similar to the findings in Biber (1988), Dimension 1 of Biber (2006a), "Oral vs. Literate Discourse," showed that all of the spoken registers (service encounters, office hours, labs, study groups, and classroom teaching) used features such as first/second-person pronouns, contractions, and adverbial clauses more frequently. The division between the use of these features in speech and writing was absolute for Dimension 1 in this study. Other languages (e.g. Somali, Korean) have been found to have a similar first dimension to that found in Biber (1988) and Biber (2006a) (see Biber and Hared 1992 for Somali and Kim and Biber 1994 for Korean).

Xiao (2009) investigated a wide range of linguistic features in a variety of English dialects (e.g. British English, Hong Kong English, Philippine English) using the ICE corpus. Xiao (2009) found a similar factor structure to that in Biber (1988). The first dimension in particular, "Interactive Casual Discourse vs. Informative Elaborate Discourse," showed that both public and private dialogic speech was associated with the use of private verbs, non-past tense, and contractions while almost all written registers were associated with greater use of prepositions, nouns, and attributive adjectives. Xiao (2009) also showed that Outer Circle speakers (particularly Indian, Philippine, and Hong Kong English speakers) use fewer features in dialogic spoken discourse that are associated with "Interactive Casual Discourse" than speakers of Inner Circle varieties (i.e. British English).

Finally, Biber and Gray (2013) applied the MD framework to second language writing and speech, using responses from the TOEFL iBT. As with the other MD analyses, Dimension 1 formed a similar division between oral and literate discourse ("Oral vs. Literate Tasks"). Spoken responses were more associated with private (mental) verbs, modal verbs, and present tense while written responses were more associated with nouns, prepositional phrases, and attributive adjectives.

Taken together, these studies show the overwhelming reliance of spoken discourse on clausal features as well as personal pronouns. By comparing speech to writing through MD analysis, it is possible to determine key characteristics of the speech, which can be used for more detailed investigation across spoken registers.

3 Distinctive features across various spoken registers

A number of more recent studies have focused on differences in the linguistic features used across spoken registers. One such study is

Friginal (2009), who investigates speech in call center interactions, phone conversations, and face-to-face conversation. Dimension 1, "Addressee Focused, Polite and Elaborated Information," shows that speakers in the call center corpus use a higher frequency of politeness and respect markers in comparison with speakers in the two other spoken corpora. An important feature of this study is the level of context provided to explain the linguistic variety found within the corpus. The social and situational factors included in the analysis include speaker role, gender, quality of service provided by the agent (identified through assessment scores on language and task performance), years of experience of the agent at the current call center, and the primary communicative task (i.e. the three types of calls: troubleshoot, inquire, purchase). The study also incorporates the level of caller expertise in technical issues (lay person or specialist) and the level of pressure or potential conflict for the communicative task.

Other studies have focused on variation across TV dialogue, movie language, and face-to-face conversation (Al-Surmi 2012; Forchini 2012; Quaglio 2009). TV show dialogue has been shown to contain even more of the features that make face-to-face conversation "involved," including first- and second-person pronouns and private verbs (e.g. *think* and *know*) (Al-Surmi 2012; Quaglio 2009). However, movie language appears to be more similar to face-to-face conversation in its use of these same features (Forchini 2012).

These studies reveal important differences in patterns of use across spoken registers. Using MD analysis allows researchers to identify differences in the use of a combination of linguistic variables for particular functions. A number of studies have investigated individual features in spoken discourse more closely, to provide an even more fine-grained analysis of the use of these features.

4 Individual features distinctive of spoken discourse

4.1 Formulaic language

Studies of lexical bundles have revealed distinctive characteristics of this type of formulaic language in speech when compared to writing. Studies show that lexical bundles are more common in speech than in writing, particularly academic writing (Biber *et al.* 1999; Biber, Conrad, and Cortes 2004; Biber 2006a). Biber *et al.* (2004) also compared the frequencies of lexical bundles used for stance, discourse organization, and referential functions in conversation and academic writing. They found that stance and discourse organizing bundles were more frequent in conversation, while referential bundles were more frequent in writing. Regarding bundle fixedness, Biber (2009) revealed that formulaic language in conversation tends to contain three fixed words in a sequence with a variable slot either preceding or succeeding it (e.g. *I don't know* *). In academic writing, on the other hand, there were more frames with internal variable slots (e.g. *the * of the*) (Biber 2009: 299). In sum, variation in the frequency, function, and fixedness of lexical bundle use suggests meaningful differences in the way that formulaic language is processed in speech as well as the functions for which it is used.

Other studies have focused on developing lists of frequent formulaic language for speech in order to inform language learning. The most well-known of such lists is probably the Academic Formulas List (Simpson-Vlach and Ellis 2010). The authors used a corpus of speech and writing but provided separate lists for each mode. Other lists have been proposed as well, including PHRASE (Martinez and Schmitt 2012), which also includes speech and writing, and provides a number of additional criteria beyond that used in Simpson-Vlach and Ellis (2010). However, their list does not distinguish across mode. Shin and Nation's (2008) list focuses solely on spoken English. Both Martinez and Schmitt (2012) and Shin and Nation (2008) rely on the BNC for their analysis, which, as discussed above, is aging. While there is some overlap in the content of the lists, variations occur, due to the different criteria employed by the researchers and the corpora chosen for analysis.

One recent innovative study focused solely on speech is Lin (2013), which investigates the use of prominence (sentence stress) in relation to formulaic language. Lin (2013) finds that while most formulaic language follows the patterns expected for prominence in general (at the end of an intonation unit), a subset of formulaic language is unstressed in final position, suggesting that the phrase in question functions more similarly to function words than to content words. Examples of formulaic language that was unstressed included *if you like* and *in other words*. As will be discussed in Section 6 below, examinations of prosody in spoken corpora are infrequent, although a growing number of studies include this important aspect of spoken discourse.

4.2 Stance features

The Longman Grammar (Biber *et al.* 1999) shows that stance features are much more common in spoken than in written contexts. It is surprising, then, that more studies have focused on the use of stance in writing rather than speech. However, a growing number of studies have looked at the use of stance in spoken contexts, including classroom teaching, office hours, call center interactions, and medical interactions (Barbieri 2008; Lindemann and Mauranen 2001; Poos and Simpson 2002; Mauranen 2003b, 2004; Swales and Burke 2003; Biber 2006b; Friginal 2008; Staples and Biber 2014). All of these studies have revealed ways in which stance features are used for important functions specific to the particular register being investigated. Mauranen (2004), for example, shows how stance features are used in academic discourse for both epistemic and strategic purposes, with the latter being focused more on interactional concerns than propositional content. Barbieri (2008) also investigated stance in classroom discourse and found that certain stance features, such as stance adverbs and modals, were used more frequently by junior and younger faculty than senior and older faculty. Staples and Biber (2014) identify a number of stance features used more frequently by nurses in medical interactions when compared with conversation (e.g. prediction and possibility modals, stance adverbs expressing likelihood).

4.3 Discourse markers

One feature examined in many corpus-based studies of speech is the use of discourse markers, most likely due to their long association with spoken as opposed to written discourse (see, e.g., Schiffrin 1989). Aijmer's (2002) book-length analysis focuses on identifying core and common functions of discourse markers on both textual and interpersonal levels. Another detailed study of discourse markers is Müller (2005), which provides insight into the different patterns of use by native and non-native speakers of English, showing that German speakers of English use particular functions of discourse markers more frequently than native speakers of English. Lam (2009) also focuses on the functions of discourse markers, and adds a comparison across registers, illustrating the connection between frequency of use for a particular function and the register under investigation. Other corpus-based studies which investigate discourse marker use include He and Kennedy (1999), which examined the *London–Lund Corpus of Spoken English* (LLC) for forms found to initiate turns in which speakers overlap. Although they did not use the term discourse marker explicitly, many of the forms they identified corresponded to those often recognized as discourse markers (e.g. *okay, well, so*). Tao (2003) examined forms used to initiate turns in the *Switchboard Corpus* and the *Cambridge University Press/Cornell University Corpus* and determined that some of the most common forms were *oh*, *yeah*, *okay*, and *well*, also forms well established as discourse markers. Register-specific studies include Swales and Malczewski (2001), which identified three discourse markers associated with denoting what they term *new episodes: so, okay*, and *now*. In their framework, new episodes are instances in classroom teaching where an instructor shifts the topic or moves from lecture to discussion. Finally, Evison (2013) analyzes turn initiators in the *Cambridge and Nottingham Corpus of Academic Discourse* (CANCAD), a subcorpus of the CANCODE, and compares them with non-academic speech in the CANCSOC, another subcorpus of the CANCODE focusing on socializing and intimate conversation. She highlights the importance of speaker role in discourse marker use, especially emphasizing the influence of power relationships (in this case, between student and teacher).

4.4 Vague language

A final area that has seen increasing activity recently is the investigation of vague language in spoken discourse, which, like discourse markers, has been identified as a distinctive feature of speech (see McCarthy 2004; Aijmer 2002). One important publicly available corpus for the study of register variation within spoken discourse is the *Hong Kong Corpus of Spoken English* (HKCSE), which contains conversation, academic, business (e.g. job placement interviews, service encounters), and public (e.g. public speeches) registers. Cheng (2007) investigated the use of vague language across registers. While vague language was used in all registers, the token *something* was found to be more frequent in conversation than in the other three registers. Evison, McCarthy, and O'Keeffe (2007) explore the different sources of reference identified in vague expressions, finding variation across registers. They also suggest that language teachers provide opportunities for learners to use vague expressions. Adolphs, Atkins, and Harvey (2007) indicate the importance of vague expressions such as *or anything* in medical interactions in order to leave questions open-ended for patients to fill in information. Finally, Fernández (2013) explores the use of vague language by L2 Spanish speakers in the *Spanish Learner Language Oral Corpora* (SPLLOC), finding that general extenders (e.g. *y eso* 'and that') were used most frequently in dialogic tasks (e.g. pair discussion and interviews) when compared with monologic tasks (e.g. narratives).

5 New directions and challenges

5.1 Fluency and prosody studies

Due to the current labor-intensive process of hand-coding fluency and especially prosodic features, few large corpora have been analyzed for fluency and prosody features. Notable exceptions include the *London–Lund Corpus* (LLC) and *Lancaster/IBM Spoken English Corpus* (SEC), both developed in the 1980s. The LLC is coded for intonation units, placement of prominence, and pitch movement (intonation). The SEC corpus is coded for these features as well as temporal alignment at the level of the phoneme. More recently, the *Intonational Variation in English* (IViE) (developed in the late 1990s) was developed to investigate dialects of British English. It includes information about pitch movement and prominence. The *Hong Kong Corpus of Spoken English* (HKCSE; Cheng, Greaves, and Warren 2008) was created specifically for the analysis of intonation, prominence, and pitch in a variety of registers (e.g. lectures, interviews, conversation, service encounters). A notable example outside English is C-ORAL ROM (Cresti and Moneglia 2005), which marks the division of utterances into intonation units (prosodic breaks) but does not indicate prominent syllables or pitch change at the boundaries of intonation units. LeaP, *Learning Prosody in a Foreign Language*, contains prosodically transcribed speech for learners of English (16 different L1s) and German (21 different L1s). The corpus contains very controlled speech (e.g. word lists and read passages) but also includes free speech in the form of interviews with speakers before and after studying abroad in a country where the target language was the primary language used. Gut (2009) both describes the corpus and conducts an analysis on the differences in use of prosodic (and phonetic) features among L1 German speakers of German, L1 German speakers of English, L1 English speakers of English, and L1 English speakers of German. One important finding is that while the overall phonological systems did not differ dramatically between native and non-native speakers (similar proportions of rising and falling intonation but more level intonation from non-native speakers), the phonetic realization of non-native speakers' intonation differed: non-native speakers' falls were shorter than native speakers'. However, it is not clear whether this finding would be the same for speakers of very different language backgrounds (e.g. English and Chinese). Gut (2009) also indicates that differences in the use of intonation and other pitch-related features were clearly tied to register differences (see p. 248).

Cheng, Greaves, and Warren (2008) provide key findings from the prosodically transcribed portions of the HKCSE, which also illustrate differences across registers. The HKCSE was compiled between 1997 and 2002 in Hong Kong in universities, businesses, and private settings. David Brazil's (1997) Discourse Intonation framework was employed in the transcription, a system which views intonation as motivated by discourse functions and pragmatic concerns rather than exclusively linked to grammatical features or emotional expression. This framework divides speech into tone units (i.e. intonation units, breath groups, thought groups) and then identifies prominent syllables within those tone units as well as their pitch height (high, mid, low). As indicated above, Cheng, Greaves, and Warren (2008) provide evidence for differences in the use of intonation across registers. Rising tone was found to be used more in conversation than in other registers (academic, business, and public) but falling tone was more frequent overall (when compared with rising and level tone) in conversation (p. 128). In other registers within the HKCSE, level tone was used more frequently than falling tone (p. 127). As a result, falling tone was also used most frequently in conversation than in other registers of the HKCSE. Level intonation seems to be used more frequently in monologic discourse, to mark continuation of a topic or to mark a focus on the language being used. Similar to the findings of Gut, Cheng, Greaves, and Warren (2008) found that Hong Kong Chinese (HKC) speakers of English used level tone slightly more than native speakers (p. 126). Notably, though, it was the most frequent tone in the corpus for both native and HKC speakers. While the HKCSE is a remarkable undertaking and provides an important resource for researchers interested in prosodic features across registers, one drawback is that the speech files are not provided with the corpus.

The automatic extraction of phonetic and phonological elements (both segmental and suprasegmental) is undoubtedly one of the major challenges facing researchers interested in using spoken corpora to investigate phonetic and prosodic patterns. A few studies offer promising developments in this area. Ferrangne (2013) provides some evidence that automatic vowel detection may be a viable tool to predict speech rate, even in non-native speech. It should be noted that the automatic detection overestimated the number of vowels when compared with manual identification of vowels. Ballier and Martin (2013) also suggest that while automated tools used to identify pitch and other suprasegmental elements are inadequate at present, they can be a useful first step when combined with manual checking of the features identified. However, they caution that the theoretical basis for such tools is questionable, and conclude that particularly for spontaneous speech, manual analysis is still the only reliable system of analysis. Finally, it should be noted that although these advancements are quite promising for the study of fluency and prosodic features, they still remain out of reach for most professionals working in this area.

Another neglected feature in the collection and study of spoken corpora has, until recently, been non-verbal behavior (e.g. gestures, eye contact). One exceptional project attempting to fill this gap is the Nottingham Multi-modal Corpus (NMMC) (see Knight *et al.* 2009 for a description of the development of this corpus). This corpus encodes hand and head movements, aligning these gestures with the linguistic elements of the transcribed corpus. Knight and Adolphs (2008) explored the possibilities of this corpus, focusing on verbal and non-verbal backchannels. They found that the duration of head nod acting as a backchannel seemed to be related to the function of the head nod (shorter nods were associated with Information Receipt while longer nods were associated with Convergence with the speaker).

5.2 Dialect studies

Along with Inner Circle varieties of English (British, New Zealand English), a growing number of corpora focus on other national varieties of English (for example, the *International Corpus of English*, discussed above in Section 1, and *VOICE–Vienna-Oxford International Corpus of English*). However, the investigation of regional dialects within national varieties has mostly focused on an "atlas" approach, which relies on words or very short stretches of speech, similar to the model discussed earlier when describing early speech "corpora." Longer stretches of speech have been recorded as part of dialect studies but often lack widespread accessibility. Exceptions include the *Survey of English Dialects* (SED), which contains sociolinguistic interviews, more or less question-and-answer sessions. An interesting recent study using this corpus is the work of Shackleton (2007), who employs a variety of multivariate techniques (e.g. cluster analysis and principle components analysis) to identify dialects based on phonetic variation, verifying some aspects of earlier dialect studies but also identifying different dialect boundaries and additional features associated with particular dialects.

Less constrained corpora have been developed more recently for the study of dialectology, including the *Freiburg English Dialect Corpus* (FRED). This corpus was created for the study of grammatical variation in dialects rather than phonetic/phonological variation. It consists of oral interviews with speakers of six dialects in Great Britain. Szmrecsanyi (2008, 2012) and Szmrecsanyi and Wolk (2011) used this corpus to classify British dialects on the basis of a large number of common morphosyntactic features. This work shows that although dialect boundaries that result from multivariate studies are less clear-cut than those identified in early dialect research, they are more accurate and powerful.

5.3 Discourse-level units

Investigation of the linguistic features used within different stretches of discourse reveals important variation *within* spoken discourse rather than across registers. The challenge, however, is identifying discourse-level units, particularly through automated methods. Few studies have attempted to automatically identify discourse-level units in speech. Passonneau and Litman (1997), however were able to automatically partition spoken narratives by using referential noun phrases, cue words (similar to discourse markers), and pauses. Another novel approach divides texts into meaningful discourse-level units by determining shifts in vocabulary patterns in discourse (Biber, Connor, and Upton 2007: ch. 6). These Vocabulary-Based Discourse Units (VBDUs) are identified by investigating the similarity and differences of surrounding words to determine areas where new vocabulary is introduced into the discourse. Using MD analysis, Csomay (2005) looks within VBDUs identified in university classroom discourse to determine the lexicogrammatical features of different phases of the lecture, across various disciplines. While all disciplines used more involved and directive language at the beginning of the lecture, Business and Engineering teachers maintained this orientation across more VBDUs. Teachers in Education, Humanities, Social Sciences, and Natural Sciences more quickly shifted into an informational focus.

While these approaches appear to be suitable for longer stretches of speech, using automated techniques on discourse-level units in highly interactive, dialogic spoken corpora is less feasible. Thus, studies that attempt such segmentation currently require a combination of top-down and bottom-up approaches, using models from previous literature but making modifications based on the actual corpus in question. One such study is Staples (2015), which applies discourse-level phases previously identified from conversation-analytic research to a corpus of nurse–patient interaction (e.g. opening and closing phases). While the identification of phases relies heavily on this previous research, it also takes into account the realization of these phases within the corpus, and thus, for example, decisions about identifying shifts into the closing phase were only possible after investigating the interactions themselves.

6 Summary

The previous sections have attempted to illustrate many of the advancements in the use of spoken corpora and the important findings that corpus-linguistics research on spoken corpora has revealed. The empirical identification of distinctive features of spoken language (primarily in English but in other languages as well) has revealed important differences in the linguistic characteristics of speech in comparison with writing. Notably, speech is characterized by the use of more verbs, adverbs, and other clausal structures, as well as personal pronouns when compared to writing. This finding has important implications not only for the description of spoken language but also for the expectations about the language produced by more proficient speakers. While a large number of studies have confirmed this finding, it still seems to not have been adopted in models of spoken discourse used within more applied settings, particularly assessment and pedagogical communities.

Identifying systematic variation across spoken registers has allowed us to understand in more detail the function of linguistic variables acting in concert (e.g. features of involvement) as well as providing a more fine-grained analysis of the features characteristic of speech (e.g. stance features, discourse markers, and vague language), offering a more subtle understanding of their functions in particular discourse contexts. There are few large or publicly available corpora for specialized discourse contexts, however, so this is an area for further development and research. In addition, corpora focusing on dialects within national varieties are rare.

While automated methods have been developed for the identification of lexico-grammatical features, a major challenge remains the investigation of fluency, prosodic, and nonverbal features as well as the segmentation of speech into discourse-level units, particularly dialogic speech. These areas are a challenge to be met by the next generation of corpus linguists focusing on spoken corpora. The advances in automated techniques are promising, but at this point still a great deal of manual labor is required.

7 Case study

This case study focuses on the use of stance features across interactional phases within nurse–patient interactions and across speaker groups (nurses and patients). Similar to studies comparing the use of stance in particular registers, it illustrates the different functions of stance features based on speaker role. Unlike many studies, however, it also investigates the use of stance features within particular phases of the nurse–patient interactions, which demonstrates the variation within medical interactions.

The motivation for this study is that no previous studies have used corpus linguistic methods to investigate differences in the use of linguistic features by patients and nurses across the phases of an interaction. The use of these features elucidates the different roles of and functions performed by the two groups within various parts of a medical interaction. The investigation of the various interactional phases provides insight into variation within medical interactions.

The primary research question in this study is: how does speaker role impact the use of stance features across the phases of a medical interaction?

7.1 Methods

The corpus

The corpus used for this study is the *American Nurse–Standardized Patient* corpus (ANSP corpus). This corpus was collected and transcribed in 2012 and includes 50 interactions between registered nurses working at a US hospital and standardized patients (SPs). SPs are actors trained to present the same case to multiple healthcare providers and are often employed to assess nurses and doctors in training. The use of SPs means that the same topics were discussed by all nurses, which allows for clearer comparisons across the interactions. The nurses included in the study were all native speakers of English and had spent most of their lives in the US. They were predominantly female (46) and white (37). The average age of the nurses was 50 years and the average number of years working as a nurse was 21 years. The 50 interactions include just over 60,000 words and just under 8½ hours of recording time. Table 15.1 provides the details of the corpus analyzed in this study.

Stance features

Table 15.2 shows the stance features included in the analysis. These features were chosen based on previous research investigating grammatical stance in spoken discourse (e.g. Biber *et al.* 1999; Biber 2006b). The features were identified using the Biber Tagger, a computational tool that

Table 15.1 *Composition of the corpus used for the study*

Speaker category	Number of texts	Number of words
Nurses	50	46,282
Patients	50	18,135

Table 15.2 *Lexico-grammatical features used for stance analyses*

1. Modal and semi-modal verbs
   - Possibility/permission/ability: *can, could, may, might*
   - Necessity/obligation: *must, should, (had) better, have to, got to, ought to*
   - Prediction/volition: *will, would, shall, be going to*
2. Stance adverbs
   - Epistemic
     Certainty: e.g. *actually, certainly, in fact*
     Likelihood: e.g. *apparently, perhaps, possibly*
   - Attitude: e.g. *amazingly, importantly, surprisingly*
     Style/Perspective: e.g. *according to, generally, typically*
3. Complement clauses controlled by stance verbs and adjectives
   3.1. Stance complement clauses controlled by verbs
      3.1a. Stance verb + *that*-clause
      3.1.b. Stance verb + *to*-clause
   3.2. Stance complement clauses controlled by adjectives
      3.2 a. Stance adjective + *that*-clause (often extraposed constructions)
         e.g. *certain, possible, amazed, essential*
      3.2b. Stance adjective + *to*-clause (often extraposed constructions)
         e.g. *certain, happy, important, able, difficult, hard*

automatically annotates texts.[1] After automatic tagging, the tags were edited using an interactive tag-checking program to ensure the accuracy of all features investigated.

Phases of the interaction

After the interactions were recorded and transcribed, they were divided into phases (opening, exam, counsel, and closing) according to previous research (Heritage and Maynard 2006; Macdonald 2007; Rosdahl and Kowalski 2008; Roter 2010). The phases were identified by two coders through an iterative process of reference to the literature, consultation with a nursing researcher, and a series of smaller (pilot) studies. Table 15.3 provides details on the content of the phases. Intercoder reliability was established on 10 percent of the data, with intraclass correlations calculated for each of the phases. The reliability ranged from ICC = .84 to .97. After establishing acceptable reliability, a second coder coded the remaining data individually.

[1] The Biber Tagger was originally developed by Biber (1988) and has undergone numerous revisions since then. It currently is based on both probabilistic and rule-based components. This tagger has been used for many large-scale corpus analyses (e.g. Biber 1988, 2006a; Biber *et al.* 1999).

Table 15.3 *Phases of the interactions*

Phase	Elements contained within phase
Opening	Greetings
	Small talk
	Orientation of patient to environment and interaction
	Acknowledgments of the patient's current condition
Exam	**History**
	Past health and medical history, family history, procedures, and treatment
	Physical exam
	Indications of the nurse's upcoming actions
	Online reports on patient's condition or reports from chart
Counsel	Diagnosis/possible diagnosis
	Health-related information
	Recommendations for treatment
	Counseling
	Reference to plan of care (e.g. doctor's follow up)
	Discussion of goals
Closing	Summary of arrangements
	Asking for further questions or concerns
	Reminder of how to contact nurse
	Expressions of future contact (e.g. *If you need anything* . . .)
	Terminal exchange (farewells, thank yous)

Data analysis

Rates of occurrence were computed for the stance features in each text of the corpus. The speech produced by the nurses and the speech produced by the patients were analyzed separately. The rates of occurrence for each of the variables investigated were normed per 100 words so that they could be compared across the different speaker groups and across the phases of the interactions.

7.2 Main findings

As Figure 15.1 shows, the most common stance feature used in the corpus was modals, used predominantly by nurses. This reflects the findings of previous studies on spoken discourse (e.g. Biber *et al.* 1999). Modals have been shown to be especially important in managing and directing discourse (see, e.g., Biber 2006a), which explains why nurses would use them the most frequently. Patients overall use fewer stance devices, most likely because they are less involved in managing the interaction and also because they have fewer opportunities to express attitudes, value judgments, and personal feelings. When they do use stance devices, patients use stance complement clauses with *that* most frequently. These findings are similar to those in Staples and Biber (2014).

However, the investigation of these trends across the phases of the interaction also shows important differences based on the interactional phase. First, modals are used the least in the exam phase, indicating that

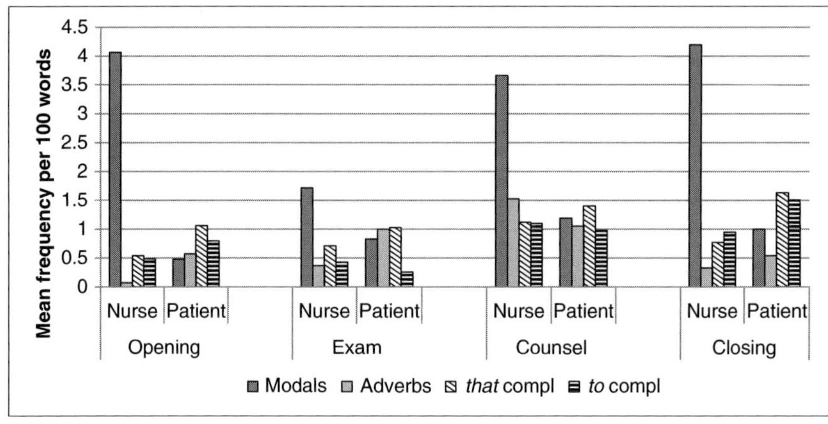

Figure 15.1 Overall trends for stance features across phases and speaker groups

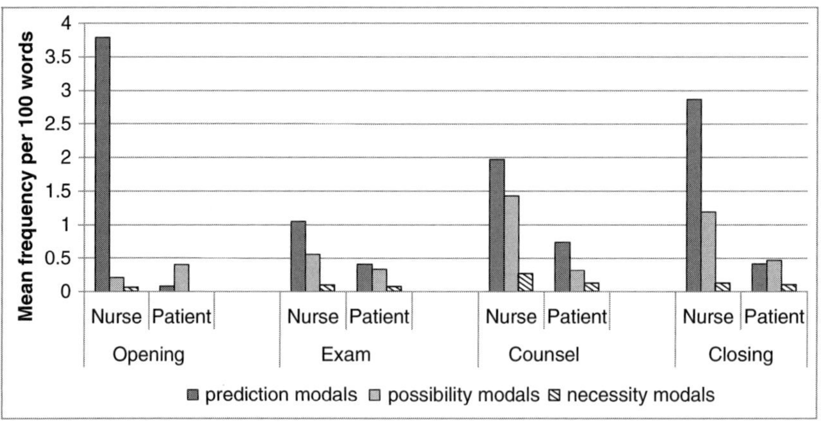

Figure 15.2 Frequency of modals used across phases and speaker groups

the functions of modals are more relevant to the other three phases. Stance adverbs pattern quite differently depending on the phase of the interaction. In the opening, exam, and closing phases they are used most frequently by patients. However, the greatest use of stance adverbials was found in the counsel phase, by nurses. Stance complement clauses were used most in the closing phase, by patients. However, they were also used frequently by both nurses and patients in the counsel phase. These patterns are discussed in more detail below.

Among the modals, prediction modals were used most frequently, particularly in the opening and closing phases. In the opening, nurses used prediction modals to establish their role in the interaction:

(Excerpt 1) N: High Elaine I'm Sue. *I'm going to* be your nurse today.

(Excerpt 2) N: Elaine is fine. Okay. Um *I'm going to* be your nurse this morning. My name is Rita. Okay.

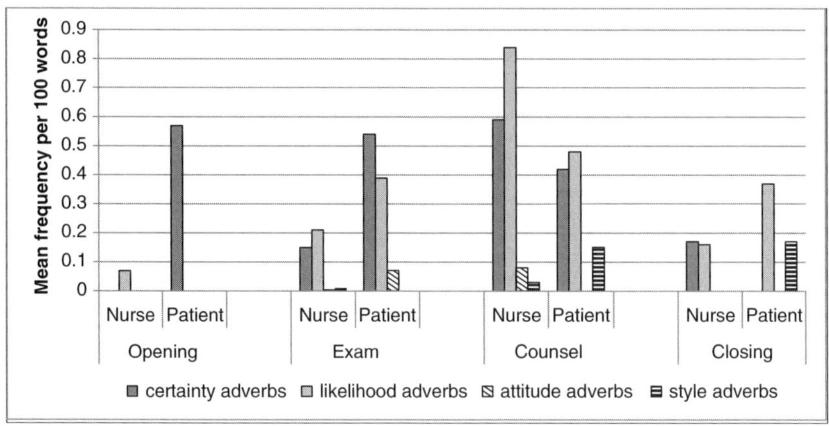

Figure 15.3 Frequency of stance adverbs used across phases and speaker groups

In the closing and to some extent the counsel phases, the nurses used prediction modals to indicate what will happen after the encounter is over:

(Excerpt 3) N: And *I'll* also have a dietician come and speak to you.
(Excerpt 4) N: Um let us see what the doctor says for today. He*'ll* be in probably later.

Possibility modals were used particularly frequently in the counsel phase by nurses, to offer options for treatment:

(Excerpt 5) N: Maybe when once the cardiologist comes in here um and clears you with your heart maybe we *can* get the psychiatrist to come and talk to you.
(Excerpt 6) N: Diet okay. And have you been instructed on carb counting? Carbohydrate counting?
P: Yeah.
N: Okay. Because we *can* get you more of that if you need that. And I *can* get you some written information on carbohydrate counting.
(Excerpt 7) N: And then for the pain I *can* get you I see on your uh medication list I *can* get you morphine or I *can* get you uh Percaset, something like that.

Patients overall used more certainty adverbs (see Staples and Biber 2014). Certainty adverbs were used by patients to express generalizations about past health history with confidence:

(Excerpt 8) N: You do. Well that's good. How are your what are your blood sugars normally?
P: Um I don't remember normal like they've *always* been good. The doctor said that they'd been good.

However, nurses also used certainty adverbs in the counsel phase, with greater frequency than patients. They did so in order to assure patients about the plan of care:

(Excerpt 9) N: Okay. Um so we'll *definitely* connect you with somebody that can get you some help with that and then maybe some you know maybe a you know some outpatient counseling you know after you leave the hospital.

(Excerpt 10) N: But there's a lot of different counseling. We can *always* like discharge before you go home. We can *always* provide you with documentation that for like outside counseling if you need. And I'll make sure that I'll let our doctors know

Likelihood adverbs were used by nurses very frequently in the counsel phase as well. For nurses, likelihood adverbs were used in a similar fashion to probability modals, to discuss possible solutions to problems:

(Excerpt 11) N: Well, I would say *maybe* talk to a counselor and take it from there and if it doesn't resolve *maybe* then you can get something from your doctor.

(Excerpt 12) N: *Maybe* it's time to *kind of* wean yourself a little bit away from chocolates.

Nurses also used likelihood adverbs to hedge about causes of patients' symptoms:

(Excerpt 13) N: So when uh you you have a low grade temperature which could *kind of* be from inflammation so we're not going to be real worried about that.

Another function of likelihood adverbs was their use in expressions of empathy. In the examples below, the nurse indicates an understanding of the patient's situation, but the likelihood adverb allows the nurse to emphasize that each person's experience with grief is different:

(Excerpt 14) N: Uh huh. There you go. And your aunt doesn't want to accept that?

P: No she think we um my mom and my brother and I we we killed him. You know we should have given him more of a chance.

N: Uh huh.

P: You know there's there's always someone that's going to upset you know?

N: Yeah. *Kind of* makes it hard when you have someone in denial with it.

P: Right.

(Excerpt 15) N: Well it's a big um it's a big loss to lose a father. And um from my own experience I can sympathize with you. And I *kind of* know what you're going through.

Patients, on the other hand, generally used likelihood adverbs to hedge about their symptoms in the exam phase:

(Excerpt 16) N: How else are you feeling physically?
P: Well um just my chest and
N: So your chest is hurting.
P: *Maybe* a little fever. I haven't slept.

In the counsel phase, likelihood adverbs were used by patients to talk about possible solutions/courses of actions, similar to nurses' use:

(Excerpt 17) P: Yeah that'd *maybe* be a good idea and get my my mother my brother involved or even my aunt if she wants to come in or we can just talk in a conference or something.

Patients also used style adverbs quite frequently in the closing phase. They did so to stress the focus of their visit and to revisit the issues discussed, to make sure that the nurse will follow up after the interaction is over.

(Excerpt 18) N: Is there anything else I can do for you right now?
P: Um not that I can think of. I *mainly* just want to make sure I'm not having a heart attack.
N: Right. Your first one was normal. We'll uh I'll uh let the doctor know that you're still having chest pain. We'll get another EKG. And uh see if he wants to draw some more labs on you and I'll get you some uh pain medication.

Finally, stance complement clauses were the most variable across interactional phases. Most frequent was the use of stance verbs + *that*-clauses by patients in the counsel phase. In fact, both nurses and patients used this construction most in the counsel phase, and stance verb + *to*-clauses were also very frequent in this phase for both nurses and patients. Interestingly, for both nurse and patient speech, the patient is the subject of the main clause. For the nurses, these patterns are used to give directives (especially with the verb *need*):

(Excerpt 19) N: So you ***need*** *to learn what your A1C is*. Okay?
(Excerpt 20) N: Um you really ***need*** *to watch your feet with the diabetes* also.
(Excerpt 21) N: And you know those are all the things that will that'll cause you to have a little bit of you know acid reflux.
P: Yes.
N: And indigestion too. You know those kinds of foods. So you know definitely you ***want*** *to kind of stay away from those*.

Notably, *need* and *want* have different impacts in these interactions, with *need* providing a stronger, more overt directive from the nurse and *want* performing the same function somewhat more indirectly.

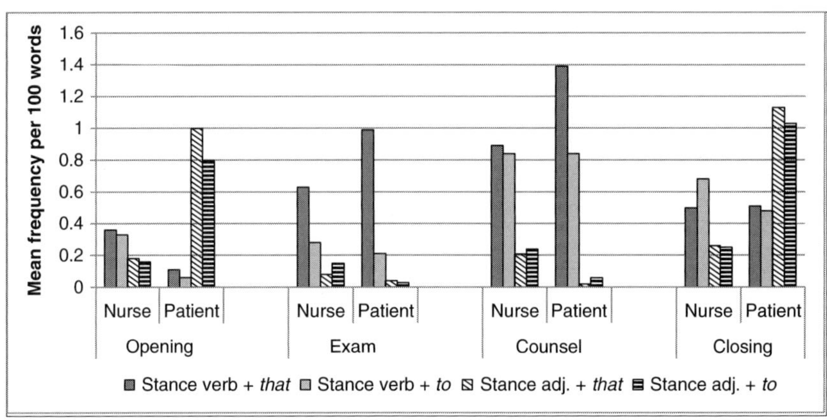

Figure 15.4 Frequency of stance complement clauses used across phases and speaker groups

Nurses also use desire verb + *to*-clause constructions to make suggestions to the patient about possible courses of action:

(Excerpt 22) N: You know in the future you might ***want*** *to check with your doctor to see if you should have that again.*

(Excerpt 23) N: Do you feel like you ***want*** *to talk to somebody?*

(Excerpt 24) N: And we also have uh uh clergical they can come here if you ***want*** *to have one of our priests or minister.*

Here, the focus is on the patient's desires and choices for solving problems, emphasizing a more patient-oriented interaction.

In contrast, patients used desire verbs at approximately the same rate as nurses, but to express their own stance, especially to convey their main reason for coming to the hospital:

(Excerpt 25) N: And what's your goal today?
P: Uh mainly just make sure my heart's okay I know I've been stressed so I just ***want*** *to make sure.*

Finally, nurses used effort verbs + *to*-clauses more frequently than patients, for the purpose of providing directives:

(Excerpt 26) N: So what doesn't help you and what isn't helpful um ***try*** *to avoid at this point in time.*

(Excerpt 27) N: ***Try*** *to take some deep breaths.* Four seconds in five seconds out. Just ***try*** *to relax a little bit.*

(Excerpt 28) N: A little high so he's going to send you home with Lisinopril. So I'm going to ***encourage*** you *to continue with that.*

Such constructions are also used to indicate the goals of the medical staff:

(Excerpt 29) N: Um and then we'll I'm going to ***try*** *to get you some counseling.*

(Excerpt 30) N: Usually we ***try*** *to do an initial exam* just to see you know make sure there are no other complications.

Interestingly, patients use adjective stance clauses much more frequently than nurses in the opening and closing phases. They do so for a similar function as the style adverbs, to emphasize their main concerns:

(Excerpt 31) P: Uh I'm just ***worried*** *that I'm having a heart attack.*
N: Well um the chest pain from what it shows is your chest x-ray's within normal limits.

They also use these patterns in polite greetings and closings, explaining the high use in the two phases:

(Excerpt 32) N: Hi I'm Molly Sue I'm going to be your nurse today.
P: Oh ***nice*** *to meet you.*
. . .
N: Alright well it was nice to meet you.
P: ***Nice*** *to meet you* thank you.

8 Conclusion

This chapter has attempted to briefly introduce important advancements and new directions in the area of spoken corpus analysis. The case study provided in Section 7 illustrated a common focus of corpus-based studies of writing and increasingly speech, namely stance devices; it also provided an example of a new direction in spoken discourse analysis in its exploration of variation within spoken interactions.

16

Corpora and written academic English

Ken Hyland

The impact of corpora in the study of written academic English over the past twenty years has been enormous, transforming how we understand, study, and teach this key area of language use. Corpora provide language data which represent a speaker's experience of language in a particular domain and so therefore offer evidence of typical patterning of academic texts. It is a method which focuses on community practices and the ways members of particular disciplines understand and talk about the world. Bringing an empirical dimension to the study of academic writing allows us not only to support intuitions, strengthen interpretations, and generally to talk about academic genres with greater confidence, but it contrasts markedly with impressionistic methods of text analysis which tend to produce partial and prescriptive findings, and with observation methods such as keystroke recording, which seek to document what writers do when they write. It also differs from methods which employ elicitation methods such as questionnaires and interviews, or introspection methods like think-aloud protocols to understand the perspectives of writers or readers on how they use texts.

Perhaps most significantly, corpus approaches to academic writing provide insights into disciplinary practices which help explain the mechanisms by which knowledge is socially constructed through language. Together, this research explicitly contradicts the view that corpus linguistics takes an impoverished, decontextualized view of texts and replaces it with a detailed picture of how students and academics write in different genres and disciplines. In this chapter I discuss some of the key studies and ideas which contribute to our understanding of academic writing in English. Section 1 offers an overview of published studies, while Section 2 describes a study which illustrates how corpus research can inform our understanding of academic writing.

1 Research into academic writing in English

This section discusses previous research, identifies a number of key studies, and provides an overview of the research methodologies that have been employed.

1.1 A brief survey of research

The textual data for studying academic writing include all the ways of using language in the academy. This is a range of genres which enact complex social activities like educating students, demonstrating learning, disseminating ideas, evaluating research, and constructing knowledge, and almost all have been collected and analyzed as corpora. Studies of these corpora reveal that all academic texts are, in one way or another, designed to persuade readers of something. In most cases this is the efficacy of an idea or piece of research, so that claims are encoded, warrants employed, arguments framed, and appropriate attitude to readers conveyed in ways that a potential audience will find most convincing. Thus, the ways academics represent themselves in bios, webpages, and prize applications, for example, seek to persuade readers of their competence and expertise as disciplinary insiders by drawing on attributes and experiences which relate the individual closely to what is valued in their community (e.g. Hyland 2012).

More specifically, the comparison of features in a corpus of 240 research articles and 56 textbooks (Table 16.1) shows how arguments are constructed to persuade different audiences in the two genres.

The greater use of *hedging*, for example, underlines the need for caution in opening up arguments in the research papers compared with the authorized certainties of the textbook, while the removal of *citation* in textbooks shows how statements are presented as facts rather than claims grounded in the literature. The greater use of *self-mention* in articles points to the personal stake that writers invest in their arguments and their desire to gain credit for claims. The higher frequency of transitions, which are conjunctions and other linking signals, in the textbooks is a result of the fact that writers need to make connections far more explicit for readers with less topic knowledge. Thus, to achieve their persuasive

Table 16.1 *Selected features in research articles and textbooks*

per 1,000 words	Hedges	Self-mention	Citation	Transitions
Research articles	15.1	3.9	6.9	12.8
University textbooks	8.1	1.6	1.7	24.9

purposes academics draw on the same repertoire of linguistic resources again and again. This is, in part, because writers try to anticipate their readers' background knowledge, processing needs, and rhetorical expectations through use of familiar rhetorical features. It is these patterns of repetition which corpus analyses seek to uncover.

Corpus analyses have, for example, been productive in identifying the structural regularities of a range of genres, describing moves in grant proposals (Connor and Upton 2004), in dissertation acknowledgments (Hyland 2003), in application statements for medical and dental school (Ding 2007), and in PhD theses (Bunton 1999). They have also described the patterns within moves, with research article introductions (e.g. Ozturk 2007) and results sections (e.g. Bruce 2009) receiving considerable attention from analysts. Beyond moves, corpus analysts have also identified a range of key features which have previously gone largely unnoticed, such as "attended and unattended *this*" (Wulff *et al.* 2012), evaluative that (Hyland and Tse 2005), code glosses (Hyland 2007), and the use of *this* and *these* as pronouns (Gray and Cortes 2011). Several studies have also shown that academic writing in English is composed far more of fixed phrases than was previously supposed (Biber *et al.* 2004).

Corpus research has also enabled researchers to make comparisons across different corpora. Thus Biber's (2006) work, for instance, confirms differences in spoken and written texts, such as the fact that lectures contain many features of conversation and comprise a series of relatively short clauses, while "university textbooks rely heavily on complex phrasal syntax rather than clausal syntax" (Biber 2006: 5). Considerable work has also sought to distinguish written genres from each other so, in research articles, abstracts differ from introductions (Samraj 2005) and features such as hedges, self-mention, and transition signals all differ considerably between articles and textbooks (Hyland 2008a). Comparisons have also been made between the ways men and women write academic texts (e.g. Tse and Hyland 2008), and how experts and novices write them, revealing, for example, differences in the use of reader engagement (Hyland 2006) and bundles (Hyland 2008b).

Perhaps comparison has been explored most extensively in the effects that culture and/or first language has on writing in English. Culture, seen as a historically transmitted and systematic network of meanings, is inextricably bound up with language and so influences writers' expectations about appropriacy, audience, ways of organizing ideas, and of structuring arguments. Corpus research has broadly supported the view that the schemata of L2 and L1 writers differ and influence how they write in English (e.g. Loi 2010; Moreno and Suárez 2008). Much of this work has focused on student genres and has identified a range of different features in first and second language writing in English (e.g. Hinkel 2002). More recent research, however, has focused on different perceptions of interpersonal appropriacy and self-representation in academic writing in different languages so that first-person pronouns, for instance, have been found to be far more frequent in English research articles than those written in Italian (Molino 2010) and Spanish (Dueñas 2007).

Yet corpus studies show discipline to be a decisive factor in the construction of academic genres. Individuals use language as members of social groups and they write essays, theses, and articles by framing problems and understanding issues in ways specific to their disciplines (Hyland 2004). While discipline is something of a contested term, corpus studies allow us to say something of how they are created and maintained, along with the knowledge they establish, through the routine rhetorical preferences of their members. They show, for example, that there is considerable variation in writers' choices of academic lexis. Hyland and Tse (2007) found that the so-called "universal" sub-technical items from the Academic Word List (Coxhead 2000) vary enormously across disciplines in terms of range, frequency, collocation, and meaning. The frequency and use of citations also differ, being about twice as frequent in the soft fields where the literature is more dispersed and the readership more heterogeneous than in the hard sciences, so writers cannot presuppose a shared context but have to build one far more through citation (Hyland 2004).

Finally, it is worth mentioning the support corpus studies have provided the view that academic writing is permeated by social interaction and intersubjectivity. These concepts have become central to language studies in recent years as we have come to realize that academics do not simply produce texts that talk about the world, but use language to acknowledge, construct, and negotiate social relations. Corpora have helped illuminate the range of features writers use to construct an appropriate authorial self. So, the considerable use of self-mention in research articles (Hyland 2001), abstracts (Bondi and Silver 2004), and undergraduate theses (Hyland 2002a, b), for example, suggests that academic writing is not a self-evidently objective and impersonal discourse. Genres such as textbooks (Bondi 2012), student essays (Matsuda and Jeffery, 2012), and book reviews (Hyland and Diani 2009) have been explored to identify how writers seek to construct and negotiate participant relationships. This has also had an impact on the development of interpretive approaches to interaction such as metadiscourse, stance, and appraisal.

Despite considerable work on genre structure, however, the ways that moves are signaled by writers and identified by readers have been far less studied. Typically, researchers have relied on changes in discourse function, or what particular stretches of a text are contributing to the overall purpose of the discourse. Often these are explicitly signaled, so that in this example from a research article abstract in biology we see a purpose statement announced by a *to* + infinitive clause and a method move indicated by a switch to past tense active verbs:

> To study the expression of ALDHs in plants we isolated and characterized a cDNA coding for a putative mitochondrial ALDH (TobAldh2A).

More generally, it is likely that particular rhetorical features cluster within particular moves to perform the specific functions of those moves, but more work needs to be done to identify these frequently occurring signals.

Another criticism of academic corpus studies is that, until fairly recently, these have been largely text-focused so that features seem rather abstract and disembodied from real users. Studies are needed that do not just analyze text corpora but which involve the authors or the readers of the texts in the analysis by also collecting interview data. Finally, there are still many gaps as researchers have been tempted to build and analyze corpora of the most publicly prominent and easily accessible genres, typically published texts and student work. This tends, however, to skew research towards a narrow area of the academy and neglects more "occluded" genres (Swales 1996). These are genres which, unlike published texts, are less public and accessible, such as those which sit behind the publication process such as reviewers' comments on submissions to journals, or applications for promotions or prizes.

1.2 Some key studies

The studies selected here represent both significant contributions to a particular area of academic writing and important moments in the evolution of corpus research in academic discourse.

Genres across the disciplines (Nesi and Gardner 2012)

This is the first detailed description of the kinds of assessed writing students do in different disciplines and in different years of their studies in UK universities. Based on the 6.5-million-word *British Academic Written English* (BAWE) corpus, the study develops a genre classification to identify and describe thirteen major types of assignment according to their purpose, stages, genre networks, and characteristic language features. Each chapter in the book discusses a "family" of genres, each with a particular social function. These are "demonstrating knowledge and understanding" (e.g. explanations and exercises); "developing powers of informed and independent reasoning" (e.g. critiques and essays); "developing research skills" (e.g. research reports and literature surveys); "preparing for professional practice" (e.g. proposals and design specifications); and writing for oneself and others (e.g. empathy writing and narrative recounts).

The study is also a good example of how corpus techniques can be used to map patterns in a large collection of texts, identifying moves in different genres, comparing frequencies of various language features, and offering detailed description of how individual words and phrases are used. The study is especially important as it provides a detailed account of undergraduate writing and descriptions of several previously disregarded genres. More importantly, it underlines the significance of disciplinary variation, showing how some genres are found almost exclusively in certain fields and how genres change as students progress through their course of study. This information is not only useful to discourse analysts, but also to teachers and those involved in syllabus and materials design for students in higher education.

University language: a corpus-based study of spoken and written registers (Biber 2006)

This book discusses the genres which confront students at US universities, both inside and outside the classroom, addressing their linguistic characteristics to provide a more representative basis for constructing and validating the TOEFL test. The study draws on the TOEFL 2000 *Spoken and Written Academic Language* (T2K-SWAL) corpus of 2.7 million words and comprises both spoken genres (such as study groups, class sessions, and service encounters) as well as 1 million words of written texts. The written genres are textbooks, course packs (lecture notes, study guides, readings, etc.), and course management materials collected from six disciplines and three levels, together with a range of varied institutional texts such as brochures, program descriptions, and student handbooks. The corpora were grammatically annotated using an automatic tagging program which identified part-of-speech categories for individual words and multi-word grammatical units such as *that is* and *for example*.

The descriptions offer important characterizations of academic writing so, for example, Biber found that over 50 percent of all nouns in the written corpus had abstract/process meanings that refer to intangible concepts or processes (*system, factor, difficulty*). The study also confirms the variation between written and spoken texts, with textbooks containing twice as many different words as classroom teaching, despite their broadly similar instructional purposes, largely due to their use of specialized lexis. The book is also interesting for its methodological approaches which include multidimensional analysis to identify sets of linguistic features that commonly co-occur with markedly high frequencies in texts. Thus institutional writing and course management texts contain high frequencies of necessity and prediction modals, second-person pronouns, and conditional adverbial clauses which push them towards the procedural end of a continuum with more content-focused genres such as textbooks and course packs at the other.

Disciplinary discourses: social interactions in academic writing (Hyland 2004)

This work presents a series of studies focusing on eight disciplines and a variety of professional, rather than student genres, examining interactional features in corpora of research articles, book reviews, abstracts, scientific letters, and undergraduate textbooks. Together, these studies explore how academics use language to both create knowledge and define their academic allegiances. They show how writers present their topics, signal disciplinary membership, and stake their claims through careful negotiations with, and considerations of, their colleagues. The book illuminates how disciplinary constraints on discourse are both restrictive and authorizing, allowing academics to construct credibility and agreement through features such as citation, hedges, and boosters, claims for novelty and significance, and metadiscourse. Methodologically the studies use the simple techniques of frequency and collocation, and combine these with interviews with academics to gain an understanding of how insiders view their literacy practices and see their participation in their disciplines. These data were collected through unstructured interviews and more focused "discourse-based interviews" about particular pieces of writing. The approach is therefore designed to focus on *discourse*, a process of social interaction, rather than just *texts*, by giving explicit attention to user perspectives and the social institutions within which they work.

Learner English on computer (Granger 1998)

This was the first book to introduce readers to the field of corpus-based research into written learner language. Edited by the founder and co-ordinator of the *International Corpus of Learner English* (ICLE), the book's chapters offer a comprehensive overview of all aspects of corpus compilation, design, and analysis, providing readers with both an understanding of methodological approaches to the field and analytical insights into aspects of academic writing by L2 students writing in English. The opening chapters review the software tools available for analyzing learner language and give examples of how they can be used. The second part of the book contains eight case studies in which computer learner corpora are analyzed for various lexical, discourse, and grammatical features such as overstatement, phraseology, direct questions, and adverbial connectors. In the third part, authors explore the application of how computer learner corpus (CLC) studies can help improve pedagogical tools, such as learner grammars, dictionaries, writing textbooks, and online writing tools. Collectively the studies offer a compelling argument for the role of corpora in SLA research, which has tended to favor introspective and experimental data.

If you look at . . . lexical bundles in university teaching and textbooks (Biber, Conrad, and Viviana Cortes 2004)

This is a pioneering corpus-based study of multi-word sequences in academic discourse. Taking a frequency-based approach, the research identifies the lexical bundles in classroom teaching and textbooks, and compares them to those in the authors' previous research on conversation and academic prose, showing that bundles are neither complete grammatical structures, or idiomatic expressions, but function as the basic blocks for the creation of discourse. The study classifies the bundles by their structural patterns and by a functional taxonomy which includes stance expressions, discourse organizers, and referential expressions. The analyses show that classroom teaching uses an extremely wide variety of different bundles in comparison to the other genres and that the written genres contained relatively few stance and organizing bundles. The study not only adds to our understanding of academic writing, but offers a clear definition of lexical bundles and a structural and pragmatic description of bundle types. While the frequency cut-offs and spread across a given number of texts in a corpus have subsequently been increased to strengthen the criteria for identifying bundles in later studies, the structural and functional descriptions have offered both teachers and researchers a useful inventory of sequences and inspired a number of further studies in the area.

Disciplinary identities (Hyland 2012)
This study extends corpus research into a new area: the relationship between author identity and disciplinary practice. Drawing on corpora which include academic bios, acknowledgments, undergraduate essays, academic homepages, book reviews, and prize applications, the analyses seek to show how we can understand identity as a performance of writers which is informed and reinscribed over time through their use of language in disciplinary communities. What we say and write aligns us with or separates us from other people and other positions, so the command of a disciplinary idiom can therefore be an assertion of oneself as a particular kind of person: one who has a right to be taken seriously in the academic world. By studying how language is routinely used in particular genres it is possible to see how disciplinary identities are performed and recognized as legitimate.

In most cases the analyses start by focusing on potentially productive items from interviews with writers or prior studies, while in other cases the task of identifying features is delegated to the computer, generating lists of high lexical items and keywords for further study. Items identified from either of these starting points then provide the basis for investigation through collocation and comparisons to see how particular academics and disciplinary communities used these features to express social identities. Such approaches reveal the regularity and repetition of what is socially ratified and independently variant and in so doing offer insights into the preferred practices of both individuals and collectivities.

1.3 Corpus methods in studies of academic writing

Perhaps most corpus studies of academic writing have followed what Tognini-Bonelli (2001) calls a *corpus-based* approach, where the researcher begins with a pre-selected list of potentially productive items and uses the corpus to examine their frequencies and the ways they behave in different contexts. This is, for example, how researchers have used corpora to study features such as self-mention (Hyland 2001) and passive voice (Xiao *et al.* 2006). Researchers have not ignored more inductive *corpus-driven* studies, however, where the corpus provides the basis for frequencies and patterns. One example is the research on lexical bundles, exemplified by Biber *et al.*'s (2004) study to identify the most common multi-word patterns in textbooks and classroom teaching discussed above. In both approaches, corpus studies of academic writing typically use the tools of frequency, keyness, concordance, and annotation.

Frequency provides evidence of non-randomness, revealing what regularities, and exceptions, exist in the language use of a group of people when engaged in a particular activity. High-frequency items represent repeated, taken-for-granted choices in academic writing as, from all the different ways of saying roughly the same thing, members of individual disciplines select the same items again and again. In-group abbreviations, acronyms, shorthand names for methods and theories, preferred argument patterns, preferences for author visibility or anonymity, particular lexical bundles, and so on, all help define and identify disciplines and genres.

Frequency can therefore lead us to what is worth discussing as it often indicates what is *salient* for groups of language users. We find, for example, that all disciplines shape words for their own uses, as demonstrated by their clear preferences for particular meanings and collocations. Thus science and engineering students, for example, are very unlikely to come across the noun *volume* in the meaning of "a book or journal series" while the noun *strategy* has different associations across disciplines, often appearing in the multi-word unit *marketing strategy* in business, *learning strategy* in applied linguistics, and *coping strategy* in sociology (Hyland and Tse 2007). Everything we know about a word is a result of our encounters with it, so that when we formulate what we want to say, our wordings are shaped by the way we regularly encounter them in similar texts. This helps to explain why it is, for example, that of all the different ways of expressing thanks, over a third of all gratitude in PhD acknowledgments is expressed as nominals (*My sincere thanks to; My gratitude to*) (Hyland 2003).

Keyness is another frequency approach often used in studies of academic writing. The basic idea is that a word form or cluster of words which are common in a given text are *key* to it, it is what the text is "about" or "what it boils down to ... once we have steamed off the verbiage, the adornment, the blah blah blah" (Scott and Tribble 2006). The text analysis program Wordsmith Tools (Scott 2013), identifies keyness by comparing frequencies in one corpus against those in another to determine which ones occur *statistically* more frequently using a log-likelihood statistic. This gives a better characterization of the differences between two corpora than simple frequency comparison as it identifies items which occur with unusually high frequency and so which are most prominent and not just common.

Keywords are therefore useful for identifying which words best distinguish the texts of a particular author or group of authors from another. Comparing different disciplines, for example, Scott and Tribble (2006), found the most frequent keywords in humanities to be *of, the, in, early, war, theory, as, century*, and *between*; in medicine to be *clinical, patients, treatment, disease, of, study*, and *diagnosis*; and in the natural sciences to be *are, Fig, shown, observe, sequence, obtained, surface*, and *analysis*. Similarly, Granger and Paquot (2009) identified the lexical verbs that are prominent in business, linguistics, and medicine compared with a one-million-word reference corpus of fiction writing. While recognizing the different meanings these might have in different fields, their keyword analysis identified potential candidates for inclusion in a list of EAP verbs, finding 106 shared key verbs. These largely consisted of verbs that typically serve organizational or rhetorical functions in academic writing: reviewing the literature (*maintain, present*), describing research (*investigate, describe*), reporting (*show, identify*), expressing cause and effect (*suggest, result*), describing tables and figures (*illustrate, highlight*) and contrasting and summarizing (*summarize, compare*).

Keyness therefore reveals a kind of interdiscursive similarity and helps build a picture of particular disciplines and how they are distinctive from each other. It also offers a starting point for *corpus-driven* investigations of academic corpora by generating list of items which can be further explored in more detail using concordance analyses.

Concordances. While frequency lists provide information about the *focus* of a collection of texts, they don't tell us how words are actually used. This is the function of concordance analyses, which provide information about users' preferred meanings by displaying repeated co-occurrence of words, allowing us to see the characteristic associations and connections they have, and how they take on specific meanings for particular individuals and in given communities. One example of this is Hyland and Tse's (2012) study of bios and how collocation allows us to see differences in the ways that senior academics and graduate students refer to themselves in the bios accompanying research articles. So, by checking the frequency of definite, indefinite and "zero" articles in a corpus of bios and then looking at concordance lines for each, we find that professors are far more likely to use naming terms that collocate with definiteness (*she is professor of, he is the author of*) which serve to uniquely identify them. In the bios of students and non-professorial faculty, on the other hand, such attributive choices signal class membership rather than a unique identity (*she is a PhD student, he is an editor of*).

Annotation refers to adding linguistic information to a corpus. While a raw corpus is a highly useful resource, annotation provides an extra layer of information, which can be counted, sorted, and compared. Lemmatizers, for example, retrieve word lemmas, the "canonical root" of a word such as *cook* from *cooking, cooks, cooked*, but while potentially useful for lexical analyses and mapping semantic relationships they are rarely used in academic writing research. POS-tagged corpora, on the other hand, are very powerful resources and have contributed to our understanding of academic writing by allowing for detailed studies of the use of grammatical categories, such as prepositions, phrasal verbs, modals, passives, etc., although the search and retrieval possibilities depend on the sensitivity of the tagset, which can range from 50 to 250 tags.

One example of how a POS tagger has been used in academic writing is Granger and Rayson's (1998) identification of salient features of interlanguage essays. Using a reduced tagset of nine major word categories and fourteen subcategories from Claws4, the analysts compared a corpus of argumentative essays by advanced French-speaking learners of English with a corpus of similar writing by native English writers. While both groups were found to use articles, adjectives, and verbs with similar frequencies, the non-native speaker writers overused determiners, pronouns, and adverbs significantly and significantly underused conjunctions, prepositions, and nouns. Hinkel's (2003) study also discovered significant differences between the structures and lexical forms used by native and non-native writers. Hinkel tagged her corpus of 1,083 essays by hand because the texts were hand-written in class. She found that advanced non-native-English-speaking students employed simple syntactic and lexical constructions, such as *be* -copula as the main verb; predicative adjectives; vague nouns; and public, private, and tentative verbs, at rates significantly higher than those found in texts by native English speakers. Both studies point to the fact that the academic writing of non-native-English-speaking learners displayed many of the stylistic features of spoken, rather than written, English.

Sinclair (1991), however, has cautioned against tagging as it disguises the interdependency between grammar and lexis by setting up artificially imposed categories on the language and so prevents researchers from seeing unnoticed patterns in the text. The "probabilistic tendencies of language" is the basis of the pattern grammar approach advocated by Hunston and Francis (2000) which encourages researchers to allow the text to throw up new insights, a philosophy which underlies the "corpus-driven" method (Tognini Bonelli 2001), discussed above, where the corpus data are not predefined in terms of a particular theory of grammar. These different ways of approaching data remind us that it is always possible to talk about the same thing in different ways and that our descriptions of language use encode particular assumptions and points of view. So, while grammatical analyses of academic writing using tagged corpora are likely to continue to offer insights into how language works in this domain, researchers should not ignore more exploratory methods which follow Sinclair's (2004) exhortation to "trust the text."

1.4 A summary of findings and gaps

Some key findings:

1. That academic texts are persuasive and structured to secure readers' agreement;
2. That there are variations in spoken and written academic genres;

3. That language groups have different ways of expressing ideas and structuring arguments;
4. That ways of producing agreement represent disciplinary specific preferences;
5. That academic persuasion depends on negotiating appropriate interpersonal relations;
6. That authors are everywhere in their texts, presenting a stance towards their topics and readers;
7. That academic texts are constructed through fixed phrases to a greater extent than we expected;
8. That academic conventions constrain both meanings and author identities, but also provide the resources for creativity and agency.

Some major research gaps which remain to be addressed:

1. We need more descriptions of the wide range of specific disciplinary genres students need to write and read.
2. We need a greater understanding of how particular genres are used within specific contexts, adding a focus on "action" to balance the focus on "language" by including research techniques such as interviews and observations in what Swales calls a "textography" (Swales 1998)
3. We need to expand corpus studies into multimodal academic genres where writing is frequently used with graphical and visual semiotic forms, such as academic websites and textbooks.
4. We need studies which focus on NNES students and how their academic writing in English is similar and distinct from each other and from NESs.
5. We need more studies to help us understand the nature of disciplinary identities and the meaning of expertise in particular fields.

2 An example study

As an illustration of corpus research, I want to consider a study which attempts to see what corpus research can contribute to the study of identity (Hyland 2002a, b). The study is important as it seeks to move away from the traditional ways of studying identity through narrative recounts or interviews to ground discussions of identity in what people actually *do* rather than what they *say* about themselves. There are two major innovations in this study: the use of interview methods to complement corpus research, adding a subjective, "emic" perspective which is not normally considered in corpus research; and the use of corpus data to "go beyond" claims made in interviews or decisions made on particular occasions of writing to explore the regularity and repetition of what is socially ratified and independently variant and therefore what represents the preferred practices of individuals and collectivities.

Background and rationale

Identity has come to be seen as something that we actively and publicly accomplish in our interactions with each other (e.g. Benwell and Stokoe 2006) so it doesn't exist *within* individuals but *between* them. But identity research is largely characterized by autobiographical and interview methods which underplay the fact that our identities must accord with the responses and behaviors of others (Hyland 2012). Language allows us to create and present a coherent self to others because it ties us into webs of commonsense, interests, and shared meanings. *Who we are* is built up through participation in social communities and linked to the rhetorical strategies and positions we adopt in engaging with others on a routine basis. We construct an identity from our consistent patterns of rhetorical choices over time.

Academic contexts obviously privilege certain ways of making meanings, but we can also see these writing conventions as options which allow writers to actively accomplish an identity through discourse choices. This is because it is through our use of community discourses that we claim or resist membership of social groups, defining who we are in relation to others. This suggests it might be productive to compare the writing of individuals with the general practices of their discipline to find evidence for identity construction. How do their choices help them achieve credibility as insiders and reputations as individuals?

The main investigative technique in this study was therefore comparison. Comparing the features of target writers' texts with a much larger reference corpus of work in the same discipline can help to determine what is general in the norms of a community and what represents more personal choices. We can, in other words, see that if a particular word, phrase or usage is common in a corpus of a particular writer's work, then it might be said to be a consistent preference which reveals something of that individual's routine expression of self: of a relatively unreflective performance of identity. To capture this I compiled a corpus from each of the published single-authored works of two experienced and well-known applied linguists, Deborah Cameron and John Swales. I selected these two academics partly because of their celebrity in the field of applied linguistics and their contrasting personalities and careers, but largely because their highly distinctive rhetorical styles seemed to offer a good starting point for this kind of analysis.

Corpora and methods

My corpus of Cameron's published writing consists of 21 single-authored papers made available by the author. It represents some twenty years of publishing and comprises 125,000 words. The Swales corpus was compiled at the Michigan ELI and consists of 14 single-authored papers together with the bulk of his three monographs, representing eighteen years of output and comprising 342,000 words. These corpora were individually compared with a larger reference corpus representing a spectrum of current published work in applied linguistics and in the same genres as the target texts. It comprises 75 research articles from 20 leading international journals and 25 chapters from 12 books totaling 750,000 words.

Wordsmith Tools 5 (Scott 2013) was used to generate word lists of the most frequent single words, and three- and four-word *lexical bundles* used by each of these two authors. I then compared each author corpus with the reference corpus using the KeyWords tool. As noted above, this program identifies words and phrases that occur statistically significantly more frequently in the smaller corpus. This meant I could identify which words best distinguished the texts of these authors from those in applied linguistics more generally as represented in the reference corpus. After reviewing the keyword lists and identifying individual words and lexical bundles, I concordanced the more frequent items to group common devices into broad pragmatic categories to capture central aspects of their writing. In other words, my approach was to use the corpora as a starting point of an investigation into the preferred rhetorical practices of these two writers. The corpus methods I used were unexceptional, but I hoped the repeated patterns they revealed would provide a basis for understanding the routine ways these writers interacted with members of their community and allow an interpretation of their discoursally constructed identities.

Main findings

The high-frequency content words and keywords indicate the niche of specialization which these academics have carved out from the mass of disciplinary subject matter. They reflect the main themes of an individual's work and serve as motifs for their contribution to the field. Items such as *women, language, gender, men, social, talk, discourse*, and *work* indicate Cameron's concern with the ways language functions to structure social relations, particularly in work contexts, and in the ways gender-linked patterns of language use are made significant in social relations. The top content items from the Swales corpus are *research, genre, English, academic, writing, non-native speakers of English*, and *the concept of discourse community* which similarly encompass his key areas of contribution.

More interesting, however, are the non-content words and phrases in the keywords lists which emerge as consistent individual choices. One example from Cameron's writing is the significantly above-average use of *is*; which was the fifth most frequent keyword in her corpus. While one of the most common words in English, in Cameron's texts it often occurs in the pattern *it is+Adj.+to infinitive* (161 times). This structure not only shifts new or complex information towards the end of a sentence, to the rheme, where it is easier for readers to process, but asserts the writer's opinion and recruits the reader into it (e.g. *It is important to*; *It is difficult to think of*). This assertiveness in Cameron's authorial positioning is also realized through the frequency with which *is* occurs in the company of *that* (230 times) in "evaluative *that*" constructions (Hyland and Tse, 2005). Here a complement clause is embedded in a superordinate clause (*It is my view that; It is problematic that*), making the attitudinal meaning the starting point of the message and the perspective from which the content of the *that*-clause is interpreted.

John Swales, on the other hand, projects a very different identity. Here is an altogether more self-effacing and conciliatory writer, projecting a cautious colleague using rhetorical choices which impart a clear personal attitude and a strong *interpersonal* connection to his readers, particularly through the use of self-mention and hedges. Both devices project the author as a participant in the text, indicating that the writer is prepared to debate issues and contribute half of a dialogue with readers. Frequent use of the first person is perhaps the most striking feature of Swales' discourse, with both *I* and *my* occurring in the top ten keywords. Self-reference, in fact, occurs 9.1 times per 1,000 words in the Swales corpus compared with 5.2 in the reference corpus, imparting a clear authorial presence of a thoughtful reflective colleague thinking through issues. An interesting aspect of Swales' identity is the extent self-mention is used in a self-deprecatory way, explicitly associated with modality, or at least a deliberative attitude. The most frequent main verbs related to *I* are *think* (86), *believe* (71), *suspect* (35), *hope* (33), *tried* (31), and *guess* (29), all of which point to some degree of tentativeness and care in handling claims and in dealing with the alternative interpretations and understandings of readers.

In Cameron's discourse then, the analyses reveal a range of features used to confidently and forcefully advocate a position, projecting a distinctive identity as a radical disciplinary expert. John Swales' choices, on the other hand, convey a clear personal attitude and a strong interpersonal, rather than intellectual, connection to readers, projecting the identity of a cautious colleague rather than a combative advocate of truth. Overall, the analyses suggest that the ways we write do not simply mimic community patterns but are a means of constructing who we are, or rather, how we would like others to see us.

Review of the study

The value of a corpus in this kind of research is that it can highlight what is common and what is individual. Stubbs (2005) puts it like this:

> individual texts can be explained only against a background of what is normal and expected in general language use, and this is precisely the comparative information that quantitative corpus data can provide. An understanding of the background of the usual and everyday - what happens millions of times - is necessary in order to understand the unique.

This methodology therefore points to new ways of understanding and exploring identity that takes us beyond what individuals say about themselves to what they do in interaction on repeated occasions, thus building a consistent persona through discourse.

In this view, identity can only be understood by close analysis of the ways writers routinely draw on the rhetorical repertoires of their communities to position themselves in recognizable ways as both individuals and members of collectivities. It might be argued, however, that using corpora in this way fails to provide sufficient context to understand identity performance as it ignores the detailed biographies of interview techniques and perhaps draws instead on assumptions about the writers which are not in their texts at all. After all, we know something of these academics and their styles and I selected two of the most rhetorically aware individuals writing in applied linguistics today. Both writers are professional discourse analysts and so are highly attentive to the effects of their choices (see Hyland 2012). My method, however, draws attention to an important aspect of corpus analysis: that although it is informed by numbers, largely frequency counts of keywords and collocations, it is ultimately constructed on interpretation. While repeated uses represent each writer's more or less conscious choices to project themselves and their work in particular ways, my take on them is necessarily subjective.

It is a methodology, however, which offers a way of exploring other unanswered questions about disciplinary constraints. Do all academic writers have a relatively consistent stylistic "signature," for example, or is this something that only develops over time? Are novice writers more tightly constrained by conventions? What changes in their repertoire with greater experience and confidence? What variations exist across disciplines and between individuals in other fields? Not least it makes sense to address the wider political operation of discourse communities and to ask, with Bizzell (1989: 225), "who gets to learn and use complex kinds of writing" and who has rights to manipulate or resist the conventions of a discipline rather than merely accommodate to them?

3 Conclusions

Corpus studies have made a considerable contribution to our understanding of academic discourse and revealed many of the ways that writers in different disciplines, genres, and languages represent themselves, their work and their readers in different ways. In particular, they have shown that a range of features occur and behave in dissimilar ways in different disciplinary environments and underlined the importance of community, context, and purpose in writing which has helped inform EAP course design and teaching.

It is this observation about students' target needs which helps clarify future directions for research. Quite clearly we need more descriptions of the specific disciplinary genres students need to write and read. Reports, essays, articles, critiques, presentations, case notes, lectures, and so on all differ across disciplines and knowledge of their structures and salient features can demystify them for learners. As corpus research into academic genres continues to grow, therefore, we can anticipate an ever increasing broadening of studies beyond texts to the talk and contexts which surround their production and use, beyond the verbal to the visual, and beyond tertiary to school and professional contexts. Corpus studies will, in tandem with other methods, have a continuing and important role to play in this endeavor.

It is important to mention, however, that generalizing from a corpus will always be an extrapolation – it provides the evidence for interpretations about how language works. Intuitions remain in the explanations analysts bring to the data that are collected, making a corpus approach a unique combination of empirical analysis, deduction, and human sensitivity.

17

Register variation

Susan Conrad

1 The importance of text categories based on situational characteristics

Long before corpus linguistics was widely known, researchers recognized that texts used in different settings and for different purposes had different distributions of linguistic features. For example, Blankenship (1962) compared individuals' speeches and magazine writing, showing that passives, word classes, sentence patterns, and other features were used to different extents. Work in sociolinguistics included frameworks for analyzing characteristics of situations that have an impact on linguistic choices, including factors such as purpose, setting, topic, participants, and mode of transmission (e.g. Hymes 1974; Brown and Fraser 1979). Today, most corpora have situation-based categories of texts. Large, general corpora usually have categories reflecting general situational context, such as conversation, fiction, and academic prose. More specialized corpora have more refined categories, such as the "speech situations" in the *Michigan Corpus of Academic Spoken English* (MICASE) – lectures, meetings, office hours, etc. (Simpson-Vlach and Leicher 2006). Thus, there seems to be widespread agreement that capturing linguistic variation requires including text categories that vary with respect to their situational characteristics – although studies vary widely in how (or if) they address the importance of these categories.

Situation-based text categories have most often been referred to as either *registers* or *genres*. Unfortunately, there has been little consistency in the use of the terms (see Biber and Conrad 2009: 15–23). Attempting to clarify the terminological morass, Biber and Conrad (2009) differentiate *register* and *genre* as two perspectives on the analysis of texts, not terms for different kinds of categories. Consistent with many previous researchers, they identify the register perspective as focusing on pervasive features – i.e. features that occur throughout texts. The genre perspective, on the other hand, focuses on features that structure complete texts. Thus, in a study of experimental research articles, a genre perspective would highlight the functions of the Introduction-Methods-Results-Discussion sections and the structuring within them, while a register perspective would highlight the frequency and function of features such as nouns, prepositions, and attributive adjectives. Importantly, too, register features are described in terms of the functions they serve and the circumstances influencing their use within the context – e.g. the dense noun phrases in research articles convey precise, concise, highly nominalized information required to convey technical information and discuss concepts for a research audience, and are possible because writers have time for careful planning and revising.

In this chapter, I use the term *register* as in Biber and Conrad (2009). To avoid confusion, I refer to all the studies reviewed as register studies and consistently refer to *registers* or *categories of texts*, even though many of the original studies use the term *genre*. All of the studies investigate distributions of linguistic features and the functions they fulfill within situational contexts. Since other chapters in this volume provide a review of specific registers (e.g. spoken English, Chapter 15, and written academic English, Chapter 16), and diachronic studies (Chapter 18), I focus here on the designs for studying synchronic register variation.

The next section reviews major approaches to corpus-based studies of register, providing an overview and exemplification of different approaches. A few additional details about English for Specific Purposes studies are then added in Section 3. Section 4 summarizes the overall accomplishments and challenges of work in register variation. The chapter then presents a sample study of registers within a specific subject area – civil engineering – to exemplify several characteristics and challenges in more detail.

2 Corpus-based approaches in studying register variation

Although register variation can be studied with many methodologies, corpus-based research is particularly well suited. A well-designed corpus can provide representative samples of registers (see Clancy 2010 on representativeness). In addition, the quantitative analysis that is typical of corpus research facilitates comparisons of linguistic features' distributions across registers and judgments about what is common or rare in a particular register.

Corpus-based studies of register variation can be analyzed along two continua based on the type of linguistic feature that is studied and the kind of text category that is emphasized (Figure 17.1). Linguistic feature emphases vary along a continuum that covers discrete individual features (words, grammatical structures, or lexico-grammatical patterns), groups of features that function to fulfill a certain discourse function or system (such

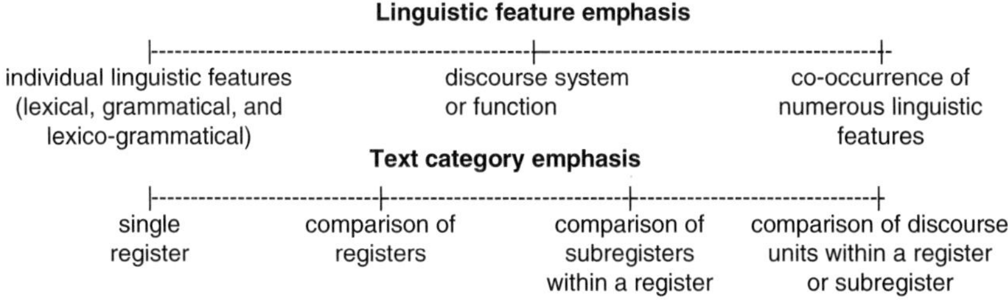

Figure 17.1 Linguistic feature and text category emphases in register variation studies

as the expression of time or evaluation), and even larger groups of features that are identified by their co-occurrence patterns in texts. With respect to text categories, a study can emphasize a single register, make comparisons between registers or between subregisters within a register, or compare specific subunits within a register or subregister (e.g. comparing the language of the different rhetorical moves in the introduction of a research article). The emphases described in Figure 17.1 are mixed in different ways to meet different purposes of register studies, as described in Sections 2.1–2.3.

The categories identified in Figure 17.1 provide a useful way to conceptualize design considerations in register studies. In truth, however, many studies fall on intermediate points on the continua or incorporate more than one emphasis. For example, Quaglio (2009) compares talk in the TV series *Friends* and conversation for all types of features – e.g. individual words such as *maybe*, the discourse function of hedging, and co-occurring features. A further categorization problem is that distinguishing categories as registers or subregisters often depends on one's perspective. For example, Hyland's (2008b) study of multi-word units in research articles, dissertations, and theses in four disciplines could be considered a study of different registers, or different subregisters, or both. Below I highlight particular aspects of studies for the sake of exemplification, not as a definitive classification of any study.

2.1 Emphasis on individual linguistic features

Studies in this category are designed to investigate linguistic features, with register a variable that accounts for variation in the use of the feature. These studies are thus not designed to describe registers themselves, but they provide a great deal of information about the linguistic features in different registers.

Numerous studies have used this approach. Table 17.1 provides a small sample to exemplify the most typical types of studies and the diversity within this approach. The studies vary from very specific items in highly specified registers – e.g. *we* in university lectures (Fortanet 2004) – to more complicated grammatical structures across multiple registers. Taken

Table 17.1 *Examples of studies focusing on individual features: single register, and comparisons of registers and subregisters*

1. Individual words	
Single registers	*We* in university lectures (Fortanet 2004), evaluative *that* in abstracts (Hyland and Tse 2005), words and acronyms in electronic gaming (Ooi 2008)
Comparisons of registers and subregisters	*Also* and *too* in 11 registers of Indian English (Balasubramanian 2009b), nouns in emerging interdisciplinary fields versus their more established disciplinary counterparts (Teich and Holz 2009), "gendered" stylistic features in two subregisters of blogs (Herrington and Paolillo 2006)
2. Multi-word sequences (*n*-grams, lexical bundles, formulaic language, phraseology)	
Comparisons of registers and subregisters	University teaching and textbooks (Biber, Conrad, and Cortes, 2004); research articles, dissertations, and theses in four disciplines (Hyland 2008b); different types of academic book reviews (Roemer 2010); interviews and academic prose in Spanish (Tracy-Ventura, Cortes, and Biber 2007); conversation and academic prose in Korean (Kim 2009); academic essays by five first language groups (Paquot 2008)
3. Grammatical features	
Single registers	Conditionals in medical discourse (Ferguson 2001); the *get*-passive in conversation (Carter and McCarthy 1999, 2006: 800)
Comparisons of registers and subregisters	*Highlighting a spoken/written distinction*: synthetic and analytic negation (Tottie 1991); *would* clauses without adjacent *if*-clauses (Frazer 2003); pronominal system in French (Fonseca-Greber and Waugh 2003). *Multiple general registers*: linking adverbials (Conrad 1999; Liu 2008); adverbial markers of stance (Conrad and Biber 2000); phrasal verbs (Liu 2011). *Subregisters*: quotative use in university speech (Barbieri 2005); conditionals in physicals and other disciplines (Louwerse, Crossley, and Jeuniaux 2008).
4. Lexico-grammatical features	
Comparisons of registers and subregisters	The verb *help* + full or bare infinitives (McEnery and Xiao 2005); noun + *that* pattern in two disciplines (Charles 2007)
5. Intonation and prosodic features	
Subregisters of speech	Monologic vs. dialogic discourse use of low pitch (Cheng, Greaves, and Warren 2008) and high pitch (Wichmann 2000)

together, this body of work contributes to our understanding of register variation in several ways. Most important, the studies demonstrate the central importance register has when accounting for language variation – for all types of features. In addition, differences between spoken and written registers are highlighted by many of the comparative studies. The work also demonstrates that broadly defined registers have subregisters within them that correspond to more specific situational characteristics. In some cases, the effect of the subregisters is even more important than previously identified dialect differences. For example, Herring and

Paolillo (2006) investigate word forms that are claimed to be associated with female authors in two subregisters of blogs (diary vs. filter). They find that personal pronouns (especially first-person pronouns), which previous studies have identified as associated with female authors, are more common in diaries by both females and males; other features such as determiners and demonstratives – previously identified as associated with males expressing more nominal rather than personal reference – are more common in filters regardless of author gender. They note that the findings for the subregisters are not surprising given their different purposes, but, as they put it, "What is surprising is that when blog genre is controlled for, the hypothesized gender differences effectively disappear" (p. 453).

A striking example of an individual feature approach is the *Longman Grammar of Spoken and Written English* (Biber *et al.* 1999). The book includes over 300 investigations of linguistic features, most of them compared across approximately 20 million words representing conversation, fiction, newspapers, and academic prose. The analyses range from simple frequency counts – such as comparing lexical word classes across registers – to more complex grammatical and lexico-grammatical studies. Several analyses consider the interaction of register with other variables that condition the choices between grammatical variants. For example, the *that* complementizer in complement clauses is the focus of several analyses. One finds that omission of *that* follows a cline from being extremely common in conversation to rare in academic prose, with fiction and newspaper writing between the two extremes. In addition, conditions that favor *that* retention in all registers (coordinated *that*-clauses, passive main verbs, and a noun phrase between the verb and *that*-clause) are found to be proportionally strongest in conversation and have less effect where *that* omission is less common. The *Longman Grammar* thus provides complex views of register's influence on grammar variation. Covering so many investigations of course makes it impossible to develop any single analysis exhaustively, but each analysis provides a solid foundation and a springboard for additional study.

Work by McCarthy and Carter also exemplifies the individual feature approach well, especially in comparing speech and writing. For example, McCarthy (1998) brings together individual feature studies of conversation, and Carter and McCarthy's (2006) comprehensive English reference guide highlights differences between speech and writing.

The individual feature approach has also been used in investigating variation across discourse units, though these studies are less common. The studies combine a genre perspective – identifying rhetorical moves in texts – with a register perspective on features used in the different moves. For example, Henry and Roseberry (2001) and Upton and Connor (2001) have examined lexical, grammatical, and lexico-grammatical features in the moves of job application letters. This type of research design is very useful for understanding discourse patterns in intra-register variation and the functions behind it. However, balancing the two perspectives can be challenging. Ding (2007) applies this design in a study of application essays, explaining that "the use of a mixed method approach" aimed "to reach a richer understanding" (p. 375); however, much of the potential remains unrealized because the register analysis consists of very brief discussion focused almost exclusively on coordinated noun phrases.

2.2 Emphasis on a discourse system

Studies that take a "discourse system" emphasis are generally concerned with how a certain type of meaning or function is expressed in discourse; they examine multiple linguistic features that can convey that type of meaning. For example, Nesselhauf (2010) takes a discourse system approach to studying the expression of future time, including six linguistic realizations: *will*, *'ll*, *shall*, *be going to*, *be to*, and the present progressive. Occasionally, a discourse system approach is used to study a more abstract characteristic, such as grammatical complexity, which Biber, Gray, and Poonpon (2011) investigate by analyzing 28 linguistic features that cover types of finite dependent clauses, non-finite dependent clauses, and dependent phrases.

A crucial issue for investigating a discourse system concerns how to operationalize the system. That is, how will realizations of the system be identified and which realizations will be included? Although always important, this issue is especially important for corpus-based studies, which generally seek to produce more generalizable results than many other approaches and to facilitate comparisons between different corpora. One strategy is to search for discrete features known to be part of the system – as in Nesselhauf's (2010) study of future time. This approach is efficient and generally allows a large amount of data to be analyzed; however, unexpected realizations of the system may be overlooked entirely. In addition, since it is necessary to verify features' use in context, practical considerations often compel researchers to exclude some features known to be part of the system. Nesselhauf, for example, excludes simple present tense from her analysis of future time due to time constraints. A second, alternative approach is to limit the size of corpus that is analyzed, but to thoroughly read through the corpus texts (or a subset of them) identifying every occurrence of the system being studied. Characteristics that require a great deal of interpretation – such as metaphor or creativity – are often studied in this way. For subregisters within conversation, McCarthy, Carter, and their colleagues have produced useful examples of this kind of work – e.g. on hyperbole (McCarthy and Carter 2004) and creativity (Carter and McCarthy 2004), as discussed further below. Given the interpretive nature of the analysis, a clear operational definition is even more important for replication or extension of the work.

Whatever their specific focus, studies of a discourse system are designed to provide a more comprehensive analysis of how the system is realized in different registers. Most discourse-system studies therefore have a comparative emphasis. General register comparisons are exemplified by the studies mentioned above: Nesselhauf (2010) compared the expression of future time across nine registers (and three centuries) and Biber, Gray, and Poonpon (2011) compared grammatical complexity in conversation and professional academic research articles. Other studies emphasize subregister variation – for example, "popularizing" features (e.g. questions, metaphor, humor) in journal editorials across two disciplines (Giannoni 2008) and interpersonal markers in office workplace talk (Koester 2006: ch. 5). Koester's findings affirm the importance of purpose as a register variable. In investigating the use of modals, vague language, hedges, intensifiers, and idioms in workplace talk, she notes that the purpose of the talk (e.g. decision-making versus procedural) is "a significant factor influencing linguistic choices . . ., in addition to other factors, such as social distance and power, which have generally been given more prominence in studies of institutional discourse" (Koester 2006: 160).

One especially popular area of study has been systems of stance or evaluation (including studies of metadiscourse, hedging, and engagement). The diverse studies include evaluation in two types of newspaper reporting (broadsheets and tabloids, Bednarek 2006a), stance features in spoken and written academic registers (Biber 2006a and b), interactional metadiscourse in job ads (Fu 2012), and evaluation in monologic vs. dialogic academic speech (Mauranen 2003a). Work by Hyland on stance and engagement in academic disciplines is especially well known (e.g. Hyland 1998, 2001, 2005).

An exemplary study for investigating a discourse system is Hyland's (2005) investigation of the ways "writers use language to express stance and relate to their readers" (p. 174). Hyland uses a corpus of approximately 1.4 million words composed of 240 research articles from leading journals in eight disciplines representing "hard" and "soft" disciplines. The procedures involve searching for 320 potential items identified mostly from previous work and examining each case to verify its use – thus illustrating the role hand-checking can play in well-designed corpus studies. Hyland also conducted interviews with experts in the fields, an important step for understanding the disciplines as cultures shaped by their epistemic and social beliefs (although the methodology description is less thorough for the interviews, omitting details such as the number of informants in each discipline). The quantitative findings are interpreted relative to disciplinary practices; for example, the higher frequency of interactional markers in the humanities and social sciences over hard sciences is tied to their more interpretative nature, less control over variables, and arguments that "recast knowledge as sympathetic understanding" (p. 187). The study also exemplifies the usefulness of studies that synthesize previous work rather than leaving individuals to synthesize diverse publications. Hyland pulls together his work from over a decade and produces a complete model of interaction in academic discourse, thereby providing a more coherent springboard for subsequent work.

Carter and McCarthy's (2004) analysis of creativity exemplifies the second approach to studying a discourse system. They use the 5-million-word CANCODE corpus of everyday spoken English to investigate creativity in interpersonal exchanges. They provide a discussion of operationalizing creativity for their study, arguing that it cannot be identified by searching for language forms but rather requires consideration of the purposes that creative language serves in everyday talk (they list eight) and then identifying occurrences by looking at participants' intended meanings and interpretations as interactions unfold. Although the definition remains somewhat abstract, it is clearly illustrated with extended examples. An important contribution of the study results from the use of a carefully designed corpus. The corpus is coded for four context types (transactional, professional, socializing, and intimate) and three interaction types (information-provision, collaborative idea, and collaborative task), allowing for sampling of twelve different sub-registers of conversation. They examine ten samples of each subregister for everyday creative use of language. They then quantitatively identify the subregisters in which creativity is most likely to take place – specifically, in socializing and intimate contexts focused on collaborative ideas. The corpus thus allows for more systematic analysis of the contextual conditions associated with creative language. Of course, as with all intensive qualitative analysis, it is possible to study only a small data set, and studies like this one require replication with other samples and other corpora – a practice that has been regrettably rare in the study of register variation.

2.3 Emphasis on the co-occurrence of multiple linguistic features

A third major approach to investigating register variation has been to analyze the co-occurrence of numerous linguistic features, investigating their patterning across multiple registers. The purpose of this approach is to investigate the range of variation in a set of registers. The approach is dominated by the multidimensional (MD) analysis technique, introduced by Biber (1986, 1988).

Biber's (1988) book covering the MD analysis of English continues to be a seminal work in register variation. Previously, no research methodology had attempted to study numerous linguistic features and registers at once; thus, by studying 67 linguistic features in 481 texts and 23 registers, Biber's work was groundbreaking. The co-occurrence patterns among features were identified quantitatively using factor analysis, resulting in six major factors. Based on the assumption that groups of features occur together because they share important communicative functions (see Biber 1988: 13–14), each factor was interpreted as a "dimension" of variation by assessing the shared functions of the features and the situational, social, and production circumstances associated with the registers that have a markedly high or low frequency of the features on the dimension. The study showed that fully understanding the relationships among registers requires considering multiple perspectives; for example, conversation and academic prose are extremely different on the dimension of "Involved vs. Informational Production," but much more similar with respect to features of "Narrative vs. Non-narrative Concerns." The study also included a description of the variability within each register for each dimension and comparisons of subregisters (e.g. disciplines within academic prose, sports vs. non-sports broadcasts, etc.).

By its nature, MD analysis is a comparative approach, and since its introduction, it has been used to make comparisons of registers, subregisters, and discourse units in several ways. First, the 1988 model of variation in English has been used in studies so that specific registers can be characterized relative to a wider range of variation (Table 17.2 row 1). This approach is exemplified further in Section 5. Second, the technique of MD analysis has been applied to new domains; as shown in Table 17.2 (row 2) these domains have varied from major languages to highly specified varieties and learner interlanguage. Third, the technique has been applied to characterize variation in the discourse units that have been identified through rhetorical analysis or through automatic analysis of vocabulary transitions (Table 17.2 row 3). Finally, some studies have added a focus on a

Table 17.2 *Examples of studies using multidimensional (MD) analysis*

Design	Example studies
(1) Application of Biber's (1988) model of variation in English to new registers (comparisons of registers and subregisters)	Academic registers and sub-registers (Biber *et al.* 2002; Conrad 1996, 2001; Nesi and Gardner 2012: ch. 2), philanthropic direct mail letters (Connor and Upton 2003), television conversation (Quaglio 2009), movie conversation (Forchini 2012)
(2) MD analysis of discourse domains and languages (comparisons of registers and subregisters)	World Englishes (Xiao 2009), written Mandarin Chinese (Zhang 2012), Somali (Biber and Hared 1992), Spanish (Biber *et al.* 2006), elementary school writing (Reppen 2001), university spoken and written registers (Biber 2006: ch. 7), outsourced call centers (Friginal 2009), blogs (Grieve *et al.* 2011), interviews of advanced ESL students and native speakers (Aguado-Jiménez, Pérez-Paredes, and Sanchez 2012)
(3) MD analysis comparing discourse units in registers or subregisters	*Comparing rhetorical moves*: biochemistry research articles (Kanoksilapatham 2007), grant proposals (Connor and Upton 2004) *Comparing vocabulary-based discourse units*: university class sessions (Csomay 2005), biology research articles (Biber and Jones 2005)
(4) MD analysis with new language focus (comparison of registers and subregisters)	Addition of metaphor types in Portuguese (Berber Sardinha 2011), bigrams in registers of English (Crossley and Louwerse 2007)

specific language form (Table 17.2 row 4), including Crossley and Louwerse's (2007) somewhat unusual MD study that used only one linguistic feature type – bigrams. Over time, the MD technique has been improved as well; for example, recent MD analyses such as Biber's (2006) study of university registers in English expanded to 90 features, especially capturing more semantic features than the 1988 study.

The MD analysis technique has been characterized as having "very sophisticated statistical analyses" and being "extremely time-consuming" (McEnery, Xiao, and Tono 2006: 308). Xiao and McEnery (2005, cf. work by Tribble) offer a "'low effort' alternative" (p. 68) to MD analysis using keyword searches. Comparing three registers, they find that many top ten keywords correspond to classes in the MD analysis (e.g. *know* represents private verbs, *I* is a first-person pronoun), and the keyword analysis approximates findings for an MD analysis. They note that the keyword analysis is not as comprehensive and not as likely to work for finer distinctions among texts, but has the advantage of ease. The article presents a carefully thought-out discussion that can be of use to analysts with only a concordancer and an untagged corpus. It would be unfortunate, however, if readers take the argument to mean that, in general, linguists should not be expected to know statistical techniques or should not expect research to take some time investment.

MD analysis is designed for large-scope comparison of registers. Like all methodologies, it cannot provide all perspectives on texts. One disappointing aspect of its application thus far is that MD analysis has rarely been incorporated with other, more qualitative techniques in research studies. Especially for educational applications, this has left implications and pedagogical applications tentative. For example, Asención-Delaney and Collentine (2011) reveal a great deal about Spanish learners' writing development by using MD analysis, but when they find a puzzling integration of features of personal involvement with features of narrative writing, they can only speculate about why. As they put it, "This involvement may be due to task requirements or to beginner-intermediate learners' tendency to produce the L2 to talk about themselves, which is typical in the Spanish curriculum" (Asención-Delaney and Collentine 2011: 319). More qualitative data analysis – such as adding interviews with the students – could offer more specific evidence of how students understand the task requirements and what their intentions were for their writing.

3 Register variation and English for Specific Purposes

The summary in the previous sections broke down register studies by aspects of their designs, using examples from a range of topic areas. It is also important to note that the study of register variation is central to one area of work – English for Specific Purposes (ESP). A foundation of the field of ESP is that language varies when it is used for different purposes, audiences, disciplines, etc. – the same concept that is central to register studies generally. (Of course, a genre perspective and a variety of other approaches not covered in this chapter also contribute greatly to our understanding of ESP.)

Many of the studies mentioned in Section 2 are part of ESP. However, a few additional features deserve mention. Most ESP work is concerned with academic contexts and teaching applications to improve second language students' success. Consequently, a number of studies that take an individual feature approach have focused on the development of word lists – i.e. identifying frequent words that are useful for students to learn for a certain context. The contexts have varied from a general academic context, as with Coxhead's (2000) Academic Word List, to very specific contexts, such as Lessard-Clouston's (2010) word list for theology lectures.

An additional purpose in some ESP studies is to compare learners with proficient speakers or writers. Table 17.3 provides examples that illustrate different types of comparisons and emphases on individual features, a discourse system, and co-occurrence patterns. Such comparisons are used to identify areas for instruction by identifying shortcomings in students' abilities to express meanings or manipulate language effectively as compared to proficient speakers/writers. For example, in her study of knowledge claims in physics, Parkinson (2011) finds students' proofs "more emphatic and less tentative" and argues that their lack of use of certain words to point out evidence in data makes "students rely on

Table 17.3 *Examples of ESP studies that compare students and proficient speakers/writers*

Emphasis	Specific focus	Comparison	Researchers
Individual features	*Word/grammar*: linking adverbials in applied linguistics writing	Chinese doctoral students vs international journal articles	Lei 2012
	Sequences of words: lexical bundles in essays	Advanced ESL students in Sweden vs. UK students	Ädel and Erman 2012
Discourse system / function	Knowledge claims in physics writing – realized by several lexical and grammatical features	Advanced ESL students in South Africa vs. journal articles	Parkinson 2011
Co-occurrence of multiple features	Multidimensional analysis of classroom presentations in business administration and education	University students' presentations vs. numerous university registers	Iberri-Shea 2011

readers to do more of the work of interpreting the data" (p. 174). She suggests activities to help students recognize the range of lexico-grammatical resources proficient writers use and the ways to construct a tighter argument that leads readers from data to knowledge claim.

Within ESP, there have also been register studies emphasizing professional discourse outside academia. For example, lexical and lexico-grammatical choices have been examined in international business earnings calls between Korean and English L1 participants (Cho and Yoon 2013) and spoken interactions on an international construction site in Hong Kong (Handford and Matous 2011). Perhaps because so many register researchers work in academic contexts, work on professional, non-academic discourse is less abundant than work on academic registers, though there are notable exceptions such as Hong Kong Polytechnic University's profession-specific corpora and associated publications (www.engl.polyu.edu.hk/RCPCE/).

4 Summary: accomplishments and challenges in register studies

Most importantly, all approaches in corpus-based register research have revealed just how important register variation is. Situational characteristics – including purpose, setting, production circumstances, mode, etc. – correspond to pervasive variation in linguistic features when studied at any level of specificity. Register studies have been especially successful in describing features that differ between registers of speech and writing (especially contrasting casual conversation and academic prose) and providing more specific descriptions of subregisters of speech and disciplines of academic prose. Variation related to the function of linguistic features in subregisters has even been found to be more important than some traditional categories in sociolinguistic studies, such as gender. Studies of new electronic registers, which pose special challenges for identifying situational characteristics and categorizing texts, are being increasingly refined (see further chapters in Hundt, Nesselhauf, and Biewer 2007 and Mehler, Sharoff, and Santini 2011). Advances in the study of register variation over the past few decades thus, in many ways, looks quite substantial.

Delving deeper into the accomplishments of register research, however, reveals significant challenges. Some concern methodology within corpus linguistics. First, even among sophisticated scholars, register variation is sometimes ignored or described in confusing ways. Biber (2012) discusses several otherwise exemplary studies that disregard register as a variable, include imprecise descriptions, or conflate variationist and text-linguistic perspectives – consequently masking the importance of register for the linguistic features being studied. In addition, few publications have been concerned with applying the findings of register studies to corpus design.

What have we learned about register variation that should be applied to better represent the variability that exists in text categories? A thorough synthesis that answers this question would be very useful to corpus linguists.

Another challenge concerns a lack of impact in other areas of linguistics. Most sociolinguistic textbooks, for example – which cover other variation in detail – do not cover register variation (see further Biber and Conrad 2009: chs. 1 and 9). Other areas of study which could benefit from incorporating corpus-based register perspectives, such as metaphor and critical discourse analysis, have only a small number of scholars who incorporate these methods (see e.g. O'Halloran 2007a on "register prosody" in hard news). Some scholars are put off by the lack of explanatory power of corpus studies, arguing they remain too descriptive (e.g. see Hood 2011 on academic disciplines). Register variation research has an unrealized potential to contribute empirical evidence to work on sociological and anthropological theories.

Many register studies are conducted in educational contexts or stem from educational needs. Despite individual teachers developing useful register-related materials, however, the impact of register research on education has been disappointing. In many countries, including the United States, register concerns are still generally considered important only in the context of ESP. A few ESL textbooks now emphasize register differences consistently (e.g. Reppen 2012; Conrad and Biber 2009), but most do not. In education more widely, there is even less impact; for example, the large native-speaker writing programs common in universities in the United States rarely expose students to the idea of register variation, let alone help students learn to adjust their language to be effective for different situational contexts (see, e.g., discussion in Beaufort 2007).

Not every register study needs to connect to a broader theory or provide concrete teaching applications; purely descriptive linguistic studies are also valuable. However, corpus-based register studies could have far greater impact than they currently do. Integrating corpus studies with other theoretical background or other research techniques would make register variation studies more applicable to other fields. The next section provides an example for applied educational research.

5 Sample study: registers in civil engineering

This sample study applies Biber's (1988) MD model of variation in English to an investigation of three registers in civil engineering: practitioner reports, student reports, and academic articles. It exemplifies the kind of ESP register study that compares students and proficient writers, but it also incorporates interview data with the register analysis, illustrating how the addition of qualitative data can result in more thorough interpretations for educational contexts and facilitate more specific applications. The analysis summarized here is part of a project that has incorporated a number of register analyses (see Conrad and Pfeiffer 2011; Conrad, Pfeiffer, and Szymoniak 2012; Conrad 2014).

The purpose of the study is to address a widely acknowledged problem in engineering education: the mismatch between students' writing proficiency and the demands of writing in the workplace. The problem has particular significance for civil engineering, where communication has been identified as the single most important factor in infrastructure project success (Thomas, Tucker, and Kelly 1998). Although there has been some previous corpus-based work in engineering, it has emphasized EFL students' needs and academic contexts (e.g. Mudraya 2006; Luzón 2009). No previous studies have used a register perspective to examine student and practitioner writing in an English-dominant country.

The study took place at Portland State University, a regional university in the northwestern United States. Most of the civil engineering students want to be practitioners when they graduate, and many course assignments mimic practitioner contexts – for example, writing to clients to document analyses, discuss design alternatives, and argue for preferred designs. In some cases the clients are real people the students interact with; in others, they are imagined. The study focuses on reports because they are a common register and represent the most in-depth projects students undertake. In addition, the study uses a small set of academic journal articles as a comparison register; this is a register that faculty and students usually have great familiarity with, but whose audience, purpose, and setting differ from practitioner reports.

Specifically, the study addresses these research questions:

1. Relative to a wide range of registers in English, how do the linguistic features of civil engineering student reports compare to practitioner reports and academic articles?
2. Which differences between the student reports and practitioner reports are likely to be the most problematic for engineering practice?

With the answers to these questions, student writers' greatest needs could be identified and teaching materials devised to address those needs.

5.1 Methodology

Because I wanted a broad perspective on the civil engineering registers, I chose to apply Biber's 1988 model of variation in English. This methodology makes it possible not just to compare the registers to each other, but also to assess more general faculty impressions – such as the claim that

Table 17.4 *Registers in civil engineering used in the study*

Register	No. of texts	No. of words	sources
Practitioner reports	60	201,700	8 engineering firms
Student reports	60	207,700	9 senior-level undergraduate courses
Academic research articles	*35*	*192,400*	10 engineering research journals
Total	155	601,800	

students write like they speak. A drawback of this approach is that the 1988 model is dated; text messages, e-mails, and blogs are undoubtedly common registers for today's students, but they are not included in the model. Nevertheless, the 1988 model is still the broadest perspective on registers in English available today.

The corpus for the study comprises 60 practitioner reports, 60 student reports, and 35 articles from engineering research journals (Table 17.4). The smaller number of journal articles reflects their more minor role in the study. All of the registers cover the same topic areas – transportation, structural engineering, geotechnical and foundation engineering, hydraulics (flow and force of water), and environmental engineering related to civil engineering projects (e.g. water quality). Compared to many corpus studies, the corpus is small. However, the number of texts and diversity of firms, classes, and journals far exceeds the coverage in previous engineering education research, and the corpus covers substantial variation for a focused educational study within one university.

The study followed typical analytical procedures for an MD study. The texts were tagged for grammatical categories (with the tagger developed by Biber), features counted, and dimension scores calculated based on the normalized counts for the 1988 registers. The registers were compared statistically with a one-way Analysis of Variance, with a post-hoc Scheffe test to determine pairwise differences.

However, the study varied from typical corpus studies in its use of interview data. Previous studies have emphasized the importance of expert informants for understanding new registers, different disciplines, and the purposes of student writing (Hyland 2005; Biber and Conrad 2009; Nesi and Gardner 2012). This study used interviews for those purposes, but it also used the interview data more specifically to inform the interpretation of the MD analysis. Specifically, interviewees were asked general questions which were analyzed for emergent themes, but they were also asked to comment on specific findings so that student, faculty, and practitioner input could be integrated into interpretations and suggested applications. Interviews with 12 students, 7 instructors, and 10 practitioners contributed to interpretations. Below, I focus on student and practitioner comments to illustrate the usefulness of the interviews.

Table 17.5 *Features on Biber's (1988) multidimensional analysis of English (with factor loadings)*

Dimension 1: Involved vs. informational production			
Positive features (involved):		Indefinite pronouns	.62
Private verbs	.96	General hedges	.58
that-deletions	.91	Amplifiers	.56
Contractions	.90	Sentence relatives	.55
Present tense verbs	.86	*wh*-questions	.52
Second-person pronouns	.86	Possibility Modals	.50
do as pro-verb	.82	Nonphrasal coordination	.48
Analytic negation	.78	*wh*-clauses	.47
Demonstrative pronouns	.76	Final prepositions	.43
General emphatics	.74	**Negative feature (informational):**	
First-person pronouns	.74	Nouns	–.80
Pronoun *it*	.71	Word length	–.58
be as main verb	.71	Prepositions	–.54
Causative subordination	.66	Type/token ratio	–.54
Discourse particles	.66	Attributive adjectives	–.47

Dimension 5: Impersonal (abstract) vs. non-impersonal style		
Positive features (impersonal):		**No negative features**
Conjuncts	.48	
Agentless passives	.43	
Past participial adverbial clauses	.42	
by passives	.41	
Past participial postnominal clauses	.40	
Other adverbial subordinators	.39	

5.2 Summary of findings

To illustrate the study findings, this section focuses on two dimensions – Dimension 1: Involved vs. Information Production and Dimension 5: Impersonal vs. Non-Impersonal Style. The linguistic features for these dimensions are listed in Table 17.5.

Figure 17.2 is a typical display in MD analysis studies showing the relationship among the registers along dimensions. In the figure, 0 corresponds to the mean register score for all the registers in Biber's 1988 study. Immediately, it is clear that the student writing is far more similar to the professional civil engineering registers than registers with very different situational characteristics. The registers differ more with respect to Dimension 5 than Dimension 1, but on both dimensions, the student reports use features far more like practitioner texts than conversation or fiction. The broad perspective from applying the 1988 model provides counter-evidence to some faculty's overall impression that student writing is like informal speech.

At the same time, when the civil engineering registers are compared, the differences are noteworthy. For Involved vs. Informational Style, the student reports were statistically significantly different from the professional

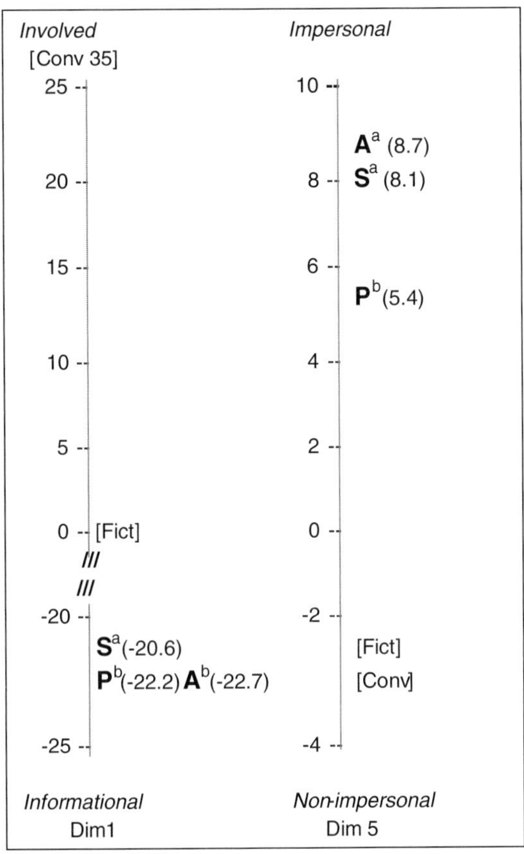

Figure 17.2 Register comparison along two dimensions
Dimension 1: involved vs. informational production
Dimension 5: abstract/impersonal vs. non-impersonal style
Conversation and Fiction scores are taken from Biber (1988). On each dimension, registers with different superscript letters were statistically significantly different from each other ($p < 05$).

registers, using fewer features of informational production, while the two professional registers did not differ significantly from each other. For Impersonal vs. Non-impersonal Style, the student reports were not significantly different from the academic articles, but both used significantly more features of impersonal style than the practitioner reports did.

An important aspect of MD studies (and all register studies) is the connection of the quantitative findings with description of the function of the features in the registers. In this study, with respect to Dimension 1, Involved vs. Informational Production, all of the civil engineering registers reflect an informational focus and a dense packing of information with nouns, prepositions, attributive adjectives, and other negative features of Dimension 1. Student writing, however, is slightly less dense with these features, while also using slightly more of the positive features of Dimension 1. The result is a difference in the information that is expressed: more concise and precise information in the professional writing than in the student writing, with more elaborate explanations in the student writing. Consider these examples that illustrate the typical patterns in professional and student writing:

Text sample 1

(a) *Practitioner report*

At your request, we have completed the field investigation, instrumentation monitoring, and slope stability analysis for the Green Glen Road landslide. The purpose of this report is to transmit the results of the field exploration, instrumentation results, and landslide analysis. We have also included a discussion of landslide repair options and recommendations for design and construction of landslide mitigation using horizontal drains.

(b) *Student report*

At the intersection of 5th and Anderson in [CityName], Oregon, a pedestrian-activated crosswalk was installed during the summer of 2009 . . . . The purpose of this project is to analyze the effectiveness of the improvements to this intersection. The analysis will provide a before and after comparison of the intersection, explore the effectiveness of the improvements, and then discuss suggested alternative solutions if necessary.

The practitioners refer to precise objects in relatively long noun phrases that incorporate adjectives, prepositions and other nouns (e.g. *the field investigation, instrumentation monitoring, and slope stability analysis for the Green Glen Road landslide* and *recommendations for design and construction of landslide mitigation using horizontal drains*). Such noun phrases are typical for the academic professional writing, too. Students use similar features, but the frequency is lower, corresponding to slightly less specific references (e.g. *a pedestrian-activated crosswalk* and *suggested alternative solutions*). Furthermore, professionals tend to coordinate noun phrases while students use more clauses; in this example, the practitioners *have completed the field investigation, instrumentation monitoring, and slope stability analysis*, while the students *will provide, explore, and discuss*. Although practitioners tend to use slightly more first- and second-person pronouns (a feature of involved production), the students tend to use other features of involved production with a much greater frequency than practitioners. This is especially true of subordinate clauses with *because* and *wh*-clauses. Often these structures occur as students describe purposes and reasoning behind procedures: *In order to properly treat and remove bacteria and contaminants, we must first determine what exactly is in the water and at what concentrations.*

To some extent, it appears that the students' different language choices reflect their school context. It is not surprising that their noun phrases are less technical as they are still learning engineering, or that they justify their reasons more explicitly when they know instructors are grading their understanding. However, the students' less informationally dense language is also, at times, not entirely accurate. For example, in text sample 1, the students state that *the analysis* will provide a comparison, explore the effectiveness, and discuss alternative solutions – but the analysis itself cannot discuss effectiveness or other solutions.

Along Dimension 5, the student reports and academic articles are similar in using a high frequency of passive structures, conjuncts, and other adverbial subordinators (the positive features in Table 17.5). Practitioner reports use these features, but to a lesser extent. The most striking difference concerns an almost complete lack of animate subjects in academic articles and student reports, whereas practitioners refer to themselves at strategic points, as exemplified in text sample 2.

Text sample 2

(a) *Academic article* (passive voice in italics)

> When comparing the behavior of the strips and bar mats, it *was observed* that the barrier displacement was about the same but the panel displacement was about three times less for the bar mats than for the strips.

(b) *Student reports* (passive voice in italics)

> Pedestrian activity *was noted* near the intersection of X Ave, Y Ave, and Z Ave. The width and unusual geometry of Z Ave made pedestrian crossings difficult. It *was recommended* that some form of pedestrian improvement was necessary to increase the safety of crossings.

(c) *Practitioner reports* (passive voice in italics, active voice + animate subject in bold)

> **We drilled** four borings on July 5, 2007, using a CME-75HT, truck-mounted drill rig using hollow-stem auger drilling techniques. Three of the borings (BH-1 to BH-3) *were drilled* within or near the footprint of the proposed power generation building and BH-4 *was located* near a corner of the control building (Figure 2A, Appendix A).
>
> **We observed** pavement and curb cracks near the intersection of Front Avenue and 47th Street . . .
>
> Due to slope stability considerations, **we recommend** that hillside excavation and wall construction *be completed* during the dry season . . .

In their passive choices, student reports look very much like academic articles, where agents are unimportant and assumed to be someone in the research group. Practitioners tend to state themselves as the agent in observations, recommendations, and the beginnings of methods. In addition, student reports and academic articles also use more adverbial subordinators, creating complex sentences where practitioners tend to have simpler sentence structure. Many student sentences contain multiple subordinated ideas:

> Text sample 3: *Student report* (subordinators in italics; other embedded structures are part of other dimensions)

> Designing the bridge to be an attraction for the garden as well as meeting ADA accessibility requirements is a priority *since* the longterm plan calls for widespread accessibility improvements to be implemented *such that* all may enjoy the beauty that the garden has to offer.

Many long student sentences have a stream-of-consciousness appearance, as though one idea just led to another during the drafting of the report and the initial draft was never revised thoroughly.

To illustrate the usefulness of the interviews, I cover just a few of their many contributions. In the practitioner interviews, the link between language use and successful engineering practice was a consistent theme. Their prime concerns were precise and accurate meaning, a lack of ambiguity, and ease of reading for clients. They saw these characteristics as necessary for conveying engineering content, maintaining client satisfaction, and managing firms' legal liability. Thus, the dense, specific noun phrases, the shorter sentences with fewer subordinate clauses, and active voice sentences are all tied to the practice of engineering. The active voice and first-person pronouns for observations, recommendations, and procedures were repeatedly noted as important because they overtly established the firm's responsibility, one way of preventing unintentional liability. Students' multiple ideas in sentences, absolute use of passives, and inaccurate meanings were all identified as serious problems for the practice of engineering.

For the student interviews, the single most important contribution concerned a belief that emerged when students were asked, based on their experience, to speculate about reasons for the study findings. Three-quarters of the interviewees immediately stated a belief that longer is better. In the words of some of the students:

> I kind of felt like I had to sound professional and smart. I mean, you want to sound really knowledgeable about things, and it seems like the easiest way to do that is to be wordy.
>
> It looks better if it's longer. I think it's that simple.
>
> Make it fancy.

This belief influenced their use of features for both dimensions summarized here. More clausal elaboration, more subordination, and more passives all contributed to longer, fancier sentences. For these students, the problem does not concern revising; it concerns their understanding of writing. They do not consider language as having an impact on content and liability, or on readers' ease of finding information. In fact, in the majority of interviews, students made no connection between engineering content and writing. They identified engineering content as something found in calculations. Writing had to do with stylistic rules learned in English composition or technical writing classes; it provided a way to give an impression of being knowledgeable through wordiness.

From the MD analysis alone, the research team would probably have developed useful materials targeting students' language needs, such as how to choose between active and passive voice and how to revise for precise content in shorter sentences. With the greater understanding from the interviews, however, we have additionally addressed students' underlying misconception that writing should sound fancy and has nothing to do with accurate engineering content. The MD analysis combined with the interviews thus not only provides information for understanding the registers as linguistic entities, but also for addressing the educational problem underlying the study.

6 Conclusion

As discussed in Section 4, register research has shown that register variation is a central concern for understanding language use. Work needs to continue to describe its importance to other linguists and to other fields where communication skills are central. Section 5 provided a brief example to illustrate the benefits of supplementing register analysis with qualitative research techniques. The combination allows for more specific applications than register analysis alone, and gives a study greater credibility among content specialists, who would otherwise be understandably skeptical of a linguist's understanding of their field. With connections like this to other fields, more integration with theoretical perspectives, and continued descriptive linguistic work, the importance of register variation can become more widely appreciated in the future.

Acknowledgments

Partial support for the sample study in Section 5 was provided by the US National Science Foundation (awards DUE-0837776 and DUE-1323259). All opinions, findings, and recommendations expressed in this material are those of the author and do not necessarily reflect the views of the National Science Foundation.

18

Diachronic registers

Merja Kytö and Erik Smitterberg

1 Introduction

The present chapter discusses the concept of register from a diachronic perspective. The terms "register" and "genre" have been used as cover terms for categories of text that are grouped together based chiefly on text-external criteria such as functions, audience expectations, and presentational conventions (see Claridge 2012: 238). The linguistic features that are characteristic of a register do not form part of its definition in this understanding of the term. However, it is important to account for the typical distribution of linguistic features in texts belonging to a register as part of register description. In Biber and Conrad (2009: 6), "[t]he description of a register" is specified as covering "three major components: the situational context, the linguistic features, and the functional relationships between the first two components."

The present chapter is structured as follows. In Section 2, an initial survey demonstrates the importance of the register factor in historical corpus linguistics and introduces a number of central matters that arise when the concept of register is applied to diachronic material. These matters include attempting to achieve comparability and representativeness, two important but sometimes mutually exclusive goals. Furthermore, we discuss the challenges that researchers face regarding the absence of, or the dearth of texts from, some registers during part of the recorded history of a language. As regards spoken language, attention is paid to the extent to which the spoken interaction of the past can be approached via speech-related registers such as drama and court records.

After this survey, we provide a more detailed examination of a selection of studies of language variation and change. We begin by considering detailed studies of single linguistic features whose distribution changes over time in specific registers or in ways apparently conditioned partly by register variation. Attention is also paid to studies that chart the development of a large number of linguistic features as they occur in different registers. The discussion of individual studies leads to an account of two important trends that have been identified in recent research on registers, viz. colloquialization and densification.

In Section 4, we provide a more in-depth account of one study where careful consideration of the register parameter has led to new insights into language variation and change: Walker's (2007) analysis of the variation in second-person pronoun usage in Early Modern English. As we will demonstrate, Walker's examination of text categories that are related to speech in different ways enables her to show how the substitution of *you* forms for *thou* forms was significantly mediated through the register parameter. The chapter concludes with a summary and a brief outline of some areas where future research on historical registers would be welcome.

2 Initial survey

As Lange (2012: 401) notes, the parameter of register "lies at the heart of every kind of corpus linguistic endeavour." As will become apparent below, this is perhaps especially true when linguistic variation, stability, and change are examined from a diachronic perspective. Kohnen (2001: 115) argues that registers "are catalysts for language change: they accelerate the spreading of a construction which already exists." Registers may of course also constrain or retard change by being resistant to the use of an innovative feature. Hundt and Mair (1999) demonstrate that late twentieth-century newspaper English is relatively open to the spread of linguistic features associated with speech, while the acceptance of such features is slower and less noticeable in academic writing. However, it is possible for a register to be agile concerning the spread of some features while remaining conservative with regard to others; for instance, Biber and Gray (2011) show that academic English has been innovative with regard to the development of the syntactic elaboration of noun phrases. In diachronic investigations, an added complication is that the linguistic features typically associated with a register may change over time (see Biber and Finegan 1997). The complex and shifting interplay of registers and their characteristic linguistic features mean that careful consideration of the register parameter is crucial in historical corpus linguistics.

The register parameter can be taken into account in two ways in diachronic investigations. In one approach, several different registers are sampled for each period analyzed, and the aim of the analysis is then typically that the corpus should be representative of a language variety so that studying the corpus "can stand proxy for the study of some entire language or language variety" (Leech 2007: 135); for instance, the LOB corpus has been taken to represent early 1960s written British English. From another perspective, the aim is rather to represent particular registers (e.g. scientific research articles), and conclusions about language change are restricted to the level of specific registers rather than of a variety as a whole (see, for instance, Biber and Gray 2011 on academic research writing). Both perspectives will be present in our discussion below.

2.1 Representativeness versus comparability in historical corpora

In this section, we discuss how two of the central desiderata in corpus linguistics apply to historical registers: *representativeness* and *comparability*. As we shall demonstrate, compiling representative and comparable (sub) corpora poses particular problems in historical linguistics; in addition, one of the desiderata may have to be sacrificed in order to achieve another.

A synchronic or diachronic corpus is representative to the extent that the study of that corpus can replace the study of the textual universe it represents. Depending on which of the two perspectives mentioned above is used, the textual universe may comprise an entire language variety or specific registers in that variety. There currently appears to be no generally agreed-upon way of operationalizing this variable. Biber (1993b) suggests that a corpus should be compiled in a cyclical process in which analyses of variation indicate where further sampling is necessary until the full range of variation in the sample universe – or in the specific register targeted – is represented in the corpus. Leech (2007) argues that proportionality can be relevant to corpus design when the aim is to represent several registers. According to Leech (2007: 138), "the basic unit to be counted in calculating the size of a given textual universe is not the text itself, but an initiator-text-receiver nexus, which we can call an ATOMIC COMMUNICATIVE EVENT (ACE)." This would mean that registers whose texts have a great many receivers (e.g. news reports) should be sampled more extensively than registers where each text is often received only by one individual (e.g. conversation), because a text from the former register enters into more atomic communicative events. Leech (2007: 140) argues that a modest degree of representativeness can be achieved through informal assessments by "professionally competent members of a speech community," and that this can be further improved upon by applying "EXTERNAL (sociocultural) criteria as formalized in a systematic typology of genres."

However, both Biber's and Leech's approaches to representativeness may lead the linguist into difficulties when s/he is confronted with historical material. Most obviously, several important registers – including the 90 percent of language use that Biber (1993b) estimates comprises conversation – are absent from the historical record. As Kohnen (2007a: np) notes, even in registers that are attested, a great many texts have of course been lost, and some of those that have survived "cannot be dated with any accuracy." If corpus linguists aim at capturing the full range of linguistic variation present in, say, thirteenth-century English, and not merely the range displayed in extant records, there is thus no reliable indicator of when this goal has been attained. There are similar difficulties with Leech's (2007) criterion; while we may be able to construct genre typologies for thirteenth-century English, there are no professionally competent members of contemporary speech communities that can be consulted.

The difficulties outlined above arguably make the register parameter even more important in historical corpus linguistics than in studies of Present-day English. If the aim is to represent a whole language variety, ensuring that appropriate registers are included in the corpus is one of the ways in which historical corpus linguists can enhance the representativeness of corpora. Including a wide range of registers and ensuring that they are proportionately represented in a corpus help to make such a corpus balanced, which improves representativeness (Kohnen 2007a: np). Regardless of whether the aim is to represent a register or a variety, including appropriate textual witnesses of the register(s) represented is of course crucial. However, different aspects of representativeness may clash in the compilation of multi-register corpora. For instance, courtroom proceedings are arguably given more space in some multi-register historical corpora than their importance to the contemporary speech communities would indicate, considering the low proportion of speakers who were involved in trials; but such measures are taken for good reasons. For instance, trial proceedings are one of the relatively few registers where women's voices are present, and the benefits to representativeness (as related to the language variety as a whole) of including linguistic material produced by an otherwise largely silenced half of the contemporary population are considered to outweigh drawbacks associated with loss of proportionality. In addition, owing to the fact that trial proceedings constitute (formal) speech taken down, such registers can open vistas into the spoken language of the past (see Section 2.3). A similar problem may arise when register-specific corpora are compiled, as the influence of different subregisters must then be taken into account.

Many historical studies within corpus linguistics are also diachronic in that the researcher wishes to study language use in two or more periods to see whether any differences over time that can be interpreted as language change are attested in the material. This, however, means that another desideratum of corpus composition must be considered, viz. comparability. Two corpora (or two samples of the same corpus) are comparable if they differ "in terms of only one parameter" (Leech 2007: 141); in diachronic linguistics, that one parameter is typically time. However, the further apart in time the sampling universes of two corpora are, the more difficult it becomes to make them comparable. If the investigation aims at capturing the language of an entire variety, one problem is that some registers are absent from parts of the attested history of English, owing to extralinguistic developments (see Section 2.2). For this reason, comparable diachronic corpora often focus partly or wholly on registers that are attested during all periods sampled. However, as Leech (2007: 142–143) notes, comparability often comes at the expense of representativeness. If only registers that are attested during the whole period studied are included in an investigation, several registers which were of considerable importance to the language during parts of that period, but which emerged too late or died out too early to be available throughout the period, may have to be excluded from consideration.

Moreover, whether the aim is to capture a register or a variety, the fact that registers change over time will affect corpus compilation. Leech and Smith (2005) discuss the consequences of this unavoidable fact. Even with a relatively modest time gap such as thirty years, problems may arise with regard to some registers; for instance, during the compilation of the BLOB-1931 corpus, it proved difficult to find early 1930s texts corresponding to the science fiction and sociology texts from 1961 present in LOB. The greater the diachronic span of the investigation, the more difficult it is likely to be to maintain the sameness of certain registers. At some point, the question arises whether researchers are looking at one register that has changed internally over time or at two different registers from two different periods, one of which has evolved into the other (see the discussion in Biber and Conrad 2009: 165–166).

Moreover, even if a register has not changed dramatically in itself, its place in the sampling universe may have done so: other registers may have taken over some of its functions, or the register may have increased or decreased in importance for other reasons. The private letter in British English is a case in point. While the register has clearly existed since the Middle English period, sociopolitical and technological change has meant that its place in the typology has varied extensively during this time. Before the introduction of the Penny Post in 1840, the expense of postage – a minimum of 4d., paid by the recipient of the letter – kept down the number of letters that were sent; in other words, several topics that would have been discussed in the form of a private letter after 1840 were either not communicated at all or communicated within the scope of another register (e.g. conversation the next time the interactants met). Conversely, in 2013, the availability of alternative channels of communication such as e-mail and Facebook messaging has drastically decreased the communicative role played by letter writing. Even registers with a great deal of diachronic stability, such as religious writing, are subject to change in this regard.

Registers may also differ in how homogeneous they are. Some registers are characterized by considerable linguistic homogeneity, something which may have developed over time; see, for instance, Görlach's (2004) study of the cookery recipe as a relatively stable register. Others, e.g. newspaper texts, are so heterogeneous that the question arises whether they can be meaningfully discussed as registers; for instance, while Moessner (2001: 136) refers to newspaper texts as a "well-established genre," Xekalakis (1999: 93) argues that "a unified and homogeneous language variety called 'newspaper language' . . . does not exist." To some extent, this is also a question of what level of abstraction is suitable for concepts such as *genre* and *register*: newspaper language may be regarded as a register incorporating several subregisters or as a hyperonymic "super-register" incorporating several registers. Two examples of how register can interact with other levels of classification will be given here. The compilers of the *Helsinki Corpus of English Texts* included the notion of a hyperonym of registers in the corpus structure. So-called diachronic text prototypes, e.g. Law and Narration, include several registers; as Moessner (2001: 134) notes, there is some similarity between these categories and Werlich's (1983) text types. Kohnen (2007a) argues that diachronic text prototypes may be one way to achieve continuity in analyses: if a certain register is not represented in a given period, it may be possible to use another register representing the same diachronic text prototype. In the *Corpus of Religious Prose*, parts of corpus texts are instead coded differently depending on which subfunctions they fulfill; for instance, a subsection of a text in the register Religious Instruction may be an instance of exhortation, exposition, exegesis, narration, or argumentation (Kohnen 2007a: np), while also retaining the register label.

Register heterogeneity becomes important when registers are sampled for diachronic corpora. If the corpus compiler or user has reason to suspect that a given register is linguistically heterogeneous, measures need to be taken to make period samples of the corpus comparable in this regard. If this aspect is not controlled for, a linguistic difference between two period samples may be interpreted as language change when in reality it is due to register-internal variation. There are different ways to control for this factor. One is simply to sample a larger number of texts, which will make it statistically more likely that the full range of internal variation is present in each period sample. Another possible solution is to stratify the register into those component subregisters that are assumed to cause the variation. If the relative importance of different subregisters has varied in diachrony, the question arises whether or not such fluctuations should be taken into account in the compilation and exploitation of corpora. For instance, it is likely that monographs occupied a more prominent place compared with journal articles in the Natural Science register in the 1800s than in the late twentieth century. If the goal is to represent Natural Science as a register at different points in time, this distinction would need to be taken into account so that different proportions of monographs and articles are sampled for the two centuries; but if the aim is to make the period samples comparable, such differences would not be reflected in sampling.

2.2 Register representation across time

There are several extralinguistic factors that influence the availability of registers for research through the history of English. If the period coverage of a study is considerable and a great deal of societal or politico-cultural change has affected language users during that time, it is likely that registers will have gained new features and conventions, developed into other registers, been replaced by new registers, or fallen into oblivion; such shifts affect the comparability of period samples. Registers may also disappear at a certain point in the history only to re-emerge later on; for instance, legal texts in English, which are represented in the Old English period (*c.* 850–1150), reappear towards the end of the Middle English period, after a gap of several centuries during which Latin and French were used instead (Claridge 2012: 240). This makes English different from, for instance, German, where legal documents in the vernacular are attested from the thirteenth (southern Germany) and fourteenth (northern Germany) centuries (see, for example, Greule, Meier, and Ziegler 2012). Such gaps in register representation constitute a major challenge for diachronic research as well as diachronic corpus compilation. For instance, special attention was paid to register continuity when the *Helsinki Corpus* was compiled (Kytö and Rissanen 1993: 13): precedence was generally given to including registers that were attested in several periods. However, a register may be and remain characteristic of a particular period to the extent that excluding it would mean seriously decreasing the extent to which the corpus would mirror the textual reality of the period. A case in point is the verse romance in the early Middle English period (1150–1250), which emerged through French influence as a new category of imaginative writing reflecting the "preoccupations of the age of chivalry and the ideals of social behaviour in aristocratic society" (Nevanlinna *et al.* 1993: 37).

There may also be variety-specific differences in register representation. For instance, the investigation of differences between language use in a mother country and its early transplanted colonies is a fascinating topic for research. However, circumstances of life in the colonies tended to promote utilitarian registers such as record keeping and letter writing, leaving less room for literary tradition and registers such as fiction and drama (Kytö 1991: 30–34). On the other hand, as Fritz (2007: 15–16) notes, the importance placed on education in several colonies also led to comparatively high literacy rates, which enabled a larger section of the population to produce texts than was the case in England (see also below).

The question of literacy constitutes a serious problem hampering the textual coverage in historical corpora: the further we go back in history, the fewer individuals could read or write. This is one of the factors contributing to the underrepresentation of texts by female authors and speakers from low socio-economic groups. Registers displaying writing habits of those with little or no formal education are valuable sources for the study of dialectal variation and language change; for instance, spelling variants produced by untutored writers can display features of early pronunciation. While spelling variation is a problem in advanced corpus linguistic analyses using historical material (e.g. keyword analysis), texts are increasingly being normalized by the application of semi-automatic techniques (e.g. VARD 2 = Variant Detector 2; see www.comp.lancs.ac.uk/~barona/vard2/; Baron and Rayson 2008). This effort can be expected to enrich register studies as it will make many historical texts and registers more accessible to corpus linguists.

A related issue concerns the form in which texts from various registers are available for inclusion in corpora: as manuscripts or in the form of text editions. Using fresh manuscript material for corpus compilation is a time-consuming enterprise: in-depth philological and computational work is often required to transfer the manuscript readings into searchable computer files. However, if text editions are used, the editorial choices made must be taken into account when the suitability of an edition for linguistic research is assessed, as "the edited text may have been altered in various ways for reasons such as facilitating the text for a particular audience whose main concern is not the language but the content of the text or other characteristics" (Kytö, Grund, and Walker 2011: 7). An increased interest in making manuscript material searchable for linguistic study is fueling editorial projects and electronic single-register editions (e.g. *An Electronic Text Edition of Witness Depositions 1560–1760*, *Corpus of Scottish Correspondence*), and multi-register corpora (e.g. *Middle English Grammar* corpus) are available or being compiled.

2.3 Speech-related registers: bad data?

One fundamental problem in the study of language change of past periods is that the material has been preserved in writing. While the study of changes unique to the written language has received a great deal of recent scholarly interest (see, for instance, Biber and Gray 2011), it remains true that a great deal of linguistic change has taken place in speech, and notably speech used in dialogue situations (Milroy 1992). Scholars have therefore devoted considerable attention to attempting to access past speech through indirect means. To shed light on the role played by spoken language in periods from which no (suitable) audio-recorded material is available, historical linguists have turned to texts containing specimens of speech-related language. For instance, the *Corpus of English Dialogues* was devoted to written sources that can be taken to contain evidence of past speech. Such evidence can appear in registers that are speech-based (trial proceedings, witness depositions), speech-like (private correspondence), and speech-purposed or written to be spoken (drama) (Culpeper and Kytö 2010: 17–18). It would be futile to claim that any such speech-related registers would render past speech "faithfully" in writing, in its verbatim form. Despite there already being stenographic systems in the early modern period, postulated accurate recordings of speech events in writing cannot be the starting point. At best, only the gist of what was said can be rendered in writing (words, phrases) (see e.g. Kytö and Walker 2003). Analyzing speech written down as if it were "real" speech would be methodologically dangerous. Instead, one of the solutions has been to place registers and their properties on an axis scaling from "communicative immediacy" to "communicative distance" (Koch 1999; Koch and Oesterreicher 1985–1986, 1990). Registers such as spontaneous everyday conversation contain features of communicative immediacy, such as privacy, familiarity of interlocutors, and so forth (Koch 1999: 400–402; for discussion and references, see Culpeper and Kytö 2010: ch. 1). To some extent, private letters can approximate the immediacy of such exchanges; this register is therefore of great interest to historical linguists and corpus compilers (see, for instance, the *Corpus of Early English Correspondence* family).

Even when the ultimate aim is to say something about the spoken language of the past, written texts thus play an important role in register comparison. According to Rissanen (1999: 188; see also Kytö and Rissanen 1983), "by a careful comparison of texts which stand at different distances from spoken language (judging by the discourse situation, the purpose of the text, the educational level of the author and other extralinguistic criteria), it is possible to present hypotheses about whether a certain construction is favoured or avoided in the spoken language of the period." In addition, it is important to consider the results of such comparative analyses in the light of developments in Present-day English and of statements about the phenomena in question in early historical grammars and language manuals (see Section 3.2; see, also, Culpeper and Kytö 2010: 14ff.).

3 Examination of specific studies

In this section, we will discuss a number of studies that represent prominent aspects of diachronic research from a register perspective. While some of the studies selected study variation among several registers, others focus on the language of a single register. In our discussion, the main division is that between studies that focus on a single linguistic feature and studies that consider the occurrence of a large number of features in the same texts. While the single-feature approach is, in principle, feasible based on the manual use of non-electronic material, the multi-feature perspective requires access to electronically stored texts and to software such as search programs.

3.1 Single-feature approaches

Impressive research on individual linguistic features was carried out in historical English linguistics even before the advent of electronic corpora. Some notable studies based on non-electronic material compared the incidence of linguistic features in several registers; for instance, Rydén and Brorström (1987) compare comedies and letters in their analysis of the variation between BE and HAVE as perfect auxiliaries. Other studies based on manually collected material focused on the distribution of the relevant feature in a single register; indeed, sometimes the language of a single author was examined. Behre's (1967, 1969) analyses of the use of multal quantifiers (e.g. *much* and *a lot [of]*) in Late Modern English may be used as an example. Behre's (1969) study is an extension of his earlier work (Behre 1967) on the same variant field in Agatha Christie's writing. Behre (1969) subjects a large number of novels to careful linguistic analysis and takes independent variables into account, such as the type of construction the quantifier occurs in and the author who produced each quantifier (which also provides indications of developments across time). However, like many studies that are not based on computerized corpora, Behre (1969) focuses on the written output of a small number of authors (Agatha Christie, John Galsworthy, Elizabeth Gaskell, George Eliot, and Anthony Trollope). This limitation makes it difficult to claim that the results are representative of the register as a whole.

The extension of the corpus-linguistic paradigm to past stages of the English language has increased the attention given to sampling issues in the above regard. Kytö and Smitterberg's (2006) and Smitterberg's (2009) analyses of multal quantifiers are based on a smaller set of material – *A Corpus of Nineteenth-century English* – than Behre (1969) used. This means that there are at times insufficient data for conclusive interpretations. However, even though the fiction register is represented by no more than 111,190 words in these studies, nine different authors publishing in three different subperiods of the nineteenth century are covered, which reduces the risk that idiosyncratic choices on the part of a single author will affect the results for the entire register. The notion of register comparison – in particular, the division of the seven registers included in the corpus into an expository and a non-expository group – is at the forefront of these analyses. Among other things, Kytö and Smitterberg (2006) are able to show that the spread of variants such as *a great deal (of)* into territory previously covered by *much* takes place chiefly in non-expository writing in the nineteenth century.

In Smitterberg (2009), this analysis is taken one step further. The register parameter is used as an independent variable in what is essentially an apparent-time framework (Mair 2009a: 1117–1118): some registers are more advanced than others in a situation where diachronic change is extrapolated from synchronic variation, an approach that was previously used by Devitt (1989) in her investigation of the standardization of Scots-English in the sixteenth and seventeenth centuries. Smitterberg shows that the distribution of the two main types of multal quantifiers, represented here by *much* and *a great deal of*, can be plotted as an S-like curve where the category axis comprises different registers that illustrate the progress of the change towards increased use of the *a great deal of* type at the expense of the *much* type. This type of study points to the interconnectedness of the two extralinguistic parameters of register and time.

3.2 Multi-feature approaches

The studies exemplified so far have all focused on what can be called single linguistic features. An alternative approach to register variation is to consider the occurrence of a large number of linguistic features as they co-occur in texts (see also Chapter 17). Such an approach requires access to computerized material, as time limitations make it nearly impossible to retrieve several different linguistic features from the same printed or handwritten documents. The computerized texts are typically also annotated to facilitate the retrieval of grammatical categories. As was first shown in factor analyses of Present-day English such as Biber (1988), the co-occurrence patterns of linguistic features form dimensions of linguistic variation like "Involved vs. Informational Production" (Dimension 1 in Biber 1988), on which registers occupy different positions; for instance, personal letters can be shown to be more involved and less informational than academic prose.

Extending the scope of multidimensional analyses to address historical register variation was a natural next step. In one such analysis, Biber and Finegan (1997) demonstrate that the Late Modern English period is characterized by increased linguistic diversity among written registers. While popular registers have become more "oral" in their linguistic make-up since at least the nineteenth century, specialist expository registers have instead developed towards a more "literate" style during the same period. Geisler (2002) applies a similar method to *A Corpus of Nineteenth-century English*, an analysis which demonstrates that historical speech-related registers need not pattern together; while both Parliamentary Debates and Trial Proceedings are based on speech taken down, the former register tends to pattern with the expository registers while the latter comes across as non-expository.

From a register perspective, it is clear that multi-dimensional techniques have a great deal to offer historical corpus linguistics. One desideratum for future research on historical registers would be not only to carry out new factor analyses, but also to start out from period-specific lists of linguistic features. One of the most important findings revealed by multi-dimensional historical register analysis is the existence of long-term trends in usage. As mentioned above, popular and specialist registers have followed different paths in this regard, leading to increased register differentiation in diachrony. The next section will be devoted to two of these trends and their significance for historical register analysis.

3.3 Register drift

Scholars have recently become interested in identifying types of linguistic change that span large periods of time. This section briefly discusses two such trends in English written registers over the past few centuries: *colloquialization* and *densification*. Mair's (2006: 187) account of twentieth-century English describes colloquialization as an important stylistic shift whereby the norms of some written registers become more similar to spoken usage and more tolerant of informality and anti-formality. This trend has been noted in late twentieth-century English (see Hundt and Mair 1999) as well as during most of the Late Modern English period (see Biber and Finegan 1997). Colloquialization has been linked to sociocultural changes such as a democratization and informalization of public discourse and to a popularization of written texts (Mair 2006; Biber and Gray 2012).

During roughly the same time span, a trend towards densification has been noted in several registers. Densification can be defined as an increase in information density; that is, more information content is expressed using a given number of words (Leech *et al.* 2009: 210, 233). Leech *et al.* (2009: 217) show that there was an increase in, for instance, [[noun] + [common noun]] sequences between the early 1960s and the early 1990s. As Biber and Gray (2011) show, however, this trend is also noticeable during much of the Late Modern English period, and it appears to be spearheaded by expository written registers. Densification and colloquialization can potentially come into conflict in a register like newspaper language, as "too much information density in this area would come at a cost to accessibility" (Leech *et al.* 2009: 218; see also Biber 2003 on newspaper discourse).

4 *Thou* vs. *you* across three registers in Early Modern English

As the language use of past periods can be expected to pattern along the register axis as it has been shown to do today, it is difficult to ignore the role played by registers in a corpus-based study of language change. Our linguistic feature selected to illustrate the influence of the register factor is the rivalry of the second-person singular pronouns *thou* and *you* in the Early Modern period when *you* forms expanded at the expense of *thou* forms. Regarding data collection, speech-related texts offer a particularly rewarding area. As mentioned in Section 2.3, the juxtaposition of several written registers with a relation to the spoken language can give us insights into the nature of past speech.

In her study based on *A Corpus of English Dialogues 1560–1760* (CED), Walker (2007) looked at the use of *thou* and *you* in three speech-related registers, viz. trial proceedings, witness depositions, and drama comedy; to complement the collection of witness depositions included in CED, additional data were drawn from manuscript material. The study was intended to fill in a gap in the field: even though there had been previous studies on the topic, Walker's project was the first large-scale quantitative and qualitative investigation into authentic registers such as trials and depositions. Drama comedy, a constructed register, was included in the study to provide a basis for comparisons with the authentic registers and with the results obtained in previous studies. Further parameters covered by the study included sociolinguistic factors (sex, age, and rank) and a number of linguistic features (e.g. closed-class vs. lexical verbs, and the pronoun forms and their syntactic functions). In addition to examining frequency distributions of the forms, Walker carried out qualitative micro-analyses to account for the choice of the forms and to discuss possible motivations behind the uses. The three major methodological frameworks that the investigation was based on were thus corpus linguistics, historical pragmatics, and historical sociolinguistics.

Looking at the dimensions of Walker's study, the texts examined totaled 400,000 words (trials: 100,000 words; depositions: 150,000 words; drama comedy: 150,000 words). Altogether close to 10,000 instances of *thou* and *you* forms were included in the study. As only singular uses of *you* were included in the analyses (to establish the *tertium comparationis*), plural uses had to be screened from the data manually; subjective, objective, and possessive determiner/pronoun uses of both forms were included in the study. Like many other studies, Walker (2007) highlights drama as a prominent source of data as regards the occurrence of dialogic features. The distribution of the relevant instances across the registers is shown in Table 18.1. In the light of the overall figures for *thou* vs. *you*, depositions emerge as the register where *thou* is the most prominent, with drama and especially trials displaying lower rates of *thou* use.

On the basis of these results, Walker's task was then to show how the change proceeded across the 200-year period (stratified into five 40-year subperiods) in the light of the register and other factors, extralinguistic and linguistic. One of her hypotheses based on previous literature was that the extralinguistic factors would influence the pronoun selection to a

Table 18.1 Thou *and* you *forms in trials, depositions, and drama 1560–1760 (Walker 2007): raw frequencies and row percentages*

	thou		you		
Register	No.	%	No.	%	Total
Trials	168	7.7	2,019	92.3	2,187
Depositions	555	43.6	719	56.4	1,274
Drama	902	14.8	5,185	85.2	6,087
Total	1,625	17.0	7,923	83.0	9,548

greater extent than the linguistic factors (the pronoun forms and their functions, closed-class vs. lexical verbs, modal vs. primary verbs, and public vs. private verbs). Differences between the registers were also expected as well as the decline of *thou*. All these hypotheses were verified in the study. As regards differences between registers, trials displayed "a marked decline after 1600" (Walker 2007: 288); depositions had higher percentages of *thou*, which declined in a zigzag pattern across the periods. Drama comedy, where *thou* was more frequent than in trials but less so than in depositions, exhibited more complicated results owing to, among other things, the relatively narrow time span covered by the texts included in the analysis and factors typical of this register, such as formulaic greetings (e.g. *your servant*) and dramatists using *thou* for characterization purposes (Walker 2007: 291). Importantly, none of the three registers investigated alone could have shown the complexity of the development across the period; several speech-related registers were needed in order to shed light on the decline of *thou* forms in Early Modern English dialogues.

Walker's study is a good example of a diachronic corpus-based investigation where the author needs to consider the special nature of his or her data and carefully assess the reliability of the data sources used. A desideratum for future research would be to incorporate all factors considered by Walker into a multifactorial analysis such as logistic regression.

5 Concluding remarks

This chapter has highlighted the growing recognition of the crucial role played by the register parameter in historical corpus linguistics. These advances have of course been made in large part by building on important pre-computerized work on language history. Research has shown that register is one of the many extralinguistic categories which lie behind the linguistic variation that is a prerequisite for language change. Moreover, careful studies of variation in the history of English based on pre-computerized text collections demonstrated the importance of taking the register parameter into account; for instance, Romaine (1982) situates register variation within a larger sociohistorical framework, and Devitt (1989) presents an account of Anglicization where the process is, to quote Hundt and Mair (1999: 236), seen "as mediated" through register. Such approaches have then been successfully adopted within the corpus-linguistic paradigm (witness, for instance, the account of Walker 2007 in Section 4 above).

However, as we have also tried to show, applying the register concept to historical stages of languages is not without complications. Not all languages are equally well represented in different registers throughout their history. Even though English, which has been our main focus in this account, does relatively well in this regard, there are conspicuous gaps in register coverage (see, for instance, the comparison of German and English with regard to early legal texts in Section 2.2). Moreover, potentially conflicting desiderata such as comparability and representativeness make it necessary for scholars to consider carefully the make-up of their corpora and the extent to which results based on a selection of registers can be generalized to the language as a whole.

Future advances in historical corpus linguistics are likely to have theoretical as well as practical effects on how scholars use registers. Challenges involved in applying the register concept across time have recently been analyzed critically in several studies. For instance, Leech (2007) problematizes notions such as comparability and representativeness; Kohnen (2007a) discusses concepts such as the distinction between "producer" registers, with identifiable addressors and short texts (e.g. private letters), and "receiver" registers, with few or anonymous authors and texts with wide circulation (e.g. biblical texts). As regards practical applications, several recent corpus projects attempt either to represent one set of registers faithfully through careful consideration of the distinctive features of registers and subregisters (for instance, for medical texts, see Taavitsainen, Pahta, and Mäkinen 2005; Taavitsainen and Pahta 2010) or to make large text collections comprising key registers available to the linguistic community (e.g. the *Corpus of Historical American English*). New corpora covering the early development of registers in transplanted varieties of English are also a promising locus of future research. Even more importantly, although significant advances have been made in recent years, many registers in languages other than English remain to be explored and made available in corpora. While our examples have been taken from English, the general points remain valid for historical corpus linguistics as a whole. As this chapter has hopefully demonstrated, register will remain a central concept in historical corpus linguistics for the foreseeable future.

Corpora

BLOB-1931 corpus. In progress. Compiled by Geoffrey Leech, Paul Rayson, and Nick Smith. See www.helsinki.fi/varieng/CoRD/corpora/BLOB-1931/index.html.

Corpus of Early English Correspondence. 1998–. Compiled by Terttu Nevalainen, Helena Raumolin-Brunberg, Jukka Keränen, Minna Nevala, Arja Nurmi, and Minna Palander-Collin (Department of English, University of Helsinki). For the corpus family, see www.helsinki.fi/varieng/CoRD/corpora/CEEC/index.html.

A Corpus of English Dialogues 1560–1760. 2006. Compiled under the supervision of Merja Kytö (Uppsala University) and Jonathan Culpeper (Lancaster University). See www.helsinki.fi/varieng/CoRD/corpora/CED/index.html.

Corpus of English Religious Prose. In progress. Compiled by Thomas Kohnen, Tanja Rütten, Ingvilt Marcoe, Kirsten Gather, and Dorothee Groeger. University of Cologne. See www.helsinki.fi/varieng/CoRD/corpora/COERP/.

Corpus of Historical American English. 2010. Compiled by Mark Davies (Brigham Young University). See http://corpus.byu.edu/coha/.

A Corpus of Nineteenth-century English. Compiled by Merja Kytö (Uppsala University) and Juhani Rudanko (University of Tampere).

Corpus of Scottish Correspondence, 1500–1715. Compiled by Anneli Meurman-Solin (University of Helsinki). See www.helsinki.fi/varieng/CoRD/corpora/CSC/index.html.

An Electronic Text Edition of Depositions 1560–1760. 2011. See Kytö, Grund and Walker (2011).

The Helsinki Corpus of English Texts. 1991. Compiled by Matti Rissanen (project leader), Merja Kytö (project secretary); Leena Kahlas-Tarkka, Matti Kilpiö (Old English); Saara Nevanlinna, Irma Taavitsainen (Middle English); Terttu Nevalainen, Helena Raumolin-Brunberg (Early Modern English) (Department of English, University of Helsinki). See www.helsinki.fi/varieng/CoRD/corpora/HelsinkiCorpus/index.html.

LOB (*Lancaster–Oslo/Bergen Corpus*). 1976 (original version), 1986 (POS-tagged version). Compiled by Geoffrey Leech, Stig Johansson, Knut Hofland, and Roger Garside. See www.helsinki.fi/varieng/CoRD/corpora/LOB/index.html.

19

Literary style and literary texts

Michaela Mahlberg

Introduction

According to Leech (2008: 55), "[t]he study of style is essentially the study of *variation* in the use of language" (emphasis in the original). The study of style in literary texts is typically seen as the remit of literary stylistics. In the same way that corpus-linguistic methods are increasingly used in a range of linguistic and language-related fields, there is also growing interest in the application of corpus methods to the study of literary texts. Over the past decade, the use of the term "corpus stylistics" has reflected this growing interest. Sometimes the term corpus stylistics indicates a disciplinary background out of which a particular study has developed. However, Biber (2011: 20) critically observes that the "spin on the historical development of corpus-stylistic research disregards the long tradition of computational and statistical research on authorship attribution and literary style." In this chapter I want to make a case for the conceptualization of corpus stylistics so that the term can serve to deliberately position work in a particular research context. For a meaningful approach to corpus stylistics it is important to discuss its relationship with related fields both in terms of methodologies and explanatory purposes.

Corpus stylistics is the study of literary texts that employs corpus-linguistic methods to support the analysis of textual meanings and the interpretation of texts. As such, corpus-stylistic research makes it possible to focus on individual texts and even text extracts – as the places where the aesthetic effects of language are best analyzed (Leech and Short 2007: 11). Crucial for corpus-stylistic work in this sense is the intrinsic explanatory purpose of the linguistic analysis. Leech (2008: 54) distinguishes between "descriptive" and "explanatory" stylistics. For the former "the purpose is just to describe the style" and for the latter "the purpose is to use stylistics to explain something" (Leech 2008: 54). An explanatory goal may be "extrinsic" or "intrinsic." An extrinsic goal is to identify the author of a text or the chronological relationship between texts, whereas an intrinsic goal is to explain the meaning of the text (Leech 2008: 54f.). The intrinsic explanatory purpose of corpus stylistics positions it closely to literary stylistics as the field where linguistic analysis and literary criticism come together. By employing corpus-linguistic methods, corpus stylistics also has an extrinsic dimension that compares texts and assesses specific linguistic features in relation to wider linguistic patterns. In this sense, quantitative methods provide the link between corpus stylistics and computational approaches to style.

To delimit the object of study for corpus stylistics it might be more useful to refer to "meanings in literary texts" than "literary style." The term "style" is used in a range of different ways. To talk about "literary style" seems to imply a clearly discernible variety that can be defined as "literary language" – in contrast to non-literary language. Typically, literary use of language is seen as creative. However, creativity is also found in "ordinary" language and literariness is best seen as a matter of degree (Carter 2004). The literariness of a text is not only determined through linguistic features; crucial is also "whether the reader (or listener) *chooses* to 'read' or respond to a text (spoken or written) in a literary way" (Carter 2004: 69, emphasis in the original). This relevance of the reader for the creation of meanings in texts is emphasized through the qualitative dimension of corpus stylistics and its aim to find links with literary criticism and hence the interpretation of literary texts in context.

The present chapter begins by situating corpus stylistics within the context of corpus linguistics (Section 1) and computational stylistics (Section 2). The relationship between corpus stylistics and literary stylistics will mainly be highlighted through the discussion of examples (Sections 3 and 6). This seems to be the most effective approach in the confines of this chapter, as in literary stylistics the analyst can draw on the full range of linguistic approaches – depending on the text under scrutiny – and the interpretative context of literary criticism will also vary with the text. After an overview of frequently used methods in corpus stylistics (Section 4), I will provide a brief summary of the current state of the art (Section 5), before the final section of the chapter (Section 6) focuses on a case study of patterns of characterization in Dickens.

1 Literary texts in corpora: register and style

Literary texts in corpora tend to be analyzed from a "register" perspective so that features of literary texts are compared to features of other varieties of the language. Biber *et al.* (1999) describe grammatical features of the English language with respect to four registers, including fiction along with conversation, news, and academic prose as a set of varieties that are both important and sufficiently diverse from one another (Biber *et al.* 1999:

15f.). Such registers are defined through situational characteristics, e.g. their interactiveness or communicative purpose. While literary texts tend to be regarded as imaginative or fictional, this is not necessarily the case and brings us back to the difficulty of defining literary language. Wales (2001: 238) observes that "it is the impossibility of defining it in any simple way that is its most defining feature." From the register point of view an important aspect of literature is the fact that it is institutionalized. Publishers, libraries, and university courses all contribute to defining what works are regarded as literature.

Biber and Conrad (2009) define a register approach to the analysis of text varieties in contrast to genre and style perspectives. A register perspective studies frequent and pervasive words and grammatical structures and interprets them in respect of situational characteristics of the variety. Because the focus is on frequent features, this approach can work with samples of texts. A genre approach in contrast, requires complete texts because it deals with conventional linguistic features that structure a text (Biber and Conrad 2009: 16). Biber and Conrad (2009: 18) see similarities between the register and the style perspective in that both are concerned with typical linguistic features that can be studied across text samples. The difference lies in the interpretation of the features. While linguistic patterns that result from the real-world situational characteristics of the registers are functional, patterns associated with styles are not. "Rather, these are features associated with aesthetic preferences" (Biber and Conrad 2009: 18). External situational characteristics, such as whether the author has the opportunity to edit a text, are less important. Crucial for the language in fiction are "the ways in which the fictional world is constructed" (Biber and Conrad 2009: 132). Because of the difference between the external world and the fictional world, in stylistics a distinction is typically made between the author and the narrator of a text (see also Stockwell 2002: 41f.). When linguistic features are seen in respect of authors' attitudes towards language, styles are often associated with authors, groups of authors, or literary periods (Biber and Conrad 2009: 18f.). Features of style can also be seen from the point of view of the reader, who responds to a text or is affected by the text as a work of art (Leech and Short 2007: 12).

Focusing on novels, Biber and Conrad (2009) argue that the communicative purpose of telling a story is reflected in register features associated with narration and the presentation of fictional discourse, such as past-tense verbs, third-person pronouns, adverbials of time, and reporting verbs. Stylistic choices on the other hand relate to how authors prefer to tell their stories. Such choices refer to the type of narrator, the extent of reported dialogue, description of people, and narrating in the past or present tense (Biber and Conrad 2009: 138).

A register rather than a style approach to literary texts reflects the aims of corpus linguistics to find generalizations – based on large collections of texts – about the way in which language is used in a range of contexts. Such generalizations are captured in dictionaries, grammars, and textbooks on the use of language. If the data contain examples that occur just once, or patterns that occur repeatedly only because they are all from the same text, these cases will usually be discarded in the search for general patterns. While the purpose of the analysis of texts may vary between corpus linguistics and studies interested in style, the methods, however, can still be similar.

2 Literary computing and computational stylistics

The application of quantitative, computational, or computer-assisted methods to literary texts has a long tradition. It can be situated within the much wider field of the digital humanities that is concerned with methods of computing to preserve, process, and make accessible a range of media and artifacts. Corpus approaches to literary texts are specifically related to work in the area of literary computing or computational stylistics. In his outline of computational stylistics, Craig (2004: 281) emphasizes that computational stylistic analysis needs to incorporate expertise from "traditional humanities disciplines" which include bibliographical, historical, and critical approaches, as well as statistics and humanities computing generally, where the latter covers expertise in corpus creation. Overall, work in the field of computational stylistics seems to be more statistical in focus and literary computing as such is still perceived as rather specialist. This is partly due to wider disciplinary developments. While methods in computing became more sophisticated, in literary criticism more generally there was a shift away from close reading to approaches that were mainly concerned with the literary theory to interpret texts.

Early applications of computer methods in the study of literature include the compilation of concordances. In reviews of historical developments in corpus linguistics, reference is often made to the fact that concordances are not an invention of corpus linguistics, but have been used in the study of literature even before computers existed, for instance, to compile concordances of the Bible or of works of Shakespeare. While in corpus linguistics concordancing has become a mainstream method, in literary criticism it does not seem to play a major role. I will return to methodological issues below.

From a literary point of view, the existence of the journal titles like *Literary and Linguistic Computing* or *Computers and the Humanities* may be regarded as a reflection of the specialist nature of literary computing. "[A]part from a general aversion to all things electronic in traditional literary criticism," Rommel (2004: 93) sees one reason for the marginal position of literary computing in the "notion of relevance" – the fact that computer-assisted methods are not perceived as making a major contribution to interpretative procedures to study aesthetic works. Literary computing is mainly seen as providing tools or adding only to a "very narrow spectrum of literary analysis – in the area of stylistic studies that focus on textual features" (Rommel 2004: 94).

The computer-assisted study of textual features often takes the form of computational stylistics "in which all the most common words … of a large set of texts are subjected to appropriate kinds of statistical analysis" (Burrows 2004: 323). One of the methods that is often employed in computational stylistics is Principal Component Analysis (PCA). This method reduces a given set of variables to a smaller number of composite variables to account for most of the relationships between the initial variables. Craig (2008) employs PCA to study relationships between Shakespeare's characters. He focuses on the fifty characters that speak more than 3,000 words and he uses the fifty most frequent words in this collection of data. He interprets the PCA results as "a sociolinguistics of character" (Craig 2008: 287). PCA shows contrasts and similarities between characters that seem to reflect the social purposes of the characters' speech. Craig (2008: 286) finds, for instance, that female characters use *I* and *me* more than *we* and *our*. The former belong to features reflecting individuality and the latter to features of impersonal, collective authority. In a similar study, Tabata (1995) uses PCA to compare first-person and third-person narratives in Dickens, using the 100 most common word types and textual segments from 10 texts (9 of which are novels). He finds that first-person and third-person narratives can differ in terms of features of "oral" vs. "literate" style. The first-person narratives show, for instance, a preference for verbal structures, the coordinate conjunctions *and* and *but*, intensifiers, and negatives. The third-person narratives, in contrast, are characterized by nominal structures (with the definite article being a strongly discriminating word), frequent hypotactic structures (as shown by the occurrence of *which* and *who*), and features that relate to the description of actions.

Stylistic studies that are concerned with the variation of a set of features across texts are similar to studies in corpus linguistics that investigate register variation with the help of statistical methods (see Biber 1988). Considerations about variation in linguistic features are also crucial to studies concerned with authorship attribution, or "stylometric" techniques. The focus on frequent words in such studies is typically justified by the assumption that "word frequencies are largely outside the author's conscious control because they result from habits that are stable enough to create a verbal fingerprint" (Hoover 2007: 176). More generally, in authorship attribution the aim is typically to find "a small number of textual characteristics that distinguish the texts of authors effectively from each other" (Hoover 2003: 261), but such characteristics are not necessarily only frequent words. For instance, Baayen *et al.* (1996) argue that the use of syntactically annotated text samples improves the performance of stylometric techniques and Hoover (2003) demonstrates the effectiveness of using collocations in authorship attribution.

Hoover (2003: 262) points out that the focus in authorship attribution differs from the aims of stylistic analysis, in that the former concentrates on small numbers of items that sufficiently differentiate texts, whereas the latter is more interested in large numbers of characteristic features to account for the styles of authors. That both are related is particularly apparent in Burrow's (1987) study on Jane Austen.

Burrows (1987) made an important contribution to showing how empirical evidence can add objectivity to the study of textual features. At the same time, one can see why it might not appeal to a general audience of literary critics. Burrows (1987) shows that frequent words play an important role in the creation of meaning in a novel and in distinguishing between different novels. He argues that frequent words – that tend to be grammatical words – do usually not receive much attention in the analysis of literary texts. He pointedly begins his study:

> It is a truth not generally acknowledged that, in most discussions of works of English fiction, we proceed as if a third, two-fifths, a half of our material were not really *there*. (Burrows 1987: 1; emphasis in the original)

Burrows (1987) argues that the top frequent (mostly grammatical) words reflect unobtrusive habits of expression – which are also what authorship studies focus on. He shows that these words differentiate idiolects of characters; they can be used to identify correlations between characters within a novel and across novels: compare Jane Austen's dialogue with other novelists', and compare dialogue and narrative. Through these comparisons, Burrows (1987) makes a major contribution to capturing patterns of Jane Austen's language. The range of comparisons that he draws on relates his work directly to concerns in corpus linguistics, where the comparison of different sets of data also plays a crucial role. While Burrows (1987) seeks links between his findings and arguments in criticism, the amount of data he deals with only allows relatively brief discussions of a range of examples. As the overall structure of his book is shaped by the different types of statistical measures that he employs (which include the chi-squared test, linear regression, and correlation-matrices), his contribution is more a methodological than an interpretative one. Methodologically, the focus is on the statistical computations and not on methods of corpus creation. In his introduction, Burrows (1987) makes it clear that the preparation of the data required considerable manual input, not only to deal with part-of-speech annotation and spelling variation, but also to mark-up the speech by characters in order to enable the comparison of character idiolects or the comparison of dialogue and narrative.

Beyond the immediate interest into patterns in Jane Austen's work, Burrows (1987) makes some fundamental observations about literary language that are of wider relevance for arguments in literary stylistics.

He draws attention to the fact that the distinction between literary and non-literary language cannot be a clear-cut one (Burrows 1987: 117), a point that is also made by Carter's (2004) approach to literariness. With the focus that Burrows (1987) puts on high-frequency words – that are grammatical words or words that are less related to content – he argues that they still will have an effect on the reader, even if at a subliminal level (Burrows 1987: 4, 32). This pervasiveness of linguistic patterning that is difficult to see without computer-assisted methods is also typically mentioned to highlight the strengths of corpus linguistic research.

3 Approaches to corpus stylistics

The previous sections have argued that corpus stylistics relates to both corpus linguistics and computational stylistics through its quantitative methods. At the same time it is set apart from these fields through its intrinsic explanatory purpose that makes it possible to focus on specific meanings in texts. In this sense, corpus stylistics requires engagement with concepts that address properties and interpretations of literary texts. In the following I want to look at four studies that exemplify principles relevant to corpus stylistics. These approaches extend or develop categories for the analysis of literary texts and/or show how corpus methods are relevant to the study of textual meanings.

Semino and Short (2004) test the model of speech and thought presentation developed by Leech and Short ([1981] 2007) by applying it systematically to a corpus that allows for comparisons between twentieth-century fictional, journalistic, and (auto)biographical narratives. From a quantitative point of view, Semino and Short's (2004) work is a corpus study into register variation where the features under analysis are determined by the categories of the speech and thought presentation model. This model was originally developed for prose fiction. Beyond the quantification of the categories, the study by Semino and Short (2004) provides further evidence of linguistic categories capturing features which are not exclusively literary or non-literary but show how literariness is a matter of degree. The extension of a model from literary to non-literary texts also underlines the point made by Sinclair (2004a) that a useful description of the language cannot exclude literary texts or only account for them by specialized categories.

In the course of their study, Semino and Short (2004) had to modify the model by modifying categories and adding new ones. In this sense, the extensive manual annotation of the texts that was necessary to enable the generation of quantitative data contributed to theoretical development (Semino and Short 2004: 40). The revised model now provides an improved set of categories for the analysis of individual texts and the explanation of their meanings. The fact that studies concerned with discourse presentation in novels are less amenable to automatic procedures had already been highlighted by Burrows (1987). Despite the sophisticated statistical methods he illustrates, the corpus he used to retrieve quantitative data required manual pre-processing. However, Burrows (1987) does not go far into the discussion of the analytical aspects of discourse presentation annotation, which would position his work more within a corpus-stylistic context.

Another book-length contribution is Toolan's (2009) approach to narrative progression in the short story. Toolan (2009) uses corpus methods to address the question of how textual signals in the form of lexico-phrasal patterning guide readers' expectations and add to their perception of the narrative progression of texts. His overall research question that is grounded in text-linguistic and narratological theory drives the corpus-linguistic methods of his approach. Toolan (2009) combines the use of automatic corpus techniques with more directed searches that are motivated by theoretical considerations. He uses a range of methods, most importantly key comparisons, but also concordance searches, cluster retrieval or tools to measure lexical novelty over the length of a text. Among the progression-signaling elements that Toolan (2009) identifies are, for instance, sentences that contain top-keyword character names, lexical keywords above a certain frequency threshold or clusters. The narrative progression parameters also include sentences containing characters' free indirect thought (FIT). The manual annotation for the study by Semino and Short (2004) highlights the present lack of an automatic FIT parser. However, Toolan (2009) suggests a sequence of three form-based rules as the basis for a semi-automatic identification of FIT. Overall, Toolan's (2009) approach shows how a specific research question guides the combination of automatic procedures with analytical methods.

Coming from the corpus-linguistic end of the spectrum, Louw (1993) illustrates the potential of the concept of "semantic prosody" in its application to stylistics. Although the paper is not exclusively concerned with literary stylistics, Louw's (1993) discussion of examples illustrates the practice of "matching texts against corpora" as a useful method for corpus stylistics. Louw (1993: 159) explains that semantic prosodies result from habitual collocates "colouring" the meanings of words they occur with. One of his examples is the semantic prosody of melancholia that surrounds the combination *days are*. Louw explains how this semantic prosody is linked to the theme of Larkin's poem "Days." Drawing on a concordance from a general corpus, Louw (1993) shows that *days are* is mostly followed by words such as *gone*, *over*, and *past*. So in Larkin's poem, the line *Days are where we live* triggers associations of melancholia that point forward to the theme of death developed in the poem. A semantic prosody as a "consistent aura of meaning with which a form is imbued by its collocates" provides a background of expectations. If an occurrence in a text departs from these expectations, it has the potential to create a specific literary effect in the reader's mind. Louw's (1993) method of matching texts against corpora is a way to provide empirical evidence for effects of foregrounding that result when uses in a text deviate from more general norms of the language. This method also shows that concordancing can in effect be more than support for close reading, which Burrows (1987, 2004) seems to regard as its main purpose in stylistic analysis.

With his study of Conrad's *Heart of Darkness*, Stubbs (2005: 5) aims to "illustrate the literary value of simple quantitative text and corpus data." He clearly acknowledges that the range of features that can be analyzed is restricted by the capabilities of the software and that the identification of features as such is only one step toward a literary interpretation. To seek links between corpus findings and literary interpretation, Stubbs (2005) begins with a brief outline of some of the observations put forward by literary critics, before he relates them to linguistic features identified with corpus methods. Features he discusses include frequencies and distributions of words, collocations, clusters, and keywords. He draws on comparative data from the imaginary prose categories of Brown, LOB, Frown, and FLOB as one reference corpus and the written component of the BNC as another. One of the examples Stubbs (2005) presents deals with the theme of unreliable knowledge. He points out that critics tend to focus on a few content words, e.g. *fog* or *indistinct* as expressions of vagueness, and disregard more grammatical words and expressions such as *something, somewhere, kind of, sort of.* He also shows for some of these vagueness words that their occurrence is higher in the novel than in the two reference corpora (Stubbs 2005: 10). With the range of examples he covers, Stubbs (2005: 22) argues that "[t]he computer does not provide a single method of text analysis, but offers a range of exploratory techniques" whose value lies in adding systematicity and detail to textual analysis and literary interpretation.

Semino and Short (2004) and Toolan (2009) are both comprehensive studies that are grounded in explicit theoretical contexts. The way in which they employ corpus methods helps them to develop models and approaches that started with or focus on properties of literary texts. The contributions by Louw (1993) and Stubbs (2005), in contrast, aim to illustrate the potential of corpus linguistic methods for the analysis of textual meaning. The influence that these articles have had seems to no small extent due to their programmatic approach, which also means that neither employs corpus methods in an in-depth study to address specific literary research questions but to illustrate the potential to do so. In practical terms, it is clear that semantic prosodies are best suited to explaining meanings in poetry or short text extracts, rather than studying a whole novel. Equally, the way in which Stubbs (2005) approaches the novel works well for the purpose of illustration. When very specific research questions are to be addressed the choice of methodology will need to be more focused which may require more manual analysis, as shown by Semino and Short (2004), or may result in a combination of corpus methods and directed searches, as illustrated by Toolan (2009). While programmatic articles can afford to offer selected examples, what makes so-called corpus-stylistic work sometimes liable to criticism is the apparent lack of motivation for the choice of a particular method.

4 Methods in corpus stylistics

Corpus-stylistic methods often draw on the standard functionalities offered by concordance packages to retrieve frequencies, study words in the form of concordances, generate collocations (e.g. Hori 2004), retrieve clusters (e.g. Starcke 2006; Viana *et al.* 2007), and perform key comparisons (e.g. O'Halloran 2007b; McIntyre 2010). As narrative texts imply that there is development of a story, tools to track the distribution of lexical items are also used (e.g. Stubbs 2001; Toolan 2009; Fischer-Starcke 2009). Corpus-stylistic studies tend to draw on corpus-linguistic techniques that allow a combination of quantitative and qualitative analysis of literary texts. Such a qualitative dimension is not always immediately apparent for methods in computational stylistics relying on large amounts of data or the analysis of high-frequency items.

Importantly, different methods are suited to different types of texts or different analytical aims. Culpeper (2009) is interested in features of characters in *Romeo and Juliet*. As dramatic text consists mainly of dialogue a key comparison can be usefully employed to identify potentially relevant differences between characters' dialogue. Similarly, for Walker's (2010) approach to Julian Barnes's novel *Talking it Over*, keyword and key semantic domain comparisons are useful methodological choices. The novel has nine first-person narrators where the format of the text makes it possible to clearly distinguish between narratorial contributions. Both Culpeper (2009) and Walker (2010) look at texts that have clear textual components which readily lend themselves to key comparisons. Similarly, O'Halloran (2006) can usefully follow Louw's (1993) method of matching texts against corpora, because he is interested in meanings in a poem that readers may perceive as "dynamic and disturbing" (O'Halloran 2006: 388). He is able to explain these effects by comparing the way in which words are used in the poem with their typical patterns in a general reference corpus.

If corpus methods are not sufficiently tailored to the research question, their usefulness is limited. Amador-Moreno (2012) is interested in the discourse marker *like* in a novel by the Irish writer Paul Howard. She claims that a corpus analysis can provide evidence for the realistic use of features of spoken Irish English in the novel. Amador-Moreno (2012) begins with a comparison of the novel and the *Limerick Corpus of Irish English* (LCIE). Focusing on *like* as a discourse marker, she shows that *like* in LCIE mainly occurs in utterance/clause-initial or final position, whereas in the novel it tends to occur in mid-clause position. As evidence for the similarity between the use of *like* in the novel and in real Irish English, Amador-Moreno (2012) then turns to functions of *like*. She illustrates examples from the novel against the background of observations made in the literature. However, the paper does not present a systematic analysis of the functions that appear in the data and there is no comparison of the functions of *like* in the novel with those found in a reference corpus. Overall, the claims made in the paper are mainly based on illustrative examples and existing literature. The recourse to corpus methods and quantitative observations does not provide strong support for the argument of the paper.

Corpus studies of literary texts often aim to demonstrate the "usefulness" of a particular methodology. Archer *et al.* (2009: 157), for instance, argue that their contribution shows how key semantic domains can provide an initial step or "a way in" to cognitive metaphor-type analysis, illustrated with the theme of love in six Shakespearean plays. In her study of Austen's novels, Fischer-Starcke (2010: 25) explicitly includes the demonstration of the usefulness of corpus-linguistic techniques among her goals, along with gaining insights into the data and developing the techniques for wider applications. Her criteria for assessing the application of corpus methods include the extent to which new insights into the data can be gained and existing interpretation can be supported or refuted (Fischer-Starcke 2010: 20). The techniques that Fischer-Starcke (2010) employs to achieve her goals are the analysis of keywords, phraseologies, and the distribution of keywords. The choice of these methods is motivated by corpus-linguistic arguments rather than the texts under analysis (Fischer-Starcke 2010: 61). The study illustrates a range of methodological possibilities rather than focusing on a theoretical approach with a literary critical starting point. In this sense it follows the model of Burrows (1987) (Fischer-Starcke 2010: 9). Examples of Fischer-Starcke's (2010) insights into the data include detail of character information provided in *Northanger Abbey* that expands on observations by literary critics (Fischer-Starcke 2010: 106), as well as a segmentation of the novel into thematic units. This segmentation based on lexical distribution and progression differs from segmentations suggested by literary critics (Fischer-Starcke 2010: 194). For Fischer-Starcke (2010: 20) an important advantage of corpus methods is the focus on objective data in contrast to the more intuitive literary critical techniques. So in the combination of qualitative and quantitative methods she emphasizes the quantitative dimension.

Overall, corpus-stylistic methods are characterized through the tension between qualitative and quantitative techniques. This tension is determined by the text(s) under analysis. Studies that employ corpus-linguistic methods to demonstrate the working of a method make selective links to literary critical arguments. This allows them to focus on the quantitative over the qualitative. While making a programmatic contribution, from the point of view of literary stylistics they only tell part of the story. On the other hand, studies that begin with research questions situated in literary stylistics may less readily be able to draw on automatic procedures, as is shown by Semino and Short (2004), or equally by Busse (2010) in her study of discourse presentation in nineteenth-century fiction. Before such studies can make claims based on quantitative data, the corpus might need extensive, typically manual, annotation. Both ways of exploring corpus methods for the analysis of literary texts are necessary for critically assessing the explanatory potential of corpus stylistics.

5 The state of the art

Because of the range of questions that are generally reflected by definitions of style and approaches to literary language, corpus research in this area can take a variety of forms. Importantly, the study of literary texts seems to be best approached through a combination of methods that makes it possible to find links between literary and linguistic concerns. The term "corpus stylistics" can be used to emphasize an intrinsic explanatory goal of stylistics that is concerned with the meaning of individual texts. Even if the goal is to focus on specific meanings in texts, these texts still need to be seen against more general patterns of the language. Computational stylistics in particular highlights the role that frequent words play in creating subliminal patterns in texts. This focus is closely related to key concerns in corpus linguistics showing that frequent patterns are not necessarily those that language users are aware of. Such frequent patterns also reflect the relationship between linguistic features of registers and the situational contexts of language production.

Corpus approaches to literary language contribute to showing that the relationship between literary and non-literary language is not a clear-cut one. This relationship is addressed by questions about what linguistic features are best regarded as register, genre or style features, but also by testing models originally designed for the analysis of literary texts on a larger corpus. In this sense, research contributes to finding a description of the language that accounts for both literary and non-literary language – not by means of different sets of categories but along a continuum.

With the focus on textual meanings, limitations of the application of corpus methods are highlighted. Effects that readers perceive may not clearly be linked to countable features. Hence, it is important to combine corpus methods with other approaches to the effects of texts; these can, for instance, include psycholinguistic approaches to gain a better understanding of how meanings are actually created in the reader's mind (Mahlberg *et al.* 2014). Moreover, the kind of research questions triggered by literary texts may require new corpus-methodological developments. Features of literary texts, such as the presentation of fictional discourse for instance, require specific annotation schemes so they can usefully be quantified.

If corpus stylistics aims to pay attention to a literary text not only as a sample of language but also as a work of art, the relevance of this research for the discipline of literary studies has to be made clear. Rommel (2004) observed that literary computing still takes a marginal place in literary studies and seems to be perceived as mainly concerned with methods. Corpus stylistics might remain equally marginal unless it engages with the theories and concerns of literary criticism. This engagement might mean that corpus linguists avoid too polemical dichotomies between the objective and the subjective interpretation of texts, as well as the design of corpus tools that are better tailored to the kind of questions that literary critics might want to ask of texts. It can also be useful to try and replicate non-corpus studies that have become influential in literary criticism (Mahlberg *et al.* 2013). By searching for new methods, critically approaching assumed differences between literary and non-literary language, and aiming to find relevant connections to literary critical concerns, corpus linguistics more generally still has plenty of room for development. The case study in the following section focuses in particular on the links between literary and linguistic concerns.

6 An example: studying patterns of characterization in Dickens

This section draws on Mahlberg (2013) to illustrate a case study. Mahlberg (2013) has two main aims. One is to outline fundamental principles of corpus stylistics as a field. In this sense the study is programmatic and similar to the work of Stubbs (2005) and Fischer-Starcke (2010). The second – and more specific – aim of the study is to analyze Dickens's fiction in order to identify textual building blocks of fictional worlds. Similarly to Toolan (2009), who deals with narrative progression in the short study, Mahlberg (2013) focuses on phenomena of literary texts, i.e. the building of fictional worlds. The study is, however, more specific than Toolan (2009) because of the focus on fictional worlds in Dickens. Mahlberg (2013) explicitly aims to combine corpus-linguistic and literary concerns and uses the concept of the corpus-stylistic circle to illustrate the relationship between the two: corpus-linguistic observations and literary insights are equally relevant to the explanation of meanings in literary texts. Methodologically, corpus methods can support the explanation of literary effects, and literary insights can help to explain corpus findings. The main research question addressed by Mahlberg (2013) is the following: in a corpus of texts by Dickens, can textual patterns be identified that have discernible functions in the creation of fictional worlds? Literary concerns provide the main motivation for this research question: to a large extent, Dickens's enduring popularity seems to be due to the memorable characters that he created and the fact that characters generally take a prominent position in his fictional worlds.

The main corpus method to address the overarching research question of the study is the analysis of clusters. This approach results from a combination of corpus-linguistic and literary arguments. Habitual phrases or specific character idiolects have been identified as important means of characterization in Dickens, hence clusters appear to be a useful starting point. At the same time, corpus linguistic studies show that very frequent clusters (more commonly referred to as "lexical bundles") are associated with discourse functions and so become important textual building blocks. From both perspectives the underlying assumption is that repeated occurrences of sequences of words reflect their functional relevance in a specific text or a register more generally. The concept of "local textual functions" allows a combination of both corpus-linguistic and literary perspectives in the analysis of clusters. Local textual functions describe the meanings of linguistic items in texts. They are local in the sense that they do not claim to capture general functions, but they account for specific (groups of) items and/or specific (groups of) texts.

The more specific corpus tools and methods that are employed comprise relatively basic techniques: the retrieval of clusters, key comparisons, concordance searches, and the identification of (significant) collocates. The major steps of the study are:

1. The retrieval of five-word clusters in a 4.5-million-word Dickens corpus and their key comparison with a nineteenth-century reference corpus.
2. The identification of groups of clusters initially on the basis of formal features (e.g. clusters that contain body-part nouns are grouped together as "body-part clusters," or clusters that include first- or second-person pronouns are collected in a group referred to as "speech clusters").
3. The different groups of clusters are analyzed more qualitatively in order to describe their functions in the creation of fictional worlds. This functional analysis also takes account of distributions across Dickens's texts and the nineteenth-century reference corpus and hones in on detailed textual examples discussed mainly from an intrinsically explanatory point of view. Especially in step 3, the analysis requires engagement with approaches in literary stylistics and Dickens studies. Methodologically, the working of the corpus-stylistic circle here means I tried to find links between the patterns that emerged from the corpus and the discussion of related examples or relevant theories in the literature on Dickens.

The study identified five groups of clusters that are associated with groups of meanings in the fictional world: in addition to clusters that refer to time and place, local textual functions specifically describe the creation of characters through their speech and body language, but also through the narrator's comments on their behavior and actions. Other patterns refer to ways of talking about characters that may or may not include names. The results indicate that local textual functions are best described along a cline of highlighting and contextualizing functions: some patterns strikingly emphasize character information, while others present the information more subtly and integrated into the wider picture of the fictional world. Added to the comparisons with fiction written by other nineteenth-century authors, this functional continuum indicates a relationship between Dickens-specific techniques of characterization and more widely used patterns.

The approach is initially limited to the focus on five-word clusters, i.e. it does not systematically take into account three- or four-word clusters or even non-contiguous sequences, which would all have added to the functional variety and can be studied in future work. Also from a computational-stylistic point of view quantitative information is assessed only in a basic way. However, at the same time, this narrow corpus-methodological focus makes it possible to systematically complement the quantitative findings with a detailed qualitative analysis. The critical engagement with approaches in literary stylistics as well as Dickens studies is a strength of the approach. Links are made, for instance, with cognitive poetics, approaches to body language in literature, or impoliteness in spoken language. Instead of providing a range of methods and linguistic examples to demonstrate the usefulness of corpus stylistics more generally, the study creates a coherent argument for a theoretical approach to characterization in Dickens. Crucial for this theoretical argument is that characterization is seen as a process in the reader's mind where information provided in the text interacts with knowledge about people in the real world (Culpeper 2001; Stockwell 2009; Palmer 2011). Thus the study provides actual evidence for the workings of the principle of text-drivenness that is relevant to cognitive stylistics.

The text-driven approach complements and develops approaches in literary criticism. It shows that habitual phrases associated with characters that have been extensively discussed by critics are part of a bigger picture. They belong to a range of patterns and textual functions for the presentation of character information. The text-driven approach also helps to show relationships between seemingly opposing critical arguments, which is shown through the detailed discussion of John's (2001) approach to Dickens's externalized techniques of characterization and Rosenberg's (1996) observations on a language of doubt. According to John (2001), Dickens's methods of characterization draw on the techniques of popular melodrama, where emotions are exaggerated and gestures and actions contribute to the externalization of character. Hence, characters are transparent. Rosenberg (1996) in contrast emphasizes the elusiveness of Dickens's characters for which he finds evidence in Dickens's language of doubt, realized for instance in comparisons with *as if*. The patterns identified in the corpus-stylistic study show that what appears to be part of a language of doubt is an interpretation of character information and not unclear character information as such.

Beyond Dickens, the study extends the stylistician's toolkit. In contrast to discourse presentation, body language in literature is still an under-explored area to which this study contributes by suggesting lexically driven categories of body language presentation.

Conclusions

This chapter has shown that corpus approaches to the study of literary style can take various forms. The variety of approaches is due to the fact that literary texts can be treated both as examples of language that are part of a register, as well as individual works of art to which the reader responds in a literary way. The more corpus approaches are interested in the literary quality of texts and intrinsic analytical goals, the more these approaches have to become interdisciplinary. Computer-assisted methods as such do not result in interpretations and the provision of data and tools alone does not convince the literary critic that the corpus linguist has something to say. In spite of the challenges that cross-disciplinary research poses, maybe now is a particularly good time for corpus stylistics? Literary stylistics has witnessed a cognitive turn that puts more emphasis on the position of the reader in the creation of meaning. In the reading process patterns in the text determine which area of background knowledge or previous experience are relevant to the creation of meaning. Hence there are obvious points of contact for cognitive-stylistic and corpus-linguistic approaches. At the same time, it seems in literary criticism close reading has started to receive more attention again. Additionally, the growing number of digitized texts is likely to increase the interest in methods of studying electronic versions of literary texts. Even more fundamentally, however, the corpus-linguistic study of language has great potential not only to show differences between literary and non-literary language but to shift the focus to the similarities between the two.

20

Dialect variation

Jack Grieve

1 Introduction

Relatively little research on dialect variation has been based on corpora of naturally occurring language. Instead, dialect variation has been studied based primarily on language elicited through questionnaires and interviews. Eliciting dialect data has several advantages, including allowing for dialectologists to select individual informants, control the communicative situation in which language is collected, elicit rare forms directly, and make high-quality audio recordings. Although far less common, a corpus-based approach to data collection also has several advantages, including allowing for dialectologists to collect large amounts of data from a large number of informants, observe dialect variation across a range of communicative situations, and analyze quantitative linguistic variation in large samples of natural language. Although both approaches allow for dialect variation to be observed, they provide different perspectives on language variation and change. The corpus-based approach to dialectology has therefore produced a number of new findings, many of which challenge traditional assumptions about the nature of dialect variation. Most important, this research has shown that dialect variation involves a wider range of linguistic variables and exists across a wider range of language varieties than has previously been assumed.

The goal of this chapter is to introduce this emerging approach to dialectology. The first part of this chapter reviews the growing body of research that analyzes dialect variation in corpora, including research on variation across nations, regions, genders, ages, and classes, in both speech and writing, and from both a synchronic and diachronic perspective, with a focus on dialect variation in the English language. Although collections of language data elicited through interviews and questionnaires are now commonly referred to as *corpora* in sociolinguistics and dialectology (e.g.

see Bauer 2002; Tagliamonte 2006; Kretzschmar *et al.* 2006; D'Arcy 2011), this review focuses on corpora of naturally occurring texts and discourse. The second part of this chapter presents the results of an analysis of variation in *not* contraction across region, gender, and time in a corpus of American English letters to the editor in order to exemplify a corpus-based approach to dialectology.

2 A review of corpus-based dialect studies

2.1 National dialect variation

The earliest corpus-based dialect studies were concerned with national variation. The first modern corpus, the Brown Corpus (Francis and Kucera 1964), contained one million words of texts from 1961 representing a range of written registers of American English. To allow for national comparison between British and American English, the *Lancaster–Oslo/Bergen Corpus* of written British English (LOB; Johansson *et al.* 1978) was compiled to be the exact British counterpart of the American Brown Corpus. Along with two more recent corpora, the Frown (Hundt *et al.* 1999) and the FLOB (Hundt *et al.* 1998), which follow the same design but represent American and British English as written in 1991, these corpora have been used for a variety of national dialect studies. For example, in an early study based on the Brown and LOB corpora, Hofland and Johansson (1982) compared word frequencies in the two corpora to identify numerous words that are more common in the two national varieties. In a functional analysis of these two corpora, Biber (1987) analyzed the relative frequencies of various lexical and grammatical features and found that American authors tend to produce texts that are more interactive and abstract than British authors across a range written registers. Hundt (1997) analyzed all four corpora to identify short-term grammatical changes in these two national varieties, finding that in many cases American English is leading change in British English, including the increasing use of the word *proven* as an intransitive verb and the declining use of the word *which* as a relative pronoun.

In addition to these American and British corpora, the *Kolhapur Corpus of Indian English* (Shastri 1988), the *Australian Corpus of English* (Collins and Peters 1988), and the *Wellington Corpus of Written New Zealand English* (Bauer 1993), also follow the same design as the Brown Corpus, although the Kolhapur Corpus contains texts from 1978, and the Australian and Wellington corpora contain texts from 1986. These corpora have also been the basis for a limited number of national comparisons. For example, Holmes (1993) analyzed the generic use of the word *man* in the Australian Corpus and the Wellington Corpus, and found that the form was less common in New Zealand English (see also Holmes 2001).

Apart from these Brown-style corpora, the *International Corpus of English* (ICE; Greenbaum 1990, 1991, 1996; Greenbaum and Nelson 1996; Hundt and Gut 2012) consists of a series of national corpora from around the world that follow the same design, which today includes corpora representing not only the varieties of all major English-speaking nations (Australia, Canada, Ireland, New Zealand, UK, US), but also national varieties from Asia (Hong Kong, India, Malaysia, Philippines, Singapore, Sri Lanka), Africa (East Africa, Nigeria, Ghana), and the Caribbean (Bahamas, Jamaica, Trinidad and Tobago), as well as in Fiji and Malta (Hundt and Gut 2012). New ICE corpora are also currently being compiled for various other national varieties, including South Africa, Namibia, and Pakistan. Much like the Brown-style corpora, the ICE corpora contain 500 texts totaling 1 million words; however, unlike the Brown-style corpora, the ICE corpora represent a different range of registers, including notably spoken registers. The ICE corpora have been the basis for numerous corpus-based studies of national variation. For example, based on an analysis of newspaper writing in several ICE corpora, Meyer (2004) found that pseudo-titles (e.g. *San Francisco Slugger* Barry Bonds, *fellow Brandeis student* Susan E. Saxe) are least common in the British press, reflecting the more conservative style of British newspapers. Mukherjee and Hoffman (2006) used the ICE corpora to compare ditransitive verb complementation patterns in Indian and British English, finding, for example, that the ditransitive verbs *give* and *send* are more likely to be used as transitive verbs in Indian English. A series of studies were also recently in published in Hundt and Gut (2012) that analyzed grammatical variation in the ICE corpora, focusing especially on the "new Englishes" spoken in Asia, Africa, and the Caribbean, comparing them both to each other and to more well-established varieties.

In addition to the Brown and ICE corpora, the much larger *British National Corpus* (BNC; Burnard 1995) and the *Longman Corpus of Written and Spoken English* (LCWSE; Biber *et al.* 1999), have also been the basis of comparisons of modern British and American English. For example, Tottie and Hoffman (2006) compared the frequency of tag questions (e.g. it's raining, *isn't it?*) in the spoken component of the BNC and the spoken American component of the LCWSE and found that tag questions are nine times more common in colloquial British English. The LCWSE was also used for numerous comparisons of the relative frequency of various lexical and grammatical features in Biber *et al.* (1999), as well other studies (e.g. Helt 2001). Finally, national corpora have been the basis for comparisons of national varieties of other pluricentric languages including Dutch (Speelman *et al.* 2003) and Portuguese (da Silva 2010).

2.2 Regional dialect variation

As opposed to national variation, there has been a limited amount of corpus-based research on regional dialect variation. The earliest collection of regional dialect speech was the *Helsinki Dialect Corpus* (Inhalainen 1988, 1990), which consists of transcribed speech collected through interviews with informants conducted by Finnish fieldworkers in parts of England in the 1970s and 1980s. Inhalainen in particular conducted numerous studies on various forms of grammatical variation in this dataset, especially in southwestern England (e.g. Inhalainen 1976, 1980). Another early collection of regional dialect data is the *Switchboard Corpus* (Godfrey *et al.* 1992), which was collected by researchers at Texas Instruments, who recorded telephone conversations between strangers selected at random by the investigators and assigned a particular topic to discuss. Despite being the earliest attempts to create dialect corpora, these datasets both consist of elicited data from rather unnatural situations and are therefore largely outside the scope of this survey.

Corpora of naturally occurring speech have only recently been used for regional dialect studies. The spontaneous spoken section of the BNC contains some regional information, which, although it has been criticized for reliability (Burnard 2002), has been used as the basis for a small number of regional dialect studies. For example, Sampson (2002) identified various regional and national patterns in verb usage in the BNC, especially involving the perfect construction, which was found to be less common in Irish speakers and speakers from southern England. Anderwald (2005) analyzed double negation in modern British English based on the BNC, finding that while double negation occurs throughout England, the pattern is most common in the South (see also Anderwald 2002).

One of the most well-known and extensively studied regional dialect corpora is the *Freiburg English Dialect Corpus* (FRED; Kortmann *et al.* 2005; Anderwald and Wagner 2007), which consists of 2.5 million words of oral histories performed by 430 elderly informants from across Great Britain recorded between 1968 and 2000. There have been several dialect studies based on this dataset. Kortmann *et al.* (2005) analyzed FRED for variation in relative clauses, verbal concord, and gendered pronouns across British dialects. Anderwald (2009) analyzed synchronic and diachronic variation in verb morphology in English in FRED as well as other corpora (BNC, as well as COLT and ARCHER, which are discussed below). Among other findings, Anderwald showed that non-standard weak verbs (e.g. *knowed, catched*) are generally more common in Scotland and in the South, although specific weak verbs are associated with various regions, including the North (e.g. *goed* for *went*), the South (e.g. *runned* for *ran*), and the West (e.g. *seed* for *saw*). In one of the first studies to provide an overall view of regional grammatical variation in British English, Szmrecsanyi (2013) analyzed FRED and identified aggregated patterns of grammatical variation in British English, inclduing a general north–south distinction, based on a multivariate analysis of the relative frequencies of 57 mostly non-standard grammatical features (see also Szmrecsanyi 2008).

Although most corpus-based research of regional linguistic variation has focused on speech and on Great Britain, recent research on regional variation in written American English has been based on the 26-million-word *Corpus of Written American Regional Dialects* (WARD; Grieve 2011; Grieve *et al.* 2011), which contains letters to the editor written by over 130,000 authors from 206 cities in the United States. Analyses of various quantitative grammatical variables in the corpus, including contractions (Grieve 2011), word order (Grieve 2012), and function word alternations (Grieve *et al.* 2011), have demonstrated that regional variation exists in written Standard American English. The WARD corpus has also been the basis for a comparison of regional variation across speech and writing, which has shown that regional variation follows similar patterns in American English regardless of medium (Grieve 2013).

There have also been a limited number of corpora with regional data compiled for other European languages, although they have not yet been the subject of regional dialect studies. Most notably, the 10-million-word corpus of spoken Dutch, *Corpus Gesproken Nederlandse* (CGN) (Schuurman *et al.* 2003), which includes a wide variety of regional information about each informant, including not only where they were born, but also where they currently reside and where they went to school. The *Scandinavian Dialect Corpus* (Johannessen 2009) is also a notable dialect corpus containing over 2 million of words of various types of data, including recordings of casual conversations, from informants in Norway, Sweden, Denmark, and Iceland.

2.3 Historical dialect variation

In addition to national variation, one of the more successful applications of the corpus-based approach to dialectology is in the field of historical sociolinguistics. Because historical writings are the only source of direct empirical data about language from before the twentieth century, historical sociolinguistics has naturally adopted a corpus-based approach to data collection, showing that complex patterns of historical dialect variation can be observed in written sources.

In the earliest systematic study of historical social dialect variation, Romaine (1982) used quantitative methods from Labovian variationist sociolinguistics to analyze social and situational variation in relative clause marking in a corpus of Middle Scots texts written between 1530 and 1550. This book is notable not only for being one of the first studies of historical dialect variation, but also for being one of the first attempts at corpus-based sociolinguistics in general. Romaine found that the alternation between various relative pronouns – including WH forms, *that*, and relative pronoun deletion – are conditioned by social, situational, and linguistic context in Middle Scots. Although the analysis focused primarily on the importance of situational and linguistic factors, in terms of social variation, Romaine compared the language of male and female writers and found that relative pronoun deletion was relatively more common in the language of women and that the relative pronoun *that* was relatively more common in the language of men.

Perhaps the most notable historical dialect corpus is the *Corpus of Early English Correspondence* (CEEC; Nevalainen and Raumolin-Brunberg 1996, 2003), which contains 2.7 millon words of personal letters written from 1410 to 1681 by both male and female authors of various classes and from across England. In the most detailed analysis of this corpus, Nevalainen and Raumolin-Brunberg (2003) analyzed variation and change in the values of 14 grammatical variables, including the alternation between *ye* and *you* and the relative frequency of paraphrastic *do*. In addition to tracking the emergence of modern forms in the corpus, this study also considered the social distribution of these variables, finding that changes are more often led by women rather than men and are more likely to originate from the capital region. Several other smaller studies have also been based on the CEEC. For example, Palander-Collin (1999) investigated the use of *I think* in male and female personal correspondence from the seventeenth century, finding that this form is consistently and considerably stronger in the language of women. A series of other studies of historical dialect variation based on the CEEC are also published in Nevalainen and Raumolin-Brunberg (1996).

In addition to the CEEC, the diachronic component of the *Helsinki Corpus* (Kytö 1996), which covers Old, Middle, and Early Modern English, and the ARCHER Corpus (Biber and Finegan, 1997), which samples texts from the seventeenth to the twentieth century, have also been the basis for similar historical dialect studies (e.g. Nevalainen 2006; Biber and Burges 2000; Biber *et al.* 2010). Among other more recent historical dialect studies, corpora have also been used to analyze the social origin of the Northern Subject Rule in Ulster (McCafferty 2003), regional variation in nineteenth-century African American correspondence (Van Herk and Walker 2005), and regional patterns in double negation in Middle English (Ingham 2006). Similar research has also been conducted on other languages, including Dutch (e.g. Vosters and Vandenbussche 2012) and German (e.g. Elspaß *et al.* 2007).

Historical dialect atlases have also been based on corpora of written language. In particular, both *The Linguistic Atlas of Older Scots* (1380–1500) (Williamson 1992) and *The Linguistic Atlas of Early Middle English* (1150–1325) (Laing and Lass 2007) are based on digitized corpora of historic texts. Alternatively, data was collected for the earlier *Linguistic Atlas of Late Mediaeval English* (1350–1450) (MacIntosh *et al.* 1986) by fieldworkers filling out questionnaires based on onsite manual analyses of original sources found in various collections; however, even though no digitized corpus was ever compiled, because this atlas was based on representative samples of naturally occurring text, it is in essence a corpus-based study as well.

2.4 Social dialect variation

Although corpus-based studies of national and historical dialect variation are common, corpus-based studies of synchronic social dialect variation, involving extralinguistic variables at such as gender, age, class, and ethnicity, which are at the core of variationist sociolinguistics (Labov 1972; Tagliamonte 2006), have been relatively uncommon until quite recently.

The corpus that has probably been the subject of the greatest number of studies of social dialect variation is the BNC, which is coded for a variety of demographic information, including age, gender, education level, and class. For example, Rayson *et al.* (1997) analyzed the socially annotated spoken component of the BNC, finding patterns in the relative frequencies of various high-frequency words across genders, ages, and classes, such as the more frequent use of female pronouns and terms relating to the family in the language of women, and the more frequent use of numbers and expletives in the language of men. Berglund (2000) analyzed the alternation between *going to* and *gonna* in the spoken component of the BNC, finding that the contracted form was more common in the lower classes, younger speakers, and women. McEnery and Xiao (2004) analyzed the relative frequency of forms of the expletive *fuck* across social groups in the BNC, finding that this word is used more by men and young adults. Xiao and Tao (2007) analyzed social variation in the relative frequencies of a large number of different amplifiers, finding that amplifiers are more common in the language of women and the highly educated. Finally, Romaine (2008) analyzed various lexical alternations across gender, age, and class in the BNC, finding, for example, that the term *sitting room* is more common among upper-class speakers, *lounge* among middle-class speakers, and *living room* among lower-class speakers (see also Romaine 2001).

As well as the BNC, other major national corpora have been the basis of social dialect studies. For example, Barbieri (2007, 2008) has analyzed social dialect variation in American English based on the spoken data from the LCSWE, identifying variation in quotative usage across age and gender (Barbieri 2007), with young women leading the introduction of the *be like* quotative, and variation in a variety of features across age groups (Barbieri 2008), with younger speakers using more slang and swearing and also more features that index their stance and personal involvement, such as personal pronouns, discourse markers, intensifiers, and stance adverbs. Barbieri (2009) also analyzed age and gender patterns in quotative *be like* in American English based on the *Cambridge Corpus of Spoken North American English*, finding that *be like* is increasing in younger speakers regardless of gender.

In addition to dialect studies that are based on general corpora, there are a growing number of dialect studies that are based on corpora built specifically for social analysis. One of the most well studied of these corpora is the *Corpus of London Teenage Language* (COLT; Andersen 2001; Stenström *et al.* 2002), which was compiled by giving tape recorders to teenagers from different age groups, ethnicities, classes, genders, and parts of London, and by then having these informants record speech from their daily lives, including interactions with friends, family, and teachers. Based on COLT, Andersen (1997) found that *like* was a very common discourse marker in the language of London teenagers including both males and females, especially those from higher classes. Similarly, Stenström *et al.* (2002) analyzed the relative frequencies of various features, including quotative *go,* which was found to be more common in younger speakers, the lower class, and minorities, and a variety of intensifiers, which were found to be generally more common in the language of women. While COLT focuses on teenage language, in a similar study, Murphy (2010) looked at age variation in the speech of Irish women in a corpus of conversations, finding variation in the relative frequencies of hedges, amplifiers, and taboo words, all of which were found to be more common in the language of young adults.

The relationship between class and linguistic variation was also analyzed in Finegan and Biber (2001), who considered the social and situational distributions of a variety of linguistic variables based on a review of previous empirical research and an analysis of the BNC (see also Finegan and Biber 1994). Finegan and Biber (2001) showed that many linguistic forms that tend to occur frequently in language produced by the lower classes also tend to occur frequently in language produced in informal situations, whereas many linguistic forms that tend to occur frequently in language produced by the middle classes also tend to occur frequently in language produced in formal situations. This relationship had already been observed (see Romaine 1980), but Finegan and Biber (2001) controversially argued that the relationship holds because situational variation is the source of much social variation. For example, the fact that reduced forms tend to occur more frequently in the language of the lower classes than in the language of the upper classes is explained as a result of the fact that lower-class speakers do not participate as frequently in the formal situations where the use of full forms is necessitated. Alternatively, traditional sociolinguists (Bell 1984; Preston 1991, 2001) have argued that this relationship holds because social variation is the source of all situational variation. For example, the fact that reduced forms tend to occur more frequently in the language of informal situations than in the language of formal situations is explained as a result of the fact that the lower classes, whose dialect is characterized by reduced forms, communicate more frequently in informal situations. This debate has not been resolved, but it provides a notable example of how corpus-based research can challenge standard assumptions about dialect variation.

In addition to spoken corpora, written corpora have also been used to analyze social dialect variation, especially computer-mediated communication. For example, Thelwall (2008) analyzed how a variety of swear words pattern across age, gender, and nation in a corpus of Myspace posts, finding that the young generally swear more often than the old in both the United States and the United Kingdom, and that men swear more often than women in the United States. Similarly, Baron (2004) analyzed linguistic variation relating to gender in instant messaging, including turn length, finding that women take longer turns than men, and that conversations between women were on average longer than conversations between men. Tagliamonte and Dennis (2008) also analyzed a corpus of instant messaging, identifying, for example, age variation in the alternation for the abbreviation for laughter, with *LOL* being more common in the language of younger informants and *haha* being more common in the language of older informants.

Similar corpora have also been analyzed in author-profiling research in forensic linguistics and natural language processing, where the social background of authors, especially their gender and age, is predicted based on the values of linguistic variables, including the relative frequency of parts-of-speech and function words (e.g. Koppel *et al.* 2002; Argamon *et al.* 2003; Schler *et al.* 2006). These researchers have analyzed gender and age across a variety of corpora – including both the BNC and specialized corpora of blogs and other registers – and have consistently found that women and the young tend to use more interactive and interpersonal features than men and the old (although see Herring and Paolillo 2006). Finally, a related field of study, authorship attribution (see Grieve 2007), analyzes language variation across individual authors using similar variables and methods to identify patterns of idiolect variation.

2.5 Summary

Although dialect studies based on corpora of naturally occurring language are far less common than studies based on elicited language, corpus-based studies have made many important contributions to the field in a relatively short time. Two general sets of findings stand out as being particularly important. First, corpus-based studies have shown that dialect variation exists across a wide range of different varieties of language, including forms of written and standard language, where dialect patterns had never been sought or even believed to exist. Corpus-based studies have therefore shown that dialect variation is far more common than had previously been assumed.

Second, corpus-based studies have shown that dialect variation can involve a much wider range of linguistic variables than is generally analyzed in dialectology and sociolinguistics. Traditional dialect studies have tended to focus on *alternation variables*, which are measured as the frequency of individual linguistic forms known as *variants* (e.g. segments, words, grammatical constructions) relative to the frequency of all synonymous linguistic forms in a sample of discourse (Labov 1972; Preston 2001; Tagliamonte 2006). For example, in his famous department store study, Labov (1972) analyzed the frequency of the deletion of postvocalic /r/ relative to the frequency of its pronunciation. Although some of the corpus-based studies reviewed above focused on alternation variables (e.g. Berglund 2000; Grieve 2011, 2012; Grieve *et al.* 2011; Romaine 1982, 2008; Nevalainen and Raumolin-Brunberg, 2003), most analyzed what can be referred to as *frequency variables* (e.g. Barbieri 2007, 2008, 2009; Biber 1987; Hofland and Johansson 1982; Rayson *et al.* 1997; Stenström *et al.* 2002; Szmrecsanyi 2013; Xiao and Tao 2007), which are measured as the frequency of linguistic forms relative to the length of a sample of discourse (e.g. the total number of words). This type of linguistic variable is commonly analyzed in quantitative corpus linguistics (e.g. Biber 1988), but has been explicitly excluded from variationist research based on the assumption that they cannot exhibit social patterns (Preston 2001). Corpus-based dialect studies have clearly shown that this assumption is false.

In addition to looking at new types of linguistic variables, corpus-based dialect studies have tended to focus on quantitative grammatical variation to a far greater extent than traditional dialect studies. In part, grammatical variation has been underresearched in traditional dialect studies because it is difficult to define legitimate grammatical alternation variables (see Lavandera 1978). By analyzing grammatical frequency variables, it has therefore been possible for corpus-based dialect studies to explore grammatical dialect variation in a much more systematic and comprehensive way than had previously been possible. In addition, by analyzing relatively large corpora of running language, corpus-based dialect studies have been able to measure grammatical variation quantitatively, which is often difficult in traditional research, where even interview transcripts are relatively short. Finally, by analyzing large numbers of grammatical variables, as reviewed in this chapter, corpus-based dialect studies have shown that there are systematic functional differences in how language is used across social groups, with different social groups, for example, using language more informally or more descriptively than other social groups. This type of *social functional linguistic variation* has generally been discounted in variationist sociolinguistics, but corpus-based research has shown that such patterns are real. Corpus-based research has therefore allowed for a more complete description of dialect variation to be obtained than was possible by analyzing data collected through elicitation and in doing so has expanded our understanding of the nature of dialect variation.

3 Dialect variation and change in *not* contraction in American letters to the editor

3.1 Research goals

In addition to reviewing previous corpus-based dialect studies, this chapter presents an analysis of dialect variation and change in *not* contraction in a corpus of American letters to the editor. In particular, the goal of this analysis is to compare *not* contraction across years, genders, and regions in the WARD corpus, which was introduced earlier in this chapter. In previous studies (e.g. Grieve 2012; Grieve *et al.* 2011), regional variation has been identified in this corpus, including regional variation in *not* contraction (Grieve 2011). In this study, the analysis of *not* contraction is extended to include variation across time and gender in addition to region so as to assess the importance of these various sources of linguistic variation and obtain a more complete understanding of how this linguistic variable is patterned in the letter to the editor register of Modern American English.

3.2 Corpus

The WARD corpus (see Grieve 2011) was compiled by downloading letters to the editor published between 2000 and 2010 in major regional newspapers from across the United States. The letters were then sorted based on their author's place of residence, as listed in the bylines of the letters. City subcorpora were then created for the 206 cities whose residents contributed at least 30,000 words of text. In total, the WARD corpus contains 26,573,826 words, spread across 159,181 letters, written by 130,659 authors – which is a far larger sample than would be possible if traditional methods for data collection had been applied. Each letter is also annotated for its date of publication, facilitating the analysis of temporal variation in this corpus.

The analysis of gender, however, is more complicated, as direct information about the gender of the authors of letters is not normally made available by newspapers. In order to analyze gender variation in this corpus, the gender of the author of each letter was predicted based on their first name, as listed in the byline of the letter. To this end, a list of the most common male and female forenames was obtained from the US Census Bureau, including the percentage of the male and female population with those names. The two lists were then cross-referenced and the unique male and female names were extracted. Based on a manual analysis of the remaining ambiguous names, it was clear that many of these names (e.g. Adam, James, Mary, Patricia) were hardly ever used by the other sex. A conservative cut-off percentage was therefore set and names that were predominantly male or female were also extracted. The other 195 ambiguous names (e.g. Pat, Shelby) were excluded from both lists. In total, this process identified 1,002 predominantly male names, and 3,965 predominately female names. The letters for each city were then sorted by gender based on these names. Letters totaling approximately 15 million words were identified as having been written by men and letters totaling 8 million words were identified as having been written by women. Letters totaling approximately 4 million words could not be identified due to ambiguous names, rare names, or joint authorship.

3.3 *Not* contraction

Four forms of *not* contraction were analyzed for this study: BE *not* contraction, HAVE *not* contraction, DO *not* contraction, and MODAL *not* contraction. Each of these variables were measured as the percentage of contracted *not* in a given corpus. This percentage was calculated by dividing the number of occurrences of contracted *not* following one of these four verb types by the number of occurrences of contracted *not* following one of these four verb types plus the number of occurrences of full *not* that could have been contracted following one of these four verbs types, and by then multiplying this value by 100. For example, if a corpus contains 80 tokens of the words *do/does/did* followed by the full form of the word *not* and 20 tokens of these verbs followed by the contracted form of the word *not*, then the DO *not* contraction rate in that corpus is 20 percent.

3.4 Temporal variation

To analyze change in *not* contraction over time, the values of the four *not* contraction variables in letters from 2002 to 2008 are plotted in Figure 20.1. Although the WARD corpus spans from 2000 to 2010, 98 percent of the words in the corpus were published between 2002 and 2008. The temporal analysis was therefore restricted to this seven-year period, as this is the period over which the values of these variables can be estimated most accurately. Figure 20.1 shows that *not* contraction has risen over this time span, with all four types of *not* contraction increasing by 6 percent to 10 percent in American letters to the editor from 2002 to 2008. It is also interesting to note that a clear hierarchy between the average rates of contraction across the four verb types is maintained here across all years, with DO *not* contraction being most common, always occurring over 50 percent of the time in any given year, and with BE *not* contraction being least common, never occurring more than 25 percent of the time in any given year.

3.5 Gender variation

To analyze gender variation in *not* contraction, the values of the four *not* contraction variables were tested for significant differences across male

Table 20.1 *Gender variation in* not *contraction*

	Female		Males		Wilcoxon Signed-rank test	
	Median	IQR	Median	IQR	W	p
BE *not* contraction	23.5%	9.3%	22.4%	7.8%	11,443	.361
DO *not* contraction	61.0%	9.1%	60.9%	8.5%	11,254	.489
HAVE *not* contraction	38.5%	25.0%	38.1%	16.3%	9,071	.191
MODAL *not* contraction	46.0%	10.5%	45.5%	7.4%	11,397	.390

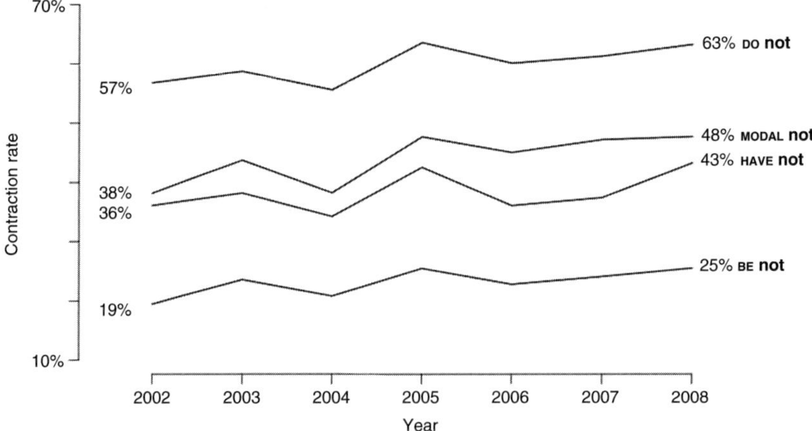

Figure 20.1 Temporal variation in *not* contraction

and female writers over the 206 cities using a non-parametric Wilcoxon signed-rank test. This analysis was restricted only to the letters for which the gender of the author could be determined. The results are presented in Table 20.1, along with the medians and interquartile ranges (IQR) for the variables in the male and female corpora. The analysis identified no significant gender differences (at a. 05 alpha level) in the median rates of *not* contraction for the four variables, indicating that *not* contraction is used at similar rates by men and women, although the median contraction rates for all four variables are slightly higher for women than for men. A more pronounced trend is visible in interquartile range, which shows that women exhibit more variability than men in their usage of *not* contraction. Boxplots for the four variables measured across male and female authors are also plotted in Figure 20.2, which clearly shows how similar these *not* contraction patterns are in letters written by men and women. Given that the temporal analysis found that *not* contraction was increasing over time, it is also interesting to note that the boxplots identify more high-value than low-value outliers, which might be indicative of the direction of a change in progress.

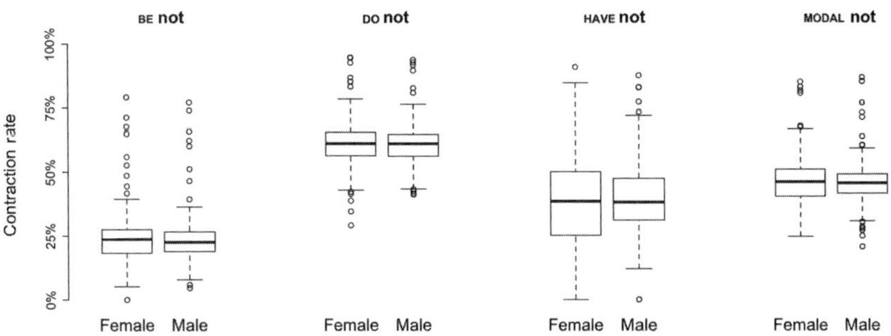

Figure 20.2 Gender variation in *not* contraction

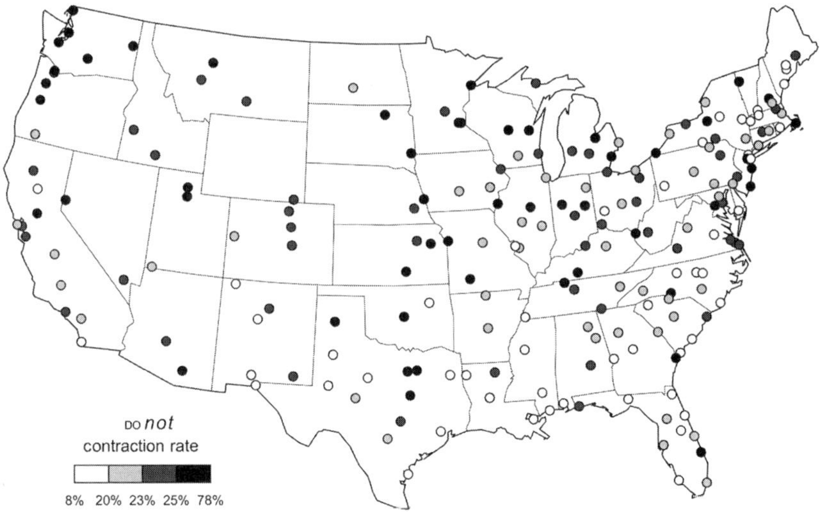

Figure 20.3 DO *not* contraction

3.6 Regional variation

To analyze regional variation in *not* contraction, the values of the four *not* contraction variables were mapped across the 206 city subcorpora. For example, DO *not* contraction is mapped in Figure 20.3, where darker dots indicate cities using a higher proportion of DO *not* contraction, and lighter dots indicate cities using a lower proportion of DO *not* contraction. There is no obvious regional pattern in this map, although upon close inspection it does appear that contraction is relatively less common in the Southeast and on the East Coast and relatively more common in the West. The maps for the other *not* contraction variables exhibit similar types of patterns.

Noisy maps such as these are very common in regional dialect studies (e.g. Labov *et al.* 2006), which is why dialectologists often draw isoglosses to divide dialect maps into regions where the different variants of the variable predominate. In this case, an isogloss could perhaps be drawn separating the Southeast and the East Coast from the rest of the United States, but it is difficult to know where to actually draw such a line or if drawing such a line is justified at all. The local spatial autocorrelation statistic Getis-Ord G_i (see Grieve 2011, 2012) was therefore used to identify statistically significant underlying patterns of regional variation in the maps for each of the variables. Given a variable measured over a series of locations, the local spatial autocorrelation analysis compares the value of that variable at each location to the values of that variable at nearby locations (in this case all locations within a 500-mile radius, following Grieve 2011) and produces a significant positive *z*-score if that location is part of a cluster of high values, a significant negative *z*-score if that location is part of a cluster of low values, or an insignificant *z*-score approaching 0 if that location is part of a region of variability. The results of the local spatial autocorrelation are then mapped to identify the locations of these spatial clusters, similar to plotting an isogloss.

The local autocorrelation maps for all four *not* contraction variables are presented in Figure 20.4. In these smoothed maps, regions with relatively high contraction rates are identified by clusters of darker locations, while regions with relatively low contraction rates are identified by clusters of lighter locations. These local spatial autocorrelation maps show clear and similar patterns of regional variation in the values of the four *not* contraction variables, with contraction being more common in the West, especially in the Midwest (BE *not* contraction, MODAL *not* contraction) and the Northwest (DO *not* contraction, HAVE *not* contraction), and with contraction being less common in the East, especially in the Northeast (DO *not* contraction, MODAL *not* contraction) and the Southeast (BE *not* contraction, HAVE *not* contraction).

In addition to analyzing the maps for the four alternation variables individually using a local spatial autocorrelation analysis, the smoothed maps for the four variables were also combined to produce a single map representing the general pattern of *not* contraction in the corpus by using a *k-means* cluster analysis to split the locations into two groups: the region where *not* contraction is relatively common and the region where *not* contraction is relatively uncommon. These two clusters are mapped in Figure 20.5. The analysis identifies an eastern region, where *not* contraction is relatively uncommon, and a western region, where *not* contraction is relatively common, with the border between these two regions roughly following the Ohio and Lower Mississippi rivers. In addition, southern Arizona and New Mexico are identified as part of the low contraction region, and southern Florida is identified as part of the high contraction region.

To verify that *not* contraction does in fact vary systematically across these two regions identified by the cluster analysis, the four alternation variables were tested for significant differences across the city subcorpora included in these two regions using a non-parametric Wilcoxon rank sum test. The results are presented in Table 20.2, along with the medians and interquartile ranges for the variables in the 98 western city subcorpora and the 108 eastern city subcorpora. The analysis identified significant regional differences (at a. 05 alpha level) in the median rates of contraction for

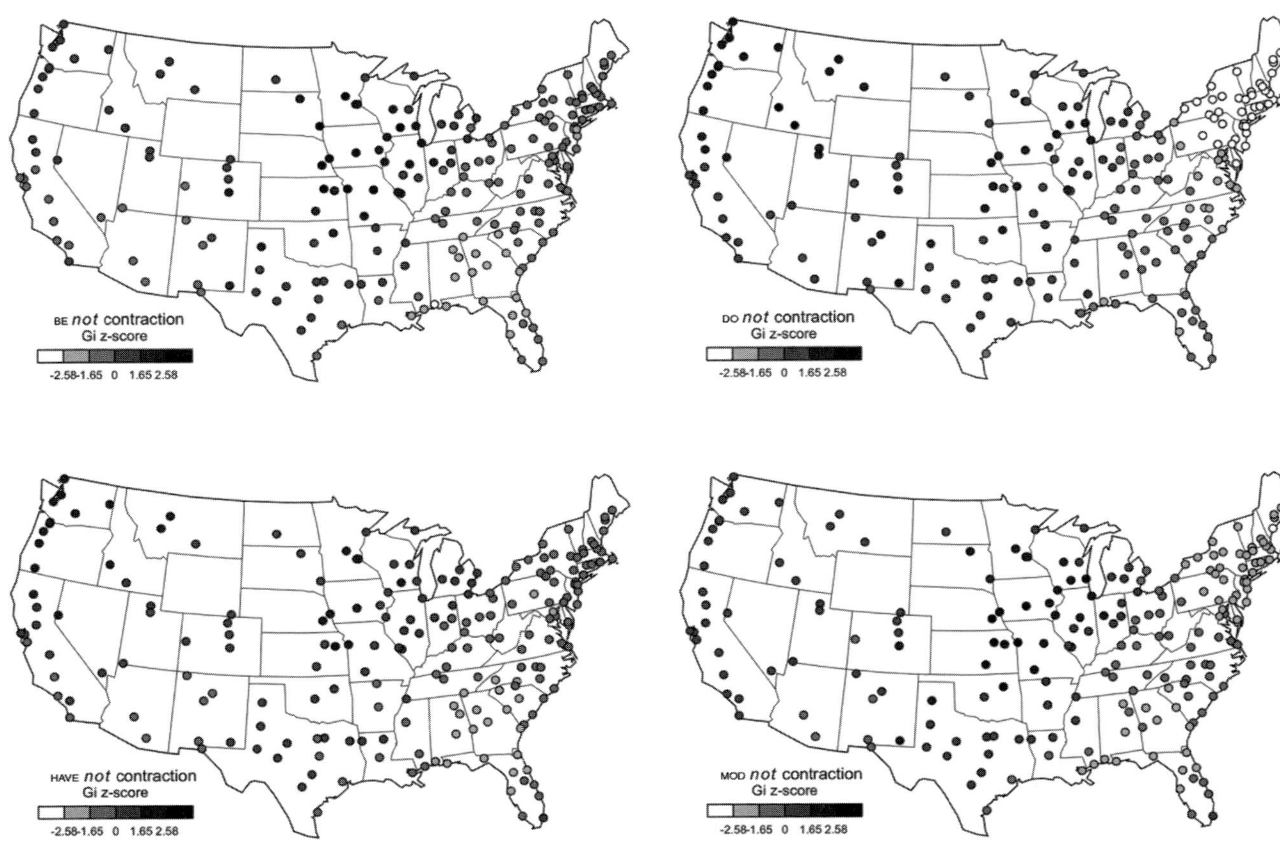

Figure 20.4 *Not* contraction local spatial autocorrelation maps

Table 20.2 *Regional variation in* not *contraction*

	West		East		Wilcoxon Rank sum test	
	Median	IQR	Median	IQR	W	p
BE *not* contraction	24.5%	4.8%	21.1%	5.8%	7,329	<.001
DO *not* contraction	62.3%	6.7%	59.0%	6.7%	7,321	<.001
HAVE *not* contraction	40.0%	12.1%	36.1%	13.6%	6,300	.018
MODAL *not* contraction	47.0%	6.3%	43.1%	7.1%	7,276	<.001

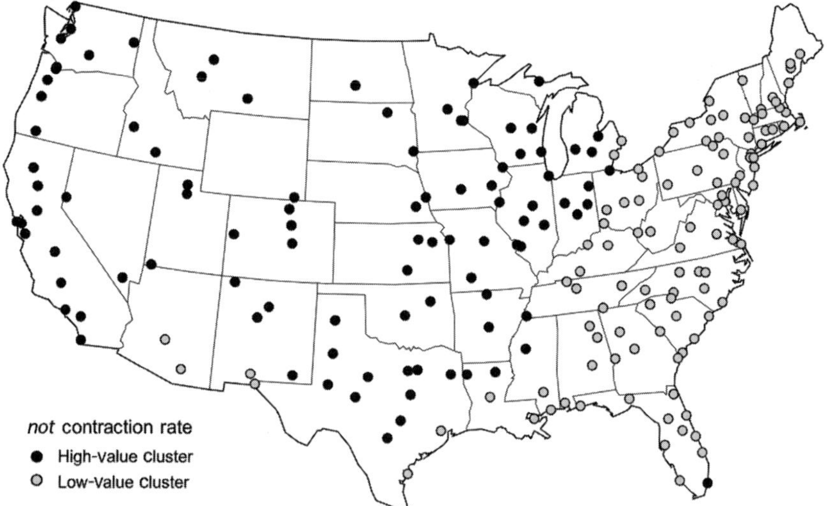

Figure 20.5 *Not* contraction clusters

the four variables, indicating that *not* contraction is used at different rates in the eastern and western United States, with all four forms being consistently more common in the West. Boxplots for the four variables measured across the two clusters are also plotted in Figure 20.6, which shows consistent differences in *not* contraction across regions. Once again, given that the temporal analysis found that *not* contraction was increasing over time, it is also interesting to note that the boxplot identify many more high-value than low-value outliers, which might be indicative of the direction of a change in progress.

3.7 Discussion

This case study analyzed variation in *not* contraction across year of publication, gender and region in a corpus of American letters to the editor. The analysis found that *not* contraction became more common in letters to the editor from 2002 to 2008 (Figure 20.1) and that *not* contraction is more

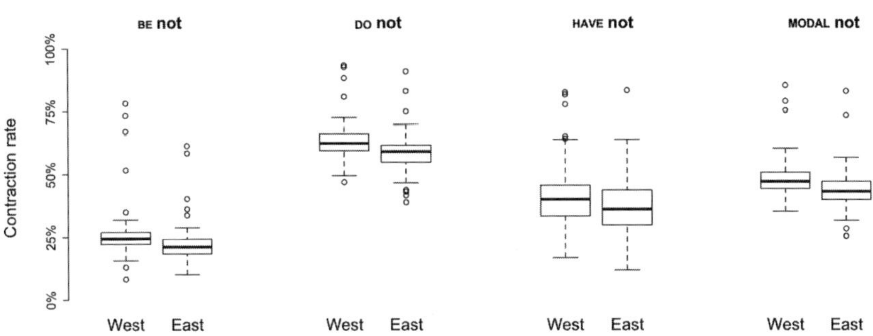

Figure 20.6 Regional variation in *not* contraction

common in letters to the editor from the West and the Midwest than from the Northeast and the Southeast (Table 20.2). Although differences were identified for time and region, no differences in *not* contraction were identified between male and female writers (Table 20.1). It would therefore appear that while the rate of *not* contraction is undergoing change in the letter to the editor register of American English, this particular change is more closely associated with region than gender.

In addition to these basic findings, because *not* contraction is generally associated with more informal language, these results suggest that letters to the editor are becoming less formal over time and that they are less formal in the western than in the eastern United States. This result is supported by several other analyses of the WARD corpus (e.g. Grieve 2011, 2012; Grieve *et al.* 2011), which have identified numerous formality differences in American letters to the editor, often with letters from the East, especially the from the Northeast, being characterized by a more formal style than letters from the West. Like many of the corpus-based dialect studies reviewed earlier in this chapter, these findings show that there are functional differences across dialects, with different groups of speakers using language in different ways. As discussed earlier in this chapter, such patterns are not predicted to exist by current standard theories of dialect variation, which assume that dialects are differentiated based on functionally equivalent forms of linguistic variation, such as alternations involving pronunciations and rare vocabulary items. Because such alternations are functionally inert, it has been assumed that dialect variation does include functional differences in language use. Social functional patterns such as those identified in this study, however, contradict this basic assumption of sociolinguistics.

4 Conclusion

This chapter has reviewed the growing field of corpus-based dialect studies, where social and regional linguistic variation is analyzed in large collections of naturally occurring language. The corpus-based approach to dialectology contrasts with the standard approach, which is based on analyzing language elicited through interviews and questionnaires. As demonstrated by the studies reviewed in this chapter, the corpus-based approach to dialectology is a growing field of inquiry that allows for new types of research questions to be pursued and new types of dialect variation to be identified. In particular, a corpus-based approach is especially conducive to the analysis of quantitative grammatical variation, because it allows for large samples of natural language to be collected for analysis, and for dialect variation to be observed and compared across a variety of communicative situations. Because of these advantages, corpus-based dialect studies have greatly expanded our knowledge of dialect variation, showing that social and regional linguistic variation are far more complex and pervasive than has previously been assumed. Nevertheless, there are disadvantages to the corpus-based approach as well. Most notably, it is difficult to obtain high-quality recordings of spoken language and to collect detailed data about the social background of informants when analyzing natural language. To a large extent, these are reasons why the corpus-based approach is not more popular in dialectology and sociolinguistics today. It is, however, only a matter of time until dialectologists will be able to download millions of high-quality audio and video posts online, along with rich social data about the posts and their audiences, and automatically transcribe and acoustically and grammatically analyze this language in order to build immense dialect corpora of spoken and written language. When this level of technology is reached, corpus-based dialect studies will become the norm.

21

World Englishes

Marianne Hundt

1 Introduction

English corpus linguistics was kick-started by the compilation of the Brown corpus of written American English (AmE) in 1961. A parallel British English (BrE) version was soon to follow. In the 1980s, the Brown-type compilation model started spreading to other parts of the English-speaking world (India, Australia, and New Zealand).[1] While Brown-type corpora are a useful resource, and their sampling frame is even extended to cover previous stages of World Englishes,[2] they are limited with respect to regional spread and, more importantly, only provide evidence on printed written language use. English corpus linguistics truly went global when, in the late 1980s, Sidney Greenbaum launched an international project that aimed at providing standard one-million-word samples of World Englishes on a hitherto unprecedented scale, the *International Corpus of English* or ICE (Greenbaum 1996). The label "standard" in this context serves two meanings, covering both the variety (educated English) that was to be sampled as well as the principled compilation designed to enable comparative research across different Englishes (see Section 2.1).

The focus in this chapter is on World Englishes that are used as first or second language varieties.[3] While some scholars have compiled their own corpora of world Englishes (e.g. by tapping into archives found on the World Wide Web),[4] the focus in this chapter is on research based on ICE, as these

[1] For an overview of research based on some of these corpora, see Fallon (2004) and Nelson (2006).

[2] For the extended Brown family covering Britain and the US, see e.g. Hundt and Leech (2012). Sebastian Hoffmann (Trier) is involved in the compilation of a historical corpus for Singapore English modeled on Brown, and Peter Collins (Sydney) is engaged in a similar project for the Philippines.

[3] Discussion of corpus-based research into English as a lingua franca (ELF) and learner Englishes can be found in Chapters 22 and 23 of this volume, respectively. For a more detailed discussion of the terminology and classification of different World Englishes, see Mesthrie and Bhatt (2008: 2–13).

[4] A publicly available web-based set of World Englishes corpora is provided by Mark Davies at http://corpus2.byu.edu/glowbe/ (last accessed 1 July 2013).

Thus, formality needs to be considered in the interpretation of findings from ICE corpora. It is a factor that plays a role at several levels. First, previous research on individual varieties (e.g. Schneider 2005; Hundt 2006) suggests that there might be less of a formality gap between written and spoken texts in ESL than in ENL corpora. Zhiming and Huaqing's (2006) study indicates that even such broad generalizations are problematic as a particular feature might be indicative of regional differences with respect to only one register (e.g. private conversation) and not even across the spoken medium as a whole. While Xiao (2009), in his multidimensional analysis of five ICE corpora (GB, India, Hong Kong, the Philippines, and Singapore), shows that there are similarities between ESL varieties with respect to stylistic parameters, he also found differences among them, e.g. that spoken and written texts are much closer in ICE-IND than in the other corpora.[14] Second, investigations into the stylistic homogeneity and heterogeneity of corpora (notably Biber 1988) have shown that there may be considerable variation within certain pre-defined text categories, on the one hand, and more similarities among texts that are grouped into different categories on the other hand; Sigley (1997: 232) therefore cautions us: "Corpus analysts are recommended to beware of treating the pre-existing text categories as natural groups, and to consider alternative text groupings which may be more relevant for their purpose." Additional studies on stylistic variation across and within ICE components are therefore needed as background information for the interpretation of findings on individual patterns.

Finally, ICE corpora have been used alongside other resources in the description of World Englishes. Especially for the study of lexicogrammatical variation, ICE provides interesting sources for hypothesis building that can then be verified against larger datasets, usually from less stratified material. Examples of such studies are Mukherjee and Hoffmann's (2006) investigation of new ditransitives in Indian English (e.g. *to gift somebody something*) or Hoffmann *et al.*'s (2012) study of light verb constructions in South Asian Englishes, where the use of the indefinite article is variable (e.g. *to take (a) look at*).

2.2 Some findings and research questions

The potential problems with cross-corpus comparability outlined in Section 2.1 do not mean that ICE does not allow for meaningful comparative research. On the contrary, ICE components (and parts thereof) have been used to investigate various linguistic features. A recurrent research question concerns ongoing change and whether a particular variety is more advanced or more conservative with respect to a particular change.

[14] Other useful studies that address the complex matter of register variation and corpus comparability are Biber (1993b), Gries (2006), and Sigley (2012).

AmE is leading the change towards a greater use of quasi- or semi-modals like *going to, want to* and is also more advanced in the decline of core modals (see e.g. Collins and Yao 2012); the continued increase of the progressive, on the other hand, is spearheaded by AusE and NZE among the ENL varieties, with some New Englishes showing higher, others showing lower frequencies of progressives (e.g. Hundt 1998; Collins 2009; Hundt and Vogel 2011). This kind of regional variation can be observed over and beyond variation across different modes (i.e. speech and writing) and registers.

Other studies focus on the relative closeness or distance between ENL and ESL varieties, looking both at how global features are used in local varieties and at evidence of structural nativization: one of the reasons that New Englishes are less advanced in the move away from core modals is that *would*, for instance, shows an extended (i.e. nativized) use (see Deuber *et al.* 2012). In the following example it has replaced ENL *will*; the example at the same time illustrates the extended use of the progressive in a context where a non-progressive VP would be used in ENL:

(3) First, I *would* be explaining about the gender inequality, which often leads to the high incidence of poverty amongst women, which is what I *would* be discussing about in the second part of this essay. (ICE-FJ, W1A-016)

Nativization is an important indicator of how far a "new" English variety has come in its development along the stages suggested in Schneider's (2007) model of new dialect evolution.

In the collection of the spoken ICE data, representative sampling did not include variables such as speaker age or gender, so there is no straightforward way in which the spontaneous spoken data in ICE could be used for apparent-time studies that allow linguists to trace ongoing change. On the assumption that written usage is generally more conservative than spoken language, a few studies have used ICE to extrapolate ongoing change from differences found in the two subsections of the corpora (e.g. van der Auwera *et al.* 2012 on the use of *need to*).

Finally, a recent trend in corpus-based research of World Englishes is the detailed statistical modeling of variation, often including ENL, ESL, and EFL varieties.[15] Szmrecsanyi and Kortmann (2011), for instance, extract information of part-of-speech frequency from the student writing sampled in five ICE components (East Africa, Hong Kong, India, Philippines, and Singapore) and the *International Corpus of Learner English* to compare degrees of analyticity and syntheticity. Their results show that, typologically speaking, ESL varieties differ from both ENL and EFL: ESL and EFL are more analytic than ENL varieties, but learner varieties are even more analytic than the institutionalized second-language varieties sampled in

[15] For more corpus-based research that bridges the "paradigm gap" between studies on first, second, and foreign language varieties, see the papers in Mukherjee and Hundt (2011).

ICE. Deshors (2014) uses a multifactorial approach in her study of the dative alternation (i.e. the choice between *Mary gave her mother a rose* and *Mary gave a rose to her mother*) to investigate potential (dis-)similarities in processing between second-language and learner Englishes: her results confirm that the preferred patterns in both ESL and EFL differ from those found in ENL varieties in more complex contexts, whereas there is little difference across the three Englishes in more routinized environments (i.e. a previously mentioned, pronominal recipient in an active clause).

3 Case study: the present perfect

The present perfect (PP) is of interest because it is an example of stable regional variation in written BrE and AmE (see e.g. Hundt and Smith 2009). At the same time, perfect constructions serve pragmatic functions in certain text types, as we will see, and show interesting patterns of nativization in New Englishes. With respect to methodological issues, the study compares results from lexical searches with data derived from syntactically annotated corpora.

For past-time reference, Present-day English (PDE) has a choice between the PP (*I have seen her*) and the simple past tense (PT) (*I saw her*). The textbook account of the PP in standard ENL varieties is that it refers to past events that have current relevance. Elsness' (1997) long-term, corpus-based study of BrE and AmE shows that the PP increases over time but starts decreasing again from the second half of the eighteenth century, a development led by AmE. In the twentieth century, there is relatively stable variation in the use of the PP, with higher levels found in BrE than in AmE (see e.g. Hundt and Smith 2009). Beyond regional differences between the two standard northern-hemisphere varieties, previous studies have found the PP to be particularly frequent in spoken Australian English (AusE) (see Engel and Ritz 2000 or Elsness 2009: 98).

As far as functions of the PP are concerned, standard PDE differs from languages such as German or French, where the perfect has grammaticalized into a form used for reference to events that are clearly in the past. However, both historical and regional varieties of English also provide evidence of the occasional narrative use of the PP in clear past-tense contexts (see e.g. Elsness 1997: 292 for historical varieties and Hughes *et al.* 2005: 12f. for dialects; this use is also attested in AusE, see Engel and Ritz 2000 and Ritz in press).[16] Engel and Ritz (2000) show how the PP has a special pragmatic function in press reportage where it serves as a framing element at the beginning or end of an article.

Elsness (2009) compares data from the Brown family of corpora with ICE data, which also include non-printed material and texts sampled from a

[16] A different subtype of the narrative function is the so-called "footballer's perfect" (Walker 2008).

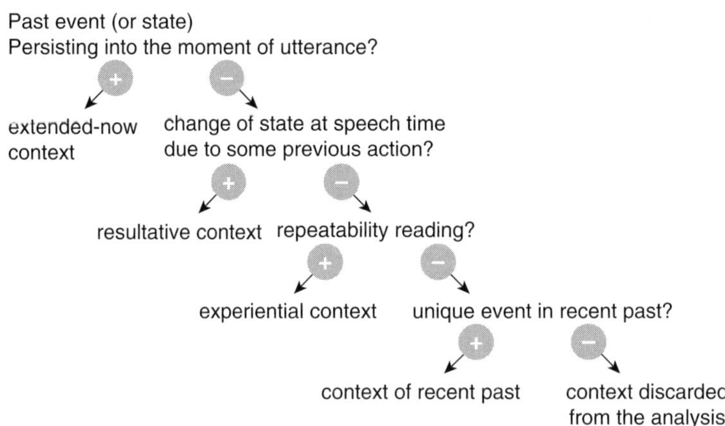

Figure 21.1 Categorization of PP contexts (Davydova 2011: 124)

slightly later date. Both factors are likely to have had an influence on the somewhat higher percentages of PPs he finds in the written parts of ICE-AUS and ICE-NZ. In other words, it is important to compare datasets that sample the same kinds of text.

Recently, a number of studies have made use of ICE to investigate the use of the PP across both ENL and ESL varieties. There are studies that look at the text frequency per million words of the PP (e.g. Bowie *et al.* 2013 or Yao and Collins 2013), but they focus on ENL Englishes only. The focus in the following survey of previous research is on studies that look at different Englishes. They model the variation in terms of variable contexts, i.e. where there is alternation between PPs and SPs. Davydova (2011) uses the spoken components of ICE-IND, East Africa, and Singapore and the *London–Lund Corpus* (LLC) of spoken BrE to study the use of PPs and SPs in "present perfect contexts," i.e. only those contexts where the PP could replace the SP (i.e. not in narrative contexts or with adverbials of definite past time references like *long ago, yesterday, the other day, in 1900,* etc.) She summarizes the procedure for defining these contexts in Figure 21.1.[17] Her data reveal that the proportion of PPs is lower in ESL varieties than in spoken BrE (Table 21.1).

Seoane and Suárez-Gómez (2013) use a similar approach but a slightly different set of ICE corpora (Hong Kong, Singapore, India, Philippines, and GB as a benchmark corpus) as well as a slightly different methodology of data retrieval and definition of the variable. Like Davydova, their focus is on spoken data, but while Davydova uses both face-to-face conversations and telephone calls, Seoane and Suárez-Gómez limit their analysis to private conversations. (The rationale for using spontaneous speech in both cases is that this is the least monitored kind of data and that, according to Miller (2004), PP and SP alternate more frequently in this type of

[17] For a more detailed discussion of this concept, see Davydova (2011: 119–131).

Table 21.1 *PP vs. SP in present perfect contexts (raw frequencies and percentages, based on Davydova 2011: 175, 223, 238, 145; infrequent additional forms not included)*

	ICE-IND	ICE-EAf	ICE-SIN	LLC
perfect	715 (53%)	247 (58%)	532 (56%)	1,812 (90%)
preterite	471 (35%)	159 (37%)	350 (36%)	197 (10%)

Table 21.2 *Forms expressing perfect meaning (i.e. experiential, recent past, resultative, and persistent situation) in Private Dialogue in Asian varieties of English (based on Seoane and Suárez-Gómez 2013: 9; PP vs. SP, only; percentages over all variants)*

	ICE-HK	ICE-SIN	ICE-PHI	ICE-IND	ICE-GB
perfect	410 (59.2%)	155 (44.4%)	169 (57.3%)	300 (77.5%)	236 (80.8%)
preterite	204 (29.5%)	174 (49.9%)	121 (41.0%)	70 (18.1%)	48 (16.4%)

language.) Seoane and Suárez-Gómez limited their analysis to the ten most frequent verbs in the Asian ICE corpora, extracting the data automatically, whereas Davydova read through the corpus files searching for PP contexts. Finally, following Huddleston and Pullum (2002: 143), Seoane and Suárez-Gómez defined the perfect semantically as expressing events covering "a time span beginning in the past and extending up to now."

This study produces different results from Davydova because of the different methodology, resulting in a more marked divide between IndE and SingE. Both studies use a semantic definition of the variable but apply different retrieval strategies. These may well give rise to diverging results despite the fact that very similar sets of data were used. The difference for BrE, in addition, is most likely due to the fact that different benchmark corpora were used: LLC was sampled earlier than ICE-GB and contains more formal conversations than those included in ICE-GB. Note, however, that while the comparison of the results for LLC and ICE-GB in Tables 21.1 and 21.2 suggests that there has been a decrease in the use of PPs, Bowie *et al.* (2013:326) report a slight increase in spoken BrE. This apparently contradictory result can be explained if we take a closer look at the definition of the variable: the percentages in the tables compare the use of the PP against the SP whereas Bowie *et al.* look at text frequency of the PP per million words (pmw). This approach avoids the difficulty of deciding which SPs could be replaced by a PP, but they report the text frequency of one construction only. Variation of PPs may actually extend beyond the SP as a variant, as a recent paper by Pfaff *et al.* (2013) indicates: they found that the past progressive (e.g. *I was just looking at this picture*) is also occasionally used in spontaneous speech to refer to recent events in past contexts. By measuring the frequency of the PP in terms of text frequency rather than against alternating constructions the question of syntactic equivalence is avoided.

With respect to suitable benchmark corpora, ICE-GB is a more suitable choice because the texts sampled, by and large, stem from the same period as those sampled in the other ICE components. Interestingly, with ICE-GB as a yardstick for comparison and a differently defined variable, IndE comes closer to BrE in Seoane and Suárez-Gómez's investigation than it was in Davydova's study and the emerging picture is one of a gradient rather than an ENL–ESL divide.

Davydova (2011: 170, 231, 253) also looks at the PP in past-tense contexts: this is actually a rare phenomenon in IndE, EAfE, and SingE (see also Balasubramanian 2009: 92).

In addition to the standard variants, i.e. the PP with auxiliary *have*, ESL ICE components also reveal traces of nativization, for instance the pattern without an auxiliary (4) or with a base form rather than a past participle (5):

(4) That's why I never looked back and had any regrets for whatever I myself *done* or decided upon with my eyes open. (ICE-IND, S1A-038; quoted from Davydova 2011:180)

(5) She *has give* four exams (ICE-IND, S1A-070, quoted from Seoane and Suárez-Gómez 2013:11)

Finally, ICE corpora yield a minority of instances with auxiliary *be*, which could be retentions of the older *be*-perfect (6). However, some of the attested examples are with transitive rather than the historically attested intransitive verbs, i.e. (7) and (8) are not simply retentions but modern "extensions" of the *be*-perfect:[18]

(6) I said to the receptionist <,> here on the desk <,> *is he gone in* to visit (ICE-IRE, S1A-008)

(7) Look I'm I'*m* almost *finished* Sacred Hunger [title of a novel; MH] (ICE-HK, S1A-047, quoted from Seoane and Suárez-Gómez 2013:12)

(8) Okay once the pieces *are been cut* and *washed* and *dried* now we connect them together. (ICE-SIN, S2A-058)

Examples (6)–(8) are all from spoken texts, overall a more likely context for nativized patterns to occur than in edited written language. While both Davydova (2011) and Seoane and Suárez-Gómez (2013) used spoken data only, the case study in the following section focuses on the use of the PP in the news sections of the ICE corpora.

[18] Note that IrE also uses the *be*-perfect with transitive verbs, a feature that McCafferty (2014) attributes to substrate influence from Irish.

3.1 Data and methodology

The case study aims to broaden the scope of previous research by including varieties of English that have not been subjected to comparative research, partly because the respective ICE components have only recently been made available or are still under construction. The ENL varieties included are BrE, AmE, CanE, NZE, and AusE; ESL varieties selected are Fiji English (FijE), PhilE, IndE, Sri Lankan English (SLE), and Ghanaian English (GhE). In addition to providing evidence on the use of PPs in some new ICE corpora, another aim is to illustrate how different approaches to data retrieval may influence the results. The analyses will be limited to the newspaper section of ICE, not only for obvious time constraints on a small-scale study and limitations on the availability of spoken data,[19] but also because newspapers are expected to be maximally comparable across different regional varieties of English. Moreover, while Miller (2004: 230) points out that "[i]n formal written English the Perfect construction is solidly fixed, in frequent use and protected by grammars of standard English and by editorial practice," this general tendency might no longer apply to newspaper texts: "with the intensive use of computers newspapers are no longer edited as rigorously as they once were" (Miller 2004:234). Finally, newspaper articles afford the possibility of investigating one of the narrative functions of the PP.

Three different approaches will be used to extract corpus data from the corpus material. The PP combines a form of the auxiliary *have* with a past participle. Because of the text frequency of auxiliary *have* and lack of grammatical annotation, previous studies tended to rely on the verb-based approach, i.e. they restricted analysis to a set of frequently used lexical verbs.[20] The ICE corpora are currently being POS-tagged and parsed at the University of Zurich, using the Tree Tagger tagset (Schmid 1994) and a probabilistic dependency parser (Pro3Gres), developed by Schneider (2008). This allows for automatic retrieval of PPs and SPs. Eight of the ten ICE components that form the basis of this study have been syntactically annotated, thus allowing for automatic retrieval of all PPs and SPs and thereby affording a bird's-eye view of the frequency of the two kinds of verb phrase.

In addition, a verb-based approach will be used for an analysis that looks at more strictly variable contexts (i.e. includes only SPs that can be replaced by a PP), making use of nine high-frequency lexical verbs (*come, finish, get, give, go, hear, see, tell, think*). A third approach will look into the co-occurrence of the PP with temporal adverbs, those that are typically associated with it (i.e. *just, (n)ever, yet*), and one that prototypically triggers the SP (*yesterday*). Finally, a qualitative analysis of the opening sections of articles in ICE-AUS, ICE-NZ, ICE-FJ, and ICE-PHI will show whether the

[19] Only written data are currently available for ICE-US, ICE-FJ, ICE-SL, and ICE-GH.

[20] Exceptions would be Hundt and Smith (2009), who retrieved PPs from the tagged version of the Brown-family corpora and Bowie *et al.* (2013), who use fuzzy tree fragments (FTFs) to retrieve their data. Davydova (2011) retrieved her data manually.

perfect is frequently used with the framing function observed by Engel and Ritz (2000).

As far as the definition of the variable is concerned, the focus is on standard variants of both the PP and the SP. Occasionally, a perfect with auxiliary *be* rather than *have* is attested even in edited, printed texts from an ESL context:

(9) The game *was* long *been seen* as a hobby . . .. (ICE-GH, W2C-004)

Such non-standard variants are not included in the counts (see Hundt forthcoming for an in-depth study of such patterns).

In interpreting the overall frequency of SPs in ESL varieties one has to be aware of the possibility that there is zero past-tense marking on verbs. The following example comes from ICE-FJ – it is a serendipitous find from a manual post-edit of co-occurrences with the adverb *yesterday*. Note that zero past-tense marking (*brave*) is used alongside regular past tense-marking (*stood*) in this example:

(10) Hundreds of students of a Suva prominent school *brave* yesterday's heat and *stood* in long queues to wait for their turn to pay their fees. (ICE-FJ, W2C-012)

While I did not systematically search for zero past-tense marking, the phenomenon seems to be rare in the newspaper data, so occurrences are not included in the counts. Similarly, PPs with a base form of the participle are not included in the present case study, partly because PPs were retrieved by searching for the standard past participle and partly because these nativized patterns, again, appeared to be typical of spoken rather than written usage. By narrowing down the envelope of variation in this way we will not have missed a large number of relevant hits: Suárez-Gómez and Seoane (2013: 167) found only 1.1 percent zero-marked SPs and 0.6 percent PPs with a base form in their written Asian English material.

While zero past-tense marking might lead to underreporting of SPs in automatically retrieved data, lack of back-shifting to past perfects in reported speech will lead to overreporting of SPs:

(11) He said his wife could have been saved if there *was* someone who knew how to apply CPR. (ICE-FJ, W2C-014)

Lack of back-shifting also occurred with PPs (and not only in the ESL varieties); these instances were not included in the counts because they are not part of the variable context investigated here, i.e. they are not typical PP contexts but variants of the past perfect:

(12) The Burnaby Lawyer noted that Bourassa *has come* to B.C. before – the most recent visit was in April, 1988. (ICE-CAN, W2C-010)

(13) While acknowledging that the Board had not lived up to its role, he emphasised that since his takeover two years ago, things *have turned* for the better. (ICE-IND, W2C-019)

Nativized patterns were also excluded from the co-occurrence data with temporal adverbs. In IndE, for instance, *yet* can be used in the sense of "still," as the following examples show:

(14) The gas emerged from a broken outlet pipe of the tanker and spread in the nearby village while people were *yet* asleep. (ICE-IND, W2C-012)

(15) Over a month having lapsed since the poll-day violence, Khan has *yet* not been arrested. (ICE-IND, W2C-004)

Finally, instances where the adverb did not modify the VP but another temporal adverb were also manually excluded from the concordances:

(16) The government *just* recently moved to dismantle the allocation of the imports of sugar under the so-called minimum access volume scheme under which a limited group corner the bulk of the importation. (ICE-PHI, W2C-006)

3.2 Findings

The automatically retrieved data is presented in two different ways. Figure 21.2a shows the overall frequency of PPs and SPs across the parsed datasets. Even though the results are presented in terms of percentages, it is important to note that these, unlike Tables 21.1 and 21.2 above, do not represent variable contexts of use, i.e. only SPs in present perfect contexts,

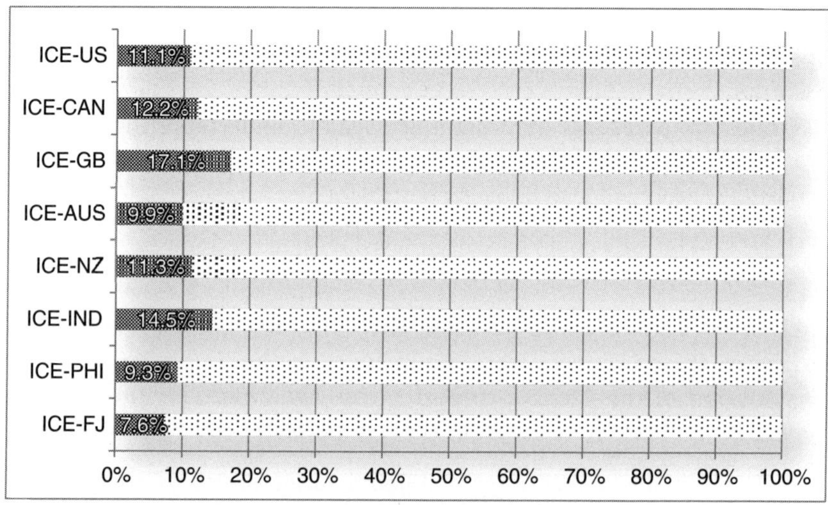

Figure 21.2a Relative frequency of PP and SP in the press section of ICE corpora (parsed) (ICE-US, N = 1890; ICE-CAN, N = 1928; ICE-GB, N = 1753; ICE-AUS, N = 2248; ICE-NZ, N = 2160; ICE-IND, N = 1584; ICE-PHI, N = 2029; ICE-FJ, N = 2145)

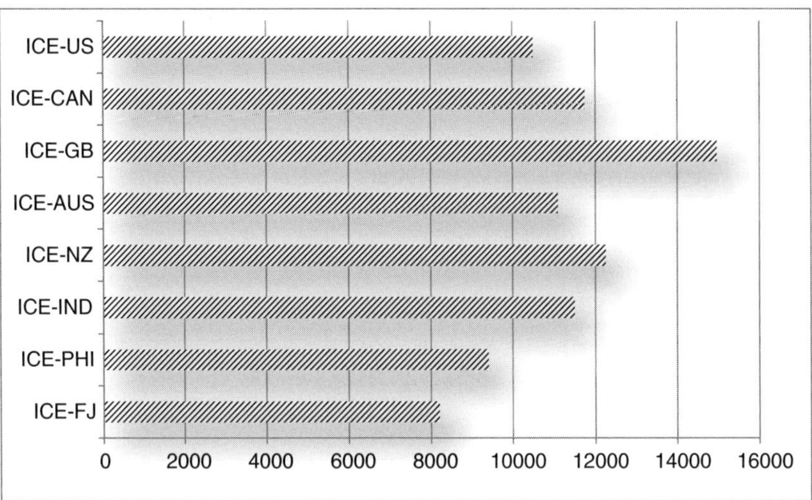

Figure 21.2b PPs (frequency pmw) in the press sections of ICE corpora (parsed)[a] (ICE-US, N = 210; ICE-CAN, N = 235; ICE-GB, N = 299; ICE-AUS, N = 222; ICE-NZ, N = 245; ICE-IND, N = 230; ICE-PHI, N = 188; ICE-FJ, N = 164;)

[a] The press sections contain approximately 20,000 words each.

but the proportion of *all* PP and SPs. The results thus simply indicate the overall distribution of the two constructions across different ICE components. The data were not manually post-edited to exclude false positives, e.g. instances of *have got (to)*.

Figure 21.2a shows that in news reporting, SPs occur with a much higher text frequency than PPs. Note, however, that the relative frequencies presented in Figure 21.2a are not directly comparable with the proportions reported in Tables 21.1 and 21.2, which only included SPs in PP contexts. The bird's-eye view also suggests that the ENL and ESL varieties do not fall into two neat groups. At 9.3 percent, PhilE yields an even lower proportion of PPs than AmE, its historical parent variety. AusE, NZE, and CanE are closer to AmE than to BrE, which has the highest relative frequency of PPs, closely followed by a historically related ESL variety, IndE. The lowest frequency of PPs is found in FijE, an ESL variety that is currently undergoing nativization (see e.g. Zipp 2014).

A somewhat different picture emerges if the frequency of PPs is measured against corpus size rather than as a proportion of PPs vs. SPs (see Figure 21.2b): ICE-AUS has slightly more rather than fewer PPs than ICE-US on this count. Text frequency counts of PPs in newspaper texts of ICE thus do not confirm Elsness's (2009) findings of a more frequent use of PPs in AusE than in the other ENL varieties.

Figure 21.3a, finally, presents the results from the verb-based approach and a variable context, i.e. only SPs that could be replaced by a PP. The

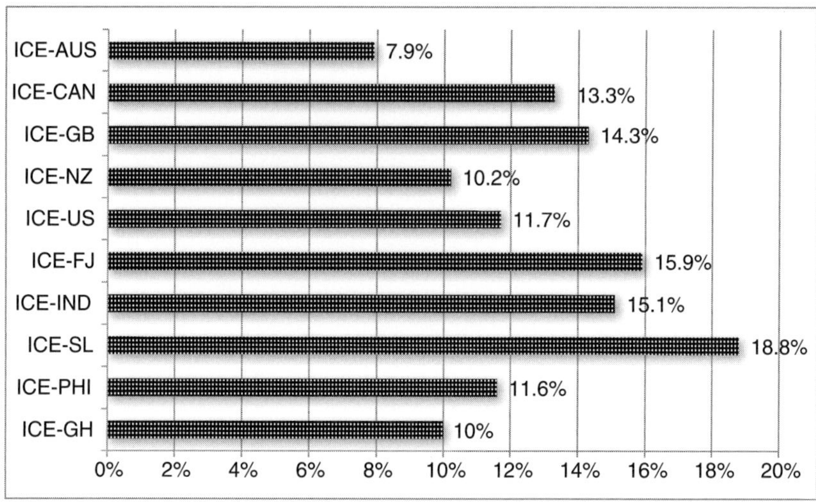

Figure 21.3a PP vs. SP with selected verbs
(ICE-AUS, N = 139; ICE-CAN, N = 98; ICE-GB, N = 112; ICE-NZ, N = 98; ICE-US, N = 120; ICE-FJ, N = 82; ICE-IND, N = 73; ICE-SL, N = 64; ICE-PHI, N = 69; ICE-GH, N = 60)

concordances were manually post-edited to exclude instances from reported speech with past-tense reporting verbs, i.e. contexts in which back-shifting rules might apply.

Even if the variable is defined differently in Figure 21.3a from the data presented in Figures 21.2a and 21.2b, and a verb-based approach is used, the proportion of PPs in newspaper texts is still much lower than in the spoken data investigated by Davydova (2011) and Seoane and Suárez-Gómez (2013) (i.e. Tables 21.1 and 21.1 above). As in Figure 21.2b, ICE-CAN and ICE-GB yield similar proportions of PPs, as do ICE-US and ICE-PHI. While the ESL varieties FijE, IndE, and SLE show a high proportion of PPs, GhE patterns more closely with PhilE here, albeit at an even lower level of PPs. AusE is now the variety with the lowest use of PPs. Note, however, that Figure 21.3a includes both active and passive VPs. Elsness (2009: 98) limits his analysis to active, positive, declarative, and non-progressive contexts, and Figure 21.3b shows that voice, for instance, appears to have an effect on the proportion of PPs and SPs as passives that may be avoided in combination with the perfect, especially in ESL varieties.

With active-only VPs, AusE and NZE show more similar usage of PPs, as do AmE and CanE; BrE has the highest proportion of PPs amongst the ENL varieties (see Figure 3b). With the exception of GhE and American-based PhilE, the ESL corpora yield relatively high proportions of PPs, with IndE showing a slightly higher proportion of PPs than BrE and the somewhat "younger" ESL varieties in Fiji and Sri Lanka producing the highest relative use of PPs. The results of this case study are thus different from those obtained from spoken data, where ESL varieties yielded overall lower proportions of PPs.

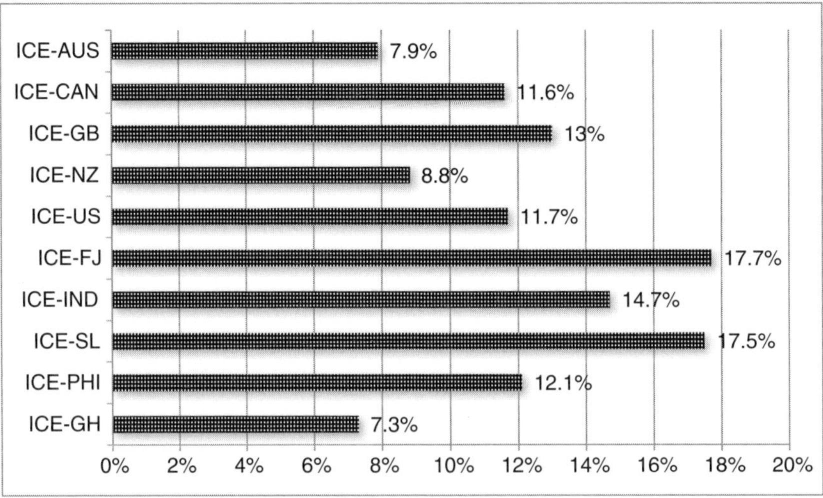

Figure 21.3b PP vs. SP with selected verbs (active only)
(ICE-AUS, N = 127; ICE-CAN, N = 86; ICE-GB, N = 100; ICE-NZ, N = 80; ICE-US, N = 120; ICE-FJ, N = 62; ICE-IND, N = 68; ICE-SL, N = 57; ICE-PHI, N = 66; ICE-GH, N = 55)

Table 21.3 *Co-occurrence of PP and SP with adverbials* just, (n)ever, yet[a]

	PP: SP	total
ICE-AUS	5 : 2	7
ICE-CAN	8 : 4	12
ICE-GB	7 : 2	9
ICE-NZ	6 : 2	8
ICE-US	8 : 7	15
ICE-FJ	2 : 2	4
ICE-IND	2 : 1	3
ICE-SL	3 : 0	3
ICE-PHI	1 : 4	5
ICE-GH	0 : 3	3

[a]Again, instances in subordinate clauses with a past-tense reporting verb are excluded.

As far as co-occurrence with temporal adverbials is concerned, the newspaper sections of ICE are too small to obtain conclusive results. However, the figures in Table 21.3 indicate some interesting trends. As predicted by previous research, SPs are more often found with adverbs expressing current relevance in AmE and in CanE, but are a real minority variant in the other ENL varieties. PhilE, again, shows the historical connection with AmE. Additional data would be needed to verify whether GhE might also be influenced by AmE or whether the absence of PPs with adverbs that typically trigger this construction has to be attributed to the overall low frequency of PPs observed in Figure 21.3b. A qualitative analysis of the data shows that the SP at times is a variant of the

PP when it co-occurs with an adverb such as *just* (17), whereas some instances are variants of the past perfect (i.e. with lack of back-shifting), as in (18):

(17) Laced with the victorious Fiji Barbarians players who *just returned* from Auckland the side has a full set of arsenal to do the damage in Vanua Levu. (ICE-FJ, W2C-018)

(18) he did not push the players hard in the first run considering the fact that *they just came* back from the festive break (ICE-FJ, W2C-020)

A systematic search for co-occurrence of the PP with a clear past-tense adverb (i.e. *yesterday*) did not yield a single incidence in any of the press sections of the ten corpora surveyed for this case study. Likewise, a qualitative analysis of the opening paragraphs of articles in ICE-AUS, ICE-NZ, ICE-FJ, and ICE-PHI did not provide any evidence of the typical framing function that Engel and Ritz (2000) describe for their spoken radio data, at least not with adverbs that have a clear past time reference.

3.3 Discussion

The different methods used to retrieve PPs from ICE and the different measures employed to compare the results make it difficult to assess them. The data presented above have shown that the envelope of variation that is studied will result in a different picture of the relation among ENL and ESL varieties: it makes a difference, for instance, whether the overall text frequency of PPs is compared or whether the variable is defined more narrowly, e.g. as an alternation between PP and SP in perfect contexts. We also saw that the results are slightly different if passive VPs are included in the counts or not.

Qualitative analyses of the corpus data show that variable use of PPs and SPs is at times difficult to categorize. In the following example, a PP is used in a clear past time context, but the choice of the PP itself suggests that the past action has current relevance:

(19) The new Prime Minister's policy declaration at the meeting of Kisan Coordination Committee on December 31 last *has given* enough indication of coming change. (ICE-IND, W2C-007)

Occasionally, ESL ICE corpora yield interesting examples of temporal expressions that typically co-occur with either a PP, a present tense or future time expression. Instead, what we find in ICE-SL is a SP:

(20) *This is the first time* Janasansadaya *came* to Anuradhapura and first a workshop is held for Maha Sangha. (ICE-SL, W2C-015)

A follow-up search showed that this is not a tense choice regularly attested in any of the ICE corpora. Previous web-based data (Hundt 2013: 194) show, however, that the present progressive outnumbers the PP with *This is the first time* in SingE and IndE. This brings us to the question of what should be included in the envelope of variation.

The results presented in the previous section used a fairly conservative definition and compared PPs and SPs only. Qualitative analyses of corpus data, however, reveal that the envelope of variation cannot only be broadened to include the nativized patterns mentioned in Section 3.1, but the present progressive, as well, as the following examples show:

(21) "Over the past five years, the number of newborns affected *is steadily increasing* which corresponds with the increase in females detected with the disease over the past five years," she said. (ICE-FJ, W2C-014)

(22) The entire hilly belt of Jammu *is experiencing* heavy snowfall since early this morning, reports say today, according to PTI –. (ICE-IND, W2C-009)

(23) "Ever since the Sakvithi and the recent Golden Key crisis erupted, we *are now experiencing* increased number of deposits than before, ..." (ICE-SL, W2C-001)[21]

These variants have not been discussed in the context of variable use of the PP so far because they are extensions of the progressive to traditional PP contexts. They are not limited to ESL varieties but also occasionally attested from ENL contexts (see Hundt and Vogel 2011: 159). This extension of the present progressive to PP contexts might be fostered by the somewhat more unobtrusive use of the past progressive in this environment (see Pfaff *et al.* 2013).

4 Conclusion and outlook

The ICE is an excellent resource for the study of standard(izing) varieties of English around the world. Due to the history of the project, certain limitations apply with respect to the diachronic bias inherent in individual components and across regional varieties. Another limitation concerns the use of spoken material, which is so far only available in orthographic transcription. For some points of fine-grained grammatical analysis (e.g. final consonant cluster reduction in past-tense VPs), availability of the original sound files would be desirable. In an ideal world, the sound files would be aligned with the transcription allowing researchers to target the particular grammatical structure retrieved from the corpus (this design feature is currently available for ICE-NIG, only, but seems to have been envisaged in the original plan for the ICE corpora, as the sound samples at the project website (http://ice-corpora.net/ice/sounds.htm) indicate). With

[21] The adverb *since* is also used as a conjunction introducing an adverbial clause of cause/reason; without *ever*, the subordinate clause would be ambiguous between the two readings and this, in turn, might have prompted the use of the present progressive in this particular example.

a few exceptions, documentation of existing ICE components remains poor even though background information is often important for the interpretation of individual corpus findings. Comparisons between ENL and ESL ICE data need to take the possibility of localization of text types into account (different narrative traditions, for instance, may affect the use of tense in fiction texts; see Biewer 2015). Van der Auwera *et al.* (2012), for instance, assume that ongoing language change tends to be more advanced in spoken than in written texts and therefore take differences between speech and writing as a proxy for ongoing change. The problem with this approach is that it must assume stylistic differences between speech and writing to be the same across different varieties of English, and this is not necessarily the case. More research, ideally in combination with real-time data or apparent-time data from sociolinguistically balanced samples is needed to verify whether these assumptions are valid.

22

New answers to familiar questions: English as a lingua franca

Anna Mauranen, Ray Carey, and Elina Ranta

English as a lingua franca (ELF) is a comparatively new domain of scholarly inquiry, which has really taken off as a research field and begun to flourish only since the middle of the first decade of this millennium. The research is overwhelmingly qualitative, as perhaps befits a field that is very much in an exploratory state. Corpus work is therefore still rare; the databases that have been collected have mostly been small, and are perhaps best counted into the very generic category of "corpus" that in traditional philology was used to describe the language data investigated for a study. Most investigations have adopted a qualitative orientation, with Conversation Analysis and various pragmatic and discourse analyses as the principal methods; most of those using large amounts of data have been surveys mainly based on questionnaires (notably Jenkins 2007; Wang 2012), apart from Jenkins's investigation into ELF accommodation in ELF phonology (2000), but even that was not based on corpus methods.

English as a lingua franca is a particular kind of language contact: a lingua franca is a vehicular language, or a contact language, used when speakers do not share a first language. Some definitions, like this one (see also, for example, Jenkins 2000 or Seidlhofer 2011) allow native speakers to be included, whereas some other ELF scholars, like Firth (1996) or House (2002), have preferred definitions that exclude native speakers altogether. Why ELF opens fresh possibilities for linguistic insights can be viewed from a theoretical, a descriptive, and an applied perspective (see Mauranen 2012). The major theoretical interest arises from the nature of ELF as a complex site of language contact: what happens to a language in a situation where virtually all other languages of the world are in contact with it? From a descriptive point of view, the interesting questions revolve around the way ELF may change English, and the features that are shared with second-language varieties and learner language. The applied interests are concerned with the ways in which language professionals should take ELF on board.

Exploration into language universals on ELF data seems particularly fruitful as ELF is an extremely rich manifestation of language contact. In a typical lingua franca situation, a multitude of different L1s come into contact with English simultaneously and, in turn, these L1-based lects are in contact with each other, making ELF what Mauranen (2012) defines as a second-order language contact between "similects." From previous research on contact linguistics we know that language universals – as unmarked, widely shared features of language – often emerge in language contact situations as speakers try to find common linguistic ground to communicate efficiently (e.g. Winford 2003). On the other hand, a fairly recent theoretical framework of so-called "vernacular universals" (see e.g. Chambers 2004) suggests that spoken varieties of languages could manifest similar kinds of non-standard forms due to the general constraints of the spoken mode – which are the same for all people. Thus, looking into L2/ELF speech from this angle can reveal whether some of the non-standard features found actually show affinities with L1 speech, and could thus be considered universals of spoken English grammar rather than L2 errors. This kind of comparative research has only recently begun to attract attention in English corpus linguistics.

Despite the somewhat bleak overall picture of the amount of corpus work completed hitherto on ELF, the first one-million-word spoken corpus, *The Corpus of English as a Lingua Franca in Academic Settings* (ELFA, www.helsinki.fi/elfa) was completed in 2008, very soon followed by *The Vienna–Oxford International Corpus of English* (VOICE, www.univie.ac.at/voice) of the same size. Also a third spoken corpus, the *Asian Corpus of English* (ACE) led by the Hong Kong Institute of Education, has now been compiled (http://corpus.ied.edu.hk/acel). Unlike many other linguistic fields, ELF research began by exploring spoken rather than written data, and genuine ELF written text databases are still missing. The rare work that discusses writing tends to be compiled in one country from speakers of the same L1, with ELF as the international contextual backdrop (e.g. Ingvarsdóttir and Arnbjörnsdóttir 2013). The first written ELF corpus has recently been completed, though: the WrELFA corpus consists of academic and popular scientific texts (www.helsinki.fi/elfa/wrelfa).

The corpus research carried out to date, although still scarce, has already been able to show features of ELF that are of a fundamental kind.

A basic question facing an ELF corpus is how different ELF is from English as a native language (ENL). As even a short fragment of ELF talk heard or seen in transcription is usually enough to tell it is not ENL, intuitions about the actual differences apart from perhaps accent are unreliable. Qualitative studies based on small samples may be deep but fall prey to the bias that intuition suffers from: is this a good reflection of the wider picture? From a corpus perspective, comparing the overall distributions of expressions, the answer is that ELF is not spectacularly different from ENL: word lists of individual words and *n*-grams show a notable overall similarity in comparable genres (Mauranen 2012). The top ends of frequency measures are the most similar to each other, as might be expected in comparing varieties of one language.

The prototypical ELF user is neither a native speaker nor a learner. Nevertheless, their English is in many ways similar to both. As we might expect, second-language varieties of English, such as World Englishes, learner language, and ELF share features that are likely to reflect the general processes of multilingual speakers using their non-first languages. When we look at these kinds of language use as situated in their social contexts, the differences become more pronounced. The social parameters of being a learner in classroom settings in particular creates rather specific settings for language use. The negotiation of norms characteristic of ELF interaction (Hynninen 2013), where non-target-like solutions may be most effective (Hülmbauer 2009), is replaced by norms and conventions of the target language mediated by a teacher. Focus on standard language form is given in a classroom setting even when methods may emphasize content. Classroom learner identities are defined by their position in the educational system, and learners cannot change the language they are seeking to acquire. Success is determined in terms of conformity to the Standard English that all major testing systems are built around. In contrast, ELF and the corpora compiled of this use embrace the language in the "real world," in the mixture of L1 backgrounds and proficiencies that constitute actual second-language use (SLU), and therefore provide data for understanding successful as well as unsuccessful English from entirely different premises to the standard-oriented learner data.

The accumulating knowledge from a large number of small-scale studies has produced a list of linguistic features that have established themselves as the set of "known" ELF features, essentially those listed in Seidlhofer (2004): omitting or inserting articles relative to ENL; dropping the third-person singular ending; confusing the relative pronouns *who* and *which*; failing to use correct forms in tag questions; inserting redundant prepositions; overusing certain verbs of high semantic generality, such as *do, have, make, put, take*; replacing infinitive constructions with *that*-clauses, as in *I want that*; overdoing explicitness (e.g. *black color* rather than just *black*). With data from the existing corpora, it has been possible to put these observations to test. Some of the findings have received support from corpus data, the clearest cases being the non-standard use of articles and prepositions (see e.g. Mauranen 2012; Cogo and Dewey 2012). In contrast, there has been no support for some of the other phenomena, notably the widespread use of the third-person zero form, a tendency to use *which* instead of *who*, and the proportional overuse of the semantically general verbs, as will be shown in more detail in the next section.

1 ELF corpus studies

ELF corpus work employs essentially similar tools to any corpus linguistic enterprise, with an emphasis on extracting the big picture with quantitative methods in combination with close reading of the relevant items in their contexts. Corpus tagging involves the same pros and cons as with other speech data and non-standard data. Where ELF is special is in certain principles of corpus compilation. In contrast to a learner corpus (see Chapter 23 this volume), an ELF corpus seeks to include speech in a natural, often complex mix, rather than selecting for given L1 backgrounds and comparable proficiency levels. Unlike World English corpora (see Chapter 21 this volume), an ELF corpus does not seek to capture a local or regional variety of English, which would then lend itself to comparisons across others of the same kind. The resulting ELF corpora do not therefore have equal amounts of given "similects" (Mauranen 2012), that is, lects of English with speakers of the same first language, and they are not intended for comparing interference phenomena or other features specific to a particular background. Since proficiency is another factor not selected for, and only authentic speech is recorded, the corpora reflect the reality of English in lingua franca use, where communication takes place between speakers of different backgrounds and skills. The result is a complex mix of Englishes in authentic co-construction of meaning.

A corpus of this kind allows us to seek answers to the question of how the situational constraints of lingua franca use shape the language. What commonalities emerge from these mixtures, and what new preference patterns can we see? Lexical, grammatical, and phraseological patterning can be either novel or show new frequency distributions. In both cases the commonalities and new preferences attested in ELF corpora show English taking shape in one of its major and fast-expanding uses in non-local environments.

1.1 Methodological issues

The earliest book-length studies based on ELF corpora – Prodromou's (2008) *English as a Lingua Franca: A Corpus-based Analysis* and Cogo and Dewey's (2012) *Analysing English as a Lingua Franca: A Corpus-driven Investigation* – illustrate the methodological orientations of early ELF research. Already in the first calls for empirical description of ELF (see e.g. Seidlhofer 2001), the need for analyzing authentic ELF data was framed from an applied linguistic perspective, with emphasis on the need for an ideological shake-up in the field of English language teaching (ELT). Unsurprisingly, many applied linguists and language teachers have been convinced by these arguments and ELF research has grown in strength as a pedagogically oriented field. The Fifth International Conference of ELF in

Istanbul in 2012 underscored this interest with "Pedagogical Implications of ELF in the Expanding Circle" as its theme. Although ELF corpora are becoming increasingly available, the trend remains toward small-scale, qualitative research.

When ELF research shifts from ideological arguments to empirical description of language in use, these pedagogical orientations can be seen to influence the corpus methodology. This is evident in the two monographs cited above, as both are based on small corpora with a bias toward experienced language professionals and language teachers in training as sources of linguistic data. In the case of Prodromou (2008), he has collected 160,000 words of transcribed ELF conversation from speakers of various professional backgrounds, but "with an emphasis on ELT professionals" (p. 98). These "successful users of English," or SUEs, were handpicked based on their already perceived, excellent command of English. Thus, language-internal criteria were applied in compiling the corpus, and Prodromou justifies this compilation principle with a pedagogical argument: these SUEs are the type of L2 users which could serve as models for learners (2008: 98–102). He furthermore assures the reader that, as the transcriber of the conversational data, "the level of English was grammatically and lexically accurate, if not necessarily 'native-like'" (2008: 101). This corpus data cannot therefore be seen as representative of the "ordinary" ELF user, nor does it capture the well-documented variability in ELF.

In the case of Cogo and Dewey's study (2012), a compilation of their respective PhD theses, they discuss their two small corpora independently. As for Cogo's data, it consists of twenty hours (no word count is given) of transcribed conversational data recorded in the shared office space of four foreign-language teachers in London, with occasional additional speakers (2012: 43). Insofar as these transcriptions of mainly four ELF speakers are subjected to a pragmatic, CA-based analysis, but not to an actual corpus methodology, they remain outside the scope of this discussion. Dewey's corpus, however, is subjected to contrastive corpus analysis using WordSmith Tools. His corpus consists of eight hours (no word count is given) of transcribed interaction recorded in a language school and an institute of higher education in London (2012: 40). Since he performs distributional analyses of his corpus in comparison with the 900,000-word demographic component of BNC Baby (2012: 62, 71), the appearance of raw frequencies without a total word count from his corpus leaves the reader in search of more information.

In an earlier publication, Dewey (2009: 83n) gives a word count of "approximately 60,000 words." However, one must turn to Dewey's (2007a) unpublished doctoral dissertation for a full account of what has been included in his corpus. In Appendix B of the dissertation (2007a: 309–317), an itemized description of the speech events and their word counts are given, along with the settings in which the recordings were made. Following the English pedagogy bias, speakers in the recordings consist of teachers and students in a language school and university MA students in an ELT and Applied Linguistics program (2007a: 63–64). Of these 61,270 transcribed words, 56 percent (34,397 words) are drawn from elicited tasks and prompt card exercises, with 44 percent (26,873 words) consisting of naturally occurring data (2007a: 309–317, based on Dewey's divisions of the data). In addition, these naturally occurring data are mainly drawn from classrooms with a focus on English and/or among MA students of English linguistics (2007a). Oddly, Cogo and Dewey suggest that Dewey's corpus has "a heavy bias towards naturally occurring non-instructional interactions" (2012: 40; see also Cogo & Dewey 2006: 63 and Dewey 2007b: 351n for similar claims).

The purpose of making these observations is twofold. First, both studies perform distributional comparisons between their data and much larger native-speaker corpora. As already mentioned, Dewey compares his 61,000 words to the 900,000-word demographic component of the BNC Baby (Cogo and Dewey 2012: 62). Prodromou also compares his 160,000 words to findings from the 5-million-word CANCODE corpus and a 5-million-word subcorpus of informal spoken English from the BNC (Prodromou 2008: 104). Neither researcher has attempted to justify the relevance of these resources for comparisons with their restricted sets of data. Second, these observations are meant to highlight the discrepancy when broad claims about "emerging trends" in ELF are based on small, unrepresentative corpora with a bias toward teachers and students of English and language professionals generally as sources of data. Dewey has yet to fully document his corpus in a published work, though statistical findings from his study continue to be reproduced without an accurate representation of his data's limitations (see e.g. Jenkins *et al.* 2011: 290).

In contrast, the one-million-word corpora of ELFA and VOICE have been meticulously compiled for balance and representativeness (see Mauranen 2006 for ELFA compilation principles and Breiteneder *et al.* 2006 for those of VOICE). Much effort has gone into the online distribution and development of VOICE, although at the time of writing the corpus awaits a comprehensive comparative analysis. In the case of ELFA, it was designed with other corpora of spoken academic English in mind (especially the *Michigan Corpus of Academic Spoken English*, or MICASE; see Mauranen 2006; Simpson *et al.* 2002) and thus lends itself more readily to a comparative analysis with a meaningful reference corpus. Like MICASE, the ELFA corpus consists of complete transcriptions of both monologic and dialogic speech events from across a wide range of disciplines. Several of these event types directly overlap (e.g. small group lectures, seminar discussions, doctoral defenses, and student presentations), and speakers are included from across the academic spectrum, from students to senior staff. Thus, Mauranen's (2012) monograph, *Exploring ELF: Academic English shaped by non-native speakers*, is so far the only published work in ELF corpus research which has combined a sound corpus methodology with sufficient quantities of comparable data. In the following sections, we consider some findings from Mauranen's work with the ELFA and MICASE corpora alongside related findings from Cogo and Dewey (2012). Questions addressed are those of lexical simplification and lexico-grammatical differences between ELF and ENL.

1.2 Lexical simplification

One of the common assumptions about ELF is that it must be a "simplified" English. While processes of simplification can indeed be observed in ELF talk, the question of lexical simplification is especially salient. Mauranen (2012: 89–93) has compared the word lists of the ELFA and MICASE corpora to determine what proportion of word types is needed to account for 50 percent of the word tokens as a gauge of lexical diversity. While MICASE requires 58 of the most common words to account for half the corpus, ELFA requires 44, clear evidence of lexical simplification (ibid.: 91). However, this difference is brought into focus when the same figure is sought from the Brown Corpus, a similarly sized corpus of written English. The Brown Corpus uses 135 word types to cover 50 percent of tokens, more than twice the number of tokens in MICASE (ibid.). Thus, when the contrast between spoken and written language is considered, the gap between ELFA and MICASE is less dramatic.

Looking more closely at these word lists making up 50 percent of the corpus data, Mauranen has compared ELFA's 44 word types with the 58 found in MICASE. She reports that 36 of these word types appear on both lists and in similar rank order, constituting 82 percent of the most common ELFA word types and 62 percent of those in the MICASE list (ibid.: 93). These figures indicate broad overlap between the most frequent items in the ELF and ENL corpora, most of which are textual organizers such as conjunctions and prepositions as opposed to content-oriented words; neither list contained a single adjective (ibid.: 94–96). While the difference in coverage of word types between the two corpora may constitute evidence of lexical simplification in ELF, it also points toward the conformity of ELF to general trends in language evolution, with the majority of these most common words being closed-class, grammatical items which are most resistant to change (see Pagel *et al.* 2007). In concluding her discussion of these high-frequency items, Mauranen suggests that ELF "is very much in line with English on the whole" (2012: 101).

In a similar vein, lexical simplification is also associated with "overuse" of general nouns and verbs as claimed by learner language research (see e.g. Altenberg and Granger 2001). However, neither the ELFA corpus nor Cogo and Dewey's data confirm this in ELF usage. Apart from a high number of repeats (*the the the, in in in*), it was largely some function words (*also, which, because*), some prepositions, and some modifiers (*quite, very, some*) that differentiated ELFA from MICASE, in addition to certain lexical nouns (*education, knowledge, democracy*) that probably reflected the topics at hand. Concerning general verbs, Mauranen finds that *make* and *get* appear with a higher frequency in MICASE than in ELFA, with keyword differentiators for MICASE including the general *get, stuff,* and *thing* (2012: 104). Cogo and Dewey also do not find overuse of general verbs in relation to the BNCB demographic subcorpus, and they confirm the strikingly higher frequency of *get* in their ENL data – 53 per 10,000 words in BNCB and 11 per 10,000 words in Dewey's ELF data, with 13 per 10,000 words in ELFA (Cogo and Dewey 2012: 70–71; Mauranen 2012: 259).

1.3 Grammatical differences

A focus of Cogo and Dewey's (2012) work has been on lexico-grammatical "innovations" in ELF, with an emphasis on qualitative analysis of their functions and underlying motives. This section discusses some of their claims concerning relative pronouns and third-person singular verb marking. Many of these grammatical questions at word level can now be clarified with a manually checked, part-of-speech tagged version of the VOICE corpus (VOICE 2013). In the case of relative pronouns, Cogo and Dewey (2012: 73–74) propose an "emergent trend" in favor of *which* over *who* in ELF generally. They obscure the significance of their figures by using raw frequencies and rank order, but when these frequencies are standardized the claimed gap in their data between ELF and ENL usage is minimal. In their BNCB demographic subcorpus, *who* and *which* each occur 11 times per 10,000 words, while *who* and *which* are found in Dewey's ELF data 9 times and 13 times per 10,000 words, respectively (ibid.). On the basis of these nominal findings, the broad claims about emerging ELF trends seem spurious.

However, the more robust ELFA corpus data in fact show an overwhelming predominance of *which* over *who* in academic ELF interaction. The pronoun *who* is distributed evenly between ELFA and MICASE, with 13 and 14 occurrences per 10,000 words, respectively, and identical positions of 104 on their respective frequency-ranked word lists (Mauranen 2012: 259). On the other hand, *which* is found 23 times per 10,000 words in MICASE, but it occurs 39 times per 10,000 words in ELFA, making it one of ELFA's top differentiating keywords with MICASE as reference corpus (ibid.: 263). The most accurate data can be found in the POS-tagged version of VOICE (2013), which distinguishes these relative pronouns from the same words in different functions, including the relative pronoun *that*, which is distinguished from its determiner role. Here the predominance of *which* (22 per 10,000 words) over *who* (10 per 10,000 words) is clear, but with an important caveat: relative pronoun *that* is preferred over all other forms, occurring 25 times per 10,000 words and accounting for 43 percent of all relative pronouns in VOICE. It is important to note that these findings are only suggestive of trends in relative pronoun usage. Only a manual examination of each relative pronoun in VOICE (n=5848), together with the animacy of the head noun, will reveal the actual rates of standard/non-standard usage.

Finally, the phenomenon of present tense third-person singular zero in place of third-person singular *-s* has been an area of interest in ELF research. Cogo and Dewey (2006, 2012) have proposed that "at least in certain types of ELF settings, 3rd person zero appears to be emerging as the default option in informal naturally occurring communications" (2012: 49). Basing this bold claim on Dewey's mainly elicited data (Dewey 2007a: 309–317, see above), they begin by identifying all instances of third-person singular verbs and excluding auxiliary verbs. Looking solely at the main verbs in third-person singular, they report that 48 percent of these employ the standard ENL *-s* morpheme, with 52 percent of these instances showing the third-person zero variant (Cogo and Dewey 2012: 49). These striking figures are mainly evidence, however, of the variability between small databases, as Breiteneder's (2005) similarly small corpus of 50,000 words of ELF interaction generates markedly different results. Among the main verbs in third-person present singular in her data, Breiteneder finds that 79 percent of these conform to the standard ENL *-s* ending, with 21 percent unmarked with third-person zero (2005: 8–9). Both studies expound on these cases with qualitative analysis, but speculations of a "default option" are clearly premature.

Again the POS-tagged VOICE corpus clarifies the situation. By providing a manually checked, dual POS tag which encodes both form and function (VOICE Project 2013), the XML corpus can be searched for all cases of an "innovative" form, in Cogo and Dewey's terms. This meticulously annotated VOICE dataset should put to rest the exaggerated claims of word-level variation in ELF, as the corpus findings are unequivocal. Of the 5,335 words in VOICE which have a VVZ function tag (i.e. third-person present singular verbs, excluding all forms of HAVE and BE), only 5.8 percent (n=310) vary from a conventional English form. The rates of variation with high-frequency HAVE and BE are even lower. Only 26 instances of third-person singular *has* are in a non-standard form, all of which are third-person plural (e.g. *somebody have to judge*). As for third-person singular *is*, a mere 19 cases in all of VOICE are non-standard, all of which are also in third-person plural form (e.g. *language which are less spoken*). When all verbs functioning in a third-person singular present tense role are taken together (n=22,428), only 1.6% of these (n=355) have an "innovative" form. In other words, 98.4% of all third-person singular present tense verb tokens in VOICE conform to standard English usage.[1]

It is useful to keep in mind that none of the ELF corpora under consideration attempt to control for the proficiency level of speakers, a major

[1] For more information on how these figures were derived, including the full Python code used to query the VOICE POS XML, see the ELFA project research blog: http://elfaproject.wordpress.com/2013/06/30/in-defense-of-good-data-the-question-of-third-person-singular-s/ (accessed 12 July 2013).

difference from the learner corpus methodology. Insofar as VOICE includes speech events outside academia (e.g. casual conversations and interactions in business/professional domains), it provides a broader snapshot of "ordinary ELF," in which speakers of various proficiency levels interact with each other as a matter of course. This low rate of variation in third-person *-s* makes Cogo and Dewey's (2012) findings appear even more anomalous, as most of their sources of linguistic data are in fact active students of English (Dewey 2007a: 309–317). In any case, these quantitative findings from VOICE do not refute qualitative analyses of the systematic ways in which innovative forms can be deployed, but it does suggest that widespread variation between ELF and ENL should be sought at a linguistic level which is broader than individual words.

1.4 Multi-word units

Phraseological sequences, under a variety of names, have been held to constitute the ultimate hurdle for the non-native speaker. It has become a generally accepted fact that L2 users get these wrong even at high proficiency levels (e.g. Nattinger and de Carrico 1992; Pawley and Syder 1983; papers in Schmitt 2004). Learner corpus work supports this interpretation (e.g. papers in Granger and Meunier 2008; Nesselhauf 2005). Such evidence has led to the building of theoretical models to explain this, notably that of Wray (2002), who has posited two different processing mechanisms for the native language and just one for other, later learned languages. On this account, native speakers can utilize either of two processing mechanisms according to need: one holistic, which operates with phraseological sequences, and which chiefly accounts for fluency and easy execution of speech. The other mechanism is analytic or compositional, operates with small components and allows for flexibility and novelty in language use. In contrast to native speakers, non-native speakers supposedly lack the first type, holistic processing. Therefore, according to Wray, they apply only compositional processing to the foreign language, construct all their expressions from scratch, and are therefore prone to error of execution in multi-word units. This position is the basis of, for instance, papers in Schmitt (2004) and developed further by Wray herself (2008).

However, if we look at ELF data, and compare the most frequent trigrams to equivalent ENL data (comparing ELFA to the MICASE corpus of academic speaking), we see striking similarities (Mauranen 2012). The higher up on the frequency list, the more similar the trigrams are: 4 of the top 5 are identical, 6 of the top 10, and 12 of the top 25 (ibid.: 145–146, 266–267). In addition, these trigrams conform to Standard English. The important point here is that although text extracts readily reveal many non-conforming features in ELF multi-word sequences, on a larger scale it is clear that ELF speech builds on very similar conventional multi-word sequences as comparable ENL speech. This is strong counterevidence to differential processing mechanisms.

Apart from the most frequent items, the frequency distributions of multi-word items – just like those of individual words – diverge in ELF relative to ENL. For instance, *in terms of* ranks 37th in ELFA, but 8th in MICASE. Also, trigrams like *would like to* (no. 14), *I would like* (no. 22), and *I would say* (no. 44) on the ELFA rank order list do not appear among the most frequent 100 trigrams in MICASE. This suggests that new preference patterns arise in ELF use, as observed in distributions. Moreover, fixed ENL patterns also suffer breaches, and new patterns develop from there. For example, in the common pattern *(let me say) a few words about (x)*, which is immutable in MICASE data, ELFA shows not only more variability, but also a new preference: *(let me say) some words about (x)* is the most frequent variant (Mauranen 2012: 153–154). New preference patterns found in independent speech events and by speakers from a variety of language backgrounds call into question the claim that deviations in ELF are irregular and idiosyncratic (for example, Mollin 2006; Prodromou 2008).

It is these incipient patterns that occur across independent events and speaker L1s that provide perhaps the most intriguing evidence of the linguistic processes that are going on as ELF is taking shape.

1.5 ELF corpus research now

As already observed at the outset, the use of English as a lingua franca is a new research field, with few actual corpus-linguistic studies so far. Corpora have nevertheless already shown their powerful potential: they have helped gain a big picture of the prominent linguistic processes in ELF, and revealed new facts about second-language use (SLU). In this last respect it complements the study of second-language varieties of English (Mukherjee and Hundt 2011). Second-language varieties in World Englishes have a recognized second-language status in their local societies, with concomitant prestige hierarchies among variants and varieties. In contrast, the unstable mixtures of ELF in international use have not developed social markers, and can be assumed to progress primarily on the basis of communicative effectiveness. This sociocultural consideration also distinguishes ELF from learner language, which is confined by classroom settings. Corpora from naturally acquired learner language could compare interestingly with ELF corpus data, which, as it stands, is based on speakers with a formal learning background.

The main contributions to linguistic description relate to the overall picture: while small-scale studies, even if taken together, have not been able to sort out the main drift from the contingent detail, corpus work has provided a sense of the degree of similarity between ENL and ELF, robust features in ELF, and new, divergent developments in frequency patterns and phraseological preferences. Corpus studies have also uncovered ongoing processes of lexical simplification, as well as morphological regularization and productivity, also showing that divergences from ENL are directional, not random. Similarly, corpora have helped settle pragmatic questions like whether there is more or less vagueness in L2 than in L1: there is somewhat more (e.g. Metsä-Ketelä 2012).

Corpus evidence has also illuminated ELF processing issues: phraseological data indicate that L2 processing is not so different from L1 processing as to allow merely bottom-up processing, leading to inevitable errors, but also top-down processing of longer sequences, just like L1. The L1–L2 difference is thus not categorical. At the same time, the distinctly greater incidence of "dysfluency" phenomena, such as hesitations and repeats, provides strong evidence that L2 is more taxing on the working memory.

Methodologically, ELF corpus work has emphasized the importance of running inter-corpus comparisons in both directions, and shown discrepancies between seemingly similar L1 corpus samples (MICASE and T2K-SWAL), which yielded different register features in comparison to ELFA (Mauranen 2012: 148–150).

A number of major gaps remain to be addressed in this new field; how do our largely European findings compare to ELF in other continents, second-language varieties, learner language, and to other lingua francas? How diffuse or differentiated are genre, register, and mode in ELF? This is an issue that has not been addressed in ELF research yet, and while it is beyond the hitherto dominant small-scale studies, it is possible to take this on board with the corpora in existence so far. Methodologically, the vital demand is for robust analytical programs that are adept at handling approximations of conventional forms.

In keeping with the theme of seeking meaningful patterns in ELF above the level of individual words, in Section 2 we report a large-scale study of verb syntax in the ELFA corpus.

2 An empirical exploration into syntactic universals of spoken ELF

Due to the aforementioned lack of large ELF corpora until very recently, methodologically sound analysis and comparisons between ELF and ENL have been difficult to carry out. This applies especially to the level of syntax in ELF (as indicated by the studies discussed above) which, on the whole, has been the least researched area of ELF so far. However, with the advent of the one-million-word spoken corpora of ELFA and VOICE, such analyses have finally become possible. This section presents an overview of a recent study and findings on four syntactic features of spoken ELF carried out on a subset of the ELFA corpus. The features looked into are the inverted word order in indirect questions (i.e. "embedded inversions"), the extended use of the progressive, the use of *would* in hypothetical *if*-clauses, and the preference for singular agreement in existential *there* constructions. A subset of the ELFA corpus was used to gain a maximal diversity of L1 backgrounds of the speakers. As the ELFA recordings were carried out in Finnish university settings, the proportion of L1 Finnish speakers in the data is inevitably somewhat higher compared to that of other L1s (although overall relatively low, as it was kept in check all through the compilation process). But for the purposes of the study it was considered important to further limit the amount of speech by Finnish speakers to avoid false conclusions based on a possible L1 Finnish effect on the results. Thus, in principle, speech events were discarded where the proportion of English produced by L1 Finnish speakers was over 50 percent. The ensuing subset of ELFA has 0.76 million words based on speech by 482 speakers from 50 different L1 backgrounds.

In the study, Ranta (2013) delves into the possibility of finding so-called "vernacular universals" in the syntactic features of spoken ELF (see p. 402 above). The study is typical of the research in the field in that it takes the spoken mode as its point of departure (as this is the unedited mode of language where possible unique features or new developments of language will most readily be discernible), but at the same time it manifests a new opening in ELF research as the first in-depth description of and exploration into the syntactic features of ELF. The reason why ELF syntax has not drawn much scholarly attention thus far may find its explanation partly in the aforementioned lack of sufficiently large databases until now, but also partly in the assumption that research into syntactic features of ELF might not reveal anything new in comparison to findings from second-language acquisition research (SLA) on English L2 syntax. However, ELF is research on language *use*, not acquisition, which calls for a different perspective on the social circumstances where the communication in L2 takes place as well as on the data investigated, even if the cognitive processes for the L2 user/learner were the same (see Mauranen 2012). Also existing learner corpora do not provide a feasible basis for comparison because they mainly comprise written language or – if compiled from spoken language – often interviews between L1 and L2 speakers.

In SLA studies the emphasis has been on the differences between L1 and L2 output with the quest for explanations why L2 speakers fail to achieve specific standard language forms. The explanations have often been found, for example, in the interference from the speakers' respective L1s or compensatory communication strategies employed by L2 speakers, and comparisons have mainly been made to standard grammars. However, ELF research looks at L2 use from the same perspective as any other natural language use, setting L1 and L2 speakers on a par. This means departure from the SLA "deficit" perspective and also renders similarities in the L1 and L2 production interesting objects of study.

Thus, Ranta (2013) looks into the above-mentioned four non-standard verb-syntactic features of spoken ELF with the question in mind whether the features are truly "ELF-specific" or if they can also be detected in comparable spoken L1 data, and if so – whether the uses are similar or different between the two speaker groups. This, on the other hand, leads to the question whether some of the observed features could actually be universal features of spoken English grammar (rather than mere L2 errors). The initial selection of the features for closer observation was purely data-driven, as the attempt was to find features in the ELF data that diverged from the standard use but that caught the researcher's eye as recurring phenomena with no link to any particular L1 background. The four features were then compared to those found in spoken L1 data.

The corpora employed in the study were the ELFA corpus for primary data, and the 1.8-million-word MICASE corpus for reference data for its close match in content and construct to ELFA, but collected in native-speaker settings. ELFA includes a handful of English native speakers and MICASE, on the other hand, some non-native English speakers, but in order to render comparisons feasible, the speaker status of all those producing non-standard forms of each feature was checked and instances produced by English native speakers in ELFA and, on the other hand, instances produced by non-native speakers in MICASE were excluded from the analysis. Both corpora derive from academic contexts, which were considered especially fit for purpose as academia uses English *de facto* as its international lingua franca with many non-native speakers using English as their daily working language. Moreover, the genre relies heavily on linguistic means for discussing abstract points, (co-)constructing arguments, defending one's views, and elaborating on ideas with not much help from the physical context. Academic speakers can, thus, be regarded as "expert users" of ELF.

The emphasis of the study was on qualitative methods, i.e. finding qualitative similarities or differences in the linguistic contexts for the non-standard features in both corpora as in the present study "universalness" was essentially understood as a similar qualitative tendency in the features, not a quantitative proportion of features that only look the same (but might actually be due to different kinds of linguistic conditioning). Quantitative frequencies and statistical significance of the differences found were computed to check whether there was a match in the proportional patterns of different qualities for each feature – which was interpreted as a sign of a universal tendency. However, for instance an identical occurrence rate was *not* considered either a sufficient or necessary condition for "universalness" of a feature. But if the proportional tendencies conflicted or the differences proved statistically significant, the universal hypothesis was dropped. The linguistic factors looked into for each of the four non-standard structures mentioned above partly arose from earlier research or from reference to standard grammars, and partly from observations on the databases themselves.

The results indicate that qualitative similarities are, indeed, to be found in the non-standard uses of the four structures studied. The affinity is the clearest in the case of **embedded inversions**, where the non-standard patterning is virtually identical in both L1 and L2 production. The non-standard indirect word order occurs both in *wh*-type questions (e.g. *I wonder when are they coming*) as well as in yes/no-type embedded questions (e.g. *I wonder are they coming*) in both ELFA and MICASE. The matrix verbs (i.e. the verbs introducing these questions, such as WONDER in the above example) that are most likely to trigger the indirect word order in *wh*-questions are WONDER, ASK, and TELL in both databases, and for yes/no questions ASK, WONDER, and KNOW. The top three interrogative words beginning a *wh*-embedded inversion are the same (in the same rank order) for both corpora: *what* (ELFA: 66% of all WH-embedded inversions, MICASE: 59%), *how* (ELFA: 15%, MICASE: 22%), and *why* (ELFA: 7%, MICASE: 10%), and for both speaker groups it is the cliticized *what's* that is especially closely associated with embedded inversions in the WH-type (*what* + BE is the most common *wh*-word + predicate combination in these embedded inversions, and in ELFA 22.6% of these are cliticized, in MICASE 29%). In yes/no-questions the top two auxiliaries appearing in the embedded inversions (in place of the standard *if/whether*) are BE and DO in equal proportions for both ELFA (72%/27%) and MICASE (70%/26%). Further, a vast majority of the matrix clauses introducing both kinds of embedded inversions are declarative clauses (almost 90% in each corpus), which seems to indicate that it is the ("interrogative-like") matrix verb (*not* e.g. an interrogative clause) preceding the indirect question that has the strongest effect on the occurrence of the non-standard formulation for both speaker groups.

Also the **extended use of the progressive** is to be found in both academic spoken corpora studied, with no clear indication of ELF speakers radically "overusing" the construction in non-standard ways compared to L1 speakers. (In ELFA, 91 percent of all progressives fell into conventional categories for the use of the progressive, for MICASE the figure was 97%.) The categories where non-standard use is to be found are almost the same for both speaker groups: stative verbs, general truths/habits, and punctual events – with the exception of "habits" not figuring in L1 data. There seems to be a slight quantitative difference, too, as L1 speakers extend the progressive most readily to stative verbs, followed by instances of general validity and even punctual events, whereas for ELF speakers most of the non-standard use falls into the category of "general truths/habits," followed by stative verbs and punctual events. However, many analogical examples of non-standard use can be detected in both databases, and the analysis also suggests exploitation of the progressive for its saliency in speech for both L1 and L2 speakers.

In the case of non-standard use of ***would* in hypothetical *if*-clauses**, both hypothetical conditionals with reference to present/future events (e.g. *I would leave immediately <u>if she would come</u>*) and those denoting past events (e.g. *I would have left immediately <u>if she would have come</u>*) were studied. In both cases a non-standard *would* construction is inserted in the *if*-clause in place of the standard past tense or past perfect tense respectively. Non-standard past conditionals appeared to be a common feature in both databases (in ELFA 55% of all past conditionals, in MICASE 15%) and for both corpora it seemed that the non-standard formulation was more likely if the *if*-clause preceded the main clause (in ELFA, 89% of the non-standard *if*-clauses came before the main clause, in MICASE 73%). For present/future conditionals, on the other hand, the quantitative and qualitative differences proved greater than similarities: non-standard present/future conditionals seem to be mainly an L2 feature (occurring more in connection with irregular verbs) and no common linguistic denominators for its appearance could be found in the L1 and ELF data.

Finally, in the results for the preference for **singular agreement in existential *there*-constructions** even with plural notional subjects (e.g. *There's people in the street*) the most striking finding was that this non-concord is overall more frequent in L1 production than in ELF production (in MICASE 34% of all instances displayed non-concord, in ELFA 19%). An explaining factor seems to be that native speakers employ *there's* as an unanalyzed and grammaticalized chunk introducing both plural and singular subjects far more frequently than non-native speakers (over 98% of the non-concord instances were introduced by *there's* in MICASE). However, also for non-native speakers the non-concord formulation is most often introduced by the cliticized *there's* (60.5% of the non-concord instances in ELFA). Also the distance between the copula BE and the head noun of the notional subject appears to increase non-concord for both speaker groups, which seems to point to similar constraints of speech production as an explaining factor behind the phenomenon for both L1 and L2 speakers.

Overall, the results – together with support from previous research literature – suggest that the non-standard features studied (with the exception of non-standard present/future conditionals) display similar enough qualitative tendencies in the use and linguistic conditioning for both native and ELF speaker production to merit consideration as "just normal" features of spoken English grammar and thus akin to "vernacular universals." Quantitatively, the non-standard use is more pronounced among ELF speakers, which is only to be expected as grammatical patterns are likely to be less deeply entrenched in L2 users' repertoire than in that of L1 speakers (see Mauranen 2012). Also, quantitatively the features are far from being "absolute" universals. But as the qualitative tendencies are in many respects the same, it seems reasonable to ascribe the occurring non-standardness to a common source: most likely the general constraints of on-line, real-time speech production and processing that are the same for all speakers, whether coming from an L1 or L2 background. Consequently, not everything that appears to be an "error" in L2 production necessarily is so. At least the data render dubious the claims that the features studied are due to transfer from the L2 speakers' first languages as L2 speakers from many typologically versatile linguistic backgrounds in ELFA end up using these features in similar non-standard ways – and also in a similar manner to that of L1 speakers.

Thus, closely comparing ELF data (ELFA) with comparable L1 data (MICASE) – and not, for example, with standard language reference grammars – has provided new insights into spoken L2 grammar and brought forth similar tendencies in L1 and L2 speech that have thus far gone unnoticed. The ELF user perspective on L2 data has proved methodologically useful in seeing familiar phenomena in a new light and showing how English used as a lingua franca, despite its indisputable own peculiarities, is in many respects as natural a language as English used as a native language (as also shown by Mauranen 2012). It takes shape under the same general circumstances of speech production and employs the resources of the language in much the same ("universal") ways as ENL to cope with the constraints. However, this does not mean that results from ENL corpus studies on actual language use would be directly transferable to ELF. As Mauranen (2012) documents, differences between ENL and ELF are also to be found (e.g. in phraseology) and ELF-specific developments discernible. Thus, it is only through a careful mapping of naturally occurring ELF that we can discover what is actually unique to L2 use and what features are shared with other (L1) varieties of English.

Primary sources

ELFA 2008. *The Corpus of English as a Lingua Franca in Academic Settings*. Director: Anna Mauranen. www.helsinki.fi/elfa/elfacorpus (25 February 2013).

Simpson, R. C., Briggs, S. L., Ovens, J., and Swales, J. M. 2002. *The Michigan Corpus of Academic spoken English*. Ann Arbor, MI: The Regents of the University of Michigan. http://quod.lib.umich.edu/m/micase/ (25 February 2013).

VOICE 2013. *The Vienna-Oxford International Corpus of English* (version POS XML 2.0). Director: Barbara Seidlhofer. www.univie.ac.at/voice/page/download_voice_xml (25 February 2013).

23

Learner language

Gaëtanelle Gilquin and Sylviane Granger

1 Learner corpus research

1.1 State-of-the-art survey

While a large range of language varieties had been explored by corpus linguists from the emergence of the field, it was only in the late 1980s that corpus linguists began to show an interest in learner language and started collecting learner corpora, i.e. electronic collections of writing or speech produced by foreign or second language learners. The new research strand, which is commonly referred to as learner corpus research (LCR), encroached on a field which until then had been the sole remit of second language acquisition (SLA). The two fields have the same object of study, i.e. learner language, but they differ markedly in their objectives and methods of analysis. One of the main differences is that SLA studies focus on competence: "[t]he main goal of SLA research is to characterize learners' underlying knowledge of the L2, i.e. to describe and explain their competence" (Ellis 1994: 13). LCR studies, on the other hand, focus on performance; their main objective is to describe the use of language by learners in actual production. To do so, they apply the tools and techniques of corpus linguistics, which, thanks to the degree of automation they involve, allow for the study of whole learner populations. This is to be contrasted with the more manual methods of analysis of traditional SLA studies, which are better suited for the investigation of a small number of individual learners. The field of LCR also has links with English as a lingua franca (ELF), although here again the perspective is different. ELF is not so much interested in the learning process itself as in the use of an L2 for communication purposes (see Mauranen 2011, also Chapter 22 this volume).

Learner corpus data

There are many different types of performance data and only some of them qualify as learner corpus data. Unlike the more experimental data types often used in SLA, where learners are forced to produce a particular form (as in fill-in-the-blanks exercises or read-aloud tasks), the focus in learner corpus data is on message conveyance and the possibility for learners to use their own wording. In principle, like any other corpora, learner corpora need to be authentic, i.e. "gathered from the genuine communications of people going about their normal business" (Sinclair 1996). However, learners, especially those who learn the target language in a country where that language is not a native or official language, rarely – if ever – use the target language in their normal everyday activities. The criterion of authenticity therefore needs to be relaxed in the case of learner corpora so as to include data, such as free compositions or informal interviews, "that are elicited for the corpus but that use procedures exerting very little control" (Nesselhauf 2004: 128). The notion of control is fluid, however, and some learner corpus researchers make use of more "peripheral types of learner corpora" (ibid.), such as picture descriptions or student translations that involve a higher degree of control (e.g. the *Giessen–Long Beach Chaplin Corpus*, a corpus of retellings of a silent Charlie Chaplin movie).

Learner corpora can be of different types, including general or specific, written or spoken, synchronic or longitudinal, mono-L1 or multi-L1 data, which can be produced by learners of different origins and different proficiency levels. A survey of the learner corpora currently available (see www.uclouvain.be/en-cecl-lcworld.html), however, reveals that some types of learner corpora are more common than others. Thus, while in principle learner corpus data can be collected from learners at all proficiency levels, most corpora to date represent the more advanced stages. This initially stemmed from a wish to fill a double-sided gap, i.e. a general neglect of the more advanced proficiency levels by both SLA researchers and designers of teaching resources, but it would now be desirable to revisit the other stages on the basis of corpus data. Another feature is that the number of written corpora by far outnumbers that of spoken corpora. This imbalance results from the difficulty of collecting and transcribing oral data produced by learners. To some extent, this focus on writing can be seen as a positive shift from SLA studies that generally prioritize L2 oral production and indeed, as will be shown below, LCR studies have greatly contributed to the analysis of learner writing. However, this balance needs to be redressed and projects such as the *Role Play Learner Corpus* and the *Louvain International Database of Spoken English Interlanguage* are particularly welcome. To take full advantage of these spoken learner corpora, which are usually released as transcriptions, it would also be advisable to have access to the audio files, so as to allow the investigation of learner pronunciation and prosody.

The majority of learner corpus studies are based on raw data, i.e. data devoid of any linguistic annotation. This is changing, however, and an increasing number of studies make use of annotated data, usually in the form of part-of-speech (POS) tagged or error-tagged data. Annotation of learner data comes with potential problems. Having been developed on the basis of native corpus data, POS-taggers may not perform as well when applied to learner texts. Studies have shown the success rate to be sensitive to errors, especially spelling errors, although for higher-proficiency-level texts which contain relatively few formal errors, the accuracy rate remains quite high (Granger *et al.* 2009: 16). Error tagging poses challenges of a different order (see also Section 1.3), having to do mainly with the manual nature of the annotation task and the variety of error typologies, which makes the results difficult to compare across LCR studies. However, annotated learner corpus data are worth the effort they involve, since they expand the possibilities of linguistic analysis (see Section 1.2, Granger and Rayson 1998).

Linguistic phenomena

Learner corpus research has tackled aspects of learner language that had been neglected until then. As against SLA studies which have traditionally prioritized morphology and grammar, LCR is characterized by a strong focus on lexis, lexico-grammar, and a range of discourse phenomena. This has been made possible by corpus software tools such as AntConc (Anthony 2004) or WordSmith Tools (Scott 2012), with which it is easy to draw up frequency lists of single words or sequences of words of a given length (bigrams, trigrams, etc.), extract all occurrences of a particular linguistic item, and identify its typical lexico-grammatical patterning. Studies using these methods have uncovered a facet of learner language which had hitherto been largely left untouched, i.e. the learner phrasicon, in particular learners' use of collocations (Nesselhauf 2005) and lexical bundles (Chen and Baker 2010). Discourse features are also strongly in evidence in learner corpus studies, in particular the use of connectors (Leńko-Szymańska 2008), discourse markers (Müller 2005), stance markers (Hasselgård 2009), and involvement features (Ädel 2008a). Grammatical features, on the other hand, have been underresearched in LCR. The reason is that the majority of researchers rely on raw learner corpus data and investigations of grammar ideally require the use of POS-tagged or parsed data. Studies of learner grammar that make use of learner corpora tend to deal with aspects of grammar that can be studied on the basis of raw data, either because they involve one specific linguistic item, such as causative *make* (Gilquin 2012) or *what*-clefts (Callies 2009), or a closed class, such as modal auxiliaries (Aijmer 2002b), articles (Díez-Bedmar and Papp 2008), or demonstrative pronouns (Petch-Tyson 2000). Studies relying on POS-tagged data are less common (Granger and Rayson 1998, Borin and Prütz 2004).

General research orientations

Unlike non-corpus-based SLA studies which are typically hypothesis-testing, LCR studies tend to be exploratory or descriptive. This general research orientation is consistent with the very nature of learner corpora which are usually collected as generic resources to be used to answer a wide range of research questions not identified at the time of collection. However, some learner corpus researchers have adopted a more explanatory research design, which uses learner corpora to revisit important SLA findings. For instance, Tono (2000) and Housen (2002) revisit, on the basis of learner corpus data, the order of acquisition of morphemes established in SLA. Studies of this type are important as they can help bridge the gap between SLA and LCR, two fields which are still distant from each other – although recent research shows signs of a rapprochement, with learner corpus data slowly earning their rightful place among standard research methods in SLA (Mackey and Gass 2012).

Another important orientation of LCR resides in its strong links with teaching, which were in evidence from the start. Several studies demonstrate how learner corpora can be used to develop pedagogical tools and methods which target more accurately the needs of the learner. Wible *et al.* (2001), for example, describe a web-based writing environment that allows for the collection and pedagogical implementation of learner corpus data. Learner corpora are also used to inform pedagogical lexicography and language testing. However, as Flowerdew (2012: 207) rightly points out, they "still seem to be 'the poor relation' as far as pedagogic applications are concerned." Most studies include a section on the pedagogical implications of the findings, but up-and-running pedagogical resources that make full use of learner corpus data are still relatively rare.

1.2 Representative studies

(1) Nesselhauf, N. 2003. The use of collocations by advanced learners of English and some implications for teaching. *Applied Linguistics* 24(2): 223–242.

This study looks into German learners' use of verb–noun collocations such as *take a break* or *shake one's head*, which were extracted manually from raw texts taken from the German component of the *International Corpus of Learner English* (ICLE) (Granger *et al.* 2009). The collocations were evaluated according to their degree of restriction (high as in *fail an exam* or low as in *exert influence*) and their degree of acceptability (correct, wrong, or dubious). The results show that about a quarter of the collocations contain one or several mistakes (mainly due to a wrong choice of verb) and that the difficulty of the collocations for the learners appears to be less affected by their degree of restriction than by the influence of the L1. The L1 seems to be responsible for over half of the incorrect collocations, and its role is visible in all types of collocational mistakes. This study is interesting because it demonstrates that collocations still represent a major problem for advanced learners and that the L1 has a significant influence on the (mis)use of collocations. It is also interesting in terms of methodology and pedagogical implications. From a methodological point of view, the article includes a thorough and honest discussion of the problems that may be involved in classifying authentic corpus data (for example, to distinguish between restricted collocations and free combinations). From a pedagogical point of view, it addresses some implications of the findings for teaching, such as the necessity of explicitly teaching some of the most difficult collocations and the desirability of adopting an L1-based approach which underlines differences between L1 and L2.

(2) Osborne, J. 2008. Adverb placement in post-intermediate learner English: A contrastive study of learner corpora. In G. Gilquin, S. Papp, and M. B. Díez-Bedmar (eds.), *Linking up contrastive and learner corpus research*, 127–146. Amsterdam: Rodopi.

This grammatical study on the placement of the adverb in learner English relies on two learner corpora, one containing essays produced by French learners only (*Chambéry Corpus*) and the other one including essays produced by learners from different mother-tongue backgrounds (ICLE). These corpora were compared with two corpora of essays written by native speakers, viz. the *Louvain Corpus of Native English Essays* (LOCNESS) and the *Essay Bank*. All four corpora were POS-tagged so as to permit the automatic extraction of adverbs. The main objective of the study is to find out whether the learners' L1 may have an influence on the use of the Verb–Adverb–Object order (e.g. *to see clearly the contrast*), which is normally not allowed in English. The large proportion of this structure among French, Italian, and Spanish learners might be explained by syntactic transfer from the L1, since French, Italian, and Spanish all allow this structure. However, the finding that learners with other L1s also produce Verb–Adverb–Object sequences suggests that transfer is not the only explanation. Besides the information it provides about adverb placement in learner English, this article is important because it clearly demonstrates that problems seemingly due to L1 transfer could in fact be shared by other learner populations and thus be attributed to other factors. This should serve as a warning against studies that hastily conclude that transfer is at work without considering further evidence such as data from other learner populations or data from the learners' L1.

(3) Flowerdew, L. 1998. Integrating "expert" and "interlanguage" computer corpora findings on causality: Discoveries for teachers and students. *English for Specific Purposes* 17(4): 329–345.

The objective of this study is to investigate the rhetorical function of causality in scientific text on the basis of an expert corpus (taken from the *MicroConcord Academic Corpus Collection*) and a learner corpus (taken from the *Hong Kong University of Science and Technology Learner Corpus*). The careful examination of concordances of 52 devices expressing reason–result, means–result, or grounds–conclusion reveals a number of features that are distinctive for the learners (as compared to the expert writers). These differences include the overuse of logical connectors as markers of local coherence, their predominantly sentence-initial position, the reliance on a small set of devices, the use of idiosyncratic phrases (e.g. *it is because*), the absence of certain grammatical patternings (like reduced relative clauses with causative verbs), and the lack of mitigating markers such as modal verbs or adverbs in the direct environment of the causal devices. The article is especially interesting for its discourse-oriented perspective, starting from a rhetorical function rather than from one or two isolated items, as well as for its focus on scientific prose and its plea for more corpus-based English for Academic/Specific Purposes textbooks. It is also a good illustration of how useful and enlightening it is to consider the functionality of items in context (qualitative approach) in addition to their overall frequency (quantitative approach).

(4) Granger, S. and Rayson, P. 1998. Automatic profiling of learner texts. In S. Granger (ed.), *Learner English on Computer*, 119–131. London and New York: Addison Wesley Longman.

The objective of this study is to establish whether it is possible to identify distinctive stylistic characteristics of learner writing fully automatically on the basis of POS-tagged corpora. The frequencies of POS categories – both major categories such as pronouns and subcategories like personal or indefinite pronouns – were compared in two similar-sized corpora, a corpus of native novice writing, LOCNESS, and the French component of ICLE. The comparison generated a number of distinctive POS configurations which highlight the speech-like nature of learner writing. The learners tend to underuse the categories typical of academic writing (e.g. nouns and prepositions) and overuse those typical of speech (e.g. indefinite determiners and pronouns, first- and second-person pronouns). The study is a good example of a fully corpus-driven analysis which allows generalizations to emerge bottom-up from the learner data. It demonstrates the interest of using POS-tagged data, an approach that is still more the exception than the rule in LCR. The study paves the way for Biber-inspired multidimensional approaches to the analysis of learner language (e.g. Asención-Delaney and Collentine 2011), typology-driven studies (Szmrecsanyi and Kortmann 2011), and natural language processing applications, in particular automatic L1 identification (Jarvis and Paquot in press).

(5) Thewissen, J. 2013. Capturing L2 accuracy developmental patterns: Insights from an error-tagged EFL learner corpus. *Modern Language Journal* 97(S1): 77–101.

This study makes use of data from ICLE to trace second language developmental trajectories in terms of accuracy. It is based on data sampled at the same point in time from learners at different proficiency levels. The data were submitted to two independent processes: they were rated by testing experts according to the *Common European Framework of Reference for Languages* (Council of Europe 2001) and fully annotated for errors on the basis of the Louvain error-tagging system (Granger 2003b). Errors were counted using a new method, called potential occasion analysis, which quantifies errors in relation to the number of times they could be produced rather than in relation to the total number of words in the corpus. The study investigates 45 error types across four proficiency levels: lower intermediate, upper intermediate, advanced, and near-native. The results show that the developmental patterns vary in function of the error category. While many error types (e.g. spelling errors or verb-dependent preposition errors) are characterized by progress followed by stabilization, others (e.g. noun number errors) show steady linear development, and others still (e.g. verb tense errors) show no sign of development. The findings generally bring support to SLA claims about the non-linear nature of language development. They also have major pedagogical implications, in particular for language testing research which has started to extract error patterns together with other features of interlanguage (accurate use, over- and underuse) from learner corpora to achieve a more accurate description of language proficiency levels.

(6) Belz, J. and Vyatkina, N. 2005. Learner corpus research and the development of L2 pragmatic competence in networked intercultural language study: The case of German modal particles. *Canadian Modern Language Review* 62(1): 17–48.

This study demonstrates that learner corpus data can be used to develop L2 pragmatic competence thanks to a methodology that fully integrates learner corpus data into normal pedagogical activities. The data used are part of *Telekorp*, a bilingual corpus that results from a telecollaborative partnership involving e-mail and synchronous chat between German-speaking learners of English and English-speaking learners of German. The corpus contains native and non-native data collected longitudinally in the two languages over a period of three weeks. The study focuses on pragmatic competence in German, and more particularly the use of modal particles such as *ja* or *doch*. Data-driven learning is at the heart of the pedagogical intervention: learners are made to reflect on L1 and L2 data directly extracted from their own telecollaborative interactions. A comparison of learners' use of modal particles before and after the experiment shows a marked increase in the number of modal particles used, improved accuracy of use, and a heightened awareness of their importance in German. One of the main advantages of using data from computer-mediated communication between native and non-native speakers is that the data are collected in the same interactions. This ensures that the native control data are fully comparable to the learner data with respect to learner and task variables.

1.3 Methodological issues for learner corpus research

While the methods generally applied in corpus linguistics can be applied in LCR too, there are a number of methods that have been specifically designed to deal with learner corpus data. They include contrastive interlanguage analysis, the integrated contrastive model, and computer-aided error analysis. New directions can (and should) also be envisaged to complement these three methods.

Contrastive interlanguage analysis

Many learner corpus studies rely (explicitly or implicitly) on a method called contrastive interlanguage analysis (CIA) (see Granger 1996). This method involves two types of comparison: one between a learner corpus and a normative reference corpus, and another one between different learner (sub)corpora.

The first type of comparison makes it possible to highlight features that are distinctive for learner language. This includes errors (which were the focus of pre-corpus interlanguage studies), but also cases of under- or overuse, i.e. the use of significantly fewer or more instances of a particular item as compared to the reference corpus. Particularly important in this type of comparison is the use of corpora that are as comparable as possible in terms of genre, topics, etc. De Cock's (2002) analysis of pragmatic prefabs in several learner and native corpora suggests that a comparison between the *Louvain International Database of Spoken English Interlanguage* (LINDSEI) and a corpus of spontaneous conversations like (the demographic component of) the *British National Corpus* would point to an overuse of *and then* in the learner corpus. Yet, a comparison with the *Louvain Corpus of Native English Conversation* (LOCNEC), which is made up of informal interviews like LINDSEI, shows that learners actually underuse *and then*. Similarly, using data produced by expert or novice writers as a control corpus may have an impact on the results of the comparison. It should also be emphasized that the reference for comparison need not necessarily be native in the strict sense (e.g. it could represent a new developing variety of World Englishes) nor need it be unique/monolithic (see Mukherjee 2005) – the most important being that this corpus-based reference is made explicit.

The second type of comparison involved in CIA is between (varieties of) interlanguages. Most commonly, this comparison is made between several learner populations with different L1s, which helps identify the possible source of certain non-standard features. Features that are limited to one L1-group (or several groups with L1s from the same language family) are likely to be due to transfer from the mother tongue (interlingual features). On the other hand, features that are shared by a large number of L1-groups are more probably linked to inherent difficulties in acquiring the target language (developmental features). This type of comparison is crucial to avoid attributing to transfer features that are common to learners from different L1s (see Section 1.2; Osborne 2008). Here again, it is important to select comparable corpora for the analysis. Multi-L1 learner corpora, which contain data produced by learners from different L1s, are usually good resources for this, as they contain subcorpora collected according to the same design criteria. However, even these may be open to several interpretations. Ädel (2008a) shows that differences in the use of involvement features in argumentative essays from ICLE, previously attributed to the learners' different mother-tongue backgrounds, may in fact result from differences in the composition of the L1 subcorpora, and more precisely the proportion of timed vs. untimed essays. This pleads in favor of going beyond the L1 investigation and taking account of other variables that have largely been neglected in LCR up to now. In ICLE no less than 21 variables are recorded per learner text (e.g. learner's age, gender, knowledge of other languages, access to reference tools), all of which can be used to compile tailor-made subsets of data. One variable that cannot accurately be controlled for in ICLE is proficiency: it is imperfectly measured in terms of number of years of English at university – a rough estimation of the learners' exact proficiency levels. Other learner corpora rely on more objective measures, like a standardized test, to establish proficiency (e.g. the *NICT JLE Corpus*). Taking such variables into consideration also opens up new ways of implementing the second type of comparison in the CIA model. Instead of comparing learners with different mother tongues, one could compare learners with different proficiency levels, learners with different degrees of exposure to the target language, learners expressing themselves in speech vs. writing, or indeed different individual learners (see Section 1.4).

Integrated contrastive model

While, as noted above, comparisons between different L1 populations help make more reliable claims about transfer, learner corpus researchers have sought to develop even more rigorous methods to identify transfer, given its central place in SLA. One such method is the integrated contrastive model (see Granger 1996; Gilquin 2000/2001), which combines CIA with a (corpus-based) contrastive analysis between the target language and the learner's mother tongue. Lack of reliable contrastive data and analysis has been shown to sometimes lead to misinterpretation of the results and misattribution of certain phenomena to transfer (see Kamimoto *et al.* 1992 on Schachter 1974). This risk can be limited by conducting a careful contrastive analysis on bilingual corpora, which allows the researcher to get a clear picture of the characteristics of the learner's L1 and the differences it presents with the target language. On the basis of such information, the researcher can predict possible occurrences of transfer or provide plausible explanations for certain characteristics of the interlanguage. This methodology is used by Demol and Hadermann (2008) to study discourse organization in learner French and Dutch. By combining the learner corpus analysis with a contrastive analysis of native French and Dutch, they are able to show, among other things, that present participles in secondary predication are more common in French than in Dutch, which could account for Dutch learners' tendency to underuse this type of structure in French. (See also the other contributions in Gilquin *et al.* 2008.)

Computer-aided error analysis

The methods described up to now do not specifically require that the learner corpora be annotated – even though annotation such as POS-tagging or parsing may enhance the possibilities of analysis (see Section 1.1). There is one method, however, that requires a specific type of annotation, namely computer-aided error analysis (Dagneaux *et al.* 1998), which relies on error-tagged corpus data, i.e. data in which learners' errors have been identified, tagged, and, usually, corrected (see Díaz-Negrillo and Fernández-Domínguez 2006 for a survey of error-tagging systems). This method is less popular than CIA, probably because it entails a number of problems at each of its stages. The stage of identification is very time-consuming because it is normally carried out manually (although there have been some attempts at automatic identification of errors). It involves making a distinction between real errors and infelicitous (but acceptable) forms. Different correctors may have different opinions on what counts as an error and it is therefore advisable to have several correctors and high inter-rater reliability for this stage of identification. Each identified error is then tagged, using a system of error tags which should be very thoroughly documented so as to ensure consistency in the assignation of the tags. The correction stage is problematic too, as it may not always be easy to reconstruct what the learner meant to say and several corrections may be equally plausible. In this respect, a multi-level error annotation system like that proposed by Lüdeling *et al.* (2005) may be useful as it allows for the multiple correction of errors. Despite these difficulties, computer-aided error analysis represents a major improvement over traditional error analysis, not least because instead of considering errors in isolation, it sees them as part of a system which includes both correct and incorrect uses.

Future directions

The methods used in LCR have gradually become more sophisticated since the first learner corpus studies conducted over twenty years ago. Yet, a number of directions should be further pursued before LCR can be said to meet the methodological requirements that are expected of corpus research and empirical research in general. A case in point is the use of statistics in LCR. As opposed to earlier LCR studies that did not include any statistics, most current studies now follow the general trend in corpus linguistics by providing some sort of statistical analysis. Most of the time, however, it merely consists in testing the statistical significance of the results (e.g. the frequency of a word in a native and learner corpus). Often this is done through the use of the well-known chi-square test – a test which, incidentally, may not even be adequate to compare word frequencies between corpora (see Bestgen 2014). More refined statistical techniques would be desirable, though, such as a multifactorial method, which allows the analyst to take into consideration the numerous factors that may affect learners' choices (see Gries and Deshors 2014). Another aspect that would benefit from further exploration is the use of multi-method approaches. In contrast to the methodological monism that tends to characterize current LCR, these make it possible to consider learner language from different (but often complementary) perspectives. The exclusive reliance on corpus data, for instance, gives a very limited access to competence, since performance can sometimes be a very imperfect window on competence. A more experimental or elicitation-based approach may therefore be necessary to bring to light what learners really know (cf. Granger 1998 on prefabricated patterns or Gilquin 2007 on *make* collocations). By triangulating findings generated by different methods including learner corpus-based methods, researchers may hope to gain new insights into the nature of interlanguage.

1.4 Advances and challenges

Since its emergence in the late 1980s LCR has established itself as a vibrant research strand at the crossroads between corpus linguistics, second language acquisition, and foreign language teaching. The advances in data collection, methodology, linguistic analysis, and applications are impressive but each of these areas still has a number of challenges to overcome before the field can truly come into its own.

Data

One of the main contributions of LCR, if not *the* main contribution, is the amount and variety of learner data it has made available to the community of researchers interested in L2 acquisition for theoretical or applied purposes. The empirical basis on which researchers can now rely, especially for writing, is more solid than in previous data collections which, in the eyes of SLA specialists themselves, suffered from a lack of representativeness. At first limited to English, the coverage in terms of L2s now includes a large number of different languages. On the downside, however, is the fact that very few learner corpora contain truly longitudinal data, with the same learners followed for an extended period of time. This dearth of longitudinal data, which is also deplored by mainstream SLA researchers (Ortega and Byrnes 2008), has begun to be addressed by the LCR community, as evidenced by some recent corpus initiatives like the LONGDALE project or the *Corpus of Advanced Learner Finnish*. Another area in which efforts should be directed is that of spoken corpora. Besides compiling new and larger spoken learner corpora with a view to countering the dominance of writing, it is time to make full use of the existing ones, i.e. analyze the sound files (when they are available) instead of relying solely on the transcripts. A last point concerns annotation. POS-tagging, though undoubtedly useful, is a very crude way to access syntax. Parsing of learner corpora is still extremely rare. This is a pity as preliminary studies that have applied shallow parsing to learner corpora (e.g. Nagata *et al.* 2011) have had encouraging results.

Methodology

Contrastive interlanguage analysis (CIA) and computer-aided error analysis (CEA) have been used successfully to analyze a wide range of linguistic phenomena and have contributed to a number of important debates in language acquisition. CIA studies raised the issue of the norm (native vs. non-native; novice vs. expert) and pointed to the benefit of relying on an explicit corpus-based norm rather than the implicit and intuitive norm that underlies many SLA studies. CEA, on the other hand, provided the opportunity to ponder on the notion of error and introduce a higher degree of standardization at each level of the error analysis process: from error identification to error interpretation through error annotation and counting methods. Another particularly positive development is the integrated contrastive model which establishes a close link between learner corpus studies and contrastive studies, thereby paving the way for more rigorous investigations of transfer. One of the major methodological weaknesses of LCR to date is the exclusive use of aggregate data. While there are undeniable benefits to be gained from pooling data from a large number of learners, the reliability of the results is not guaranteed if possible differences between individual learners are disregarded. This methodological weakness can be addressed by the use of statistical techniques like the analysis of variance (ANOVA), which compares the between-group variation to the within-group variation. The combination of learner corpus data and experimental data is another area in need of further exploration.

Linguistic analysis

Learner corpus research has put in evidence an aspect of interlanguage which had hitherto been intractable, i.e. frequency of use. It has amply demonstrated that interlanguages are characterized by patterns of under- and overuse which are as distinctive as, if not more than, downright errors. The shift of focus from morphosyntax to lexis and discourse has proved to be particularly fruitful for the analysis of advanced interlanguage. A number of features related to lexical expansion and genre diversification have been identified and found to be systematic across different L1 populations (Cobb 2003). A question that still remains largely open, however, is how these features develop across time. To answer this question we need more longitudinal studies covering the full interlanguage continuum – from beginner to advanced – to complement the cross-sectional studies that have been the backbone of LCR to date. The corpus-based study of interlanguage should also be expanded to include less computationally tractable phenomena, including grammatical aspects such as tense and aspect or the complexity of NPs or VPs, as well as phonetic aspects like pronunciation and prosody – two types of aspects that have received relatively little attention in LCR up to now. Another criticism that can be leveled at LCR is that it has so far been relatively weak on interpretation. Myles (2005: 380), for example, deplores that learner corpus studies "often remain rather descriptive, documenting differences between learner and native language rather than attempting to explain them" and that studies "are also often not sufficiently informed by SLA theory." The few SLA-informed studies relying on learner corpora have shown that these provide a solid empirical basis to revisit some of the main findings of SLA research that were established on limited (often non-electronic) samples of language and/or experimental data. The influence of the full range of factors that affect learners' behavior should also be investigated. To date, the influence of the L1 has often been discussed, although there has been a lack of baseline L1 corpora to confirm the presence of transfer. However, other factors have been largely neglected. The collection of a wide variety of metadata, together with the learner data themselves, should therefore be encouraged, and so should the inclusion of these metadata in the analysis, for example in the form of a multifactorial approach that seeks to assess the relative effect of each of a number of variables.

Applications

Potential applications of LCR are extremely varied: they include materials and syllabus design, language testing, lexicography, data-driven learning, as well as a number of natural language processing (NLP) applications. One of the earliest applications is the integration of error warnings into monolingual learners' dictionaries (Gillard and Gadsby 1998). Language testing was also prompt to use learner corpus data for development and validation purposes (Hawkey and Barker 2004). Automatic error detection, which had been identified as a promising application very early on (Granger and Meunier 1994), is making increased use of learner corpus data to develop more efficient algorithms (Leacock *et al.* in press). Other NLP applications involve automated scoring (Briscoe *et al.* 2010) and automatic L1 identification (Jarvis and Paquot in press). Sadly, however, progress has been very slow, if at all visible, in the area where advances had been most ardently expected by early learner corpus researchers, that of textbooks and other pedagogical tools, in particular grammars. One reason for this is that the LCR field is still very young and that one should not expect too much too soon. That said, the field has already generated a wealth of relevant findings, but they are scattered and therefore not easy to integrate into pedagogical resources. There is a pressing need for a synthesis of current findings, which could result in a learner corpus-informed follow-up to Swan and Smith's (1987) intuition-based volume on the characteristic difficulties of learners from several mother-tongue backgrounds.

2 Empirical study: two-word discourse markers in native and non-native speech

Some of the aspects discussed above will now be illustrated by means of a study of two-word discourse markers (DMs) in native and non-native speech. Through this study, we were interested in finding out how learners of English from different mother-tongue backgrounds use DMs, and how their use compares to that of native speakers (quantitatively and qualitatively), but we also wanted to demonstrate that when doing learner corpus research one should consider individual data in addition to pooled data. The role of DMs in efficient communication has often been underlined, both in native speech (e.g. Erman 1987) and non-native speech (e.g. Hasselgren 2002), and the problems foreign learners encounter when using (or not using) them have been brought to light repeatedly, often on the basis of corpora. However, studies of DMs in LCR tend to be limited in two ways: first, they are usually restricted to one learner population (e.g. German learners in Müller 2005, French-speaking learners in Gilquin 2008, Swedish learners in Aijmer 2011); and second, they adopt a global approach that does not take account of individual variation (Götz 2013 is a major exception to this). Our study departs from these in that it examines data produced by learners from eleven L1s and considers them both as groups and as individual learners. The investigation of several learner populations (rather than just one) makes it possible to determine the influence of the mother tongue on the use of DMs. As for the analysis at the level of individual speakers, it follows a recent trend in corpus linguistics that recognizes that "corpora are inherently variable internally" (Gries 2006: 110) and that comparing "native and non-native corpora as wholes . . . runs the risk of disguising differences between individual texts, and may therefore potentially produce misleading results" (Durrant and Schmitt 2009: 168).

Two corpora lie at the basis of our study, namely LINDSEI, which is made up of informal interviews with higher intermediate to advanced foreign learners of English (Gilquin *et al.* 2010), and LOCNEC, which is an exact replica of LINDSEI but with native speakers of English (De Cock 2004). In total, twelve L1 groups are represented: Bulgarian, Chinese, Dutch, French, German, Greek, Italian, Japanese, Polish, Spanish, and Swedish (each corresponding to a subcorpus of LINDSEI consisting of some 50 interviews), as well as British English (corresponding to the 50 interviews of LOCNEC). We applied a corpus-driven method to select the DMs. After extracting all bigrams from LINDSEI and LOCNEC, we selected those bigrams occurring with a minimum frequency of 200 occurrences in at least one of the L1 subcorpora. We then identified the DMs among these, for a total of six different DMs, viz. *and so, and then, I mean, in fact, sort of,* and *you know*. Finally, we manually excluded the concordance lines where the bigram did not behave as a syntactically non-obligatory string, keeping a sentence like *You can't start doing things like that* ***you know*** but excluding one like ***you know*** *everything about them*. The data were analyzed by means of a contrastive interlanguage analysis, of which we exploited the two types of comparison: a comparison between learners and native speakers and a within-learner comparison (comparison between different learner populations and between different learners).

Considering the corpora as aggregates reveals a general underuse of DMs among learners: *you know, sort of, I mean* and *and then* are significantly more frequent in LOCNEC than in LINDSEI, while the frequency of *and so* is not significantly different between the two corpora; *in fact* is the only exception, being significantly overused by the learners (see Table 23.1).

There is however a great deal of variation between the subcorpora, depending on the learners' L1. For instance, *sort of* (Figure 23.1) is rarely used among most learner groups, but the Swedish (SW) group displays a very high frequency which brings it close to the level of the native speakers (EN). On the other hand, a DM like *in fact* (Figure 23.2) shows three main peaks of frequency for Bulgarian (BG), French (FR), and Italian (IT) learners,

Table 23.1 *Relative frequency per 100,000 words of DMs in LOCNEC and LINDSEI*

	LOCNEC	LINDSEI
you know	514.9	266.8
sort of	487.2	56.1
I mean	372.7	159.2
and then	291.3	184.3
and so	65.9	79.4
in fact	5.2	55.3

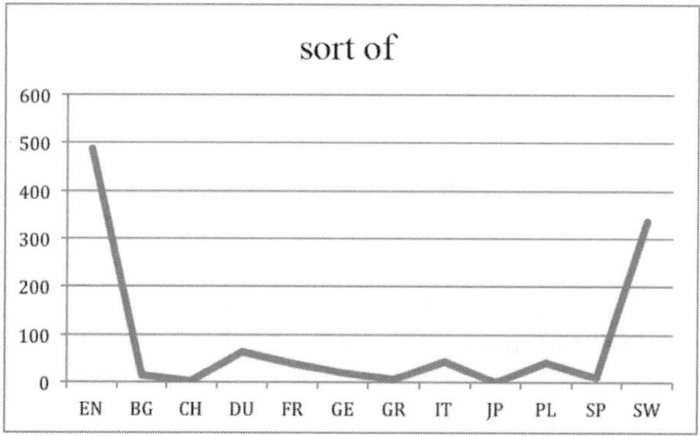

Figure 23.1 Relative frequency per 100,000 words of *sort of* in the different subcorpora

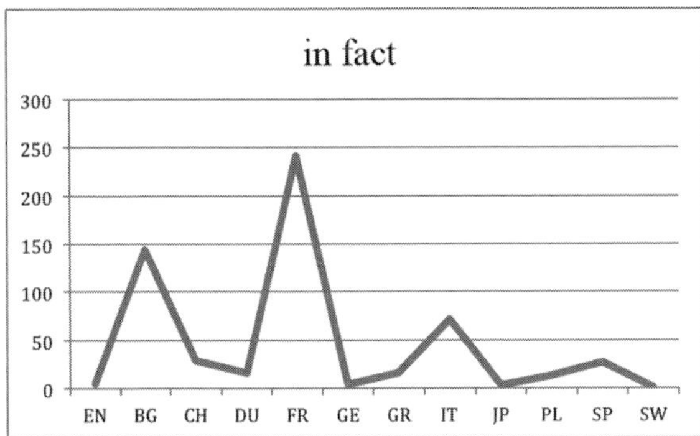

Figure 23.2 Relative frequency per 100,000 words of *in fact* in the different subcorpora

whereas all the other populations (including the native speakers) display a rather low frequency.

An ANOVA test reveals the presence of interesting clusters of L1 populations for each of the six DMs, which demonstrates the relevance of the L1 variable. It should be emphasized, however, that the variation is not necessarily a direct reflection of the L1 influence. The overuse of *in fact* among the French-speaking learners, for example, is very probably a consequence of the frequent use of the equivalent French DM *en fait*, but the high frequency of *sort of* among the Swedish learners may simply be due to these learners' high proficiency in speaking skills.

At the last level of analysis, that of the individual interviews, we also found marked variation, in the form of speakers' idiolectal preferences for certain DMs. Interestingly, this variability also appears in the native corpus, where it is actually the most marked of all (sub)corpora. While some native speakers have a strong preference for *sort of*, for instance, others clearly prefer *you know*. The same is true of the learners, who may have strong preferences for certain DMs. The main difference between the two groups, however, is that the learners' preferences tend to be exclusive: they show a preference for one or two DMs to the exclusion of the others, which they do not (or at least hardly ever) use; the native speakers, by contrast, may display certain preferences but usually still use the whole range of DMs (except for *and so* and *in fact*, which are less common in LOCNEC). This corpus-internal variability should be taken into account when doing LCR. More generally, one should bear in mind that the native norm is not unique, nor is the learner behavior.

It may be tempting, in corpus linguistics in general and in LCR in particular, to limit the analysis to a quantitative approach. While quantitative results provide interesting insights into certain aspects of interlanguage, they may also hide some qualitative trends that are worthy of interest. In the case of two-word DMs, we wanted to go beyond the simple equation between high frequency of DMs and fluency (as established, e.g., in Hasselgren 2002) to see how native-like learners' use of DMs was. With this aim in mind, we selected two groups of learners whose use of *you know* showed different tendencies, namely the French-speaking learners who use relatively few occurrences of *you know* (228 per 100,000 words) and the Polish learners who use many occurrences of it (715 per 100,000 words), and we compared these two populations with the native group (relative frequency of *you know*: 515 per 100,000 words). By making a distinction between cases where *you know* does not interrupt any structure (e.g. *it's just like a curtain* ***you know*** *so you've gotta change it*) and cases where it interrupts phrases or closely knit structures (e.g. *if we* ***you know*** *make some= something legal*), we noticed that the French-speaking learners' behavior was closer to the native norm than that of the Polish learners. While the French-speaking learners use *you know* in an interrupted structure in 37 percent of the cases (to be compared with 35 percent in LOCNEC), the Polish learners interrupt closely knit structures in 60 percent of the cases. In other words, it turns out that the French-speaking learners underuse *you know* but when they do use it, the breakdown of interrupted vs. non-interrupted structures is very similar to that found among the native speakers. On the other hand, the Polish learners use *you know* very often (more, in fact, than the native speakers) but they tend to use it within strings that should in principle have been uttered as uninterrupted chunks. Especially striking are the interruptions between a copula (usually *be*) and the nominal part of the predicate (as in *he stopped being* ***you know*** *humorous*) and the interruptions between a preposition and the rest of the prepositional phrase (as in *that was some guy from* ***you know*** *the upper classes*). Such uses, rather than contributing to the fluency of the Polish learners' speech, mark it as particularly disfluent and non-native-like, contrary to what the quantitative analysis would have suggested.

While both the quantitative and qualitative analyses should be expanded to provide a full picture of the use of two-word DMs by foreign learners of English, this study shows the potential of LCR to bring to light linguistic features typical of certain (groups of) learners. The exploitation of a native corpus, used in combination with the learner corpora, makes it possible to see how the learner data are situated in relation to a certain reference norm (without being limited by it), whereas the inclusion of the L1 variable gives a glimpse of the possible influence of the mother tongue. This "classic" application of the CIA model is furthermore refined by also adopting a more individual approach, which considers the speakers individually and underlines the idiolectal variation that can be found within corpora. Like many other learner corpus-based studies, however, this one does not examine the wide range of variables that are available in learner corpora like LINDSEI and that may have an effect on the learners' use of DMs (such as the time spent in an English-speaking country or the knowledge of other languages), nor does it consider the general context in which the learners acquire English (e.g. input-rich vs. input-poor environment). It also fails to fully exploit the spoken corpus at hand, since we did not use the audio files, even though these would have been useful, for example, to disambiguate between the DM and non-DM uses of the six bigrams under study. In addition, since we only worked on the basis of the (transcribed) utterances produced by the interviewees, without looking at the interviewers' turns, we could not adopt a more pragmatic perspective, which would have consisted in investigating how interaction is created between speakers by means of DMs, nor a sociolinguistic perspective, which could, for instance, have studied whether the interviewer's profile (e.g. male or female, native or non-native speaker of English) might have an impact or not on the presence of DMs in the learner's language. Finally, this study is mainly descriptive and does not seek to establish links with two fields which can be seen as close (and complementary) to LCR, namely second language acquisition (SLA) and foreign language teaching (FLT). An SLA approach would, for example, favor a more interpretative perspective and a more pronounced focus on competence than is the case with learner corpora (which may give an indication of what learners know or fail to know about the target language but strictly speaking only provide access to performance). An FLT approach would look into the ways in which the corpus findings can be applied for pedagogical purposes; in the case of our study, this could start with the question of whether (and how) DMs should be taught in the classroom. A combined LCR-SLA-FLT approach would thus result in an integrated descriptive/interpretative/applied perspective which is still largely lacking in the field of interlanguage studies.

Part IV

Other applications of corpus analysis

24

Vocabulary

Ron Martinez and Norbert Schmitt

In both L1 and L2 pedagogy, the question of which lexis should be taught and in which order of priority has long been asked (Nation 2001), with researchers increasingly turning to corpora for the answer. As reviewed in Leech (2011b), one reason is the longstanding perception that the most common words should be taught first, and indeed there is a good body of research to support that notion (e.g. Laufer and Ravenhorst-Kalovski 2010; Nation 2006; Stæhr 2009). As this frequency–usefulness lexical relationship has both notionally and empirically endured the test of time, so too have researchers' attempts to identify and list vocabulary using frequency information informed by corpus evidence. This chapter will take a critical look at the development of some key corpus-informed vocabulary lists in detail, including older ones for the lessons they provide (e.g. the General Service List, the Academic Word List), and some newer ones to review what advances have been made (e.g. the New General Service List (Brezina and Gablasova 2013), the Academic Vocabulary List (Gardner and Davies, 2013), the Academic Formulas List (Simpson-Vlach and Ellis 2010)). Finally, we will present a detailed account of the development of our own corpus-derived multi-word vocabulary list – the PHRASE List (Martinez and Schmitt 2012) – reflecting on and building from the lessons learned from other important lists – both old and new.

1 Introduction

The size of the adult native-speaker lexicon has been estimated at tens of thousands (e.g. Goulden, Nation, and Read 1990; Zechmeister, Chronis, Cull, D'Anna, and Healy 1995). While few would expect that all learners' vocabulary should reach that size, it is fairly well established that a strong relationship exists between vocabulary knowledge and general L2 proficiency, reading comprehension in particular (e.g. Laufer and Ravenhorst-Kalovski 2010; Nation 2006), and not unlike someone who needs to tidy up a house before dinner guests arrive, there is a sense that one should approach that daunting task strategically, prioritizing that which will make the biggest "dent." Common sense (and Zipf's law) has traditionally dictated that one should focus on the most common vocabulary first.

What corpus linguistics has contributed, in essence, is making the identification of those most common lexical items much easier and more data-informed than would have been possible without such a tool. With massive amounts of computerized texts – now more easily obtained than ever before – at a keystroke one can generate a frequency list in a fraction of the time it would have taken to achieve the same task by hand. Indeed, it was by hand that the early work in frequency lists was carried out; moreover, it will be suggested in this chapter that while there can be no doubt that computerized corpora have made an invaluable contribution to our understanding of the frequency–usefulness relationship, some of the earliest work in list-making may hold some important lessons.

2 "Old" wordlists

2.1 The General Service List (West 1953)

Although the use of computerized corpora to enhance the analysis of lexis seems a rather recent phenomenon, the perceived need to use a corpus to help put some order into the apparent lexical vastness of English for pedagogical purposes has actually existed for some time. The General Service List (or GSL), a list of 2,000 lexical items deemed to be especially useful for the purposes of language pedagogy, was first published by Michael West in 1953, but the groundwork for the GSL goes back to the early 1910s and Edward Thorndike, who realized that "even expert teachers have very inadequate and inaccurate notions of the relative frequency and importance of words" (Thorndike 1921: 360).

Much has changed since Thorndike's manual tabulation of 5 million words from children's schoolbooks. Nonetheless, on a qualitative level, the corpus research and concomitant issues taken on by Thorndike and colleagues over a century ago remain largely the same. Much like today, the researchers had to make decisions about what corpus size was needed (or adequate), and how and why they would choose the texts that comprised the corpus. One question that was asked, however, that was often not asked as much in the wake of computerized corpus linguistics: *Is it enough to simply provide a list of words?* Or, as put by Michael West in his report on the early Thorndike work, "Are we to count 'Apply for a job' and 'Apply a cup to the lips' as one word or two? . . . We shall certainly teach 'large' ('a large box'). Shall we teach 'at large'?" (West 1937: 436).

Recognizing the importance of such questions, Thorndike teamed up with colleague Irving Lorge to enhance the existing list. The researchers

GAME	638e	(1)	(*amusement, children's play*) Fun and games It's not serious; it's just a game	9%
		(2)	(*with the idea of competition, e.g., cards, football, etc.*) A game of football Indoor games; out-door games	38%
		(3)	(a particular contest) We won, six games to three I played a poor game Play a losing game (10-5%)	23%
		(4)	(games = athletic contest) Olympic Games	8%
		?	[=*animals*, 11%; game -/, game-birds, etc., 5%] [=fun, Make game of, - 05%]	

Figure 24.1 Entry for *game* in the West (1953) General Service List

went back to the original Thorndike (1932) data and cross-tabulated each word with individual senses in the *Oxford English Dictionary*, so that the word *game*, for example, was listed with a raw frequency of 638 (in the corpus of 5 million words), but was "semanticized" (West 1953: xii) into 29 separate units – or what are also known as "lexemes" – each unit with its own token frequency. This work culminated in the seminal *A Semantic Count of English Words* (Lorge and Thorndike 1938).

To help make the list more user-friendly, West applied the Lorge and Thorndike semantic frequency data to a 2,000-word subset of words (judged as especially pedagogically relevant due to features related to usefulness, difficulty, and style), and further enhanced it by dividing the individual senses "more coarsely" (West 1953: vii).

As can be seen in Figure 24.1, the 29 semantic divisions in the Lorge and Thorndike (1938) list are broken down into an arguably much more digestible 4 lexemes. Moreover, the list is made even more accessible by the addition of percentages, facilitating the prioritization of which sense to teach/target first. It is this version of the list, published under the title *A General Service List of English Words* (West 1953), that proved to be the one of the most enduring and influential corpus-informed lists of English vocabulary. One might guess that it was West's ability to make the list more "digestible" that helped make the list so successful; as will be seen later in this chapter, however, it may also be this very same attribute that would eventually be considered one of the list's main weaknesses.

2.2 The Academic Word List (Coxhead 2000)

In less than a decade after the publication of the GSL, the nature of corpus linguistics began to change in the wake of the increasing capability (and availability) of computers to do the work that was once done by hand. Notably, Henry Kučera and Nelson Francis of Brown University in 1961 developed the Brown Corpus, at just 1 million words substantially smaller than the corpora used by Thorndike and colleagues, but generally considered the first "modern" corpus of English since the text was digitized and inputted into a computer. Kučera and Francis published word lists based on computerized analyses of the corpus (Kučera and Francis 1967), and included valuable dispersion data in the lists. They also made use of part-of-speech (POS) tagging, but it was very crude and required manual proofreading. Absent from their lists, however, were some of the important developments present in the GSL, such as a more refined separation of the lexemes, and a user (i.e. layperson) friendly presentation.

Another list that benefitted from the use of a computer was Avril Coxhead's *Academic Word List* (Coxhead 2000). Not unlike Thorndike and colleagues' motivations for their lists, Coxhead wanted to identify words that students needed to know in order to function in school; in the case of the *Academic Word List* (AWL), the interest was more centered on success in higher education. Prior to the AWL, there were other academic lists that had been published and which did not use computerized corpora, such as the *University Word List* (Xue and Nation 1984), which in turn was informed by the Campion and Elley (1971) *Academic Vocabulary List*[1] and the *American University Word List*[2] (Praninskas 1972). However, Coxhead's corpus was collected in electronic form, and was much larger than most predecessors at 3.5 million words, made up of four balanced subcorpora (arts, commerce, law, and science). Words were included in the corpus if they were shown to not be on the GSL (West, 1953), and occurred at least 10 times in each of the subcorpora (and in at least 15 of the 28 subject areas).

Much like Thorndike and those that followed him, the unit of counting was not word forms but "base" forms that included any inflected and/or derived forms, or what Bauer and Nation (1993) called a "word family." Coxhead's analysis ultimately rendered a total of 570 word families that met the criteria for inclusion in the AWL. However, arguments can be made against the assumption that if one understands a lemmatized word it is reasonable to assume that changes in morphology should not present too much difficulty. This is true for the general English corpora from which the Thorndike, Lorge, and West vocabulary lists emerged, and is probably even truer for vocabulary for specific genres of English, as is the case of the AWL. Consider,

[1] A list designed for overseas students in New Zealand, constructed using a corpus of 301,800 words based on published material (i.e. textbooks, academic journal papers) and a selection of university examination papers, covering the most important academic disciplines at New Zealand universities in the 1970s (Campion and Elley, 1971).

[2] Compiled using an academic-textbook-derived corpus of 272,466 words, aimed for use by non-native speakers at American universities. The list excluded words from the General Service List (West 1953).

for example, the case of the word *drama* in the AWL: it is clear that it features in the list because of the words *dramatic* and *dramatically* when discussing trends and statistics in academic texts (e.g. *dramatic change, increased dramatically*); less clear is the extent to which the word *drama* alone is semantically related to those forms.

In the next section, we will look at "new" versions of the lists so far discussed, to later evaluate how far we have actually advanced as a field.

3 "New" word lists

3.1 The New General Service List (Brezina and Gabraslova 2013)

Although the West's (1953) GSL has served teachers and researchers well for a number of years, issues with the list have emerged over time. One issue is obvious: age. West's GSL, as discussed in Section 2, was a selection of words extracted from a much longer word list that had been derived from (mostly) schoolbook corpora dating back over a century ago. It goes without saying that the lexicon suffers changes over time, and it therefore stands to reason that the list should be updated. However, there is another issue that has plagued the old GSL as well. West, in his desire to make the list as pedagogically useful as possible, did not base his selection criteria for the GSL on raw frequency alone, but instead wanted to especially include those items which were likely to present less of a learning burden, likely to provide the most coverage (e.g. superordinates), and exclude lexis that might "mark" a learner somehow (for example, too formal and informal). The problem is that such judgments, while no doubt made with the best of intentions and the experience of a classroom teacher (West himself), also make the list less replicable.

With those issues in mind, Brezina and Gablasova (2013) gathered four large corpora together – the 1960s Lancaster–Oslo/Bergen Corpus (LOB – 1 million words), the 1990s *British National Corpus* (BNC – 100 million words), the *BE06 Corpus of British English* (BE06 – 1 million words), and the monitor-type *EnTenTen* corpus available in SketchEngine (12 billion web-gathered words) – to extract the core overlapping high-frequency vocabulary (top 3,000 words) across the four corpora with a view to creating a new GSL. In addition to frequency of the words, Brezina and Gablasova also ensured that the final ranking took into account the items' dispersion in the corpora (i.e. the diversity of corpus files in which the words appear). Importantly, the unit of counting was not the word family, but word lemmas (headword with inflectional rather than derivational morphological variants). Once created, the new GSL was compared to the old GSL, in addition to the AWL, with the rationale that the AWL is really an extension of the GSL and would help observe any differences in the frequency distributions between the words in the two lists.

Table 24.1 *Comparison of new GSL to West GSL and AWL (Brezina and Gablasova 2013)*

	Number of items		
Word list	Types	Lemmas	Word families
New GSL	5,115	2,494	
West GSL	7,826	4,114	2,000
AWL	3,099		570

Some interesting and important differences were found. Brezina and Gablasova identified 2,116 core lexical items that overlapped across the lists of 3,000 words extracted from the four corpora. (In addition, the new GSL also contains 378 items identified as "current vocabulary" [p. 14], i.e. words emerging in the English lexicon in more recent years.) Some of the quantitative differences are shown in Table 24.1.

As can be seen in Table 24.1, perhaps the most obvious difference is in lemma size. Brezina and Gabraslova contend that this reduction represents an improvement on at least two levels. First, for those who would use the list, it means a much more manageable figure. Second, with lemmas listed instead of whole word families, there is no assumption that knowledge of a baseword can be extended to derived forms (e.g. *puzzle* → *puzzling*, *price* → *priceless*).

Without a doubt, the new GSL benefits from a number of improvements upon the old, including accounting for dispersion and not frequency alone, and being informed by far larger corpora than were available in the West's day.

3.2 The New Academic Vocabulary List (Gardner and Davies 2013)

As discussed in Section 2.2, the Academic Word List represented an important advancement in corpus-informed vocabulary research in academic English; however, not unlike the GSL, some potential issues with the list have been pointed out by researchers since its initial publication. One such issue – again, like the GSL – is the AWL's inclusion of word families. Gardner and Davies (2013) cite the example of *react*, listed in the AWL only as a stem ("headword"), but which subsumes such disparate derived forms as *reactionary, reactivation*, and *reactor* (Gardner and Davies 2013: 3).

Another shortcoming Gardner and Davies find with the original AWL is its exclusion of the GSL, when in fact many high-frequency "general" words are also important in academic genres. Consider the following extract from a business academic journal (from Bhuian, Menguc, and Bell, 2005: 9):

Table 24.2 *Coverage of AVL and AWL in COCA academic and BNC academic (Gardner and Davies 2013: 19)*

List	Coverage of COCA academic	Coverage of BNC academic
AVL (570)	13.8%	13.7%
AWL (570	7.2%	6.9%

Abstract
Within the **literature** of marketing and management, researchers have explored different **models** that examine the **relationships** between market orientation, entrepreneurship, and performance. In this **paper**, we offer a new model that includes curvilinearity in the moderating effect of entrepreneurship on the relationship between market orientation and performance.

The four words in boldface are those which are in the GSL but were not included in the AWL. They are also words that are employed in this academic genre in a more specialized way that deviates from their more canonical and dominant senses in the GSL.

With these points in mind especially, Gardner and Davies conceived of a new list, one that would include lemmas and not word families, and not necessarily exclude general high-frequency words if they were found in academic English corpora. The corpora, in turn, would be much larger than the AWL's 3.5 million. Hence, gathering texts from a wide swath of academic disciplines, Gardner and Davies extracted a "core" academic list from a corpus of over 120 million words. Taking into account important data related to each lemma's range (its frequency across academic disciplines) and dispersion, the researchers arrived at a new Academic Vocabulary List (AVL) of just over 3,000 words (the full list can be explored at www.wordandphrase.info/academic). Taking the top 570 word families (and not lemmas) from the AVL, one can see that it compares favourably to the AWL in terms of its coverage of academic text (Table 24.2).

As Gardner and Davies (2013) point out, it is interesting that this apparent advantage holds true not only for the academic portion of the *Corpus of Contemporary American English* (COCA), but also for the BNC. The authors therefore appear justified in their assertion that the AVL can now be considered "the most current, accurate, and comprehensive list of core academic vocabulary in existence today" (p. 21).

4 Discussion of "old" versus "new"

So, how exactly have word lists improved? At least three important aspects can be mentioned. The first one is related to corpus size.

Clearly, the new GSL and new AVL are based on corpora many times the sizes of their respective predecessors, not to mention better sampling methods. A second aspect is to do with subjective decisions regarding what should be included and excluded. The original GSL excluded important lexical items solely on the basis of *a priori* assumptions regarding what was pedagogically most useful; the new GSL takes greater care to ensure replicability. In the case of the AWL, there was a presumption made that it should exist "on top of" the GSL, but the AVL shows us that there is some important overlap between general and academic English. Finally, probably the most important development in the new lists has been the decision to include lemmas rather than word families. There is no doubt that listing word-family headwords can belie an important underlying semantic complexity.

We believe, however, that a note of caution may be in order before concluding that the lemma should be what all lists should consist of. For one, the lemmatization process employed in the new GSL and AVL research involved automated part-of-speech (POS) tagging, which has error rates often hovering around 4 percent (Schmid, 1994). In practical terms, that means that approximately 480 million of the words in a corpus like the one compiled for the new GSL may have actually been assigned the wrong word class. However, there is a greater conundrum still. In the new GSL, the word *as* is listed as one of the most common (both as adverb and conjunction). Separately, it also lists *well* as one of the most common lemmas. However, corpus evidence tells us that *as well* (not to mention *as well as*) is also very common – and clearly has its own meaning. The problem is the frequency of *as* is clearly being influenced by items such as the following (listed with their respective BNC counts):

1. such as 30,857
2. as well as 18,041
3. as if 14,470
4. as to 11,535
5. as well 11,519
6. as a result 7,939
7. as soon as 5,323
8. as long as 5,084
9. as though 4,988
10. as far as 4,619
11. as a whole 3,615
12. as for 3,157
13. in so far as 2,344
14. as such 2,290
15. so as to 1,954
16. as opposed to 1,615

17. as yet 1,423
18. might as well 1,348
19. as usual 1,287
20. as of 1,069

A consultation of BNC – one of the corpora used in the new GSL – reveals that the total frequency of *as* in that corpus is 653,947. However, the multi-word lexemes above – only the top 20 – already add up to 134,477, or over 20 percent of all occurrences of *as*. The same can be said of a great many items in the new GSL (for example, Gardner and Davies [2007] point out that 70 percent of all instances of *pick* are actually in phrasal verbs).

Indeed, a similar issue can be found in the new AVL. As an example, the lemma *result* is presented with *result* as a noun (72,083), as a verb (20,138), and derived adjectival forms (*resulting/resultant*). However, in the academic portion of COCA, *result* occurs in *as a result* (i.e. "therefore"/"because of") 11,407 times – over 15 percent of the noun total. Perhaps even more compelling, the bigram *result in* (i.e. "cause") occurs in that same academic subcorpus 16,446 times – or over 80 percent of the verb total. At the same time, there may be issue with some items that were not included in the AVL. Gardner and Davies (2013) included a "ratio" criterion when compiling their list, which meant that a lemma had to be at least 50 percent more frequent in the academic than in the non-academic corpus in order to help exclude general high-frequency words with little specific academic value. The authors cite the words *way, part, take, know*, and *large* (p. 11) as examples of words that did not make that cut, but we also know that academic discourse contains such items as *in the same* ***way***, *in large* ***part***, ***take*** *account of, is* ***known*** *to*, and *to a* ***large*** *degree* – which also means that these items were excluded from consideration.

In other words, while the newer lists should be lauded for their more careful compilation and choice of lemma over word family for its superior discrimination of different senses of meaning, perhaps a way forward is to explore the lexicon beyond single orthographic words, to aim instead for the lexeme over the lemma. *Collins Dictionary*[3] defines a lexeme as

> *a minimal meaningful unit of language, the meaning of which cannot be understood from that of its component morphemes.* Take off *(in the senses to mimic, to become airborne, etc.) is a lexeme, as well as the independent morphemes* take *and* off

Such a construct may ultimately bring us closer to a pedagogically relevant list of the most important vocabulary. After all, we know from research (e.g. Martinez and Murphy 2010) that when L2 readers (especially) encounter such multi-word lexemes their comprehension is often adversely affected. It stands to reason that a list that is inclusive of both single and multi-word lexical items would be more accurately reflective of the nature of the vocabulary.

[3] Retrieved from www.collinsdictionary.com/dictionary/english/lexeme on 21 November 2013.

5 Lists that go beyond "words"

Indeed, there have already been a number of attempts at developing lists of multi-word items. Biber *et al.* (1999), for instance, using the term "lexical bundle" to describe "sequences of word forms that commonly go together" with the only requirement being that the items "recur" a certain number of times in a corpus (p. 990), list a good number of such items in their seminal *Longman Grammar of Written and Spoken English*. Although lexical bundles are not always complete grammatical structures or idiomatic, according to proponents of lexical bundle research, they can be considered "basic building blocks of discourse" (Biber, Conrad, and Cortes 2004: 371).

Biber *et al.* (2004), using a corpus of over 2 million words of university teaching and textbooks, sought to identify the most common lexical bundles in the academic genre. For example, the researchers identified the following as belonging to the functional category of "referential expressions" (p. 387):

- that's one of the
- and this is a
- and this is the
- is one of the
- was one of the
- one of the things
- and one of the
- one of the most
- those of you who
- of the things that

The fact that these expressions recur in the corpus is no doubt important, and potentially of great pedagogic value. Although in and of themselves these bundles may not appear to have much meaning, that is not the point; as Biber *et al.* point out, lexical bundles should be thought of as "descriptive facts that require explanation" (2004: 400). On the other hand, it could also be said that such a list is probably of not much obvious use to the average classroom language teacher or student, and therefore is perhaps of limited pedagogic value in practical terms.

A more recent list of academic expressions is the *Academic Formulas List* (Simpson-Vlach and Ellis 2010). Much like Biber *et al.* (2004), Simpson-Vlach and Ellis (2010) sought to compile a list of the most useful formulaic sequences used in both written and spoken academic English. In order to do so, the authors used a combination of corpora, including the *Michigan Corpus of Academic Spoken English* (MICASE) and the BNC files that contained academic spoken English, then went about choosing a method of identifying the phrases for their list. The researchers decided to avoid the pure "lexical bundle approach of Biber and colleagues" (Simpson-Vlach and Ellis 2010: 490), as lexical bundles present sequences like *at the same time* and *to do with the* as having equal psycholinguistic salience even though they instinctively do not (ibid.). On the other hand, the authors continue, methods of phrase identification that prioritize pure intuition can be too open to subjectivity. Therefore, Simpson-Vlach and Ellis attempted to arrive at a metric to reconcile both approaches.

The authors first extracted *n*-grams[4] from their corpora and then calculated mutual information[5] (MI) – a measure of strength of association between words – for each of the phrase candidates. However, as pointed out by the authors, although MI can help separate more meaningful *n*-grams from pure lexical bundles, one reason for this is that MI also tends to identify relatively infrequent words that co-occur.

Therefore, in order to determine which quantitative information (e.g. frequency, *n*-gram length, MI score, or combination) would help them best inform their ultimate metric, Simpson-Vlach and Ellis recruited twenty native-speaker judges (with language testing and teaching experience) to rate a stratified random sample of the formulas on the basis of the following criteria (2004: 496):

A. whether or not they thought the phrase constituted "a formulaic expression, or fixed phrase, or chunk" [...];
B. whether or not they thought the phrase has "a cohesive meaning or functions, as a phrase" [...];
C. whether or not they thought the phrase was "worth teaching, as a bona fide phrase or expression" [...].

The researchers were then able to correlate the qualitative judgment data with the quantitative statistics and, through multiple regression, arrive at a metric could be applied to all quantitatively derived formulas and predict which ones would be worth teaching (or "formula teaching worth" – FTW), which ended up mostly being MI, with some influence from frequency (β 0.56 MI + β 0.31 frequency). Therefore, the items in the Academic Formulas List (AFL) are in theory prioritized by this FTW metric (Table 24.3), with formulaic sequences most likely to be deemed useful listed first.

As the authors point out, such strict adherence to pure statistical selection criteria virtually eliminates possible "claims of subjectivity" (p. 490); however, as the criteria (A, B, C above) did not actually guide the selection, many items in the AFL – particularly those with lower FTW ratings, might

[4] Word combinations that recur in a corpus, identified by specialized software. *N*-grams can be of any length, usually determined by the researcher.

[5] According to Manning and Schutze (1999), MI is a kind of "measure of how much one word tells us about another" (p. 178). In practical terms, a high MI score indicates that when one word appears it is likely that it will also appear with the other. An example is the word *torrential* which is strongly associated with *rain*, and therefore *torrential rain* would usually be assigned a high MI score in most corpora.

Table 24.3 *Spoken AFL top 10*

		Speech		Writing		
		Raw freq	Freq per million	Raw freq	Freq per million	FTW
1	be able to	551	256	209	99	2.96
2	blah blah blah	62	29	0	0	2.92
3	this is the	732	340	127	60	2.77
4	you know what I mean	137	64	4	2	2.27
5	you can see	449	209	2	1	2.12
6	trying to figure out	41	19	2	1	2.05
7	a little bit about	101	47	0	0	2.00
8	does that make sense	63	29	0	0	1.99
9	you know what	491	228	4	2	1.99
10	the University of Michigan	76	35	1	0	1.98

be seen as only marginally having "cohesive meaning" as a "bona fide phrase." In the end it is unclear the extent to which many expressions in the AFL offer a more practical, pedagogical tool than the lexical bundles in the Biber *et al.* (2004) work.

Perhaps we should turn once again to the original GSL. Although clearly out of date now and fraught with a number of issues, including the corpus on which it was based, and subjective decisions regarding what should be included or not, there may be a baby in that bathwater. While the subjectivity can be seen as problematic, at the same time there was some value, we believe, in the (laborious) qualitative analysis that went into the work. That meticulous counting method resulted in what was probably a more accurate representation of the nature of the lexis in the corpus from which the 1953 GSL was derived, with counts that reflected separate lexemes, including multi-word expressions. Moreover, in our view, one thing the West GSL did well was present information in a way that made sense to classroom practitioners, teasing out semantics and including contextualizing example sentences. In the section that follows, we present our own contribution to vocabulary list research, one which we hope has benefited from the successes and lessons to be gained from other list work, both old and new.

6 The *PHRASE List* (Martinez and Schmitt 2012)

So far, we have reviewed selected previous corpus-informed vocabulary list projects that we judge noteworthy for the valuable lessons that each has added over the years, including (1) the importance of not taking raw frequency counts at face value (i.e. the importance of also considering semantics), and (2) how the answer to the early question of whether multi-word lexical units should be counted in vocabulary lists in addition to the conventional, single orthographic words, seems to be "yes." Finally, it has been our assessment that West's (1953) General Service List may present a model worth emulating because it not only incorporated both those attributes, but it also was a list not intended to be comprehensive in nature; the list took 30,000 words with thousands more semantic frequencies and broke those down into what was subjectively deemed the "nitty gritty" for the purposes of English language teaching, presenting it all in a format that was accessible by the non-specialist user. It is therefore in a similar vein that we strived to design our own list of selected multi-word expressions; expressions carefully picked, not unlike the items in the GSL, from a list of thousands of other candidates for their pedagogical relevance. The final product, the *PHRASal Expressions List* (or *PHRASE List*), and fuller explication of its rationale are presented in full in Martinez and Schmitt (2012). This section provides greater detail on how the actual list was compiled, reflecting on the issues raised earlier in this chapter.

6.1 Revisiting issues of frequency and semantics

Our main objective was to create a list which would have pedagogic utility, mirroring purposes similar to the GSL and AWL lists, but for multi-word expressions, to be ultimately juxtaposed and even integrated with such lists. Indeed, the proposal itself is not really a new one:

> Some items larger than a word behave like high frequency words. That is, they occur frequently as multiword units (*good morning, never mind*), and their meaning is often not clear from the meaning of the parts (*at once, set out*). If the frequency of such items is high enough to get them into a general service list in direct competition with single words, then perhaps they should be included. (Nation and Waring 1997: 18)

Nation and Waring seem to suggest that the two most important criteria for inclusion of multi-word expressions in a GSL-like list is (high) frequency and semantics – semantic opacity, in particular ("meaning . . . not clear from the meaning of the parts"). We concur with both these suggestions.

However, while 2,000 entries seemed "a large vocabulary" (West 1937: 433) when the GSL was written, the new GSL and AVL show us that "core" general and academic vocabularies are comprised of at least 3,000 words. In fact, research shows that 5,000 words is probably a better estimate of a pedagogically relevant (e.g. "adequate reading comprehension") functional threshold (Laufer and Ravenhorst-Kalovski 2010; Milton 2009: 180). We therefore decided that multi-word expressions that came within the same frequency range as the first 5,000 words in a single-word frequency list might be a sensible target.

6.2 Using the corpus data

The next step was to decide on the corpus source of the language data for the list. After careful consideration, the full 100-million-word BNC was deemed the best choice from among the publicly available large corpora for a number of reasons, including its size, diversity, and reputation. Of course, a corpus of the size of the BNC cannot be easily analyzed without the use of some kind of specialized software to be able to observe patterns using all the data contained in it. WordSmith Tools (version 5.0) was chosen, among other reasons, due to its compatibility with the latest BNC XML edition (used in our study) and ability to generate both word frequency lists and lists on recurring strings of words (or "*n*-grams").

WordSmith Tools was then used to upload all the texts (over 4,000) and construct what is called an "index" of all the words in the corpus. An index analysis collects vital information about each word in the corpus (e.g. dispersion, collocation, and so on), and is necessary if one wishes to run an analysis of recurrent word strings.

Once the index was complete, the list was further analyzed and restructured in a process of lemmatization. This process allowed us to arrive at the crucial frequency band cut-off points with the 5,000-word frequency level, mentioned earlier, already established as a target range (Table 24.4).

With the frequency cut-off bands now established, we began the actual extraction process by using WordSmith Tools to interrogate the original indexed list for any and all *n*-grams (or bundles) between two and four words long repeated in the corpus at least five times. This search rendered a list of over 4.2 million *n*-grams. It is interesting to contrast this figure with the single-word index list. As our frequency cut-off exercise indicated that we only needed to search for items recurring at least 787 times in the corpus, our candidate pool was limited to 14,500 *n*-grams – which, as can be seen in Figure 24.2, would have to be vetted manually.

The time-consuming qualitative stage of analysis then began, involving a line-by-line data deletion phase (Figure 24.3). The first author meticulously went down the *n*-gram list item-by-item looking for "plausibly

Table 24.4 *1,000-level frequency cut-offs (BNC)*

Frequency band	Token frequency cut-off[a]	Frequency band	Token frequency cut-off
1,000	12,271 +	8,000	434 +
2,000	4,455 +	9,000	356 +
3,000	2,089 +	10,000	295 +
4,000	1,217 +	11,000	249 +
5,000	787 +	12,000	213 +
6,000	620 +	13,000	184 +
7,000	547 +	14,000	162 +

[a]Per 100 million, including all tokens within a word family

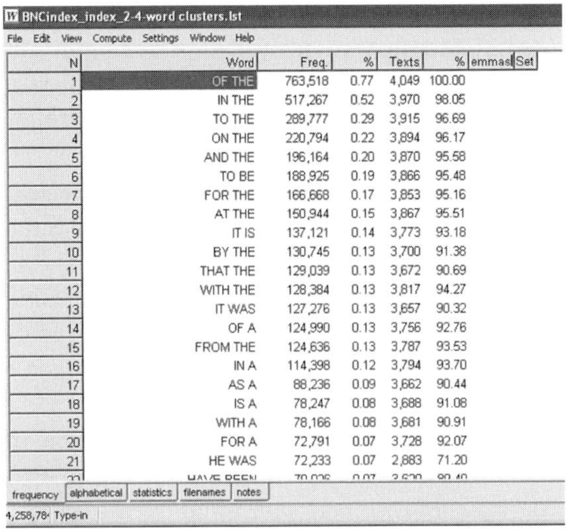

BNCindex_index_2-4-word clusters.lst

File Edit View Compute Settings Window Help

N	Word	Freq.	%	Texts	%	emmas	Set
1	OF THE	763,518	0.77	4,049	100.00		
2	IN THE	517,267	0.52	3,970	98.05		
3	TO THE	289,777	0.29	3,915	96.69		
4	ON THE	220,794	0.22	3,894	96.17		
5	AND THE	196,164	0.20	3,870	95.58		
6	TO BE	188,925	0.19	3,866	95.48		
7	FOR THE	166,668	0.17	3,853	95.16		
8	AT THE	150,944	0.15	3,867	95.51		
9	IT IS	137,121	0.14	3,773	93.18		
10	BY THE	130,745	0.13	3,700	91.38		
11	THAT THE	129,039	0.13	3,672	90.69		
12	WITH THE	128,384	0.13	3,817	94.27		
13	IT WAS	127,276	0.13	3,657	90.32		
14	OF A	124,990	0.13	3,756	92.76		
15	FROM THE	124,636	0.13	3,787	93.53		
16	IN A	114,398	0.12	3,794	93.70		
17	AS A	88,236	0.09	3,662	90.44		
18	IS A	78,247	0.08	3,688	91.08		
19	WITH A	78,166	0.08	3,681	90.91		
20	FOR A	72,791	0.07	3,728	92.07		
21	HE WAS	72,233	0.07	2,883	71.20		

frequency | alphabetical | statistics | filenames | notes

4,258,78‹ Type-in

Figure 24.2 A sample of unedited 2–4 grams list derived from BNC

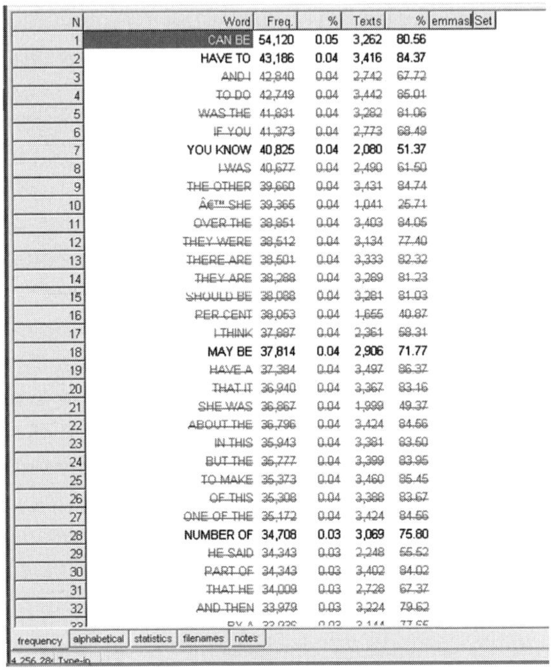

N	Word	Freq.	%	Texts	%	emmas	Set
1	CAN BE	54,120	0.05	3,262	80.56		
2	HAVE TO	43,186	0.04	3,416	84.37		
3	~~AND I~~	~~42,840~~	~~0.04~~	~~2,742~~	~~67.72~~		
4	~~TO DO~~	~~42,749~~	~~0.04~~	~~3,442~~	~~85.01~~		
5	~~WAS THE~~	~~41,831~~	~~0.04~~	~~3,282~~	~~81.06~~		
6	~~IF YOU~~	~~41,373~~	~~0.04~~	~~2,773~~	~~68.49~~		
7	YOU KNOW	40,825	0.04	2,080	51.37		
8	~~I WAS~~	~~40,677~~	~~0.04~~	~~2,490~~	~~61.50~~		
9	~~THE OTHER~~	~~39,660~~	~~0.04~~	~~3,431~~	~~84.74~~		
10	~~Â€™ SHE~~	~~39,365~~	~~0.04~~	~~1,041~~	~~25.71~~		
11	~~OVER THE~~	~~38,851~~	~~0.04~~	~~3,403~~	~~84.05~~		
12	~~THEY WERE~~	~~38,512~~	~~0.04~~	~~3,134~~	~~77.40~~		
13	~~THERE ARE~~	~~38,501~~	~~0.04~~	~~3,333~~	~~82.32~~		
14	~~THEY ARE~~	~~38,288~~	~~0.04~~	~~3,289~~	~~81.23~~		
15	~~SHOULD BE~~	~~38,088~~	~~0.04~~	~~3,281~~	~~81.03~~		
16	~~PER CENT~~	~~38,053~~	~~0.04~~	~~1,655~~	~~40.87~~		
17	~~I THINK~~	~~37,887~~	~~0.04~~	~~2,361~~	~~58.31~~		
18	MAY BE	37,814	0.04	2,906	71.77		
19	~~HAVE A~~	~~37,384~~	~~0.04~~	~~3,497~~	~~86.37~~		
20	~~THAT IT~~	~~36,940~~	~~0.04~~	~~3,367~~	~~83.16~~		
21	~~SHE WAS~~	~~36,867~~	~~0.04~~	~~1,999~~	~~49.37~~		
22	~~ABOUT THE~~	~~36,796~~	~~0.04~~	~~3,424~~	~~84.56~~		
23	~~IN THIS~~	~~35,943~~	~~0.04~~	~~3,381~~	~~83.50~~		
24	~~BUT THE~~	~~35,777~~	~~0.04~~	~~3,399~~	~~83.95~~		
25	~~TO MAKE~~	~~35,373~~	~~0.04~~	~~3,460~~	~~85.45~~		
26	~~OF THIS~~	~~35,308~~	~~0.04~~	~~3,388~~	~~83.67~~		
27	~~ONE OF THE~~	~~35,172~~	~~0.04~~	~~3,424~~	~~84.56~~		
28	NUMBER OF	34,708	0.03	3,069	75.80		
29	~~HE SAID~~	~~34,343~~	~~0.03~~	~~2,248~~	~~55.52~~		
30	~~PART OF~~	~~34,343~~	~~0.03~~	~~3,402~~	~~84.02~~		
31	~~THAT HE~~	~~34,009~~	~~0.03~~	~~2,728~~	~~67.37~~		
32	~~AND THEN~~	~~33,979~~	~~0.03~~	~~3,224~~	~~79.62~~		

frequency | alphabetical | statistics | filenames | notes

4,256,28‹ Type-in

Figure 24.3 Example of initial data deletion phase (faded *n*-grams are deleted ones)

formulaic" multi-word items (Wray 2009: 41), guided by carefully pre-established selection (and exclusion) criteria, explained in full in Martinez and Schmitt (2012), but in essence, as cited earlier (Nation and Waring 1997: 18), choosing items whose "meaning (is) not clear from the meaning of the parts."

Naturally there were far more lines deleted in the *n*-gram data than those retained, and even when potential items were identified, it was often just the beginning of a new search; it was quickly discovered that the number of phrasal expressions with unique form–meaning mappings was relatively limited.

An example is the phrasal expression *at first.* At a glance, it may seem clear that *at first* is an adverbial expression ("initially"), but with each potential phrasal expression identified an additional concordance of that item was run, and then it would become clear that *at first* also has non-phrasal expression manifestations, as in *love at first sight.* However, since an item like *at first* has a frequency of over 5,000 in the corpus, line-by-line searching was not a viable option. Therefore, a random sampling method was employed instead.

What the random sampling entailed was simply generating a concordance of the potential phrasal expression in question using the entire BNC corpus. Once generated, the concordance was saved and then a special command – "delete to N" – was used to reduce the concordance lines to a random sample of just 100. Each line was then scrutinized and deleted if necessary until the percentage of lines reflecting the desired sense of the multi-word item was arrived at. In the case of *at first*, out of 100 randomly selected concordance lines, 84 exemplars of *at first* in its phrasal adverbial sense remained – or 84 percent of the original total.

In order to validate this percentage, a second random sample was generated to check consistency. This method produced stable results, and in cases of minor discrepancies the lower of the two percentages was used (e.g. the two random concordances for *at first* yielded 84 and 85 percent, so the 84 percent figure was used). In the rare cases in which the figures did not match so closely, additional random samples were generated until a reliable percentage figure could be derived. Finally, the frequency figure for each multi-word item was calculated by multiplying the total frequency figure by the percentage figure as explained above. For *at first,* this calculation was 5,090 (raw frequency) × .84 (% of desired sense) = 4,275 (adjusted final frequency). The lines in the actual WordSmith word list were then edited to reflect the adjustment.

Also, frequency figures sometimes increased from their original levels. Since the current BNC-derived word lists are lemmatized and organized into word families, it was decided the same construct should remain in the multi-word item list. The expression *take place*, for example, in its uninflected form had a frequency count of just 3,248. However, the form can also be lemmatized:

take place → takes place, taking place, taken place, took place

In the case of *take place*, after conflating all of the inflected forms, the count increased from 3,248 to 10,556.

On other occasions, a subtractive method could be employed in order to arrive at a more accurate frequency figure. For example, *opposed to* essentially has two manifestations: *(be) opposed to sth*, and *as opposed to*. The *n*-gram list is not much help on its own since the program was asked to identify all recurring 2-to-4-word strings, and therefore *opposed to* is subsumed in *as opposed to*. In order to focus on just *opposed to*, it was possible to simply subtract the number of occurrences of the string *as opposed to* (1,615) from the number of times the bigram *opposed to* appears in the corpus (2,674), which rendered a difference of 1,059. In other words, the true frequency of just *opposed to* is 1,059.

Finally, expressions were sometimes encountered that contained variable components. For example, in the BNC, the first exemplar of *shake one's head* is actually *shook his head* (1,698 occurrences). When a phrase with a variable component such as this one was identified (in this case, mainly the pronoun), a careful follow-up search was conducted in order to identify all variable forms of that expression and arrive at a more accurate frequency count of it. Therefore, after considering *shook his head* (1,698), *shook her head* (1,241), *shook my head* (114), *shake my head* (30), *shaking my head* (17), and so on, the final frequency tally was 3,250.

In all, 505 phrasal expressions were identified that occurred at least 787 times in the BNC – matching the single-word frequency range of the top 5,000 words in that corpus – and which also met the semantic criteria.

6.3 Presenting the corpus data

Following the analysis presented in Section 6.2, the first version of the PHRASE List was produced. However, the list eventually underwent a number of changes as a result of further analyses and consideration. The first version (Figure 24.4) lacked some of the desirable features found in the West (1953) GSL.

For example, colleagues and peer reviewers commented that while certain phrases were readily recognizable as lexical items (e.g. *might as well, in the first place, take for granted*) with clear, discrete form–meaning mappings, some other phrases eluded immediate interpretation (e.g. *or so, all but, yet to*) not unlike the expressions listed in the Biber *et al.* (2004) and Simpson-Vlach and Ellis (2010) research – which we wished to avoid.

IN CONTRAST	2229
THIS STAGE	2223
ALL BUT	2214
ABOVE ALL	2212
RID OF	2212
IN ANY CASE	2159
THANKS TO	2159
GO AWAY	2150
ONCE MORE	2146
OH WELL	2129

Figure 24.4 A sample from the first draft of the PHRASE List

Integrated list rank	Phrase	Frequency (per 100 million)	Example
3149	IN CONTRAST (TO)	2229	The inside was amazing **in contrast**.
3152	THIS STAGE	2223	We can't at **this stage.**
3157	ALL BUT	2214	She **all but** gave up when she saw her test score.
3160	ABOVE ALL	2212	It is **above all** what people care most about.
3162	RID OF	2212	She was happy to be **rid of** it.
3197	IN ANY CASE	2159	It's not due till tomorrow **in any case**.
3199	THANKS TO	2159	And it's **thanks to** her research that we know that.
3205	GO AWAY	2150	The problem won't just **go away**.
3207	ONCE MORE	2146	I call on you **once more** my fellow citizens.
3220	OH WELL	2129	It was due yesterday? **Oh well**.

Figure 24.5 A sample from a later revision of the PHRASE List

BEFORE

RANK		FREQUENCY
4719.	CULT	1061
4720.	DESCENT	1061
4721.	STOCKING	1061
4722.	BELLY	1060
4723.	NUTRITION	1060
4724.	BRACKET	1059
4725.	SOFA	1059

AFTER

RANK		FREQUENCY
4719.	CULT	1061
4720.	DESCENT	1061
4721.	FOR GOOD ('FOREVER')	1061
4722.	STOCKING	1061
4723.	BELLY	1060
4724.	NUTRITION	1060
4725.	BRACKET	1059
4726.	(BE) OPPOSED TO	1059
4727.	SOFA	1059

Figure 24.6 Example of integrated list of phrasal expressions and single words

Therefore, much in the same way Michael West did for the original (1953) GSL, the decision was taken to contextualize the vocabulary in example sentences (Figure 24.5).

As shown in Figure 24.5, the contextualization of the phrases seems to have enhanced the interpretability of the items in all cases, with the meaning of a phrasal expression like *all but* becoming much clearer. What is more, the example sentences also help illustrate the intended sense of phrases. For example, the phrase *oh well* on its own in a list could look like some kind of incomplete stem of a longer sentence (e.g. *Oh well that's interesting*); however, the contextualization helps to show that it is an item in its own right.

The frequency column remained the same, but in Figure 24.5 there is the addition of the "Integrated List Rank." What this last figure indicates is where the phrasal expression would rank on a frequency-ranked word list derived from the BNC, as exemplified in Figure 24.6. These data were added as it was felt they helped to conceptualize the relative importance of the phrasal expressions, even more than the raw frequency data.

As seen in other lists reviewed in this chapter, we also saw the value of distinguishing genre and modality (written/spoken) information, and wanted to do the same with the PHRASE List. However, the BNC is

Integrated list rank	Phrase	Frequency (per 100 million)	Spoken general	Written general	Written academic	Example
107	HAVE TO	83092	**1479**	**502**	**89**	I exercise because I **have to.**
165	THERE IS/ARE	59833	**1133**	**997**	**668**	**There are** some problems.
415	SUCH AS	30857	**130**	**591**	**620**	We have questions, **such as** how it happened.
463	GOING TO (FUTURE)	28259	**587**	**194**	**12**	I'm **going to** think about it.
483	OF COURSE	26966	**511**	**327**	**41**	He said he'd come **of course.**

Figure 24.7 Sample of the PHRASE List with numerical genre-sensitive frequency information

composed of hundreds of different subcorpora, and there is no easy way to isolate, say, just general spoken conversation and investigate the frequency of a given phrase in those files. Furthermore, even the individual files in the BNC that are tagged as representing "spoken" English, for example, are not what one would immediately think of with respect to that modality of communication, with many BNC files actually containing data of memorized and/or written language that has been read aloud. This problem of genre mislabeling in the BNC has actually long been recognized by users of that corpus (Lee 2002). Fortunately, an index entitled "The BNC World Edition (Bibliographical) Index," which exists in the form of a publicly available Excel file, has been developed to address this issue (Lee 2002: 1).

Initially, it was hoped that four genres could be isolated and investigated for the PHRASE List: spoken general English (i.e. general conversation), written general English, spoken academic English, and written academic English. However, upon closer examination of the BNCW Index, it was decided that there were not enough corpora of the spoken academic genre present in the corpus to allow for a representative and comparable sample to be generated. Therefore, 2 million words of the other genres were isolated from the BNC, and merged to form three subcorpora for further analysis. The 505 phrasal expressions in the PHRASE List were then individually checked for their relative frequency. An example of the data that resulted, and the alterations that took place as a result in the PHRASE List, can be seen in Figure 24.7.

However, as presented, these new frequency data pertaining to genre were ultimately found to be more of a hindrance than a help, unfortunately. Every person who had the opportunity to look at the new version of the list found the new numbers confusing, and understandably so. First of all, the original data columns containing frequency information are still in the list, so the addition of three new sets of numbers is somewhat daunting. Second, the new sets of frequency information actually are uninterpretable in practical terms. As an example, the phrase *such as* is shown to have 130 attested examples in the spoken general corpora analyzed.

Integrated list rank	Phrase	Frequency (per 100 million)	Spoken general	Written general	Written academic	Example
107	HAVE TO	83092	* * *	* *	*	I exercise because I **have to**.
165	THERE IS/ARE	59833	* * *	* * *	* *	**There are** some problems.
415	SUCH AS	30857	*	* * *	* * *	We have questions, **such as** how it happened.
463	GOING TO (FUTURE)	28259	* * *	* *	x	I'm **going to** think about it.
483	OF COURSE	26966	* * *	* *	*	He said he'd come **of course**.

Figure 24.8 Genre-sensitive frequency information represented by system of symbols

However, even when juxtaposed with the subsequent two columns with higher figures, what does that number of 130 mean? To a user picking up the list for the first time, one can imagine it would be very difficult to determine if that figure of 130 means that it is rare, and if it is, how rare it is relative to the other genres.

This led to the development of a new, non-numerical system (also used in Biber *et al.* 2004), which is the one used in the final version of the PHRASE List (sample provided in Figure 24.8).

As seen in Figure 24.8, a system of four symbols was devised which correspond to the frequencies of each item, previously represented numerically. Each phrasal expression now has at least three stars (***) in at least one genre, representing the genre in which that phrase occurs the most. If the frequency of that same phrase in another genre was found to be the same (within 30 percent), the same number of stars was assigned. However, if the token frequency was between 30 and 70 percent less than the highest value at three stars, it was assigned two stars, and if it represented only between 5 and 29 percent of the highest value, just one star. Anything less frequent than 5 percent of the highest value was assigned an X, designating the phrase as rare or non-existent in that genre.

7 Conclusion

It has been our aim in this chapter to review what we believe have been important lessons learned (or that should be learned) over various attempts to use linguistic corpora to identify and prioritize vocabulary for English language teaching and learning, so that current and future related research can remain mindful of them. Although it is clear that, with the help of computers, the trail blazed by Thorndike and colleagues a century ago when they painstakingly labored for years through a dense timberland of millions of printed words has since been turned into a veritable superhighway, the lexical forest still needs to be occasionally traversed unhurriedly and observantly in order to be properly appreciated.

As evidenced by the enduring influence of Michael West's (1953) General Service List, vocabulary lists driven by pure quantitative data are more likely to find their way into practical applications when they are complemented by qualitative judgments in a user-friendly presentation. At the same time, the new GSL and AVL teach us that we must be careful with subjective judgments, as those lists show how careful sampling and methodology can lead to more reliable lists of the most important vocabulary. However, the new GSL and AVL also remind us of the importance of considering semantic as well as frequency data to avoid potentially presenting a skewed picture of the lexicon. We believe that our list has benefited from the legacy of successes and caveats that each corpus-informed vocabulary list provides. Nonetheless, we must also recognize that in developing and releasing our own list, we become a part of that legacy. We do not expect that our research as presented here should dictate the design of future similar studies, but we hope to have contributed to the ever-evolving understanding of how corpora can enhance the study of vocabulary. As West himself said so many years ago:

> it is undesirable that there should ever be any one prescriptive list, for that would tend to hamper the liberty of teachers and writers, and do more harm than good. What is needed is a standard form from which infinite divergences may be made, as well as a set of criteria, so that those who diverge may do so with reasoned intention. (West 1937: 433)

25

Lexicography and phraseology

Magali Paquot

1 Introduction

Corpus linguistics has contributed to lexicography in a number of ways. It has provided the methods and tools for lexicographers to better assess the relative importance of different words and their different uses. It has led to the development of innovative approaches to the lexicographical treatment of meaning, grammar, and pragmatics, and extended the entire scope of lexicographic research (Teubert 2001; Hanks 2009, 2012a). However, it is probably in the lexicographical description of phraseology that corpus linguistics has had the most revolutionary effect. Evidence of word use in corpora has shown to an unprecedented extent that words are not isolates but rather combine with each other in preferred syntagmatic patterns to acquire meaning (e.g. Sinclair 1991; Hanks 2012b).

This distinctive vision of language (and language study) is rooted in Firth's contextual theory of meaning and developed in the work of M. A. K. Halliday, J. Sinclair, and M. Hoey. Stubbs (1993: 2–3) lists nine principles underlying British linguistics in the Firthian tradition, four of which general ideas are of particular significance for the lexicographical treatment of phraseology: (1) language should be studied in actual, attested, authentic instances of use, not as intuitive, invented, isolated sentences; (2) linguistics is concerned with the study of meaning: form and meaning are inseparable; (3) there is no boundary between lexis and syntax: lexis and syntax are interdependent; and (4) much language use is routine. The latter principle places collocation, i.e. "a relation of affinity which holds between words in a language, and which is revealed by the typical co-occurrence of words" (Seretan 2011: 10) (see also Chapter 6, this volume), at the forefront of any linguistic or lexicographic description of language and has been articulated by Sinclair in the form of the "idiom principle":

> The principle of idiom is that a language user has available to him or her a large number of semi-preconstructed phrases that constitute single choices, even though they might appear to be analysable into segments. (Sinclair 1991:110)

In Sinclair's view of language, phraseology is central: phraseological items, whatever their nature, take precedence over single words (Granger and Paquot 2008: 29). This is perhaps best illustrated in the tendency of very frequent words such as *make, know*, or *fact* to derive their meanings from the context in which they occur. As put by Moon (2007: 168), "Evidence shows that their most frequent uses are often delexicalized: thus semantically independent meanings of *take* such as 'remove, move, steal, escort' are less common than its use in structures such as *take a step, take part, take a long time*."

Sinclair's pioneering corpus work was first put into practice lexicographically in the *Collins COBUILD English Language Dictionary* (CCELD), a monolingual dictionary for learners of English published in 1987. The concern for word combinations was not new in pedagogical lexicography: phraseology had long been recognized as an essential component of native-like fluency and idiomatic language use (Pawley and Syder 1983) and an early and groundbreaking attempt to help learners to encode meaning in a native-like way by focusing on collocations, idioms, and speech formulae can be traced back to Hornby *et al.*'s (1942) *Idiomatic and Syntactic English Dictionary* (see Cowie 1999: 42), though the word combinations "were identified from experience of language and language teaching" (Moon 2007: 168).

Since the CCELD's publication in 1987, the use of corpus data has spread rapidly to English pedagogical lexicography. Dictionaries for other languages, specialized dictionaries, and bilingual dictionaries are now also following suit. The aim of this chapter is to assess the impact of corpus data on the description of phraseology in various types of English dictionaries.[1] The focus is on electronic dictionaries as "Today lexicography is largely synonymous with electronic lexicography and many specialists predict the disappearance of paper dictionaries in the near future" (Granger 2012: 2). Section 2 starts with a brief description of the Sketch Engine, probably one of the corpus query systems most frequently used by lexicographers today to analyze the preferred environment of words. It then shows how the use of corpora has been instrumental in developing new access routes to phraseological units in learners' dictionaries, before providing an overview of studies that have dealt with word combinations in English lexicography, and more particularly their coverage, i.e. how many and which word combinations are listed in dictionaries. Section 3 reports on a study that investigates the usefulness of phraseological information in learners' dictionaries to answer the specific needs of non-native

[1] Moon (2008: 314b) has examples of corpus-based lexicographic projects in other languages.

students and researchers who have to write in academic settings and makes out a case for the use of a wider range of specialized corpora in dictionary making. The chapter ends with suggestions for further and better integration of corpus data (and corpus query tools) to improve the coverage of and access to phraseology in dictionaries.

2 In search of phraseology: from dictionary making to the study of dictionaries

A wide range of software tools and resources are available today to assist in the identification and analysis of word combinations. The Sketch Engine is a corpus tool originally developed to answer the specific needs of lexicographers. It features all the characteristics of a good concordancer, i.e. display of concordance lines in KWIC format, sorting options, frequency distribution, collocation statistics (see Chapters 2 and 6 this volume) as well as unique components such as Word sketches. These are corpus-based summaries of a word's collocational behavior and provide separate lists of collocates ordered by decreasing frequency or statistical significance for each grammatical relation a word participates in. Figure 25.1, for example, provides a sample of the Word sketch for the verb *suggest*. The first two columns display the most frequent subjects and objects of the verb *suggest*. The third column shows that *suggest* is commonly used in the past participle form followed by the preposition *by* and lists the nouns that are typically introduced by the preposition. The fourth column provides a list of adverbs that typically follow the verb *suggest*.

suggest *(verb)* Corpus of Academic Journal Articles (CAJA) freq = 64485 (683.4 per million)

subj_NP	20787	4.5	NP	15017	2.3	PP_by-i	1748	4.5	AVP	948	0.7
evidence	1350	45.28	role	436	29.96	study	57	14.96	here	135	40.9
study	916	28.09	possibility	254	31.75	theory	36	16.41	otherwise	69	42.5
research	644	32.2	way	218	19.89	analysis	32	11.53	earlier	62	38.15
result	601	24.86	presence	207	26.69	fact	27	15.0	above	58	38.61
analysis	417	20.69	relationship	205	20.18	model	26	8.21	only	52	20.8
finding	375	32.25	need	169	24.46	observation	21	15.85	either	38	29.98
literature	306	29.38	mechanism	161	21.51	literature	19	14.06	strongly	36	27.92
theory	298	22.93	effect	159	11.29	finding	18	13.63	instead	34	27.1
model	285	13.43	existence	157	29.01	result	18	7.05	in	23	26.26
datum	215	13.55	approach	134	15.04	author	16	15.12	previously	22	20.6
author	197	28.49	model	132	8.47	datum	16	6.64	further	21	19.67
work	190	15.79	importance	119	21.93	research	15	8.67	not	21	6.18
observation	162	22.93	difference	112	11.61	presence	13	10.85	again	20	20.41
researcher	116	22.72	use	109	13.53	experiment	12	8.87	that	18	28.03
article	99	17.43	link	93	22.48	evidence	12	7.8	much	18	16.1
paper	99	15.96	change	93	9.47	researcher	10	11.52	elsewhere	17	24.12
approach	96	9.68	reason	83	14.85	Figure	9	11.63	below	16	22.27
hypothesis	95	16.53	involvement	82	22.62	work	9	5.02	also	16	7.83
Research	93	24.72	factor	73	8.61	referee	8	19.81	therefore	12	13.15
report	90	16.85	degree	72	14.89	example	8	5.34	perhaps	10	14.92

Figure 25.1 A sample of the WordSketch for the verb *suggest*

Other features of the Sketch Engine that are particularly useful for the lexicographic description of phraseology include:

1. A thesaurus which provides a list of "nearest neighbors" for a word, i.e. words that share collocates with the search word and may therefore be potential synonyms (or possibly antonyms). For example, the ten nearest neighbors for the noun *argument* are *claim, idea, view, theory, interpretation, explanation, account, concept, principle* and *reason.*
2. The Sketch-Diff option compares word sketches for two words and identifies the collocates that they have in common and those that are unique to each word.

See Kilgarriff and Kosem (2012) for a comprehensive overview of the Sketch Engine.

Lexicographers can also make use of admirable online corpus-based resources such as the *Database of Analysed Texts of English* (DANTE) and the *Pattern Dictionary of English Verbs* (PDEV). DANTE is a lexical database that provides a fine-grained description of the meanings, grammatical and collocational behavior, and text type characteristics of over 42,000 English words. It was created for lexicographers and computational linguists, using a custom-built corpus of 1.7 billion words uploaded in the Sketch Engine. The PDEV is an ongoing corpus-driven project in which a procedure called Corpus Pattern Analysis (CPA) is applied to identify the various patterns in which a verb is used and then discover how exactly meanings arise from each of the patterns. The completed project will contain around 5,800 verb entries (Hanks 2012b: 424–429). See Hanks (2013) for a detailed discussion of Corpus Pattern Analysis.

The systematic exploitation of corpus data in the process of dictionary making, together with the advent of electronic dictionaries, has resulted in the reshaping of lexical entries. This is especially true of electronic learners' dictionaries where phraseological information may surface in various elements of the microstructure:

1. The full-sentence definition format in which words are defined in context "to represent the match between phraseology and meaning" (Moon 2008a: 251) as illustrated in the following example from the *Collins COBUILD Advanced Learner's English Dictionary* (6th edition):

    If you **make an issue of** something, you try to make other people think about it or discuss it, because you are concerned or annoyed about it. (CCAD6)

2. The use of corpus-derived examples which indicate typical lexicogrammatical patterns and collocations. In the *Oxford Advanced Learner's Dictionary* (8th edition), for example, a selected list of adjective and verb collocates are highlighted in the examples that are used to illustrate sense 1 of the noun *issue*:

1 [**countable**] an important topic that people are discussing or arguing about

*a **key/sensitive/controversial issue***
*This is a **big issue**; we need more time to think about it.*
She usually writes about environmental issues.
*The union plans to **raise the issue** of overtime.*
The party was divided on this issue.
*You're just **avoiding the issue**.*
*Don't **confuse the issue**.* (*OALD8*)

3. The display of a restricted set of collocations and fixed phrases in the body of a lexical entry. In the *Macmillan English Dictionary for Advanced Learners* (2nd edition), for example, each example sentence is preceded by the collocation it illustrates highlighted in bold, as shown with sense 22 of the verb *take*:

   22 [transitive] to have or to show a feeling or opinion
   take offence I'm afraid she took offence at my remarks.
   take (an) interest He's never taken much interest in his kids.
   take a view/attitude I take the view that children should be told the truth. (*MEDAL2*)

   Fixed phrases (most particularly idioms and phrasal verbs) are often treated as subentries. In the *Longman Dictionary of Contemporary English* (5th edition), for example, fixed phrases with the noun *point* are listed as separate senses of the word:

   14 to the point dealing only with the important subject or idea, and not including any unnecessary discussions:
   Her comment were brief and to the point.
   15 make a point of doing something to do something deliberately, even when it *involves making a special effort:*
   He made a point of spending Saturdays with his children.
   I always make a point of being early. (*LDOCE5*)

4. Collocation boxes where salient collocates as identified by a statistical analysis of corpus data are organized by part of speech. *LDOCE5* is the only dictionary that provides collocation boxes and phrase banks for almost each word, while *MEDAL2* deserves special mention for offering collocation boxes at the level of a word sense rather than for the word in general.

Some of these features are typical of just one dictionary: the full sentence definition format, for example, is a hallmark of the Collins COBUILD series (Hanks 1987). Features such as corpus-based examples are mainstream in today's electronic pedagogical lexicography, while a selected list of specific collocations and phrases is often offered in bilingual dictionaries.

Lexicographic research has addressed the question of accessibility of phraseological information in dictionaries (e.g. De Cock and Granger

2004; Herbst and Mittmann 2008) and a few studies of dictionary use have investigated whether dictionary users were able to locate in different dictionaries the collocations they needed to perform a given task (e.g. Lew 2012). However, most research has concentrated on aspects of coverage, i.e. how many and which phraseological units are listed in dictionaries (e.g. De Cock 2002; Coffey 2006; Siepmann 2008; Götz-Votteler and Herbst 2009).

Two studies by Walker (2009) and Moon (2008b) stand out as they compare different types of dictionaries. Walker (2009) examined the way in which collocations are treated in three learners' dictionaries (*COBUILD5*, *LDOCE4*, and *OALD7*), three collocation dictionaries (i.e. the *Oxford Collocations Dictionary for Students of English*, 2002; the *BBI Dictionary (revised edition) of English Word Combinations*, 1997 (*BBI*); the *LTP Dictionary of Selected Collocations*, 1999 (*LTP*)) and two dictionaries of business English (the *Oxford Business English Dictionary for Learners of English*, 2005 (*OBED*); the *Longman Business English Dictionary*, 2000 (*LBED*)). The selected dictionaries are corpus-based except for two collocation dictionaries, i.e. *BBI* and *LTP*. The study focused on eighteen semantically related nouns (e.g. *issue, aspect*, and *factor*) and verbs (e.g. *run, head*, and *manage*) from the domain of business English. Findings from a corpus-based analysis of the collocational behavior of these lexical items were used as a benchmark for assessing the treatment of collocations in the different dictionaries. Two corpora were queried, i.e. the *Bank of English* and a more specialized corpus of business English made up of the commercial and financial data files from the *British National Corpus* (6.3 million words). The collocations included in the entries for each of the eighteen selected items in the different dictionaries were listed and compared with those revealed by the corpus-based analysis. Major findings include:

1. There is a lack of consistency in the collocations recorded in the three learners' dictionaries. Only 5 percent of all the collocates listed in the learners' dictionaries appear in the three dictionaries and 24 percent appear in two of the three dictionaries. Put differently, 71 percent of the collocates appear in just one of the three dictionaries (see also Coffey 2006).
2. Most of the collocations included in the learners' dictionaries correspond to those identified in the corpora but the dictionaries tend to record the most frequent collocates (e.g. *key/main issue* rather than *contentious issue*). Walker (2009: 290) argued that, as a result, the learners' dictionaries often include the same collocates in entries for near synonyms, thus failing to highlight the differences in their semantics.
3. A similar picture emerges from the analysis of the two dictionaries of business English. *OBED* and *LBED* include many more collocations from the field of business and commerce (e.g. *growth target, earnings target*) but, like the learners' dictionaries, they prioritize the most frequent collocates.

4. There is very little agreement in the collocates recorded in the three collocation dictionaries: only 3 percent of the total number of collocates listed are found in all three dictionaries, and 82 percent appear in only one of the three dictionaries.
5. The *Oxford Collocations Dictionary for Students of English* is the only one of the three collocation dictionaries which is corpus-based. Not surprisingly then, it was found to contain the largest number of collocates which were the same or similar to those revealed by the corpus analysis (Walker 2009: 295).

One year earlier than Walker, Moon (2008b) adopted a similar methodological framework to evaluate the coverage of collocations in monolingual dictionaries for native speakers of English, monolingual learners' dictionaries and bilingual French–English dictionaries. After a general description of the collocational behavior of the three English words *river, rivet*, and *riven*, as observed in the 450-million-word *Bank of English*, the study examined how it is represented in the different types of dictionaries. Moon's analysis is particularly enlightening in that it offers a diachronic perspective to current lexicographic practice and places emphasis on "the function of phraseological information in relation to the needs and interests of the target users" (2008b: 333). The analysis of the *Collins English Dictionary* (2003) and the *New Oxford Dictionary of English* (1998) showed that dictionaries for native speakers scarcely represent the phraseological patterns of *river, rivet*, and *riven* as identified in the *Bank of English*. This lack of phraseological information most probably stems from the fact that, in a monolingual dictionary for native speakers, information presented has essentially been for decoding: "a primary role of a native-speaker dictionary is to list and explain the lexical items of a language" (Moon 2008b: 318). Learners' dictionaries, on the other hand, have from the outset taken proactive steps to help learners encode in idiomatic English (see Rundell 1999). Moon (2008b) found that preferred collocates, prepositional selections, and pattern structures are incorporated into definitions and examples in the *OALD7*, the *LDOCE4*, and the *COBUILD2* (see also De Cock and Granger (2005) for a discussion of how learner corpora can be used to identify learners' difficulties and improve aspects of prevention of error in learners' dictionaries). Although bilingual dictionaries have always shown more awareness of phraseology than monolingual native-speaker dictionaries, Moon (2008b) found that the phraseology of French nouns such as *fleuve* and *rivière* is poorly covered in the *Collins–Robert French–English English-French Dictionary* (2002, 6th edition) and the *Oxford–Hachette French Dictionary* (2001, 3rd edition). The two dictionaries focus primarily on the translations of compounds (e.g. *river basin* and *bassin fluvial*) and not on other types of phraseological units such as collocations.

The evidence of current research clearly shows that learners' dictionaries have played a pioneering role in the description of phraseology and that other kinds of dictionaries have lagged behind. Today, however, the most exciting developments are to be found in bilingual lexicographic research. The lack of large corpora for languages other than English is one of the greatest impediments to the successful treatment of bilingual phraseology and Ferraresi *et al.*'s (2010) study is particularly important in that it presents Web corpora as viable alternatives and valid reference resources for lexicographic purposes. In the first part of the study, the authors made use of a very large Web-derived corpus of British English (ukWac, 1.9 billion words) and the BNC to extract collocational pairs with three English lexical headwords, i.e. the adjective *hard*, the noun *point*, and the verb *charge*. The extracted pairs were ranked according to the log-likelihood measure and the top thirty pairs for each headword extracted from the ukWaC and the BNC were merged into a single alphabetically ordered list. A lexicographer was then asked to flag the 129 different collocational pairs that he believed could be included in the English half of an English–French bilingual dictionary. The results of the expert validation indicate that over 70 percent of these pairs automatically taken from the two corpora could well be relevant. While the BNC and ukWaC share 45 percent of the validated collocational pairs (e.g. *melting* + *point, hard* + *cash, charge* + *offence*), each corpus also contains between 25 and 30 percent of validated collocational pairs not found in the other. A closer look at these pairs revealed that the ukWaC performs slightly better than the BNC: it offers a better coverage of different word senses and provides "a more up-to-date snapshot of language in use" (Ferraresi *et al.* 2010: 353). For example, the ukWaC includes more instances of collocations illustrating the "take as payment" sense of the verb *charge* as in *charge* + *fee, VAT, penalty* or *rent*, as well as instances of the pattern "*charge* + PERSON" (e.g. *customer*), a pattern that is not found in the BNC.

In the second part of the study, they show that data of high linguistic quality can also be obtained from a Web-derived corpus of French (frWaC, 1 billion words). For example, they used the frWaC to extract a list of the sixty most frequent noun collocates in a span of 1 to 3 words to the right of two translation equivalents of the verb *charge*, namely *inculper* and *accuser*. Potential translation equivalents for 12 out of 16 collocational pairs found in the ukWaC were found in the resulting list (e.g. *charge* + *burglary* ~ *inculper/accuser* + *vol, charge* + *connection* ~ *inculper/accuser* + *complicité, charge* + *conspiracy* ~ *inculper* + *conspiration*). They were all validated by an English to French professional translator with French as a native language. The corpus also proved particularly useful for identifying preferred collocational pairs and lexicogrammatical patterns in the target language as well as larger but perhaps less lexicalized phrases such as "*faire payer* + NOUN."

Apart from collocations, a wide range of less salient word combinations remain largely disregarded in current lexicographic practice. Corpus-based approaches to phraseology, however, have uncovered the essential functions played in language by *n*-grams or lexical bundles, i.e. "recurrent expressions, regardless of their idiomaticity, and regardless of their structural status" (Biber *et al.* 1999: 990) such as *he is, is that the, I don't know what, can I have a, as suggested by*, and *if it were accepted that* (see also Chapter 7 this volume). Granger and Lefer (2012) investigate whether the *n*-gram method can be used to enhance the quality of English–French bilingual dictionaries. They used the French part of the *Label France* translation corpus, i.e. a 1-million-word parallel corpus made up of French magazine articles translated into English, to extract automatically a list of *c.* 6,000 2- to 5-grams with a minimum frequency of 20, which they analysed manually: only complete sequences were retained and lemmatized (e.g. the sequences *dans le cadre de/du/d'/des* put under the phrasal lemma *dans le cadre de*). Granger and Lefer (2012) came up with a final list of 425 *n*-grams which they then checked against two online subscription-based dictionaries, i.e. *Le Grand Robert–Collins* version 2.0 (*RC*) and *Hachette–Oxford* (*HO*). They found that 15 percent of the selected lexical bundles are absent from the French-to-English parts of both dictionaries. The majority of "absent" lexical bundles are longer units of 3 to 5 words which function as discourse organizers or complex adverbs of time/space (e.g. *avant même que, ce n'est sans doute pas, de ce point de vue*). The authors also showed that more than a quarter of the lexical bundles appear in an example with no particular highlighting, e.g. *au quotidien, loin d'être, on assiste à, sous la direction de.*

In the second part of the study, Granger and Lefer (2012) used the English part of the *Label France* translation corpus to identify frequent translation equivalents of two lexical bundles, i.e. *de plus en plus (de)* and *sur le plan (de)*, and compare corpus-derived translation equivalents with those found in three French–English bilingual dictionaries: *RC*, *HO*, and the *Larousse French–English Dictionary* (*LA*). They found that bilingual dictionaries offer two main translations for *de plus en plus: more and more* and "comparative + comparative" (e.g. *hotter and hotter*). However, the most frequent equivalent in the translation corpus is *increasingly*, which is only mentioned in the *LA*. The translation corpus also revealed a translation equivalent which is conspicuous by its absence from the three dictionary entries, "*ever* + comparative." Granger and Lefer's study thus also provides compelling evidence that parallel corpora can be used to improve the number and accuracy of translation equivalents.

Summary and critical standpoint

The treatment of phraseological units differs significantly across dictionaries both in terms of coverage and access. Co-occurrence analysis lay at the core of the pioneering COBUILD project and collocations now feature prominently in (at least) British pedagogical lexicography. By contrast, a whole range of recurrent phrases with essential discourse functions have yet to find the place they deserve in learners' dictionaries, dictionaries for native speakers, and bilingual dictionaries alike. As regards access, techniques range from highlighting a restricted number of word sequences in examples to providing lists of salient collocates in collocation boxes.

There are many different types of English corpora (see Chapter 1 this volume) but the most widely used corpus in lexicography is the large monolingual reference corpus. Today, lexicographers at Oxford, for example, have at their disposal a corpus of over 2 billion words that represent a range of material from different subject areas (e.g. business, computing, law), regions of the world (e.g. Australian English, Canadian English as well as new varieties such as Hong Kong English), and types of writing (e.g. academic papers, newspapers, novels, blogs).[2] Lexicographers often compare the different parts of a reference corpus so as to label the words that are more typical of informal, formal, spoken, literary, or technical English, or to flag the words that are only used in specific geographical varieties of English. By contrast, so far, the lexicographical treatment of phraseology has largely been undifferentiated: no domain, genre or register labels are attached to phraseological units in dictionaries. Corpus-based studies have, however, shown that different genres and text types are characterized by different phraseological profiles (e.g. Biber and Conrad 1999; Luzón Marco 2000; Gledhill, 2000).

While the large monolingual reference corpus is an extraordinary source of lexicographic data, other types of corpora certainly deserve a more prominent place on the lexicographer's computer: specialized corpora, parallel corpora, and learner corpora. As regards the use of learner corpora, they certainly have a major role to play in the prevention of phraseological errors. Learner corpus research has revealed the huge impact of the first language on the learner phrasicon (see Paquot and Granger (2012) for a review of studies of formulaic language in learner corpora; also Chapter 23 this volume) and, until very recently, L1-orientation was still considered as unrealistic from the perspective of publishers (see Gilquin *et al.* 2007). Recent research has, however, illustrated the clear necessity to adapt dictionaries to users' needs and with the advent of electronic dictionaries, L1-orientation appears to be one way forward to answer the call for more customization of lexicographic data (see De Schryver 2003: 182–185).

In the words of Granger (2012: 2), "The innovations afforded by the electronic medium can radically transform every facet of dictionary design and use" (see Granger and Paquot (2012) for a discussion of significant innovations in electronic lexicography). In the area of phraseology, however, publishers have at best used the opportunities opened up by the shift of dictionaries towards the electronic so as to offer more collocations and phrases and improve search options to find these word combinations.

[2] http://oxforddictionaries.com/words/about-the-oxford-english-corpus

3 Towards a genre-based approach to the lexicographical treatment of phraseology in electronic monolingual learners' dictionaries

Corpus-based studies have highlighted the crucial role of recurrent word combinations such as *prime example*, *final point*, *noted above*, *worth noting*, *as follows*, *as a result*, *the evidence suggests that*, *it is possible to*, or *in the case of* in academic texts (e.g. Curado Fuentes, 2001; Biber *et al.* 2004; Biber and Barbieri 2007; Pecman, 2008). They have generally supported Gledhill's view that "there is a shared scientific voice or 'phraseological accent' which leads much technical writing to polarize around a number of stock phrases" (Gledhill 2000: 204). As put by Nation (2001: 178), "vocabulary choice is a strong indicator of whether the writer has adopted the conventions of the relevant discourse community." Mastery of these word combinations is therefore particularly important, especially for the large proportion of students and researchers for whom English is a non-native language. A growing number of university students have to write term papers, reports or their MA/PhD dissertations in English. For researchers worldwide, the stakes are even higher as they need to write and publish in English to achieve international recognition in their field.

Electronic monolingual learners' dictionaries today often use as a selling point the fact that they provide a variety of resources to help users produce written texts, especially in academic or professional settings. These features typically include a focus on academic words, vocabulary expansion material, special notes for helping learners avoid common errors, mid-matter sections focusing on specific discourse functions, exercises to enable users to practice what they have learned as well as collocation boxes. The study reported on here assesses the usefulness of collocation boxes for academic writing in the latest editions of the "Big Five," i.e. the five major electronic monolingual learners' dictionaries of English:

1. *Cambridge Advanced Learner's Dictionary* (3rd edition, 2008) [*CALD3*]
2. *Oxford Advanced Learner's Dictionary* (8th edition, 2010) [*OALD8*]
3. *Collins-Cobuild Advanced Learner's English Dictionary* (6th edition, 2009) [*CCAD6*]
4. *Macmillan English Dictionary for Advanced Learners* (2nd edition, 2007) [*MEDAL2*]
5. *Longman Dictionary of Contemporary English* (5th edition, 2009) [*LDOCE5*]

It focuses on collocation boxes for ten high-frequency verbs – *argue*, *demonstrate*, *illustrate*, *imply*, *indicate*, *prove*, *reveal*, *show*, *suggest*, and *support* – that center around the production of knowledge in the process of academic investigation (see Meyer 1997). Their pervasiveness in academic discourse is further supported by the fact that they belong to Paquot's (2010) *Academic Keyword List* (AKL). This is a list of 930 potential academic words, i.e. "words that are reasonably frequent in a wide range of academic texts but relatively uncommon in other kinds of texts and which, as such, might be used to refer to those activities that characterize academic work, organize scientific discourse and build the rhetoric of academic texts, and so be granted the status of academic vocabulary" (Paquot 2010: 29).[3] I refer to the ten verbs as "verbs of evidence" as they enable writers to show that a phenomenon or fact (e.g. the data or research mentioned) constitutes or has produced evidence for something.

In terms of quantity and access route, the treatment of collocations varies considerably across the five learners' dictionaries. In *OALD8* and *CALD3*, there is no collocation box for verbs of evidence: a limited number of collocations and phraseological units are highlighted in bold in example sentences. As shown in Table 25.1, *CCAD6* provides access to a selected list of collocates for the verbs *argue, imply, indicate, prove*, and *suggest*, while *MEDAL2* offers collocation boxes for *argue, show, suggest*, and *support*. *LDOCE5* is the only dictionary that systematically provides collocation boxes for all lexical entries. For each word, users can generally check: (1) a list of all the collocations that appear in the entry (generally in bold in examples); (2) a list of all the collocations that include that particular word but in other entries; and (3) a list of corpus-derived collocations for that particular word.

In the electronic age, dictionary lookup is often described as an information retrieval activity (Bothma 2011; Heid 2011; Lorentzen and Theilgaard 2012). In information retrieval, retrieval effectiveness has commonly been assessed by means of the measures of *recall* and *precision* (Salton 1989; Ponte and Croft 1998; Shafi and Rather 2005). Recall is defined as the proportion of relevant materials retrieved and precision is the proportion of retrieved materials that are relevant. Applied to dictionary lookup, and

Table 25.1 *Collocation boxes for verbs of evidence in the Big Five*

	CALD3	*OALD8*	*CCAD6*	*MEDAL2*	*LDOCE5*
argue			√	√	√
demonstrate					√
illustrate					√
imply			√		√
indicate			√		√
prove			√		√
reveal					√
show				√	√
suggest			√	√	√
support				√	√

[3] Unlike Coxhead's (2000) *Academic Word List*, the *Academic Keyword List* includes the 2,000 most frequent words in English, thus making it possible to appreciate the paramount importance of core English words in academic prose. The *Academic Keyword List* is available from www.uclouvain.be/en-372126.html

more specifically to the purposes of finding collocations in monolingual learners' dictionaries, *recall* may be defined as the proportion of relevant collocations retrieved in a specific dictionary and computed as follows:

$$\text{Recall rate of relevant collocations} = \frac{\text{Relevant collocations found in dictionary}}{\text{Relevant collocations as found in corpus}}$$

Precision is the proportion of collocations listed in a specific dictionary that are relevant:

$$\text{Precision rate of relevant collocations} = \frac{\text{Relevant collocations found in dictionary}}{\text{Collocations found in dictionary}}$$

To investigate the usefulness for academic writing of the collocation boxes available in *CCAD6*, *MEDAL2*, and *LDOCE5*, I assessed the recall and precision rates of the ten most typical academic collocations of each verb of evidence as found in the *Corpus of Academic Journal Articles* (CAJA), i.e. a 90-million-word corpus of research articles published in peer-reviewed journals (Kosem 2010). I used the CAJA as the standard against which to evaluate the collocations reported in the learners' dictionaries as (1) it is the largest corpus of academic writing available, (2) it was compiled in recent years, (3) it represents a wide variety of academic disciplines, and (4) unlike the academic component of the BNC, for example, it only includes full texts – not samples. As such, it is deemed to be a unique model of academic writing.

Using the Sketch Engine, I extracted Word Sketches for the verbs *argue, demonstrate, illustrate, imply, indicate, prove, reveal, show, suggest*, and *support.* To operationalize the concept of "relevant collocations," collocates were ordered by decreasing frequency to identify the most frequent "general" academic collocations rather than by statistical score as the latter option retrieved too many discipline-specific collocations (e.g. *prove* + *theorem, plaintiff* + *prove*). The analysis was restricted to the ten most frequent collocates in subject and object positions as these two syntactic relations are clearly identifiable in *CCAD6*, *MEDAL2*, and *LDOCE5*, and thus comparable between the Word Sketches and the three dictionaries.

Recall and precision rates were computed for each verb in *CCAD6*, *MEDAL2*, and *LDOCE5*. Recall rates range from 10 percent for the verb *prove* in LDOCE5 to 65 percent for the verb *illustrate* in the same dictionary, with a mean of 29.76 percent. In the case of the verb *support*, for example, only 7 collocates out of the 20 academic collocates as found in the CAJA are listed in *LDOCE5*. As shown in Table 25.2, the recall rate is thus 35 percent. No figures are given for *COBUILD* as there is no collocation box under the entry for the verb *support*. *MEDAL2* only lists 6 collocates in the verb–object relation and its recall rate is thus of 30 percent. When the two syntactic

Table 25.2 Recall rates for the collocates of the verb *support* in *LDOCE5, CCAD6,* and *MEDAL2*

CAJA collocates	*LDOCE5*	*CCAD6*	*MEDAL2*
NP (= object)			
argument			√
claim	√		√
conclusion	√		√
finding, model, role			
hypothesis	√		√
idea			√
notion	√		
view	√		√
Subj_NP			
analysis, argument, data, fact, finding, observation, result, study			
evidence	√		
research	√		
Total	7/20		6/20
Recall	(35%)	not applicable	(30%)

relations are considered separately, the minimum recall rate drops to 0 percent (for the verb *prove* in a subject–verb relation in *LDOCE5*) and the maximum recall rate reaches 90% (for the verb *show* in a subject–verb relation in *LDOCE5*).

MEDAL2 does not provide many collocation boxes for verbs of evidence but when it does, recall is often relatively good, as the dictionary innovates by offering collocation boxes at the level of the word sense, rather than for the word in general. For example, the collocation box under Sense 4 of the verb *support* ("to show that an idea, statement, theory etc. is true or correct") lists eight abstract nouns that are frequently used as objects of the verb in academic texts: *argument, claim, conclusion, contention, hypothesis, idea, theory*, and *view*. Among those nouns, six are typical academic collocations as found in CAJA (see Table 25.2).

Precision rates range from 6.8 percent for the verb *prove* in *LDOCE5* to 75 percent for the verb *support* in *MEDAL2* (Table 25.3). Academic collocations are often listed together with a number of collocations that are more typical of other text types and genres. In *LDOCE5*, for example, the 31 collocates of the verb *support* only include 6 highly frequent general academic collocates (*claim, evidence, hypothesis, idea, research*, and *view*) together with nouns such as *accusation, cause, charity, effort, event, family, government, team, weight*, etc. Precision is particularly low in *LDOCE5* with a mean of 23.9 percent.[4] The list of "collocations from other entries" proves particularly problematic: different uses of the headword are juxtaposed and users are

[4] The policy of *LDOCE5* to divide collocations into different lists on the basis of the source of information makes the collocation lists become in part repetitive (see Götz-Votteler and Herbst 2009 for a critical overview). Collocates that are repeated in the different collocation lists were, however, only counted once.

Table 25.3 Precision rates for subject and object collocations of verbs of evidence in *LDOCE5, CCAD6,* and *MEDAL2*

	LDOCE5			*CCAD6*			*MEDAL2*		
	CAJA	Total	Precision	CAJA	Total	Precision	CAJA	Total	Precision
argue	4	7	57.1	2	4	50	0	0	
demonstrate	6	19	31.6						
illustrate	13	26	50.0						
imply	5	7	71.4	–	–				
indicate	9	17	52.9	3	8	37.5			
prove	3	44	6.8	–	–				
reveal	5	16	31.3						
show	11	99	11.1				–	–	
suggest	6	19	31.6	4	8	50	–	–	
support	6	31	19.4				6	8	75

sometimes forced to scan through lists that may consist of more than 100 collocations (in the case of the lemma *show* for example) to find the appropriate collocation. In addition, verb and noun uses of lemmas such as *show* and *support* are listed together. Precision rates were not computed for the verbs *imply* and *prove* in *CCAD6* and the verbs *argue, show*, and *suggest* in *MEDAL2*. The collocation boxes for these verbs in the two dictionaries do not list nouns but mainly adverbs. There is a collocation box with object nouns for the verb *show* in *MEDAL2* but it appears under a sense that is clearly not academic-like, i.e. "to behave in a way that allows people to know your feelings, opinions, or personal qualities," and was therefore not included in the analysis.

The results of a precision and recall analysis of the collocations included in a dictionary are crucially dependent on the definition of "relevant collocations" put forward and may even vary according to (the quality of) the corpus data used to identify the relevant collocations. Recall and precision nevertheless prove particularly instructive tools for measuring how well a dictionary answers specific users' needs.

Precision is most probably also an appropriate measure to quantify what has been variously called "information stress" or "information overload" in the literature. As put by Tarp (2009: 26), "a major problem in the present information age is not the absence of data from which the needed information can be retrieved, but the abundance of unstructured data." Quite clearly, collocations in learners' dictionaries generally are unstructured data. They cover a wide range of meanings that are often characteristic of different genres and text types. The list of collocations for the verb *show* in *LDOCE5*, for example, includes word combinations and senses as varied as *show sth's limitations, show compassion, show a disposition to do sth, show a correlation, show a desire, show contempt, show mastery, show symptoms,* and *show your amusement*. More importantly perhaps, academic collocations are listed along with other word combinations that are not appropriate for academic writing. In *MEDAL2*, for example, there is a collocation box for the verb *argue*, sense 2 ("to give reasons why you believe that something is right or true"), a sense that is also quite common in academic writing, which offers the following list of adverb collocates: *consistently, convincingly, forcefully, passionately, persuasively, plausibly,* and *strongly*. Non-native writers can be seriously misled by this presentation of collocations as they are not given any help in deciding which word combinations are most appropriate in academic writing. Put differently, the treatment of phraseology in electronic learners' dictionaries may lead non-native writers to believe that all collocations and phrases are suitable for all purposes (e.g. writing a research article or a short story, writing a letter to a friend or to a human resources manager). This echoes a question that was well formulated by Williams in 2006: "Learner's dictionaries are made for learners, but who are the learners in question?" To really help EFL learners write in English, future dictionaries must show greater awareness of the many different types of writing, genres, and styles. Not only does this hold for the phraseological description of words, but also for other features of the microstructure such as sense ordering and example sentences (see Paquot 2012: 165–166).

4 Conclusion

The use of corpus data has considerably improved the coverage of phraseology in electronic dictionaries, but its lexicographical treatment has "still not found an adequate balance between the parameters of quantity and quality" (Götz-Votteler and Herbst 2009: 57). In fact, much remains to be done. In terms of quantity, for example, the use of corpus-derived collocation boxes needs to be systematized. Today, they are often restricted to a limited set of highly frequent nouns or verbs. When available, collocation boxes are devoted to a small class of morpho-syntactic relationships such as "adjective + noun" or "verb + noun." Word Sketches provide different lists of collocates for the different patterns of a word (e.g. *argue + case, point* vs. *argue + for + importance, existence, view* or *suggest* + Ving: *using, adding, considering* vs. *suggest + as+ cause, explanation, factor*) and these combinations should also make their way into dictionaries. Ideally, phrase banks should also feature more prominently in electronic dictionaries to address the current paucity of lexical bundles, especially when they are cohesive markers that fulfill a range of functions (see Granger and Lefer 2012: 163).

In terms of quality, a wider range of multi-word expressions certainly deserves to be granted headword status (see Heid and Gouws 2006) and we are still very far away from Sinclair's "ultimate dictionary" that would contain "all the lexical items of a language, each one in its canonical form with a list of possible variations" (Sinclair 2004b: xxiv). It is also essential that the lexicographical treatment of collocations and other phraseological units be context sensitive. The *Macmillan English Dictionary for Advanced Learners* (1st edition, 2002) broke new ground by providing sense-differentiated collocations. Context, however, also includes other aspects of "collocational normality." Over fifteen years ago, Partington (1998: 17) wrote that "collocational normality is dependent on genre, register and style i.e. what is normal in one kind of text may be quite unusual in another." This significant statement has not yet found an echo in commercial lexicography. It has, however, recently been put into practice in a number of innovative corpus-based academic lexicographical projects. The *Louvain English for Academic Purposes Dictionary* (*LEAD*), for example, is an integrated dictionary and corpus tool intended to help non-native speakers write academic texts in English (see Granger and Paquot 2010; Paquot 2012). Context-sensitivity is addressed by selective use of corpus data in the *LEAD*: according to the users' profiles, collocations and lexical bundles are linked to relevant concordance lines in discipline-specific corpora. As the corpus-query tool is fully integrated into the *LEAD*, users also have direct access to these specialized corpora and can therefore "participate in the social activity of negotiating meanings in a committed and informed way" (Teubert 2001: 151–2).

The field of lexicography has been very much part and parcel of the corpus revolution and very few would argue today against the statement that, unlike many contemporary revolutions, it has been a real success story. The part played by corpora has become increasingly important and "no serious compiler would undertake a large dictionary project nowadays without one (and preferably several) at hand" (De Schryver 2003: 167). Like many other fields, lexicography is now witnessing a second and extraordinarily rapid turnabout with the "internet revolution." The consequences for dictionaries and dictionary making are unprecedented and a discussion clearly falls beyond the scope of this chapter (see Granger and Paquot 2012). However, I would like to pinpoint two fundamental characteristics of the Web 2.0 that will undoubtedly have an impact on the role of corpus data in future lexicography. First, given the potential levels of connectivity and interoperability now available, it is to be expected (and desired) that future online dictionaries will feature more integration of corpus-query tools (see Asmussen 2013). Users should be able to navigate to and fro and use the best resource to answer each of their specific linguistic needs. To search for the most appropriate collocation, for example, a simplified and more user-friendly version of a Word Sketch could well fit the bill. Second, in the quest for more user-oriented and context-sensitive data in lexicography, there is scope for new forms of online collaboration. The time is ripe for a dictionary-cum-corpus platform where users can upload their own corpora, so as to visualize patterns of word use in a context which reflects their individual field of interest.

Dictionaries

CALD3 Cambridge Advanced Learner's Dictionary, 3rd edition, 2008.
CCAD6 Collins–COBUILD Advanced Learner's English Dictionary, 6th edition, 2009.
LDOCE5 Longman Dictionary of Contemporary English, 5th edition, 2009.
MEDAL2 Macmillan English Dictionary for Advanced Learners, 2nd edition, 2007.
OALD8 Oxford Advanced Learner's Dictionary, 8th edition 2010.

Web resources

DANTE	www.webdante.com/index.html
Pattern Dictionary of English Verbs	http://deb.fi.muni.cz/pdev/
Sketch Engine	http://www.sketchengine.co.uk/

26

Classroom applications of corpus analysis

Thomas Cobb and Alex Boulton

1 Introduction

Corpus linguistics is almost by definition *applied* linguistics, as was tacitly acknowledged when the American Association of Applied Corpus Linguistics (AAACL) dropped its third A in 2008. Its methodologies can be applied far beyond the discipline itself (see McEnery *et al.* 2006: 8), not least in language teaching and learning, where its influence has been of three main types. The first lies in improved descriptions of language varieties and features which can inform aspects of the language to be taught; the second makes corpora and tools for analyzing them available to the teacher; the third puts them directly into the learner's hands. We begin this chapter with an overview of all three types before concentrating mainly on the third type in the final sections, since other chapters in this volume deal in more detail with corpora and vocabulary, lexicography and phraseology, pedagogical materials, and translation.

1.1 Upstream use

Early instantiations of the first approach predate modern electronic corpora, with famous examples including Thorndike and Lorge's *Teacher's Wordbook of 30,000 Words* (1944) or West's *General Service List* (1953) for English, and Gougenheim and colleagues' *Dictionnaire fondamental de la langue française* (1958) for French. Work on frequency lists continues to this day derived from ever larger, electronic corpora, such as the British National Corpus (BNC: Oxford, 1995) and the Corpus of Contemporary American English (COCA: Davies, 2009), and has spread to other languages, as seen in recent series of lists from Routledge based on corpora of Spanish, German, Portuguese, Chinese, Czech, Arabic, French, and Japanese. Of course, frequency applies not only to words, but also to larger units like phrases and chunks, as in Martinez and Schmitt's BNC-based phrasal expressions list (2012). While by no means the only criterion, the basic idea is that frequency of form and meaning is the most reliable predictor of what can be most usefully taught at different points in the learning process, as argued by Cobb (2007) for the early stages, or Schmitt and Schmitt (2014) for later stages. This type of work can thus inform syllabus design and testing, as the choice and sequence of forms and meanings to teach and test become more empirically based, for example in the design of TOEFL tests (Biber *et al.* 2004) and frequency-based vocabulary tests (Nation and Beglar 2007). Frequency analysis of learner corpora can also help to determine what learners of different backgrounds typically can and cannot do at different levels, again feeding into syllabus design more effectively than previous attempts at contrastive analysis based on qualitative structural differences, as argued by Granger (e.g. 2009). The *English Profile* project from Cambridge University is a major example of this type of work informed by both native-speaker and learner corpora.

Corpus research has not only informed syllabus and testing but has also been the driving force behind many other tools in language description, one of the most influential being the COBUILD project at Birmingham University (see Sinclair 1987). This large monitor corpus was specifically designed with pedagogical aims in mind, including a radically new type of dictionary with the entries chosen and organized according to frequency, and uncompromisingly authentic examples taken from the corpus. All the large publishing houses have followed this lead, and today it is inconceivable to produce a dictionary in a major language without substantial corpus input. The influence does not stop at lexis but can also be exploited in the production of usage manuals and grammar books, such as the *Longman Grammar of Spoken and Written English* (*LGSWE*: Biber *et al.* 1999). Corpora have also been used in the construction of teaching materials, though in many cases (e.g. *Touchstone*; McCarthy *et al.* 2006) the activities are indistinguishable from those in traditional books; the innovation is that the language taught is based on "real" usage and frequency data rather than depending on the authors' (often fallible) intuitions or fortuitous occurrences in the language inputs selected for learners' attention.

But it is possible to go further still and make direct use of corpus material with learners. Reppen (2010b: ch. 2) and Bennett (2010: ch. 3) discuss activities that make explicit use of the corpus information featured in grammar books such as the *LGSWE*, sensitizing learners to issues of frequency, morphology, chunking, collocations, register, and so on. A small quantity of published materials include corpus data too, from grammar books (e.g. Thornbury 2004) to supplementary materials (e.g. Thurstun and Candlin 1997) and even full courses (e.g. Mohamed and Acklam 1995). In books like these, concordance lines and other corpus data are turned into activities that students can use to explore the language, either deductively (e.g. to test a rule or categorize different uses), or inductively (i.e. to formulate their own hypotheses about usage).

1.2 Teacher use

This brings us to the second major use of corpora in the language classroom, when teachers consult corpus data directly rather than relying on decision-makers upstream. First, corpus tools can be applied to individual texts, in helping decide whether a text is appropriate and what elements to focus on. Free software such as VocabProfile online (www.lexutor.ca/vp) or AntWordProfiler offline (www.antlab.sci.waseda.ac.jp/) allows a teacher to input a text which is then returned with the lexis color-coded according to the frequency of each word in the BNC or COCA corpus. Such information can help with decisions about which items to teach in a given text, for example, ignoring or glossing over less frequent items while using the highly visible multiple occurrences of others as an aid to teaching in context (Cobb 2007).

From the teacher's perspective, corpora can help in deciding what to teach. Often the corpora used for this purpose are not large modern corpora like the BNC or COCA but rather smallish corpora like the Brown (Kučera and Francis 1979), or else purpose-built and sometimes level-appropriate text collections not necessarily meant to be representative of a language in its entirety. Such corpora can be particularly useful in teaching languages for specific purposes where published materials are difficult to come by. Frequency of occurrence and typical usage can be a useful guide, though of course these need to be tempered by pedagogical considerations. Corpora can also provide a useful source of authentic language, as the teacher can select typical language *samples* to complement or replace the invented language *examples* often found in teaching materials (Gavioli 2005: 7). This applies not just to teaching, but also to testing: Stevens (1991) found the use of multiple authentic concordance lines especially beneficial in gap-fill tests, effectively allowing English for specific purposes (ESP) tests to be constructed from authentic rather than made-up language.

Native and non-native teachers can also turn to corpora when they have a language question, as intuition is notoriously unreliable in many cases (even textbook rules are at times quite inadequate descriptions of actual language use; e.g. Carter *et al.* 1998). This can be helpful in correcting work outside the class, but can also serve as an in-class "informant" when responding to unforeseen language points. Where no explanation comes readily to mind, it gives the teacher a way to test intuitions, and an alternative to inventing a spurious rule or simply replying "because" (see Johns 1990). Finally, teachers can use corpus data in similar ways to the manuals outlined above, selecting corpus data (concordance lines, distributions, collocates, clusters, and so on) to create focused activities.

1.3 Learner use

Here we come to the third and final major use of corpora by language learners themselves. Corpus-based learning tasks and activities can be designed along a wide spectrum from "hard" to "soft" (see Gabrielatos 2005), beginning with totally controlled exercises as in the examples above: the teacher can decide the question, query a relevant corpus, and choose the appropriate information, which is then modeled into an activity with focused instructions and closed answers leading to predetermined outcomes. With time, any or all of these decisions and stages can, however, be taken over by learners themselves. The learner querying of corpora involves techniques that are essentially akin to the activities of corpus linguists: "Like a researcher, the learner has to form preliminary hypotheses on the basis of intuition or scanty evidence; those hypotheses then have to be tested and rejected or refined against further evidence, and finally integrated within an overall model" (Johns 1988: 14). Corpus consultation in this manner may focus on learning *per se*, or it may use a corpus as a reference tool alongside dictionaries and other resources in both comprehension and production, especially of written language. In reading, learners can quickly check specific patterns that may not be frequent enough to warrant a mention in dictionaries, or they can access all the occurrences of unknown words or uses in a given text, thus providing more relevant and focused contexts than may be found in a dictionary (Cobb *et al.* 2001). In drafting or revising texts or translations, learners can also check their tentative work against "normal" use in large or specialized corpora (e.g. O'Sullivan and Chambers 2006; Gaskell and Cobb, 2004).

Clearly in its most open-ended form, such activity can be quite demanding on the learner, who is likely to need intensive training or, perhaps preferably, scaffolding during extensive practice over a period of time in order to reap the full benefits of corpus consultation. We therefore need sound theoretical reasons to introduce work of this type, to be clear we are not doing so for contrived reasons (Chambers *et al.* 2004). The basic idea is that massive but controlled exposure to authentic input is of major importance, as learners gradually respond to and reproduce the underlying lexical, grammatical, pragmatic, and other patterns implicit in the languages they encounter. This can be through unconscious habit-formation from a behaviorist/emergentist perspective – see Hoey's (2005) theory of priming, or Taylor's (2012) account of implicit accumulated memories in Mental Corpus theory – or through some element of conscious noticing from a language awareness perspective. Other proposed benefits include the motivation inherent in use of ICT for individualized, relevant purposes where the learners build their knowledge based on their own needs and interests; learner corpus work is thus a generally constructivist and inductive approach to language learning, the discovery and problem-solving procedures favoring cognitive and metacognitive development, critical thinking and noticing skills, language awareness and sensitivity in dealing with authentic text, as well as autonomy and life-long learning (see e.g. Römer 2006: 26; O'Sullivan 2007: 277–278).

All of these would appear to be desirable elements in current applied linguistic thinking. The question of course is whether corpus work really lives up to expectations, with benefits sufficient to justify the investment. For this, we need to look at research to date, which is the purpose of the rest of this chapter. The following section takes an overview of the research field as a whole, then focuses in on a number of studies we have conducted. The subsequent section takes the form of a preliminary meta-analysis in order to assess more broadly the benefits derived (or costs incurred) from the direct use of corpora by learners.

2 Empirical research in L2 corpus use

Getting learners to explore language is nothing new: they are frequently asked to compare example sentences on the blackboard, or identify features of written or spoken texts (Boulton and Tyne 2014). Using corpora merely moves it up a level, increasing the quantity of data available for examination, systematizing the querying procedures and output language, and potentially allowing learners a greater role in the process. According to McEnery and Wilson (1997: 12), the first such uses of corpora go back to the late 1960s at Aston University in Birmingham; other beginnings can be found in ESP courses at the University of Nottingham in the early 1970s (Butler 1974). The first published paper to our knowledge is by McKay (1980) at San Francisco University, describing learner use of printed corpus-based materials; the first description of hands-on concordancing can be found in Ahmad *et al.* (1985) at the University of Surrey. But the approach is largely associated with Tim Johns at the University of Birmingham, where he and other colleagues allowed their students access to COBUILD and other corpora and software in the 1980s for pedagogical purposes (see Johns and King 1991). Since then, there have been tremendous advances: many large corpora are available free on the Web (e.g. bncweb.lancs.ac.uk or corpus.byu.edu), as is software to aid rapid compilation from internet sources in just a few minutes (e.g. bootcat.sslmit.unibo.it), not to mention simple, stable, fast, and free tools with user-friendly interfaces (e.g. www.antlab.sci.waseda.ac.jp), often accompanied by video tutorials and online help.

Most of the early academic publications emanating from all this activity were descriptive and argumentative in nature; the first empirical evaluation comes from Baten *et al.* (1989). A much-lamented paradox of data-driven learning (another term for corpus-based learning) has been the slow appearance of very much research data investigating whether learners do actually benefit from corpus consultation as a part of their language learning (e.g. Flowerdew 2012: 206). There are some reasons for this apparent lack of empirical support (e.g. the long-term nature of some of its goals are hard to operationalize, such as fostering autonomy, noticing, pattern induction, and language awareness). Nonetheless, our consultation of various databases, intensive trawls of individual journals, and serendipitous findings brings together a total of 132 papers which seek to empirically evaluate some aspect of corpus use in foreign or second language (L2) learning and teaching;[1] eliminating duplicates reduces the number to 116 (i.e. where the same study was presented in more than one paper). This is a not inconsiderable body of work.

Of these 116 publications, 76 were published in 36 different journals, 53 of them ranked on the 2011 *European Reference Index for the Humanities* (*ERIH*) lists; 35 were book chapters, some from major publishers, often resulting from thematic conferences (11 include the word *proceedings* in the title); the remainder are "fugitive" literature in the form of unpublished PhDs and working papers. Though they spread from 1989 to 2012, the increasing interest can be seen in that nearly half the papers were published in the last five years. Virtually all the publications are in English; though this might be due in part to search bias, we have only found five in French, which suggests that publications in other languages are likely to be comparatively rare too. About half of the total were conducted within the European Union, and half of the rest in Asia; most were in a foreign language environment, but about a third comprised mixed L1 classes in a second language context. English was the target language in 95 cases, though some feature learners of French (eight studies) or another European language, and in one case Chinese.

Over 100 of the studies are from higher education settings, though only about half seem to feature students majoring in languages (such basic meta-data are often frustratingly missing). There are at present only nine studies in secondary education, and a handful of other contexts such as language schools. Unsurprisingly, perhaps, many of the participants have quite substantial language proficiency: advanced or upper-intermediate in just over half, but lower levels in at least fifty studies. The language objectives generally tend towards the level of vocabulary or lexico-grammar (including clusters and collocations, i.e. word usage in context), but there are attempts to use corpora in learning grammar and syntax, and even occasionally in phonetics or semantics. A recent development is an increase in studies at the level of text, including discourse and critical analysis, genres, sensitivity to text type or sociolinguistic variation. Some go further still, using corpora in courses on literature or cultural studies

[1] References to studies in most of these categories can be found in the meta-analysis that follows. A complete and evolving list can be found in the supplement to Boulton (2010a) at bit.ly/DDLsurvey

with non-native students who thus combine linguistic and non-linguistic uses of corpora.

The Web is used as a corpus in ten studies, whether through a general-purpose search engine (e.g. Google) or a dedicated concordancer (e.g. www.webcorp.org.uk). Large corpora such as the BNC or COCA feature in about a third of all studies, but about half use locally built corpora, especially where the students have specific disciplinary or language needs such as writing research articles. These are sometimes created by the learners themselves, and can comprise as few as 2,000 words. It is worth noting that only 26 studies use corpora that are available free online, which means that many students would not be able to continue their explorations after the end of their courses. Mostly these corpora are explored on computer, only 24 using exclusively or in part printed activities derived from a corpus. WordSmith Tools is used in 18 studies despite its relatively advanced features and interface; AntConc and LexTutor are also popular, and a small number use purpose-built concordancing software.

The study duration varies from just a few minutes in some experimental contexts to a semester or more in five cases; the majority involve part of a course that lasts several hours over a few weeks. There is an average of 40 participants (including control or comparison groups), ranging from case studies with just one participant to quite large-scale studies with 100 or more. This gives rise to considerable methodological heterogeneity, with statistical analysis of quantitative results in 49 studies, raw figures and percentages in 41 more, and the remaining 26 favoring a purely qualitative approach.

This factual description of the work to date can do little more than scratch the surface. The rest of this section presents a small selection of our own empirical studies featuring a variety of research designs and objectives. They provide a flavor of research in this area and prepare the reader for a synthesis of some of the more general outcomes in the section that follows.

2.1 Learning with corpora (Cobb 1997b, 1999b)

This sequence of studies gathers together several of the themes introduced above: it uses an in-house corpus of learners' existing materials and purpose-built concordancing software; it responds to a specific learning need within an ESP context (English for commerce); it involves a mainly semantic analysis of concordance lines over a reasonably longitudinal exposure; and it measures its outcomes in both within- and between-subjects comparisons. It is also one of the earliest confirmations of "measurable learning from hands-on concordancing."

Cobb's (1997b) work with a corpus as a vocabulary learning tool took place in the context of a new university in a developing country (Sultan

Qaboos University, in Oman) that wished to use English as the medium of instruction but whose students were seriously underprepared for such a venture. This was particularly true with regard to the vocabulary needed for academic reading. The students' average vocabulary size was under 1,000 word families, while 3,000 families is typically reckoned a bare minimum (Cobb 2007). The goal of this project was to use corpus and concordance as a way for these students to meet and learn a relatively large number of words, for use in reading comprehension, in a relatively short time. The rationale for using a corpus was that the presence of meta-language could make a purely definitional approach unsuitable, while the shortness of time available would not allow sufficient encounters with new words in context for natural word learning to occur. The corpus was a digitization of all the ESL materials that the students were using to prepare them for forthcoming English-medium study.

A target set of 240 word families was chosen as a 12-week test of a corpus-based approach to word learning. In a within-groups design, 11 learners met 20 new words per week via game-like computer activities that used either concordances or short definitions as an information source, on alternate weeks. A post-test of the 240 new words showed that 75.9 percent of the words met through concordances were retained, but only 63.9 percent of those met via definitions, an advantage for concordancing of more than one standard deviation.

Following this indication that corpus work could help these learners expand their lexicons, a scaled-up version of the project was prepared using two levels of learner, both experimental and control groups, two outcome measures corresponding to experimental and control conditions, and a learning target of 200 new word families per week for twelve weeks (or 2,400 words, roughly the number these learners would need to have a chance of reading for content in English). Experimental subjects used concordances to work with their new words exclusively, inferring meanings from multiple concordance lines and only using a dictionary to confirm their inferences, while controls used the same software but with a bilingual dictionary as the information source.

Weekly and pre–post tests recorded word knowledge on both definitional and novel-text gap-fill measures. It was hypothesized that learning words via concordances would facilitate the gap-fill task. The results showed that both experimental and control groups made significant and substantial pre–post gains on the definitional measures (4 to 8 percent), but only concordancers made significant gains on the novel-text/gap-fill measure. This was true for both lower (13 percent gain) and upper intermediate concordancers (16 percent gain), gains of just under and just over one standard deviation, respectively. Further, a delayed post-test showed that even definitional knowledge was quick to decay for definitional learners, but the opposite was true for concordance learners (reported from different perspectives in Cobb 1999a, b). The advantages for concordance-based vocabulary expansion seem clear, at least in these circumstances, though the generalizability of this finding remains to be determined.

2.2 Types of learning, types of learner (Boulton 2009, 2010b, 2011, 2012b)

As with Cobb, most of Boulton's work with corpora involves students who are not majoring in languages; this particular series of experiments involves first-year architecture students in France. For learners such as these, English classes are compulsory, but are not a major interest nor a priority within their overall degree; consequently, many have relatively low levels of English proficiency and lack inherent motivation for studying the language. Their overt objective for the end of their three-year degree is to attain at least an intermediate level (B1 on the Common European Framework of Reference for Languages); without independent certification for this they cannot graduate – also a source of some resentment. They are, however, intelligent, creative, and autonomous students; the question then was whether a discovery approach might help not only with their level of English but also in their motivation for the language, empowering them in their learning. A major difference with the work by Cobb is that here we were concerned to provide only publicly accessible corpora and tools, namely the BNC and COCA, 100 million and 400 million words of British and American English respectively.

In the first study in this series (Boulton 2010b), 62 learners were given a five-minute introduction to concordancing, then spent thirty minutes working in groups on printed corpus-based materials for five language items (inductively in pairs, feeding back to the whole group), and five others using standard dictionary entries, the instructions being as close as possible between the two groups. These problematic grammar/usage points had been collected from their own written productions earlier in the year, and featured in an earlier pre-test as well as a post-test the following week. The post-test showed significant improvement from both treatments (unlike for five untreated items). Although the improvement was greatest for the experimental treatments, the difference between the two was not significant. The students with lower levels did relatively better using corpora, while the more advanced ones maintained their advantage using the traditional approach. A final questionnaire showed very positive reactions to the experimental treatment. Overall, this study was taken to show that this student body could achieve results at least as good working with concordance lines as with other methods, without substantial training, and more importantly were open to the discovery approach in corpus use, especially those who had been less successful with traditional teaching methods in the past.

A subsequent question was whether such learners could cope with online corpus work. This allows greater learner responsibility and less programmatic input, but also greater room for problems. In this longer-term study (Boulton 2012b), 40 students were again briefly introduced to corpus work, then experienced a variety of corpus activities on problem lexico-grammar points for a few minutes over ten weekly classes, alternating between paper-based and computer-based concordancing activities similar to the within-subjects design in Cobb (1997b) above. A test in the final session gave a small but not significant advantage to paper-based activities, though questionnaires showed the students had a slight preference for computer-based activities. They were generally receptive to hands-on corpus work as a whole, but surprisingly this did not seem to correlate with learning outcomes. A link was found between proficiency and outcomes from the paper-based treatment, but this can be interpreted as meaning computer-based data-driven learning is open to all levels even among these lower-intermediate learners.

In both these studies, the learners were generally receptive to working with corpora, but it was noted that there were quite substantial individual differences, suggesting that corpus work might not be equally appropriate for all learners. In the next study (Boulton 2009), 34 learners experienced hands-on concordancing as part of their class over twelve weeks, and then completed the Index of Learning Styles questionnaire adapted for French (Soloman and Felder 1996). This widely used psychometric instrument assesses respondents on four dimensions: Active–Reflective, Sensing–Intuitive, Visual–Verbal, and Sequential–Global. The objective here was to see if any of these proclivities correlated significantly with receptivity to using corpora, as rated by the participants themselves in a separate questionnaire. Of the learners who had the strongest feelings towards corpus use (positive or negative preference), the only significant correlation was that the most receptive were more likely to have a strong Visual learning style. This is consistent with a smaller pilot study (Boulton 2010c), though that suggested that liking corpus work and doing it well are not necessarily connected: those with an Active learning style achieved better outcomes. Though significant, these correlations are not very large, and the general conclusion is that learners with different learning styles can work successfully and enjoyably with corpora.

The final study was inspired by Allan (2006) and Johns *et al.* (2008), who independently found that corpus work seemed to lead to improved performance not only on targeted language items, but also in other areas. As neither study specifically focused on this, Boulton (2011) focused on noticing ability following corpus work in the same context as the previous studies with both paper-based and hands-on corpus work. At the end of the year, both experimental and control groups were given a short text to read for five minutes, then tested on whether they had noticed a number of language points (focus on form and on meaning) entirely unrelated to any work conducted during the year. The results show the experimental group performing better in noticing than the control group, though the difference did not quite reach statistical significance but suggest it could do in a further better-targeted study.

The questions at the end of this discussion of some reasonably encouraging studies of learning from corpora are: how typical are these research studies? How typical are the results? Do enough of the larger cull of studies have the design criteria and data to support any sort of generalization about outcomes, and if so, what is the generalization? To answer these questions we assemble as much of the learner concordancing research as possible into a preliminary meta-analysis of findings.

3 A meta-analysis of corpus results

This chapter has so far surveyed various uses of corpora for language teaching/learning purposes. This type of "literature review" is common in the introductory sections of research articles, and the effects of corpus use have been the object of several extensive narrative syntheses (e.g. Chambers 2007; Boulton 2010a). This involves selecting the papers to review, deciding on their relative importance, interpreting the results, and putting everything back together to arrive at general conclusions, thus inevitably concealing a substantial degree of subjectivity. It is, however, possible to conduct a more rigorous survey in the form of a meta-analysis, which entails a near-exhaustive collection of studies in a given area (see Norris and Ortega 2006). The quantitative results are combined to provide a statistically meaningful picture over the many different situations covered, which clearly has advantages over the traditional narrative review in that it attempts to systematically reduce the bias inherent in subjective evaluation (Jeon and Kaya 2006), providing a way to "accumulate the results of the studies, the empirical findings, in as objective and data-driven a fashion as is possible" (Ellis 2006: 303). As with corpus linguistics itself, the adage "there's no data like more data" applies, and several non-significant results may, when combined, nevertheless contribute to substantial and significant findings. This methodology allows us to iron out many of the minor flaws in individual studies (assuming that the flaws in each are different); the counterpoint of course is that important differences can be lost, and great care is needed to avoid the trap of identifying the overarching research question with a single figure as a measure of its value.

Rather than providing new experimental data, this part of the chapter provides a preliminary meta-analysis of research in the field so far. For present purposes, the research questions are kept as simple as possible:

- Is corpus use *effective* for L2 learners – i.e. does it have a demonstrable effect?
- Is corpus use *efficient* for L2 learners – i.e. compared to other forms of learning?

While this may appear reductionist to an extent, it does respond to a clear desire on the part of researchers and practitioners to have simple answers to complex questions, and allows us to make some kind of sense of a highly heterogeneous collection of studies as objectively as possible.

3.1 Methodology

The procedures and criteria of meta-analysis in second language acquisition (SLA) are now well established, and the present consideration of the empirical work on integrating corpora in language teaching and learning will follow those of Norris and Ortega (2000) and Spada and Tomita (2010) as much as possible, although in less detail for this preliminary survey of research. The procedure will be to amass the greatest number of research studies with descriptive statistics (and ideally a control group) to calculate their standardized mean differences on the common scale of standard deviation units, or effect size, as measured by Cohen's *d*. This measure of effect size is, simply stated, the difference between two means (whether of the same group pre- and post-treatment, or experimental and control groups after treatment) divided by the combined standard deviation.

When an effect size has been calculated for each study (where this is possible), then a provisional average effect size and standard deviation can be calculated and the overall effect assessed within acceptable confidence limits. Upper and lower confidence intervals can be determined for the range within which the mean should statistically occur 95 percent of the time; if this range does not include zero, then the results can be deemed reliable. All things being equal, the larger the effect size, the more confident we can be that the focus variable is indeed statistically dependable. Traditionally, effect sizes up to $d = .2$ are considered small, $d = .5$ medium, and over $d = .8$ strong (Cohen 1988), though Oswald and Plonsky (2010: 99) suggest revising these up to $d = .4$, $d = .7$, and $d = 1.0$, respectively, to cater for the specificities of research in language teaching/learning.

The data considered here are drawn from the corpus of 116 individual studies described in the previous section. These date from 1989 to 2012, and include journal papers and book chapters, but also PhDs and conference proceedings (published as text and not just slides or oral presentations). Some meta-analyses avoid such "fugitive literature" (Norris and Ortega 2000: 431), but given the likelihood of a smallish number of eligible studies in the present meta-analysis, such studies are included here. However, the aim is not to pass judgment on the quality of individual studies, and all are weighted equally in the meta-analysis itself.

For this preliminary meta-analysis we retained only studies that focused on some kind of broadly defined "outcome" in terms of learning or of performance, in order to include, for example, using concordances as an aid to translation or in retrieving lexical items, which are not strictly speaking learning outcomes. In other words, this meta-analysis investigates whether corpus use can have an effect over a wide range of variables, including vocabulary and grammar learning, error correction, lexical retrieval, and translation success.

Further exclusion criteria are needed for the purposes of a meta-analysis of this type; in particular, only experimental or quasi-experimental studies with a pre/post-test or a treatment/control group design, or both, can provide appropriate comparative data. It should also be noted that few studies assign students randomly to treatment groups, though the intact groups they use may themselves be randomly assigned; and the distinction between control and comparison groups is blurred.

It is precisely this type of quantitative reporting that is likely to be consistent over many studies, thus lending itself to comparison and synthesis. However, application of the exclusion criteria unfortunately means that many valuable qualitative studies cannot be represented – especially regarding such un- or under-operationalized variables like awareness, noticing, and autonomy which, as already mentioned, are difficult or impossible to quantify (Boulton 2012a). Even among the studies reporting quantitative data, essential information is often missing, from group sizes to means, or more frequently standard deviations, which in most cases cannot be calculated from the results. Following application of the exclusion criteria, the final number of papers included in this preliminary meta-analysis is thus reduced to just 21. This proportion of 18.1 percent (21 out of 116) is just over half of Norris and Ortega's 30.8 percent (77 out of 250) and Spada and Tomita's 33.0 percent (34 out of 103), both drawing on the more established research area of mainstream SLA. Where a single study reports several data sets, only the one representing the most relevant or concrete language learning or performance objective is included.

The pre/post-test and experimental/control studies were kept separate for the purposes of analysis, for the reasons outlined below. However, no other variables will be considered at this stage of the meta-analysis, such as participant meta-data (e.g. age, L1, L2, level of proficiency), instructional design (e.g. duration, hands-on or mediated interaction with various corpus types) or experiment design (e.g. immediate or delayed post-test). Many of these outcome types and conditions could be coded and investigated separately as moderating variables in a fuller meta-analysis, but that is beyond the scope of the present chapter. To conclude: while our meta-analysis will depart from the standard model on several points, the basic idea of the meta-analysis model is preserved.

Furthermore, this model is particularly suited to help us understand the state of research in this area, even in its nascent state. That is because studies are particularly vulnerable to the problems inherent in the significance-testing type of research, where the credibility of experiments depends so much on their *n*-sizes (see Norris and Ortega 2000; Ellis 2006), which in this area are often bound by the number of posts in a computer room.

3.2 Results

The 21 studies are summarized in Tables 26.1 and 26.2. These separate within-subject studies (comparing pre- and post-tests) and between-subjects studies (i.e. comparing treatment and control groups), as the different designs tend to produce rather different results. The former show whether the treatment is *effective* (whether or not there is a difference before and after), while the latter show whether the treatment is *efficient* (whether or not there is a difference compared to the comparison group). Since almost any form of instruction is likely to lead to some effect (the main conclusion from Hattie's 2009 meta-analysis of meta-analyses), it is to be expected that the results of a within-groups analysis will be markedly higher than a between-groups analysis. This is indeed precisely what Oswald and Plonsky (2010) found in their survey of 27 meta-analyses in second language acquisition.

The answers to our two main research questions are drawn from the information in Tables 26.1 and 26.2, which show the authors and year of publication in the first column, followed by the essential research focus in simplified form, and then the basic data necessary to calculate the effect size (number of participants, means, standard deviations and pooled standard deviations) for the 21 studies. At the bottom is the combined effect size along with its standard deviation, and the 95 percent confidence intervals.

The mean gain effect size as shown in Table 26.1 is 1.68 standard deviation units (with its own standard deviation (or SD d) of .84, and a reasonably narrow 95 percent confidence interval of 1.36–2.00 (note too that this does not contain 0). This is extremely high even by Oswald and Plonsky's (2010) more exacting limits (strong ≥ 1.0), showing that corpora can be effective in the sense that the results are significantly higher following treatment (see Research Question 1). For Table 26.2, the effect size is predictably somewhat lower at 1.04 (SD d = .73). However, it is still well within the confidence limits (.83–1.25) and can be characterized as "very strong" by conventional estimates, showing that corpus-based learning is more *efficient* than traditional treatments (see Research Question 2).

These effect sizes of 1.69 and 1.04 compare favorably with Norris and Ortega's (2000) average effect size of .96 (SD d = .87; CI = .78–1.14) for focused or explicit L2 instruction, over unfocused or minimally focused instruction. They also compare favorably to Spada and Tomita's (2010) effect sizes of .86 (SE = .14) for the effect of explicit instruction on complex grammatical constructions, and .63 (SD d = .11) for simpler constructions. And they compare particularly favorably with Grgurović *et al.*'s (2013) average effect size for the efficiency of CALL (computer-assisted language learning) over non-CALL of .35 within groups and .24 between groups. In other words, research evidence is stronger for using corpora in language teaching and learning than it is for explicit instruction or for use of computers in language learning.

Table 26.1 *Within-groups effect size (k = 8), sorted by effect size*

			Pre-test		Post-test			
Study	Research question	n	Mean	SD	Mean	SD	Pooled SD	Cohen's d
Chang & Sun 2009	Does scaffolded corpus work improve proof-reading performance?	13	56.15	16.35	91.54	8.26	12.95	2.73
Chan & Liou 2005	Can a bilingual concordancer assist learning of verb–noun collocations?	32	10.59	3.26	19.53	3.95	3.62	2.47
Lin 2008	Does corpus work increase the accuracy rate of academic vocabulary in writing?	25	68.88	3.57	80.64	5.72	4.77	2.47
Moreno Jaén 2010	Do corpus materials improve learners' collo-cational knowledge?	21	48.02	11.18	67.97	11.31	11.25	1.77
Chang 2012	Does corpus work help improve use of stance and move in writing?	7	8.43	3.79	13.57	2.08	3.06	1.68
Cobb 1997a	Does corpus work lead to vocabulary gains?	11	63.90	14.80	75.90	7.10	11.61	1.03
Huang & Liou 2007	Does corpus work help receptive and pro-ductive vocabulary learning?	38	39.00	17.13	49.50	15.41	16.29	0.64
Liou *et al.* 2006	Does corpus work lead to vocabulary gains?	38	39.00	17.13	49.50	15.41	16.29	0.64
					Effect size (mean gain)			**1.68**
					SD *d*			**0.84**
					95% CI lower			**1.36**
					95% CI upper			**2.00**

Table 26.2 *Between-groups effect size ($k = 13$), sorted by effect size*

		Control group			Experimental group				
Study	Research question	n	Mean	SD	n	Mean	SD	Pooled SD	Cohen's d
Stevens 1991[a]	Do multiple concordance lines aid comprehension?	20	49.10	15.00	20	90.00	18.60	16.90	2.42
Supatranont 2005[b]	Does corpus work lead to vocabulary gains?	50	27.46		50	20.04			2.00
Gordani 2012	Does autonomous corpus work have a positive effect on lexical knowledge?	35	17.77	3.37	35	22.97	3.22	3.30	1.58
Johns *et al.* 2008	Does concordancing with a novel lead to improved reading ability?	11	60.00	16.73	11	83.64	13.62	15.25	1.55
Cobb 1999b	Does corpus work lead to vocabulary gains?	12	70.75	12.35	12	86.83	8.90	10.76	1.49
Gan *et al.* 1996	Does corpus work help vocabulary skills development?	24	9.36	2.55	24	13.04	3.16	2.87	1.28
Sun & Wang 2003	Does corpus work help with learning collocation patterns?	40	48.50	21.25	41	65.00	24.57	22.97	0.72
Tian 2005	Is corpus work an effective approach for grammar?	48	67.39	27.13	50	80.52	12.20	21.03	0.62
Rapti 2010	Does corpus work impact the teaching and learning of grammar?	14	48.29	28.59	14	60.89	21.74	25.40	0.50
Boulton 2011	Does corpus work help with noticing skills?	25	18.84	3.78	34	20.50	3.37	3.58	0.46
Kaur & Hegelheimer 2005	Does corpus work lead to correct use of new vocabulary in writing?	9	44.22	12.94	9	49.00	12.12	12.54	0.38
Boulton 2010a[a]	Can learners use corpus worksheets to help with problem items?	62	5.68	1.70	62	6.39	2.10	1.91	0.37
Sripicharn 2003[c]	Does corpus work transfer to new tasks?	22	25.00	5.24	48	25.36	3.80	4.58	0.08
					Effect size (mean difference)				**1.04**
					SD *d*				**0.73**
					95% CI lower				**0.83**
					95% CI upper				**1.25**

[a]Control provided by within-group design.
[b]SDs not given, ES calculated by researchers from original data.
[c]Data combined from two studies.

3.3 Discussion

The overall effect sizes reported here of 1.68 (within subjects) and 1.04 (between subjects) is respectable in educational terms, suggesting not only that corpora can be effective but that they can be efficient compared to other treatments. In other words, the answers to both our research questions (Is corpus use *effective* for L2 learners – i.e. does it have a demonstrable effect? Is corpus use *efficient* for L2 learners – i.e. compared to other forms of learning?) are clearly Yes and Yes, based on the studies available to date. Given the broad sweep of focus in the various primary studies, it seems that corpora can be of benefit to L2 users for a range of purposes: learning and use of language anywhere on the lexico-grammatical continuum (including collocation and idiom) for both receptive and productive purposes, as well as in more extensive reading and writing tasks or in translation. It seems particularly appropriate in the usual problem areas that feature prominently in these studies (i.e. where conventional transmission-based teaching has been found ineffective). It can be useful in both controlled, paper-based work and in more autonomous, hands-on concordancing, and can be suited to both general and specific purposes. The evidence suggests that corpus work is now ready to expand beyond the university ESP class, where it has largely been used to date, into mainstream second and foreign language learning – where, of course, its effects can continue to be investigated and the conditions of its success elaborated.

Yet, inevitably, a note of caution must be added. Attaching a single figure to a meta-analysis helps to make sense of a body of research with limited risk of bias or subjectivity, provides a convenient yardstick by which to gauge individual studies past and future, and may be politically expedient for attracting interest to the area (see Grgurović *et al.* 2013: 2). On the downside, it may lead some to suppose that this is the final word, and that no future research is necessary. However, quite the opposite is the case (Norris and Ortega 2006: 10–11).

First, in the meta-analysis presented here, we have attempted only a preliminary study, and further work would be required to come to more reliable conclusions. In particular, it is essential to note the variation within the studies, which by no means all produce the same results: the details are as important as the major findings (Ellis 2006: 308). A "wish list" for a fully fledged meta-analysis would include a more principled and extensive trawl of papers from databases and other journals, as well as more fugitive literature; better coding for each paper to see more easily what they have (or do not have) in common, and developing this for more rigorous inclusion/exclusion criteria; weighting the studies according to their design; combining effect sizes where more than one is provided in a given study, and allowing more than one effect from the same study where the population samples are different; teasing out more data from studies which include t-scores or F-scores, for example. Graphic displays should further help to visualize the variation in effect sizes between individual studies, and maybe suggest leads as to what the biggest effect sizes have in common and, conversely, what subvariables are most worth following up.

Finally, and perhaps most importantly, our aim here is to suggest avenues for future work. This includes areas that are underrepresented at the present time. First, in terms of research focus, we would hope the future would bring more discourse-level studies with a focus on text and associated features of genre, stance, etc., to complement the current dominance of studies on lexis and specific grammar points. It will be interesting to see what multimodal or multimedia corpora can bring to the table, and their impact on speaking and listening skills. The ways corpora are used and integrated are also in need of further study: how do controlled, teacher-led corpus tasks compare with the type of more serendipitous, independent hands-on corpus work traditionally associated with Johns' data-driven learning? And how do these relate to learner profiles (such as motivations, styles, or levels of proficiency), i.e. are there some learners for whom corpus work is more or less suitable? Perhaps most strikingly in need of study are the longer-term or secondary effects of regular concordance work on language awareness and sensitivity, autonomy, motivation, noticing, and other cognitive and metacognitive skills, and so on; their virtual absence in the studies covered here is no doubt due in large measure to the difficulty of assessing such features over time.

Second, in terms of study design, we would hope for more longitudinal studies with delayed post-tests to balance the short-term focus on very specific target items often found in the work reviewed here. We would strongly encourage the authors of studies to publish their results whatever the outcomes, as experience suggests that many conference presentations in particular are subject to the "file-drawer" problem where they elicit undesired or non-significant results – of all the studies included here, only Boulton (2011) admits to not showing a significant *p*-value. And we would very much hope that empirical research will become steadily more rigorous, with the use of true control or comparison groups, more regular reporting of the essential meta-data (even L1, group size, duration, etc. are missing on occasion), descriptive statistics (means and especially standard deviations), and more extensive use of inferential statistics. Indeed, it has become traditional to conclude works of meta-analysis with a scolding about sloppy research and an exhortation to do better in future (e.g. Norris and Ortega 2000: 497–498), at least in research domains that have been long established and should have more to show for a large amount of effort expended and a large number of studies published. In a newish domain such as ours, a nudge for more, more differentiated, and yet also more replicated, and in all cases better-reported studies is probably sufficient.

4 Conclusion

Corpora have found many uses in the field of language teaching and learning in the hands of decision-makers, teachers, and learners. Published research covers classroom applications for a wide variety of learner profiles and for extremely different uses, from highly controlled to entirely autonomous work, from paper-based materials to hands-on concordancing, from reference resource to learning tool. This variety underlines the highly flexible role of corpora – there is no single "right" way to use them. From a research perspective, this may lead to a perceived fragmentation of the field, which a thorough meta-analysis may go some way to resolving.

The meta-analysis as a research form is by definition exploratory rather than confirmatory, starting from questions (to be explored) rather than hypotheses (to be confirmed or denied). Of course, few researchers, meta-analysts or otherwise, would deny hoping that their questions would be answered in a certain way, and take steps to ensure objectivity. In the survey presented here, we were gratified to uncover a measure of confirmation from research to date that corpora have been not only effective in language teaching and learning, but also efficient, insofar as they produce fairly regular advantages of a standard deviation or more over other methods of achieving the same goals. Our meta-analysis is only exploratory; further work will be needed to exploit current research fully, especially in exploring the mediator variables that are likely to be worth investigating.

The synthesis presented in this chapter has shown that there is more research in the area than sometimes claimed, but of highly varying rigor both for qualitative and especially quantitative studies. Further, the questions addressed, though varied, tend towards the short-term and experimental with a focus on specific language items; more longitudinal, ecological, open-ended studies are needed, especially addressing the alleged benefits of corpus work in promoting learning to learn and, consequently, in producing "better learners."

A final word. Traditional corpus consultation is in some ways a relatively marginal activity, to be found in few classrooms around the world. However, it is in many ways analogous with internet searches and use of other technologies for querying the vast stores of data available, which has arguably become the dominant learning mode in our culture. Learners regularly Google up internet-as-corpus data to help with collocations, grammar choices, and many other matters, particularly in their writing (see Boulton, in press). Indeed "Googling" is largely an invention of corpus linguists (Crystal 2012) and the majority of internet users are busy becoming knowledge co-constructors from corpus data. This, of course, is definitely *not* to say that all search-based learning is accurate, permanent or worthwhile – far from it – in language learning or any other area. That is why research is needed to show us how to take best advantage. How much training is needed? How much ongoing scaffolding? Are certain learning or personal styles favored or disfavored? How is the success of such learning best measured? What is the ideal complementarity between search-based and other forms of instruction? We now see that these questions are central rather than peripheral to language learning; and in our meta-analysis we have seen that ways of answering them are under development.

27

Corpus versus non-corpus-informed pedagogical materials: grammar as the focus

Fanny Meunier and Randi Reppen

Introduction

In 2000, TESOL Quarterly published an article by Susan Conrad titled "Will corpus linguistics revolutionize grammar teaching in the 21st century?" Conrad argued that three changes prompted by corpus-based studies of grammar had "the potential to revolutionize the teaching of grammar" (2000: 549): first, monolithic descriptions of English grammar would be replaced by register-specific descriptions; second, the teaching of grammar would become more integrated with the teaching of vocabulary; and third, the emphasis would shift from structural accuracy to the appropriate conditions of use for alternative grammatical constructions. The article also ended with a number of thought provoking questions, viz. whether or not corpus-based research had reached the right audiences; how research applications were presented; how and how much corpus research had been incorporated into materials; and finally, how teachers reacted to the use of corpus research.

The present chapter aims to check whether the changes predicted by Conrad have actually taken place and how exactly they have materialized in pedagogical materials. Section 1 presents some of the key issues in the writing of corpus-informed materials. In Section 2, we briefly present eight grammar textbooks (four corpus-informed and four non-corpus-informed); these textbooks are analyzed with a view to finding out the similarities and differences between these two types of materials and to answering the research questions presented in the introduction. We carry out a more in-depth analysis of two of the four research questions listed above, namely how corpus-based research applications are presented, and how (and how much) corpus-based research has been incorporated into materials. As numerous corpus studies have investigated the passive, we have selected that topic as a candidate for the comparison of corpus-informed versus non-corpus-informed pedagogical materials. Some suggestions for the future are presented in the concluding section.

1 Creating corpus-based/corpus-informed materials: some key issues

1.1 Terminology

On his "Bookmarks for Corpus-based Linguists" page,[1] David Lee writes that one of the reasons why he uses the CBL (i.e. corpus-based linguistics) acronym is to put the focus on linguistics and adds that "what we primarily do is 'linguistics': it just happens to be corpus-based, or 'corpus-driven,' 'corpus-informed,' whatever you want to call it." Whilst several labels are indeed found in the literature, and are sometimes considered as relatively synonymous (as exemplified by Lee's quote), we have a preference for the term corpus-informed when it comes to referring to pedagogical materials. Linguistic research can be corpus-based or corpus-driven (or a mix of the two). In a corpus-driven approach the corpus serves as an empirical basis from which researchers extract their data and detect linguistic phenomena without [too many] [*our addition*] prior assumptions and expectations (Tognini-Bonelli 2001). The conclusions are drawn exclusively on the basis of corpus observations. In a corpus-based approach, in contrast, linguistic information (frequencies, collocations, etc.) is extracted from a corpus to check expectations or confirm linguistic theories. In most cases, researchers motivated by a research question about a particular aspect of language use or a particular structure, use a combination of both corpus-driven and corpus-informed approaches when analyzing a corpus. As the writing of pedagogical materials demands that pedagogical decisions be taken, we find the "corpus-informed" label more appropriate as it encompasses:

- the inclusion of results, conclusions, discoveries from research carried out on a variety of corpora (e.g. native or learner corpora, spoken or written, from different genres, produced by expert or novice writers/speakers);
- the selection of what exactly should be included (e.g. structures, vocabulary, contexts of use, collocational and colligational patterns, frequency);
- the decisions linked to the presentation of the corpus information (e.g. text, graphs, concordances, data-driven approach, other);
- and, when the materials focus on skills, the selection of suitable texts (oral or written) as a prompt for instruction.

[1] www.uow.edu.au/~dlee/CBLLinks.htm

1.2 Authenticity

Numerous studies have stressed the need to include authentic (use-based) lexico-syntactic features of language in language-teaching materials. The importance of specifying contextual and register or genre specificities has also been put forward as a key factor in the acquisition of communicative competence, both receptively and productively (e.g. Gilmore 2007 and 2011; Mukherjee and Rohrbach 2006; Römer 2006; Friedman 2009).

When it comes to instructed second language acquisition, however, the use of authentic vs. simplified/didacticized materials is still hotly debated, with some arguing that authenticity is key to language teaching (Römer 2005 suggests that texts included in textbooks should mirror the frequencies and uses of present progressives in native-speaker corpora), others presenting the pros of simplified/didactized materials (e.g. Illes 2009; Widdowson 2003), and others adopting a more balanced view stressing the need for authentication above that of authenticity (e.g. Mishdan 2004; Belz and Vyatkina 2008). Instead of adopting a dichotomous approach or arguing for or against a specific type of materials, we would suggest a more integrated/holistic view and follow Bündgens-Kosten (2013: 272), who considers authenticity as "the result of a social negotiation process rather than an innate feature of a text, object, person, or activity." Although the article focuses on computer-aided language learning (CALL), the author distinguishes between three domains of authenticity that we consider relevant to our research: authenticity through language (linguistic authenticity), authenticity through origin (cultural authenticity), and authenticity through daily life experiences (functional authenticity).

In favor of the use of fully authentic texts as input texts is the fact that linguistic authenticity is de facto guaranteed (on the condition, however, that the texts be truly representative of the particular genre that is being tackled); in favor of the use of simplified/didactized materials as input texts is the fact that learning can be better scaffolded according to learners' levels and also the fact that contrived texts/dialogues can incorporate natural discourse features. Throughout this debate the fact that learners should aim at a good level of linguistic authenticity in their communicative competence is much more consensual.

Although the debate on authenticity will no doubt continue, no publisher, teacher, or learner would claim that linguistic inauthenticity is a learning goal. As an attempt to consider how corpus research can be incorporated into materials to reflect authenticity we propose a number of ways in which corpus research can be used to inform materials. These factors will be influenced by several considerations including: the communicative or linguistic skill(s) being taught (e.g. speaking, reading, vocabulary, grammar), the proficiency level of the students and the course content (i.e. is this a general English course or an ESP course?). Considering these factors, we propose that corpus research can be used to inform materials development in the following ways:

- in helping select the linguistic target features (e.g. vocabulary, lexico-grammar; grammar);
- the amount of space in the text devoted to the features;
- in the sequencing of materials;
- through the inclusion of actual corpus data (e.g. lists of vocabulary or common lexico-grammar patterns);
- through the inclusion of information on register differences (e.g. conversation and academic prose);
- in the selection of the texts used in examples (e.g. do the texts accurately reflect the use of the target feature?).

1.3 Accessing linguistic authenticity: the use of corpora

Representing, explaining, or describing linguistic authenticity has been made possible through the use of corpus analysis. Linguistic descriptions have shown that intuition is often unreliable when it comes to matters related to patterns of language use. Linguistic descriptions based on both large comprehensive corpora and descriptions of specialized corpora have greatly contributed to knowledge of the linguistic characteristics of language use across different situations and production circumstances. When it comes to grammar, Quirk *et al.*'s 1985 *Comprehensive Grammar of the English Language* was probably the first grammar to use corpus data (i.e. the London–Lund Corpus) in a systematic way. Biber's work on variation across speech and writing (see 1988 and subsequent publications) has paved the way for the use of complex computational techniques to analyze the linguistic characteristics of spoken and written genres, and to facilitate the identification of basic, underlying dimensions of variation in English (see also Chapters 14, 16, and 17 this volume for more information on how corpus analysis can help uncover linguistic authenticity through frequency, context, colligational patterns, genre and registers, form–meaning pairings/mappings, pragmatic appropriacy, etc.).

In the last decade there has been a significant increase in corpus-informed teaching materials. Meunier and Gouverneur (2008) write that corpora have found their way to the offices of major ELT publishers and that the use of corpora has even become a selling point (special logos to advertise corpus-based publications) and publishers explain how the use of corpora helps them present real, authentic English as it is "really used," as it is "written and spoken now." Less explicit in the publishers' discourse, however, is a clear description of the corpus analysis carried out to decide what information to present, be it quantitatively or qualitatively.

In Sections 2.1. to 2.4., we first introduce and briefly describe four corpus-informed grammar (text)books: the *Longman Student Grammar of Spoken and Written English* (Biber, Conrad, and Leech 2002), *Real Grammar* (Conrad and Biber 2009), *English Grammar Today* (Carter, McCarthy, Mark, and O'Keeffe 2011), and the *Grammar and Beyond* series (Blass, Iannuzzi, Savage, and Reppen 2012). We then also present four non-corpus-informed textbooks (Sections 2.5. to 2.8.) which will be used as comparative materials for the case study on the passive (Section 3).

2 Review of grammar materials

In this section we first review four corpus-informed ELT grammar "books" which we consider as representative of current corpus-informed materials. We use the generic term "book" on purpose as the titles we have selected are not homogeneous in type, with some being closer to reference grammars, some others to pedagogical grammars, while the last type deals with grammar integrated with other language skills (reading, writing, etc.). This choice of books that are not all meant for the same audiences, nor have the same purposes, naturally implies that differences are to be expected in terms of granularity, precision, and amount of grammatical metalanguage used, and also in the actual structure of the books or space devoted to specific grammatical topics. These differences notwithstanding, we opted for variety rather than homogeneity of material types as this variety is more representative of the impact of corpus research on teaching materials. We decided to choose books which were aimed at upper-intermediate to advanced learners of English. In addition to the corpus-informed books, we will also review four popular non-corpus-informed grammar books at this same upper-intermediate to advanced level. These are: *Understanding and Using English Grammar*, 4th edition,[2] international edition (Azar and Hagen 2009); *Focus on Grammar*, 4th edition (Fuchs and Bonner 2011); *Grammar in Context*, 5th edition (Elbaum 2009); and *Grammar Dimensions*, 4th edition (Wisniewska 2009). We will then compare the two types of materials (corpus-informed vs. non-corpus-informed) through a case study of the presentation of the passive to find out the similarities and differences in the treatment of that topic in the two types of materials, and to see how corpus findings have been included in corpus-based materials. A brief summary of each book is provided below.

[2] The Azar book series is not initially known for being corpus-based. However, there is a short note in the introduction to the fourth edition which specifies that the edition contains corpus-informed content (2009: xi): "Based on the findings of our corpus researcher, Gena Bennett, grammar content has been added, deleted, or modified to reflect the discourse patterns of spoken and written English." However, clear indications are missing as to which corpus has been used.

2.1 *The Longman Student Grammar of Spoken and Written English* (*LSG*), (Biber, Conrad, and Leech 2002)

The *LSG* is based on research carried out on the *Longman Spoken and Written English* corpus (LSWE). It is described as a pedagogical grammar for students and their teachers. It is based on the *Longman Grammar of Spoken and Written English* (*LGSWE*, Biber *et al.* 1999). The authors (three of the five original authors of the *LGSWE*) have simplified and reorganized its content to avoid much technical detail and to make it accessible to students and teachers. Similarly to the *LGSWE*, the *LSG* contains over 3,000 authentic examples of English (often simpler examples and extracts than those included in *LGSWE*) and contrasts the major patterns of use in spoken and written registers. Some examples have been truncated to save space (and those are marked with the *t* symbol). The book begins with the basics in the opening chapters, and moves progressively into more advanced territory. It ends with a chapter devoted to the special characteristics of conversational grammar. A glossary of grammatical terms and an index are also provided. The *LSG* does not contain any exercises or activities for students; these are all found in the accompanying workbook.

2.2 *Real Grammar* (*RG*) (Conrad and Biber 2009)

Like the *LSG* described above, *Real Grammar* (*RG*) is based on research carried out on the *Longman Spoken and Written English* corpus (LSWE). This supplemental resource is intended for advanced students to use as a self-study book or in class as a supplement to grammar instruction. The fifty units can be used in any order and provide students with contextualized practice for the target grammar features. Register plays a central role in the presentation and practice of the target grammar features. Each unit is coded for its use in spoken or written contexts. All of the examples and texts used in the exercises come from the corpus used in the analyses. In the note to the teacher (p. ix), the authors explain modifications that were made. For example, difficult vocabulary was replaced with a simpler form, but one that maintained the same part of speech. Extremely long or complex sentences were modified by removing certain elements such as optional adverbials. In the conversation examples, false starts and excessive fillers were removed. Lists of frequent forms are presented as in Unit 3's presentation of common discovery verbs used in the present perfect in academic writing (p. 7).

2.3 *English Grammar Today* (*EGT*) (Carter, McCarthy, Mark, and O'Keeffe 2011)

English Grammar Today (*EGT*) is described as a guide to contemporary English grammar and usage. It is supported by a practical Workbook for grammar practice and comes with a CD-ROM which provides access to the book content, 200 additional grammar explanations in a fully searchable format, and audio recordings for all examples and dialogues. It is organized into an A–Z structure. Many of the examples included in the book come from the *Cambridge International Corpus* (CIC), which contains written and spoken text from different national varieties of English (e.g. British, Irish, American) and genres (newspapers, popular journalism, advertising, letters, literary texts, debates and discussions, service encounters, university tutorials, formal speeches, friends talking in restaurants, families talking at home). The emphasis is on standard modern British English but differences between British and American English are discussed. Whilst mostly informed by corpus research, the guidance to English grammar use and understanding is also informed by the authors' and their colleagues' own experience as teachers of English. Some of the entries contain (usually at the end of the entry) information about the typical errors made by learners and those errors come from the *Cambridge Learner Corpus*. The target audience is described as intermediate learners of English at the B1–B2 levels of the Common European Framework of Reference for Languages (CEFR).

2.4 *Grammar and Beyond* (*G&B*), level 3 (Blass, Iannuzzi, Savage, and Reppen 2012)

Grammar and Beyond (G&B) is a recent contextualized grammar series with a strong emphasis on practice. As is the case for the previously described book, it is based on research and analysis of the *Cambridge International Corpus* (CIC) and the *Cambridge Learner Corpus* (CLC). Words from the Academic Word List (Coxhead 2000) that are used in *G&B* texts are included in an appendix. *G&B* has four levels. We have selected level 3 as it is meant for high intermediate students (levels B1–B2 of the CEFR). The emphasis is on modern North American English as it is actually spoken and written. It identifies and teaches differences between the grammar of spoken and written English and focuses more attention on the structures that are commonly used. The book is also informed by experienced classroom teachers and reading and writing topics that will naturally elicit examples of the target grammar structure have been included in the book.

2.5 *Understanding and Using English Grammar* (*UUEG*), 4th edition, international edition (Azar and Hagen 2009)

Understanding and Using English Grammar (*UUEG*) is a developmental skills textbook for intermediate to advanced English language learners. The book is divided into twenty core chapters (each representing a grammar point) and an appendix including seven smaller units (e.g. grammar terminology, contractions, or troublesome verbs). It uses a grammar-based approach but also promotes the development of all language skills. It contains warm-up exercises for each grammar point, grammar charts, and grammar exercises, but also some listening, reading, and expanding speaking activities.

2.6 *Focus on Grammar* (*FoG*), 4th edition (Fuchs and Bonner 2011)

Focus on Grammar (*FoG*) is a five-level series. In addition to a student book and workbook, other resources are also available, including: audio files, an online component for additional practice, placement and achievement tests, and test-generating software. The series focuses on grammar, but includes all skills. After presentation, the target grammar features are practiced in a range of contexts to help students master the form and use of the target structure. Practice moves from controlled practice to more open-ended activities. For our case study we have selected level 4 since it is designed for high intermediate-level students.

2.7 *Grammar in Context* (*GiC*), 5th edition (Elbaum 2009)

Grammar in Context (*GiC*) is a three-level grammar series. In addition to extensive controlled practice it includes information about American culture. Level 2 was used in our case study. This level has fourteen units. Units are theme based and use an integrated skills approach.

2.8 *Grammar Dimensions* (*GD*), 4th edition (Wisniewska 2009)

In addition to presenting grammar, each unit in *Grammar Dimensions* (*GD*) has sections focusing on form, meaning, and use. This three-prong approach provides a contextualized presentation of the grammar forms. This same focus drives the integrated practice in each unit. All four skills are addressed and practiced in context in this series. For the case study, we selected Level 2 from this four-level series.

3 The case study: corpus-informed vs. non-corpus-informed treatment of the passive in grammar textbooks

3.1 Overall comparison

In this section we analyze the treatment of the passive in the four corpus-informed books and four non-corpus-informed grammar books presented in Section 2. Our aim in comparing those two types of grammar books is twofold, viz. to find out the similarities and differences between these materials, and see which corpus findings have been included in corpus-informed materials. To do so, we have opted for a case study approach and have chosen to work on the passive. This topic has been extensively researched in corpus studies and, therefore, much is known about the use and also the lexical associations of the passive. We designed a checklist to help us compare the materials. The first column lists items based on knowledge that has been accumulated in the past ten years from research on the passive. The checklist for corpus-informed materials will be presented first and will then be followed by the non-corpus materials one. Intermediate conclusions will be provided after each checklist and general conclusions will be given in Section 4.

Granger (2013) recaps the findings of native corpus-based studies devoted to the passive. She mainly refers to Svartvik's (1966) study of written registers and to a similar study she conducted (Granger 1983) on spoken registers. She also uses Biber's (1988) multidimensional analysis of variations in spoken and written English, and Biber *et al.* (1999) and Gries and Stefanowitsch (2004) for collostructional information. The key results that she refers to are the following:

- 80–90 percent of the passives are agentless;
- *get*-passives are rare;
- the frequency of use of the passive is subject to strong register associations with the highest rate of passives found in academic/scientific writing and the lowest in informal conversation;
- there are strong associations between active–passive constructions and lexical choices with some verbs displaying strong passive attraction or repulsion.

In the same article Granger (2013: 12) also presents the major findings of a detailed analysis she carried out of "the passive sections in 11 recent pedagogical grammars for higher intermediate/advanced learners of English." Her main conclusion is that "corpus-based studies of the passive have had relatively little impact on pedagogical grammars." More specifically, she finds that in most pedagogical grammars:

- the information on the dominance of the agentless passive, whilst mentioned, is usually backgrounded;
- the *get*-passive tends to be presented as very frequent and interchangeable with the *be*-passive;
- register preferences are either totally absent or given very cursory treatment;
- lexical aspects are nearly always presented negatively as lists of verbs that cannot passivize (and the examples are sometimes surprising as they include structures rarely found in learner language, such as *A nice house is had by them*, *I'm fitted by my shoes*, or *Tact is lacked by your mother*, which are found in Swan (2005).

We have decided to check the issues listed above in the eight grammar books that we have selected to see if we find the same patterns as Granger. General tables will first be presented, with a view to highlighting general trends in terms of overall structure and contents. Basically, this will help

Table 27.1 *The passive in four corpus-informed grammar books*

Corpus-informed passive	*RG*	*EGT*	*G&B*	*LSG*
Dominance of the agentless passive mentioned	Y	Y	*Briefly*	
mentioned	Y			
Get-passive as infrequent	N/A **Comments** The focus is the use of the passive in writing so GET is not mentioned, since it is not common in academic writing	Y	Y	Y
Register preferences indicated	Y	Y	Y	Y
Lexical information (e.g. common vocab patterns)	Y	Y	Y	Y
Contextualized examples	Y	In passing (but more is in the workbook)	Y	In passing
Integrated practice within skills[a]	Y	N	Y	N
Learner corpus data (typical errors, etc.) included	In passing	Some treatment in the workbook	Y	N

[a] This feature has been added as it will be further exploited in the qualitative analysis (Y = yes, N = no, N/A = non-applicable)

us answer the following question: do "corpus-informed" and more traditional grammar books present different types of descriptions of one and the same grammatical feature?

We will then provide more details on exactly which type of information is presented in the corpus-informed books, but also how is it presented. In 2008, Meunier and Gouverneur stated that publishers seem to acknowledge the importance of corpora in ELT but fail to give precise information on how exactly the corpus is used. A more qualitative analysis (Section 3.2.) will help us answer those questions.

Although not part of the checklist, it is worth pointing that all the books covered offer sections on how to form the passive (typical structure, various tenses, etc.). They also include a discussion on the main reasons for using a passive structure (e.g. agent unknown or not interesting). The number of pages devoted to the passive varies from one book to another but, as explained in Section 2, as the books are not fully comparable in types, we will not comment on that aspect here.

What the checklist reveals is that some corpus-based information is rather coherent across the various books (*get*-passives are rare and are more commonly found in speech; agentless passives are more frequent than passives with *by*-agent, etc.). When lexical preferences are mentioned, however, there are differences in the degree to which these are covered. For example, the number of verbs mentioned as frequent in the passive varies greatly (from 4 to 46).

Another difference (which is due to the inherent variety of the books selected) is the integration, or lack thereof, of the grammatical topic with(in) skills. The integration of learner corpus data (and use of error correction exercises) is another case in point. Apart from *G&B*, which presents error correction exercises as one of the key features of the approach adopted, most books either avoid that aspect completely (*LSG*), or only refer to errors in passing.

We will now turn to Table 27.2 which summarizes the treatment of the passive in non-corpus-informed textbooks.

Table 27.2 *The passive in four non-corpus-informed grammar books*

Non-corpus-informed passive	*Understanding and Using English Grammar*	*Focus on Grammar*	*Grammar in Context 2*	*Grammar Dimensions 2*
Dominance of the agentless passive mentioned	Y	Mentioned briefly	Mentioned briefly	Y
Get-passive as infrequent	N	N/A Comments: *Get*-passives are not mentioned	N/A Comments: *Get*-passives are not mentioned	In passing Comments: States that *get*-passive is more common in conversation but nothing about it being relatively rare
Register preferences indicated	Mentioned briefly	N	N	Y
Lexical information (e.g. common vocab patterns)	In passing	N	Somewhat Comments: Gives a list of verbs that cannot occur in the passive	N
Contextualized examples	Minimally	Y	Y	Y
Integrated within skills	Y	Y	Minimally	Y
Learner corpus data (typical errors, etc.) included	N	N	N	N

(Y = yes, N = no, N/A = non applicable)

Table 27.3 *Comparison of the responses per category in Tables 27.1 and 27.2*

	Table 27.1 – corpus-informed	Table 27.2 – non-corpus-informed
Yes	19 (68%)	9 (32%)
No	3 (11%)	9 (32%)
Mixed	6 (21%)	10 (36%)
Total	*28*	*28*

The results for non-corpus-informed books are radically different from those obtained in Table 27.1. As can be seen from Table 27.2, only a minority of clear *Yes* were found (9 out of a possible total of 28; versus 19/28 for corpus-informed books). Table 27.3 compares the number of answers per category in the two tables.

Granger's (2013) conclusion that corpus-based studies of the passive have had relatively little impact on pedagogical grammars is thus confirmed for the non-corpus-informed books that we have selected in our study (which, apart from one book, were different from those in Granger's study). Non-corpus-informed pedagogical grammars fail to include important information on the passive.

Granger's results are, however, disconfirmed for the corpus-informed materials as we obtained a clear *Yes* for almost 70 percent of the cells on the checklist. There nonetheless remains room for improvement as 11 percent of the cells received a negative evaluation.

Non-corpus-informed materials slightly outperform corpus-informed materials on two fronts: the contextualization of the examples (in 3 cases out of 4, versus 2 out of 4 for corpus-informed books) and the integration of grammar within skills (in 3 cases out of 4, versus 2 out of 4 in corpus-informed books). This said, the new generation of corpus-informed grammar books also works toward integrating grammar in a more holistic and communicative skills-based approach.

A rather surprising result for us was the fact that none of the non-corpus-informed books dealt with errors. The fact that information from learner corpora was absent was to be expected, but much less so was the total absence of focus on errors.

3.2 A more qualitative analysis: zooming in on lexical information and exercises

In this section, we will carry out a more in-depth and qualitative analysis of one of the features that distinguish corpus-informed from non-corpus-informed ones, i.e. the inclusion of lexical information. Analysis will also be provided on the types of exercises presented in the textbooks and some of the accompanying workbooks. Due to limitations of space, not all aspects will be addressed for all the books but we will zoom in on a number of focal illustrations.

Lexical information

Vocabulary is an important cornerstone of language learning and proficiency. During the last decade we have become more aware of the intimate relationship between vocabulary and grammar. The passive is no exception to this. Lexical information is one area where the corpus-informed books have a clear advantage over the non-corpus-informed books. Corpus-informed books can provide accurate lists of verbs that are frequent in the passive based on information found in corpora. These books can also provide information on lexical relationships including: prepositions that are frequent with the passive (e.g. *be associated with*, *be composed of*); passive verbs that are common with a non-human *by*-phrase (e.g. *Real Grammar*: 50). These all highlight the relationship between lexis and grammar and are useful to a language learner.

Exercises

Authors of corpus-informed materials stress the importance of using authentic and "real" language, thereby providing the learners with linguistic authenticity (see Section 1.2). Through the types of exercises included, it is also possible to assess the two other types of authenticity presented by Bündgens-Kosten (2013), namely authenticity through origin (cultural authenticity), and authenticity through daily life experiences (functional authenticity). We would also like to add the notion of pedagogic task authenticity, defined by Breen (1987: 23) as "any structured language learning endeavor which has a particular objective, appropriate content, a specified working procedure, and a range of outcomes for those who undertake the task." As Joy (2011: 14) puts it, in such cases, we deviate from the "reality jinx in order to facilitate better learning conditions" and even if the activities do not represent an authentic purpose at the micro level, they are intended to help students master the language for future communicative demands.

We have analyzed the place devoted to exercises on the basis of the number of exercises (and exercise items) and the types of exercises proposed. Table 27.4 summarizes the various results for the corpus-informed books.

Depending on their audience and aims, some textbooks devote much more space to exercises than others (see, for instance, *G&B* with 21 exercises vs. the *LSG* 4 exercises). The various columns describing the types of exercises are not mutually exclusive. For instance, an exercise can include both focus on form aspects and discussions on contexts of use (which consequently means that the total percentages in columns 4 to 8 can exceed 100 percent if one adds up all the categories). Focus on form exercises still constitute an important proportion (minimum one-third of the exercises) with some including at least some sort of focus on form (e.g. identification

Table 27.4 *Exercises on the passive in the four corpus-informed books*

	No. of pages referring to the passive[a] in book	Overall no. of exercises	Exs relating to form	Exs relating to context of use	Error correction exs	Passive to active switch	Active to passive switch	No. of exercises with textual coherence (i.e. no isolated and unrelated sentences	Origin of exercise sentences
RG	9	10	7/10 (70%)	8/10 (80%)	0	1/10 (10%)	2/10 (20%)	5/10 (50%)	All authentic
EGT	13	13 77 ex. items	4/13 (31%)	3/13 (23%)	1/13 (8%)	2/13 (16%)	3/13 (23%)	4/13 (31%)	Unknown
G&B	29	21 118 ex. items + 4 skills-oriented exercises	10/21 (48%)	8/21 (38%)	4/21 (19%)	1/21 (5%)	4/21 (19%)	21/21 (100%)	Some authentic / some unknown
LSG(+workbook)	38	4 17 ex. items	4/4 (100%)	3/4 (75%)				2/4 (50%)	All authentic (corpus ref)

[a] Keywords used for the search in the index: passive/passive voice/passives and . . . (verbs, forms, typical errors, etc.)

of the form) in all the exercises. Despite some differences in percentages, all the books also include exercises relating to the context of use of the passive (up to 75 percent for the *LSG*).

When it comes to textual coherence (understood here as exercises which do not contain isolated and unrelated sentences), we note marked differences between the books, with *EGT* featuring only one-third of the exercises with textual coherence and *G&B* offering 100 percent of exercises displaying textual coherence (even if in some exercise sentences are numbered individually, they form a text or relate to one coherent topic).

G&B is the only book which includes exercises integrating focus on form and skills (listening, writing, discussing). It is also the only one which regularly[3] proposes error correction exercises (including self-editing ones).

Almost all the books include exercises that ask students to contrast the forms being presented. Most of the time those involve rewriting exercises from active to passive. Two of the exercises proposed by *EGT* did, however, strike us as being particularly unnatural. In exercise 4, students are presented with five sentences in the passive and are asked to rewrite the underlined sections as active voice forms using the words given in brackets as subjects of the sentence:

- e.g.: "Can you believe how much footballers <u>are paid</u> these days"? (they . . .)
- expected answer: "Can you believe how much they pay footballers these days?"

If the exercise can help students better master the shift from one voice to another, the validity of the answer can be debated as the active form does not sound particularly better. Exercise 5 is the reverse type of exercise (i.e. students are asked to rewrite newspaper headlines presented in the active form as full passive sentences):

- e.g. "Major bank announces 200 job losses."
- expected answer: "200 job losses have been announced by a major bank."

Here again, whilst we agree that newspapers usually contain more passive forms than some other text types and that many learners (who often underuse the passive) need practice in using passive sentences, we feel that the exercise presented here might be counterproductive. As was the case for exercise 4, the expected answer does not come out as being a very natural/authentic option for a newspaper headline.

As mentioned earlier, the workbook accompanying the *LSG* contains fewer exercises than the other books. It must be noted, however, that it is the only book where all the examples are clearly identified as coming from corpora (the text type is always listed). This book does not offer any

[3] *EGT* offered only one error correction exercise.

"shifting" exercise, which does not come as a surprise as all examples are authentic and shifting would make the examples less authentic.

Apart from a few exceptions mentioned above, a vast majority of the exercises presented in the four books can be said to have pedagogic task authenticity. In terms of linguistic authenticity, some are "more authentic" than others as all the examples come from corpora. For some other books, the examples may have been slightly adapted, and for some others the origin is not mentioned.

The authenticity through origin (cultural authenticity) is more difficult to assess here and will not be discussed. As for the authenticity through daily life experiences (functional authenticity), it seems to be present only in *G&B*, thanks to the reading, speaking, listening, and writing activities suggested.

4 Conclusion

This chapter first addressed the value of using native and learner corpora in second/foreign language teaching and showed that it was both possible and desirable to adopt corpus approaches in the design and development of language teaching materials. We then briefly presented a number of corpus- and non-corpus-informed grammar books and carried out a case study on the treatment of the passive in those two types of grammar books. The comparison revealed that non-corpus-informed materials fail to include important information on the passive.

Our aim in carrying out the case study was not to come up with the conclusion that all grammar textbooks should include corpus-based information on all grammar points. Whilst corpus-based information on article usage might not add much to the treatment of articles in grammar books, we believe that some areas would really benefit from the inclusion of the results of corpus studies. These areas include, among others, the passive, the conditionals, the use of relative clauses and the treatment of aspectuality (and notably the use of the progressive). Corpus information on registers, frequency, and lexical preferences is key to a good understanding and use of grammar, and that is why they should no longer be ignored and should find their way into all types of grammar books. The results of corpus studies carried out on native and learner corpora can help textbook designers prioritize features, be it on the basis of frequency of use (native corpora) or of difficulty in acquisition (learner corpora).

Finding exactly the right amount of corpus information (frequency, registers, lexical preferences, etc.) in sufficient detail is probably an elusive goal as each user/learner has different needs. But, as shown in the case study carried out in this chapter, it should be feasible to draw up a list of core corpus findings worth including in all types of grammar books.

Also, as pointed out by Lee and McGarrell (2011: 95) "Perhaps the lack of available guidance is, at least in part, to blame for the finding that not all textbooks . . . equally reflect findings of corpus research." It should therefore also be part of the corpus linguists' agenda to provide textbook writers with clear guidelines as to which type of core grammatical information is worth including in textbooks. In line with Lee and McGarrell (2011), we also hope that the availability of descriptive grammars based on corpus research will be helpful to materials writers to "portray a more accurate picture of the language rather than convey an inaccurate picture and misleading prescriptive rules."

Appendix 1: List of ELT grammar books (Granger 2013)

Azar, B. S. 1999. *Understanding and using English Grammar*. New York: Longman.

Carter, R., Hughes, R., and McCarthy, M. 2000. *Exploring grammar in context: Grammar reference and practice upper-intermediate and advanced*. Cambridge University Press.

Celce-Murcia, M. and Larsen-Freeman, D. 1999. *The grammar book: An ESL/EFL teacher's course*. Boston, MA: Heinle & Heinle.

Cowan, R. 2008. *The teacher's grammar of English: A coursebook and reference guide*. New York: Cambridge University Press.

Eastwood, J. 2006. *Oxford practice grammar*. Oxford University Press.

Foley, M. and Hall, D. 2003. *Longman advanced learners' grammar: A self-study reference and practice book with answers*. Harlow: Longman.

Hewings, M. 2005. *Advanced grammar in use: A self-study reference and practice book for advanced students of English*. 2nd edition. Cambridge University Press.

Lester, M. 2008. *McGraw-Hill's essential ESL grammar: A handbook for intermediate and advanced ESL students*. New York: McGraw-Hill.

Penston, T. 2005. *A concise grammar for English language teachers*. Greystones: TP Publications.

Swan, M. 2005. *Practical English usage*. Oxford University Press.

Vince, M. 2008. *Macmillan English grammar in context: Advanced*. Oxford: Macmillan.

28

Translation

Silvia Bernardini

1 Introduction

The empirical study of translation has traditionally been text-based, typically focusing on the comparison of single originals and their translations. In this way, linguists have looked for examples of translation shifts, or "departures from formal correspondence" in the process of going from the source language (SL) to the target language (TL; Catford 1965 in Venuti 2000: 141ff.), or else have viewed translations as contextualized instances of cross-linguistic correspondences, and analyzed them so as to identify ways in which "the differences in the expressive power of two languages may be overcome" (Doherty 2002: 1). Classicists and literary study scholars have painstakingly combed translations, particularly of canonical works, looking for "rocks on which [past translators] have split, and the right objects on which a translator . . . should fix his attention" (Arnold 1861: 2). On this basis, proposals have been made for an analytic of translation based on "deforming tendencies" (*tendances déformantes*), or "universals of deformation inherent in translation as such" (Berman 1985 in Venuti 2000: 296).

This is admittedly an oversimplified account, which nonetheless may help to establish a backdrop for the emergence of the corpus-based approach in the early 1990s. Three factors acted as catalysts. First, the quantitative focus afforded by corpus methods could provide an alternative to "pick and choose" observations – i.e. those "subjective, largely intuitive and impressionist methods" that some researchers had grown dissatisfied with (Holmes 1978 in Weissbort and Eysteinsson 2006: 421). Second, the 1980s and early 1990s saw an upsurge of interest in the specificities of (the language used in) translation, variously termed *translationese* (Gellerstam 1996) or *third code* (Frawley 1984). Translation scholars grew interested in the set of "fingerprints" that one language leaves on another when texts are translated between the two (Gellerstam 1996), or in the "third code which arises out of the bilateral consideration of the matrix and target codes" (Frawley 1984: 168). The research agenda thus opened up to consideration coherent *sets* of texts (or corpora), as opposed to *single* originals and their translations. Third, the theoretical shift away from the primacy of the source text (ST) and the notion of equivalence, and toward the target text (TT) and the notion of appropriateness, brought with it the need for studies focusing on translated texts within their contexts of reception, with a view to exploring "the nature of translational norms as compared to those governing non-translational kinds of text production" (Toury 1995: 61). Corpus linguistics provided an appropriate toolkit for the monolingual comparison of translated texts and comparable texts originating from the receiving culture.

The first part of this chapter surveys the development of *corpus-based translation studies* (CBTS), from the programmatic proposals in the early 1990s to recent developments and trends. Section 2.1 briefly outlines the theoretical and methodological bases of CBTS, in particular as concerns the types of corpora and the research questions specific to translation research, as opposed to other uses of corpora in translation (e.g. for translation teaching or practice) and to bordering disciplines such as contrastive linguistics. Section 2.2 digs deeper into five studies that have been especially influential and/or that embody especially sound research practices, while Section 2.3 concludes by summarizing the state of the art in CBTS and the major questions still requiring to be addressed. In the second part (Section 3), a case study is presented which aims to test whether translated texts are more or less collocational than comparable non-translated texts, using a combination of comparable, parallel, and reference corpora.

2.1 The theoretical and methodological bases of CBTS

2.1.1 Textual patterning, norms, and universals of translation

The application of corpus methodologies to translation research can be traced back to Mona Baker's seminal paper in which she argues that:

> the most important task that awaits the application of corpus techniques in translation studies . . . is the elucidation of the nature of translated text as a mediated communicative event. In order to do this, it will be necessary to develop tools that will enable us to identify universal features of translation, that is features which typically occur in translated text rather than original utterances and which are not the result of interference from specific linguistic systems. (Baker 1993: 243)

Following Baker's influential proposal, several translation researchers set out to construct and analyze monolingual comparable corpora, i.e. collections of texts in the same language, similar in all respects but for the existence vs. the absence of a constraining ST. So, the main issue was no longer a question of how a particular ST had been manipulated in translation. Rather, the focus shifted to the general description of translated language, treated as any other language variety and compared monolingually against the benchmark of non-translated language. Investigations could then be carried out using the whole expanse of methods being developed for corpus analysis at large, including corpus-driven observations such as type–token ratio, ratio of lexical to function words, sentence length (Laviosa 1998; Xiao 2010) as well as corpus-based ones such as relative frequencies of specific words, word classes, collocations, lexico-syntactic structures and so forth (Dayrell 2007; Mauranen 2002; Olohan and Baker 2000). In this way, evidence could be gathered of "patterning which is specific to translated texts, irrespective of the source or target languages involved" (Baker 1995: 234), which could in turn bring to light tendencies inherent in all types of translation. Proposed *universals* of translation include simplification, explicitation, normalization, or conservatism, and leveling out or convergence – the latter referring to the fact that sets of translated texts in a corpus display less variance than comparable sets of non-translated texts (Laviosa 1998).

This body of research has provided a wealth of insights about typical features of translated texts, going beyond a particularistic approach and shedding light on tendencies common to sets of translations, even though there is still no consensus as to whether these tendencies are in fact universal, and whether it makes sense to speak of universality in the first place. Methodological doubts have been raised about issues of corpus (in)comparability (Bernardini and Zanettin 2004) and theoretical doubts about universality, representativeness and causality of descriptive universals (Chesterman 2004). Empirical findings such as those of Becher (2011: 42) concerning explicitation in translation between English and German also suggest that some hypothesized universals of translation may in fact be explained in terms of "previously established cross-linguistic differences in terms of syntax, lexis, and communicative norms" between the two languages involved, such that "it is unnecessary to assume that translators follow a 'universal strategy' of explicitation, as it has often been done in the literature" (Becher 2011: 26). Despite these criticisms, we may concur with Chesterman (2004: 11) that "[w]hat ultimately matters is perhaps not the universals, which we can never finally confirm anyway, but new knowledge of the patterns, and patterns of patterns, which helps us to make sense of what we are looking at."

2.1.2 The analysis of translation shifts

Parallel corpora have not been central to CBTS so far, due to the concurrent general shift away from the ST (see introduction) and to methodological reasons. Bilingual or multilingual parallel-corpus analysis is inherently more complex than monolingual corpus analysis, requiring a descriptive framework including – crucially – a *tertium comparationis*, or common platform of comparison, and for this reason mostly relying on the direct observation of parallel concordances.

Translation research using parallel corpora has focused on translation *shifts*, or the small changes "that build up cumulatively over a whole text as a result of the choices taken by or imposed on the translator" (Munday 1998: 542). At its most basic, this involves comparing STs and their TTs, as in Munday (1998), which analyzes the first part of a novel by Gabriel García Márquez and its English translation and finds evidence of shifts in narrative point of view and cohesion, or Shih (2012) who studies the rendering of prepositions in translation from English to Chinese and highlights the effects of cross-linguistic differences, textual functions, and translator preferences on the observed shifts.

A more complex parallel design is used by Øveras (1998), who searches for shifts in cohesion/coherence in the *English–Norwegian Parallel Corpus*, a bidirectional corpus including STs in English and their Norwegian TTs and (comparable) STs in Norwegian and their English TTs. By carrying out the analysis in both translation directions, she can factor out language-specific effects. She concludes that, in both translation directions, explicitating shifts (i.e. cases in which co-textually recoverable ST material is made explicit in the TT, e.g. when ellipsis in the ST is replaced by a noun in the TT) are more common than implicitating ones (in which an explicit ST item is rendered by one that relies more on the co-text for reader interpretation, e.g. when a lexical word in the ST is translated as a proform in the TT). This work thus provides support for the explicitation hypothesis. A similar corpus setup (a bidirectional parallel corpus of French and Dutch) is used by Vanderbauwhede *et al.* (2011) in their study of demonstrative determiners, which shows that around 30 percent of translation shifts occurring in either direction are due to omissions, additions, or reformulations motivated by translator preferences.

Less central to CBTS than monolingual comparable corpora, parallel corpora – simple ones, bidirectional ones including STs and TTs in two directions, multi-target ones with one source and many targets, and so forth – have been used extensively in research carried out at the crossroads of corpus-based translation studies and contrastive linguistics. Where the latter focus predominates, the purpose is to highlight systemic differences between languages, the very aspect that CBTS attempt to factor out in their attempt to highlight translation-specific shifts that occur regardless of the languages involved. According to Johansson (2007: 5), who pioneered work on contrastive corpus research with the creation of the *English–Norwegian Parallel Corpus*, the use of parallel corpora increases the validity of cross-linguistic comparisons, since it allows for "the systematic exploitation of the bilingual intuition of translators, as it is reflected in the pairing of source and target language expressions in the corpus texts."

2.1.3 The stylistic fingerprints of translators

Translator style has emerged in the last decade as one of the research objects in CBTS, investigated either by means of comparable or parallel corpora. Studies adopting the monolingual comparable design borrow insights from literary stylistics to bring to the fore "the translator's characteristic use of language, his or her individual profile of linguistic habits, compared to other translators" (Baker 2000: 245). Objections have been raised, however, against the total neglect of the ST, since "many important questions about writer motivation ... may not arise in the case of translated texts unless the texts are seen in the context of their source texts" (Malmkjær 2004: 22).

A more promising approach to the analysis of translator style involves a multi-target parallel structure, i.e. an ST and two (or more) TTs, as in the case of Ji's (2010) study of phraseology and translator's profiles in two translations of *Don Quixote* into Chinese, and Marco's (2004) analysis of translator style in two translations of Poe's *The Fall of the House of Usher* into Catalan, in which the style displayed by Catalan translators in their own writing as well as aspects of the contemporary literary canon are also factored in.

2.1.4 Summing up

Three main objectives of descriptive research have drawn the attention of CBTS researchers: first and foremost, the search for textual patterning supporting hypotheses about the existence of norms or universals of translation; second, the analysis of translation shifts; and, third, the identification of stylistic fingerprints left by translators. These issues have been investigated by means of monolingual comparable and parallel corpora, the former being seen as more innovative and powerful than the latter. After initial enthusiasm, however, it has become clear that source-language and source-text specific effects should not be ignored *by design* (Pym 2008). More composite corpus designs and more sophisticated techniques for data analysis have emerged, counteracting the excessive downplay of the ST through a triangulation of "different components of multilingual corpora as well as of reference corpora not originally created for translation-oriented purposes" (Zanettin 2012: 12), and/or through the use of techniques borrowed from bordering research communities, e.g. those employed for authorship attribution and stylometry (Oakes and Ji 2012).

Focusing mainly on textual patterning, norms, and universals of translation, and adopting a varied array of corpus resources including monolingual comparable and parallel ones, the five empirical studies presented in the next section have all played a central role in first establishing CBTS as a discipline with its theoretically motivated research agenda and methodology, and then buttressing its foundations and bringing it forward.

2.2 CBTS: selected studies

2.2.1 Laviosa (1998)

The obvious starting point for any survey of key CBTS studies is Laviosa's (1998) article describing the *English Comparable Corpus* (ECC) and investigating simplification in its narrative subcorpus. The ECC is the first and best-known attempt to construct a corpus of translated and non-translated texts. Two subcorpora are included, one of newspaper texts (from *The Guardian* and *The European*) and the other of narrative (fiction and biography) texts. Despite attempts to match texts in the two components as closely as possible (e.g. in terms of author gender and publication date), the extent of their comparability remains an open question. Relevant variables uncontrolled for include differences in topic (difficult to control in fictional works) as well as the fact that the non-translated subcorpus contains text samples while the translated subcorpus contains full texts (Laviosa 2002: 39–40).

In Laviosa's study, the fiction subcorpus of the ECC is searched for evidence supporting the simplification hypothesis, i.e. the idea that translated texts are simpler than comparable non-translated texts in the same language. Based on previous analysis of the newspaper subcorpus, Laviosa (1998: 560) turns this general assumption into the following working hypotheses:

> The translational component of the comparable corpus of narrative texts has a lower lexical density and mean sentence length than the non-translational component.
>
> The translational component of the comparable corpus of narrative texts contains a higher proportion of high-frequency words and its list head covers a greater percentage of text with fewer lemmas than the non-translational component.

The first hypothesis is confirmed with respect to lexical density, significantly lower in translated texts, but not with respect to mean sentence length. Differently from the newspaper corpus, this turns out to be significantly higher, with higher variance, in translated fiction. The second hypothesis is confirmed for both observations: in the translated component, the most frequent word forms account for a significantly higher percentage of the corpus and the proportion of high-frequency to low-frequency words is significantly higher.

On the basis of this study and of a previous analysis of newspaper language, Laviosa proposes four "core patterns of lexical use" potentially applying to translated English in general, namely that:

> Translated texts have a relatively lower percentage of content words versus grammatical words (i.e. their lexical density is lower); the proportion of high frequency words versus low frequency words is relatively higher in translated texts; the list head of a corpus of translated texts

> accounts for a larger area of the corpus (i.e. the most frequent words are repeated more often); The list head of translated texts contains fewer lemmas. (Laviosa 1998: 564)

As for sentence length, Laviosa (1998: 564) concludes that it "may be particularly sensitive, in the narrative subject domain, to the influence of different source languages, as well as the author's particular style."

Laviosa's work from the late 1990s has been extremely influential in paving the way for the construction of translation corpora for languages other than English (e.g. the corpus of translated Finnish at the university of Savonlinna) and for the search for core patterns of translated language. Xiao (2010) is a recent example of a corpus analysis comparing translated and non-translated Mandarin Chinese in terms of the core lexical features proposed by Laviosa, and finding that they are "essentially also applicable in translated Chinese, which suggests that translated Chinese also demonstrates a tendency for simplification at lexical level" (Xiao 2010: 22–23).

2.2.2 Kenny (2001)

Kenny's study of lexical creativity (2001) takes as its starting point the observation that translators opt for conventional TL solutions when faced with creative or unusual SL expressions (Øverås 1998; Vanderauwera 1985). Kenny looks for confirmation of this normalizing tendency in a parallel corpus of contemporary German novels and their English translations. Her method consists in identifying, in the ST corpus, creative word hapaxes and creative patterns of word co-occurrence. Creativity is evaluated with reference to attestation and frequency in a reference corpus of German (the written part of the Mannheim *Deutsches Referenzkorpus*), supplemented with lexicographic resources and native-speaker judgments. The corresponding translated segments are then retrieved and their level of creativity is checked in the same way (attestation and frequency in the *British National Corpus*).

To give an example (Kenny 2001: 149–150), the German corpus contains the manner adverbial *adamsäpfelnd*, which Kenny glosses as "adamsappling" in English. The word is not attested in the German reference corpus, and is therefore classified as a creative hapax coined by the author to describe (presumably) an act of swallowing in which one's Adam's apple moves prominently. Looking at the TT, the translator has resorted to a full clause to render this creative adverbial, i.e. "His Adam's apple bobs," which includes the collocation, attested in the *British National Corpus*, "Adam's apple" + "bob." Kenny finds substantial evidence of normalization of this kind: about 40 percent of the creative hapaxes and 20 percent of the unusual collocations selected for analysis are normalized in translation.

The approach adopted by Kenny relies on (informed) subjective evaluation and manual inspection of concordance lines. This is arguably unavoidable given the focus on atypicality and creativity, but it also follows from the adoption of a parallel perspective that prioritizes translation shifts. As such, it occupies the opposite end of the methodological spectrum from Laviosa's (1998) study discussed in Section 2.2.1. Since translator's choices are directly accessible through the analysis of aligned parallel corpora, Kenny can establish with certainty when and how translators normalize (not so in the case of Laviosa, who can only *speculate* that the use of simpler language is causally related to the translation process, since source texts are not included in her corpus). On the other hand, Kenny's method does not allow her to draw conclusions on the normal-ness of translated texts with respect to comparable non-translated texts, while Laviosa's does. Other approaches have attempted to combine the best of both worlds.

2.2.3 Teich (2003)

For her study of cross-linguistic (English/German) variation in system and text, Teich (2003) resorts to a register-controlled bidirectional corpus of scientific texts (expert to educated layperson) in translated and non-translated English and German. This corpus design combines the comparable and the parallel perspectives, and permits analyses in two languages/language directions.

Teich's aim is to determine whether, in the two translation directions, there is evidence of SL *shining through* (or interference) or, conversely, of TL *normalization*. The selection of features for analysis – transitivity and agency, voice, grammatical metaphor, the theme system, and nominal pre- and post-modification – is made on the basis of a preliminary contrastive account of the two languages rooted in systemic functional linguistics, and of previous research contrasting the registerial features of scientific English and scientific German. The distribution of each feature is first observed in the non-translated subcorpora, and then comparisons are made at the monolingual comparable level (translated and non-translated English and German) and the parallel level (English–German translations; German–English translations).

The general picture emerging from this study is a complex one. Both SL shining through and TL normalization are found: translations "appear to be a particular kind of register that tends towards an extreme of registerial typicality concerning some features and at the same time lets the SL interfere with regard to other features" (Teich 2003: 223). German shows more effects than English, and, coherent with her approach, Teich explains this finding in terms of systemic differences between the two languages: if a language has more options available in a given grammatical system, it can afford to let the SL interfere; if it has fewer options, it has to compensate, and if similar means of compensations are used often, the result is TL normalization.

At the intersection between translation studies and contrastive linguistics, Teich's study focuses more on cross-linguistic systemic differences than on the role of the translator and of the translation process. Nonetheless it is of interest to translation scholars because of its selection of features for analysis based on solid theoretical foundations, its careful contrastive observations, and the adoption of corpus resources that afford a multiple perspective on the data (parallel/comparable, English/German), while limiting the number of variables by resorting to a single genre. An approach along these lines has been used by other researchers and has provided relevant insights about, among others, patterns of collocation (Nilsson 2006) and explicitation (Hansen-Schirra *et al.* 2007).

2.2.4 Kanter *et al.* (2006)

Though less well known than the studies surveyed so far, Kanter *et al.*'s (2006) work is included here because of its intriguing proposal of a new, truly corpus-driven, universal of translation. They use a monolingual comparable corpus consisting of four subcorpora of English texts from the *International Herald Tribune*: one of non-translated English texts, and three of texts translated into English from Greek, Hebrew, and Korean respectively. The subcorpora are matched for size (230,000 words each), and include texts from the same newspaper sections (news, arts and leisure, business and finance, and opinion).

The authors count the number of types unique to each subcorpus and calculate the extent of the overlap between each pair of subcorpora. They find "a remarkable similarity in (a) the number of types unique to each translated corpus and (b) the number of types common to the original-English corpus and each of the translated corpora" (Kanter *et al.* 2006: 39). These similarities are reflected in the number of tokens and consequently in the type/token ratios, which are similar for all subcorpora translated into English and lower by about 20 percent than in non-translated English. They suggest that these insights can be used to distinguish a translated text/corpus from a non-translated one automatically.

While this study does not offer any motivation, social, cognitive or otherwise, nor any explanation for the observed patterns, it does confirm that translated (English in this case) and non-translated language differs in objective, quantifiable ways. Baroni and Bernardini (2006) arrive at similar conclusions using *n*-gram-based text representations and machine learning techniques on a closely comparable corpus of translated and non-translated Italian articles taken from a single magazine on geopolitics.

2.2.5 Delaere *et al.* (2012)

The study by Delaere *et al.* (2012) nicely epitomizes the current status of the discipline (at its best) and the progress made since its beginnings. The object of analysis is Toury's law of growing standardization (another name for normalization), and evidence is sought in a corpus of non-translated Dutch and Dutch translated from English and French. A number of patterns are selected for investigation that have at least two variants, one belonging to standard Belgian Dutch, the other being non-standard according to normative sources. These patterns/variants are searched for in an annotated corpus and manually validated.

On the basis of these counts, a profile-based correspondence analysis is applied to nine language varieties identified within the corpus. Six of these are text types (instructive, administrative, etc.) and three are translation-related varieties (non-translated, translated from English, translated from French). Profile-based chi-square distances are calculated for the different varieties, distances are mapped on a two-dimensional plot, and confidence ellipses are drawn around each variety: lack of overlap indicates a statistically significant distance. The interaction between text type and translation-related variety is also calculated and displayed graphically.

Ellipses for the three translation-related varieties do not overlap, i.e. they are significantly different in terms of use of (non-)standard variants. More specifically, non-translated Belgian Dutch is (slightly) less standard than Belgian Dutch translated from English and substantially less standard than Belgian Dutch translated from French. Apart from the general picture, Delaere *et al.*'s results indicate that not all translated texts are standardized to the same extent: translated fiction, external communication, and administrative texts confirm the general trend, while journalistic texts and non-fiction texts do not.

Despite some limitations (gaps in the corpus for certain text types, as acknowledged by the authors, but also lack of reference to STs and parallel observations), this study is an example of best practice, nicely combining a careful corpus design, a linguistically motivated choice of patterns, solid grounding in theory, and sophisticated statistical techniques complemented by intuitive graphic representations. And, crucially, it raises more questions than it answers, as good research should:

> What is the role of the publishing houses? . . . Can we attribute the use of standard language in certain text types . . . to a process of editorial control? What is the influence of the status of, for example, a literary translator versus a technical translator? (Delaere *et al.* 2012: 221)

2.3 Summing up: CBTS today

The body of research surveyed so far has provided us with a wealth of hypotheses about the typical features of translated language. Even though none of these features has been uncontroversially proved to be universal, several seem to be candidates for statistical universality testing. For instance, it has been shown that translated texts in languages as different as English and Chinese are more likely to be simpler, more normal, more standard, more explicit than comparable texts in the same language. It has also been pointed out that translated texts share basic linguistic traits that tell them apart from comparable non-translated texts (e.g. number of unique words, *n*-gram patterns).

These findings provide empirical confirmation for theoretical claims that predate the 1990s and the corpus-based approach: Teich's (2003) interpretation of her results as suggesting that translated texts form a particular kind of register *within* a register, for instance, resonates with views voiced by philosopher and translation theorist Ortega y Gasset (1937, in Venuti 2000: 61), who maintained that "translation doesn't even belong to the same literary genre as the text to be translated ... translation is a literary genre apart, different from the rest, with its own norms and its own ends."

Alongside typical features shared by translated texts, TTs also carry with them imprints of the SLs from which they were translated, as shown by CBTS using parallel/bidirectional corpora and reference corpora. These studies have also suggested that interference, like other typical features, is register- and language-dependent. The parallel perspective therefore cannot be bypassed.

Going back to the typical features of translated language (simple, normal, standard, explicit), it is clear that they do not form an arbitrary list, but rather point to a common unifying factor. Pym (2008: 326) has hypothesized that this is to be found in translators' risk aversion: "[t]ranslators will tend to avoid risk by standardizing language and/or channelling interference, if and when there are no rewards for them to do otherwise." Be that as it may, the question is still open as to whether translators make self-conscious, strategic decisions to normalize, explicitate, etc., or whether normalization, explicitation, etc. lie beyond translators' control or even awareness, and should be therefore construed as inherent in the translation process. The obvious next step requires that hypotheses based on corpus evidence be integrated with process-oriented studies, to shed light on motivations and causality, along the lines, for example, of Alves *et al.* (2010).

3 Case study: collocations in translated (and non-translated) language

3.1 Introduction and aims

This case study investigates the use of English collocations by authors and translators of financial texts. The topic seems an especially rewarding one for CBTS. Evidence from research on second language learning and translator performance (Bahumaid 2006), as well as recommendations in textbooks of translation (Hatim and Mason 1997), lend support to the view that mastering collocations is a crucial aspect of foreign language and translation competence, and that it is not easily achieved, even when translating into one's own native language. As happens with non-native language production (Nesselhauf 2005), one could expect translations to show evidence of interference at the collocational level. However, the tendency has also been observed for translators to reduce the creative potential of unusual words and phrases found in their STs, resorting to a stock of familiar TL phrases whenever possible and producing normalized TTs (Øverås 1998; Kenny 2001).

Despite the interest, the notion has so far been mainly touched upon in pursuit of other research aims, and/or addressed using a selective keyword approach – describing the collocational patterning of a handful of interesting words (e.g. Olohan 2004). The few studies that have attempted to go beyond have been faced with problems of data-sparseness.

Danielsson (2001) aims to identify "units of translation" (i.e. bilingual collocation pairings) in parallel corpora on the basis of "units of meaning" extracted from monolingual corpora of English and Swedish. Out of about 2,000 units of meaning identified in a monolingual reference corpus, only two occur five times or more in a 400,000 word corpus of Swedish narrative texts.

Using a corpus of Brazilian Portuguese narrative texts (eight non-translated and five translated from English), Dayrell (2007: 377) tries to determine whether "collocational patterns tend to be less diverse (i.e. reduced in range) in translated texts in comparison with non-translated texts." The comparison is limited to ten word forms that occur 200 times or more in either subcorpus, since less frequent words would be unlikely to provide enough evidence about their typical collocational patternings.

In general, translation-driven corpora are costly to assemble, requiring ingenious design decisions to guarantee comparability and/or, in the case of parallel corpora, the collection and alignment of two versions for each text. As a consequence they tend to be small compared to monolingual corpora – usually measured in hundreds of thousands rather than millions of words.

To bypass the data-sparseness bottleneck experienced by previous studies of collocational patternings in translation, in this study collocations are identified in, and compared across, monolingual comparable subcorpora (English only) based on lexical association data obtained from reference corpora. In a nutshell, bigram *types* are first obtained from the corpora of translated and non-translated texts used for the study; they are then matched with frequency and Mutual Information data obtained from a reference corpus of English, and ranked according to these data. Lastly, rankings for the same part-of-speech pattern are compared across translated and non-translated subcorpora, to see if they differ significantly.

Taking the reference corpus to represent "the collective linguistic experience of a language community" (Howarth 1996: 72), it is thus possible to fulfill the aim of this study, i.e. find out if translated texts display higher/lower levels of collocativeness than non-translated texts, regardless of the fact that either subcorpus will inevitably use different, not directly comparable, collocations. Section 3.2 describes the corpus setup and provides a step-by-step account of the method.

3.2 Corpora and method

3.2.1 Corpora

Two corpora were built specifically for this study. The FINREP corpus is a corpus of corporate financial reports, i.e. reports issued annually by companies providing financial information as well as commentaries about operational and financial performance. The SHARLET corpus covers a prominent subgenre within the corporate financial report, namely that of shareholders' letters. These are short texts (about one page on average), appearing in the introductory (non-audited) part of the report, normally preceding the more technical chief executive report on operations. Previous research has singled out this subgenre as especially worthy of attention because of its wide readership of both experts and lay people, its inherent promotional nature, and its role in shaping financial analysts' opinions and investor decisions (Bhana 2009).

Both corpora have three components: English texts translated from Italian, their Italian STs, and comparable texts in non-translated English. English translated reports and shareholders' letters are downloaded first, selecting companies based in Italy and whose CEOs/chairpersons are of Italian origin and upbringing. Then their Italian STs are also downloaded, and comparable English texts are sought. These should be published by companies based in countries where English is a first language, and cover a range of business types and years of publication roughly comparable to those in the translated subcorpus.

Tables 28.1 and 28.2 summarize basic information about these corpora. The central columns (EN-NT and EN-TR) are the most important ones,

Table 28.1 *The* FINREP *corpus*

	FINREP-EN-NT	FINREP-EN-TR	FINREP-IT-NT
Number of texts	27	27	27
Number of tokens	692,046	704,567	740,542
Number of types	27,865	32,226	39,056
Time span	2009–2012	2011	2011
Language	English	English	Italian
Origin	23 UK, 3 US, 1 IE	IT	IT
Parallel tokens	1,445,109		
Comparable tokens	1,396,613		
Total corpus size (tokens)	2,841,722		

Table 28.2 *The* SHARLET *corpus*

	SHARLET-EN-NT	SHARLET-EN-TR	SHARLET-IT-NT
Number of texts	35	35	35
Number of tokens	37,335	38,473	38,745
Number of types	5,247	5,304	6,532
Time span	2001–2009	2000–2009	2000–2009
Language	English	English	Italian
Origin	17 UK, 12 US, 2 AU, 2CA, 2 IE	IT	IT
Parallel tokens	77,218		
Comparable tokens	75,808		
Total corpus size (tokens)	114,553		

since the main comparison in this study is monolingual comparable, contrasting translated and non-translated English. The Italian source texts (IT-NT) are only checked in case higher levels of collocativeness are found, to ensure that these are due to translation and not to unrelated variables.

As a reference corpus, the ukWaC corpus was used. This is a general-purpose corpus of (British) English built in 2007 by web crawling (Baroni *et al.* 2009), containing 2.69 million texts, 1.9 billion word tokens, and 3.8 million word types. While not ideal – it was designed so as to sample mainly British English, while the texts in the translation-driven corpora are not limited to the British variety of English – this corpus was judged to provide the best trade-off between quantity, quality, and availability.

Both translation-driven and reference corpora are tagged and lemmatized using the TreeTagger and indexed with the Corpus WorkBench.

3.2.2 Method

For the purposes of this study collocations are defined, adopting a *pattern* rather than *keyword* method (Stubbs 2002: 230), as lexical clusters made of two word forms matching a given part-of-speech (POS) pattern, e.g. Adjective–Noun (*intangible assets, forward-looking statements*). Several patterns are identified that are likely to form lexical collocations in English (see Table 28.3). There is no claim that these patterns retrieve *all* collocations, but only that they provide a principled way to select potential collocation candidates. Other patterns can be targeted in future studies, using the same method.

Eight POS patterns are formed of contiguous lexical words (a Noun followed by a Noun, e.g. *operating profit*, a Verb followed by an Adverb, e.g. *act swiftly*, and so forth), while five are formed of lexical words separated by one or two function words (a Noun followed by a Conjunction or Preposition followed by a Noun, e.g. *board [of] directors*;

Table 28.3 *POS patterns used for candidate collocation extraction*

POS	Example
Adjective–Adjective	*uncertain economic*
Adjective–Noun	*intangible assets*
Adverb–Adjective	*mutually supportive*
Adverb–Verb	*really matters*
Noun–Noun	*operating profit*
Noun–Verb	*economy recovers*
Verb–Noun	*quench thirsts*
Verb–Adverb	*act swiftly*
Adjective–[Conjunction|Preposition]– Adjective	*effective [. . .] efficient*
Noun–[Conjunction|Preposition]–Noun	*board [. . .]directors*
Verb–[Determiner|Preposition]–Noun	*unleashing [. . .] power*
Noun–[Preposition]–Determiner|Pronoun|Number]–Noun	*answer [. . .][. . .]question*
Verb–[Particle|Preposition|Pronoun]–[Determiner|Pronoun]–Noun	*respond [. . .] [. . .]challenges*

a Verb followed by a Particle or Preposition or Pronoun, followed by a Determiner or Pronoun, followed by a Noun, e.g. *respond [to] [the] challenges*). The intervening function words are used to constrain searches but are not retained in the subsequent phases: only the association between lexical words is tested against the reference corpus.

All word pairs matching the POS patterns in Table 28.3 are extracted from FINREP-EN-TR, FINREP-EN-NT, SHARLET-EN-TR, and SHARLET-EN-NT. All subcorpora contain English texts only, therefore there is no cross-linguistic comparability issue. Before disposing of duplicates in order to produce lists of *types*, the lists of bigram tokens for each pair of subcorpora are randomly trimmed to exactly the same size, so as to control for any bias due to differences in subcorpus size.

The lists of types from the translation-driven corpora are then filtered on the basis of attestedness in ukWaC. Word pairs are ranked according to their bare frequency of co-occurrence in the latter corpus, and according to their MI score, setting a cut-off point of MI>2 with FQ≥2 to exclude hapaxes and extremely low MI values. These two separate rankings are meant to account for both very common and (less common but) strongly associated word pairs (Krenn 2000). Table 28.4 shows the top of the MI ranking and the top of the frequency ranking for the Adverb–Verb pattern in the FINREP-EN-TR and FINREP-EN-NT corpus. MI is calculated using the UCS toolkit (Evert 2004).

Similar rankings are produced for all the patterns in Table 28.3, for both subcorpus comparisons (translated and non-translated FINREP, translated and non-translated SHARLET). The significance of differences between each pair of rankings is tested, using the Mann–Whitney–Wilcoxon ranks test. Descriptive statistics are also calculated and plotted graphically to get an impressionistic image of the data distributions for

Table 28.4 *Adverb–Verb rankings (bigrams from translated and non-translated English financial reports, with frequency and MI data from* ukWaC*)*

Frequency ranking				MI ranking			
bigram (FINREP-EN-NT)	FQ (ukWaC)	bigram (FINREP-EN-TR)	FQ (ukWaC)	bigram (FINREP-EN-NT)	MI (ukWaC)	bigram (FINREP-EN-TR)	MI (ukWaC)
as follows	70,418	*as follows*	70,418	*visually impaired*	4.72	*densely populated*	5.05
well known	38,888	*well known*	38,888	*eagerly awaited*	4.65	*competitively priced*	4.62
as opposed	20,400	*widely used*	12,175	*competitively priced*	4.62	*substantively enacted*	3.97
very pleased	12,715	*commonly used*	11,881	*classically styled*	4.47	*aforementioned*	3.86
commonly used	11,881	*as regards*	9,862	*expressly disclaims*	4.45	*harshly penalised*	3.82

significantly different ranking pairs (p<.05). Where the translated component turns out to use more/stronger collocations than the non-translated component, parallel concordances (English TTs and their Italian STs) are consulted to establish a causal link between the observed patterns and the translation process. The Italian subcorpora comprising the source texts of the English translations and described in Tables 28.1 and 28.2 (FINREP-IT-NT and SHARLET-IT-NT), are only used in this (last and crucial) step of the analysis.

3.3 Results and discussion

3.3.1 Corporate financial reports

Three frequency-based rankings (**Adjective–Noun, Adverb–Verb** and **Noun**–[Preposition|Conjunction]–**Noun**) and two MI rankings (**Adverb–Adjective** and **Adverb–Verb**) are found to differ significantly (Table 28.5). As also shown in Figures 28.1–28.4 (minimum and maximum values are not shown to improve plot readability), these differences reflect the fact that non-translated texts display consistently higher levels of collocativeness than translated texts with respect to the patterns under consideration. Furthermore, the non-translated rankings are in all cases longer than the translated rankings, on average by as much as 15 percent. It will be remembered that the token list pairs were trimmed to identical sizes. Length differences therefore may be taken to indicate either that the token lists contain more repetitions, or that they contain fewer pairs attested in ukWaC with frequency and/or MI values above the set thresholds. While the method employed cannot shed light on this issue, both explanations reinforce the pattern observed in Figures 28.1–28.4, i.e. that non-translated reports make greater use of (a wider range of) more frequent and/or more strongly associated collocations than comparable translated texts.

Table 28.5 *Results of significance testing (comparison of rankings from the* FINREP-NT-EN *and* FINREP-TR-EN *subcorpora)*

Pattern	W	p-value	Ranking criterion	Higher in
Adverb–Verb	83,344	0.0091	MI	NT
	82,263.5	0.02366	LOG FQ	NT
Adverb–Adjective	24,376.5	0.02910	MI	NT
Adjective–Noun	4,187,781	0.0001706	LOG FQ	NT
Noun–Preposition OR Conjunction–Noun	292,238.5	0.006704	LOG FQ	NT

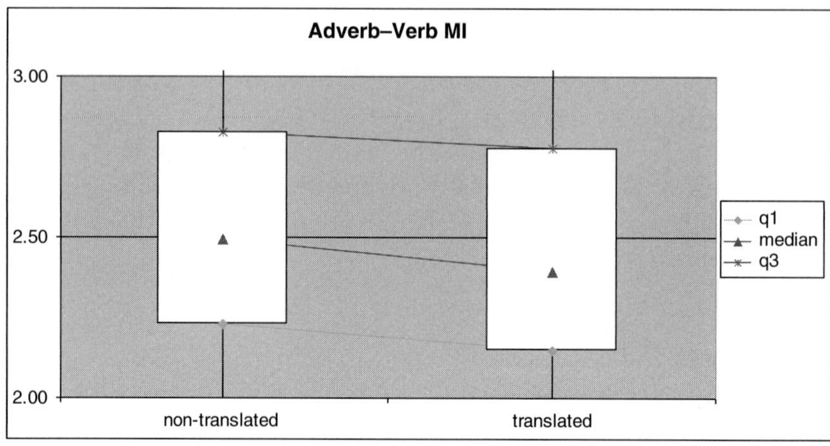

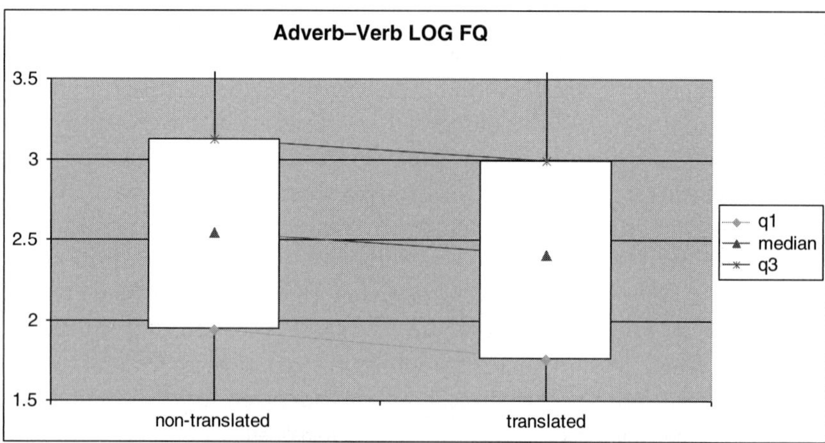

Figure 28.1 Box plots for **Adverb–Verb** (MI and LOG FQ)

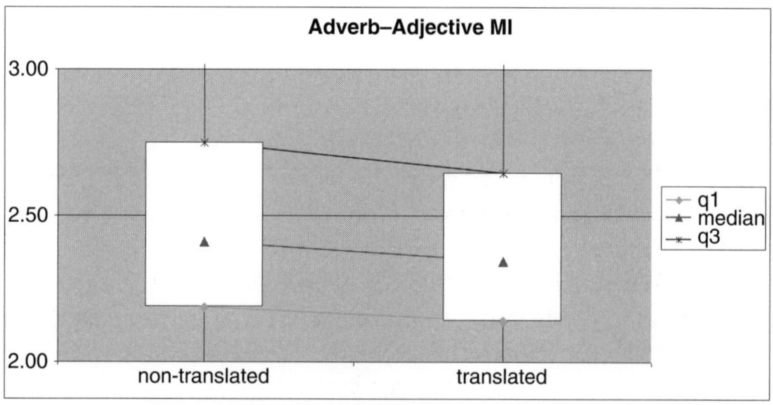

Figure 28.2 Box plot for **Adverb–Adjective** (MI)

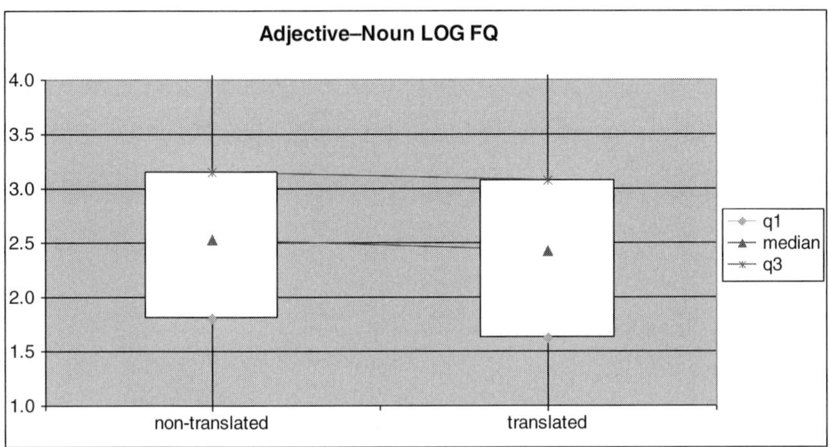

Figure 28.3 Box plot for **Adjective–Noun** (LOG FQ)

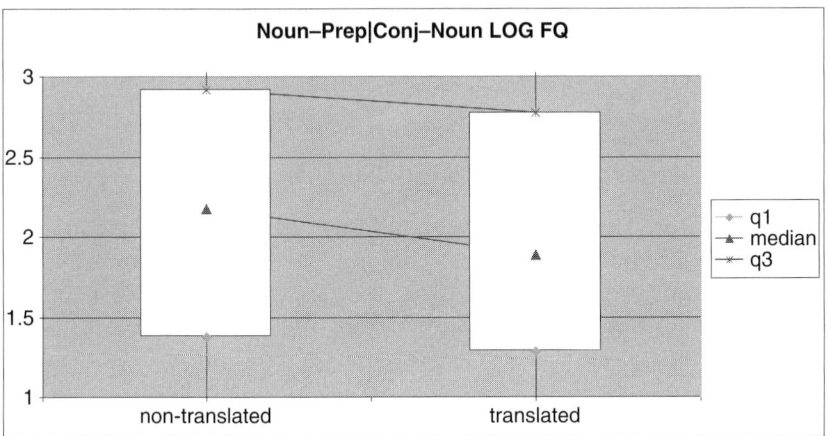

Figure 28.4 Box plot for **Noun**–(Preposition OR Conjunction)–**Noun** (LOG FQ)

3.3.2 Shareholders' letters

Only one ranking comparison returned a significant difference, namely that for the **Adverb–Verb** pattern and the MI values. This result may be taken to suggest that the method is not ideal for very small text collections, or that different parameters and thresholds should be used in these cases. Results for this comparison are summarized in Table 28.6 and represented graphically in Figure 28.5.

Differently from the FINREP corpus, in which both the frequency and the MI rankings for this pattern showed significantly lower levels of collocativeness in translation, in this case translation displays *higher* levels of collocativeness. The actual rankings are both rather short, but the NT one contains 33 percent more collocations than the TR ranking (58 collocations

Table 28.6 *Results of significance testing (comparison of rankings from the* SHARLET-NT-EN *and* SHARLET-TR-EN *subcorpora)*

Pattern	W	p-value	Ranking criterion	Higher in
Adverb–Verb	810	0.01837	MI	TR

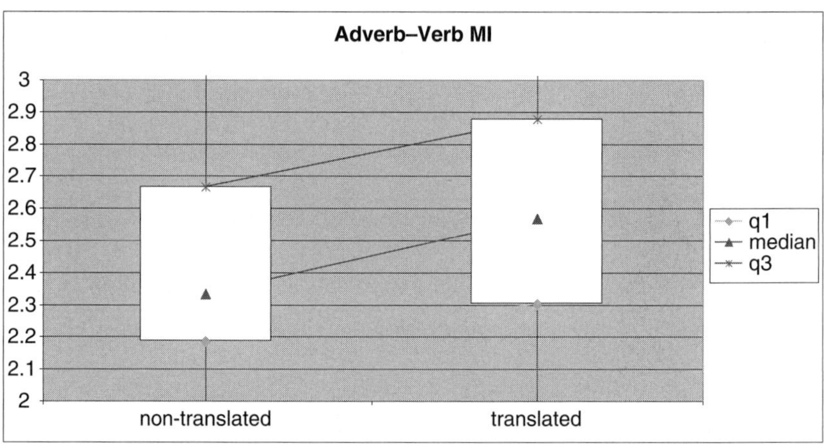

Figure 28.5 Box plot for **Adverb–Verb** (MI)

in NT vs. 39 in TR), suggesting that a longer ranking is not necessarily associated with higher MI values, as might be hypothesized looking at the FINREP corpus results. Both rankings contain many (positively evaluating) degree and manner adverbs, but the NT ranking also includes technical terms (*fully franked, heavily over-subscribed*), which are absent from the TR ranking. Since the TR subcorpus turns out to be more collocational, we can search the parallel subcorpus for motivating shifts.

In several cases, this pattern seems to result from non-obligatory explicitating shifts (examples 1–4).

(1) <snam-05> infrastructures that can transport **ever increasing** volumes of gas
infrastrutture per trasportare volumi **crescenti** di gas [*increasing*]

(2) <finmec-09> Finmeccanica has been **negatively affected** to a limited extent
Finmeccanica ha **risentito** in maniera limitata [*affected*]

(3) <interpump-08> with the **widely publicized** defaulting of subprime mortgages
con la **nota** vicenda dei mutui subprime [*known, familiar*]

(4) <barilla-06> Our goal is to identify **newly discovered** benefits
per dare **nuovi** benefici [*new*]

In these examples, one element in the collocation is added by the translator (typically the adverb, more rarely the past participle, as in example (4)), which is neither given in the ST nor required specifically by the TT or TL (i.e. it does not compensate for information lost in translation, nor does it fill cultural gaps). About 18 percent of the collocations in the TR ranking result from explicitating shifts of this kind.

A near-significant difference (p=.07) was also found for the Verb–Noun ranking comparison, similarly suggesting that translated texts are more collocational. Several shifts are once again explicitating ones: translators add premodifiers that are not present in the ST (*unwavering commitment* to render Italian "impegno," simply meaning *commitment*) and resort to light-verb constructions to render a logical relation expressed by a simple preposition in the ST (*forming part of* to render Italian "del," meaning *of*). Light-verb constructions are also employed to render a wide range of ST expressions, including figurative ones. For instance, *take advantage* is used to translate Italian dictionary equivalents like "sfruttare" and "approfittare di," but also to render two figurative verbs literally meaning *hook the economic recovery* and *grab the opportunity*. These shifts seem indicative of a normalizing tendency whereby translators opt for standard, frequent phrases offered by the TL to render a variety of less lexicalized ST expressions. Further studies on larger corpora are necessary to ascertain that these findings are in fact statistically significant and thus generalizable.

3.4 Conclusion

A method for comparing use of collocations in translated and non-translated texts was applied to two monolingual comparable corpora of texts from the same domain and in the same language (finance/English) but varying in size and genre (a largish corpus of financial reports and a tiny corpus of shareholders' letters). Relying on frequency data obtained from a large monolingual corpus, it was possible to show that translated financial reports are less collocational than comparable non-translated reports, while translated shareholders' letters seem to go in the opposite direction: they feature stronger collocations than non-translated letters, often resulting from explicitating or normalizing shifts. The latter can be observed thanks to the corpus design, which includes a parallel component.

Even though the data available for the second genre are too few to allow confident generalizations (suggesting that some tuning of the method would be required for very small corpora), the picture emerging from this study is one in which (a) both interference and normalization occur in translation, and (b) they do not occur at random. The technical collocations that make the bulk of the FINREP rankings are more subject to interference, while the less technical, often figurative language found in SHARLET is more likely to be rendered in translation with standard, even stereotyped collocations. These findings reinforce a view of the translation process as a norm-governed activity, rather than one that is subject to universal constraints.

Observations about non-technical translation are also in line with corpus studies comparing native and non-native written production (Durrant and Schmitt 2009: 174), which suggest that learners "over-rely on forms which are . . . common in the language." These commonalities between use of collocations by translators translating into their own language and by learners writing in a foreign language point to fascinating new research directions, to be pursued through solid yet ingenious research methodologies, sensitive to the situational context of translation and integrating product- and process-oriented approaches, as discussed in the first part of this chapter.

References

Aarts, B. 2007. *Syntactic gradience: The nature of grammatical indeterminacy.* Oxford University Press.

Aarts, B., Close, J., Leech, G., and Wallis, S. (eds.). 2013. *The verb phrase in English: Investigating recent language change with corpora.* Cambridge University Press.

Aarts, B., Close, J., and Wallis, S. 2013. Choices over time: Methodological issues in investigating current change. In Aarts, Close, Leech, and Wallis (eds.), 14–45.

Aarts, F. G. A. M. 1971. On the distribution of noun-phrase types in English clause-structure. *Lingua* 26(3): 281–293.

Aarts, J. 1999. The description of language use. In H. Hasselgård and S. Oksefjell (eds.), *Out of corpora: Studies in honour of Stig Johansson*, 3–20. Amsterdam and Atlanta: Rodopi.

Ädel, A. 2008a. Involvement features in writing: Do time and interaction trump register awareness? In G. Gilquin, S. Papp, and M. B. Díez-Bedmar (eds.), *Linking up contrastive and learner corpus research*, 35–53. Amsterdam: Rodopi.

2008b. *Metadiscourse in L1 and L2 English.* Amsterdam: John Benjamins.

Ädel, A. and Erman, B. 2012. Recurrent word combinations in academic writing by native and non-native speakers of English: A lexical bundles approach. *English for Specific Purposes* 31: 81–92.

Adger, D. and Smith, J. 2010. Variation in agreement: A lexical feature-based approach. *Lingua* 120: 1109–1134.

Adolphs, S. 2008. *Corpus and context.* Amsterdam: John Benjamins.

Adolphs, S. and Knight, D. 2010. Building a spoken corpus: what are the basics? In A. O'Keeffe and M. McCarthy (eds.), *The Routledge handbook of corpus linguistics*, 38–52. London: Routledge.

Adolphs, S., Atkins, S., and Harvey, K. 2007. Caught between professional requirements and interpersonal needs: Vague language in healthcare contexts. In J. Cutting (ed.), *Vague language explored*, 62–78. New York: Palgrave Macmillan.

Afida, M. A. 2007. Semantic fields of problem in business English: Malaysian and British journalistic business texts. *Corpora* 2(2): 211–239.

Aguado-Jiménez, P., Pérez-Paredes, P., and Sanchez, P. 2012. Exploring the use of multidimensional analysis of learner language to promote register awareness. *System* 40: 90–103.

Ahmad, K., Corbett, G., and Rogers, M. 1985. Using computers with advanced language learners: An example. *Language Teacher* (Tokyo) 9(3): 4–7.

Aijmer, K. 2002a. *English discourse particles: Evidence from corpora*. Amsterdam: John Benjamins.

2002b. Modality in advanced Swedish learners' written interlanguage. In S. Granger, J. Hung, and S. Petch-Tyson (eds.), *Computer learner corpora, second language acquisition and foreign language teaching*, 55–76. Amsterdam: John Benjamins.

2011. *Well I'm not sure I think . . .*: The use of *well* by non-native speakers. *International Journal of Corpus Linguistics* 16(2): 231–254.

2013. *Understanding pragmatic markers: A variational pragmatic approach*. Edinburgh University Press.

Aijmer, K. and Simon-Vandenbergen, A.-M. (eds.). 2006. *Pragmatic markers in contrast*. Oxford: Elsevier.

Allan, R. 2006. *Data-driven learning and vocabulary: Investigating the use of concordances with advanced learners of English*. Centre for Language and Communication Studies, Occasional Paper, 66. Dublin: Trinity College Dublin.

Alonso-Almeida, F., Ortega-Barrera, I., and Quintana-Toledo, E. 2012. Corpus of Early English Recipes: Design and implementation. In Vázquez (ed.), 37–50.

Al-Surmi, M. 2012. Authenticity and TV shows: A multidimensional analysis perspective. *TESOL Quarterly*, 46(4): 671–694.

Altenberg, B. 1998. On the phraseology of spoken English: The evidence of recurrent word combinations. In A. Cowie (ed.), *Phraseology: Theory, analysis and applications*, 101–122. Oxford University Press.

Altenberg, B. and Granger, S. 2001. The grammatical and lexical patterning of MAKE in native and non-native student writing. *Applied Linguistics* 22 (2), 173–194.

Alves, F., Pagano, A., Neumann, S., Steiner, E., and Hansen-Schirra, S. 2010. Translation units and grammatical shifts: Towards an integration of product- and process-based translation research. In G. Shreve and E. Angelone (eds.), *Translation and cognition*, 109–142. Amsterdam: John Benjamins.

Amador-Moreno, C. 2012. A corpus-based approach to contemporary Irish writing: Ross O'Carroll-Kelly's use of *like* as a discourse marker. *International Journal of English Studies* 12(2): 19–38.

Andersen, G. 1997. *They like wanna see like how we talk and all that*: The use of *like* as a discourse marker in London teenage speech. In M. Ljung (ed.), *Corpus-based studies in English*, 37–48. Amsterdam: Rodopi.

2001. *Pragmatic markers and sociolinguistic variation: A relevance-theoretic approach to the language of adolescents*. Amsterdam: John Benjamins.

Andersen, G. and Bech, K. (eds.). 2013. *English corpus linguistics: Variation in time, space and genre*. Amsterdam and New York: Rodopi.

Anderwald, L. 2002. *Negation in non-standard British English: Gaps, regularizations and asymmetrics*. London: Routledge.

2005. Negative concord in British English dialects. In Y. Iyeiri (ed.), *Aspects of English negation*, 113–137. Amsterdam: John Benjamins.

2009. *The morphology of English dialects: Verb formation in non-standard English*. Cambridge University Press.

Anderwald, L. and Wagner, S. 2007. *FRED – The Freiburg English Dialect Corpus*: Applying corpus-linguistic research tools to the analysis of dialect data. Creating and digitizing language corpora. *Synchronic Databases* 1: 35–53.

Anshen, F. and Aronoff, M. 1999. Using dictionaries to study the mental lexicon. *Brain and Language* 68(1–2): 16–26.

AntConc. 2007–2013. Anthony, L. Tokyo, Japan: Waseda University. See www.antlab.sci.waseda.ac.jp/index.html (accessed 28 February 2013).

Anthony, L. 2004. AntConc: A learner and classroom friendly, multi-platform corpus analysis toolkit. *Proceedings of IWLeL 2004: An Interactive Workshop on Language e-Learning* 7–13.

Archer, D. 2005. *Questions and answers in the English courtroom (1640–1760): A sociopragmatic analysis*. Amsterdam: John Benjamins.

(ed.). 2009. *What's in a word-list? Investigating word frequency and keyword extraction*. Farnham, Surrey: Ashgate.

2014. Exploring verbal aggression in English historical texts using USAS: The possibilities, the problems and potential solutions. In Taavitsainen, Jucker, and Tuominen (eds.), 277–302.

Archer, D., Aijmer, K., and Wichmann, A. 2012. *Pragmatics: An advanced resource book for students*. London: Routledge.

Archer, D. and Bousfield, D. 2010. See better, Lear? See Lear better! A corpus-based pragma-stylistic investigation of Shakespeare's *King Lear*. In McIntyre and Busse (eds.), 183–203.

Archer, D., Culpeper, J., and Rayson, P. 2009. Love – a familiar or a devil? An exploration of key domains in Shakespeare's comedies and tragedies. In Archer (ed.), 137–157.

Argamon, S., Koppel, M., Fine, J., and Shimoni, A. R. 2003. Gender, genre, and writing style in formal written texts. *Text*, 23: 321–346.

Arnold, M. 1861. *On translating Homer*. London: Longman, Green, Longman, and Roberts.

Arnovick, L. K. 1999. *Diachronic pragmatics: Seven case studies in English illocutionary development*. Amsterdam: John Benjamins.

Asención-Delaney, Y. and Collentine, J. 2011. A multidimensional analysis of written L2 Spanish. *Applied Linguistics* 32: 299–322.

Asmussen, J. 2013. Combined products: Dictionary and corpus. In R. H. Gouws, U. Heid, W. Schweickard, and H. E. Wiegand (eds.), *Dictionaries: An international encyclopedia of lexicography*, vol. 5.4 (suppl.): *Recent developments with focus on electronic and computational lexicography*, 1081–1090. Berlin and New York: Walter de Gruyter.

Aston, G. and Burnard, L. 1998. *The BNC handbook*. Edinburgh University Press.

Azar, B. S. and Hagen, S. A. 2009. *Understanding and using English grammar*, 4th edn. White Plains, NY: Pearson Longman.

Baayen, R. H. 1993. On frequency, transparency, and productivity. In G. E. Booij and J. van Marle (eds.), *Yearbook of Morphology 1992*, 181–208. Dordrecht: Kluwer Academic Publishers.

1994. Productivity in language production. *Language and Cognitive Processes* 9(3), 447–469.

2008. *Analyzing linguistic data: A practical introduction to statistics using R*. Cambridge University Press.

2010. A real experiment is a factorial experiment. *The Mental Lexicon* 5(1): 149–157.

2011. Corpus linguistics and naïve discriminative learning. *Brazilian Journal of Applied Linguistics* 11(2): 295–328.

Baayen, H., van Halteren, H., and Tweedie, F. 1996. Outside the cave of shadows: Using syntactic annotation to enhance authorship attribution. *Literary and Linguistic Computing* 11(3): 121–131.

Bachmann, I. 2011. Civil partnership – "Gay marriage in all but name": A corpus-driven analysis of discourses of same-sex relationships in the UK Parliament. *Corpora* 6(1): 77–105.

Bahumaid, S. 2006. Collocation in English-Arabic translation. *Babel* 52(2): 133–152.

Baker, M. 1993. Corpus linguistics and translation studies: Implications and applications. In M. Baker, G. Francis, and E. Tognini Bonelli (eds.), *Text and technology*, 223–50. Amsterdam: John Benjamins.

1995. Corpora in translation studies: An overview and some suggestions for future research. *Target* 7(2): 223–243.

2000. Towards a methodology for investigating the style of a literary translator. *Target* 12(2): 241–266.

Baker, P. 2004. Querying keywords: Questions of difference, frequency and sense in keywords analysis. *Journal of English Linguistics* 32(4): 346–359.

2005. *The public discourses of gay men*. London: Routledge.

2006. *Using corpora in discourse analysis*. London: Continuum.

2008. "Eligible" bachelors and "frustrated" spinsters: Corpus linguistics, gender and language. In J. Sunderland, K. Harrington, and H. Stantson (eds.), 73–84. *Gender and language research methodologies*. London: Palgrave.

2009a. The BE06 Corpus of British English and recent language change. *International Journal of Corpus Linguistics* 14(3): 312–337.

2009b. The question is, how cruel is it? Keywords, fox hunting and the House of Commons. In Archer (ed.), 125–136.

2010. *Sociolinguistics and corpus linguistics*. Edinburgh University Press.

2011. Times may change, but we will always have money: Diachronic variation in recent British English, *Journal of English Linguistics* 39(1): 65–88.

Baker, P., Gabrielatos, C., Khosravinik, M., Krzyzanowski, M., McEnery, T., and Wodak, R. 2008. A useful methodological synergy? Combining critical discourse analysis and corpus linguistics to examine discourses of refugees and asylum seekers in the UK press. *Discourse and Society* 19(3): 273–306.

Baker, P., Gabrielatos, C., and McEnery, T. 2013. Sketching Muslims: A corpus driven analysis of representations around the word "Muslim" in the British press 1998–2009. *Applied Linguistics* 34(3): 255–278.

Baker, P. and McEnery, T. 2005. A corpus-based approach to discourses of refugees and asylum seekers in UN and newspaper texts. *Journal of Language and Politics* 4(2): 197–226.

Balasubramanian, C. 2009a. *Register variation in Indian English*. Amsterdam: John Benjamins.

2009b. Circumstance adverbials in registers of Indian English. *World Englishes* 28: 485–508.

Ballier, N. and Martin, P. 2013. Developing corpus interoperability for phonetic investigation of learner corpora. In Ana Diaz-Negrillo, N. Ballier, and P. Thompson (eds.), *Automatic treatment and analysis of learner corpus data*, 33–64. Amsterdam: John Benjamins.

Barbieri, F. 2005. Quotative use in American English: A corpus-based, cross-register comparison. *Journal of English Linguistics* 33: 222–256.

2007. Older men and younger women: A corpus-based study of quotative use in American English. *English World-Wide* 28: 23–45.

2008a. Patterns of age-based linguistic variation in American English. *Journal of Sociolinguistics* 12: 58–88.

2008b. Involvement in university classroom discourse. Unpublished dissertation, Northern Arizona University.

2009. Quotative *be like* in American English: Ephemeral or here to stay? *English World-Wide* 30: 68–90.

Barbieri, F. and Eckhardt, S. 2007. Applying corpus-based findings to form-focused instruction: The case of reported speech. *Language Teaching Research* 11(3): 319–346.

Barnbrook, G. 2002. *Defining language: A local grammar of definition sentences*. Amsterdam: John Benjamins.

Baron, A. and Rayson, P. 2008. VARD 2: A tool for dealing with spelling variation in historical corpora. *Proceedings of the Postgraduate Conference in Corpus Linguistics, Aston University, Birmingham, 22 May 2008*. Available at http://acorn.aston.ac.uk/conf_proceedings.html

Baron, N. S. 2004. See you online: Gender issues in college student use of instant messaging. *Journal of Language and Social Psychology* 23: 397–423.

Baroni, M. and Bernardini, S. 2004. BootCaT: Bootstrapping corpora and terms from the web. *Proceedings of LREC 2004*.

2006. A new approach to the study of translationese: Machine-learning the difference between original and translated text. *Literary and Linguistic Computing* 21(3): 259–274.

Baroni, M., Bernardini, S., Ferraresi, A., and Zanchetta, E. 2009. The WaCky Wide Web: A collection of very large linguistically processed web-crawled corpora. *Language Resources and Evaluation* 43(3) 209–226.

Baroni, M., Kilgarriff, A., Pomikálek, J., and Rychlý, P. 2006. WebBootCaT: A web tool for instant corpora. In *Proceedings of Euralex 2006*. Turin.

Bartsch, S. 2004. *Structural and functional properties of collocations in English: A corpus study of lexical and pragmatic constraints on lexical co-occurrence*. Tübingen: Gunter Narr.

Baten, L., Cornu, A-M., and Engels, L. 1989. The use of concordances in vocabulary acquisition. In C. Laurent and M. Nordman (eds.), *Special language: From humans thinking to thinking machines*, 452–467. Clevedon: Multilingual Matters.

Bauer, L. 1993. *Manual of information to accompany the Wellington Corpus of Written New Zealand English*. Wellington: Victoria University, Department of Linguistics.

2001. *Morphological productivity*. Cambridge University Press.

2002. Inferring variation and change from public corpora. In J. K. Chambers, P. Trudgill, and N. Schilling-Estes (eds.), *The handbook of language variation and change*, 97–114. Malden, MA, and Oxford: Blackwell.

Bauer, L. and Nation, P. 1993. Word families. *International Journal of Lexicography*, 6(4): 253–279.

Bayley, P. and Williams, G. 2012. *European identity: What the media say*. Oxford University Press.

Beaufort, A. 2007. *College writing and beyond*. Logan: Utah State University Press.

Becher, V. 2011. When and why do translators add connectives? A corpus-based study. *Target* 23(1): 26–47.

Beckman, M. E., Hirschberg, J., and Shattuck-Hufnagel, S. 2005. The original ToBI system and the evolution of the ToBI framework. In S.-A. Jun (ed.), *15th International Congress of Phonetic Sciences (ICPhS15), Barcelona, Spain, 2–9 August 2003*, 9–14.

Bednarek, M. 2006a. *Evaluation in media discourse: Analysis of a newspaper corpus*. London: Continuum.

2006b. Evaluating Europe: Parameters of evaluation in the British press. In C. Leung and J. Jenkins (eds.), *Reconfiguring Europe: The contribution of applied linguistics*, 137–156. London: BAAL/Equinox.

2008. *Emotion talk across corpora*. London: Palgrave.
2010. *The language of fictional television: Drama and identity*. London: Continuum.

Bednarek, M and Caple, H. 2012. *News discourse*. London: Continuum.

Behre, F. 1955. *Meditative-polemic* SHOULD *in Modern English* THAT*-clauses*. Stockholm: Almqvist & Wiksell.
1967. *Studies in Agatha Christie's writings: The behaviour of* A GOOD (GREAT) DEAL, A LOT, LOTS, MUCH, PLENTY, MANY, A GOOD (GREAT) MANY. Stockholm, Gothenburg, and Uppsala: Almqvist & Wiksell.
1969. Variation and change in the distribution of *lot(s)*, *deal*, *much*, *many*, etc. *English Studies* 50: 435–451.

Bell, A. 1984. Language style as audience design. *Language in Society* 13: 145–204.

Belz, J. and Vyatkina, N. 2005. Learner corpus research and the development of L2 pragmatic competence in networked intercultural language study: The case of German modal particles. *Canadian Modern Language Review* 62(1): 17–48.
2008. The pedagogical mediation of a developmental learner corpus for classroom-based language instruction. *Language Learning & Technology*, 12(3): 33–52.

Bennett, G. 2010. *Using corpora in the language learning classroom: Corpus linguistics for teachers*. University of Michigan Press.

Benson, M. 1990. Collocation and general-purpose dictionaries. *International Journal of Lexicography* 3(1): 23–34.

Benson, M., Benson, E., and Ilson, R. 1986/2010. *The BBI combinatory dictionary of English* (3rd edn.). Amsterdam: John Benjamins.

Benwell, B. and Stokoe, E. 2006. *Discourse and identity*. Edinburgh University Press.

Berber Sardinha, T. 2011. Metaphor and corpus linguistics. *RBLA, Belo Horizonte* 11: 329–360.

Berglund, Y. 2000. *Gonna* and *going to* in the spoken component of the British National Corpus. *Language and Computers* 33: 35–50.

Berman, A. 1985. La traduction comme épreuve de l'étranger. *Texte* 4: 67–81.

Bernaisch, T., Gries, S. Th., and Mukherjee, J. 2014. The dative alternation in South Asian English(es): Modelling predictors and predicting prototypes. *English World-Wide* 35(1): 7–31.

Bernardini, S. and Zanettin, F. 2004. When is a universal not a universal? Some limits of current corpus-based methodologies for the investigation of translation universals. In A. Mauranen and P. Kujamäki (eds.), *Translation universals: Do they exist?*, 51–62. Amsterdam: John Benjamins.

Bertuccelli Papi, M. 2000. Is a diachronic speech act theory possible? *Journal of Historical Pragmatics* 1(1): 57–66.

Bestgen, Y. 2013. Inadequacy of the chi-squared test to examine vocabulary differences between corpora. *Literary and Linguistic Computing* 29(2): 164–170.

Bhana, N. 2009. The chairman's statements and annual reports: Are they reporting the same company performance to investors? *Investment Analysts Journal* 70: 32–46.

Bhuian, S. N., Menguc, B., and Bell, S. J. 2005. Just entrepreneurial enough: the moderating effect of entrepreneurship on the relationship between market orientation and performance. *Journal of Business Research* 58: 9–17.

Biber, D. 1986. Spoken and written textual dimensions in English: Resolving the contradictory findings. *Language* 62: 384–414.

1987. A textual comparison of British and American writing. *American Speech* 62: 99–119.

1988. *Variation across speech and writing*. Cambridge University Press.

1993a. Co-occurrence patterns among collocations: A tool for corpus-based lexical knowledge acquisition. *Computational Linguistics* 19(3): 531–538.

1993b. Representativeness in corpus design. *Literary and Linguistic Computing* 8(4), 243–257.

1995. *Dimensions of register variation*. Cambridge University Press.

2003. Compressed noun-phrase structures in newspaper discourse: The competing demands of popularization vs. economy. In J. Aitchison and D. M. Lewis (eds.), *New media language*, 169–181. London: Routledge.

2004. Historical patterns for the grammatical marking of stance: A cross-register comparison. *Journal of Historical Pragmatics* 5(1): 107–135.

2006a. *University language: A corpus-based study of spoken and written registers*. Amsterdam: John Benjamins.

2006b. Stance in spoken and written university registers. *Journal of English for Academic Purposes* 5: 97–116.

2009. A corpus-driven approach to formulaic language in English: Multi-word patterns in speech and writing. *International Journal of Corpus Linguistics* 14(3): 275–311.

2011. Corpus linguistics and the scientific study of literature: Back to the future? *Scientific Study of Literature* 1(1): 15–23.

2012. Register as a predictor of linguistic variation. *Corpus Linguistics and Linguistic Theory* 8: 9–37.

Biber, D. and Barbieri, F. 2007. Lexical bundles in university spoken and written registers. *English for Specific Purposes* 26: 263–86.

Biber, D. and Burges, J. 2000. Historical change in the language use of women and men: Gender differences in dramatic dialogue. *Journal of English Linguistics* 28: 21–37.

Biber, D., Connor, U., and Upton T. 2007. *Discourse on the move: Using corpus analysis to describe discourse structure*. Amsterdam and Philadelphia: John Benjamins.

Biber, D. and Conrad, S. 1999. Lexical bundles in conversation and academic prose. In H. Hasselgård and S. Oksefjell (eds.), *Out of corpora: Studies in honour of Stig Johansson*, 181–190. Amsterdam: Rodopi.

2009. *Register, genre, and style*. Cambridge University Press.

Biber, D., Conrad, S., and Cortes, V. 2004. "If you look at . . . ": Lexical bundles in university teaching and textbooks. *Applied Linguistics* 25: 371–405.

Biber, D., Conrad, S., and Leech, G. 2002. *The Longman student grammar of spoken and written English*. London: Longman.

Biber, D., Conrad, S., and Reppen, R. 1998. *Corpus linguistics: Investigating language structure and use*. Cambridge University Press.

Biber, D., Conrad, S., Reppen, R., Byrd, P., and Helt, M. 2002. Speaking and writing in the university: A multi-dimensional comparison. *TESOL Quarterly* 36: 9–48.

Biber, D., Conrad, S., Reppen, R., Byrd, P., Helt, M., Clark, V., Cortez, V., Csomay, E., and Urzua, A. 2004. *Representing language use in the university: Analysis of the TOEFL 2000 spoken and written academic language corpus*. Princeton: ETS/TOEFL.

Biber, D., Davies, M., Jones, J., and Tracy-Ventura, N. 2006. Spoken and written register variation in Spanish: A multi-dimensional analysis. *Corpora* 1: 1–37.

Biber, D., Egbert, J. A., Gray, B., Oppliger, R., and Szmrecsanyi, B. Forthcoming. Variationist versus text-linguistic approaches to grammatical change in English: Nominal modifiers of head nouns. *Handbook of English historical linguistics*.

Biber, D. and Finegan, E. 1989. Drift and the evolution of English style: A history of three genres. *Language* 65: 487–517.

1997. Diachronic relations among speech-based and written registers in English. In T. Nevalainen and L. Kahlas-Tarkka (eds.), *To explain the present: Studies in the changing English language in honour of Matti Rissanen*, 253–275. Helsinki: Société Néophilologique.

Biber, D. and Gray, B. 2011. Grammatical change in the noun phrase: The influence of written language use. *English Language and Linguistics* 15(2): 223–250.

2012. The competing demands of popularization vs. economy: Written language in the age of mass literacy. In T. Nevalainen and E. C. Traugott (eds.), *The Oxford handbook of the history of English*, 314–328. Oxford University Press.

2013. *Discourse characteristics of writing and speaking task types on the TOEFL iBT test: A lexico-grammatical analysis* (TOEFL iBT Research Report No. 19). Princeton, NJ: Educational Testing Service.

Biber, D., Gray, B., and Poonpon, K. 2011. Should we use characteristics of conversation to measure grammatical complexity in L2 writing development? *TESOL Quarterly* 45: 5–35.

Biber D., Grieve J., and Iberri-Shea, G. 2010. Noun phrase modification. In G. Rohdenburg and J. Schlüter (eds.), *One language, two grammars? Differences between British and American English*, 182–193. Cambridge University Press.

Biber, D. and Hared, M. 1992. Dimensions of register variation in Somali. *Language Variation and Change* 4: 41–75.

Biber, D., Johansson, S., Leech, G., Conrad, S., and Finegan, E. 1999. *Longman grammar of spoken and written English.* Harlow: Pearson Education.

Biber, D. and Jones, J. 2005. Merging corpus linguistic and discourse analytic research goals: Discourse units in biology research articles. *Corpus Linguistics and Linguistic Theory* 1: 151–182.

Biber, D., Kim, Y-J., and Tracy-Ventura, N. 2010. A corpus-driven approach to comparative phraseology: Lexical bundles in English, Spanish, and Korean. In S. Iwasaki, H. Hoji, P. M. Clancy, and S-O. Sohn (eds.), *Japanese/Korean linguistics*, vol. 17: 75–94. Stanford: Center for the Study of Language and Information (CSLI).

Biewer, C. 2015. *A Sociolinguistic and morphosyntactic profile of Fiji English, Samoan English and Cook Island English.* Amsterdam: John Benjamins.

Biewer, C., Hundt, M., and Zipp, L. 2010. How a Fiji corpus? Challenges in the compilation of an ESL ICE component. *ICAME Journal* 34: 5–23.

Bigi, S. and Greco Morasso, S. 2006. Focus on cultural keywords. *Studies in Communication Sciences* 6(1): 157–174.

2012. Keywords, frames and the reconstruction of material starting points in argumentation. *Journal of Pragmatics* 44(10),1135–1149.

Bizzell, P. 1989. Cultural criticism: a social approach to studying writing. *Rhetoric Review* 7: 224–230.

Blackwell, S. 1987. Syntax versus orthography: Problems in the automatic parsing of idioms. In R. Garside, G. Leech, and G. Sampson (eds.), *The computational analysis of English*, 110–119. Harlow: Longman.

Blankenship, J. 1962. A linguistic analysis of oral and written style. *Quarterly Journal of Speech* 48: 419–422.

Blass, L., Iannuzzi, S., Savage, A., and Reppen, R. 2012. *Grammar and beyond: Level 3.* Cambridge University Press.

Bloomfield, L. 1933. *Language*. New York: Henry Holt.

Blum-Kulka, S. 1997. *Dinner talk: Cultural patterns of sociability and socialization in family discourse*. Mahwah, NJ: Lawrence Erlbaum.

Bolinger, D. 1961. *Generality, gradience, and the all-or-none*. The Hague: Mouton.

Bondi, M. 2008. Emphatics in academic discourse: Integrating corpus and discourse tools in the study of cross-disciplinary variation. In A. Ädel and R. Reppen (eds.), *Exploring discourse through corpora*, 31–55. Amsterdam and Philadelphia: John Benjamins.

2012. Voice in textbooks: Between exposition and argument. In K. Hyland and C. Sancho Guinda (eds.), *Stance and voice in written academic genres*, 101–117. London: Palgrave.

Bondi, M. and Scott, M. (eds.). 2010. *Keyness in texts*. Amsterdam: John Benjamins.

Bondi, M. and Silver, M. 2004. Textual voices: A cross disciplinary study of attribution in academic discourse. In L. Anderson and J. Bamford (eds.), *Evaluation in oral and written discourse*, 117–136. Rome: Officina Edizioni.

Borin, L. and Prütz, K. 2004. New wine in old skins? A corpus investigation of L1 syntactic transfer in learner language. In G. Aston, S. Bernardini, and D. Stewart (eds.), *Corpora and language learners*, 45.66. Amsterdam and Philadelphia: John Benjamins.

Bothma, T. J. D. 2011. Filtering and adapting data and information in an online environment in response to user needs. In Fuertes-Olivera and Bergenholtz (eds.), 71–102.

Boulton, A. 2009. Corpora for all? Learning styles and data-driven learning. In M. Mahlberg, V. González-Díaz, and C. Smith (eds.), *Proceedings of the 5th Corpus Linguistics Conference*. Downloaded from http://ucrel.lancs.ac.uk/publications/cl2009

2010a. Learning outcomes from corpus consultation. In M. Moreno Jaén, F. Serrano Valverde, and M. Calzada Pérez (eds.), *Exploring new paths in language pedagogy: Lexis and corpus-based language teaching*, 129–144. London: Equinox.

2010b. Data-driven learning: Taking the computer out of the equation. *Language Learning* 60(3): 534–572.

2010c. Consultation de corpus et styles d'apprentissage. *Cahiers de l'APLIUT* 29(1): 98–115.

2011. Language awareness and medium-term benefits of corpus consultation. In A. Gimeno Sanz (ed.), *New trends in computer-assisted language learning: Working together*, 39–46. Madrid: Macmillan ELT.

2012a. Computer corpora in language learning: DST approaches to research. *Mélanges Crapel* 33: 79–91.

2012b. Hands-on/hands-off: Alternative approaches to data-driven learning. In J. Thomas and A. Boulton (eds.), *Input, process and product: Developments in teaching and language corpora*, 153–169. Brno: Masaryk University Press.

In press. Applying data-driven learning to the web. In A. Leńko-Szymańska and A. Boulton (eds.), *Multiple affordances of language corpora for data-driven learning*. Amsterdam: John Benjamins.

Boulton, A. and Tyne, H. 2014. *Méthodologie de la découverte en didactique des langues: Des documents authentiques aux corpus*. Paris: Didier.

Bowie, J., Wallis, S., and Aarts, B. 2013. The perfect in spoken British English. In Aarts *et al.* (eds.), 318–352.

Brazil, D. 1994. *Pronunciation for advanced learners of English*. Cambridge University Press.

1994. *Pronunciation for advanced learners of English*. Cambridge University Press.

1995. *A grammar of speech*. Oxford University Press.

1997. *The communicative value of intonation in English.* Cambridge University Press.

Breen, M. 1987. Learner contributions to task design. In C. Candlin and D. Murphy (eds.), *Language learning tasks*, 23–46. Englewood Cliffs, NJ: Prentice Hall.

Breiteneder, A. 2005. The naturalness of English as a European lingua franca: The case of the 'third person -s'. *VIEWS* 14(2): 3–26. Downloaded from http://anglistik.univie.ac.at/fileadmin/user_upload/dep_anglist/weitere_Uploads/Views/Views0502ALL_new.pdf (accessed 9 July 2013).

Breiteneder, A., Pitzl, M. L., Majewski, S., and Klimpfinger, T. 2006. VOICE recording: Methodological challenges in the compilation of a corpus of spoken ELF. *Nordic Journal of English Studies* 5(2): 161–187.

Brems, L. 2011. *Measure noun constructions: An instance of semantically-driven grammaticalization.* Berlin: Mouton de Gruyter.

Bresnan, J. 2007. Is syntactic knowledge probabilistic? Experiments with the English dative alternation. In S. Featherston and W. Sternefeld (eds.), *Roots: Linguistics in search of its evidential base*, 77–96. Berlin: Mouton de Gruyter.

Bresnan, J., Cueni, A., Nikitina, T., and Baayen, H. R. 2007. Predicting the dative alternation. In G. Boume, I. Kraemer, and J. Zwarts (eds.), *Cognitive foundations of interpretation*, 69–94. Amsterdam: Royal Netherlands Academy of Science.

Bresnan, J. and Ford, M. 2010. Predicting syntax: Processing dative constructions in American and Australian varieties of English. *Language* 86/1: 186–213.

Bretz, F., Hothorn, T., and Pestfall, P. 2010. *Multiple comparisons using R.* Boca Raton, FL: Chapman & Hall/CRC.

Brezina, V. and Gablasova, D. 2013. Is there a core general vocabulary? Introducing the New General Service List. *Applied Linguistics.*

Brinton, L. J. 2007. The development of *I mean*: Implications for the study of historical pragmatics. In Fitzmaurice and Taavitsainen (eds.), 37–79.

2010. Discourse markers. In Jucker and Taavitsainen (eds.), 285–314.

2015. Interjection-based delocutive verbs in the history of English. In I. Taavitsainen *et al.* (eds.), *Developments in English: Expanding electronic evidence*, 140–161. Cambridge University Press.

Briscoe, T., Medlock, B., and Andersen, Ø. 2010. Automated assessment of ESOL free text examinations. *Cambridge ESOL.* University of Cambridge Computer Laboratory. www.cl.cam.ac.uk/techreports/UCAM-CL-TR-790.pdf

Brown, A. and Deterding, D. 2005. A checklist of Singapore English pronunciation features. In D. Deterding, A. Brown, and L. Ee Ling (eds.), *English in Singapore: Phonetic research on a corpus*, 7–13. Singapore: McGraw-Hill.

Brown, P. and Fraser, C. 1979. Speech as a marker of situation. In K. Scherer and H. Giles (eds.), *Social markers in speech*, 33–62. Cambridge University Press.

Brown, P. and Levinson, S. 1987. *Politeness: Some universals in language usage*. Cambridge University Press.

Brown, R. and Gilman, A. 1960. The pronouns of power and solidarity. In T. Sebeok (ed.), *Style in language*, 253–276. Cambridge, MA: MIT Press.

Bruce, I. 2009. Results sections in sociology and organic chemistry articles: A genre analysis *English for Specific Purposes* 28(2): 105–124.

Bryson, B. 1991. *Neither here nor there: Travels in Europe*. London: Secker & Warburg.

Buchstaller, I. 2011. Quotations across the generations: A multivariate analysis of speech and thought introducers across 5 decades of Tyneside speech. *Corpus Linguistics and Linguistic Theory* 7(1): 59–92.

Bündgens-Kosten, J. 2013. Authenticity in CALL: Three domains of "realness" *ReCALL*, 25/2, 272–285.

Bunton, D. 1999. The use of higher level metatext in PhD theses. *English for Specific Purposes* 18: S41–S56.

Burnard, L. (ed.). 1995. *British National Corpus: Users reference guide British National Corpus Version 1.0*. Oxford University Computing Service.

2002. Where did we go wrong? A retrospective look at the British National Corpus. *Language and Computers* 42: 51–70.

Burrows, J. F. 1987. *Computation into criticism: A study of Jane Austen's novels and an experiment in method*. Oxford: Clarendon.

Busse, B. 2006. *Vocative constructions in the language of Shakespeare* (Pragmatics & Beyond new series 150). Amsterdam: John Benjamins.

2010. Speech, writing and thought presentation in a corpus of nineteenth-century English narrative fiction. University of Bern.

Busse, U. and Hübler, A. (eds.). 2012. *The meta-communicative lexicon of English now and then: A historical pragmatics approach*. Amsterdam: John Benjamins.

Butler, C. 1974. German for chemists: Teaching languages to adults for special purposes. *CILT Reports and Papers* 11: 50–53.

1998. Collocational frameworks in Spanish. *International Journal of Corpus Linguistics* 3(1): 1–32.

Bybee, J. 2007. *Frequency of use and the organization of language*. New York: Oxford University Press.

Caldas-Coulthard, C. and Coulthard, M. (eds.). 1996. *Texts and practices: Readings in critical discourse analysis*. London: Routledge.

Calhoun, S. 2010. How does informativeness affect prosodic prominence? *Language and Cognitive Processes* 25(7–9): 1099–1140.

Callies, M. 2009. "What is even more alarming is . . . " A contrastive learner-corpus study of what-clefts in advanced German and Polish L2 writing.

In M. Wysocka (ed.), *On Language structure, acquisition and teaching. Studies in honour of Janusz Arabski on the occasion of his 70th birthday*, 283–292. Katowice: Wydawnictwo Uniwersyetu Slaskiego.

Campion, M. and Elley, W. 1971. *An academic vocabulary list*. Wellington, New Zealand: Council for Educational Research.

Carter, R. 2004. *Language and creativity: The art of common talk*. London: Routledge.

Carter, R., Hughes, R., and McCarthy, M. 1998. Telling tails: Grammar, the spoken language and materials development. In B. Tomlinson (ed.), *Materials development in language teaching*, 67–89. Cambridge University Press.

Carter, R. and McCarthy, M. 1995. Grammar and the spoken language. *Applied Linguistics* 16.2: 141–58.

1997. *Exploring spoken English*. Cambridge University Press.

1999. The English *get*-passive in spoken discourse: Description and implications for an interpersonal grammar. *English Language and Linguistics* 3: 41–58.

2004. Talking, creating: Interactional language, creativity, and context. *Applied Linguistics* 25: 62–88.

2006. *Cambridge grammar of English: A comprehensive guide*. Cambridge University Press.

Carter, R., McCarthy, M., Mark, G., and O'Keeffe, A. 2011. *English grammar today*. Cambridge University Press.

Catford, J. C. 1965. *A linguistic theory of translation: An essay in applied linguistics*. Oxford University Press.

Cauldwell, R. T. 2003a. *Streaming speech: Listening and pronunciation for advanced learners of English* (Windows CD-ROM). Birmingham: Speechinaction.

2003b. *Streaming speech: Listening and pronunciation for advanced learners of English* (Student's book). Birmingham: Speechinaction.

2007. SpeechinAction Research Centre (SPARC). (www.speechinaction.com/, accessed 18 March 2013.)

2013. *Phonology for listeners: Teaching the stream of speech*. Birmingham: Speechinaction.

Cauldwell, R. T. and Hewings, M. 1996. Intonation rules in ELP textbooks. *ELT Journal* 50:4, 327–334.

Chambers, A. 2007. Popularising corpus consultation by language learners and teachers. In E. Hidalgo, L. Quereda, and J. Santana (eds.), *Corpora in the foreign language classroom*, 3–16. Amsterdam: Rodopi.

Chambers, A., Conacher, J., and Littlemore, J. (eds.). 2004. *ICT and language learning: Integrating pedagogy and practice*. University of Birmingham Press.

Chambers, J. K. 2004. Dynamic typology and vernacular roots. In B. Kortmann (ed.), *Dialectology meets typology: Dialect grammar from a cross-linguistic perspective*, 127–145. New York: Mouton de Gruyter.

Chan, T-P. and Liou, H-C. 2005. Effects of web-based concordancing instruction on EFL students' learning of verb-noun collocations. *Computer Assisted Language Learning* 18(3): 231–251.

Chang, P. 2012. Using a stance corpus to learn about effective authorial stance-taking: A textlinguistic approach. *ReCALL* 24(2): 209–236.

Chang, W-L. and Sun, Y-C. 2009. Scaffolding and web concordancers as support for language learning. *Computer Assisted Language Learning* 22 (4): 283–302.

Charles, M. 2006a. Phraseological patterns in reporting clauses used in citation: a corpus-based study of theses in two disciplines. *English for Specific Purposes* 25: 310–331.

2006b. The construction of stance in reporting clauses: a cross-disciplinary study of theses. *Applied Linguistics* 27: 492–518.

2007. Argument or evidence? Disciplinary variation in the use of the noun *that* pattern. *English for Specific Purposes* 26: 203–18.

Chen, Y.-H. and Baker, P. 2010. Lexical bundles in L1 and L2 academic writing. *Language Learning and Technology* 14(2): 30–49.

Cheng, W. 2007. The use of vague language across genres in an International Hong Kong Corpus. In J. Cutting (ed.), *Vague language explored*, 161–181. New York: Palgrave Macmillan.

2012. *Exploring corpus linguistics*. London: Routledge.

Cheng, W., Greaves, C., Sinclair, J., and Warren, M. 2008. Uncovering the extent of the phraseological tendency: Towards a systematic analysis of concgrams. *Applied Linguistics* 30(2): 236–52.

Cheng, W., Greaves, C., and Warren, M. 2006. From n-gram to skipgram to concgram. *International Journal of Corpus Linguistics* 11(4): 411–433.

2008. *A corpus-driven study of discourse intonation*. Amsterdam: John Benjamins.

Chesterman, A. 2004. Hypotheses about translation universals. In G. Hansen, K. Malmkjær, and D. Gile (eds.), *Claims, changes and challenges in translation studies*, 1–13. Amsterdam: John Benjamins.

Cho, H. and Yoon, H. 2013. A corpus-assisted comparative genre analysis of corporate earnings calls between Korean and native-English speakers. *English for Specific Purposes* 32: 170–185.

Chomsky, N. 1957. *Syntactic structures*. The Hague: Mouton.

1962/1964. A transformational approach to syntax. In A. A. Hill (ed.), *Proceedings of the Third Texas Conference on Problems of Linguistics Analysis*, 124–58. Austin: University of Texas, 1962. Reprinted in J. A. Fodor and J. J. Katz, *The Structure of language*, 211–241. Englewood Cliffs, NJ: Prentice-Hall, 1964.

Chomsky, N. and Halle, M. 1968. *The sound pattern of English*. New York: Harper and Row.

Chun, D. M. 2002. *Discourse intonation in L2: From theory and research to practice*. Amsterdam and Philadelphia: John Benjamins.

Church, K. and Hanks, P. 1990. Word association norms, mutual information and lexicography. *Computational Linguistics* 16(1): 22–29.

Clancy, B. 2005. "You're fat. You'll eat them all." Politeness strategies in family discourse. In K. P. Schneider and A. Barron (eds.), *The pragmatics of Irish English*, 177–197. Berlin: Mouton de Gruyter.

2010. Building a corpus to represent a variety of language. In A. O'Keeffe and M. McCarthy (eds.), *The Routledge handbook of corpus linguistics*, 80–92. Abingdon, Oxon: Routledge.

Forthcoming. Hurry up baby son all the boys is finished their breakfast: Examining the use of vocatives as pragmatic markers in Irish Traveller and settled family discourse. In C. Amador Moreno, K. McCafferty, and E. Vaughan (eds.), *Pragmatic markers in Irish English*. Amsterdam: John Benjamins.

Clancy, B. and McCarthy, M. 2015. Co-constructed turn-taking. In K. Aijmer and C. Rühlemann (eds.), *Corpus pragmatics*, 430–453. Cambridge University Press.

Clancy, B. and Vaughan, E. 2012. It's lunacy now: A corpus-based pragmatic analysis of the use of now in contemporary Irish English. In B. Migge and M. Ní Chiosáin (eds.), *New perspectives on Irish English*, 225–246. Amsterdam: John Benjamins.

Claridge, C. 2008. Historical corpora. In A. Lüdeling and M. Kytö (eds.), *Corpus linguistics*. Handbücher zur Sprach- und Kommunikationswissenschaft, 242–259. Berlin: Mouton de Gruyter.

2012. Chapter 16. Linguistic levels: Styles, registers, genres, text types. In A. Bergs and L. J. Brinton (eds.), *English historical linguistics: An international handbook*, vol. 1: 237–253. Berlin and Boston: Walter de Gruyter.

Claridge, C. and Arnovick, L. 2010. Pragmaticalisation and discursisation. In Jucker and Taavitsainen (eds.), 165–192.

Clark, H. H. 1973. The language-as-fixed-effect fallacy: a critique of language statistics in psychological research. *Journal of Verbal Learning and Verbal Behavior* 12(4). 335–359.

Cobb, T. 1997a. From concord to lexicon: Development and test of a corpus-based lexical tutor. Unpublished PhD thesis, Concordia University.

1997b. Is there any measurable learning from hands-on concordancing? *System* 25(3): 301–315.

1999a. Applying constructivism: A test for the learner-as-scientist. *Educational Technology Research & Development* 47(3): 15–33.

1999b. Breadth and depth of lexical acquisition with hands-on concordancing. *Computer Assisted Language Learning* 12(4): 345–360.

2003. Analyzing late interlanguage with learner corpora: Québec replications of three European studies. *The Canadian Modern Language Review* 59(3) 393–423.

2007. Computing the vocabulary demands of L2 reading. *Language Learning & Technology* 11(3): 38–63.

Cobb, T., Greaves, C., and Horst, M. 2001. Can the rate of lexical acquisition from reading be increased? An experiment in reading French with a suite of on-line resources. In P. Raymond and C. Cornaire (eds.), *Regards sur la didactique des langues secondes*, 133–153. Montreal: Editions Logique.

Cochran, W. G. 1954. Some methods for strengthening the common 2 tests. *Biometrics* 10: 417–451.

Coffey, S. 2006. "Delexical verb + noun" phrases in monolingual English learners' dictionaries. *Proceedings of the XII EURALEX Congress*. Downloaded from www.euralex.org/elx_proceedings/Euralex2006/

Cogo, A. and Dewey, M. 2006. Efficiency in ELF communication: From pragmatic motives to lexico-grammatical innovation. *Nordic Journal of English Studies* 5(2): 59–93.

2012. *Analysing English as a lingua franca: A corpus-driven investigation*. London: Continuum.

Cohen, J. 1988. *Statistical power analysis for the behavioral sciences*, 2nd edn. Hillsdale, NJ: Erlbaum.

Cole, J., Mo, Y., and Baek, S. 2010. The role of syntactic structure in guiding prosody perception with ordinary listeners and everyday speech. *Language and Cognitives Processes* 25(7–9), 1141–1177.

Cole, J., Mo, Y., and Hasegawa-Johnson, M. 2010. Signal-based and expectation-based factors in the perception of prosodic prominence. *Laboratory Phonology* 1, 425–452.

Collins, P. 2009. *The progressive in English*. In Peters *et al.* (eds.), 115–123.

Collins, P. and Peters, P. 1988. The Australian corpus project. In M. Kytö, O. Ihalainen, and M. Rissanen (eds.), *Corpus linguistics, hard and soft*, 103–121. Amsterdam: Rodopi.

Collins, P. and Yao, X. 2012. Modals and quasi-modals in New Englishes. In Hundt and Gut (eds.), 35–53.

Connor, U. and Upton, T. 2003. Linguistic dimensions of direct mail letters. In C. Meyer and P. Leistyna (eds.), *Corpus analysis: Language structure and language use*, 71–86. Amsterdam: Rodopi.

2004. The genre of grant proposals: A corpus linguistic analysis. In U. Connor and T. Upton (eds.), *Discourse in the professions: Perspectives from corpus linguistics*, 235–256. Amsterdam: John Benjamins.

Conrad, S. 1996. Investigating academic texts with corpus-based techniques: An example from biology. *Linguistics and Education* 8: 299–326.

1999. The importance of corpus-based research for language teachers. *System* 27: 1–18.

2000. Will corpus linguistics revolutionize grammar teaching in the 21st century? *TESOL Quarterly* 34: 548–560.

2001. Variation among disciplinary texts: A comparison of textbooks and journal articles in biology and history. In S. Conrad and D. Biber (eds.), *Multi-dimensional studies of register variation in English*, 94–107. Harlow: Pearson Education.

2014. Expanding multi-dimensional analysis with qualitative research techniques. In T. Berber Sardinha and M. Veirano Pinto (eds.), *Multi-dimensional analysis 25 years on: A tribute to Douglas Biber*, 273–295. Amsterdam: John Benjamins.

Conrad, S. and Biber, D. 2000. Adverbial marking of stance in speech and writing. In S. Hunston and G. Thompson (eds.), *Evaluation in text: Authorial stance and the construction of discourse*, 56–73. Oxford University Press.

2009. *Real grammar: A corpus-based approach to English grammar*. New York: Pearson Education.

Conrad, S. and Pfeiffer T. 2011. *A preliminary analysis of student and workplace writing in civil engineering. Proceedings of the 2012 American Society for Engineering Education Conference*. Downloaded from www.asee.org/search/proceedings

Conrad, S., Pfeiffer, T., and Szymoniak, T. 2012. *Preparing students for writing in civil engineering practice. Proceedings of the 2012 American Society for Engineering Education Conference*. Downloaded from www.asee.org/search/proceedings

Conzett, J. 1997. Integrating collocation into a reading and writing course. In J. Coady and T. Huckin (eds.), *Second language vocabulary acquisition*, 70–87. Cambridge University Press.

Cortes, V. 2004. Lexical bundles in published and student disciplinary writing: Examples from history and biology. *English for Specific Purposes* 23: 397–423.

2008. A comparative analysis of lexical bundles in academic history writing in English and Spanish. *Corpora* 3: 43–58.

2013. *The purpose of this study is to*: Connecting lexical bundles and moves in research article introductions. *Journal of English for Academic Purposes* 12: 33–43.

Cotter, C. 2010. *News talk: Investigating the language of journalism*. Cambridge University Press.

Council of Europe 2001. *Common European Framework of Reference for Languages*. Cambridge University Press.

Cowden-Clarke, M. V. 1881. *The complete concordance to Shakespeare: Being a verbal index to all the passages in the dramatic works of the poet*, new and rev. edn. Bickers & Son, London.

Cowie, A. P. 1999. *English dictionaries for foreign learners: A history*. Oxford University Press.

Cowie, C. 2010. Researching and understanding accent shifts in Indian call centre agents. In G. Forey and J. Lockwood (eds.), *Globalization, communication and the workplace: Talking across the world*, 125–144. London: Continuum.

Coxhead, A. 2000. A new academic word list. *TESOL Quarterly* 34: 213–238.

Craig, H. 2004. Stylistic analysis and authorship studies. In S. Schreibman, R. Siemens, and J. Unsworth (eds.), *A companion to digital humanities*, 273–288. Oxford: Blackwell.

2008. "Speak, that I may see thee": Shakespeare characters and common words. *Shakespeare Survey* 61: 281–288.

Craig, W. J. 1914. William Shakespeare (1564–1616). *The Oxford Shakespeare*. Oxford University Press. www.bartleby.com/70/ (accessed 5 March 2013).

Cresti, E. and Moneglia, M. 2005. *C-Oral-Rom Integrated Reference Corpora for Spoken Languages*. Amsterdam: John Benjamins.

Crombie, A. C. 1995. Commitments and styles of European scientific thinking. *History of science* 33: 225–38.

Crossley, S. and Louwerse, M. 2007. Multi-dimensional register classification using bigrams. *International Journal of Corpus Linguistics* 12: 453–478.

Cruttenden, A. 1997. *Intonation*, 2nd edn. Cambridge University Press.

Crystal, D. 1975. *The English tone of voice*. London: Edward Arnold.

1995. *The Cambridge encyclopedia of the English language*. Cambridge University Press.

2012. Searchlinguistics. In C. Chapelle (ed.), *The encyclopedia of applied linguistics*. New York: Wiley.

Csomay, E. 2005. Linguistic variation within university classroom talk: A corpus-based perspective. *Linguistics and Education* 15: 243–274.

2013. Lexical bundles in discourse structure: A corpus-based study of classroom discourse. *Applied Linguistics* 34(3): 369–88.

Culpeper, J. 2001. *Language and characterization: People in plays and other texts*. Harlow: Pearson Education.

2002. Computers, language and characterisation: An analysis of six characters in *Romeo and Juliet*. In U. Melander-Marttala, C. Ostman, and M. Kytö (eds.), *Conversation in life and in literature: Papers from the ASLA Symposium* (Association Suédoise de Linguistique Appliquée (ASLA), 15), 11–30. Uppsala: Universitetstryckeriet. See www.lexically.net/wordsmith/corpus_linguistics_links/Keywords-Culpeper.pdf (accessed 5 March 2013).

2009a. Historical sociopragmatics: An introduction. *Journal of Historical Pragmatics* 10(2): 179–186; rpt *Historical Sociopragmatics*. Amsterdam: John Benjamins.

2009b. Keyness: Words, parts-of-speech and semantic categories in the character-talk of Shakespeare's *Romeo and Juliet*. *International Journal of Corpus Linguistics* 14(1): 29–59.

2011. *Impoliteness: Using language to cause offence*. Cambridge University Press.

Culpeper, J. and Kytö, M. 2010. *Early Modern English dialogues: Spoken interaction as writing*. Cambridge University Press.

Curado Fuentes, A. 2001. Lexical behaviour in academic and technical corpora: Implications for ESP development. *Language Learning and Technology* 5(3):106–129.

Curzan, A. 2012. Interdisciplinarity and historiography: periodization in the history of the English language. In A. Bergs and L. Brinton (eds.), *Historical linguistics of English*, vol. 2:1233–1256. Berlin: Mouton de Gruyter.

Cutler, A., Dahan, D., and van Donselaar, W. 1997. Prosody in the comprehension of spoken language: A literature review. *Language and Speech* 40: 141–201.

Dagneaux, E., Denness, S., and Granger, S. 1998. Computer-aided error analysis. *System* 26: 163–174.

Dalton-Puffer, C. 1996. *The French influence on Middle English morphology: A corpus-based study of derivation*. Berlin: Mouton de Gruyter.

Damerau, F. J. 1993. Generating and evaluating domain-oriented multi-word terms from texts. *Information Processing and Management* 29: 433–447.

Danielsson, P. 2001. The automatic identification of meaningful units in language. Unpublished doctoral dissertation, Göteborg University.

D'Arcy, A. 2011. Corpora: Capturing language in use. In W. Maguire and A. McMahon (eds.), *Analysing variation in English*, 49–72. Cambridge University Press.

2012. The diachrony of quotation: Evidence from New Zealand English. *Language Variation and Change* 24(3): 343–369.

da Silva, A. S. 2010. Measuring and parameterizing lexical convergence and divergence between European and Brazilian Portuguese. In D. Geeraerts, G. Kristiansen, and Y. Peirsman (eds.), *Advances in cognitive sociolinguistics*, 41–84. Berlin and New York: Mouton de Gruyter.

da Silva, J. F., Dias, G., Guilloré, S., and Pereira Lopes, J. G. 1999. Using LocalMaxs Algorithm for the extraction of contiguous and non-contiguous multiword lexical units. *Proceedings of the 9th Portuguese Conference on Artificial Intelligence: Progress in Artificial Intelligence*, 113–132. Berlin: Springer.

Daudaravičius, V. and Marcinkevičienė, R. 2004. Gravity counts for the boundaries of collocations. *International Journal of Corpus Linguistics* 9 (2): 321–348.

Davies, M. 2007. *The TIME Magazine Corpus (100 million words, 1920s–2000s)*. Available online at http://corpus.byu.edu/time

2008. *The Corpus of Contemporary American English (COCA): 400+ million words, 1990-present*. Available online at www.americancorpus.org

2009. The 385+ million word *Corpus of Contemporary American English* (1990–2008+): Design, architecture, and linguistic insights. *International Journal of Corpus Linguistics* 14: 159–90.

2010. *The Corpus of Historical American English (COHA): 400+ million words, 1810–2009*. http://corpus.byu.edu/coha

2011. *The Corpus of Contemporary American English* as the first reliable monitor corpus of English. *Literary and Linguistic Computing* 25: 447–65.

2012a. Expanding horizons in historical linguistics with the 400 million word *Corpus of Historical American English. Corpora* 7: 121–57.

2012b. Examining recent changes in English: Some methodological issues. In T. Nevalainen and E. C. Traugott (eds.), *Handbook on the history of English: Rethinking approaches to the history of English*, 263–87. Oxford University Press.

2013. Recent shifts with three nonfinite verbal complements in English: data from the 100-million-word *Time* corpus (1920s-2000s). In Aarts *et al.* (eds.), 46–67.

Forthcoming. A corpus-based study of lexical developments in Early and Late Modern English. In Merja Kytö and Päivi Pahta (eds.), *Handbook of English historical linguistics*. Cambridge University Press.

Davydova, J. 2011. *The present perfect in non-native Englishes: A corpus-based study of variation*. Berlin: De Gruyter.

Dayrell, C. 2007. A quantitative approach to compare collocational patterns in translated and non-translated texts. *International Journal of Corpus Linguistics* 12(3): 375–414.

De Cock, S. 2002. *Pragmatic prefabs in learners' dictionaries. Proceedings of the X EURALEX Congress*. Downloaded from www.euralex.org/elx_proceedings/Euralex2002/

2004. Preferred sequences of words in NS and NNS speech. *Belgian Journal of English Language and Literatures (BELL)*, New Series 2: 225–246.

De Cock, S. and Granger, S. 2004. High frequency words: The bête noire of lexicographers and learners alike. A close look at the verb "make" in five monolingual learners' dictionaries of English. *Proceedings of the XI EURALEX Congress*. Downloaded from www.euralex.org/elx_proceedings/Euralex2004/

2005. Computer learner corpora and monolingual learners' dictionaries: The perfect match. *Lexicographica* 20: 72–86.

de Haan, P. 1989. *Postmodifying clauses in the English noun phrase: A corpus-based study*. Amsterdam: Rodopi.

Dehé, N. 2009. Clausal parentheticals, intonational phrasing, and prosodic theory. *Journal of Linguistics* 45(3):569–615.

Dehé, N. and Wichmann, A. 2010. The multifunctionality of epistemic parentheticals in Discourse: Prosodic cues to the semantic–pragmatic boundary. *Functions of Language* 17(1): 1–28.

Deignan, A. and Semino, E. 2010. Corpus techniques for metaphor analysis. In L. Cameron and R. Maslen (eds.), *Metaphor analysis: Research practice in applied linguistics, social sciences and the humanities*, 161–179. London: Equinox.

Delaere, I., De Sutter, G., and Plevoets, K. 2012. Is translated language more standardized than non-translated language? *Target* 24(2): 203–224.

Demol, A. and Hadermann, P. 2008. An exploratory study of discourse organisation in French L1, Dutch L1, French L2 and Dutch L2 written narratives. In G. Gilquin, S. Papp, and M. B. Díez-Bedmar (eds.), *Linking up contrastive and learner corpus research*, 255–282. Amsterdam: Rodopi.

de Schryver, G.-M. 2003. Lexicographer's dreams in the electronic-dictionary age. *International Journal of Lexicography* 16(2): 143–199.

Deshors, S. C. 2014. A case for a unified treatment of EFL and ESL: A multifactorial approach. *English World-Wide* 35(3): 277–305.

Deshors, S. C. and Gries, S. Th. Forthcoming. A case for the multifactorial assessment of learner language: The uses of *may* and *can* in French-English interlanguage. In D. Glynn and J. Robinson (eds.), *Polysemy and synonymy: Corpus methods and applications in cognitive linguistics*. Amsterdam and Philadelphia: John Benjamins.

de Smet, Hendrik. 2012a. The course of actualization. *Language* 88(3): 601–633.

2012b. *Spreading patterns: Diffusional change in the English system of complementation*. Oxford University Press.

de Smet, H. and Cuyckens, H. 2005. Pragmatic strengthening and the meaning of complement constructions: The case of *like* and *love* with the *to*-infinitive. *Journal of English Linguistics* 33: 3–34.

Deuber, D., Biewer, C., Hackert, S., and Hilbert, M. 2012. *Will* and *would* in selected New Englishes: General and variety-specific tendencies. In Hundt and Gut (eds.), 77–102.

Devitt, A. J. 1989. *Standardizing written English: Diffusion in the case of Scotland 1520–1659*. Cambridge University Press.

Dewey, M. 2007a. English as a lingua franca: An empirical study of innovation in lexis and grammar. PhD thesis, King's College London.

2007b. English as a lingua franca and globalization: An interconnected perspective. *International Journal of Applied Linguistics* 17(3): 332–54.

2009. English as a lingua franca: Heightened variability and theoretical implications. In A. Mauranen and E. Ranta (eds.), *English as a lingua franca: Studies and findings*, 60–83. Newcastle upon Tyne: Cambridge Scholars Press.

Díaz-Negrillo, A. and Fernández-Domínguez, J. 2006. Error tagging systems for learner corpora. *RESLA* 19: 83–102.

Diessel, H. and Tomasello, M. 2005. Particle placement in early child language: A multifactorial analysis. *Corpus Linguistics and Linguistic Theory* 1(1): 89–112.

Díez-Bedmar, M. B. and Papp, S. 2008. The use of the English article system by Chinese and Spanish learners. In G. Gilquin, S. Papp, and M. B. Díez-Bedmar (eds.), *Linking up contrastive and learner corpus research*, 147–175. Amsterdam: Rodopi.

Ding, Huiling. 2007. Genre analysis of personal statements: Analysis of moves in application essays to medical and dental schools. *English for Specific Purposes* 26: 368–392.

Divjak, Dagmar S. and Gries, Stefan Th. 2006. Ways of trying in Russian: Clustering behavioral profiles. *Corpus Linguistics and Linguistic Theory* 2(1): 23–60.

2008. Clusters in the mind? Converging evidence from near synonymy in Russian. *The Mental Lexicon* 3(2): 188–213.

Dodd, B. 2000. Introduction: The relevance of corpora in German studies. In B. Dodd (ed.), *Working with German corpora*, 1–39. University of Birmingham Press.

Doherty, M. 2002. *Language processing in discourse*. London: Routledge.

Dor, D. 2005. Toward a semantic account of *that*-deletion in English. *Linguistics* 43: 345-382.

Dorgeloh, H. and Wanner, A. (eds.). 2010. *Syntactic variation and genre*. Berlin and New York: De Gruyter Mouton.

Drew, P. and Heritage, J. 1992. *Talk at work: Interaction in institutional settings*. Cambridge University Press.

Dueñas, P. M. 2007. "I/we focus on . . .": A cross-cultural analysis of self-mentions in business management research articles. *Journal of English for Academic Purposes* 6(2): 143–162.

Duguid, A. 2007. Men at work: How those at Number 10 construct their working identity. In G. Garzone and S. Sarangi (eds.), *Discourse, ideology and specialized communication*, 453–484 Bern: Peter Lang.

2009. Insistent voices: Government messages. In Morley and Bayley (eds.), 234–260.

2010a. Investigating *anti* and some reflections on Modern Diachronic Corpus-Assisted Discourse Studies (MD-CADS). *Corpora* 5(2): 191–220.

2010b. Newspapers discourse informalisation: A diachronic comparison from keywords. *Corpora* 5(2): 109–138.

Dunning, T. 1993. Accurate methods for the statistics of surprise and coincidence. *Computational Linguistics* 19(1): 61–74.

Durrant, P. and Schmitt, N. 2009. To what extent do native and non-native writers make use of collocations? *International Review of Applied Linguistics* 47(2): 157–177.

Ebeling, J., Ebeling, S., and Hasselgård, H. 2013. Using recurrent word-combinations to explore cross-linguistic differences. In K. Aijmer and B. Altenberg (eds.), *Advances in corpus-based contrastive linguistics: Studies in honour of Stig Johansson*, 177–200. Amsterdam: John Benjamins.

Eeg-Olofsson, M. and Altenberg, B. 1994. Discontinuous recurrent word combinations in the London–Lund Corpus. In U. Fries, G. Tottie, and P. Schneider (eds.), *Creating and using English language corpora: Papers from the fourteenth international conference on English language research on computerized corpora*, 63–77. Amsterdam: Rodopi.

Egan, T. 2012. Through seen through the looking glass of translation equivalence: a proposed method for determining closeness of word senses. In

Sebastian Hoffmann, Paul Rayson, and Geoffrey N. Leech (eds.), *English corpus linguistics: Looking back, moving forward*, 41–56. Amsterdam: Rodopi.
Elbaum, S. N. 2009. *Grammar in context*, 5th edn. Boston, MA: HeinleCengage.
Ellis, N. 2006. Meta-analysis, human cognition, and language learning. In J. Norris and L. Ortega (eds.), *Synthesizing research on language learning and teaching*, 301–322. Amsterdam: John Benjamins.
2007. Language acquisition as rational cue-contingency learning. *Applied Linguistics* 27(1): 1–24.
Ellis, N. C. and Ferreira-Junior, F. 2009. Constructions and their acquisition: Islands and the distinctiveness of their occupancy. *Annual Review of Cognitive Linguistics* 7: 187–220.
Ellis, N., Simpson-Vlach, R., and Maynard, C. 2008. Formulaic language in native and second language speakers: Psycholinguistics, corpus linguistics, and TESOL. *TESOL Quarterly* 42: 375–396.
Ellis, R. 1994. *The study of second language acquisition*. Oxford University Press.
Elsness, J. 1997. *The perfect and the preterite in contemporary and earlier English*. Berlin and New York: Mouton de Gruyter.
2009. The perfect and the preterite in Australian and New Zealand English. In Peters *et al.* (eds.), 89–114.
Elspaß, S., Langer, N., Scharloth, J., and Vandenbussche. 2007. *Germanic language histories "from below" (1700–2000)*. Berlin: De Gruyter.
Engel, D. M. and Ritz, M. E. 2000. The use of the present perfect in Australian English. *Australian Journal of Linguistics* 20(2): 119–140.
Enkvist, N. E. 1964. On defining style. In N. E. Enkvist, J. Spencer, and M. Gregory (eds.), *Linguistics and style*, 1–56. Oxford University Press.
Erman, B. 1987. *Pragmatic expressions in English: A study of* you know, you see *and* I mean *in face-to-face conversation*. Stockholm: Almqvist & Wiksell.
Ervin-Tripp, S. 1971. Sociolinguistics. In J. Fishman (ed.), *Advances in the sociology of language*, 15–91. The Hague: Mouton de Gruyter.
Everitt, B. and Hothorn, T. 2011. *An introduction to applied multivariate analysis with R*. Berlin and New York: Springer.
Evert, S. 2004. The statistics of word cooccurrences: Word pairs and collocations. Unpublished PhD dissertation, University of Stuttgart.
2008. Corpora and collocations. In A. Lüdeling and M. Kytö (eds.), *Corpus linguistics: An international handbook*, 1212–1248. Berlin: Mouton de Gruyter.
Evert, S. and Lüdeling, A. 2001. Measuring morphological productivity: Is automatic preprocessing sufficient? In P. Rayson, A. Wilson, T. McEnery, A. Hardie, and S. Khoja (eds.), *Proceedings of the Corpus Linguistics Conference 2001*, 167–175.
Evison, J. 2013. Turn openings in academic talk: Where goals and roles intersect. *Classroom Discourse* 4(1): 3–26.
Evison, J., McCarthy, M., and O'Keeffe, A. 2007. "Looking out for love and all the rest of it": Vague category markers as shared social space. In

J. Cutting (ed.), *Vague language explored*, 138–160. New York: Palgrave Macmillan.

Fairclough, N. 1989. *Language and power*. London: Longman.

1996. Technologisation of discourse. In Caldas-Coulthard and Coulthard (eds.), 71–83.

2000. *New Labour, new language?* London: Routledge.

Fallon, H. 2004. Comparing World Englishes: A research guide. *World Englishes* 23(2): 309–316.

Farr, F. and O'Keeffe, A. 2002. Would as a hedging device in an Irish context: An intra-varietal comparison of institutionalised spoken interaction. In R. Reppen, S. Fitzmaurice, and D. Biber (eds.), *Using corpora to explore linguistic variation*, 25–48. Amsterdam: John Benjamins.

Ferguson, G. 2001. If you pop over there: A corpus-based study of conditionals in medical discourse. *English for Specific Purposes* 20: 61–82.

Fernández, J. 2013. A corpus-based study of vague language use by learners of Spanish in a study abroad context. In C. Kinginger (ed.), *Social and cultural aspects of language learning in study abroad*, 299–332. Amsterdam: John Benjamins.

Ferrangne, E. 2013. Automatic suprasegmental parameter extraction in learner corpora. In Ana Diaz-Negrillo, N. Ballier, and P. Thompson (eds.), *Automatic treatment and analysis of learner corpus data*, 151–168. Amsterdam: John Benjamins.

Ferraresi, A., Bernardini, S., Picci, G., and Baroni, M. 2010. Web corpora for bilingual lexicography: A pilot study of English/French collocation extraction and translation. In R. Xiao (ed.), *Using corpora in contrastive and translation studies*, 337–359. Newcastle upon Tyne: Cambridge Scholars Press.

Fillmore, C. J. 1985. Syntactic intrusions and the notion of grammatical construction. In M. Niepokuj, M. VanClay, V. Nikiforidou, and D. Feder (eds.), *Proceedings of the eleventh annual meeting of the Berkeley Linguistics Society*, 73–86. University of California, Berkeley: Berkeley Linguistics Society.

Fillmore, C. J., Johnson, C. R., and Petruck, M. R. L. 2003. Background to Framenet. *International Journal of Lexicography* 16: 235–250.

Finegan, E. and Biber, D. 1994. Register and social dialect variation: An integrated approach. In D. Biber and E. Finegan. (eds.), *Sociolinguistic perspectives on register*, 315–347. Oxford University Press.

2001. Register variation and social dialect variation. In P. Eckert and J. R. Rickford (eds.), *Style and sociolinguistic variation*, 235–267. Cambridge University Press.

Firth, A. 1996. The discursive accomplishment of normality: On "lingua franca" English and conversation analysis. *Journal of Pragmatics* 26(2): 237–259.

1957. *Papers in Linguistics 1934–1951*. London: Oxford University Press.

1968. A synopsis of linguistic theory 1930–1955. In F. R. Palmer (ed.), *Selected papers of J. R. Firth 1952–59*, 1–32. Bloomington: Indiana University Press.

Fischer-Starcke, B. 2009. Keywords and frequent phrases of Jane Austen's *Pride and Prejudice*: A corpus-stylistic analysis. *International Journal of Corpus Linguistics* 14(4): 492–523.

2010. *Corpus linguistics in literary analysis: Jane Austen and her contemporaries*. London: Continuum.

Fitzmaurice, S. M. and Taavitsainen, I. (eds.). 2007. *Methods in historical pragmatics*. Berlin: Mouton de Gruyter.

Flamson, T., Bryant, G. A., and Barrett, H. C. 2011. Prosody in spontaneous humor: Evidence for encryption. *Pragmatics & Cognition* 19(2), 248–267.

Fletcher, W. 2013. Corpus analysis of the World Wide Web. In C. A Chapelle (ed.), *Encyclopedia of applied linguistics*, 339–347. Wiley-Blackwell.

Flowerdew, L. 1998. Integrating "expert" and "interlanguage" computer corpora findings on causality: Discoveries for teachers and students. *English for Specific Purposes* 17(4): 329–345.

2012. *Corpora and language education*. Basingstoke: Palgrave Macmillan.

Fonseca-Greber, B. and Waugh, L. 2003. On the radical difference between the subject personal pronouns in written and spoken European French. In P. Leistyna and C. Meyer (eds.), *Corpus analysis: Language structure and language use*, 225–240. Amsterdam: Rodopi.

Forchini, P. 2012. *Movie language revisited: Evidence from multi-dimensional analysis and corpora*. Bern: Peter Lang.

Fortanet, I. 2004. The use of "we" in university lectures: Reference and function. *English for Specific Purposes* 23: 45–66.

Fox, B. 1987. *Discourse structure and anaphora*. Cambridge University Press.

Fox, B. and Thompson, S. 1990. A discourse explanation of the grammar of relative clauses in English conversation. *Language* 66: 297–316.

Francis, G., Hunston, S., and Manning, E. 1996. *Collins COBUILD grammar patterns 1: Verbs*. London: HarperCollins.

1998. *Collins COBUILD grammar patterns 2: Nouns and Adjectives*. London: HarperCollins.

Francis, W. N. and Kučera H. 1964. *Manual of information to accompany "A Standard Sample of Present-Day Edited American English, for use with Digital Computers."* Providence, RI: Brown University.

1982. *Frequency analysis of English usage: Lexicon and grammar*. Boston: Houghton Mifflin.

Franconi, M. 2011. L'ingegneria linguistica dei briefings: Come viene gestito il dibattito tra la Casa Bianca e *La Stampa* sulle sommosse arabe. Dissertation, Faculty of Political Science, Bologna University.

Frawley, W. 1984. Prolegomenon to a theory of translation. In W. Frawley (ed.), *Translation: literary, linguistic, and philosophical perspectives*, 159–175. Cranbury, NJ: Associated University Presses.

Fraysse-Kim, Soon Hee. 2010. Keywords in Korean national consciousness: A corpus-based analysis of school textbooks. In Bondi and Scott (eds.), 219–33.

Frazier, Stefan. 2003. A corpus analysis of *would*-clauses without adjacent *if*-clauses. *TESOL Quarterly* 37: 443–466.

Friedman, G. L. 2009. Learner-created lexical databases using web-based source material. *ELT Journal* 63(2): 126–136.

Fries, C. C. 1940. *American English grammar: The grammatical structure of present-day American English with especial reference to social differences or class dialects* (National Council of Teachers of English: English monograph). New York: Appleton-Century-Crofts.

1952. *The structure of English: An introduction to the construction of English sentences*. London: Longman.

Friginal, E. 2009. *The language of outsourced call centers: A corpus-based study of cross-cultural interaction*. Amsterdam: John Benjamins.

2010. Call centre training and language in the Philippines. In G. Forey and J. Lockwood (eds.), *Globalization, communication and the workplace: Talking across the world*, 190–203. London: Continuum.

Fritz, C. W. A. 2007. *From English in Australia to Australian English: 1788–1900*. Frankfurt am Main: Peter Lang.

Fu, X. 2012. The use of interactional metadiscourse in job postings. *Discourse Studies* 14: 399–417.

Fuchs, M. and Bonner, M. 2011. *Focus on grammar*, 4th edn. White Plains, NY: Pearson Education.

Fuertes-Olivera, P. A. and Bergenholtz, H. (eds.). 2011. *e-Lexicography: The internet, digital initiatives and lexicography*. London and New York: Continuum.

Fung, L. and Carter R. 2007. Discourse markers and spoken English: Native and learner use in pedagogic settings. *Applied Linguistics* 28: 410–439.

Gabrielatos, C. 2005. Corpora and language teaching: Just a fling or wedding bells? *Teaching English as a Second Language – Electronic Journal* 8(4): 1–35. Downloaded from http://tesl-ej.org/ej32/a1.html

Gabrielatos, C. and Baker, P. 2008. *Fleeing, sneaking, flooding*: A corpus analysis of discursive constructions of refugees and asylum seekers in the UK press, 1996–2005. *Journal of English Linguistics* 36(1): 5–38.

Gan, S-L., Low, F., and Yaakub, N. 1996. Modeling teaching with a computer-based concordancer in a TESL preservice teacher education program. *Journal of Computing in Teacher Education* 12(4): 28–32.

Gardner, D. and Davies, M. 2007. Pointing out frequent phrasal verbs: A corpus-based analysis. *TESOL Quarterly* 41: 339–359.

2013. A new academic vocabulary list. *Applied Linguistics* 34(5): 1–24.

Garside, R. 1987. The CLAWS word-tagging system. In R. Garside, G. Leech, and G. Sampson (eds.), *The computational analysis of English: A corpus-based approach*, 30–41. London: Longman.

1993. The marking of cohesive relationships: Tools for the construction of a large bank of anaphoric data. *ICAME Journal* 17: 5–27.

Garside, R., Leech, G., and McEnery, T. (eds.) 1997. *Corpus annotation: Linguistic information from computer text corpora*. Harlow: Longman.

Gaskell, D. and Cobb, T. 2004. Can learners use concordance feedback for writing errors? *System* 32(3): 301–319.

Gavioli, L. 2005. *Exploring corpora for ESP learning*. Amsterdam: John Benjamins.

Geisler, C. 2002. Investigating register variation in nineteenth-century English: A multi-dimensional comparison. In R. Reppen, S. M. Fitzmaurice, and D. Biber (eds.), *Using corpora to explore linguistic variation*, 249–271. Amsterdam and Philadelphia: John Benjamins.

Gellerstam, M. 1996. Translations as a source for cross-linguistic studies. In K. Aijmer, B. Altenberg, and M. Johansson (eds.), *Languages in contrast*, 53–61. Lund University Press.

Gelman, A., Hill, J., and Yajima, M. 2012. Why we (usually) don't have to worry about multiple comparisons. *Journal of Research on Educational Effectiveness* 5: 189–211.

Gerbig, A. 2010. Key words and key phrases in a corpus of travel writing: From early modern English to contemporary "blooks." In Bondi and Scott (eds.), 147–168.

Giannoni, D. 2008. Popularizing features in English journal editorials. *English for Specific Purposes* 27: 212–232.

Gillard, P. and Gadsby, A. 1998. Using a learners' corpus in compiling ELT dictionaries. In S. Granger (ed.), *Learner English on computer*, 159–171. London: Longman.

Gilmore, A. 2007. Authentic materials and authenticity in foreign language learning. *Language Teaching* 40, 97–118.

2011, "I prefer not text": Developing Japanese learners' communicative competence with authentic materials. *Language Learning* 61: 786–819.

Gilquin, G. 2000/2001. The integrated contrastive model: Spicing up your data. *Languages in Contrast* 3(1): 95–123.

2002. Automatic retrieval of syntactic structures: The quest for the Holy Grail. *International Journal of Corpus Linguistics* 7(2): 183–214.

2007. To err is not all: What corpus and elicitation can reveal about the use of collocations by learners. *Zeitschrift für Anglistik und Amerikanistik* 55(3): 273–291.

2008. Hesitation markers among EFL learners: Pragmatic deficiency or difference? In J. Romero-Trillo (ed.), *Pragmatics and corpus linguistics: A mutualistic entente*, 119–149. Berlin: Mouton de Gruyter.

2012. Lexical infelicity in English causative constructions: Comparing native and learner collostructions. In J. Leino and R. von Waldenfels (eds.), *Analytical causatives: From 'give' and 'come' to 'let' and 'make'*, 41–63. Munich: Lincom Europa.

Gilquin, G., De Cock, S., and Granger, S. 2010. *Louvain International Database of Spoken English Interlanguage. Handbook and CD-ROM*. Louvain-la-Neuve: Presses universitaires de Louvain.

Gilquin, G., Granger, S., and Paquot, M. 2007. Learner corpora: The missing link in EAP pedagogy. *Journal of English for Academic Purposes* 6(4): 319–335.

Gilquin, G., Papp, S., and Díez-Bedmar, M. B. (eds.). 2008. *Linking up contrastive and learner corpus research*. Amsterdam: Rodopi.

Gledhill, C. 2000. *Collocations in science writing*. Tübingen: Gunter Narr Verlag.

Glynn, D. 2010. Testing the hypothesis: objectivity and verification in usage-based Cognitive Semantics. In D. Glynn and K. Fischer (eds.), *Quantitative methods in cognitive semantics: Corpus-driven approaches*, 239–629. Berlin and New York: De Gruyter Mouton.

Goatly, A. 2004. Corpus linguistics, systemic-functional grammar and literary meaning: A critical analysis of Harry Potter and the Philosopher's Stone. *Revista Ilha do Desterro: A Journal of English Language, Literatures in English and Cultural Studies* 46: 115–154.

Godfrey, J., Holliman, E., and McDaniel, J. 1992. SWITCHBOARD: Telephone speech corpus for research and development. In *Proceedings of ICASSP*, 517–520. San Francisco, CA: IEEE Signal Processing Society.

Goh, C. 1998. The level tone in Singapore English. *English Today* 14(1): 50–53.

2000. A discourse approach to the description of intonation in Singapore English. In A. Brown, D. Deterding, and L. E. Ling (eds.), *The English language in Singapore: Research on pronunciation*, 35–45. Singapore Association for Applied Linguistics.

Goldberg, A. E. 1995. *Constructions: A construction grammar approach to argument structure*. Chicago University Press.

1999. The emergence of the semantics of argument structure constructions. In B. MacWhinney (ed.), *The emergence of language*, 197–212. Mahwah, NJ: Lawrence Erlbaum.

(ed.). 1995. *Conceptual structure, discourse and language*. Stanford: CSLI Publications.

2006. *Constructions at work: The nature of generalization in language*. Oxford University Press.

Gordani, Y. 2012. The effect of the integration of corpora in reading comprehension classrooms on English as a foreign language learners' vocabulary development. *Computer Assisted Language Learning, i-First article*. DOI:10.1080/09588221.2012.685078.

Görlach, M. 2004. *Text types and the history of English*. Berlin and New York: Mouton de Gruyter.

Götz, S. 2013. *Fluency in native and nonnative English speech*. Amsterdam: John Benjamins.

Götz-Votteler, K. and Herbst, T. 2009. Innovation in advanced learners' dictionaries of English. *Lexicographica* 25: 47–66.

Gougenheim, G. 1958. *Dictionnaire fondamental de la langue française*. Paris: Didier.

Goulden, R., Nation, P., and Read, J. 1990. How large can a receptive vocabulary be? *Applied Linguistics* 11: 358–359.

Grabe, E. and Post, B. 2002. *The transcribed IViE corpus*. University of Oxford, Phonetics Laboratory.

Grafmiller, J. 2014. Variation in English genitives across modality and genre. *English Language and Linguistics* 18(3), 471–496.

Granger, S. 1983. *The* be + *past participle construction in spoken English with special emphasis on the passive*. Amsterdam: Elsevier Science Publishers.

1996. From CA to CIA and back: An integrated approach to computerized bilingual and learner corpora. In K. Aijmer, B. Altenberg, and M. Johansson (eds.), *Languages in contrast*, 37–51. Lund University Press.

1998 Prefabricated patterns in advanced EFL writing: Collocations and formulae. In A. P. Cowie (ed.), *Phraseology: Theory, analysis, and applications*, 145–160. Oxford University Press.

(ed.). 1998b. *Learner English on computer*. London: Longman.

2003a. The International Corpus of Learner English: A new resource for foreign language learning and teaching and second language acquisition research. *TESOL Quarterly*, 37: 538–546.

2003b. Error-tagged learner corpora and CALL: A promising synergy. *CALICO* 20(3): 465–480.

2009. The contribution of learner corpora to second language acquisition and foreign language teaching: A critical evaluation. In K. Aijmer (ed.), *Corpora and language teaching*, 13–32. Amsterdam: John Benjamins.

2012. *Introduction: Electronic lexicography – from challenge to opportunity*. In Granger and Paquot (eds.), 1–11.

2013. The passive in learner English: Corpus insights and implications for pedagogical grammar. In S. Ishikawa (ed.), *Learner corpus studies in Asia and the world*, vol. 1: *Papers from LCSAW2013*, 5–15. Kobe: School of Languages and Communication, Kobe University.

Granger, S., Dagneaux, E., and Meunier, F. 2002. *The International Corpus of Learner English: Handbook and CD-ROM*. Louvain-la-Neuve: Presses universitaires de Louvain.

Granger, S., Dagneaux, E., Meunier, F., and Paquot, M. 2009. *The International Corpus of Learner English. Version 2: Handbook and CD-Rom*, Louvain-la-Neuve: Presses universitaires de Louvain.

Granger, S., Hung, J., and Petch-Tyson, S. (eds.). 2002. *Computer learner corpora, second language acquisition and foreign language teaching*. Amsterdam: John Benjamins.

Granger, S. and Lefer, M.-A. 2012. *Towards more and better phrasal entries in bilingual dictionaries. Proceedings of the XV EURALEX Congress.* Downloaded from www.euralex.org/proceedings-toc/euralex_2012/

Granger, S. and Meunier, F. 1994. Towards a grammar checker for learners of English. In U. Fries and G. Tottie (eds.), *Creating and using English language corpora*, 79–91. Amsterdam: Rodopi.

(eds.). 2008. *Phraseology: An interdisciplinary perspective*. Amsterdam: John Benjamins.

Granger, S. and Paquot, M. 2008. *Disentangling the phraseological web.* In Granger and Meunier (eds.), 27–49.

2009. In search of General Academic English: A corpus driven study. In K. Katsampoxaki-Hodgetts (ed.), *Options and practices of LSP practitioners conference proceedings*, 94–108. University of Crete.

2010. Customising a general EAP dictionary to meet learner needs. In S. Granger and M. Paquot (eds.), *eLexicography in the 21st century: New challenges, new applications*, 87–96. Louvain-la-Neuve: Presses universitaires de Louvain.

(eds.). 2012. *Electronic lexicography*. Oxford University Press.

Granger, S. and Rayson, P. 1998. Automatic profiling of learner texts. In S. Granger (ed.), *Learner English on computer*, 119–131. London and New York: Longman.

Gray, B. and Biber, D. 2013. Lexical frames in academic prose and conversation. *International Journal of Corpus Linguistics* 18: 109–135.

Gray, B., Biber, D., and Hiltunen, T. 2011. The expression of stance in early (1665–1712) publications of the *Philosophical Transactions* and other contemporary medical prose: Innovations in a pioneering discourse. In I. Taavitsainen and P. Pahta (eds.), *Medical writing in Early Modern English*, 221–257. Cambridge University Press.

Gray, B. and Cortes, V. 2011. Perception vs. evidence: An analysis of *this* and *these* in academic prose. *English for Specific Purposes* 30, 1: 31–43.

Greaves, C. 2009. *ConcGram 1.0: A phraseological search engine*. Amsterdam: John Benjamins.

Greenacre, M. 2007. *Correspondence analysis in practice*. 2nd edn. Boca Raton, FL: Chapman & Hall/CRC.

Greenbaum, S. 1969. *Studies in English adverbial usage*. London: Longman.

1974. Some verb-intensifier collocations in American and British English. *American Speech* 49: 79–89.

1990. Standard English and the international corpus of English. *World Englishes* 9: 79–83.

1991. ICE: The International Corpus of English. *English Today* 28: 3–7.

(ed.). 1996. *Comparing English Worldwide: The International Corpus of English*. Oxford: Clarendon Press.

Greenbaum S. and Nelson, G. 1996. The International Corpus of English (ICE) Project. *World Englishes* 15: 3–15.

Greene, B. B. and Rubin, G. M. 1971. *Automatic grammatical tagging of English*. Providence, RI: Department of Linguistics, Brown University.

Greule, A., Meier, J., and Ziegler, A. (eds.). 2012. *Kanzleisprachenforschung: Ein internationales Handbuch*. Berlin: Walter de Gruyter.

Grgurović, M., Chapelle, C. A., and Shelley, M. C. 2013. A meta-analysis of effectiveness studies on computer technology supported language learning. *ReCALL* 25(2): 165–198.

Gries, S. Th. 2000. Multifactorial analysis in corpus linguistics: The case of particle placement. PhD dissertation, University of Hamburg.

2003a. *Multifactorial analysis in corpus linguistics: A study of particle placement*. London and New York: Continuum.

2003b. Towards a corpus-based identification of prototypical instances of constructions. *Annual Review of Cognitive Linguistics* 1: 1–27.

2004. HCFA 3.2. A program for R. Downloaded from: www.linguistics.ucsb.edu/faculty/stgries/

2005a. Syntactic priming: A corpus-based approach. *Journal of Psycholinguistic Research* 34: 365–399.

2005b. Null-hypothesis significance testing of word frequencies: A follow-up on Kilgarriff. *Corpus Linguistics and Linguistic Theory* 1(2): 277–294.

2006. Exploring variability within and between corpora: Some methodological considerations. *Corpora* 1(2): 109–151.

2008. Dispersions and adjusted frequencies in corpora. *International Journal of Corpus Linguistics* 13: 403–37.

2009. *Quantitative corpus linguistics with R: A practical introduction*. London: Routledge.

2010a. Corpus linguistics and theoretical linguistics: A love–hate relationship? Not necessarily … *International Journal of Corpus Linguistics* 15(3): 327–343.

2010b. Useful statistics for corpus linguistics. In A. Sánchez and M. Almela (eds.), *A mosaic of corpus linguistics: selected approaches*, 269–291. Frankfurt am Main: Peter Lang.

2010c. Dispersions and adjusted frequencies in corpora: Further explorations. In S. Th. Gries, S. Wulff, and M. Davies (eds.), *Corpus linguistic applications: Current studies, new directions*, 197–212. Amsterdam: Rodopi.

2012a. Frequencies, probabilities, association measures in usage-/exemplar-based linguistics: Some necessary clarifications. *Studies in Language* 36(3): 477–510.

2012b. Corpus linguistics, theoretical linguistics and cognitive/psycholinguistics: Towards more and more fruitful exchanges. In J. Mukherjee and M. Huber (eds.), *Corpus linguistics and variation in English: Theory and description*, 41–63. Amsterdam: Rodopi.

2013a. *Statistics for linguistics using R*, 2nd rev. and ext. edn. Berlin and New York: De Gruyter Mouton.

2013b. 50-something years of work on collocations: what is or should be next ... *International Journal of Corpus Linguistics* 18(1): 137–165.

2014b. Quantitative corpus approaches to linguistic analysis: Seven or eight levels of resolution and the lessons they teach us. In I. Taavitsainen, M. Kytö, C. Claridge, and J. Smith (eds.), *Developments in English: Expanding electronic evidence*, Cambridge University Press.

Forthcoming. Statistics for learner corpus research. G. Gilquin, S. Granger, and F. Meunier (eds.), *The Cambridge handbook of learner corpus research*. Cambridge University Press.

Gries, S. Th. and Deshors, S. C. 2014. Using regressions to explore deviations between corpus data and a standard/target: two suggestions. *Corpora* 9(1): 109–136.

Gries, S. Th. and Hilpert, M. 2008. The identification of stages in diachronic data: variability-based neighbor clustering. *Corpora* 3(1): 59–81.

2010. Modeling diachronic change in the third person singular: a multifactorial, verb- and author-specific exploratory approach. *English Language and Linguistics* 14(3): 293–320.

2012. Variability-based neighbor clustering: a bottom-up approach to periodization in historical linguistics. In T. Nevalainen and E. C. Traugott (eds.), *The Oxford handbook of the history of English*, 134–144. Oxford University Press.

Gries, S. Th. and Mukherjee, J. 2010. Lexical gravity across varieties of English: An ICE-based study of n-grams in Asian Englishes. *International Journal of Corpus Linguistics* 15(4): 520–548.

Gries, S. and Stefanowitsch, A. 2004. Extending collostructional analysis: A corpus-based perspective on "alternations." *International Journal of Corpus Linguistics* 9(1): 97–129.

Grieve, J. 2007. Quantitative authorship attribution: An evaluation of techniques. *Literary and Linguistic Computing* 22: 251–270.

2011. A regional analysis of contraction rate in written Standard American English. *International Journal of Corpus Linguistics* 16: 514–546.

2012. A statistical analysis of regional variation in adverb position in a corpus of written Standard American English. *Corpus Linguistics and Linguistic Theory* 8: 39–72.

2013. A statistical comparison of regional phonetic and lexical variation in American English. *Literary and Linguistic Computing* 28(1): 39–72.

Grieve, J., Biber, D., Friginal, E., and Nekrasova, T. 2011. Variation among blogs: A multi-dimensional analysis. In A. Mehler, S. Sharoff, and M. Santini (eds.), *Genres on the web*, 303–322. Dordrecht: Springer.

Grieve, J., Speelman D., and Geeraerts, D. 2011. A statistical method for the identification and aggregation of regional linguistic variation. *Language Variation and Change* 23: 193–221.

Grondelaers, S., and Speelman, D. 2007. A variationist account of constituent ordering in presentative sentences in Belgian Dutch. *Corpus Linguistics and Linguistic Theory* 3: 161–193.

Groom, N. 2010. Closed-class keywords and corpus-driven discourse analysis. In Bondi and Scott (eds.), pp. 59–78.

Grundmann, R. and Krishnamurthy, R. 2010. The discourse of climate change: A corpus-based approach. *Critical Approaches to Discourse Analysis across Disciplines* 4(2): 125–146.

Gu, Y. G. 2002. Towards an understanding of workplace discourse. In C. Candlin (ed.), *Research and practice in professional discourse*, 137–186. City University of Hong Kong Press.

Guiraud, P. 1954. *Les caractères statistiques du vocabulaire*, pages 64–7 reprinted 1975 in P. Guiraud and P. Kuentz (eds.), *La stylistique: Lectures*. Paris: Klincksieck.

Gut, U. 2009. *Non-native speech: A corpus-based analysis of phonological and phonetic properties of L2 English and German*. Oxford: Peter Lang.

Hakuta, K. 1974. Prefabricated patterns and the emergence of structure in second language acquisition. *Language Learning* 24: 287–97.

Halliday, M. A. K. 1961. Categories of the theory of grammar. *Word* 17(2): 241–92.

1963. The tones of English. *Archivum Linguisticum* 15: 1–28.

1966. Lexis as a linguistic level. In C. Bazell, J. Catford, M. A. K. Halliday, and R. Robins (eds.), *In memory of J. R. Firth*, 148–162. London: Longman.

1967. *Intonation and grammar in British English*. The Hague: Mouton.

1968. Notes on transitivity and theme in English: Part 3. *Journal of Linguistics* 4: 179–215.

1976. *System and function in language*. Oxford University Press.

1985. *An introduction to functional grammar*. London: Edward Arnold.

1994. *An introduction to functional grammar*, 2nd edn. London: Edward Arnold.

Halliday, M. A. K. and Hasan, R. 1976. *Cohesion in English*. London: Longman.

Han, W., Arppe, A., and Newman, J. Forthcoming. Topic marking in a Shanghainese corpus: From observation to prediction. *Corpus Linguistics and Linguistic Theory*.

Handford, M. 2010. *The language of business meetings*. Cambridge University press.

Handford, M. and Matous, P. 2011. Lexicogrammar in the international construction industry: A corpus-based case study of Japanese–Hong-Kongese on-site interactions in English. *English for Specific Purposes* 30: 87–100.

Hanks, P. 1987. Definitions and explanations. In J. Sinclair (ed.), *Looking up: An account of the COBUILD project in lexical computing*, 116–36. London and Glasgow: Collins.

2009. The impact of corpora on dictionaries. In P. Baker (ed.), *Contemporary corpus linguistics*, 214–36. London and New York: Continuum.

2012a. The corpus revolution in lexicography. *International Journal of Lexicography* 25(4): 398–436.

2012b. *Corpus evidence and electronic lexicography*. In Granger and Paquot (eds.), 57–82.

2013. *Lexical analysis: norms and exploitations*. Cambridge, MA: MIT Press.

Hansen-Schirra, S., Neumann, S., and Steiner, E. 2007. Cohesive explicitness and explicitation in an English–German translation corpus. *Languages in Contrast* 7(2): 241–265.

Hassall, P. 2006. Developing an International Corpus of Creative English. *World Englishes* 25(1): 131–151.

Hasselgård, H. 2009. Thematic choice and expressions of stance in English argumentative texts by Norwegian learners. In K. Aijmer (ed.), *Corpora and language teaching*, 120–39. Amsterdam: John Benjamins.

2010. *Adjunct adverbials in English*. Cambridge University Press.

Hasselgård, H. and Johansson, S. 2012. Learner corpora and contrastive interlanguage analysis. In F. Meunier, S. De Cock, G. Gilquin, and M. Paquot (eds.), *A taste for corpora: In honour of Sylviane Granger*, 33–61. Amsterdam and Philadelphia: John Benjamins.

Hasselgren, A. 2002. Learner corpora and language testing. Small words as markers of learner fluency. In S. Granger, J. Hung, and S. Petch-Tyson (eds.), *Computer learner corpora, second language acquisition and foreign language teaching*, 143–173. Amsterdam: John Benjamins.

Hastie, T., Tibshirani, R., and Friedman, J. 2009. *The elements of statistical learning: Data mining, inference, and prediction*. Berlin and New York: Springer.

Hatim, B. and Mason, I. 1997. *The translator as communicator*. London: Routledge.

Hattie, J. 2009. *Visible learning: A synthesis of meta-analyses relating to achievement*. New York: Routledge.

Hawkey, R. and Barker, F. 2004. Developing a common scale for the assessment of writing. *Assessing Writing* 9: 122–159.

Hawkins, J. A. 2003. Why are zero-marked phrases closer to their heads? In G. Rohdenburg and B. Mondorf (eds.), *Determinants of grammatical variation in English*, 175–204. Berlin and New York: Mouton de Gruyter.

Hay, J. and Baayen, H. 2005. Shifting paradigms: gradient structure in morphology. *Trends in Cognitive Sciences* 9: 342–348.

He, A. and Kennedy G. 1999. Successful turn-bidding in English conversation. *International Journal of Corpus Linguistics* 4: 1–27.

Heid, U. 2011. Electronic dictionaries as tools: Towards an assessment of usability. In Fuertes-Olivera and Bergenholtz (eds.), 287–304.

Heid, U. and Gouws, R. 2006. A model for a multifunctional electronic dictionary of collocations. *Proceedings of the XII EURALEX Congress*. Downloaded from www.euralex.org/elx_proceedings/Euralex2006/

Helt, M. 2001. A comparison of British and American spoken English. In S. Conrad and D. Biber (eds.), *Multi-dimensional studies of register variation in English*, 171–184. London: Longman.

Henry, A. and Roseberry, R. 2001. A narrow-angled corpus analysis of moves and strategies of the genre: "Letter of Application." *English for Specific Purposes* 20: 153–167.

Herbst, T. 2009. Valency – item-specificity and idiom principle. In U. Römer and R. Schulze (eds.), *Exploring the lexis-grammar interface*, 49–68. Amsterdam: John Benjamins.

Herbst, T., Heath, D., and Roe, I. 2004. *A valency dictionary of English*. Berlin: De Gruyter.

Herbst, T. and Mittmann, B. 2008. Collocation in English dictionaries at the beginning of the twenty-first century. *Lexicographica: International Annual for Lexicography*, 103–19.

Heritage, J. and Maynard, D. 2006. *Communication in medical care: Interaction between primary care physicians and patients*. Cambridge University Press.

Hernández, N., Kolbe, D., and Schulz, M. E. (eds.). 2011. *A comparative grammar of British English dialects*, vol. 2: *Modals, pronouns and complement clauses*. Berlin and Boston: De Gruyter.

Hernándes-Campoy, J. M. and Condre-Silvestre, J. C. (eds.). 2012. *The handbook of historical sociolinguistics*. Oxford: Wiley-Blackwell.

Hernández, N. 2006. *User's guide to FRED*. Downloaded from www.freidok.uni-freiburg.de/volltexte/2489/pdf/Userguide_neu.pdf

Herring, S. C. and Paolillo, J. C. 2006. Gender and genre variation in weblogs. *Journal of Sociolinguistics* 10: 439–459.

Hewings, M. 1986. Problems of intonation in classroom interaction. *Guidelines* 2(1): 45–51.

(ed.). 1990. *Papers in discourse intonation*. Birmingham: English Language Research.

Hewings, M. and Cauldwell, R. 1997. Foreword. In D. Brazil (ed.), *The communicative value of intonation in English*, v–vii. Cambridge University Press.

Hilpert, M. 2008. *Germanic future constructions: A usage-based approach to language change*. Amsterdam: John Benjamins.

2011. Dynamic visualizations of language change: Motion charts on the basis of bivariate and multivariate data from diachronic corpora. *International Journal of Corpus Linguistics* 16(4): 435–461.

2013. *Constructional change in English: Developments in allomorphy, word formation, and syntax*. Cambridge University Press.

Hilpert, M. and Gries, S. Th. 2009. Assessing frequency changes in multistage diachronic corpora: Applications for historical corpus linguistics and the study of language acquisition. *Literary and Linguistic Computing* 24(4): 385–401.

Hiltunen, T. 2010. *Grammar and disciplinary culture: A corpus-based study*. Helsinki: University of Helsinki.

Hindmarsh, R. 1980. *Cambridge English lexicon*. Cambridge University Press.

Hinrichs, L. and Szmrecsanyi, B. 2007. Recent changes in the function and frequency of Standard English genitive constructions: A multivariate analysis of tagged corpora. *English Language and Linguistics* 11(3): 437–474.

Hinkel, E. 2002. *Second language writers' text*. Mahwah, NJ: Lawrence Erlbaum.

2003. Simplicity without elegance: Features of sentences in L1 and L2 academic texts. *TESOL Quarterly*. 37(2): 275–302.

Höhn, N. 2012. "And they were all like 'What's going on?'": New quotatives in Jamaican and Irish English. In Hundt and Gut (eds.), 263–289.

Hochberg, Y. 1988. A sharper Bonferroni procedure for multiple tests of significance. *Biometrika* 75(4): 800–802.

Hoey, M. 1991. *Pattern of lexis in text*. Oxford University Press.

2004a. Lexical priming and the properties of text. In A. Partington, J. Morley, and L. Haarman (eds.), *Corpora and discourse*, 385–412. Bern: Peter Lang.

2004b. Language as choice: what is chosen? In G. Thompson and S. Hunston (eds.), *System and corpus: Exploring connections*, 37–54. London: Continuum.

2005. *Lexical priming: A new theory of words and language*. London: Routledge.

Hoffmann, S. 2005. *Grammaticalization and English complex prepositions: A corpus-based study*. London: Routledge.

2007. Processing Internet-derived text – creating a corpus of Usenet messages. *Literary and Linguistic Computing* 22(2): 151–165.

Hoffmann, S., Evert, S., Smith, N., Lee, D., and Berglund Prytz, Y. 2008. *Corpus linguistics with BNCweb – a practical guide*. Frankfurt am Main: Lang.

Hoffmann, S., Hundt, M., and Mukherjee, J. 2012. Indian English – an emerging epicentre? A pilot study on light verbs in web-derived corpora of South Asian Englishes. *Anglia* 129(3–4): 258–280.

Hoffmann, S. and Mukherjee, J. 2007. Ditransitive verbs in Indian English and British English: A corpus-linguistic study. *Arbeiten aus Anglistik und Amerikanistik* 32: 5–24.

Hoffmann, T. and Siebers, L. (eds.). *World Englishes: Problems, properties and prospects*. Amsterdam and Philadelphia: John Benjamins.

Hofland, K. and Johansson, S. 1982. *Word frequencies in British and American English*. Bergen: Norwegian Computing Centre for the Humanities.

Holm, S. 1979. A simple sequentially rejective multiple test procedure. *Scandinavian Journal of Statistics* 6(2): 65–70.

Holmes, J. 1988. Paying compliments: A sex preferential politeness strategy. *Journal of Pragmatics* 12(4): 445–465.

1993. Chairpersons and goddesses: Non-sexist usages in New Zealand English. *Te Reo* 36: 99–113.

2001. A corpus-based view of gender in New Zealand English. In M. Hellinger and H. Bußmann (eds.), *Gender across languages: The linguistic representation of women and men*, vol. 1: 115–136. Amsterdam and Philadelphia: John Benjamins.

Holmes, J. and Stubbe, M. 2003. *Power and politeness in the workplace*. London: Longman.

Holmes, J. S. 1978. Describing literary translations: Models and methods. In J. S. Holmes, J. Lambert, and R. van den Broek (eds.), *Literature and translation*, 69–83. Leuven: ACCO.

Holtz, M. 2007. Corpus-based analysis of verb/noun collocations in interdisciplinary registers. *Proceedings of the Corpus Linguistics Conference 2007*. http://ucrel.lancs.ac.uk/publications/CL2007/paper/14_Paper.pdf (accessed 2 August 2011).

Hommel, G. 1988. A stagewise rejective multiple test procedure based on a modified Bonferroni test. *Biometrika* 75(2): 383–386.

Hood, S. 2011. Writing discipline: Comparing inscriptions of knowledge and knowers in academic writing. In F. Christie and K. Maton (eds.), *Disciplinarity: Functional linguistic and sociological perspectives*, 106–128. London: Continuum.

Hoover, D. L. 1999. *Language and style in "The Inheritors."* Lanham, MD: University Press of America.

2003. Frequent collocations and authorial style. *Literary and Linguistic Computing* 18(3): 261–286.

2007. Corpus stylistics, stylometry, and the styles of Henry James. *Style* 41(2): 174–255.

Hopper, P. J. and Traugott, E. C. 2003. *Grammaticalization*, 2nd edn. Cambridge University Press.

Hori, M. 2004. *Investigating Dickens' style: A collocational analysis*. Basingstoke: Palgrave Macmillan.

Horn, L. R. and Ward, G. (eds.). 2004. *The handbook of pragmatics*. Oxford: Blackwell.

House, J. 2002. Developing pragmatic competence in English as a lingua franca. In K. Knapp and C. Meierkord (eds.), *Lingua franca communication*, 245–267. Frankfurt: Peter Lang.

Housen, A. 2002. A corpus-based study of the L2-acquisition of the English verb system. In S. Granger, J. Hung, and S. Petch-Tyson (eds.), *Computer learner corpora, second language acquisition and foreign language teaching*, 77–116. Amsterdam: John Benjamins.

Howarth, P. 1996. *Phraseology in English academic writing: Some implications for language learning and dictionary making*. Tübingen: Max Niemeyer.

1998a. Phraseology and second language proficiency. *Applied Linguistics* 19(1): 24–44.

1998b. The phraseology of learners' academic writing. In A. P. Cowie (ed.), *Phraseology: Theory, analysis, and applications*, 161–86. Oxford: Clarendon Press.

Hülmbauer, C. 2009. "We don't take the right way. We just take the way we think you will understand": The shifting relationship between correctness and effectiveness in ELF. In A. Mauranen and E. Ranta (eds.), *English as a lingua franca: Studies and findings*, 323–47. Newcastle upon Tyne: Cambridge Scholars Publishing.

Huang, H-T. and Liou, H-C. 2007. Vocabulary learning in an automated graded reading program. *Language Learning & Technology* 11(3): 64–82.

Huang, Y. 2007. *Pragmatics*. Oxford University Press.

Huber, M. 2007. The Old Bailey Proceedings, 1674–1834: Evaluating and annotating a corpus of 18th- and 19th-century spoken English. In A. Meurman-Solin and A. Nurmi (eds.), *Annotating variation and change* (Studies in Variation, Contacts and Change in English 1). University of Helsinki. Downloaded from www.helsinki.fi/varieng/journal/volumes/01/

Huckin, T. and Coady, J. 1999. Incidental vocabulary acquisition in a second language: A review. *Studies in Second Language Acquisition* 21: 121–138.

Huckvale, M. and Fang, A. C. 1996. *PROSICE: A spoken English database for prosody research*. In Greenbaum (ed.), 262–279.

Huddleston, R. and Pullum, G. K. 2002. *The Cambridge grammar of the English language*. Cambridge University Press.

Hudson, R.1994. About 37% of word-tokens are nouns. *Language* 70: 331–9.

Hughes, A., Trudgill, P., and Watt, D. 2005. *English accents and dialects: An introduction to social and regional varieties of English in the British Isles*, 4th edn. London: Hodder Arnold.

Hultgren, A. K. 2011. "Building rapport" with customers across the world: The global diffusion of a call centre speech style. *Journal of Sociolinguistics* 15(19): 36–64.

Hundt, M. 1997. Has BrE been catching up with AmE over the past 30 years? In Ljung (ed.), *Corpus-based Studies in English*, 135–151. Amsterdam: Rodopi.

1998. *New Zealand English grammar. Fact or fiction?* Amsterdam: John Benjamins.

2004. Animacy, agentivity, and the spread of the progressive in Modern English. *English Language and Linguistics* 8: 47–69.

2006. "The committee has/have decided . . .": On concord patterns with collective nouns in inner and outer circle varieties of English. *Journal of English Linguistics* 34(3): 206–232.

2013. The diversification of English: old, new and emerging epicentres. In D. Schreier and M. Hundt (eds.), *English as a contact language*, 182–203. Cambridge University Press.

Forthcoming. Error, feature, (ongoing) grammatical change or something else altogether? In E. Seoane Posse and C. Suárez Gómez (eds.), *Englishes today: Theoretical and methodological issues*. Amsterdam: John Benjamins.

Hundt, M. and Gut, U. (eds.). 2012. *Mapping unity and diversity worldwide: Corpus-based Studies of New Englishes*. Amsterdam: John Benjamins.

Hundt, M. and Leech, G. 2012. Small is Beautiful – on the value of standard reference corpora for observing recent grammatical change. In T. Nevalainen and E. Traugott (eds.), *The Oxford handbook of the history of English*, 175–188. Oxford University Press.

Hundt, M. and Mair, C. 1999. "Agile" and "uptight" genres: The corpus-based approach to language change in progress. *International Journal of Corpus Linguistics* 4(2): 221–242.

Hundt, M., Nesselhauf, N., and Biewer, C. (eds.). 2007. *Corpus linguistics and the web*. Amsterdam: Rodopi.

Hundt, M., Sand, A., and Siemund, R. 1998. *Manual of Information to Accompany the Freiburg–LOB Corpus of British English ("FLOB")*. Freiburg University.

Hundt, M., Sand, A., and Skandera, P. 1999. *Manual of information to accompany the Freiburg–Brown Corpus of American English*. University of Freiburg.

Hundt, M. and Smith, N. 2009. The present perfect in British and American English: Has there been any change, recently? *ICAME Journal* 33: 45–63.

Hundt, M. and Vogel, K. 2011. Overuse of the progressive in ESL and learner Englishes – fact or fiction? In Mukherjee and Hundt (eds.), 145–166.

Hunston, S. 2002. *Corpora in applied linguistics*. Cambridge University Press.

2003. Lexis, wordform and complementation pattern: A corpus study. *Functions of Language* 10: 31–60.

2011. *Corpus approaches to evaluation: Phraseology and evaluative language*. London: Routledge.

Hunston, S. and Francis, G. 1998. Verbs observed: A corpus-driven pedagogic grammar. *Applied Linguistics* 19(1): 45–72.

2000. *Pattern grammar: A corpus-driven approach to the lexical grammar of English*. Amsterdam: John Benjamins.

Hunston, S., Francis, G., and Manning, E. 1997. Grammar and vocabulary: Showing the connections. *ELT Journal* 51: 208–216.

Hunston, S. and Sinclair, J. 2000. A local grammar of evaluation. In S. Hunston and G. Thompson (eds.), *Evaluation in text: Authorial stance and the construction of discourse*, 75–100. Oxford University Press.

Hyland, K. 1998. *Hedging in scientific research articles*. Amsterdam: John Benjamins.

2001. Humble servants of the discipline? Self-mention in research articles. *English for Specific Purposes* 20: 207–226.

2002a. Options of identity in academic writing. *ELT Journal* 56: 351–358.

2002b. Authority and invisibility: authorial identity in academic writing. *Journal of Pragmatics* 34(8): 1091–1112.

2003. Dissertation acknowledgments: The anatomy of a Cinderella genre. *Written Communication* 20(3): 242–268.

2004. *Disciplinary discourses: social interactions in academic writing*. Ann Arbor, MI: University of Michigan Press.

2004. *Genre and second language writers*. Ann Arbor, MI: Michigan University Press.

2005. Stance and engagement: A model of interaction in academic discourse. *Discourse Studies* 7: 173–192.

2006. Representing readers in writing: Student and expert practices. *Linguistics and Education* 16: 363–377.

2007. Applying a gloss: Exemplifying and reformulating in academic discourse. *Applied Linguistics*. 28: 266–285.

2008a. Genre and academic writing in the disciplines. *Language Teaching* 41(4): 543–562.

2008b. As can be seen: Lexical bundles and disciplinary variation. *English for Specific Purposes* 27(1): 4–21.

2012. *Disciplinary identities*. Cambridge University Press.

Hyland, K. and Diani, G. (eds). 2009. *Academic evaluation: Review genres in university settings*. London: Palgrave Macmillan.

Hyland, K. and Tse, P. 2005. Evaluative *that* constructions: Signalling stance in research abstracts. *Functions of Language* 12: 39–64.

2007. Is there an "academic vocabulary"? *TESOL Quarterly* 41(2): 235–254.

2012. "She has received many honours": Identity construction in article bio statements. *Journal of English for Academic Purposes* 11: 155–165.

Hymes, D. 1974. *Foundations in sociolinguistics*. University of Philadelphia Press.

Hynninen, N. 2013. Language regulation in English as a lingua franca: Exploring language-regulatory practices in academic spoken discourse. PhD dissertation, University of Helsinki. Downloaded from http://urn.fi/URN:ISBN:978-952-10-8639-7 (30 July 2013).

Iberri-Shea, G. 2011. Speaking in front of the class: A multi-dimensional comparison of university students' public speech and university language. *Classroom Discourse* 2: 251–267.

Ihalainen, O. 1976. Periphrastic DO in affirmative sentences in the dialect of east Somerset. *Neuphilologische Mitteilungen* 77: 608–622.

1980. Relative clauses in the dialect of Somerset. *Neuphilologische Mitteilungen* 81: 187–196.

1988. Creating linguistic databases from machine-readable dialect texts. In A. R. Thomas (ed.), *Methods in dialectology*, 569–584. Clevedon: Multilingual Matters.

1990. A source of data for the study of English dialect syntax: The Helsinki Corpus. In J. Aarts and W. Meijs (eds.), *Theory and practice in corpus linguistics*, 83–103. Amsterdam: Rodopi.

Ikehara, S., Shirai, S., and Uchino, H. 1996. A statistical method for extracting uninterrupted and interrupted collocations from very large corpora. *Proceedings of the 16th Conference on Computational Linguistics*, vol. 1: 574–579.

Illes, E. 2009. What makes a coursebook series stand the test of time? *ELT Journal* 63(2): 145–153.

Ingham R. 2006. On two negative concord dialects in early English. *Language Variation and Change* 18: 241–266.

Ingvarsdóttir, H. and Arnbjörnsdóttir, B. 2013. ELF and academic writing: A perspective from the Expanding Circle. *Journal of English as a Lingua Franca* 2(1): 123–45.

Ishikawa, S. 2011. A new horizon in learner corpus studies: The aim of the ICNALE project. In G. Weir, S. Ishikawa, and K. Poonpon (eds.), *Corpora and language technologies in teaching, learning and research*, 3–11. Glasgow: University of Strathclyde Publishing.

Israel, M. 1996. The way constructions grow. In A. E. Goldberg (ed.), *Conceptual structure, discourse and language*, 217–230. Stanford: CSLI Publications.

Jacobs, A. and Jucker, A. H. 1995. The historical perspective in pragmatics. In Jucker (ed.), 3–33.

Jaeger, T. F. 2006. Redundancy and syntactic reduction in spontaneous speech. PhD thesis, Stanford University.

Jaeger, T. F. and Snider, N. 2008. Implicit learning and syntactic persistence: Surprisal and cumulativity. *Proceedings of the Annual Meeting of the Cognitive Science Society*.

Jarvis, S. and Paquot, M. In press. Native language identification. In S. Granger, G. Gilquin, and F. Meunier (eds.), *The Cambridge handbook of learner corpus research*. Cambridge University Press.

Jaworski, A., Coupland, N., and Galanski, D. 2004. *Metalanguage: Social and ideological perspectives*. Berlin: Mouton de Gruyter.

Jeffries, L. and Walker, B. 2012. Key words in the press. *English Text Construction* 5(2): 208–29.

Jenkins, J. 2000. *The phonology of English as an international language*. Oxford University Press.

2007. *English as a lingua franca: Attitude and identity*. Oxford University Press.

Jenkins, J., Cogo, A., and Dewey, M. 2011. Review of developments in research into English as a lingua franca. *Language Teaching* 44(3): 281–315.

Jeon, E. H. and Kaya, T. 2006. Effects of L2 instruction on interlanguage pragmatic development. In J. M. Norris and L. Ortega (eds.), *Synthesizing research on language learning and teaching*, 165–211. Amsterdam: John Benjamins.

Jespersen, O. 1909–49. *A modern English grammar on historical principles*. 7 vols. Copenhagen: E. Munksgaard; London: Allen and Unwin.

Ji, M. 2010. *Phraseology in corpus-based translation studies*. Bern: Peter Lang.

Johannessen, J. B., Priestley, J., Hagen, K., Afarli, T. A., and Vangsnes, Ø. A. 2009. The Nordic Dialect Corpus – an advanced research tool. In

Proceedings of the 17th Nordic Conference of Computational Linguistics NODALIDA 2009, 73–80.

Johansson, S. 1985. Grammatical tagging and total accountability. In S. Bäckman and G. Kjellmer (eds.), *Papers on language and literature presented to Alvar Ellegdrd and Erik Frykman*, 208–220. Gothenburg: Acta Universitatis Gothoburgensis.

2007. *Seeing through multilingual corpora*. Amsterdam: John Benjamins.

Johansson, S. and Hofland, K. 1989. *Frequency analysis of English vocabulary and grammar*, vols. 1–2 Oxford: Clarendon Press.

Johansson, S., Leech, G., and Goodluck, H. 1978. *Manual of information to accompany the Lancaster–Olso/Bergen Corpus of British English, for use with digital computers*. Department of English, University of Oslo.

John, J. 2001. *Dickens's villains: Melodrama, character, popular culture*. Oxford University Press.

Johns, T. 1988. Whence and whither classroom concordancing? In T. Bongaerts, P. de Haan, S. Lobbe, and H. Wekker (eds.), *Computer applications in language learning*, 9–27. Dordrecht: Foris.

1990. From printout to handout: Grammar and vocabulary teaching in the context of data-driven learning. *CALL Austria* 10: 14–34.

Johns, T. and King, P. (eds.). 1991. *Classroom concordancing. English Language Research Journal* 4.

Johns, T., Lee, H., and Wang, L. 2008. Integrating corpus-based CALL programs and teaching English through children's literature. *Computer Assisted Language Learning* 21(5): 483–506.

Johnson, D. E. 2008. Getting off the GoldVarb Standard: Introducing Rbrul for mixed-effects variable rule analysis. *Language and linguistics compass* 3: 359–383.

Johnson, J. 2012. What are these corpus linguists talking about? An MD-CADS content analysis of the IJCL. Talk given at CADS Conf 2011, Bologna University, 13–14 September 2012.

Johnson, S., Culpeper, J., and Suhr, S. 2003. From politically correct councillors to Blairite nonsense: Discourses of political correctness in three British newspapers. *Discourse and Society* 14(1): 28–47.

Jones, M., Rayson, P., and Leech, G. 2004. Key category analysis of a spoken corpus for EAP presented at the 2nd Inter-Varietal Applied Corpus Studies (IVACS) International Conference on "Analyzing Discourse in Context." The Graduate School of Education, Queen's University, Belfast, Northern Ireland, 25–26 June 2004.

Joy, J. 2011. The duality of authenticity in ELT. *Journal of Language and Linguistic Studies*, 7(2):7–23.

Jucker, A. H. (ed.). 1995. *Historical pragmatics: Pragmatic developments in the history of English*. Amsterdam: John Benjamins.

2002. Discourse markers in Early Modern English. In R. Watts and P. Trudgill (eds.), *Alternative histories of English*, 210–230. London and New York: Routledge.

2006. Historical pragmatics. In K. Brown (ed.), *Encyclopedia of language and linguistics*, 2nd edn., 329–332. Oxford: Elsevier. Rpt. 2009. In J. L. Mey (ed.), *Concise encyclopedia of pragmatics*, 2nd edn. Amsterdam: Elsevier.

2008. Historical pragmatics. *Language and Linguistics Compass* 2(5): 894–906.

2013. Corpus pragmatics. In J-O. Östman and J. Verschueren in collaboration with E. Versluys (eds.), *Handbook of pragmatics*, 1–17. Amsterdam: John Benjamins.

Jucker, A. H., Schneider, G., Taavitsainen, I., and Breustedt, B. 2008. *Fishing for compliments: Precision and recall in corpus-linguistic compliment research*. In Jucker and Taavitsainen, 273–294.

Jucker, A. H., Schreier, D., and Hundt, M. (eds.). 2009. *Corpora: Pragmatics and discourse*. Amsterdam: Rodopi.

Jucker, A. H. and Taavitsainen, I. 2000. Diachronic speech act analysis: Insults from flyting to flaming. *Journal of Historical Pragmatics* 1(1): 67–95.

(eds.). 2008a. *Speech acts in the history of English*. Amsterdam: John Benjamins.

2008b. Apologies in the history of English. Routinized and lexicalized expressions of responsibility and regret. In Jucker and Taavitsainen, 229–244.

(eds.). 2010. *Historical pragmatics* (Handbooks of Pragmatics 8). Berlin: De Gruyter Mouton.

2012. Pragmatic variables. In Hernández-Campoy and Condre-Silvestre (eds.), 303–317.

2013. *English historical pragmatics*. Edinburgh University Press.

2014a. Diachronic corpus pragmatics: Intersections and interactions. In Taavitsainen, Jucker, and Tuominen (eds.), 3–26.

2014b. Complimenting in the history of American English: A metacommunicative expression analysis. In Taavitsainen, Jucker, and Tuominen (eds.), 2057–2276.

Jucker, A. H., Taavitsainen, I., and Schneider, G. 2012. Semantic corpus trawling: Expressions of "courtesy" and "politeness" in the Helsinki Corpus. In C. Suhr and I. Taavitsainen (eds.), *Developing corpus methodology for historical pragmatics*. www.helsinki.fi/varieng/journal/volumes/11/jucker_taavitsainen_schneider/

Kallen, J. and Kirk, J. 2008. *ICE-Ireland: A user's guide*. Belfast: Cló Ollscoil na Banríona.

2012. *SPICE-Ireland: A user's guide*. Belfast: Cló Ollscoil na Banríona.

Kaltenböck, G. 2008. Prosody and function of English comment clauses. *Folia Linguistica* 42(1): 83–134.

Kamimoto T., Shimura, A., and Kellerman, E. 1992. A second language classic reconsidered: The case of Schachter's avoidance. *Second Language Research* 8(3): 251–277.

Kanoksilapatham, B. 2007. Rhetorical moves in biochemistry research articles. In D. Biber, U. Connor, and T. Upton (eds.), *Discourse on the move*, 73–103. Amsterdam: John Benjamins.

Kanter, I., Kfir, H., Malkiel, B., and Shlesinger, M. 2006. Identifying universals of text translation. *Journal of Quantitative Linguistics* 13(1): 35–43.

Kaur, J. and Hegelheimer, V. 2005. ESL students' use of concordance in the transfer of academic word knowledge: An exploratory study. *Computer Assisted Language Learning* 18(4): 287–310.

Kemmer, S. and Barlow, M. 2000. Introduction: A usage-based conception of language. In M. Barlow and S. Kemmer (eds.), *Usage-based models of language*, vii–xxvii. Stanford, CA: CSLI Publications.

Kendall, T., Bresnan, J., and van Herk, G. 2011. The dative alternation in African American English researching syntactic variation and change across sociolinguistic datasets. *Corpus Linguistics and Linguistic Theory* 7 (2): 229–244.

Kennedy, G. 1998. *An introduction to corpus linguistics*. London: Longman.

Kenny, D. 2001. *Lexis and creativity in translation*. Manchester: St. Jerome.

Kerekes, J. 2007. The co-construction of a gate-keeping encounter: An inventory of verbal actions. *Journal of Pragmatics* 39: 1942–1973.

Kilgarriff, A. 1996. Why chi-square doesn't work, and an improved LOB-Brown comparison. In *Proceedings of the ALLC-ACH Conference*, 169–172. Bergen, Norway.

2005. Language is never ever ever random. *Corpus Linguistics and Linguistic Theory* 1(2): 263–276.

2007. Googleology is bad science. *Computational Linguistics* 33: 147–151.

Kilgarriff, A. and Kosem, I. 2012. *Corpus tools for lexicographers*. In Granger and Paquot (eds), 31–56.

Kilgarriff, A. and Tugwell, D. 2002. Sketching words. In M.-H. Corréard (ed.), *Lexicography and natural language processing: A Festschrift in honour of B.T.S. Atkins*, 125–137. EURALEX.

Kim, Y. and Biber, D. 2009. Korean lexical bundles in conversation and academic texts. *Corpora* 4: 135–165.

Kim, Y.-J. and Biber, D. 1994. A corpus-based analysis of register variation in Korean. In D. Biber and E. Finegan (eds.), *Sociolinguistic perspectives on register variation*, 157–81. New York: Oxford University Press.

Kita, K., Kato, Y., Omoto, T., and Yano, Y. 1994. Automatically extracting collocations from corpora for language learning. *Journal of Natural Language Processing* 1(1): 21–33.

Knight, D. and Adolphs, S. 2008. Multi-modal corpus pragmatics: The case of listenership. In J. Romero-Trillo (ed.), *Pragmatics and corpus linguistics: A mutualistic entente*, 175–190. Berlin: De Gruyter.

Knight, D., Evans, D., Carter, R., and Svenja A. 2009. HeadTalk, HandTalk and the corpus: Towards a framework for multi-modal, multi-media corpus development. *Corpora* 4(1): 1–32.

Knowles, G., Wichmann, A., and Alderson, P. (eds.). 1996. *Working with speech*. London: Longman.

Koch, P. 1999. Court records and cartoons: Reflections of spontaneous dialogue in early Romance texts. In A. H. Jucker, G. Fritz, and F. Lebsanft (eds.), *Historical dialogue analysis*, 399–429. Amsterdam and Philadelphia: John Benjamins.

Koch, P. and Oesterreicher, W. 1985–1986. Sprache der Nähe – Sprache der Distanz. Mündlichkeit und Schriftlichkeit im Spannungsfeld von Sprachtheorie und Sprachgeschichte. *Romanistisches Jahrbuch* 36: 15–43.

1990. *Gesprochene Sprache in der Romania: Französisch, Italienisch, Spanisch* (Romanistische Arbeitshefte 31). Tübingen: Max Niemeyer.

Koester, A. 2006. *Investigating workplace discourse*. London: Routledge.

2010. Building small specialised corpora. In A. O'Keeffe and M. McCarthy (eds.), *The Routledge handbook of corpus linguistics*, 66–79. London: Routledge.

Kohnen, T. 2001. Text types as catalysts for language change: The example of the adverbial first participle construction. In H.-J. Diller, and M. Görlach (eds.), *Towards a history of English as a history of genres*, 111–124. Heidelberg: Winter.

2007a. From Helsinki through the centuries: The design and development of English diachronic corpora. In P. Pahta, I. Taavitsainen, T. Nevalainen, and J. Tyrkkö (eds.), *Towards multimedia in corpus studies*. Helsinki: Research Unit for Variation, Contacts and Change in English (VARIENG), University of Helsinki. Available at www.helsinki.fi/varieng/journal/volumes/02/kohnen/ (accessed 13 February 2013).

2007b. Text types and the methodology of diachronic speech act analysis. In Fitzmaurice and Taavitsainen, 139–166.

2008. Tracing directives through text and time. Towards a methodology of a corpus-based diachronic speech act analysis. In A. Jucker and I. Taavitsainen (eds.), *Speech acts in the history of English*, 295–310. Amsterdam: John Benjamins.

2009. Historical corpus pragmatics: Focus on speech acts and texts. In Jucker, Schreier, and Hundt (eds.), 13–36.

Kolbe, D. 2008. Complement clauses in British Englishes. PhD thesis, University of Trier.

Koller, V., Hardie, A., Rayson, P., and Semino, E. 2008. Using a semantic annotation tool for the analysis of metaphor in discourse. www.metaphorik.de/15/koller.pdf (accessed 5 March 2013).

Koppel, M., Argamon, S., and Shimoni, A. R. 2002. Automatically categorizing written texts by author gender. *Literary and Linguistic Computing* 17: 401–412.

Kortmann, B., Herrmann, T., Pietsch, L., and Wagner, S. 2005. *A comparative grammar of British English dialects: Agreement, gender, relative clauses*. Berlin: Mouton de Gruyter.

Kosem, I. 2010. Designing a model for a corpus-driven dictionary of academic English. PhD thesis. Aston University, Birmingham, UK. Downloaded from http://eprints.aston.ac.uk/14664/

Krenn, B. 2000. *The usual suspects: Data-oriented models for the identification and representation of lexical collocations*. Saarbrücken: DFKI and Universität des Saarlandes.

Kretzschmar Jr., W. A., Anderson, J., Beal, J. C., Corrigan, K. P., Opas-Hänninen, L. L., and Plichta, B. 2006. Collaboration on corpora for regional and social analysis. *Journal of English Linguistics*, 34: 172–205.

Krishnamurthy, R. 1996. Ethnic, racial and tribal: the language of racism? In Caldas-Coulthard and Coulthard (eds.), 129–49.

2000. Collocation: From *silly ass* to lexical sets. In C. Heffer, H. Sauntson, and G. Fox (eds.), *Words in context: A tribute to John Sinclair on his retirement*. University of Birmingham.

2002. Corpus, collocation, and lexical sets. In B. Hollosy and J. Kiss-Gulyas (eds.), *Studies in linguistics*, vol. VI, part I: 7–42. University of Debrecen.

Krug, M. 2000. *Emerging English modals: A corpus-based study of grammaticalization*. Berlin: Mouton de Gruyter.

Kruisinga, E. 1909–11/1931–2. *A handbook of present-day English*. Groningen: Noordhoff.

Kučera, H. and Francis, W. M. 1967. *Computational analysis of Present-Day American English*. Providence, RI: Brown University Press.

1979. *A standard corpus of present-day edited American English, for use with digital computers* (Revised and amplified from 1967 version). Providence, RI: Brown University Press.

Kytö, M. 1991. *Variation and diachrony, with Early American English in focus: Studies on* CAN/MAY *and* SHALL/WILL. Frankfurt am Main.: Peter Lang.

1993. Third-person singular verb inflection in early British and American English. *Language Variation and Change* 5(2): 113–39.

1996. *Manual to the diachronic part of the Helsinki Corpus of English Texts. Coding conventions and lists of source texts*. Department of English, University of Helsinki.

Kytö, M., Grund, P. J., and Walker, T. 2011. *Testifying to language and life in Early Modern England. Including CD-ROM: An Electronic Text Edition of Depositions 1560–1760 (ETED)*. Amsterdam: John Benjamins.

Kytö, M. and Rissanen, M. 1983. The syntactic study of Early American English: The variationist at the mercy of his corpus? *Neuphilologische Mitteilungen* 84(4): 470–490.

1993. General introduction. In M. Rissanen, M. Kytö, and M. Palander-Collin (eds.), *Early English in the computer age: Explorations through the Helsinki Corpus*, 1–17. Berlin: Mouton de Gruyter.

Kytö, M. and Smitterberg, E. 2006. 19th-century English: An age of stability or a period of change? In R. Facchinetti and M. Rissanen (eds.), *Corpus-based studies of diachronic English*, 199–230. Bern: Peter Lang.

Kytö, M. and Walker, T. 2003. The linguistic study of Early Modern English speech-related texts: How "bad" can "bad" data be? *Journal of English Linguistics* 31(3): 221–248.

Labov, W. 1972. *Sociolinguistic patterns*. Philadelphia, PA: University of Pennsylvania Press.

Lacheret, A., Simon, A. C., Goldman, J.-P., and Avanzi, M. 2013. Prominence perception and accent detection in French: From phonetic processing to grammatical analysis. *Language Sciences* 39: 95–106.

Laing, M. and Lass, R. 2007. *A linguistic atlas of Early Middle English, 1150–1325*. Available at www.lel.ed.ac.uk/ihd/laeme2/laeme2.html.

Lam, P. W. Y. 2009. The effect of text type on the use of so as a discourse particle. *Discourse Studies* 11(3): 353–372.

Lange, C. 2012. Text types, language change, and historical corpus linguistics. In C. Lange, B. Weber, and G. Wolf (eds.), *Communicative spaces: Variation, contact, and change. Papers in honour of Ursula Schaefer*, 401–416. Frankfurt am Main: Peter Lang.

Laufer, B. and Ravenhorst-Kalovski, G. C. 2010. Lexical threshold revisited: Lexical text coverage, learners' vocabulary size and reading comprehension. *Reading in a Foreign Language* 22(1): 15–30.

Laufer, B. and Waldman, T. 2011. Verb-noun collocations in second language writing: A corpus analysis of learners' English. *Language Learning* 61(2): 647–672.

Lavandera, B. 1978. Where does the linguistic variable stop? *Language in Society* 7: 171–182.

Laviosa, S. 1998. Core patterns of lexical use in a comparable corpus of English narrative prose. *Meta* 43(4): 557–570.

2002. *Corpus-based translation studies: Theory, findings, applications*. Amsterdam: Rodopi.

Leacock, C., Chodorow, M., and Tetreault, J. In press. Automatic spell- and grammar-checking. In S. Granger, G. Gilquin, and F. Meunier (eds.), *The Cambridge handbook of learner corpus research*. Cambridge University Press.

Lee, D. 2002. Notes to accompany the BNC Word edition (bibliographical) index. Available at www.uow.edu.au/~dlee/home/BNCWIndexNotes.pdf

Lee, D. and McGarrell, H. 2011. Corpus-based/corpus-informed English language learner grammar textbooks: An example of how research informs pedagogy. *CONTACT, TESOL Ontario* 37(2): 78–100.

Leech, G. 1992. Corpora and theories of linguistic performance. In J. Svartvik (ed.), *Directions in corpus linguistics: Proceedings of Nobel Symposium, 4–8 August 1991*, 105–122. Berlin: Mouton de Gruyter.

1996. Foreword: The spoken English corpus in its context. In G. Knowles, A. Wichmann, and P. Alderson (eds.), *Working with speech: Perspectives on research into the Lancaster/IBM Spoken English Corpus*, ix–xii. London: Longman.

1999. The distribution and function of vocatives in American and British English conversation. In H. Hasselgård and S. Oksefjell (eds.), *Out of corpora: Studies in honour of Stig Johansson*, 107–120. Amsterdam: Rodopi.

2000. Same grammar or different grammar? Contrasting approaches to the grammar of spoken discourse. In S. Sarangi and M. Coulthard (eds.), *Discourse and social life*, 48–65. London: Longman.

2003. Modality on the move: the English modal auxiliaries 1961–1992. In R. Facchinetti, M. Krug, and F. Palmer (eds.), *Modality in contemporary English*, 223–240. Berlin: Mouton de Gruyter.

2007. New resources, or just better old ones? The holy grail of representativeness. In M. Hundt, N. Nesselhauf, and C. Biewer (eds.), *Corpus linguistics and the Web*, 133–151. Amsterdam: Rodopi.

2008. *Language in literature: Style and foregrounding*. Harlow: Pearson Education.

2011a. The modals ARE declining: Reply to Neil Millar's "Modal verbs in TIME: Frequency changes 1923–2006," *International Journal of Corpus Linguistics* 14:2 (2009), 191–220. *International Journal of Corpus Linguistics* 16/4: 547–564.

2011b. Frequency, corpora and language learning. In F. Meunier, S. De Cock, G. Gilquin, and M. Paquot (eds.), *A taste for corpora: In honour of Sylviane Granger*, 7–31. Amsterdam: John Benjamins.

Leech, G., Francis, B., and Xu, X. 1994. The use of computer corpora in the textual demonstrability of gradience in linguistic categories. In C. Fuchs and B. Victorri (eds.), *Continuity in linguistic semantics*, 57–76. Amsterdam: Benjamins.

Leech, G., Garside, R., and Bryant, M. 1994. CLAWS 4: The tagging of the British National Corpus. In *Proceedings of the 15th International Conference on Computational Linguistics (COLING 94)*, 622–628. Kyoto, Japan.

Leech, G., Hundt, M., Mair, C., and Smith, N. 2009. *Change in contemporary English: A grammatical study*. Cambridge University Press.

Leech, G., Rayson, P., and Wilson, A. 2001. *Word frequencies in written and spoken English: Based on the British National Corpus*. London: Longman.

Leech, G. and Short, M. [1981] 2007. *Style in fiction: A linguistic introduction to English fictional prose*. Harlow: Pearson Education.

Leech, G. and Smith, N. 2005. Extending the possibilities of corpus-based research on English in the twentieth century: A prequel to LOB and FLOB. *ICAME Journal* 29: 83–98.

Lehto, A., Baron, A., Ratia, M., and Rayson, P. 2010. Improving the precision of corpus methods: The standardized version of Early Modern English Medical Texts. In Taavitsainen and Pahta (eds.), 279–289.

Lei, L. 2012. Linking adverbials in academic writing on applied linguistics by Chinese doctoral students. *Journal of English for Academic Purposes* 11: 267–275.

Leńko-Szymańska, A. 2008. Non-native or non-expert? The use of connectors in native and foreign language learners' texts. *Acquisition et interaction en langue étrangère* 27: 91–108. http://aile.revues.org/4213

Lessard-Clouston, M. 2010. Theology lectures as lexical environments: A case study of technical vocabulary use. *Journal of English for Academic Purposes* 9: 308–321.

Levinson, S. 2004. Deixis. In L. Horn and G. Ward (eds.), *The handbook of pragmatics*, 97–121. Oxford: Blackwell.

Lew, R. 2012. The role of syntactic class, frequency, and word order in looking up English multi-word expressions. *Lexikos* 22: 243–60.

Liberman, M. and Prince, A. 1977. On stress and linguistic rhythm. *Linguistic Inquiry* 8: 249–336.

Lin, M-C. 2008. Building a lexical syllabus on Moodle with web concordancers for EFL productive academic vocabulary. *Proceedings of WorldCALL 2008*. Fukuoka University. Downloaded from www.ntnu.edu.tw/acad/rep/r97/a4/a405-1.pdf

Lin, P. 2013. The prosody of formulaic expression in the IBM/Lancaster Spoken English Corpus. *International Journal of Corpus Linguistics* 18(4): 561–588.

Lindemann, S. and Mauranen, A. 2001. "It's just real messy": The occurrence and function of *just* in a corpus of academic speech. *English for Specific Purposes* 20: 459–475.

Lindquist, H. 2009. *Corpus linguistics and the description of English*. Edinburgh University Press.

Liou, H-C., Chang, J. S., Chen, H-J., Lin, C-C., Liaw, M-L., Gao, Z-M., Jang, J-Y. R., Yeh, Y., Chuang, T. C., and You, G-N. 2006. Corpora processing and computational scaffolding for an innovative web-based English learning environment: The CANDLE project. *CALICO Journal* 24(1): 77–95.

Liu, D. 2008. Linking adverbials: An across-register corpus study and its implications. *International Journal of Corpus Linguistics* 13: 491–518.

2011. The most frequently used English phrasal verbs in American and British English: A multicorpus examination. *TESOL Quarterly* 45: 661–688.

Lohmann, A. 2011. Help vs help to: A multifactorial, mixed-effects account of infinitive marker omission. *English Language and Linguistics* 15(3): 499–521.

Loi, C. K. 2010. Research article introductions in Chinese and English: A comparative genre-based study. *Journal of English for Academic Purposes* 9(4): 267–279.

Longman Dictionary of Contemporary English. 1987. Harlow: Longman.

López-Couso, M. J. 2010. Subjectification and intersubjectification. In Jucker and Taavitsainen (eds.), 127–163.

Lorentzen, H. and Theilgaard, L. 2012. Online dictionaries – how do users find them and what do they do once they have? *Proceedings of the XV*

EURALEX Congress. Downloaded from www.euralex.org/proceedings-toc/euralex_2012/

Lorenz, D. 2012. Semi-modal constructions in English: Emancipation through frequency. PhD thesis, University of Freiburg.

Lorge, I. and Thorndike, E. L. 1938. *A semantic count of English words*. New York: Teachers College, Columbia University.

Louw, B. 1993. Irony in the text or insincerity in the writer? The diagnostic potential of semantic prosodies. In M. Baker, G. Francis, and E. Tognini-Bonelli (eds.), *Text and technology*, 157–176. Philadelphia and Amsterdam: John Benjamins.

2000. Contextual prosodic theory: Bringing semantic prosodies to life. In C. Heffer, H. Sauntson, and G. Fox (eds.), *Words in context: A tribute to John Sinclair on his retirement*. University of Birmingham.

Louwerse, M., Crossley, S., and Jeuniaux, P. 2008. What if? Conditionals in educational registers. *Linguistics and Education* 19: 56–69.

Lüdeling, A., Walter, M., Kroymann, E., and Adolphs, P. 2005. Multi-level error annotation in learner corpora. In *Proceedings from the Corpus Linguistics Series* 1(1). www.birmingham.ac.uk/research/activity/corpus/publications/conference-archives/2005-conf-e-journal.aspx

Lutzky, U. 2012. *Discourse markers in Early Modern English*. Amsterdam: John Benjamins.

Luzón, M. 2009. The use of *we* in a learner corpus of reports written by EFL Engineering students. *Journal of English for Academic Purposes* 8: 192–206.

Luzón Marco, M. J. 2000. Collocational frameworks in medical research papers: a genre-based study. *English for Specific Purposes* 19(1): 63–86.

Macalister, J. 2011. Flower-girl and bugler-boy no more: Changing gender representation in writing for children. *Corpora* 6: 25–44.

Macdonald, L. M. 2007. Nurse talk: Features of effective verbal communication used by expert district nurses. Unpublished Master's thesis, Victoria University of Wellington, Wellington, NZ.

MacIntosh, A., Samuels, M. L., and Benskin, M. 1986. *A linguistic atlas of late mediaeval English*. Aberdeen University Press.

MacKenzie, L. 2013. Variation in English auxiliary realization: A new take on contraction. *Language Variation and Change* 25: 1–25.

Mackey, A. and Gass, S. (eds.) 2012. *Research methods in second language acquisition: A practical guide*. Chichester: Wiley-Blackwell.

Mackin, R. 1978. On collocations: "Words shall be known by the company they keep." In P. Strevens (ed.), *In honour of A. S. Hornby*, 149–165. Oxford University Press.

Mahlberg, M. 2007. Clusters, key clusters and local textual functions in Dickens. *Corpora* 2(1): 1–31.

2013. *Corpus stylistics and Dickens's Fiction*. New York and London: Routledge.

Mahlberg, M. Conklin, K., and Bisson, M. 2014. Reading Dickens's characters: Employing psycholinguistic methods to investigate the cognitive reality of patterns in texts. *Language and Literature* 23(4): 369–388.

Mahlberg, M., Smith, C., and Preston, S. 2013. Phrases in literary contexts: Patterns and distributions of suspensions in Dickens's novels. *International Journal of Corpus Linguistics* 18(1): 35–56.

Mair, C. 2002. Three changing patterns of verb complementation in Late Modern English: A real-time study based on matching text corpora. *English Language and Linguistics* 6(1): 105–31.

Mair, C. 2006. *Twentieth-century English: History, variation, and standardization.* Cambridge University Press.

2009a. Corpora and the study of recent change in language. In A. Lüdeling and M. Kytö (eds.), *Corpus linguistics: An international handbook*, vol. 2: 1109–1125. Berlin and New York: Walter de Gruyter.

2009b. Corpus linguistics meets sociolinguistics: Studying educated spoken usage in Jamaica on the basis of the International Corpus of English. In Hoffmann and Siebers (eds.), 39–60.

2011. Grammaticalization and corpus linguistics. In H. Narrog and B. Heine (eds.), *The Oxford handbook of grammaticalization*, 239–250. Oxford University Press.

Mair, C. and Winkle, C. 2012. Change from *to*-infinitive to bare infinitive in specificational cleft sentences: Apparent-time data from World Englishes. In Hundt and Gut (eds.), 243–262.

Malmkjær, K. 2004. Translational stylistics: Dulcken's translations of Hans Christian Andersen. *Language and Literature* 13(1): 13–24.

Manes, J. and Wolfson, N. 1981. The compliment formula. In F. Coulmas (ed.), *Conversational routine: Explorations in standardized communication situations and prepatterned speech*, 115–132. The Hague: Mouton.

Manhire, T. 2012. *The Arab Spring*. London: Guardian Books.

Manning, C. and Schütze, H. 1999. *Foundations of statistical natural language processing*. Cambridge, MA: MIT Press.

Marchi, A. 2010. "The moral in the story": A diachronic investigation of lexicalised morality in the UK press. *Corpora* 5(2): 161–190.

Marchi, A. and Taylor, C. 2009. "If on a winter's night two researchers": A challenge to assumptions of soundness of interpretation. *CADAAD Journal* 3(1): 1–20.

Marco, J. 2004. Translating style and styles of translating: Henry James and Edgar Allan Poe in Catalan. *Language and Literature* 13(1): 73–90.

Marco, M. 2000. Collocational frameworks in medical research papers: A genre-based study. *English for Specific Purposes* 19: 63–86.

Marcus, M. P., Santorini, B., and Marcinowicz, M. A. 1993. Building a large annotated corpus of English: The Penn Treebank. *Computational Linguistics* 19(2): 313–30.

Marshall, I. 1983. Tagging words in the LOB Corpus. *Computers and the Humanities* 17: 139–50.

Martinez, R. and Murphy, V. 2010. Effect of frequency and idiomaticity on second language reading comprehension. *TESOL Quarterly* 45(2): 267–290.

Martinez, R. and Schmitt, N. 2012. A phrasal expressions list. *Applied Linguistics* 33(3): 299–320.

Marttila, V. 2014. Creating digital editions for corpus linguistics: The case of Potage Dyvers, a family of six Middle English recipe collections. Dissertation, University of Helsinki.

Mason, O. 1997. The weight of words: an investigation of lexical gravity. *Proceedings of PALC'97*, 361–375.

1999. Parameters of collocation: the word in the centre of gravity. In John M. Kirk (ed.), *Corpora galore: Analyses and techniques in describing English*, 267–280. Amsterdam: Rodopi.

2000. *Programming for corpus linguistics: How to do text analysis with Java.* Edinburgh University Press.

Matoré, G. 1953. *La méthode en lexicologie: Domaine français.* Paris: Marcel Didier.

Matsuda, P. and Jeffery, J. 2012. Voice in student essays. In K. Hyland and C. Sancho Guinda (eds.), *Stance and voice in written academic genres*, 151–165. London: Palgrave.

Mauranen, A. 2002. Where's cultural adaptation? InTRAlinea. Downloaded from www.intralinea.it/ (accessed 26 March 2013).

2003a. "But here's a flawed argument": Socialisation into and through metadiscourse. In P. Leistyna and C. Meyer (eds.), *Corpus analysis: Language structure and language use*, 19–34. New York: Rodopi.

2003b. "A good question." Expressing evaluation in academic speech. In G. Cortese and P. Riley (eds.), *Domain specific English: Textual practices across communities and classrooms*, 115–140. New York: Peter Lang.

2004. "They're a little bit different": Observations on hedges in academic talk. In K. Aijmer and A. B. Stenström, *Discourse patterns in spoken and written corpora*, 173–198. Amsterdam: John Benjamins.

2006. A rich domain of ELF – the ELFA Corpus of Academic Discourse. *Nordic Journal of English Studies* 5(2): 145–59.

2011. Learners and users – Who do we want corpus data from? In F. Meunier, S. De Cock, G. Gilquin, and M. Paquot (eds.), *A taste for corpora: In honour of Sylviane Granger*, 155–171. Amsterdam: John Benjamins.

2012. *Exploring ELF: Academic English shaped by non-native speakers.* Cambridge University Press.

McCafferty, K. 2003. The Northern subject rule in Ulster: How Scots, how English? *Language Variation and Change* 15: 105–139.

2014. "[W]ell are you not got over thinking about going to Ireland yet": The *be*-perfect in eighteenth- and nineteenth-century Irish English. In M. Hundt (ed.), *Late modern English syntax*, 333–351. Cambridge University Press.

McCarthy, M. 1998. *Spoken language and applied linguistics.* Cambridge University Press.

2000. Captive audiences: The discourse of close contact service encounters. In J. Coupland (ed.), *Small talk*, 84–109. London: Longman.

2003. Talking back: Interactional response tokens in everyday conversation. *Research on Language and Social Interaction* 36(1): 33–63.

2004. Lessons from the analysis of chunks. *The Language Teacher* 28(7): 9–12.

McCarthy, M. and Carter, R. 2002. "This that and other": Multi-word clusters in spoken English as visible patterns of interaction. *Teanga* 21: 30–52.

2004. There's millions of them: Hyperbole in everyday conversation. *Journal of Pragmatics* 36: 149–184.

McCarthy, M., McCarten, J., and Sandiford, H. 2006. *Touchstone 4* (Teacher's Edition). Cambridge University Press.

McCarthy, M. and O'Dell, F. 2004. *English phrasal verbs in use*. Cambridge University Press.

2005. *English collocations in use*. Cambridge University Press.

McCarthy, M. and O'Keeffe A. 2003. "What's in a name?" Vocatives in casual conversation and radio phone-in calls. In P. Leistyna and C. Meyer (eds.), *Corpus analysis: Language structure and language use*, 153–185. Amsterdam: Rodopi.

McEnery, T. 2006a. *Swearing in English: Bad language, purity and power from 1586 to the present*. London: Routledge.

2006b. The moral panic about bad language in England, 1691–1745. *Journal of Historical Pragmatics* 7(1): 89–113.

2009. Keywords and moral panics: Mary Whitehouse and media censorship. In D. Archer (ed.), pp. 93–124.

McEnery, T. and Hardie, A. 2012. *Corpus linguistics: Method, theory and practice*. Cambridge University Press.

McEnery, T. and Wilson, A. 1997. Teaching and language corpora. *ReCALL* 9(1): 5–14.

McEnery, T. and Xiao, R. 2004. Swearing in modern British English: The case of *fuck* in the BNC. *Language and Literature* 13: 235–268.

2005. HELP or HELP *to*: What do corpora have to say? *English Studies* 86: 161–187.

McEnery, A., Xiao, R., and Mo, L. 2003. Aspect marking in English and Chinese: Using the Lancaster Corpus of Mandarin Chinese for contrastive language study. *Literary and Linguistic Computing* 18(4): 361–378.

McEnery, T., Xiao, R., and Tono, Y. 2006. *Corpus-based language studies*. London: Routledge.

McIntyre, D. 2010. Dialogue and characterization in Quentin Tarantino's *Reservoir Dogs*: A corpus stylistic analysis. In McIntyre and Busse (eds.), pp. 162–183.

McIntyre, D. and Archer, D. 2010. A corpus-based approach to mind style. *Journal of Literary Semantics* 39(2): 167–182.

McIntyre, D. and Busse, B. (eds.). 2010. *Language and style*. Basingstoke: Palgrave Macmillan.
McKay, S. 1980. Teaching the syntactic, semantic and pragmatic dimensions of verbs. *TESOL Quarterly* 14(1): 17–26.
McKeown, K. and Radev, D. 2000. Collocations. In R. Dale, H. Moisl, and H. Somers (eds.), *A handbook of natural language processing*. New York: Marcel Dekker.
Mehler, A., Sharoff, S., and Santini, M. (eds.). 2011. *Genres on the web*. Dordrecht: Springer.
Mesthrie, R. and Bhatt, R. M. 2008. *World Englishes: The study of new linguistic varieties*. Cambridge University Press.
Metsä-Ketelä, M. 2012. Frequencies of vague expressions in English as an academic lingua franca. *Journal of English as a Lingua Franca* 1(2): 263–285.
Meunier, F. and Gouverneur, C. 2008. New types of corpora for new educational challenges: Collecting, annotating and exploiting a corpus of textbook material. In K. Aijmer (ed.), *Corpora and language teaching*, 179–201. Amsterdam and Philadelphia: John Benjamins.
Meunier, F. and Granger, S. (eds.). 2008. *Phraseology in foreign language learning and teaching*. Amsterdam and Philadelphia: John Benjamins.
Meurman-Solin, A. 2013. Visual prosody in manuscript letters in the study of syntax and discourse. www.helsinki.fi/varieng/journal/volumes/14/meurman-solin_a/
Meurman-Solin, A. and Tyrkkö, J. 2013. Introduction. In A. Meurman-Solin and J. Tyrkkö (eds.), *Principles and practices for the digital editing and annotation of diachronic data*. www.helsinki.fi/varieng/journal/volumes/14/introduction.html
Mey, J. 2001. *Pragmatics: An introduction*. Oxford: Blackwell.
Meyer, C. 2002. *English corpus linguistics: An introduction*. Cambridge University Press.
2004. ADS Annual Lecture: Can you really study language variation in linguistic corpora? *American Speech* 79: 339–355.
Meyer, P. G. 1997. *Coming to know: Studies in the lexical semantics and pragmatics of academic English*. Tübingen: Gunter Narr Verlag.
Michel, J.-B., Shen, Y. K., Presser Aiden, A., Veres, A., Gray, M. K., The Google Books Team, Pickett, J. P., Hoiberg, D., Clancy, D., Norvig, P., Orwant, J., Pinker, S., Nowak, M. A., and Lieberman Aiden, E. 2011. Quantitative analysis of culture using millions of digitized books. *Science* 331: 176–182.
Michelbacher, L., Evert, S., and Schütze, H. 2011. Asymmetry in corpus-derived and human word associations. *Corpus Linguistics and Linguistic Theory* 5(1): 79–103.
Millar, N. 2009. Modal verbs in TIME: Frequency changes 1923–2006. *International Journal of Corpus Linguistics* 14(2): 191–220.

Miller, D. 2006. From concordance to text: Appraising "giving" in Alma Mater donation requests. In G. Thompson and S. Hunston (eds.), *System and corpus: Exploring connections*, 248–268. London: Equinox.

Miller, J. 2004. Perfect and resultative constructions in spoken and non-spoken English. In O. Fischer, M. Norde, and H. Perridon (eds.), *Up and down the cline – the nature of grammaticalization*, 229–246. Amsterdam: Benjamins.

Milroy, J. 1992. A social model for the interpretation of language change. In M. Rissanen, O. Ihalainen, T. Nevalainen, and I. Taavitsainen (eds.), *History of Englishes: New methods and interpretations in historical linguistics*, 72–91. Berlin and New York: Mouton de Gruyter.

Milton, J. 2009. *Measuring second language vocabulary acquisition.* Bristol: Multilingual Matters.

Miranda-García, A. and Calle-Martín, J. 2012. Compiling the Málaga Corpus of Late Middle English Scientific Prose. In Vázquez (ed.), 51–66.

Mishan, F. 2004. Authenticating corpora for language learning: A problem and its resolution. *ELT Journal* 58(3): 219–227.

Mitkov, R. (ed.). 2003. *Oxford handbook of computational linguistics.* Oxford University Press.

Moessner, L. 2001. Genre, text type, style, register: A terminological maze? *European Journal of English Studies* 5(2): 131–138.

Mohamed, S. and Acklam, R. 1995. *Intermediate choice* (Students' Book). Harlow: Longman.

Moisl, H. 2009. Exploratory multivariate analysis. In A. Lüdeling and M. Kytö (eds.), *Corpus linguistics: An international handbook*, vol. 2: 874–899. Berlin and New York: Mouton De Gruyter.

Morino, A. 2010. Personal and impersonal authorial references: A contrastive study of English and Italian linguistics research articles. *Journal of English for Academic Purposes* 9(2): 86–101.

Mollin, S. 2006. English as a lingua franca: A new variety in the new Expanding Circle? In A. Mauranen and M. Metsä-Ketelä (eds.), *English as a lingua franca*. Special Issue of *The Nordic Journal of English Studies* 5(2): 41–58.

Moon, R. 1998. Frequencies and forms of phrasal lexemes in English. In A. P. Cowie (ed.), *Phraseology: Theory, analysis, and applications*, 79–100. Oxford: Clarendon Press.

2007. Sinclair, lexicography, and the Cobuild Project: The application of theory. *International Journal of Corpus Linguistics* 12(2): 159–181.

2008a. Sinclair, phraseology, and lexicography. *International Journal of Lexicography* 21(3): 243–254.

2008b. *Dictionaries and collocation.* In Granger and Meunier (eds.), 313–336.

Moreno, A. and Suárez, L. 2008. A study of critical attitude across English and Spanish academic book reviews. *Journal of English for Academic Purposes* 7(1): 15–26.

Moreno Jaén, M. 2010. Developing university learners' collocational competence: An empirical corpus-based investigation. In M. Moreno Jaén, F. Serrano Valverde, and M. Calzada Pérez (eds.), *Exploring new paths in language pedagogy: Lexis and corpus-based language teaching*, 229–243. London: Equinox.

Morley, J. and Bayley, P. (eds.). 2009. *Corpus-assisted discourse studies on the Iraq conflict: Wording the war*. London: Routledge.

Moskowich, I. and Crespo, B. (eds.). 2012. *Astronomy "playne and simple": The writing of science between 1700 and 1900*. Amsterdam: John Benjamins.

Müller, S. 2005. *Discourse markers in native and non-native English discourse*. Amsterdam: John Benjamins.

Mudraya, O. 2006. Engineering English: A lexical frequency instructional model. *English for Specific Purposes* 25: 235–256.

Mukherjee, J. 2005. The native speaker is alive and kicking: Linguistic and language-pedagogical perspectives. *Anglistik* 16(2): 7–23.

2009. The lexicogrammar of present-day Indian English: Corpus-based perspectives on structural nativisation. In U. Römer and R. Schulze (eds.), *Exploring the lexis–grammar interface*, 117–136. Amsterdam: John Benjamins.

Mukherjee, J. and Gries, S. 2009. Collostructional nativisation in New Englishes: Verb-construction associations in the International Corpus of English. *English World-Wide* 30: 27–51.

Mukherjee, J. and Hoffmann, S. 2006. Describing verb-complementation profiles of New Englishes: A pilot study of Indian English. *English World-Wide* 27: 147–173.

Mukherjee, J. and Hundt, M. (eds.). 2011. *Exploring second-language varieties of English and learner Englishes: Bridging a paradigm gap*. Amsterdam: John Benjamins.

Mukherjee, J. and Rohrbach, J.-M. 2006. Rethinking applied corpus linguistics from a language–pedagogical perspective: New departures in learner corpus research. In B. Kettemann and G. Marko (eds.), *Planning, gluing and painting corpora: Inside the applied corpus linguist's workshop*, 205–232. Frankfurt: Peter Lang.

Mukherjee, J. and Schilk, M. 2012. Exploring variation and change in New Englishes: Looking into the International Corpus of English (ICE) and beyond. In Nevalainen and Traugott (eds.), 189–199.

Mulderrig, J. 2011. The grammar of governance. *Critical Discourse Studies* 8: 45–68.

Munday, J. 1998. A computer-assisted approach to the analysis of translation shifts. *Meta* 43(4): 542–56.

Murphy, B. 2010. *Corpus and sociolinguistics: Investigating age and gender in female talk*. Amsterdam: John Benjamins.

Murray, N. 2010. Pragmatics, awareness raising, and the cooperative principle. *ELT Journal* 64(3): 293–301.

Myles, F. 2005. Interlanguage corpora and second language acquisition research. *Second Language Research* 21(4): 373–391.

Nagao, M. and Mori, S. 1994. A new method of n-gram statistics for large number of n and automatic extraction of words and phrases from large text data of Japanese. *Proceedings of the 15th Conference on Computational Linguistics*, 611–615.

Nagata, R., Whittaker, E., and Sheinman, V. 2011. Creating a manually error-tagged and shallow-parsed learner corpus. *Proceedings of the 49th Annual Meeting of the Association for Computational Linguistics, Portland, Oregon, June 19–24 2011*, 1210–1219.

Nation, P. 2001. *Learning vocabulary in another language*. Cambridge University Press.

2006. How large a vocabulary is needed for reading and listening? *The Canadian Modern Language Review* 63(1): 59–82.

Nation, P. and Beglar, D. 2007. A vocabulary size test. *The Language Teacher* 31(7): 9–13.

Nation, P. and Waring, R. 1997. Vocabulary size, text coverage and word lists. In N. Schmitt and M. McCarthy (eds.), *Vocabulary: Description, acquisition and pedagogy*, 6–19. Cambridge University Press.

Nattinger, J. and DeCarrico, J. 1992. *Lexical phrases and language teaching*. Oxford University Press.

Nekrasova, T. M. 2009. English L1 and L2 speakers' knowledge of lexical bundles. *Language Learning* 59(3): 647–686.

Nelson, G. 1996. The design of the corpus. In Greenbaum (ed.), 27–35.

2006. World Englishes and corpora studies. In B. B. Kachru, Y. Kachru, and C. L. Nelson (eds.), *The handbook of World Englishes*. Oxford: Blackwell, 733–50.

Nelson, G., Wallis, S., and Aarts, B. 2002. *Exploring natural language. Working with the British component of the International Corpus of English*. Amsterdam: John Benjamins.

Nelson, M. 2010. Building a written corpus: what are the basics? In A. O'Keeffe and M. McCarthy (eds.), *The Routledge handbook of corpus linguistics*, 53–65. London: Routledge.

Nesi, H. and Basturkmen, H. 2006. Lexical bundles and discourse signaling in academic lectures. *International Journal of Corpus Linguistics* 11(3): 283–304.

Nesi, H. and Gardner, S. 2012. *Genres across the disciplines: Student writing in higher education*. Cambridge University Press.

Nesselhauf, N. 2003. The use of collocations by advanced learners of English and some implications for teaching. *Applied Linguistics* 24(2): 223–242.

2004. Learner corpora and their potential for language teaching. In J. McH. Sinclair (ed.), *How to use corpora in language teaching*, 125–152. Amsterdam: John Benjamins.

2005. *Collocations in a learner corpus*. Amsterdam: John Benjamins.

2010. The development of future time expressions in Late Modern English: Redistribution of forms or change in discourse? *English Language and Linguistics* 14: 163–186.

Nesselhauf, N. and Römer, U. 2007. Lexical-grammatical patterns in spoken English: The case of the progressive with future time reference. *International Journal of Corpus Linguistics* 12: 297–333.

Nevalainen, T. 1996. Gender difference. In T. Nevalainen and H. Raumolin-Brunberg (eds.), *Sociolinguistics and language history: Studies based on the Corpus of Early English Correspondence*, 77–91. Amsterdam: Rodopi.

2006. Corpora, historical sociolinguistics and the transmission of language change. In A. M. Hornero, M. J. Luzón, and S. Murillo (eds.), *Corpus linguistics: Applications for the study of English*, 23–37. Bern and Berlin: Peter Lang.

Nevalainen, T. and Raumolin-Brunberg, H. (eds.). 1996. *Sociolinguistics and language history: Studies based on the Corpus of Early English Correspondence.* Amsterdam: Rodopi.

2003. *Historical sociolinguistics: Language change in Tudor and Stuart England.* London: Pearson Education.

Nevalainen, T. and Traugott, E. (eds.). *The Oxford handbook of the history of English.* Oxford University Press.

Nevanlinna, S., Pahta, P., Peitsara, K., and Taavitsainen, I. 1993. Middle English. In M. Rissanen, M. Kytö, and M. Palander-Collin (eds.), *Early English in the computer age: Explorations through the Helsinki Corpus*, 33–51. Berlin and New York: Mouton de Gruyter.

Newman, J. and Columbus, G. 2009. Education as an over-represented topic in the ICE corpora? Paper presented at the 15th Conference of the International Association for World Englishes, Cebu City, Philippines, 22 to 24 October 2009.

Nilsson, P-O. 2006. A multidimensional perspective on collocational patterning in Swedish fiction texts translated from English. *Literary and Linguistic Computing* 21: 113–126.

Noël, D. and Colleman, T. 2010. Believe-type raising-to-object and raising-to-subject verbs in English and Dutch: A contrastive investigation in diachronic construction grammar. *International Journal of Corpus Linguistics* 15: 157–182.

Norris, J. and Ortega, L. 2000. Effectiveness of L2 instruction: A research synthesis and quantitative meta-analysis. *Language Learning* 50(3): 417–528.

(eds.). 2006. *Synthesizing research on language learning and teaching.* Amsterdam: John Benjamins.

Oakes, M. P. 2009. Corpus linguistics and language variation. In P. Baker (ed.), *Contemporary corpus linguistics*, 159–183. London: Continuum.

Oakes, M. and Ji, M. (eds.). 2012. *Quantitative research methods in corpus-based translation studies.* Amsterdam: John Benjamins.

O'Connor, J. D. O. and Arnold, G. F. 1973. *Intonation of colloquial English: A practical handbook*, 2nd edn. London: Longman.

O'Donnell, M. B. 2011. The adjusted frequency list: A method to produce cluster-sensitive frequency lists. *ICAME Journal* 35: 135–169.

O'Donnell, M. B., Scott, M., Mahlberg, M., and Hoey, M. 2012. Exploring text-initial words, clusters and concgrams in a newspaper corpus. *Corpus Linguistics and Linguistic theory* 8(1): 73–101.

O'Halloran, K. 2006. The literary mind. In S. Goodman and K. O'Halloran (eds.), *The art of English: Literary creativity*, 364–389. Basingstoke: Palgrave Macmillan.

2007a. Critical discourse analysis and the corpus-informed interpretation of metaphor at the register level. *Applied Linguistics* 28: 1–24.

2007b. The subconscious in James Joyce's "Eveline": A corpus stylistic analysis that chews on the "Fish hook." *Language and Literature* 16(3): 227–244.

O'Keeffe, A. 2006. *Investigating media discourse*. London: Routledge.

O'Keeffe, A., Clancy, B., and Adolphs, S. 2011. *Introducing pragmatics in use*. London: Routledge.

O'Keeffe, A., McCarthy, M., and Carter, R. 2007. *From corpus to classroom: Language use and language teaching*. Cambridge University Press.

Oldham, P., Hall, S., and Burton, G. 2012. Synthetic biology: Mapping the scientific landscape. *PLoS ONE* 7(4): e34368.

Olohan, M. 2004. *Introducing corpora in translation studies*. London: Routledge.

Olohan, M. and Baker, M. 2000. Reporting *that* in translated English. *Across Languages and Cultures* 1(2): 141–58.

Onnis, L. and Thiessen, E. 2012. Language-induced biases on human sequential learning. Paper presented at the 34th Annual Meeting of the Cognitive Science Society, Sapporo, Japan.

Ooi, V. 2008. The lexis of electronic gaming on the web: A Sinclairian approach. *International Journal of Lexicography* 21: 311–323.

Ortega, L. and Byrnes, H. (eds.). 2008. *The longitudinal study of advanced L2 capacities*. New York and London: Routledge.

Ortega y Gasset, J. 1937. The misery and splendor of translation. In R. Schulte and J. Biguenet (eds.), *Theories of translation: An anthology of essays from Dryden to Derrida*, 1992, 93–112. University of Chicago Press.

Osborne, J. 2008. Adverb placement in post-intermediate learner English: A contrastive study of learner corpora. In G. Gilquin, S. Papp, and M. B. Díez-Bedmar (eds.), *Linking up contrastive and learner corpus research*, 127–146. Amsterdam: Rodopi.

O'Sullivan, I. 2007. Enhancing a process-oriented approach to literacy and language learning: The role of corpus consultation literacy. *ReCALL* 19(3): 269–286.

O'Sullivan, I. and Chambers, A. 2006. Learners' writing skills in French: Corpus consultation and learner evaluation. *Journal of Second Language Writing* 15(1): 49–68.

Oswald, F. and Plonsky, L. 2010. Meta-analysis in second language research: Choices and challenges. *Annual Review of Applied Linguistics* 30: 85–110.

Øverås, L. 1998. In search of the third code. An investigation of norms in literary translation. *Meta* 43(4): 571–588.

Oxford University Computing Services. 1995. *The British National Corpus*. Oxford University Press.

Ozturk, I. 2007. The textual organization of research article introductions in applied linguistics: Variability within a single discipline. *English for Specific Purposes* 26 (1): 25–38.

Pagel, M., Atkinson, D. Q., and Meade, A. 2007. Frequency of word-use predicts rates of lexical evolution throughout Indo-European history. *Nature* 449(11): 717–720.

Palander-Collin, M. 1999. Male and female styles in seventeenth-century correspondence: I think. *Language Variation and Change* 11: 123–141.

Palmer, A. 2011. Social minds in fiction and criticism. *Style* 45(2): 196–240.

Paquot, M. 2008. Exemplification in learner writing: A cross-linguistic perspective. In F. Meunier and S. Granger (eds.), *Phraseology in foreign language learning and teaching*, 101–119. Amsterdam: John Benjamins.

2010. *Academic vocabulary in learner writing: From extraction to analysis*. London and New York: Continuum.

2012. The LEAD dictionary-cum-writing aid: An integrated dictionary and corpus tool. In Granger and Paquot (eds.), 163–185.

Paquot, M. and Bestgen, Y. 2009. Distinctive words in academic writing: A comparison of three statistical tests for keyword extraction. In A. Jucker, D. Schreier, and M. Hundt (eds.), *Corpora: Pragmatics and discourse*, 247–269. Amsterdam: Rodopi.

Paquot, M. and Granger, S. 2012. Formulaic language in learner corpora. *Annual Review of Applied Linguistics* 32: 130–149.

Parkinson, J. 2011. The Discussion section as argument: The language used to prove knowledge claims. *English for Specific Purposes* 30: 164–175.

Partington, A. 1998. *Patterns and meanings*. Amsterdam: John Benjamins.

2003. *The linguistics of political argument*. London: Routledge.

2004. "Utterly content in each other's company": Semantic prosody and semantic preference. *International Journal of Corpus Linguistics* 9(1): 131–156.

2009. Evaluating evaluation and some concluding thoughts on CADS. In Morley and Bayley (eds.), 261–303.

(ed.). 2010a. *Modern diachronic corpus-assisted studies*, special edition, *Corpora* 5(2). Edinburgh University Press.

2010b. Modern diachronic corpus-assisted discourse studies (MD-CADS) on UK newspapers: An overview of the project. *Corpora* 5(2): 83–108.

2012. The changing discourses on antisemitism in the UK press from 1993 to 2009: A modern-diachronic corpus-assisted discourse study. *Journal of Language and Politics* 11(1): 51–76.

Partington, A., Duguid, A., and Taylor, C. 2013. *Patterns and meanings in discourse: Theory and practice in corpus-assisted discourse studies.* Amsterdam: John Benjamins.

Passonneau, R., and Litman, D. 1997. Discourse segmentation by human and automated means. *Computational Linguistics* 23(1): 103–140.

Pawley, A. and Syder, F. H. 1983. Two puzzles for linguistic theory: Nativelike selection and nativelike fluency. In J. C. Richards and R. W. Schmidt (eds.), *Language and communication*, 191–225. London: Longman.

Pearce, M. 2008. Investigating the collocational behaviour of man and woman in the BNC using Sketch Engine1. *Corpora* 3(1): 1–29.

Pecina, P. 2010. Lexical association measures and collocation extraction. *Language Resources and Evaluation* 44(1–2): 137–158.

Pecman, M. 2008. Compilation, formalisation and presentation of bilingual phraseology: Problems and possible solutions. In Meunier and Granger (eds), 203–222.

Peters, P., Collins, P., and Smith, A. (eds.). 2009. *Comparative studies in Australian and New Zealand English: Grammar and beyond.* Amsterdam: John Benjamins.

Petch-Tyson, S. 2000. Demonstrative expressions in argumentative discourse: A computer-based comparison of non-native and native English. In S. Botley and A. M. McEnery (eds.), *Corpus-based and computational approaches to discourse anaphora*, 43–64. Amsterdam: John Benjamins.

Pfaff, M., Bergs, A., and Hoffmann, T. 2013. "I was just reading this article": On the expression of recentness and the English past progressive. In Aarts *et al.* (eds.), 217–238.

Philip, G. 2010. Metaphorical keyness in specialised corpora. In Bondi and Scott (eds.), pp. 185–203.

Pickering, L. 2001. The role of tone choice in improving ITA communication in the classroom. *TESOL Quarterly* 35: 233–255.

2012. Suprasegmentals: Discourse intonation. In C. A. Chapelle (ed.), *The encyclopedia of applied linguistics*, 5437–5443. Hoboken, NJ: Wiley-Blackwell.

Pierrehumbert, J. 1980. The phonology and phonetics of English intonation. PhD dissertation, MIT.

Pierrehumbert, J. and Hirschberg, J. 1990. The meaning of intonational contours in the interpretation of discourse. In P. R. Cohen, J. Morgan, and M. E. Pollack (eds.), *Intentions in communication*, 271–311. Cambridge, MA: MIT Press.

Pike, K. L. 1945. *The intonation of American English.* Ann Arbor: University of Michigan Press.

Ponte, J. M. and Croft, W. B. 1998. A language modeling approach to information retrieval. *Computer and Information Science* 98(3): 275–281.

Poos, D. and Simpson, R. 2002. Cross-disciplinary comparisons of hedging: Some findings from the Michigan Corpus of Academic Spoken English. In R. Reppen, S. Fitzmaurice, and D. Biber (eds.), *Using corpora to explore linguistic variation*, 3–21. Philadelphia: John Benjamins.

Poplack, S. and Dion, N. 2009. Prescription vs. praxis: The evolution of future temporal reference in French. *Language* 85: 557–587.

Poplack, S. and Tagliamonte, S. 1996. Nothing in context: Variation, grammaticization and past time marking in Nigerian Pidgin English. In P. Baker and A. Syea (eds.), *Changing meanings, changing functions: Papers relating to grammaticalization in contact languages*, 71–94. Westminster: University Press.

Poutsma, H. 1929. *A grammar of late Modern English*. 4 vols. Groningen: Noordhoff.

Praninskas, J. 1972. *American university word list*. London: Longman.

Prentice, S. and Hardie, A. 2009. Empowerment and disempowerment in the Glencairn Uprising: A corpus-based critical analysis of Early Modern English news discourse. *Journal of Historical Pragmatics* 10(1): 23–55.

Preston, D. 1991. Sorting out the variables in sociolinguistic theory. *American Speech* 66: 3–26.

2001. Style and the psycholinguistics of sociolinguistics: The logical problem of language variation. In P. Eckert and J. R. Rickford (eds.), *Style and sociolinguistic variation*, 279–304. Cambridge University Press.

Prince, E. 1978. A comparison of *wh*-clefts and *it*-clefts in discourse. *Language* 54: 883–906.

Prodromou, L. 2008. *English as a lingua franca: A corpus-based analysis*. London: Continuum.

Pym, A. 2008. On Toury's laws of how translators translate. In A. Pym, M. Shlesinger and D. Simeoni (eds.), *Descriptive translation studies and beyond*, 311–28. Amsterdam: John Benjamins.

Quaglio, P. 2009. *Television dialogue: The sitcom Friends vs. natural conversation*. Amsterdam and Philadelphia: John Benjamins.

Quirk, R. 1965. Descriptive statement and serial relationship. *Language* 41: 205–17.

1968. *Essays on the English language medieval and modern*. London: Longman.

Quirk, R., Greenbaum, S., Leech, G., and Svartvik, J. 1972. *A grammar of contemporary English*. Harlow: Longman.

1985. *A comprehensive grammar of the English language*. London and New York: Longman.

R Development Core Team. 2013. *R: A language and environment for statistical computing*. R Foundation for Statistical Computing, Vienna, Austria.

Ranta, E. 2013. Universals in a universal language? Exploring verb-syntactic features in English as a lingua franca. PhD thesis, University of Tampere. *Acta Electronica Universitatis Tamperensis*. Available from: //urn.fi/URN:ISBN:978-951-44-9299-0.

Rapti, N. 2010. A study of classroom concordancing in the Greek context: Data-driven grammar teaching and adolescent EFL learners. PhD thesis, University of Nottingham.

Raumolin-Brunberg, H. 2005. The diffusion of subject YOU: A case study in historical sociolinguistics. *Language Variation and Change* 17: 55–73.

Rayson, P. 2003. Matrix: A statistical method and software tool for linguistic analysis through corpus comparison. PhD thesis, Lancaster University.

2008. From key words to key semantic domains. *International Journal of Corpus Linguistics* 13(4): 519–549.

2009. *WMatrix: A Web-based Corpus Processing Environment*. Computing Department: Lancaster University. //ucrel.lancs.ac.uk/wmatrix/ (accessed 28 February 2013).

Rayson, P. and Archer, D. 2008. Key domain analysis: Mining text in the humanities and social sciences. Paper presented at the workshop on "Text mining and the social sciences," 4th International Conference on e-Social Science, University of Manchester.

Rayson, P., Archer, D., Piao, S. L., and McEnery, T. 2004a. The UCREL semantic analysis system. In *Proceedings of the Workshop on Beyond Named Entity Recognition Semantic Labelling for NLP Tasks in Association with 4th International Conference on Language Resources and Evaluation (LREC 2004)*, 25 May 2004, Lisbon, Portugal, 7–12. Paris: European Language Resources Association.

Rayson, P., Berridge, D., and Francis, B. 2004b. Extending the Cochran rule for the comparison of word frequencies between corpora. In G. Purnelle, C. Fairon, and A. Dister (eds.), *Le poids des mots: Proceedings of the 7th International Conference on Statistical Analysis of Textual Data* (JADT 2004), 10–12 March 2004, vol. 2: 926–936. Louvain-la-Neuve, Belgium: Presses universitaires de Louvain.

Rayson, P., Leech G., and Hodges, M. 1997. Social differentiation in the use of English vocabulary. *International Journal of Corpus Linguistics* 2: 133–152.

Reed, B. S. 2006. *Prosodic orientation in English conversation*. London: Palgrave.

Reitter, D., Moore, J. D., and Keller, F. 2010. Priming of syntactic rules in task-oriented dialogue and spontaneous conversation. *Proceedings of the 28th Annual Conference of the Cognitive Science Society*, 685–690.

Renouf, A. and Sinclair, J. 1991. Collocational frameworks in English. In K. Aijmer and B. Altenberg (eds.), *English corpus linguistics*, 128–144. London: Longman.

Reppen, R. 2001. Register variation in student and adult speech and writing. In S. Conrad and D. Biber (eds.), *Multi-dimensional studies of register variation in English*, 187–199. Harlow: Pearson Education.

2010a. Building a corpus: What are the key considerations? In A. O'Keeffe and M. McCarthy (eds.), *The Routledge handbook of corpus linguistics*, 31–37. London: Routledge.

2010b. *Using corpora in the classroom*. Cambridge University Press.
2012. *Grammar and beyond - level 2*. Cambridge University Press.

Riccio, G. 2009. White House press briefings as a message to the world. In Morley and Bayley (eds.), 108–140.

Rice, S. and Newman, J. 2008. Beyond the lemma: Inflection-specific constructions in English. Paper given at the AACL conference, Brigham Young University, Utah.

Rietveld, T., van Hout, R. and Ernestus, M. 2004. Pitfalls in corpus research. *Computers and the Humanities* 38(4): 343–362.

Rissanen, M. 1999. Syntax. In R. Lass (ed.), *The Cambridge history of the English language*, vol. III: *1476–1776*, 187–331. Cambridge University Press.

Ritz, E-M. In press. *Relationship between event, reference time and time of utterance and the representation of present perfect sentences in Australian English narratives* (Cahiers Chronos). Amsterdam: Rodopi.

Römer, U. 2005. *Progressives, patterns, pedagogy: A corpus-driven approach to English progressive forms, functions, contexts and didactics*. Amsterdam: John Benjamins.
2006. Pedagogical applications of corpora: Some reflections on the current scope and a wish list for future developments. *Zeitschrift für Anglistik und Amerikanistik* 54(2): 121–134.
2010. Establishing the phraseological profile of a text type: The construction of meaning in academic book reviews. *English Text Construction* 3: 95–119.

Rohdenburg, G. 1996. Cognitive complexity and increased grammatical explicitness in English. *Cognitive Linguistics* 7: 149–182.
1999. Clausal complementation and cognitive complexity in English. In F.-W. Neumann and S. Schülting (eds.), *Anglistentag 1998 Erfurt*, 101–112. Trier: Wissenschaftlicher Verlag.

Roland, D., Elman, J. L., and Ferreira, V. S. 2006. Why is *that*? Structural prediction and ambiguity resolution in a very large corpus of English sentences. *Cognition* 98: 245–272.

Romaine, S. 1980. Stylistic variation and evaluative reactions to speech: problems in the investigation of linguistic attitudes in Scotland. *Language and Speech* 23: 213–232.
1982. *Socio-historical linguistics: Its status and methodology*. Cambridge University Press.
2001. A corpus-based view of Gender in British and American English. In M. Hellinger and H. Bussmann (eds.), *Gender across language*, vol. 1: 153–175. Amsterdam: John Benjamins.
2008. Corpus linguistics and sociolinguistics. In A. Lüdeling and M. Kytö (eds)., *Corpus linguistics. An international handbook*, 96–111. Berlin: Mouton de Gruyter.

Romero-Trillo, J. (ed.). 2008. *Pragmatics and corpus linguistics: A mutualistic entente*. Berlin: Mouton de Gruyter.

Rommel, T. 2004. Literary studies. In S. Schreibman, R. Siemens, and J. Unsworth (eds.), *A companion to digital humanities*, 88–96. Oxford: Blackwell.

Rosch, E. 1975. Cognitive representation of semantic categories. *Journal of Experimental Psychology: General* 104: 192–233.

1976. Principles of categorization. In E. Rosch and B. B. Lloyd (eds.), *Cognition and categorization*, 27–48. Hillsdale, NJ: Lawrence Erlbaum.

Rosdahl, C. B. and Kowalski, M. T. 2008. *Textbook of basic nursing*. Philadelphia: Lippincott, Williams & Wilkins.

Rosenberg, B. 1996. *Little Dorrit's shadows: Character and contradiction in Dickens*. Columbia and London: University of Missouri Press.

Rosenfelder, I. 2009. *Rhoticity in educated Jamaican English*. In Hoffmann and Siebers (eds.), 61–82.

Ross, J. R. 1973. A fake NP squish. In C.-J. Bailey and R. W. Shuy (eds.), *New ways of analyzing variation in English*, 96–140. Washington, DC: Georgetown University Press.

Roter, D. 2010. The Roter method of interaction process analysis. Unpublished manual.

Rühlemann, C. 2007. *Conversation in context: A corpus-driven approach*. London: Continuum.

2010. What can a corpus tell us about pragmatics? In A. O'Keeffe and M. McCarthy (eds.), *The Routledge handbook of corpus linguistics*, 288–301. London: Routledge.

Rudanko, J. 2006. Watching English grammar change: A case study on complement selection in British and American English. *English Language and Linguistics* 10(1): 31–48.

Rundell, M. 1999. Dictionary use in production. *International Journal of Lexicography* 12(1): 35–53.

Rydén, M. and Brorström, S. 1987. *The be/have variation with intransitives in English: With special reference to the Late Modern Period*. Stockholm: Almqvist & Wiksell International.

Sagi, E., Kaufmann, S., and Clark, B. 2011. Tracing semantic change with Latent Semantic Analysis. In J. Robynson and K. Allan (eds.), *Current methods in historical semantics*, 161–183. Berlin and New York: Mouton de Gruyter.

Salem, A. 1987. *Pratique des segments répétés*. Paris: Institut National de la Langue Française.

Salton, G. 1989. *Automatic text processing*. Reading, MA: Addison-Wesley.

Salsbury, T. and Crummer, C. 2008. Using teacher-developed corpora in the CBI classroom. *English Teaching Forum* 2: 28–37.

Sampson, G. 1987. The grammatical database and parsing scheme. In R. Garside, G. Leech, and G. Sampson (eds.), *The computational analysis of English: A corpus-based approach*, 82–96. London and New York: Longman.

2002. Regional variation in the English verb qualifier system. *English Language and Linguistics* 6: 17–30.

Samraj, B. 2005. An exploration of a genre set: Research article abstracts and introductions in two disciplines. *English for Specific Purposes* 24: 141–156.

Sardinha, T. 2000. Semantic prosodies in English and Portuguese: A contrastive study. *Cuadernos de Filología Inglesa* 9(1): 93–110.

Schachter, J. 1974. An error in error analysis. *Language Learning* 24(2): 205–214.

Schauer, G. and Adolphs, S. 2006. Expressions of gratitude in corpus and DCT data: Vocabulary, formulaic sequences and pedagogy. *System* 34: 119–134.

Scherre, M. and Naro, A. 1991. Marking in discourse: "Birds of a feather." *Language Variation and Change* 3: 23–32.

Schiffrin, D. 1987. *Discourse markers*. Cambridge University Press.

Schler, J., Koppel, M., Argamon, S., and Pennebaker, J. 2006. Effects of age and gender on blogging. In N. Nicolov, F. Salvetti, M. Liberman, and J. H. Martin (eds.), *Proceedings of 2006 AAAI Spring Symposium on Computational Approaches for Analyzing Weblogs*, 199–205.

Schmid, H. 1994. Probabilistic part-of-speech tagging using decision trees. In *Proceedings of International Conference on New Methods in Language Processing, Manchester*, 44–49.

Schmitt, N. (ed.). 2004. *Formulaic sequences: Acquisition, processing and use*. Amsterdam: John Benjamins.

Schmitt, N. and Carter, R. 2004. Formulaic sequences in action: An introduction. In N. Schmitt (ed.), *Formulaic sequences*,1–22. Amsterdam: John Benjamins.

Schmitt, N. and Redwood, S. 2011. Learner knowledge of phrasal verbs: A corpus-informed study. In F. Meunier, S. De Cock, G. Gilquin, and M. Paquot (eds.), *A taste for corpora: In honor of Sylviane Granger*, 173–207. Amsterdam and Philadelphia: John Benjamins.

Schmitt, N. and Schmitt, D. 2014. A reassessment of frequency and vocabulary size in L2 vocabulary teaching. *Language Teaching* 47(4): 484–503.

Schneider, E. W. 2005. The subjunctive in Philippine English. In D. T. Dayag and J. S. Quakenbusch (eds.), *Linguistics and language education in the Philippines and beyond: A Festschrift in honor of Ma. Lourdes S. Bautista*. Manila: Linguistic Society of the Philippines, 27–40.

2007. *Postcolonial English*. Cambridge University Press.

Schneider, G. 2008. Hybrid long-distance functional dependency parsing. PhD dissertation, University of Zurich.

Schneider, K. 2012. Appropriate behaviour across varieties of English. *Journal of Pragmatics* 44: 1022–1037.

Schulze, R. and Römer, U. 2009. Introduction: Zooming in. In U. Römer and R. Schulze (eds.), *Exploring the lexis-grammar interface*, 1–14. Amsterdam: John Benjamins.

Schuurman, I., Schouppe, M., Hoekstra, H., and van der Wouden, T. 2003. CGN, an annotated corpus of spoken Dutch. In *Proceedings of the 4th International Workshop on Linguistically Interpreted Corpora*, 340–347.

Scott, M. 1996–2013. *WordSmith Tools*. Oxford University Press/Lexical Analysis Software Ltd. See www.lexically.net/wordsmith/index.html (accessed 4 March 2013).

1997. PC analysis of key words – and key key words. *System* 25(2): 233–245.

2000. Focusing on the text and its key words. In L. Burnard and T. McEnery (eds.), *Rethinking language pedagogy from a corpus perspective*, vol. 2: 103–122. Frankfurt: Peter Lang.

2004. *Oxford WordSmith Tools*. Version 4.0. Oxford University Press.

2009. In search of a bad reference corpus. In Archer (ed.), 79–91.

2010. Problems in investigating keyness. In Bondi and Scott (eds.), 43–57.

2013. *WordSmith Tools Manual*. Version 6.0. Liverpool: Lexical Analysis Software Ltd. See www.lexically.net/downloads/version6/wordsmith6.pdf (accessed 4 March 2013).

Scott, M. and Tribble, C. 2006. *Key words and corpus analysis in language education*. Amsterdam: John Benjamins.

Sedlatschek, A. 2009. *Contemporary Indian English: Variation and change*. Amsterdam: John Benjamins.

Seidlhofer, B. 2001. Closing a conceptual gap: The case for a description of English as a lingua franca. *International Journal of Applied Linguistics* 11(2): 133–158.

2004. Research perspectives on teaching English as a lingua franca. *Annual Review of Applied Linguistics* 24: 209–239.

2011. *Understanding English as a lingua franca*. Oxford University Press.

Semino, E. and Short, M. 2004. *Corpus stylistics: Speech, writing and thought presentation in a corpus of English writing*. London: Routledge.

Seoane, E. and Suárez-Gómez, C. 2013. The expression of the perfect in East and South-East Asian Englishes. *English World-Wide* 34(1): 1–25.

Seretan, V. 2011. *Syntax-based collocation extraction*. Berlin: Springer.

Shackleton, R. G. 2007. Phonetic variation in the traditional English dialects: A computational analysis. *Journal of English Linguistics* 35(1): 30–102.

Shafi, S. M. and Rather, R. A. 2005. Precision and recall of five search engines for retrieval of scholarly information in the field of biotechnology. *Webology* 2(2). Downloaded from www.webology.org/2005/v2n2/a12.html

Shastri, S. V. 1988. The Kolhapur Corpus of Indian English and work done on its basis so far. *ICAME Journal* 12: 15–26.

Shih, C-L. 2012. A corpus-aided study of shifts in English-to-Chinese translation of prepositions. *International Journal of English Linguistics* 2 (6): 50–62.

Shiina, M. 2005. How playwrights construct their dramatic worlds: A corpus-based study of vocatives in early modern English comedies. In C. R. Caldas-Coulthard and M. Toolan (eds.), *The writer's craft, the culture's technology*, 209–224. Amsterdam: Rodopi.

Shimohata, S., Sugio, T., and Nagata, J. 1997. Retrieving collocations by co-occurrences and word order constraints. *Proceedings of the 35th Annual Meeting of the Association for Computational Linguistics*, 476–481.

Shin, D. and Nation, P. 2008. Beyond single words: The most frequent collocations in spoken English. *ELT Journal* 62(4): 339–348.

Shirato, J. and Stapleton, P. 2007. Comparing English vocabulary in a spoken learner corpus with a native speaker corpus: Pedagogical implications arising from an empirical study in Japan, *Language Teaching Research* 11(4): 393–412.

Siepmann, D. 2008. Phraseology in learners' dictionaries: what, where and how? In Meunier and Granger (eds.), 185–202.

Sigley, R. J. 1997. Text categories and where you can stick them: A crude formality index. *International Journal of Corpus Linguistics* 2(2): 199–237.

2012. Assessing corpus comparability using a formality index: The case of the Brown and LOB clones. In S. Yamazaki and R. J. Sigley (eds.), *Approaching language variation through corpora: A Festschrift in honour of Toshio Saito*, 65–114. Bern: Peter Lang.

Simpson, R., Briggs, S. L., Ovens, J., and Swales, J. M. 2002. *The Michigan Corpus of Academic Spoken English*. Ann Arbor: The Regents of the University of Michigan.

Simpson, R. and Mendis, D. 2003. A corpus based study of idioms in academic speech. *TESOL Quarterly* 3: 419–41.

Simpson-Vlach, R. and Ellis, N. C. 2010. An academic formulas list: New methods in phraseology research. *Applied Linguistics* 31(4): 487–512.

Simpson-Vlach, R. and Leicher, S. 2006. *The MICASE handbook: A resource for users of the Michigan Corpus of Academic Spoken English*. Ann Arbor: University of Michigan Press.

Sinclair, J. 1966. Beginning the study of lexis. In C. Bazell, J. Catford, M. A. K. Halliday, and R. Robins (eds.), *In memory of J. R. Firth*, 148–162. London: Longman.

(ed.). 1987. *Looking up: An account of the COBUILD project in lexical computing*. London: Collins.

1988. Mirror for a text. *Journal of English and Foreign Languages* 1: 15–44.

1991. *Corpus, Concordance, Collocation*: Oxford University Press.

1996. Preliminary recommendations on corpus typology, technical report, EAGLES (Expert Advisory Group on Language Engineering Standards). www.ilc.cnr.it/EAGLES96/corpustyp/corpustyp.html

2004a. *Trust the text: Language, corpus, and discourse*. London: Routledge.

2004b. Interview with John Sinclair conducted by Wolfgang Teubert. In R. Krishnamurthy (ed.), *English collocation studies: The OSTI report*, xvii–xxix. London and New York: Continuum.

2006. Aboutness 2. Manuscript, Tuscan Word Centre, Italy.

Sinclair, J. *et al.* (eds.). 1987. *Collins COBUILD English language dictionary*. London: Harper Collins.

(eds.). 1990. *Collins COBUILD English Grammar*. London: HarperCollins.

(eds.). 1995. *Collins COBUILD English Dictionary*. London: HarperCollins.

Skandera, P. 2003. *Drawing a map of Africa: Idiom in Kenyan English*. Tübingen: Narr.

Smith, A. 2013. Complex prepositions and variation within the PNP construction. In H. Hasselgård, J. Ebeling, and S. Oksefjell Ebeling (eds.), *Corpus perspectives: On patterns of lexis*, 153–174. Amsterdam and Philadelphia: Benjamins.

Smith, N., Hoffmann, S., and Rayson, P. 2008. Corpus tools and methods, today and tomorrow: Incorporating linguists' manual annotations. *Literary and Linguistic Computing* 23(2): 163–180.

Smith, N. and Leech, G. 2013. Verb structures in twentieth-century British English. In Aarts, Close, Leech, and Wallis (eds.), 68–98.

Smitterberg, E. 2009. Multal adverbs in nineteenth-century English. *Studia Neophilologica* 81(2): 121–144.

Soloman, B. and Felder, R. 1996. *Index of learning styles questionnaire*. Raleigh: North Carolina State University. Downloaded from www.engr.ncsu.edu/learningstyles/ilsweb.html

Spada, N. and Tomita, Y. 2010. Interactions between type of instruction and type of language feature: A meta-analysis. *Language Learning* 60(2): 263–308.

Speelman, D., Grondelaers, S., and Geeraerts, D. 2003. Profile-based linguistic uniformity as a generic method for comparing language varieties. *Computers and the Humanities* 37: 317–337.

Sripicharn, P. 2003. Evaluating classroom concordancing: The use of corpus-based materials by a group of Thai students. *Thammasat Review* 8(1): 203–236.

Stæhr, L. S. 2009. Vocabulary size and the skills of listening, reading and writing. *Language Learning Journal* 36(2): 139–152.

Staples, S. 2014. Linguistic characteristics of international and US nurse discourse. Unpublished dissertation, Northern Arizona University.

Staples, S. and Biber, D. 2014. The expression of stance in nurse–patient interactions: An ESP perspective. In M. Gotti and D.S. Giannoni (eds.), *Corpus analysis for descriptive and pedagogical purposes: ESP perspectives*, 123–142. Bern: Peter Lang.

Staples, S., Egbert, J., Biber, D., and McClair, A. 2013. Formulaic sequences and EAP writing development: Lexical bundles in the TOEFL iBT writing section. *Journal of English for Academic Purposes* 12: 214–25.

Starcke, B. 2006. The phraseology of Jane Austen's *Persuasion*: Phraseological units as carriers of meaning. *ICAME Journal* 30: 87–104.

Staum, L. 2005. When stylistic and social effects fail to converge: A variation study of complementizer choice. MS, Stanford University.

Stefanowitsch, A. and Gries, S. 2003. Collostructions: Investigating the interaction between words and constructions. *International Journal of Corpus Linguistics* 8(2): 209–243.

Steger, M. and Schneider, E. W. 2012. Complexity as a function of iconicity: The case of complement clause constructions in New Englishes. In B. Kortmann and B. Szmrecsanyi (eds.), *Linguistic complexity*, 156–191. Berlin and Boston: De Gruyter.

Stenström, A. B., Andersen, G., and Hasund, I. K. 2002. *Trends in teenage talk: Corpus compilation, analysis and findings*. Amsterdam: John Benjamins.

Stevens, V. 1991. Concordance-based vocabulary exercises: A viable alternative to gap-filling. In T. Johns and P. King (eds.), *Classroom concordancing, special issue of ELR Journal* 4: 47–61.

Stewart, D. 2009. *Semantic prosody: A critical evaluation*. London: Routledge.

Stockwell, P. 2002. *Cognitive poetics: An introduction*. London: Routledge.

2009. *Texture: A cognitive aesthetics of reading*. Edinburgh University Press.

Stockwell, R. P., Schachter, P., and Partee, B. H. 1973. *The major syntactic structures of English*.

Stubbs, M. 1983. *Discourse analysis*. Oxford: Blackwell.

1993. British traditions in text analysis: From Firth to Sinclair. In M. Baker, F. Francis, and E. Tognini-Bonelli (eds.), *Text and technology: In honour of John Sinclair*, 1–36. Amsterdam: John Benjamins.

1995. Collocations and semantic profiles: On the cause of the trouble with quantitative methods. *Function of Language* 2(1): 1–33.

1996. *Text and corpus linguistics*. Oxford: Blackwell.

2000. Using very large text collections to study semantic schemas: A research note. In C. Heffer and S. Hunston (eds.), *Words in context*, 1–9. University of Birmingham ELR Monograph 18.

2001a. On inference theories and code theories: Corpus evidence for semantic schemas *Text* 21(3): 437–465.

2001b. *Words and phrases*. Oxford: Blackwell.

2002. Two quantitative methods of studying phraseology in English. *International Journal of Corpus Linguistics* 7(2): 215–244.

2005. Conrad in the computer: Examples of quantitative stylistic methods. *Language and Literature* 14(1): 5–24.

2006. Corpus analysis: The state of the art and three types of unanswered questions. In G. Thompson and S. Hunston (eds.), *Style and corpus: Exploring connections*, 15–36. London: Equinox.

2009. The search for units of meaning: Sinclair on empirical semantics. *Applied Linguistics* 30(1): 115–137.

2010. Three concepts of keywords. In Bondi and Scott (eds.), 21–42.

Stubbs, M. and Gerbig, A. 1993. Human and inhuman geography: On the computer-assisted analysis of long texts. In M. Hoey (ed.), *Data, description, discourse: Papers on the English Language in honour of John McH. Sinclair on his sixtieth birthday*, 64–85. London: HarperCollins.

Suárez-Gómez, C. and Seoane, E, 2013. They have published a new cultural policy that just come out: Competing forms in spoken and written New Englishes. In Andersen and Bech (eds.), 163–182.

Sun, Y-C. and Wang, L-Y. 2003. Concordancers in the EFL classroom: Cognitive approaches and collocation difficulty. *Computer Assisted Language Learning* 16(1): 83–94.

Supatranont, P. 2005. A comparison of the effects of the concordance-based and the conventional teaching methods on engineering students' English vocabulary learning. PhD thesis, Chulalongkorn University.

Svartvik, J. 1966. *On voice in the English verb*. The Hague: Mouton.

(ed.). 1990. *The London–Lund Corpus of Spoken English: Description and research* (Lund Studies in English 82). University of Lund.

Swales, J. M. 1990. *Genre analysis: English in academic and research settings*. Cambridge University Press.

1996. Occluded genres in the academy: The case of the submission letter. In E. Ventola and A. Mauranen (eds.), *Academic writing: Intercultural and textual issues*. 45–58. Amsterdam: John Benjamins.

1998. Other Floors, *Other voices: A textography of a small university building*. Mahwah, NJ: Lawrence Erlbaum.

2002. Integrated and fragmented worlds: EAP materials and corpus linguistics. In J. Flowerdew (ed.), *Academic discourse*, 150–164. London: Longman, Pearson Education.

Swales, J. M. and Burke, A. (2003). It's really fascinating work: Differences in evaluative adjectives across academic registers. In P. Leistyna and C. F. Meyer (eds.), *Corpus analysis: Language structure and language use*, 1–18. New York: Rodopi.

Swales, J. and Malczewski, B. 2001. Discourse management and new-episode flags in MICASE. In R. C. Simpson and J. M. Swales (eds.), *Corpus linguistics in North America: Selections from the 1999 symposium*, 145–164. Ann Arbor: University of Michigan Press.

Swan, M. and Smith, B. 1987. *Learner English: A teacher's guide to interference and other problems*. Cambridge University Press.

Sweetser, E. 1990. *From etymology to pragmatics*. Cambridge University Press.

Szmrecsanyi, B. 2005. Language users as creatures of habit: A corpus-based analysis of persistence in spoken English. *Corpus Linguistics and Linguistic Theory* 1(1): 113–150.

2006. *Morphosyntactic persistence in spoken English: A study at the intersection of variationist sociolinguistics, psycholinguistics, and discourse analysis*. Berlin: Mouton de Gruyter.

2008. Corpus-based dialectometry: aggregate morphosyntactic variability in British English dialects. *International Journal of Humanities and Arts Computing*, 2: 279–296.

2013. *Grammatical variation in British English dialects: A study in corpus-based dialectometry*. Cambridge University Press.

Szmrecsanyi, B. and Hernández, N. 2007. *Manual of information to accompany the Freiburg Corpus of English Dialects sampler ("FRED-S")*. Downloaded from: urn:nbn:de:bsz:25-opus-28598, www.freidok.uni-freiburg.de/volltexte/2859/

Szmrecsanyi, B. and Kortmann, B. 2011. Typological profiling: Learner Englishes versus indigenized L2 varieties of English. In Mukherjee and Hundt (eds.), 167–187.

Szmrecsanyi, B. and Wolk, C. 2011. Holistic corpus-based dialectology. *Revista Brasileira de Linguística Aplicada* 11(2): 561–592.

Taavitsainen, I. 2009. The pragmatics of knowledge and meaning: Corpus linguistic approaches to changing thought-styles in early modern medical discourse. In Jucker, Schreier, and Hundt (eds.), 37–62.

2012. Historical pragmatics. In A. Bergs and L. Brinton (eds.), *Handbook of historical linguistics*, 1457–1474. Berlin: De Gruyter Mouton.

Taavitsainen, I. and Fitzmaurice, S. 2007. Historical pragmatics: What it is and how to do it. In Fitzmaurice and Taavitsainen (eds.), 11–36.

Taavitsainen, I. and Jucker, A. H. 2007. Speech act verbs and speech acts in the history of English. In Fitzmaurice and Taavitsainen (eds.), 107–138.

2008. "Methinks you seem more beautiful than ever": Compliments and gender in the history of English. In Jucker and Taavitsainen (eds.), 195–228.

2010. Expressive speech acts and politeness in eighteenth-century English. In R. Hickey (ed.), *Eighteenth-century English: Ideology and change*, 159–181. Cambridge University Press.

Taavitsainen, I., Jucker, A. H., and Tuominen, J. (eds.). 2014. *Diachronic corpus pragmatics* (Pragmatics & Beyond New Series 243). Amsterdam: John Benjamins.

Taavitsainen, I. and Pahta, P. 1998. Vernacularisation of medical writing in English: A corpus-based study of scholasticism. *Early Science and Medicine*. 3(2): 157–185.

(eds.). 2010. *Early Modern English medical texts: Corpus description and studies*. Amsterdam: John Benjamins.

Taavitsainen, I., Pahta, P., and Mäkinen, M. 2005. *A Collection of Middle English Medical Text*. Amsterdam: John Benjamins (CD Rom).

Taavitsainen, I. and Suhr, C. 2012. *Developing historical corpus pragmatics towards multimodality*. www.helsinki.fi/varieng/journal/volumes/11/taavitsainen_suhr.html

Tabata, T. 1995. Narrative style and the frequencies of very common words: A corpus-based approach to Dickens's first person and third person narratives. *English Corpus Studies* 2: 91–109.

Tagliamonte, S. A. 2006. *Analysing sociolinguistic variation*. Cambridge University Press.

2007. Representing real language: Consistency, trade-offs and thinking ahead! In J. Beal, K. Corrigan, and H. Moisl (eds)., *Using unconventional digital language corpora*, vol. 1: *Synchronic corpora*, 205–240. Basingstoke: Palgrave Macmillan.

Tagliamonte, S. A. and Denis, D. 2008. Linguistic ruin? LOL! Instant messaging and teen language. *American Speech* 83: 3–34.

Tagliamonte, S. A. and Lawrence, H. 2000. *I used to dance, but I don't dance now*: The habitual past in English. *Journal of English Linguistics* 28: 324–353.

Tagliamonte, S. A. and Smith, J. 2002. *Either it isn't or it's not*: NEG/AUX contraction in British dialects. *English World Wide* 23: 251–281.

Tagliamonte, S. A. and Temple, R. 2005. New perspectives on an ol' variable: (t,d) in British English. *Language Variation and Change* 17: 281–302.

Tannen, D. 1985. Relative focus on involvement in oral and written discourse. In D. Olsen, N. Torrence, and A. Hildyard (eds.), *Literacy, language, and learning: The nature and consequences of reading and writing*, 124–147. Cambridge University Press.

Tao, H. 2003. Turn initiators in spoken English: A corpus-based approach to interaction and grammar. *Language and Computers* 46: 187–207.

Tarp, S. 2009. Beyond lexicography: new visions and challenges in the information age. In H. Bergenholtz, S. Nielsen, and S. Tarp (eds.), *Lexicography at a crossroads: Dictionaries and encyclopedias today, lexicographical tools tomorrow*, 17–32. Bern: Peter Lang.

Taylor, A. 2008. Contact effects of translation: Distinguishing two kinds of influence in Old English. *Language Variation and Change* 20: 341–365.

Taylor, C. 2009. Interacting with conflicting goals: Facework and impoliteness in hostile cross-examination. In J. Morley and P. Bayley (eds.), *Corpus-assisted discourse studies on the Iraq conflict: Wording the war*, 208–233. New York: Routledge.

2010. Science in the news: A diachronic perspective. *Corpora* 5(2): 221–250.

2012. And there isn't: (How) can we access the absent using CADS? Talk given at CADS Conf 2011, Bologna University, 13–14 September 2012.

2013. Searching for similarity using corpus-assisted discourse studies. *Corpora* 8: 81–113.

Taylor, J. 2012. *The mental corpus: How language is represented in the mind.* Oxford University Press.

Taylor, L. 1996. The compilation of the Spoken English Corpus. In G. R. Knowles, A. L. Wichmann, and P. E. Alderson (eds.), *Working with speech: Perspectives on research into the Lancaster/IBM spoken English corpus*, 20–37. London: Longman.

Teich, E. 2003. *Cross-linguistic variation in system and text.* Berlin: Mouton de Gruyter.

Teich, E. and Holtz, M. 2009. Scientific registers in contact: An exploration of the lexico-grammatical properties of interdisciplinary discourses. *International Journal of Corpus Linguistics* 14: 524–548.

Teubert, W. 2001. Corpus linguistics and lexicography. *International Journal of Corpus Linguistics* 6: 125–53.

2004. Corpus linguistics and lexicography: The beginning of a beautiful friendship. *Lexicographica: International Annual for Lexicography*, 1–19.

2005. My version of corpus linguistics. *International Journal of Corpus Linguistics* 10: 1–13.

Thelwall, M. 2008. Fk yea I swear: Cursing and gender in a corpus of MySpace pages. *Corpora* 3: 83–107.

Thewissen, J. 2013. Capturing L2 accuracy developmental patterns: Insights from an error-tagged EFL learner corpus. *Modern Language Journal* 97(S1): 77–101.

Thomas, S., Tucker, R., and Kelly, W. 1998. Critical communication variables. *Journal of Construction Engineering and Management* 124, 58–66.

Thompson, G. 1996a. *Introducing functional grammar*. London: Arnold.

1996b. Voices in the text: discourse perspectives on language reports. *Applied Linguistics* 17(4): 501–530.

Thompson, S. A. and Mulac, A. 1991. Discourse uses of *that* in English. *Journal of Pragmatics* 15: 237–251.

Thornbury, S. 2004. *Natural grammar: The keywords of English and how they work*. Oxford University Press.

Thorndike, E. L. 1921. Word knowledge in elementary school. *Teachers College Record*, 22(4): 334–370.

1932. *A teacher's word book of the 20,000 words found most frequently and widely in general reading for children and young people*. New York: Teachers College, Columbia University.

Thorndike, E. and Lorge, I. 1944. *The teacher's word book of 30,000 words*. New York: Columbia University.

Thurstun, J. and Candlin, C. 1997. *Exploring academic English: A workbook for student essay writing*. Sydney: CELTR.

Tian, S. 2005. The impact of learning tasks and learner proficiency on the effectiveness of data-driven learning. *Journal of Pan-Pacific Association of Applied Linguistics* 9(2): 263–275.

ToBI (n. d.). The Ohio State University, Department of Linguistics. www.ling.ohio-state.edu/~tobi/ (accessed 18 April 2013).

Tognini-Bonelli, E. 2001. *Corpus linguistics at work*. Amsterdam: John Benjamins.

Tono, Y. 2000. A computer learner corpus-based analysis of the acquisition order of English grammatical morphemes. In L. Burnard and T. McEnery (eds.), *Rethinking language pedagogy from a corpus perspective. Papers from the Third International Conference on Teaching and Language Corpora*, 123–132. Frankfurt am Main: Peter Lang.

2004. Multiple comparisons of IL, L1 and TL corpora: The case of L2 acquisition of verb subcategorization patterns by Japanese learners of English. In G. Aston, S. Bernardini, and D. Stewart (eds.), *Corpora and language learners*, 45–66. Amsterdam: John Benjamins.

Toolan, M. 2009. *Narrative progression in the short story: A corpus stylistic approach*. Amsterdam: John Benjamins.

Torgo, L. 2011. *Data mining with R: Learning with case studies*. Boca Raton, FL: Chapman & Hall/CRC.

Torres Cacoullos, R. and Walker, J. A. 2009a. The present of the English future: Grammatical variation and collocations in discourse. *Language* 85: 321–354.

2009b. On the persistence of grammar in discourse formulas: A variationist study of *that*. *Linguistics* 47: 1–43.

Tottie, G. 1991. *Negation in English speech and writing: A study in variation*. San Diego: Academic Press.

Tottie, G. and Hoffmann, S. 2006. The tag questions in American and British English. *Journal of English Linguistics* 34(4): 283–311.

Toury, G. 1995. *Descriptive translation studies and beyond*. Amsterdam: John Benjamins.

Tracy-Ventura, N., Cortes, V., and Biber, D. 2007. Lexical bundles in speech and writing. In G. Parodi (ed.), *Working with Spanish corpora*, 217–231. London: Continuum.

Traugott, E. C. 1982. From propositional to textual and expressive meanings: Some semantic-pragmatic aspects of grammaticalization. In W. P. Lehmann and M. Yakov (eds.), *Perspectives on historical linguistics*, 245–271. Amsterdam: John Benjamins.

2003. Constructions in grammaticalization. In B. D. Joseph and R. D. Janda (eds.), *The handbook of historical linguistics*, 624–647. Oxford: Blackwell.

2004. Historical pragmatics. In Horn and Ward (eds.), 538–561.

2008. Testing the hypothesis that priming is a motivation for change. *Theoretical Linguistics* 34: 135–142.

2010. Grammaticalization. In Jucker and Taavitsainen (eds.), 97–126.

Traugott, E. C. and Dasher, R. B. 2005. *Regularity in semantic change*. Cambridge University Press.

Travis, C. E. 2007. Genre effects on subject expression in Spanish: Priming in narrative and conversation. *Language Variation and Change* 19: 101–135.

Tribble, C. 2000. Genres, keywords, teaching: Towards a pedagogic account of the language of project proposals. In L. Burnard and T. McEnery (eds.), *Rethinking language pedagogy from a corpus perspective*, 75–90. Frankfurt am Main: Peter Lang.

Tse, P. and Hyland, K. 2008. "Robot Kung fu": Gender and the performance of a professional identity. *Journal of Pragmatics*. 40(7): 1232–1248.

Ullmann, S. 1973. *Meaning and style: Collected papers*. Oxford: Blackwell.

Upton, T. and Connor, U. 2001. Using computerized corpus analysis to investigate the text linguistic discourse moves of a genre. *English for Specific Purposes* 20: 313–329.

Valkonen, P. 2008. Showing a little promise: Identifying and retrieving explicit illocutionary acts from a corpus of written prose. In Jucker and Taavitsainen (eds.), 247–272.

Van Bogaert, J. 2010. A constructional taxonomy of I think and related expressions: accounting for the variability of complement-taking mental predicates. *English Language and Linguistics* 14: 399–427.

van der Auwera, J., Noël, D., and De Wit, A. 2012. The diverging *need(to)*'s of Asian Englishes. In Hundt and Gut (eds.), 55–75.

Vanderauwera, Ria 1985. *Dutch novels translated into English*. Amsterdam: Rodopi.

Vanderbauwhede, G., Desmet, P., and Lauwers, P. 2011. The shifting of the demonstrative determiner in French and Dutch in parallel corpora. *Meta* 56(2): 443–64.

Van Ek, J. A. 1966. *Four complementary structures of predication in contemporary British English*. Groningen: J. B. Wolters.

Van Herk, G. and Walker, J. 2005. S marks the spot? Regional variation and early African American correspondence. *Language Variation and Change* 17: 113–131.

van Rooy, B., Terblanche, L., Haase, C., and Schmied, J. 2010. Register differentiation in East African English: A multidimensional study. *English World-Wide* 31(3): 311–349.

Vaughan, E. 2007. "I think we should just accept ... our horrible lowly status": Analysing teacher-teacher talk within the context of community of practice. *Language Awareness* 16(3): 173–189.

Vaughan E. and Clancy, B. 2011. The pragmatics of Irish English. *English Today* 27(2): 47–52.

2013. Small corpora and pragmatics. In J. Romero-Trillo (ed.), *Yearbook of Corpus Linguistics and Pragmatics 2013: New domains and methodologies*, 53–73. Berlin: Springer.

Vázquez, N. (ed.). 2012. *Creation and use of historical English corpora in Spain*. Newcastle upon Tyne: Cambridge Scholars.

Venuti, L. (ed.). 2000. *The translation studies reader*. London: Routledge.

Verschueren, J. 1999. *Understanding pragmatics*. London: Arnold.

2003. The pragmatic perspective. In J. Verschueren, J.-O. Östman, J. Blommaert, and C. Bulcaen (eds.), *The handbook of pragmatics online*. Amsterdam: John Benjamins.

Viana, V., Fausto, F., and Zyngier, S., 2007. Corpus linguistics and literature: A contrastive analysis of Dan Brown and Machado de Assis. In S. Zyngier, V. Viana, and J. Jandre (eds.), *Textos e leituras: Estudos empíricos de língua e literatura*, 233–256. Rio de Janeiro: Publit.

Vine, B. 1999. *Guide to The New Zealand component of the International Corpus of English*. Wellington: School of Linguistics and Applied Language Studies, Victoria University of Wellington.

VOICE Project. 2013. *VOICE Part-of-Speech Tagging and Lemmatization Manual*. Downloaded from www.univie.ac.at/voice/documents/ VOICE_tagging_manual.pdf (accessed 25 February 2013).

von Eye, A. 1990. *Introduction to Configural Frequency Analysis: The search for types and antitypes in cross-classifications*. Cambridge University Press.

Vosberg, U. 2006. *Die große Komplementverschiebung: Außersemantische Einflüsse auf die Entwicklung satzwertiger Ergänzungen im Neuenglischen*. Tübingen: Gunter Narr.

Vosters, R. and Vandenbussche, W. 2012. Bipartite negation in 18th and early 19th century Southern Dutch: Sociolinguistic aspects of norms and variation. *Neuphilologische Mitteilungen* 3: 343–64.

Wales, K. 2001. *A dictionary of stylistics*. Harlow: Pearson Education.

Walker, B. 2010. Wmatrix, key concepts and the narrator in Julian Barnes's *Talking it over*. In B. Busse and D. McIntyre (eds.), *Language and style*, 364–387. Basingstoke: Palgrave Education.

2012. Character and characterisation in Julian Barnes' *Talking It Over*: A corpus stylistic analysis. PhD thesis, Lancaster University.

Walker, C. 2009. The treatment of collocation by learners' dictionaries, collocational dictionaries and dictionaries of business English. *International Journal of Lexicography* 22:(3), 281–299.

Walker, J. 2008. The footballer's perfect – are footballers leading the way? In E. Lavric, G. Pisek, A. Skinner, and W. Stadler (eds.), *The linguistics of football*, 295–303. Tübingen: Gunter Narr.

Walker, T. 2007. *Thou and you in Early Modern English dialogues: Trials, depositions, and drama comedy*. Amsterdam and Philadelphia: John Benjamins.

Walker, T. and Kytö, M. 2013. Features of layout and other visual effects in the source manuscripts of An Electronic Text Edition of Depositions 1560–1760 (ETED). www.helsinki.fi/varieng/journal/volumes/14/ walker_kyto/

Wallis, S., Aarts, B., Ozon, G., and Kavalova, Y. 2006. *DCPSE: The Diachronic Corpus of Present-Day Spoken English*. London: Survey of English Usage, UCL.

Walsh, S. 2013. Corpus linguistics and conversation analysis at the interface: Theoretical perspectives, practical outcomes. In J. Romero-Trillo (ed.), *Yearbook of Corpus Linguistics and Pragmatics 2013: New domains and methodologies*, 37–52. Berlin: Springer.

Wang, Y. 2012. Chinese speakers' perceptions of their English in intercultural communication. PhD thesis, University of Southampton.

Warren, M. 2010. Identifying aboutgrams in engineering texts. In Bondi and Scott (eds.), 113–126.

Wei, N. and Li, X. 2014. Exploring semantic preference and semantic prosody across English and Chinese: Their roles for cross-linguistic equivalence. *Corpus Linguistics and Linguistics Theory*, special Issue on *Corpus-Based Translation and Contrastive Linguistic Studies* 10(1): 103–138.

Weiner, J. and Labov, W. 1983. Constraints on the agentless passive. *Journal of Linguistics* 19: 29–58.
Weinert, R. 1995. The role of formulaic language in second language acquisition: A review. *Applied Linguistics* 16(2): 180–205.
Weissbort, D. and Eysteinsson, A. (eds.). 2006. *Translation – theory and practice: A historical reader*. Oxford University Press.
Wekker, H. Chr. 1976. *The expression of future time in contemporary British English*. Amsterdam: North-Holland.
Werlich, E. 1983. *A text grammar of English*. Heidelberg: Quelle & Meyer.
West, M. 1937. The present position in vocabulary selection for foreign language teaching. *Modern Language Journal* 21(6): 433–437.
1953. *A general service list of English words*. London: Longman.
Wible, D., Kuo, C. H., Chien, F.-Y., Liu, A., and Tsao, N.-L. 2001. A web-based EFL writing environment: Integrating information for learners, teachers, and researchers. *Computers and Education* 37(3–4): 297–315.
Wible, D. and Tsao, N-L. 2011. Towards a new-generation of corpus-derived lexical resources for language learning. In F. Meunier, S. De Cock, G. Gilquin, and M. Paquot (eds.), *A taste for corpora: In honor of Sylviane Granger*, 237–255. Amsterdam and Philadelphia: John Benjamins.
Wichmann, A. 2000. *Intonation in text and discourse: Beginnings, middles, and ends*. London: Longman.
2004. The intonation of Please-requests: a corpus-based study. *Journal of Pragmatics* 36: 1521–1549.
Wichmann, A. and Culpeper, J. 2003. Sociopragmatic annotation: New directions and possibilities in historical corpus linguistics. In A. Wilson, P. Rayson, and T. McEnery (eds.), *Corpus linguistics by the Lune: A festschrift for Geoffrey Leech*, 37–58. Frankfurt am Main: Peter Lang.
Widdowson, H. 2003. *Defining issues in English language teaching*. Oxford University Press.
Wiechmann, D. 2008. On the computation of collostruction strength: testing measures of association as expressions of lexical bias. *Corpus Linguistics and Linguistic Theory* 4(2): 253–290.
Wilkinson, L. and the Task Force on Statistical Inference. 1999. Statistical methods in psychology journals: Guidelines and expectations. *American Psychologist* 54(8): 594–604.
Williams, G. 2001. Mediating between lexis and texts: Collocational networks in specialised corpora. *ASp* 31–33: 63–76.
2006. Advanced ESP and the learner's dictionary: Tools for the non-language specialist. *Proceedings of the XII EURALEX Congress*. Available from www.euralex.org/elx_proceedings/Euralex2006/
Williams, R. [1976] 1983. *Keywords*. London: Fontana.
Williamson, K. 1992. A computer-aided method for making a linguistic atlas of Older Scots. *Scottish Language* 11/12: 138–73.

Wilson, A. 2013. Embracing Bayes factors for key item analysis in corpus linguistics. In A. Koll-Stobbe and M. Bieswanger (eds.), *New approaches to the study of linguistic variability*, 3–11. Frankfurt am Main: Peter Lang.

Wilson, A. and Zeitlyn, D. 1995. The distribution of person-referring expressions in natural conversation. *Research on Language and Social Interaction* 28(1): 61–92.

Winford, D. 2003. *An introduction to contact linguistics*. Oxford: Blackwell.

Wisniewska, I. 2009. *Grammar dimensions*, 4th edn. Boston, MA: Heinle Cengage.

Wodak, R. 2007. Pragmatics and critical discourse analysis: A cross-disciplinary inquiry. *Journal of Pragmatics and Cognition* 15(1): 203–227.

Wolk, C. 2014. Integrating aggregational and probabilistic approaches to dialectometry and language variation. PhD dissertation, University of Freiburg.

Wolk, C., Bresnan, J., Rosenbach, A., and Szmrecsanyi, B. 2013. Dative and genitive variability in Late Modern English: Exploring cross-constructional variation and change. *Diachronica* 30(3): 382–419.

Wray, A. 2002. *Formulaic language and the lexicon*. Cambridge University Press.

2008. *Formulaic language: Pushing the boundaries*. Oxford University Press.

2009. Identifying formulaic language: Persistent challenges and new opportunities. In R. Corrigan, E. A. Moravcsik, H. Ouali, and K. M. Wheatley (eds.), *Formulaic language*, vol. 1: *Distribution and historical change*, 27–51. Amsterdam: John Benjamins.

Wray, A. and Perkins, M. 2000. The functions of formulaic language: An integrated model. *Language and Communication* 20: 1–28.

Wulff, S., Ellis, N. C., Römer, U., Bardovi-Harlig, K., and LeBlanc, C. 2009. The acquisition of tense-aspect: Converging evidence from corpora and telicity ratings. *Modern Language Journal* 93(3). 354–369.

Wulff, S., Römer, U., and Swales, J. 2012. Attended/unattended this in academic student writing: Quantitative and qualitative perspectives. *Corpus Linguistics and Linguistic Theory* 8: 129–157.

Wunder, E-M., Voormann, H., and Gut, U. 2010. The ICE Nigeria corpus project: Creating an open, rich and accurate corpus. *ICAME Journal* 34: 78–88.

Wynne, M. (ed.). 2005. *Developing linguistic corpora: A guide to good practice*. Oxford: Oxbow Books. Downloaded from www.ahds.ac.uk/creating/guides/linguistic-corpora/index.htm

Xekalakis, E. 1999. *Newspapers through the times: Foreign reports from the 18th to the 20th centuries*. Zurich (no publisher).

Xiao, R. 2009. Multidimensional analysis and the study of world Englishes. *World Englishes* 28: 421–450.

2010. How different is translated Chinese from native Chinese? *International Journal of Corpus Linguistics* 15, 1: 5–35.

Xiao, R. and McEnery, T. 2005. Two approaches to genre analysis: Three genres in modern American English. *Journal of English Linguistics* 33: 62–82.

Xiao, R. and McEnery, T. 2006. Collocation, semantic prosody and near synonymy: A cross-linguistic perspective. *Applied Linguistics*, 27(1): 103–129.

Xiao, R., McEnery, T., and Qian, Y. 2006. Passive constructions in English and Chinese: A corpus-based contrastive study. *Languages in Contrast*, 6(1): 109–149.

Xiao, R. and Tao, H. 2007. A corpus-based sociolinguistic study of amplifiers in British English. *Sociolinguistic Studies* 1: 241–273.

Xue, G. and Nation, I. S. P. 1984. A university word list. *Language Learning and Communication* 3: 215–229.

Yao, X. and Collins, P. 2013. *Functional variation in the English present perfect: A cross-varietal study.* In Andersen and Bech (eds.), 91–111.

Yorio, C. 1980. Conventionalized language forms and the development of communicative competence. *TESOL Quarterly* 14(4): 433–42.

Zadeh, L. 1965. Fuzzy sets. *Information and Control* 8: 338–53.

Zanettin, F. 2012. *Translation-driven corpora*. Manchester: St. Jerome.

Zechmeister, E. B., Chronis, A. M., Cull, W. L., D'Anna, C. A., and Healy, N. A. 1995. Growth of a functionally important lexicon. *Journal of Literacy Research* 27(2): 201–212.

Zeldes, A. 2012. *Productivity in argument selection: From morphology to syntax.* Berlin and New York: De Gruyter Mouton.

Zhang, W., Yoshida, T., Tang, X., and Ho, T-B. 2009. Improving effectiveness of mutual information for substantival multiword expression extraction. *Expert Systems with Applications* 36: 10919–10930.

Zhang, Z-S. 2012. A corpus study of variation in written Chinese. *Corpus Linguistics and Linguistic Theory* 8: 209–240.

Zhiming, B. and Huaqing, H. 2006. Diglossia and register variation in Singapore English. *World Englishes* 25(1): 105–114.

Zipp, L. 2014. *Educated Fiji English: Lexico-grammar and variety status.* Amsterdam: John Benjamins.

Zuur, A. F., Ieno, E. N., Walker, N., and Saveliev, A. A. 2009. *Mixed effects models and extensions in ecology with R.* Berlin and New York: Springer.

Index